T0189682

Lecture Notes of the Institute for Computer Sciences, Social Informatics and Telecommunications Engineering 465

More information about this series at https://link.springer.com/bookseries/8197

Mian Ahmad Jan · Fazlullah Khan (Eds.)

Application of Big Data, Blockchain, and Internet of Things for Education Informatization

Second EAI International Conference, BigIoT-EDU 2022
Virtual Event, July 29–31, 2022
Proceedings, Part I

 Springer

Editors
Mian Ahmad Jan ⓘ
Department of Computer Science
Abdul Wali Khan University Mardan
Mardan, Pakistan

Fazlullah Khan ⓘ
Department of Computer Science
Abdul Wali Khan University Mardan
Mardan, Pakistan

ISSN 1867-8211   ISSN 1867-822X (electronic)
Lecture Notes of the Institute for Computer Sciences, Social Informatics
and Telecommunications Engineering
ISBN 978-3-031-23949-6   ISBN 978-3-031-23950-2 (eBook)
https://doi.org/10.1007/978-3-031-23950-2

This Springer imprint is published by the registered company Springer Nature Switzerland AG
The registered company address is: Gewerbestrasse 11, 6330 Cham, Switzerland

Preface

We are delighted to introduce the proceedings of the second edition of the European Alliance for Innovation (EAI) International Conference on Application of Big Data, Blockchain, and Internet of Things for Education Informatization (BigIoT-EDU 2022). BigIoT-EDU aims to provide a platform for international cooperation and exchange, enabling big data and information education experts, scholars, and enterprise developers to share research results, discuss existing problems and challenges, and explore cutting-edge science and technology. The conference focuses on research fields such as big data and information education. The use of artificial intelligence (AI), blockchain, and network security lies at the heart of this conference as we focus on these emerging technologies to excel the progress of Big Data and information education.

BigIoT-EDU has three tracks: the Main Track, the Late Track, and a Workshop Track. BigIoT-EDU 2022 attracted over 700 submissions, and Each submission was reviewed by at least Three Program Committee members in a double blind process, resulting in the acceptance of only 205 papers across all three tracks. The workshop was titled "International Workshop on IoT-enabled Big Data Analytics using Machine Learning for Smart Societies" and co-chaired by Muhammad Babar and Mian Muhammad Aimal from Allama Iqbal Open University Islamabad, Pakistan, and the Virtual University Lahore, Pakistan, respectively. The workshop aimed to focus on advanced techniques and algorithms to excel big data analytics and machine learning for advancement of smart societies.

Coordination with the steering chair, Imrich Chlamtac, was essential for the success of the conference. We sincerely appreciate his constant support and guidance. It was also a great pleasure to work with such an excellent organizing committee team for their hard work in organizing and supporting the conference. In particular, we are grateful to the Technical Program Committee, who completed the peer-review process for the technical papers and helped to put together a high-quality technical program. We are also grateful to Conference Manager Martin Vojtek for his constant support along with the whole of the EAI team involved in the conference. We must say that they have been wonderful and it is always a pleasant experience to work with them. Also, we would like to thank all the authors who submitted their papers to the BigIoT-EDU 2022 conference.

We strongly believe that the BigIoT-EDU conference provides a good forum for all researchers, developers, and practitioners to discuss all science and technology aspects that are relevant to big data and information education. We also expect that the future

BigIoT-EDU conferences will be as successful and stimulating as this year's, as indicated by the contributions presented in this volume.

Mian Ahmad Jan
Fazlullah Khan
Mengji Chen
Walayat Hussain
Shah Nazir

Organization

Steering Committee

Imrich Chlamtac	University of Trento, Italy
Mian Ahmad Jan	Abdul Wali Khan University Mardan, Pakistan
Fazlullah Khan	RoZetta Institute, Australia

Organizing Committee

General Chairs

Mian Ahmad Jan	Abdul Wali Khan University Mardan, Pakistan
Fazlullah Khan	RoZetta Institute, Australia
Mengji Chen	Guangxi Science and Technology Normal University, China

Technical Program Committee Chairs

Fazlullah Khan	RoZetta Institute, Australia
Mian Ahmad Jan	Abdul Wali Khan University Mardan, Pakistan
Walayat Hussain	Victoria University, Australia
Shah Nazir	University of Swabi, Pakistan

Sponsorship and Exhibit Chairs

Sahil Verma	Chandigarh University, India
Lan Zimian	Harbin Institute of Technology, China
Izaz Ur Rehman	Abdul Wali Khan University Mardan, Pakistan
Sara Karim	Abdul Wali Khan University Mardan, Pakistan

Local Chairs

Huang Yufei	Hechi Normal University, China
Wan Haoran	Shanghai University, China

Workshops Chairs

Zhang Yinjun	Guangxi Science and Technology Normal University, China
Rahim Khan	Abdul Wali Khan University Mardan, Pakistan

Abid Yahya	Botswana International University of Science and Technology, Botswana
Syed Roohullah Jan	Abdul Wali Khan University Mardan, Pakistan

Publicity and Social Media Chairs

Varun G. Menon	SCMS Group of Educational Institutions, India
Aamir Akbar	Abdul Wali Khan University Mardan, Pakistan

Publications Chairs

Mian Ahmad Jan	Abdul Wali Khan University Mardan, Pakistan
Fazlullah Khan	RoZetta Institute, Australia

Web Chairs

Mohammad Imran	Abdul Wali Khan University Mardan, Pakistan
Yar Muhammad	Abdul Wali Khan University Mardan, Pakistan

Posters and PhD Track Chairs

Mengji Chen	Guangxi Science and Technology Normal University, China
Ateeq ur Rehman	University of Haripur, Pakistan

Panels Chairs

Kong Linxiang	Hefei University of Technology, China
Muhammad Usman	Federation University, Australia

Demos Chairs

Ryan Alturki	Umm Al-Qura University, Saudi Arabia
Rahim Khan	Abdul Wali Khan University Mardan, Pakistan

Tutorials Chairs

Wei Rongchang	Guangxi Science and Technology Normal University, China
Muhammad Zakarya	Abdul Wali Khan University Mardan, Pakistan
Mukhtaj Khan	University of Haripur, Pakistan

Session Chairs

Ryan Alturki	Umm Al-Qura University, Saudi Arabia
Aamir Akbar	Abdul Wali Khan University Mardan, Pakistan
Mengji Chen	Hechi University, China

Vinh Troung Hoang	Ho Chi Minh City Open University, Vietnam
Muhammad Zakarya	Abdul Wali Khan University Mardan, Pakistan
Yu Uunshi	Shanxi Normal University, China
Ateeq ur Rehman	University of Haripur, Pakistan
Su Linna	Guangxi University, China
Shah Nazir	University of Swabi, Pakistan
Mohammad Dahman Alshehri	Taif University, Saudi Arabia
Chen Zhi	Shanghai University, China
Syed Roohullah Jan	Abdul Wali Khan University Mardan, Pakistan
Qin Shitian	Guangxi Normal University, China
Sara	Abdul Wali Khan University Mardan, Pakistan
Mohammad Wedyan	Al-Balqa Applied University, Jordan
Lin Hang	Beijin Linye University, China
Arjumand Yar Khan	Abdul Wali Khan University Mardan, Pakistan
Liu Cheng	Wuxi Technology University, China
Rahim Khan	Abdul Wali Khan University Mardan, Pakistan
Muhammad Tahir	Saudi Electronics University, Saudi Arabia
Tan Zhide	Anhui University, China

Technical Program Committee

Mian Yasir Jan	CECOS University, Pakistan
Abid Yahya	Botswana International University of Science and Technology, Botswana
Noor Zaman Jhanjhi	Taylor's University, Malaysia
Mian Muhammad Aimal	Virtual University, Pakistan
Muhammad Babar	Iqra University, Pakistan
Mamoun Alazab	Charles Darwin University, Australia
Tao Liao	Anhui University of Science and Technology, China
Ryan Alturki	Umm Al-Qura University, Saudi Arabia
Dinh-Thuan Do	Asia University, Taiwan
Huan Du	Shanghai University, China
Sahil Verma	Chandigarh University, India
Abusufyan Sher	Abdul Wali Khan University Mardan, Pakistan
Mohammad S. Khan	East Tennessee State University, USA
Ali Kashif Bashir	Manchester Metropolitan University, UK
Nadir Shah	COMSATS University Islamabad, Pakistan
Aamir Akbar	Abdul Wali Khan University Mardan, Pakistan
Vinh Troung Hoang	Ho Chi Minh City Open University, Vietnam
Shunxiang Zhang	Anhui University of Science and Technology, China

Guangli Zhu	Anhui University of Science and Technology, China
Kuien Liu	Pivotal Inc., USA
Kinan Sher	Abdul Wali Khan University Mardan, Pakistan
Feng Lu	Chinese Academy of Sciences, China
Ateeq ur Rehman	University of Haripur, Pakistan
Wei Xu	Renmin University of China, China
Ming Hu	Shanghai University, China
Abbas K. Zaidi	George Mason University, USA
Amine Chohra	Paris-East Créteil University (UPEC), France
Davood Izadi	Deakin University, Australia
Sara	Abdul Wali Khan University Mardan, Pakistan
Xiaobo Yin	Anhui University of Science and Technology, China
Mohammad Dahman Alshehri	Taif University, Saudi Arabia
Filip Zavoral	Charles University in Prague, Czech Republic
Zhiguo Yan	Fudan University, China
Florin Pop	Politehnica University of Bucharest, Romania
Gustavo Rossi	Universidad Nacional de La Plata, Argentina
Habib Shah	Islamic University of Medina, Saudi Arabia
Hocine Cherifi	University of Burgundy, France
Yinjun Zhang	Guangxi Science and Technology Normal University, China
Irina Mocanu	University Politehnica of Bucharest, Romania
Jakub Yaghob	Charles University in Prague, Czech Republic
Ke Gong	Chongqing Jiaotong University, China
Roohullah Jan	Abdul Wali Khan University Mardan, Pakistan
Kun-Ming Yu	Chung Hua University, China
Laxmisha Rai	Shandong University of Science and Technology, China
Lena Wiese	University of Göttingen, Germany
Ma Xiuqin	Northwest Normal University, China
Oguz Kaynar	Sivas Cumhuriyet University, Turkey
Qin Hongwu	Northwest Normal University, China
Pit Pichappan	Al-Imam University, Saudi Arabia
Prima Vitasari	National Institute of Technology, Indonesia
Simon Fong	University of Macau, China
Shah Rukh	Abdul Wali Khan University Mardan, Pakistan
Somjit Arch-int	Khon Kaen University, Thailand
Sud Sudirman	Liverpool John Moores University, UK
Tuncay Ercan	Yasar University, Turkey
Wang Bo	Hechi University, China

Contents – Part I

Contents – Part II

Contents – Part III

A Study of College English Writing from the Perspective of Deep Learning

Jianliang Guo[✉]

Nanchang Institute of Technology, Jiangxi 330044, China
guoshuaige2020@163.com

Abstract. Deep learning is to let students perceive, experience, understand and apply knowledge and take the initiative to learn. As a form of language output, writing needs to be combined with in-depth learning. This paper mainly analyzes how to carry out college English Writing Teaching under in-depth learning, including how to deal with the teaching design of several links before, during and after class, and how to effectively use personal feedback, peer feedback and teacher feedback to improve students' critical thinking, strengthen their in-depth learning and finally improve their writing ability.

Keywords: Deep learning · College English writing · Multidimensional feedback

1 Introduction

The improvement of students' writing level has always been one of the focuses of second language teaching. Due to the fear that students will make some mistakes in writing repeatedly, teachers in traditional college English writing teaching often correct and feed back every mistake in students' exercises, but this correction method will make students pay more attention to spelling, word selection The shallow learning of syntax, grammar and punctuation leads to the lack of control over the consistency, coherence and cohesion of writing texts and the depth of expression, which is not conducive to the cultivation of students' in-depth learning ability.

Deep learning refers to allowing students to actively process, understand and apply the knowledge they have learned, which is opposite to the relatively superficial passive acceptance of shallow knowledge learning. This means that in College English writing teaching, teachers should strive to guide students to have a critical understanding of what they have learned, make a positive transfer of previous knowledge and experience, and deeply process it. In recent years, the rise of text writing such as diary writing and the use of various feedback mechanisms in writing teaching have made many foreign language teachers pay more attention to how to effectively teach and feedback students' personalized and long text writing in writing teaching, so as to enable students to more actively and effectively understand their own language use errors, Stimulate their dialectical thinking ability and active learning ability, so as to improve their writing ability[1].

M. A. Jan and F. Khan (Eds.): BigIoT-EDU 2022, LNICST 465, pp. 1–9, 2023.
https://doi.org/10.1007/978-3-031-23950-2_1

This paper mainly discusses the research on learning English writing based on deep learning, so as to enable students to gradually improve their deep learning ability and improve their English writing level.

In fact, College English writing is very know-how. It depends on whether you are willing to remember something. If you are taking CET-4, you are suggested to buy a composition book by wangchangxi or Xinghuo. Do you know the skills of College English writing? Next, Xiaobian will tell you the skills of College English writing.

1. Be good at imitation

    For most students studying English, the accumulation of vocabulary and sentence patterns in English is still extremely limited, and it is far from being able to express smoothly and freely in English. It is appropriate to create at this stage. If you have to create, you can only write words like long time no see. Therefore, imitation is the only way at this stage.

    When it comes to imitation, some students' method is to recite a pile of model essays, and then go to the examination room to cut and paste them. The effect can be imagined. This is not imitation in the real sense. At best, it is writing the text from memory. How to imitate?

    First, the goal of imitation should be clear. The focus of imitation should always be on certain sentence structures rather than individual vocabulary. The reason is very simple: a word, with the change of the content of the article, may not be used; The sentence structure is a universal thing, which can be applied to a wide range of areas, and learning to help writing is obvious.

    Secondly, the imitated material should be tunnel. Textbooks like new concept English provide many original English expressions. Blindly choose articles to learn, remember some sentences that are not Chinese or foreign, spread false rumors and waste time.

    Finally, imitation should be reflected in the actual writing. For example, the third book of new concepts has a sentence pattern that says: &for the * * * reason& it means what is the cause of a certain phenomenon. When used in the College English test, we can explain why bicycles are so popular in China. The expression is: the bicycles very popular in China for the * * * reason&. However, many students often recite these sentence patterns without using them. When it comes to the reason, it is still &because&, and so on.

2. Be flexible

    In the process of correcting English compositions, we often find some expressions that translate Chinese rigidly into English. Due to the differences between Chinese and English and the insufficient accumulation of vocabulary and expression methods, it is quite normal to find it difficult to express. The key question is how to deal with it. There is a saying that determination is like a mountain and the path is like water. It is appropriate to apply it to this topic. To write an English composition, one must have the determination to write it well and the confidence to express the meaning clearly. This is a mountain of ambition; But the key is to have a flexible attitude when encountering problems, and be able to solve problems flexibly like running water.

2 Related Work

2.1 Current Situation of College English Writing Teaching

Foreign language writing teaching models and teaching methods are constantly emerging, such as controlled composition model, contrastive rhetoric model, writing process model, process method, genre method, result method, inquiry teaching method and so on, which have promoted the development of English writing teaching theory and practice to a certain extent. However, due to the serious disconnection between theory and practice and the limitation of class hours, the traditional result teaching method is still the main teaching method in College English writing teaching, and the teaching effect is not prominent. Most teachers only focus on correcting students' writing assignments, focusing on correcting students' spelling errors, grammatical errors, vocabulary use errors, whether the content is inconsistent with the requirements, etc., ignoring to explore the causes of students' repeated errors of the same type in completing writing tasks and the difficulties encountered in writing, and how to take corresponding countermeasures to solve these problems. This kind of correction of "treating symptoms but not improving the foundation" eventually leads to teachers' "time-consuming" correction and students' learning "low efficiency". In addition, due to the lack of teaching hours, most teachers only provide students with several writing model articles to recite before the exam, and the students' writing performance is still low. At present, there is no special writing textbook for College English, especially for undergraduates. There is no authoritative guidance textbook specially published by the national education department for the "need to master the writing skills of practical articles and essays" stipulated in the general requirements of College English curriculum requirements. Taking the author's school as an example, in the New Horizon College English reading and writing course) currently used, although writing exercises are set in each unit, due to class hour constraints, the teachers are limited to simply summarizing the writing structure through the taught reading chapters and giving rough writing guidance to students, and students do not really master and flexibly use this writing skill. It is not difficult to imagine that for professional English students, it is necessary to set up a writing class for more than one semester to teach writing knowledge and skills, and non-English majors can not master and apply them skillfully through the sporadic instructions of teachers [2].

For a long time, one of the important manifestations restricting the development of College English students' writing ability is that the input and output of students' English corpus are seriously out of proportion. Although college English reading and writing course contains writing exercises, it still focuses on the cultivation of students' reading ability. Theoretically, in College English reading class (including intensive reading class and fast reading class), students will be exposed to a large number of real corpus. The input of such a large number of corpora failed to improve the students' writing ability in the study of the two academic years. Most students are extremely short of writing vocabulary, have a lot of grammatical structure errors, lack the necessary connection between sentences, can not use the learned grammatical knowledge and vocabulary to form sentences and paragraphs, and can not skillfully use Chapter writing skills, Unable to write a qualified composition with authentic expression within the specified time.

1. Careful examination
   It is absolutely not allowed to write without writing. Instead, you should carefully review the topic, see the requirements and tips of the topic, make full use of the information provided by the topic and the scope delineated by the key words, and start writing after the topic is established. For example, according to the title of the missery of shyness, candidates should not only explain shyness, but also highlight the missery brought by shyness So far, the essay will focus on what it brings, misery
2. Full coverage of test sites
   No matter what form of writing, there are requirements for writing content, generally in three aspects. Before writing, candidates must see clearly the requirements of the writing content to ensure that the article covers all test sites.
3. Fluent language
   The scoring standard has clearly told the examinee that the article should be fluent in language, fluent in words and sentences, and accurate in expression, which is the basis for getting high scores.
4. Prominent theme

If the title is pollution from cars or air pollution, the descriptions in the following paragraphs are somewhat verbose:

1. Part of this problem is the world'Sexploding population.
2. A growing population undoubtedly means more factories polluting the air.
3. Besides, land and water pollution has also increased.
4. Pollutionis, in fact, threatening our health, our happiness, and our civilization.

2.2 The Relationship Between Deep Learning and College English Writing

In the aspect of computer artificial intelligence, deep learning actually refers to an algorithmic thinking. Its core is that the computer simulates the deep thinking of the human brain, so as to realize the complex operation of data. In the field of artificial intelligence, computer processing information is a process of automatic coding and automatic decoding, from data extraction, abstract cognition to optimal selection. Human brain processes information layer by layer. Computer artificial intelligence simulates human brain cognitive structure to process complex information. Artificial intelligence does not rely solely on data model, Artificial intelligence simulation is also structured from symbol reception, decoding, connection establishment to optimal selection. Deep learning is the closest research to human brain learning in the field of computer. Deep learning has made a breakthrough in the problem field of solving abstract problems, as evidenced by the great victory of alphgo go. The significant progress made by in-depth learning in the computer field has made a breakthrough in artificial intelligence, promoted the major development of relevant academic research, and its application performance in relevant practical application fields is also very strong. The industry began to put a large number of artificial intelligence products into production. With the continuous development of artificial intelligence and the continuous advancement of subject technology, in the 1980s and 1990s, deep learning was continuously promoted and applied in the field of education.

The breakthrough of artificial intelligence in the field of computer has attracted attention and profound reflection in the field of education. Computer can also simulate human brain: neural network for in-depth learning, so what cognitive style should people adopt for knowledge, and whether students' learning of knowledge has the difference between shallow learning and deep learning has aroused educators' continuous reflection [3]. How students' cognition of knowledge is established step by step, how students transition from shallow knowledge to deep knowledge, and how to realize deep processing of knowledge. At present, many educational researchers are interested in how to realize deep learning under the technology support environment. Among them, scholars in educational technology pay more attention to the related research of deep learning under the technology support, and deep learning plays a certain role in the research of educational technology.

In the field of education, many scholars agree with the definition of deep learning: deep learning is based on learners' self-learning interests and needs, comprehensible and scientifically critical digestion and absorption of new knowledge and ideas, and the use of diversified learning strategies to integrate discipline knowledge structure, deeply process knowledge information Establish the relationship between old and new knowledge, and effectively transfer and use knowledge information to solve complex practical problems in the real field of vision. In short, deep learning is an active inquiry, high-level thinking, effective transfer and use of knowledge to solve practical problems. The goal of in-depth learning is to enable students to be creative and imaginative, establish partnerships with others, develop the ability to explore and solve practical problems on their own initiative, and use the power of digital tools to connect knowledge with the world in the process of receiving knowledge and information. In this extremely rich knowledge and increasingly rapid innovation and development It is a kind of learning with contribution and innovation in the era of increasingly close worldwide ties. The research results of in-depth learning design supported by technology are becoming richer and richer. The design process of College English Writing Classroom Based on deep learning is shown in Fig. 1.

3 English Writing Teaching Under Deep Learning

Each link of writing task arrangement needs to set corresponding learning tasks for students to avoid directly giving a composition. In this way, students may not be familiar with the topic or think deeply enough, resulting in writing only from a superficial level, or some logical errors.

For example, in the pre writing stage, teachers can provide various forms of background information such as video text, so that students can fully accumulate and think about the pre writing background knowledge. Taking the argumentative writing of "whether the Internet makes people more lonely" as an example, teachers can provide students with background knowledge related to writing topics such as Ted speeches, news reports, research papers and English original magazines in advance[4]. The materials involved should involve the positive and negative contents of the impact of the Internet on people as a preview task, Students can be asked to summarize the given materials, including the author's views, the author's arguments, and the corresponding good language expressions, so that students can not only develop ideas, but also have

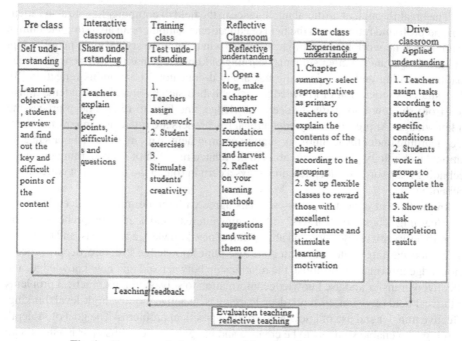

Fig. 1. Classroom design process of deep learning English Writing

a more comprehensive and profound understanding of the topics discussed, but also accumulate the corresponding language expressions.

In the writing stage, teachers can first organize students to use cloud class and other online platforms to write the outline and comment on each other's views. Teachers can comment and feed back on situations existing in the outline writing, such as poor logic, insufficient pertinence of topic sentence writing, or inconsistency between arguments and arguments, so as to provide immediate feedback, To help students set up an effective writing framework and promote peer learning. Compared with teachers' unilateral feedback, it can effectively reduce students' psychological anxiety.

In addition, teachers can also require multiple drafts of one writing task to be revised. In the process of writing task, the multi-dimensional evaluation methods of self feedback, peer evaluation and teacher evaluation are adopted to monitor the whole writing process. In order to help students complete their self feedback more effectively, teachers should provide corresponding checklists in advance according to the writing purpose of this chapter, so as to help students make clear and effective comparison and self correction from the aspects of wording, grammar, syntax, cohesion and content.

After completing the first draft, students will also conduct peer review. In this link, students can put forward corresponding suggestions from the perspective of readers to help modify the second draft. After writing, teachers can divide the class into two groups for debate according to different writing positions, which can better promote the integration of views and the presentation of arguments between the students in the same group. At the same time, they can think more seriously about the views of the opposing students and find out the possible omissions or loopholes in their own argumentation. Taking the argumentative paper "whether the Internet makes people more lonely" as an example, some students think that modern people should learn to enjoy loneliness and think that loneliness is a kind of growth experience, while the opposite side questions whether the concept of "loneliness" proposed here is generated because of the existence of the "Internet" or applicable in all environments, In this way, we can better think about the given conditions of the writing topic, and better carry out our own writing demonstration around the conditions.

4 Establish a Multi-dimensional Teaching Feedback Mechanism

4.1 Self Feedback

Self feedback is also called self correction or self-assessment. According to Charles (1990)'s self-monitoring theory, let students actively express their puzzles and existing problems in the writing process, so that teachers can have a more direct and specific understanding of some common problems in students' writing and make corresponding feedback; At the same time, it can also enable students to make a critical analysis of writing from the perspective of readers, and realize that writing is a careful process that needs multi manuscript revision. In the process of implementing self feedback, teachers need to provide a certain checklist according to the deep-seated writing training purpose they want to achieve in writing, so as to avoid students staying in the modification of shallow spelling and grammar.

4.2 Peer Review

The enthusiasm of peer feedback in foreign language writing classroom has been widely recognized. This feedback method can indeed improve students' writing accuracy. Comments from the perspective of peers can reduce students' writing anxiety. At the same time, in the process of peer feedback, students can also find problems in their own writing, so as to promote the revision of their own writing.

However, peer feedback also has some problems, such as feedback standard, feedback accuracy, proficiency and English level of team members. To solve these problems, teachers first need to formulate a detailed and accurate standard list of feedback, so that students can give feedback to their peers' writing from shallow people to deep; At the same time, feedback expression should also focus on positive expression as much as possible, and encourage feeders to provide constructive modification suggestions from the perspective of readers, so as to stimulate the critical thinking of those participating in peer feedback. In grouping, students with different English levels should be divided into the same group. At the same time, teachers also need to organize students to carry out corresponding exercises, provide model analysis and explanation, and monitor the feedback process to ensure that students can master the feedback standard as soon as possible and skillfully carry out peer feedback.

4.3 Teacher Feedback

Teachers can give feedback in written and oral forms, which can better provide students with modification suggestions at all levels from words and sentences to chapters. Combined with the first two feedback methods, teachers can give feedback to students' second draft writing, and focus on the text structure and content, so as to help students more critically modify the third draft writing, So as to improve people's learning ability. In the final work presentation, if it is in the form of debate, teachers can also participate in it, and consciously put forward the logical problems that students may ignore to stimulate everyone's thinking. For the analysis and explanation of the model text, in addition to good sentences and expressions, teachers should also focus more on the cohesion and coherence of the text, so that students can understand that a good article does not mean a pile of gorgeous words, nor is it only a way of commonly used cohesive words, so as to gradually reduce the occurrence of Chinese expression and thinking, the teaching effect is shown in Fig. 2.

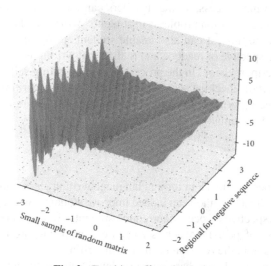

Fig. 2. Teaching effect simulation

5 Conclusion

As a communicative way of transmitting and expressing information in writing, writing ability has always been valued by people. The ultimate goal of English writing teaching is to improve students' ability to use the language. How to provide effective background knowledge input, help students look at thinking problems more comprehensively, stimulate their writing enthusiasm, so as to write independently, and how to monitor the whole writing process through a variety of feedback methods and evaluate it in a variety of ways, so as to further stimulate students' dialectical thinking and improve their in-depth learning ability, It is worth every writing teacher to think about.

References

1. Wei, Z.: Smart English classroom design based on deep learning [J]. Educational academic monthly **10**, 99–104 (2019)
2. Shuai, Z.: a case study on the characteristics and effects of teacher feedback in English writing [J]. Foreign Lang. Testing Teach. **1**, 43–52 (2020)
3. Shangzhen, K.: Discussion on college english writing teaching strategies based on online automatic evaluation system [J]. Sci. Tech. Inf. **17**(34), 119–120 (2019)
4. Yunan, Z.: A study on the effectiveness of peer feedback in College English Writing Teaching. Harbin Normal University (2019)
5. Liu, Z., Jingjing, X., Cheng, Q., Zhao, Y., Pei, Y., Yang, C.: Trajectory planning with minimum synthesis error for industrial robots using screw theory. Int. J. Precis. Eng. Manuf. **19**(2), 183–193 (2018). https://doi.org/10.1007/s12541-018-0021-3
6. Du, Z., Ouyang, G.Y., Xue, J., Yao, Y. B.: A review on kinematic, workspace, trajectory planning and path planning of hyper-redundant manipulators. In: Proceedings of the lectrical and Electronics Engineers International on Cyber Technology in Automation, Control, and Intelligent Systems (CYBER), pp. 444–449, IEEE, Xi'an, China, October 2020.
7. Torres, F.J., Ramirez-Paredes, J.P., Garcia-Murillo, M.A., Martinez-Ramirez, I.G.V.A.: A tracking control of a flexible-robot including the dynamics of the induction motor as actuator. IEEE Access 9, 82373–82379 (2021)
8. Zhengm, X., Wu, G.: Kinodynamic planning with reachability prediction for PTL maintenance robot. In: Proceedings of the Institution of Mechanical Engineers - Part I: Journal of Systems & Control Engineering, vol. 235, no. 8, pp. 1417–1432 (2021)
9. Liu, F., Huang, H., Li, B., Hu, Y.H.: Design and analysis of a cable-driven rigid-flexible coupling parallel mechanism with variable stiffness. Mech. Mach. Theor. **153**, 104030 (2020)
10. Wang, Z., Chen, Z., Mao, C., Zhang, X.: An ANN-based precision compensation method for industrial manipulators via optimization of point selection. Math. Prob. Eng. **2**, 32 (2020)
11. Guo, F., Cheng, G., Pang, Y.: Explicit dynamic modeling with joint friction and coupling analysis of a 5-DOF hybrid polishing robot. Mech. Mach. Theor. **167**, 104509 (2022)
12. Lavín-delgado, J.E., Chávez-vázquez, S., Gómez-aguilar, J.F., Delgado-Reyes, G., Ruíz-jaimes, M.A.: Fractional-order passivity-based adaptive controller for a robot manipulator type s. Fractals **28**(8), 2040008 (2020)
13. Rong, B., Rui, X., Tao, L., Wang, G.: Theoretical modeling and numerical solution methods for flexible multibody system dynamics. Nonlinear Dyn. **98**(2), 1519–1553 (2019)
14. Jia, L., Huang, Y., Chen, T., Guo, Y., Yin, Y., Chen, J.: MDA + RRT: a general approach for resolving the problem of angle constraint for hyper-redundant manipulator. Expert Syst. Appl. **193**, 116379 (2022)

Design and Implementation of English Teaching Analysis System Based on Data Mining

Bei Yu[✉]

Guangzhou College of Technology and Business, Guangzhou 510850, Guangdong, China
yongjiegui@sina.com.cn

Abstract. Driven by the current situation of teaching management, teaching managers at colleges and universities at all levels generally hope to build a more functional teaching analysis system by using advanced information technology, so as to provide more comprehensive historical data analysis functions for teaching managers. The design and implementation of English teaching analysis system based on data mining in this paper improves the management and teaching level of the whole school in the process of English teaching, and finally improves the ability of English subject management in teaching decision-making.

Keywords: Data mining · English teaching · Analysis system

1 Introduction

Since the new century, with the substantial adjustment of the national enrollment policy, China's higher education has been in the fast lane of adjustment and development. The development level of informatization and modernization in the field of education has also entered a new stage of development. Based on the basic theory of modern management information system, various colleges and universities have made great progress and achievements in management information. The most common is all kinds of information management systems for schools, students and teachers. Among the many information-based teaching systems used at present, there are many systems that can provide services for the daily teaching of the school. Therefore, how to realize the unified utilization of daily accumulated data, analyze and mine some laws in the data, and provide more real and specific basis and analysis results for decision-making and management in school teaching has become a problem and difficulty to be solved [1]. In this paper, the design and implementation of English teaching analysis system based on data mining is to improve the management and teaching level of the whole school in the process of English teaching, and finally improve the ability of English subject management in teaching decision-making.

With the development of globalization and the deepening of communication among countries, multilingual learning has been paid more and more attention, and it is very important to master a foreign language. Among them, English, as a widely used foreign language, has been included in the basic courses of education in Colleges and universities

M. A. Jan and F. Khan (Eds.): BigIoT-EDU 2022, LNICST 465, pp. 10–18, 2023.
https://doi.org/10.1007/978-3-031-23950-2_2

in China. In the process of English Teaching in Colleges and universities, due to the large number of students, weak interaction, single teaching mode and language environment, the imbalance between the written and oral education in the process of English education has been caused. Students often have high written test scores, but lack the oral ability to communicate in English, It is very important to strengthen the interactive process and oral learning in the learning process, and to explain words and sentences in an interesting teaching form. However, most of the current English teaching systems use simple audio-visual multimedia to assist teaching, which can not provide targeted learning programs for students' oral ability and classroom performance, and the interactivity is not strong.

To sum up, it is an urgent problem for technical personnel in the field to provide an English teaching system to assist teachers in multi-mode English teaching, which is highly interactive, can effectively improve teaching quality, accurately analyze students' oral ability, and assist teachers in targeted teaching.

2 Data Analysis System

2.1 Data Analysis System Concept

Nowadays, the widely used data analysis system, supported by a variety of modern disciplines and basic theories, provides intelligent support and assistance for various types of management processes by using comprehensive technologies such as computer, informatization and virtual simulation, aiming at solving semi-structured decision-making problems. A well-designed data analysis system can provide managers with more detailed supporting data, information and relevant background materials in use, and realize the identification of relevant problems through further clarifying the decision-making objectives; Then, the data analysis model can be modified and adjusted to provide alternative alternative schemes for decision-makers, evaluate and optimize different schemes, provide managers with all-round analysis, comparison and comprehensive judgment based on real-time human-computer interaction technology, and finally provide users with correct decision-making services and support.

Aiming at the problems and needs mentioned above, this scheme proposes an English teaching system for English learning, which can solve the above technical problems due to the following technical solutions. In order to achieve the above purpose, the invention provides the following technical scheme: an English teaching system for English learning, including: a signal acquisition and statistics module, an intelligent analysis module, a management module, a scenario simulation module, a power supply module and a wearable mobile terminal; The signal acquisition and statistics module includes a signal acquisition unit and a statistics unit. The signal acquisition unit is used to collect the start time and end time of the key signal and voice signal of the intelligent learning terminal. The signal acquisition unit sends the key signal and the collected time information to the statistics unit, The statistical unit is used to receive the key signal sent by the signal acquisition unit and the collected time information, and classify and count the signals and information; The intelligent analysis module is connected with the signal acquisition and statistics module. The intelligent analysis module is used to receive the data output by the statistics unit, perform intelligent analysis on the data, and generate the incentive learning scheme with the highest matching degree according to the incentive scheme in the teaching database; The management module is used to receive intelligent analysis data and store it in the teaching database, evaluate teaching assessment scores, and manage intelligent learning terminals and wearable mobile terminal devices; The scenario simulation module is connected with the management module. The scenario simulation module is used to generate simulated dialogue roles and virtual scenes according to the input teaching content and the collected scenario simulation indoor object location information, indoor space information and student information.

The wearable mobile terminal is used to collect students' identity information and perform login verification. The wearable mobile terminal is wirelessly connected with the scenario simulation module to assist students in oral English scenario simulation learning. Further, the signal acquisition unit generates a signal object and a voice acquisition object according to the current teaching mode selected by the user, the signal object is used to express the key attribute and the key signal source number, the voice acquisition object is used to express the attribute and the voice signal source number of the voice signal, and sorts the key signals corresponding to the signal object according to the timestamp order, And recording the start time and end time of the voice signal corresponding to the voice acquisition object, and sending the sorting data and the recorded time data to the statistical unit for classification statistics. The specific steps of the classification statistics are as follows:

Step S1: monitor the statistical signal. When the statistical signal is monitored, judge whether the current statistical signal is used for key signal statistics. When it is used for key signal statistics, the key signals with different attributes and different key signal source numbers are counted according to the order of key signals to form the first attribute sorting list;

Step S2: otherwise, the start time and end time of voice signals with different attributes are statistically classified according to the voice signal source number, and the voice signal source number with voice overlapping time period greater than 30% is marked to form a second attribute sorting list;

Step S3: send the acquired first attribute sorting list and the second attribute sorting list to the intelligent analysis module for learning interest analysis, and display the classification results on the display in a visual form to assist teachers in teaching.

2.2 Development Analysis of Data Analysis System

The modern data analysis system, which has been widely used in various fields, originates from the emergence and development of management information system. Here, based on the database platform, the management information system can provide services for all kinds of managers, and deal with all kinds of events in the real environment with the support of modern information and network technology; Accordingly, the data analysis system can provide more efficient decision-making assistance for managers and users at all levels according to various data stored in the system [2]. Since the 1970s, artificial intelligence and computer technology have made great progress, making the auxiliary management of various strategies and development plans based on such technology widely used. In the process of auxiliary decision-making, there are many problems to be considered and the factors involved are more complex, so it is necessary to consider the comprehensive results of various schemes, so as to It also promotes the emergence and rapid development of data analysis system.

In fact, the concept of data analysis system originated in the 1980s and has been developed for more than 30 years. As early as the 1980s, some scholars proposed a data analysis system based on three-tier structure, and the three-tier structure of this system corresponds to the dialogue components, data components and model components of the whole system respectively. Among them, the data component is the main component The data analysis system based on three-tier structure further defines the basic composition of the data analysis system, and gives the related technologies that can play an important role in the data analysis system, such as common model base management technology and complex components It is precisely because of the emergence of the three component structure that further promotes the considerable development and progress of the data analysis system supporting decision-making. After that, some scholars put forward the data analysis system based on the three system structure, namely language system, problem processing system and knowledge system. The data analysis system with this structure is more widely used It is a problem processing system, or knowledge system, which is different from the expert system based on artificial intelligence.

Driven by the increasing complexity of the problems that the data analysis system needs to deal with, the number of various models used to provide services is also increasing, which makes it more difficult to realize the whole between different service models; at the same time, due to the continuous improvement of researchers' understanding of information processing concepts and development laws in the field, in the context of more diverse changes in reality Driven by the environment, data analysis systems with higher levels and functions are needed to provide services, which further stimulates people's enthusiasm for the research of data analysis systems. Especially since this century, the scale of databases and the amount of data stored in various information systems have also shown an increasing trend; based on these huge amounts of data, all kinds of personnel responsible for management We hope to find and find deeper information and knowledge, and then serve the decision-making process.

3   Data Mining Technology

3.1   Data Mining Concept

Data mining refers to the process of extracting hidden, unknown but potentially useful information and knowledge from a large number of incomplete, noisy, fuzzy and random actual data. Data mining is also called knowledge discovery.

Data mining has become a useful and practical tool to discover the potential relationship between patterns and the amount of existing data. In addition, the combination of machine learning, statistical analysis, modeling technology and database technology, data pattern discovery, data relations and derivation rules used in data mining can help predict future trends, conditions and behaviors, and enable enterprises to make aggressive and knowledge driven decisions. Typical enterprises apply data mining technology, including market analysis, customer analysis, fraud detection, evaluation of retail promotion and credit risk analysis. A complete data mining tool set not only supports multiple methods of pattern discovery and relationship, but also provides tools to evaluate the statistical quality and confidence [3].

Further, the specific steps of intelligent analysis include:

Step S1: record the collected key signal of the same student as R, the start time of the voice signal as T1, and the completion time of the voice signal as T2, then the duration of the voice signal is TC = T1–T2;

Step S2: record the intelligent learning terminal number of the input voice signal of the same student, the number of times N1 of the voice module used in the intelligent learning terminal and the number of hours T1 of the voice module used, and the interval of the use hours C1, and record the number of the intelligent learning terminal of the input key signal R of the same student, the number of times N2 of the key module used in the intelligent learning terminal and the number of hours T2 of the key module used, The interval of using class hours is recorded as C2. The interval of class hours C1 and C2 respectively represent the interval of using key module and voice module by the same student;

Step S3: calculate the duration TB of the historical average speech signal of the same student, the average values CB1 and CB2 of the class interval, and assign the preset weight values W1, W2, W3, W4 and W5 for the number of class hours T1, the number of class hours T2, the duration TB of the historical average speech signal, the average value CB1 of the class interval and the average value CB2 of the class interval, W1 = W2 "W4 = W5" W3;

Step S4: according to the formula P = (t1*w1 + t2*w2 + tb*w3 + cb1*w4 + cb2*w5)/5, a matching value p is generated, and the corresponding learning interest level is obtained according to the generated matching value P. from the learning interest level, the highest matching encouraged learning scheme is obtained from the encouraged learning scheme in the teaching database.

Further, the management module comprises a teaching management unit for managing teaching information, student information and scoring classroom assessment, and a device management unit for managing intelligent learning terminals and wearable mobile terminals;

The teaching management unit includes a mode selection module, a teaching resource management module, a teacher information management module and an assessment scoring module. The mode selection module is used for teachers to select ordinary teaching modes and scenario simulation teaching modes. The teaching resource management module is used for teachers to upload independently edited English teaching resources, English teaching content, Download ar data templates and the students' classroom learning data, The teacher information management module is used to verify the identity of the teaching teacher and record the teaching content introduction, teacher name and professional title. Mode selection and equipment control can be carried out only after the authentication is successful. The assessment scoring module is used to obtain the matching value p of each student according to the preset scoring division range, and give the assessment score according to the scoring division range of the matching value p;

3.2 Data Mining Classification

The knowledge that can be found by data mining is as follows:

(1) Generalized knowledge refers to the general description knowledge of category characteristics. Finding universal, meso and macro knowledge according to the micro nature of data, reflecting the common nature of similar things, is the generalization, refinement and abstraction of data.
(2) Classified knowledge is the characteristic knowledge that reflects the common nature of similar things and the knowledge of attribute differences between different things. For example, decision tree algorithm is a commonly used classification method.
(3) Clustering knowledge, clustering is to achieve "birds of a feather flock together", not the same kind. The whole database is divided into different classes. The data between the same class are as similar as possible, and the differences between classes should be obvious.
(4) Correlation knowledge reflects the dependence or correlation between one event and other events. The information of another data object can be inferred from the information of one data object.
(5) Predictive knowledge, which infers future data based on historical and current data, can be considered as time series data.
(6) Deviant knowledge, the description of differences and extreme special cases, reveals the abnormal phenomenon of things deviating from the Convention.

3.3 Data Mining Steps

The whole data mining process is composed of several steps. The main steps are:

(1) Data cleaning: its function is to remove data noise and eliminate incomplete and inconsistent data.
(2) Data integration: its function is to combine data from multiple data sources and store them in a consistent data store.
(3) Data conversion: its function is to convert data into a data storage form suitable for data mining.
(4) Data mining: select the appropriate mining algorithm to obtain the corresponding rules. Its function is to use mining algorithm technology to mine relevant knowledge laws.
(5) Result analysis: the function of interpreting and evaluating the results is to screen out effective potential knowledge from the mining results according to certain evaluation criteria.
(6) Knowledge representation: its function is to integrate the knowledge obtained from analysis into the organizational structure of information system by using visualization and knowledge expression.

The specific process of data mining is shown in Fig. 1.

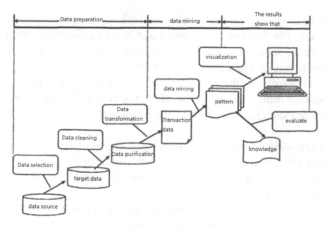

Fig. 1. Data mining process

4 Design and Implementation of English Teaching Analysis System Based on Data Mining

The existing college English teaching data analysis system is based on the database accumulated in the existing various information management systems of the school, and makes an in-depth analysis of the contents of the school in each link of the English teaching process with the help of data warehouse, online analysis, data mining and other technologies widely used in the field of information processing. For various processing processes, the one that focuses on the operation process can be called transaction processing process, which is also a common operation in the online operation and use of the database. It mainly queries and modifies the records in the database, and more serves the specific application of the school in the implementation process of English teaching. The focus is mainly on the response time of the operation Data security and integrity of processed data. It is because there are different operation modes in form and content that the demand for data in the system is also different. Specifically, the data analysis system used to assist decision-making realizes the analysis and query process based on data [4]. The system stores a large amount of massive data in different periods. Due to the lack of analysis process supported by historical data, it can not get accurate results. At the same time, considering that the composition of various historical data in the system is the integration of information data in various business systems before the school, it is difficult to accurately estimate the time consumed by the data analysis system in query and analysis, which usually requires continuous operation for multiple hours and consumes more system resources. Different from the data analysis system, in the operation system, the data is mainly the process data used in the system operation. Each operation in the business operation process is recorded. The operated data is also mainly the dynamic update data, and the relevant data needs to be processed in real time. Therefore, it is precisely because of this fundamental difference in data requirements that there are fundamental differences in the process of data management. Therefore, in order to effectively solve this difficult contradiction, it is necessary to divide the two data management systems with different properties, and construct their corresponding data application environment on the basis of the division, and then provide support for different levels of applications. As shown in Fig. 2, it is the specific application architecture of such solutions in the field of education.

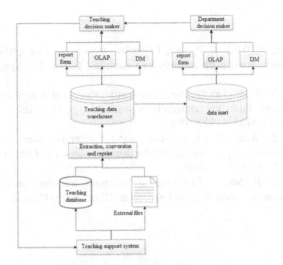

Fig. 2. Structure of English teaching analysis system

Using the system architecture shown in Fig. 2, external data can be introduced into the analysis environment, and through the extraction and conversion of data in the database, the errors and formats in the data can be corrected and unified to ensure that the data can meet the data format and quality standards required by the data warehouse. Then, the data can be stored in the data warehouse. In use, for different functional institutions and departments of the school, we can make full use of the data mart to realize daily management and decision-making.

5   Conclusion

Based on the comprehensive summary and analysis of the research background and current situation of relevant topics, this paper makes a targeted research on the data analysis system, and constructs a teaching data operation center and data analysis system with relatively perfect functions, so as to provide a more comprehensive historical data analysis function for English teaching managers. In this way, the school's English teaching managers can timely understand the information at all levels, so that the historical data stored in the database can play a full role; Through the multi-dimensional analysis and mining of multi-source data, some potential conclusions and laws are obtained, which can assist the implementation process of English teaching, improve the English teaching level of the whole school, and finally improve the ability of discipline management in teaching management and decision-making.

Acknowledgement. Guangxi Higher Education Undergraduate Teaching Reform Project in 2020, Research and Practice on flipped Classroom teaching of Business English Listening and Speaking course based on mobile platform,serial number 2020JGB456.

References

1. Maier, C., Laumer, S., Wirth, J., Weitzel, T.: Technostress and the hierarchical levels of personality: a two-wave study with multiple data samples. Eur. J. Inf. Syst. **28**(5), 496–522 (2019)
2. Zhang, H., Liang, Y., Su, H., Liu, C.: Event-driven guaranteed cost control design for nonlinear systems with actuator faults via reinforcement learning algorithm. IEEE Trans. Syst. Man Cybern. Syst. **50**(11), 4135–4150 (2020)
3. Shen, B., Wang, Z., Wang, D., Li, Q.: State-saturated recursive filter design for stochastic time-varying nonlinear complex networks under deception attacks. IEEE Trans. Neural Netw. Learn. Syst. **31**(10), 3788–3800 (2020)
4. Yao, D., Li, H., Lu, R., Shi, Y.: Distributed sliding-mode tracking control of second-order nonlinear m systems: an event-triggered approach. IEEE Trans. Cybern. **50**(9), 3892–3902 (2020)

Research on the Design of Modern Music Creation System Under Data Technology

Qin Du[✉] and Xiaojun Yu

College of Science and Technology, Jiangxi Normal University, 78 Youth Avenue, Gongqing 332020, Jiangxi, China
duqin19880122@163.com

Abstract. The innovative and diverse nature of modern musical composition has become an indisputable fact. With the rapid development of modern information technology, the corresponding computer music composition has also emerged, and the application of artificial intelligence in the field of music has become an emerging field of research, which poses a new challenge for music sociology. But while computer music poses challenges, it also presents many opportunities for musicians. This paper presents a study of modern music composition based on deep learning algorithms, analysing the trends and characteristics of this new approach, in the hope that such research will make technology work better for music.

Keywords: Deep learning algorithms · Modern music · Music composition

1 Introduction

With the development of science and technology, computers are playing an important role in music composition, and computer music composition has become a style of music. In terms of the current practice of composing computer music, there are two different conceptual tendencies: one is to use the computer as a tool to imitate or partially replace the traditional musical forms and acoustic characteristics with innovative ones. Most of the popular music and film scores are created under this concept. The other is to use the computer as a tool, but to break away from the traditional musical forms and acoustic characteristics, seeking new timbre design, acoustics and musical expression. The music created under this concept is often performed live in concert (with computers and electronic instruments on stage in real time), sometimes in conjunction with traditional acoustic instruments, but in a way that breaks away from traditional techniques to play new sounds. These two different conceptions of music, the former belonging to the category of popular or practical music and the latter belonging to the category of serious or experimental music.

Whatever the composer's conception, whether his music is popular or practical or serious or experimental, as long as he is composing on a computer, he must follow the technical procedures of computer music, and it is this specific technical procedure that

M. A. Jan and F. Khan (Eds.): BigIoT-EDU 2022, LNICST 465, pp. 19–24, 2023.
https://doi.org/10.1007/978-3-031-23950-2_3

distinguishes this composition from traditional composition in its approach (not only in its means) [1]. The computer has not only changed the technical means of music, but also the way in which it is composed, enriching the forms and increasing the scope of computer music composition. Computer music composition has obvious advantages for breaking through existing musical styles, and this is the focus of computer composition research. This paper presents a study of modern music composition based on deep learning algorithms, analysing the trends and characteristics of this new approach, in the hope that such research will make technology work better for music.

2 Deep Learning Algorithms

2.1 Overview of Deep Learning

Deep learning is the simulation of the biological brain by building deep, mesh-like computer models, which in some ways resemble bionics. It is an important branch of machine learning. The development of neural networks has experienced three high points. The first climax was in the 1940s. During this period, scholars introduced many new concepts that formed the prototype of deep learning, such as the concept of perceptual machines and adaptive linear units. A perceptual machine refers to a model that can learn model weights based on each category of input, while an adaptive linear unit can simply learn data patterns to predict new data, and its method of training weights is, with minor improvements, the stochastic gradient descent method that is very popular today. The second high point was from the 1980s to the 1990s. Some of the ideas developed during this time are very important to present-day deep learning, such as the backward conduction algorithm which began to be used successfully and which is still the dominant method in neural network training today. For the problem of temporal modelling, the Long Short Term Memory Network (LSTM) came to prominence [2]. A third high point began in 2006. During this time, deep learning techniques were not only perfected at a much faster pace, but began to be applied to real, widespread life, with breakthroughs in the structure and performance of convolutional and temporal neural networks, for example, which have beaten humans in the fields of computer vision, speech recognition and natural language processing. Even in areas of human intelligence that were previously beyond the reach of machines.

2.2 Deep Generative Models

A deep generative model is a deep network model that can learn the joint probability distribution of observed data samples and labels. It is generally a probabilistic graph-based model. A trained deep generative model is able to generate new data that matches the probability distribution of that sample. Labeled data is not necessary in some generative models (e.g. restricted Boltzmann machines, deep belief networks) which learn the probability distribution of observed data samples through their unique network structure and training methods. As such, it can be applied to both supervised and unsupervised learning. Some of the more representative models of deep generative models are Restricted Boltzmann Machines (RBM), Deep Belief Network (DBN), and Generative Adversarial

Network (GAN). The probability distributions of RBMs and DBNs are calculated based on the energy function of their own networks, and they both maximize the probability value of the data in the visible layer or the probability value of the input data of the network in the previous layer by maximizing the likelihood method. The approximate inference of DBNs is a top-down process of mutual feedback, as the human brain itself uses many top-down.

2.3 Models for Deep Learning and their Training

A restricted Boltzmann machine is a modification of the Boltzmann machine, which is a stochastic network with a slow training process due to the interconnections between the cells within its layers as shown in Fig. 1(a). 1986 Somlensky introduced a restricted Boltzmann machine, which contains one visible layer and one hidden layer, with no interconnections between the cells within the layers as shown in Fig. 1(b). This is shown in Fig. 1(b). This makes the use of RBMs for inference calculations very efficient.

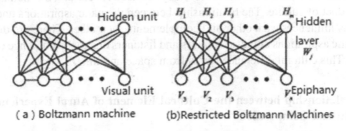

Fig. 1. Boltzmann machine and restricted Boltzmann machine

Suppose an RBM contains n visible units and M hidden units, we can use vectors v and h to represent the states of visible units and hidden units respectively, where v_i represents the state of the ith visible unit and h_j represents the state of the jth hidden unit. Then, for a given set of states v, h, the joint probability distribution of RBM as a system can be expressed by energy function:

$$E(v,h) = -\sum_{i=1}^{m}\sum_{j=1}^{m} W_{ij}v_ih_j - \sum_{i=1}^{m} v_ib_i - \sum_{j=1}^{m} h_jc_i \tag{1}$$

where w_{ij} and c_i are the parameters of RBM. Where w_{ij} is the connection strength between the visible unit i and the hidden unit j, b_i is the offset of the visible unit i, and c_j is the offset of the hidden unit j. The task of learning RBM is to get the values of these parameters to fit the given training data.

3 Elements of Musical Composition

3.1 The Relationship Between the Cultural Elements of Thematic Appeal and Musical Composition

Thematic appeal refers to the fact that every composer pours out his or her feelings through beautiful lyrics in the process of creating music, the purpose of which is to express personal feelings. The motivation for thematic appeal stems from the writer's personal cultural literacy and need for culture. Of course, different regions and time periods, influenced by different cultural and historical contexts, will show different thematic demands. Firstly, in terms of different geographical areas, the thematic aspirations change with the region. During the Second World War Madusovsky's musical work 'Evening outside Moscow' was a song composed to commemorate the defence of Moscow. The words of the young man's heartfelt feelings of victory, budding love and pre-dawn farewell are cleverly blended with the beauty of nature. From different time periods, the thematic aspirations change over time. For example, most of the lyrics in our ancient times were intended to express love for the great, simple, and peaceful landscape. During the period when our country was invaded, red songs were widely popular in the country, and the words were all about the people's yearning for peace. And most of the thematic appeals of modern songs involve the need for love [3].

Musical composition refers to an expression and innovation of the culture of the region in which the music creator lives. So the thematic demands of each musical composition are different. As the creator is driven by the need for culture, the thematic appeal is also a product of culture. The relationship between thematic aspirations and musical compositions influences each other and complements each other. There are differences in the thematic aspirations of music creators and listeners due to the influence of cultural differences. This cultural difference stems from space and time.

3.2 The Relationship between the Cultural Element of Aural Experience and Musical Composition

Aural experience refers to the accumulation of the creator's experience of various instruments and songs in his or her life. In the process of accumulation, the composer needs to rely on his or her own musicianship to summarise what he or she has heard, that is, to remove the dross and absorb the essence. Music composers often need to travel to different regions to listen to and record music with a distinctive musical style for future compositions. These recordings can be of great use in later compositions. But if we, as ordinary people, were to listen to and record this music, we would only end up remembering the simple melodies.

One of the reasons why this article considers the aural experience as a cultural element that influences musical composition is because in musical composition, the aural experience, like the linguistic experience, is a concrete expression of the cultural and musical literacy of the creator. The second reason is that music itself is a cultural product of its time, and the most common way to improve one's cultural literacy is through listening, seeing, touching and other sensory actions to obtain information and to expand and accumulate it. As a result of the influence of different cultural backgrounds, different creators will have different musical listening experiences. The difference in listening experience leads to different compositions.

4 Modern Music Composition Based on Deep Learning Algorithms

4.1 Integration of the Compositional Process

In traditional music composition, it is mainly the composer who uses the score to encode the musical information, and the singer and performer decode it according to the composer's encoding, which is to restore the performance to its true effect. In this process, the score process is very important because it does not capture the entire process, so there may be gaps in the composer's encoding, and the singer and performer may add a lot of innovation or understanding to the decoding process, resulting in the actual song not being the same as the one presented by the composer.

Modern music composition based on deep learning algorithms does not have these differences, as the computer makes the coding process easier for the composer and provides a true and detailed record of the composer's information. At the same time, the computer reduces the difficulty of decoding for the singer and the performer, and the conversion is done by the computer. All the composer has to do is to perform his or her regular performance on the keys and this information is automatically encoded on the computer, which is what digital coding really is. The computer is capable of automatic decoding, a process in which the digital signal is converted into an analogue signal. When composing on a computer, the composer has to form a unified whole of conception, composition and performance, to be able to process the acoustics in time and to be able to arrange the best possible finished product with quality.

4.2 Integration of Aural and Visual Sensations

Once the computer has received the signals from the composer, it is able to convert the information into sound signals in time for the composer to perceive the song through headphones or speakers. The computer presents these sound signals in the sequencer software interface, displaying a wide range of graphics consistent with the sound, including MIDI event tables, multitrack graphics, scores, sound frequencies, time codes and other indicators, which make composing a dynamic process [4]. The composer can see the invisible music directly and compose it at the same time, by merging, copying, cutting, deleting, copying, etc., in the same way as word processing, without the need to anticipate the sound from memory as in traditional composition, but in a visual and aural experience.

4.3 Expanding the Possibilities of the Material

Traditional compositions are usually written and composed orally with expressiveness, range and timbre as the main focus. Computer-based songwriting breaks away from this mode of composition and allows the composer to imitate conventional instrumental timbres, use non-instrumental sound materials as inspiration, and create and invent compositional timbres. The composer can capture sounds from nature, from the chirping and roaring of animals, to the sound of wind and water, the sound of the sea and even industrial noises. Based on deep learning algorithms, the synthesizer is able to collect a wide variety of sound materials and create distorted sounds from a variety of simulated sounds, breaking the limits of time and range. Anything a composer can think of can be created using a synthesiser. The composer can also use music from radio and television, VCD, CD, etc. to create his or her own musical material. The composer is able to find the most desirable sound effects through actual simulations, breaking the traditional songwriting model and increasing the infinite possibilities of music.

5 Conclusion

Computer music composition is an important component of songwriting and occupies a more important position. Modern music composition based on deep learning algorithms is an important way of creating music that breaks with the original compositional paradigm, increases the plasticity and infinitude of music, and makes music composition more flexible.

References

1. Tianxing, Z.: The development and teaching characteristics of computer music. Art Res. J. Harbin Normal Univ. **32**(01), 2251–2264 (2012)
2. Hongyuan, Z.: Research on automatic composition and arrangement based on deep learning. Master's thesis, University of Science and Technology of China, Hefei (2019)
3. Xiaomei, Q.: Research on the teaching characteristics and application of computer music, **16**(04), 887–899 (2012)
4. Pengyun, L.: "Flying beyond the boundary":A study of Liu Jian's interactive electronic music composition. J. Nanjing Arts College (Music and Performance Edition) March 2013

A Study on the Scoring Method of Oral English Test in College English Online Computer Test

Wen Hu[✉]

Hezhou University, Guangxi 542899, China
huwen4431@163.com

Abstract. With the change of English teaching methods, English examination methods have gradually changed from paper examination to computer examination. The online scoring of oral English test is more in line with the needs of teaching reform, and how to score online reasonably is more important. At present, the domestic scoring system technology for Chinese has been quite perfect, and the international scoring method technology for spoken English is not mature. Even if some scoring systems evaluate the scores, there are still some doubts about the accuracy of the scores. In view of the above background and the needs of English proficiency test teaching reform, this paper mainly studies the scoring method of College English online computer-based oral test. At present, most of the scoring methods of spoken English at home and abroad are based on HMM model, which gives a simple machine probability score through the training of corpus, but does not give an objective and specific score. The scoring method of parameter comparison mainly reflects the difference between standard spoken English and standard spoken English, which can not represent the specific score. In view of the above problems, based on the existing achievements and technologies, this paper studies the scoring method of College English online computer-based oral test.

Keywords: College English · Oral test · Network computer test · Scoring method

1 Introduction

Interactive computer-aided language learning system based on speech processing technology is one of the research hotspots of speech technology. It will change the existing language learning environment and teaching mode and greatly improve the efficiency of language learning. The development of the second generation of intelligent voice interaction technology makes our thinking mode no longer single. Whether we can apply voice processing technology to English online examination and realize online English intelligent interactive scoring is the focus of this research. In order to apply the computer-based English test model to college oral English test, it is necessary to study the methods and principles of English scoring [1].

Since the beginning of the pilot work of College English teaching reform of the Ministry of education's College English teaching model based on network and computer in

M. A. Jan and F. Khan (Eds.): BigIoT-EDU 2022, LNICST 465, pp. 25–36, 2023.
https://doi.org/10.1007/978-3-031-23950-2_4

February 2004, there has been a revolution in College English teaching and examination in Colleges and universities across the country. In terms of teaching methods, the school has broken the traditional teaching mode and teaching concept [2]. Computer teaching has gone deep into every teaching explanation, vigorously promoted Experiential English, and let students participate in classroom teaching, which fully reflects the interactive teaching concept. In the form of examination, it tends to use the network computer test instead of the paper test, especially in the College English listening and speaking test. It is worth studying whether we can successfully extend the College English online computer test to the College English test. In order to realize the popularization and application of college oral English test online computer test, it is necessary to study how to score the oral English test reasonably and the related principles and algorithms in application [3].

In April 2010, the national "high level Forum on Deepening College English teaching reform and innovating talent training mode" was held in Southeast University. The high-level forum was attended by Liu Xianghong, director of the Liberal Arts Department of the Higher Education Department of the Ministry of education, Jin Guibao, deputy director of the Higher Education Department of the Ministry of education, Professor Jin Yan, director of the CET-4 and CET-6 examination committee, Professor Wang Shouren, director of the college foreign Language Education Steering Committee of the Ministry of education, Professor Yang Zhizhong, President of the National College Foreign Language Teaching Research Association, and Comrade Cao Xiaoying of the College English teaching reform Liaison Office of the Ministry of education, And more than 20 guests from more than 10 universities, including Tsinghua University, Peking University, Nanjing University, Chongqing University, Huazhong University of science and technology, Wuhan University and South China University of technology [4]. Liu Xianghong, director of the liberal arts division of the Department of higher education, from the strategic position of education, the fundamental requirements of education, the strong driving force of education development, the national basic education development policy and the core task of education reform and development, The outline of the national medium and long term education reform and development plan (2010–2020) was publicized in terms of the objectives of the outline of the national medium and long term education reform and development plan. Director Liu Xianghong stressed at the conference to speed up the process of educational informatization and promote the computer teaching and examination mode of College English [5].

In foreign countries, in recent years, more and more investment and achievements have been made in the application research of intelligent voice technology in oral education research. The achievements of English pronunciation evaluation application technology based on the first generation of intelligent voice technology such as MIT and the University of California have been applied in English Autonomous Learning: Several well-known foreign companies include Rosetta stone, aurolog Pearson and others have invested heavily in the research and development of the application of oral English speech testing technology, and some achievements have been industrialized in the market. At the same time, the U.S. government has issued policies to strongly support the R & D and industrialization of English pronunciation evaluation technology, and has adopted American native technology (phonepass) to test the oral English level of government officials [6].

Based on the educational background described above, this topic is applied under this background. In order to meet the teaching reform of College English grade examination, it will be the final trend to score the examinee's oral English pronunciation by computer. If we can overcome the relevant technical problems, it will have a good market application prospect. Aiming at CET-4 and CET-6, the online computer test is conducted for college students' oral English pronunciation level, and an objective and reasonable evaluation score is given to reflect the candidates' oral English pronunciation level [7]. At present, tablet computers are very popular in the market. If this technology can be embedded into tablet computers to make an application software for scoring oral English pronunciation, which is similar to the form of Chinese learning machine, it will have a good market prospect in China, especially in the field of primary and secondary school students. In addition, there are many promising examples in this list, which shows that the subject is still very promising and worthy of in-depth study.

2   Related work

2.1   Characteristics of Oral English

(1)   The emergence and characteristics of oral English

Spoken English refers to the speaker's English pronunciation. Generally speaking, the pronunciation will vibrate. The vibration will compress and expand the air, form sound waves, and spread in the air at a speed of 340 m/s. When the sound wave reaches the human ear, the eardrum will feel the pressure signal of stretching and pressing, and the inner ear nerve will transmit this signal to the human brain, which will recognize the meaning of spoken English. The waveform of oral English pronunciation is irregular for a long time, and the waveform parameters change with time. Therefore, from a macro point of view, oral English pronunciation is a non-stationary state. However, oral pronunciation is generally a certain shape formed by the movement of human oral muscles to form the vocal tract. From this point of view, oral English pronunciation has short-term stability in a certain period of time, which is generally 10 ms 30 ms. For example, the consonants in spoken English can be extracted without regularity by using the characteristics of short-term consonants [8]. The short-term stability of spoken English pronunciation runs through the analysis and processing of spoken English signals. In the process of analyzing and processing spoken English, relevant analysis and research are carried out on this basis. Divide spoken English words into small segments, called frames. The relevant data sampling and feature parameter extraction are carried out for the framing speech.

(2)   Acoustic characteristics of spoken English

Spoken English is emitted by the pronunciation organ and has certain physical characteristics, that is, the so-called acoustic characteristics. Aurally speaking, spoken English has the following four characteristics: pitch, length, intensity, and timbre. The sound intensity represents the intensity of the sound. The sound intensity depends on the vibration amplitude of the pronunciation body. The greater the amplitude, the stronger the pronunciation. In spoken English signal analysis and processing, the energy of speech is expressed by evolving into volume. It can be expressed by the amplitude in a sound frame. Generally, there are two ways to express it as follows:

① The volume is represented by the sum of the absolute values of the sampling points of each sound frame;

② The sum of the squares of the sampling points of each sound frame, then take the logarithm with the base of 10 and multiply by 10.

(3) Pronunciation characteristics of spoken English words.

English: oral pronunciation is a special sound, including sound and language. Spoken English will have a very obvious loud center when speaking, and the voice segments that can be obviously felt are called syllables. Phoneme is a distinguishable basic syllable unit. A syllable of English can contain one or more phonemes. Phonetics uses phonons to represent a concrete realization of phonemes in pronunciation. The phonemes of spoken English words can be divided into vowels and consonants. When the exhaled air flows from the throat, pharyngeal cavity into the mouth and from the lips, these vocal channels are completely open, and the air flow can pass smoothly without obstruction. The phonemes emitted at this time are called vowels. When the air flow is exhaled from the lungs, when a part of the vocal tract is closed, the air flow is blocked, and the air flow cannot pass smoothly. The phonemes that overcome the obstruction of the vocal organs are called consonants. Different phonemes can be distinguished according to the different pronunciation characteristics of vocal tract and vocal cord. The pronunciation characteristics corresponding to these two points include: the state of vocal tract, that is, whether the vocal cord belongs to vibration or opening; The position and height of the tongue, and the specific position of the tongue in the upper jaw, such as the front, middle or rear. Whether the tongue contracts partially or completely. In detail, phonemes are divided into vowels, consonants, diphthongs, affricates and semivowels. If divided according to the type of excitation sound source, the oral English pronunciation generated by periodic glottic wave excitation is called vowel [9]. This kind of oral English signal is driven by vocal cord tension to produce a quasi periodic pulse air flow, which excites the vocal tract. If the vocal cord does not vibrate, but the vocal tract contracts somewhere, forcing the air flow to pass through this contracted part at a higher speed and generating other sound sources, the English pronunciation generated by excitation is called consonant. From the analysis of oral English pronunciation process from a physiological point of view, it can be seen that sound source and vocal tract are the decisive factors of oral English pronunciation.

2.2 Pitch Extraction in Spoken English

Oral English pronunciation is divided into vowels and consonants. The vowel part of English syllable has quasi periodicity, so it can be extracted by pitch. Pitch in spoken English pronunciation is a periodic feature expressed by pronouncing vowels. During oral English pronunciation, the air flow in the lungs passes through the glottis in the throat, causing periodic vibration of the vocal cords. The periodic pulse train enters the sound channel, and the generated quasi periodic waveform is called pitch. Different pitch reflects different phoneme contents, which can be used as the basis for phoneme identification. On the other hand, rhythm plays an important role in spoken English. English rhythm is based on stress. From the perspective of pronunciation process, the acoustic parameters that play a role in stress perception include at least intensity, duration and pitch change. When comparing the characteristic parameters used at the same time, we also introduce the fundamental frequency trajectory. Therefore, how to extract the pitch of the syllable part of spoken English signal is very important.

Pitch extraction of spoken English signals is mainly divided into time domain method, frequency domain method and time-frequency hybrid method. The time domain method is to estimate the spoken English signal directly to analyze the periodic peak of the waveform, mainly including short-time autocorrelation method, short-time average amplitude difference function method and so on. This paper presents an improved algorithm for pitch extraction of spoken English signals based on autocorrelation (ACF) and average amplitude difference (AMDF). Frequency domain introduces the cepstrum method for pitch extraction. This section will study how to extract the pitch of spoken English signals from time domain and frequency domain.

The pitch extraction method of spoken English signal in time domain focuses on the autocorrelation method (ACF) and average amplitude difference method (AMDF), as well as the improved new algorithm. Based on the principles of ACF and AMDF, the new algorithm makes full use of the clipping idea, and carries out amplitude clipping on the reciprocal of the modified autocorrelation function and the modified average amplitude difference function. The unnecessary extreme value is removed, leaving only the extreme value of the pitch period position. Finally, the extreme value is more prominent through the product of the two to improve the extraction effect.

$$Fn(k) = N + m_1 m_4 \frac{1 - e^{(pk_f + m_2 + m_3 - \lambda)t}}{pk_f + m_2 + m_3 - \lambda} \tag{1}$$

N is the length of the short-time signal. It is easy to see that the autocorrelation function R (k) has a peak at the integer multiple of the pitch period, and the average amplitude difference function f (k) is at the integer multiple of the pitch period A valley value appears on the. Similarly, the modified autocorrelation function RN (k) will have a peak at the integer multiple of the pitch period, while the modified average amplitude difference function fn (k) will have a valley at the integer multiple of the pitch period. If FN (k) is divided by RN (k), the valley will be more obvious. The improved algorithm uses this idea and central clipping to accurately extract the pitch of spoken English signals.

No matter doing short-time autocorrelation analysis or calculating the average amplitude difference, the interference caused by the formant characteristics of the channel will lead to the inconsistency between the peak or valley value and the pitch period, which will bring errors to the detection results In order to solve this problem, two methods can be adopted. The first is filtering. First, let the oral English signal pass through a band-pass filter to remove the influence of most formants; the second is central clipping. The low amplitude part of spoken English signal contains a lot of formant information, while the high amplitude part contains a lot of pitch information. The influence of formant on the detection results can be effectively reduced by central clipping.

In recent years, an improved pitch extraction algorithm based on cepstrum has been proposed. The idea of improved algorithm can be divided into three categories: 1. The idea and method of statistical detection; 2. The idea of nonlinear channel system model; 3. The method of combining single-sided ACF in cepstrum domain. Figure 1 is a block diagram of an improved pitch extraction algorithm based on cepstrum. This algorithm combines LPC analysis and inverse filtering, and can accurately obtain pitch information.

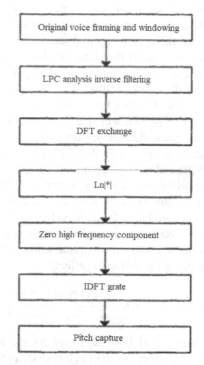

Fig. 1. Pitch extraction based on Cepstrum

3   Research on Spoken English Scoring Algorithm Based on HMM

This paper studies how to score oral English pronunciation. Based on HMM model, two new algorithms are proposed and studied. One of the two new scoring methods is based on phoneme level, the other is based on log likelihood distribution, and the two algorithms are verified by experiments. HMM scoring method is a scoring method based on statistical model. It mainly scores phonemes according to the recognition results of acoustic model, and then scores the whole sentence. Most of the scoring methods based on HMM model are used to score phonemes. At present, the common methods mainly include log likelihood score and log a posteriori probability score. The difference between this scoring method and the feature comparison scoring method with reference oral English is that this scoring method reflects the reader's oral English pronunciation ability to some extent, not just the feature difference between the standard oral English and the standard oral English.

3.1 Evaluation Algorithm of Spoken English Pronunciation

At present, there are many scoring methods for oral English. The more common ones are: log likelihood scoring, log a posteriori probability scoring, segment classification scoring, segment length scoring, fluency scoring, etc. All these scores are known standard spoken English, and the scores are obtained by comparing the similarity between the tested spoken English and it. The given machine scores are required to be reliable and have a good correlation with the scores of experts. The scores obtained in this way only reflect the readers' oral English pronunciation ability, not the best similarity with the standard oral English pronunciation.

Period duration here refers to the duration of phoneme segments in oral English pronunciation. From the perspective of psychology and linguistics, the dullness of oral English pronunciation will affect the fluency of pronunciation and the unnaturalness of pronunciation. The difference of pronunciation between native speakers and non-native speakers will also affect the duration of the period. In addition, a series of errors such as phoneme insertion, deletion and substitution will also occur when readers pronounce oral English, which will also affect the duration of the period. Therefore, the length of time can also be used to evaluate the quality of pronunciation, especially the fluency and naturalness of oral pronunciation. This requires the standard English corpus to calculate the discrete probability distribution of the duration of the relevant phonemes[10].

3.2 Improved Phoneme Scoring Method Based on HMM

Generally speaking, the evaluation of readers' oral English pronunciation mainly focuses on the characteristics of paragraph and supraparagraph. The proposed scoring method is mainly based on the characteristics of readers' oral pronunciation. The scoring method is based on phonemes and has nothing to do with the content of pronunciation. This text independent scoring method is mainly realized by using the standard oral English pronunciation statistical model and confidence measure algorithm. The statistical model usually adopts the HMM model we are familiar with. The confidence measure algorithm mainly gives the final oral English pronunciation score according to the recognition results of the corpus recognizer, that is, the corresponding score is given according to the recognition results. Generally, we call the score obtained in this way as the machine score, which is usually tested for consistency with the score of experts to reflect the reliability of the machine score.

This section proposes a new phoneme based pronunciation scoring method. The algorithm uses Markov distance to define a new pronunciation score from the phoneme level combined with the log likelihood ratio and speed normalized segment length information given by corpus recognition. In order to score spoken English as a whole and get the phoneme score by weighted average, in order to better understand the algorithm, we first introduce the relevant concepts of HMM model.

(1) Hidden Markov model (HM) physical meaning

Hidden Markov model (HMM) is a statistical model, which is a probability model used to describe the statistical characteristics of a random process. HMM is a double random process. One is the observation sequence that can be obtained through observation, and the other is the transition between the state generators that generate these observation sequences, but the observer cannot see the state transition between these state generators. Therefore, such a double stochastic process is called hidden Markov model. Hidden Markov model "can evolve through Markov chain. The speech signal is generated by the sound source through the sound channel processing. The human voice channel characteristics are divided into a limited number of parts or states with stable characteristics, and the short-time signal generated by each state acting on the sound signal depends on the channel physical parameters or speech probability distribution If the characteristic change of the channel is described by the state transition probability of HMM, it can be expressed as: the probability distribution of the observed value of the generated short-term speech signal is expressed by the generation probability of HMM state, then the HMM model can effectively describe the time-varying speech signal. HMM uses the principles of probability and statistics to successfully characterize the overall time-varying nonstationarity and local short-term stationarity of speech signals. It is widely used in speech recognition and scoring English.

(2) Markov chain

Markov chain is a special case of Markov random process, that is, Markov chain is a Markov process with discrete state and time parameters.

$$\Delta x_{k+1}(t) = \int_0^t e^{(pk_f + m_2 + m_3)(t-\tau)} (m_1 \Delta u_k(\tau) + pd) d\tau \qquad (2)$$

The random observation sequence described by Markov chain reflects the future state probability, which is only related to the current state probability, but has nothing to do with the past state.

(3) Principle of improved phoneme scoring algorithm

The phoneme scoring algorithm first extracts the feature parameters of spoken English. In this section, 39 dimensional MFCC feature parameters are selected. Then, according to the content that readers need to pronounce, the phoneme HMM model is spliced into a forced linear matching network, which is recorded as FA. At the same time, a phoneme cycle recognition network without grammatical model restriction is also generated, which is abbreviated as pl. The output of FA network indicates the matching between the reader's oral pronunciation and the standard spoken language on the phoneme. PL network is the background model needed to construct confidence measure, and its output represents the phoneme recognition results of readers' oral pronunciation. The pronunciation evaluation module is used to comprehensively score the phoneme segmentation, likelihood score and segment length information output by FA and PL networks.

4 Research on Oral English Scoring Algorithm Based on Feature Comparison

4.1 Overview of Feature Comparison Algorithm

If the standard spoken English pronunciation is known, we will use it as the reference standard for scoring. Since there will be one standard pronunciation when listening is played in the oral English computer test, usually the standard spoken English pronunciation, the oral English entered by the reader during follow-up reading will be used as the reference oral English, and the similarity between it and the standard oral English will be compared for scoring basis. This method uses the idea of template matching in speech recognition. The more similar the reader is to the standard spoken pronunciation, the higher the score is given. DTW algorithm or dynamic programming algorithm can be used to calculate the difference of characteristic parameters between them.

In the specific operation, the feature comparison algorithm is mainly used. Compare the acoustic characteristic parameters of the reader's oral English with the standard oral English characteristic parameters, calculate the degree of difference between the reader and the standard oral English, and score the reader's oral English accordingly. The specific flow chart of scoring with standard spoken language is shown in Fig. 2 below, which is mainly divided into three parts: the - part is the extraction of feature parameters, which mainly carries out pitch extraction and MFCC extraction for standard spoken language and reader spoken language. The second part compares the features.

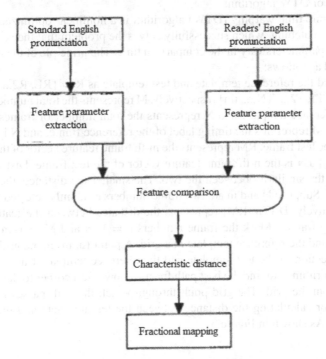

Fig. 2. Block diagram of oral English scoring based on feature comparison

According to the acoustic features extracted above, the common DTW algorithm '6 is used to calculate its similarity. Because the feature parameters are extracted by frame, and there is a time length difference between standard spoken language and reader spoken language pronunciation, it is necessary to normalize it, and DTW algorithm is mainly to complete this part of work, carry out template matching and calculate the degree of difference. The third part uses the function mapping method to map the calculated difference distance vector to the objective score, and calculates the correlation coefficient between the score obtained by the algorithm and Mr. Liu of the foreign language department to verify the reliability of the algorithm. The algorithm flow chart is shown in Fig. 2:

4.2 Feature Comparison Algorithm

There are time differences between readers' oral English and standard oral English. What methods should be adopted to avoid the influence of this difference. When extracting the feature parameters of the phoneme level of spoken English signal, the frame number obtained by the same phoneme may only be different between the standard spoken English and the reader's spoken English, or there is a time difference between the standard spoken English and the reader's spoken English. How to reasonably extract and compare the effective frame is very important, The following focuses on the common methods used to deal with such problems, DTW algorithm and its improved algorithm.

(1) Principle of DTW algorithm

Dynamic time warping (DTW) algorithm is a nonlinear optimization method of pattern matching, which successfully solves the problem that the acoustic characteristic parameters vary in the comparison time. The principle of the algorithm is described as follows:

Record the reference template and test template as $R = \{RL, R2... RM.. RM\}$ and $T = \{T1, T2..., TN,..., tin\}$ respectively. M represents the total number of frames of the reference template and N represents the total number of frames of the test template. M represents the timing label of the reference frame, and N is the timing label of the test frame. RM represents the m-th frame feature vector of the reference frame, and TN is the n-th frame feature vector of the test frame. Distance is used to reflect the similarity between the two. The smaller the distance, the higher the similarity. Suppose N and m are two frame numbers randomly selected from T and R, respectively. D $[Tn, RM]$ represents the distance between the feature vectors of the two frames. Mark the frame numbers $n = 1–N$ and $M = 1–m$ of the test template and the reference template in a grid. A point (n, m) in the grid represents the intersection of the test template and the reference template frame. Therefore, DTW algorithm is to find the best path from the lower left corner to the upper right corner from the grid. The grid point through which the path passes is the frame number for calculating the distance between the test template and the reference template. As shown in Figure 3

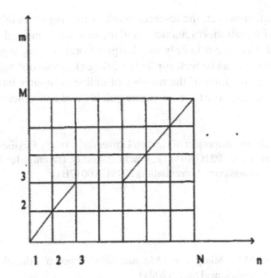

Fig. 3. Schematic diagram of DTW algorithm

The pitch characteristic curve of spoken English intonation is to extract the pitch of the vowel part of the syllable unit. Pitch frequency can be used as all the features of word intonation, but in continuous oral English pronunciation, the intonation of each word syllable unit is affected by the context. The calculation of intonation curve can obtain the pitch frequency of syllable unit, but the conversion information between the front and rear syllables is ignored, that is, the intonation of vowel part does not contain the track characteristics of all intonation. The pitch value of the vowel can be obtained by the pitch frequency of the syllable. Therefore, if the phoneme of the current syllable is a vowel, the frequency between it and the previous syllable is continuous, and the information between the two syllables can be described. If the phoneme of the current syllable is a consonant, the frequency between it and the previous syllable will be separated, which will lose the frequency transfer feature between the two syllable units.

5 Conclusion

Due to the reform of English teaching mode, the way of examination has gradually shifted from paper examination to network computer examination. With the development of the second generation intelligent voice interaction technology, combined with the development needs of domestic English level examination. This paper makes an in-depth study on how to score online in College English online examination. This paper introduces the design of scoring algorithm in detail, and gives some simulation diagram description and data analysis of relevant algorithms, mainly from the two aspects of reference oral English corpus and no reference oral English corpus. Because the oral pronunciation of English is different from that of Chinese, and the components of English words are mainly composed of phonemes. This paper deeply studies the scoring method of spoken English, and puts forward some new algorithms on parameter extraction and scoring algorithm. However, the research work of this paper mainly focuses on the scoring of some oral English short sentences, and the scoring of an English short passage has not been studied. Because it is only the design of oral scoring algorithm, it is still worth exploring whether it can be well applied to college English online computer-based examination. The diversification of the number of online computer-based examination and the huge voice database how to score online quickly and conveniently are still worth exploring.

Acknowledgements. Horizontalproject of Hezhou University: College English Teaching Reform Innovations in Informatization(2021GX0117) ; Practical Ability Trainings for English Majors of Normal Universities in Professional Accreditation(2019GX0017B) .

References

1. Kido, K., Takahashi, M.: A Study on the Measurement Method of Educational Capability of High School Teachers - ScienceDirect (2021)
2. Zabala-Delgado, J.: A Mixed-Methods Approach to Study the Effects of Rater Training on the Scoring Validity of Local University High-Stakes Writing Tests in Spain (2021)
3. Kim, B.J., Lee, S.B.: A study on the evaluation method of autonomous vehicle for fixed targets (2021)
4. Luo, B.J.: A Study on the innovative design method of rural microlandscape taking edible fungi as an example. E3S Web Conf. **236**(1), 04049 (2021)
5. Park, S.: A study on the method of reflective writing class for korean learners -based on the case of a liberal arts writing subject. Korean Assoc. Gener. Educ. **15**(1), 121–134 (2021)
6. Back, J.D., Jeong, W.M., Lee, J.I., et al.: A Study on the method of calculating the number of working days for harbor construction using the wave of ulsan new port. J. Korean Soc. Coastal Ocean Eng. **33**(2), 80–91 (2021)
7. Hwang, H.J., Khan, J.B., Ji, H.S., et al.: A study on the method of setting the water quality target level for integrated environmental management. J. Korean Soc. Water. Wastewater **35**(3), 187–196 (2021)
8. Cho, S., Lee, J.H.: A study on the usability test method of collaborative robot based on ECG measurement (2021)
9. Hongyan, D., Yangyang, L., Yan, Z., et al.: Correction to: Study on the methodology of striae gravidarum severity evaluation. Biomed. Eng. Online **20**(1), 1–12 (2021)
10. Shi, R.: The role and application of situational teaching in teaching chinese as a foreign language-a case study of primary oral english class. J. Contemp. Educ. Res. **5**(10), 6 (2021)

Design and Implementation of Key Modules of English Teaching System Based on J2EE

Wang Aju(⊠)

School of Foreign Languages, Dalian Polytechnic University, Dalian 116034, Liaoning, China
tsingxiaozhu@sina.com

Abstract. With the development of Internet technology, online English teaching system came into being and developed rapidly. Now there are all kinds of online learning systems popular on the network, and their basic functions are generally the same. They mainly realize the sharing of a large amount of information and the online communication between teachers and students. The module discussed in this paper belongs to a complete English teaching system, which solves the two problems mentioned above. It not only provides a simulated classroom environment in the network and combines English network teaching with classroom teaching, but also provides a platform for teachers to manage English learning materials through the reasonable design of reading, writing and Translation module, On the other hand, through the reasonable annotation of existing materials and the application of text analysis function, the guiding ability of network materials for students' learning is enhanced.

Keywords: J2EE · English teaching · Key module design

1 Introduction

At present, the popular online English teaching systems on the Internet mainly focus on students' self-study and teachers' offline answers. Students can find the resources they need for learning from the network for self-study. In case of problems, they can seek the help of teachers by email. This way makes great use of the rich resources on the network and greatly expands students' autonomy in learning, However, the learning methods provided by many websites are relatively limited, and the real-time communication with teachers is also constrained. Moreover, these online English learning systems are often not combined with the school's teaching courses, which is not conducive to teachers' unified teaching activities using the network.

With the rapid development of information technology and the wide popularization of computers, more and more fields have realized informatization and automation. The advantages of computer are becoming more and more obvious. It can not only provide more, more comprehensive and cutting-edge information, but also better manage information and make the access and update of information more convenient [1]. On the other hand, people gradually realize the importance of information in today's society.

M. A. Jan and F. Khan (Eds.): BigIoT-EDU 2022, LNICST 465, pp. 37–45, 2023.
https://doi.org/10.1007/978-3-031-23950-2_5

How to collect more information, how to correctly and reasonably manage and use this information, and how to make computers serve the industry to the greatest extent have become the focus of many people. This paper discusses an information-based process in the field of teaching. Taking English teaching as the starting point, this paper discusses some new ideas and models in the process of realizing English network teaching. The focus of this paper is how to reasonably organize the rich available teaching materials in English teaching and how to help students use the network for English learning.

Lynn Vanderzyl was new to learning senior high school computer science (Cs), and she wentout at this logical area— learning a programming class using Visual Basic, Python, and Java.Alas, this way wasn't engaging her students: " my grades were too small and they threw mysystem. " The next year, this class was redesigned with the emphasis on game design, withstudents working together to create video games and teach CS in this process.And it went!Games are more than simply the gateway into CS; they will also serve as long-term educationinstruments. James Staffen, an undergraduate CS study in Penn State and the former Zulamastudent, is the huge believer in teaching Cs by planning games.He began programming athighschool and knows how challenging the education process will be.

Everyone is involved in creating the next step in education but in all the levels that guarantees thepipeline which is shown in Fig. 1 and 2.

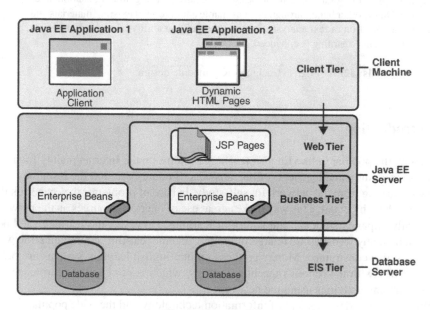

Fig. 1. Overall client

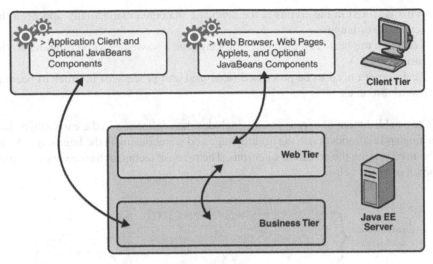

Fig. 2. J2EE servicer

2 Related Work

College English teaching in China still adopts the traditional cramming teaching mode, which cannot improve students' English ability quickly. In view of this problem [1] take professional college English teaching as a supplement to ordinary college English teaching. [2] propose a method of building cognitive student model in the network-based intelligent teaching system. [4]discuss the technology, architecture and implementation of J2EE, and discusses the technology and implementation of J2EE. In order to further improve the enthusiasm of students in distance teaching [5] propose an interactive College English distance teaching system based on multimedia technology. [6] develop an online English teaching system in comparison with the common teaching auxiliary system. [7] use the Noticing Hypothesis theory to try to solve the problems emerged from artificial intelligence teaching courses. [8] propose an English hybrid intelligent teaching assistant model based on mobile information system development, which integrates massive English teaching resources. Other influential work includes [8–10].

2.1 Corpus Related Technical Research

In the process of English language teaching and linguistics research, linguists and educators have been looking for an ideal method to study natural language and its laws. Corpus linguistics was born in this process. Corpus, also known as language material, is a collection of naturally occurring language materials. Corpus is a special database for research and use, which is composed of a large number of language information used in real situations. According to certain language principles, it uses random sampling method to collect naturally occurring continuous languages, and uses text or discourse fragments to build a large-scale electronic text database with a certain capacity. Its characteristics can be summarized as the following three points:

(1) What is stored in the corpus is the language materials that actually appear in the actual use of language;
(2) Corpus is the basic resource carrying language knowledge with computer as the carrier;
(3) Real corpora need to be processed (analyzed and processed) in order to become useful resources.

The establishment of corpus mainly includes data collection in the early stage, data screening and classification in the middle stage and warehousing in the later stage. XML can be used to store the resources of corpus. The relevant technical framework of corpus is shown in Fig. 3 below.

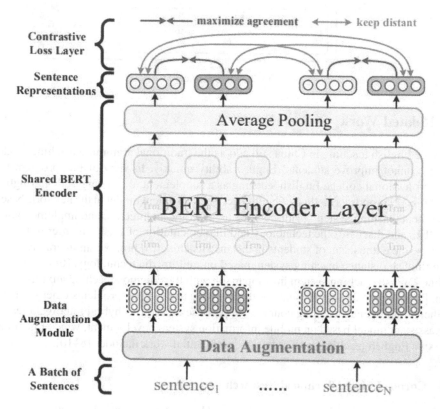

Fig. 3. Corpus related technical framework

Corpus production is simple and complex. In addition to considering the representativeness and preprocessing of corpus, large-scale corpus production also needs to rely on technologies such as network database and structured query (SQL). These productions are demanding and difficult, and serve specific research purposes, such as the development and research of parallel corpus and audio corpus. At present, with the development of retrieval tools, there are many successful sharing software, such as wordsmith toolsv4, concordancev3, monoconcord and word Cruncher; There are also many free software, such as mircconcord, tact2.1 (based on DOS platform), wconcord, concap, MLCT concordancer, word pilot, tantconc, paraconc, etc. most of these software take KWIC (context keyword) index technology as the core function, and have the functions of vocabulary statistics and collocation statistics, which are suitable for word-based analysis [2]. Because many retrieval software can retrieve plain text, as long as the language materials to be retrieved are saved in the form of plain text (txt), the production of simple corpus can be realized, and then the retrieval can be carried out by using tools such as wordsmith toolsv4. If the retrieved corpus needs to be classified or multi-layer classified, it can be realized through the hierarchy of folders. If the corpus is classified into two types: Humanities and popular science, and each type contains 10 different topics, the folder layout can adopt the structure shown in the figure below. If you need to store files in different folders according to certain file specifications, you can locate them in the index through the file path.

Even though OKCoin based in China, they have launched separate site for English speakingcountries and users—OKCoin.com. This platform is easy to use in Europe and some other countries, such as Great Britain, Ireland, Canada, Australia, New Zealand. OKCoin.com interfaceand technical support entirely in English, so there won t be any problems in resolving possibleissues. OKCoin offers both LTC and BTC trading pairs into USD. Below, Ill share a few tips forworking with English and Japanese type together on the web.

2.2 J2EE Technology

Choosing J2EE as the development framework of the system is mainly considered from the development cost and the availability, scalability and reliability of the development process.

J2EE is an architecture that uses Java 2 platform to simplify the development, deployment and management of enterprise solutions. The foundation of J2EE technology is the standard version of the core Java platform or Java2 platform. J2EE not only consolidates many advantages of the Standard Version, such as the feature of "write once, run anywhere", JDBC API for easy access to database, CORBA technology and security mode that can protect data in Internet applications, but also provides support for EJB (Enterprise JavaBeans), javaservlet API JSP (Java Server Pages) and XML technology. Its ultimate goal is to become an architecture that can greatly shorten the launch time of enterprise developers.

J2EE technology not only has architecture, but also provides middle tier integration framework to meet the needs of applications that do not need too much cost and need high availability, high reliability and scalability. By providing a unified development platform, J2EE reduces the cost and complexity of developing multi-layer applications. At the same time, it provides strong support for existing application integration, fully supports Enterprise JavaBeans, has good wizards, supports packaging and deploying applications, adds directory support, strengthens the security mechanism and improves performance.

3   Overall Demand Analysis of English Teaching System

In traditional English teaching, teachers generally use the way from vocabulary to phrase, then to sentence, followed by text analysis and learning. Therefore, vocabulary, phrases and sentences are the basis of English learning. The Internet-based English teaching system should also follow this Law and provide teachers and students with a step-by-step and hierarchical learning platform of vocabulary, phrases and sentences. The relevant modules discussed in this paper belong to the vocal analysis function of the reading, writing and translation part of the English online teaching system [3, 4]. This part mainly provides a platform for teachers and students to teach and learn English words, phrases, sentences and chapters. The platform mainly includes four parts: vocabulary learning platform, phrase learning platform, sentence learning platform and text learning platform, which correspond to the vocabulary library management module, phrase library management module, sentence library management module and text analysis module [5]. For different user identities, each module also adds the control of permission management, so that different users have different use permissions and different function entries. For example, for teacher users, their permissions include add, modify, delete, view, search, etc. for student users, their permissions are only view and search [6]. The reason for this design is that due to the large number of student users, if the permission to modify and delete is given, it is not easy to manage, and a large amount of data will be generated, which will bring great pressure to the server. The overall structure of this part is shown in Fig. 4.

Based on our proven experience of working with data driven solution, 2018 will see greateremphasis on having a more data-centered approaches to the projects we work on.Be it a workflow system, management information system or a web dashboards that we work on, ourfocus will be on using relevant technologies to harness the power of data and apply the datascience approach to provide deeper insights to our clients and users. The first step in a successful audio visual presentation system integration is finding the right avsolution to meet your needs. Those unfamiliar with key aspects of audio visual technology mightsettle on the lowest cost option or the biggest screen possible for the space.After all, the biggest,most affordable TV on the market is the best option, right? Well, not exactly [7].

In this classification, network security obligations would incorporate building system interfacecard hardware for switches, switches or PC motherboards, on the equipment side.Another illustration would be a system design who takes a shot at the TCP/P convention stack and relatedadministrations (DNS, DHCP et cetera) for a working framework like Windows, Linux or Macos.

The system users targeted by the voice analysis function are mainly teachers and students. Teachers use this function to mainly complete the maintenance and updating of systematic teaching resources such as words, phrases and sentences [8]. Vocabulary-analysis provides teachers with the entrance of resource input, resource management and resource retrieval; Students mainly use this function to realize English self-learning, including access to resources such as words, phrases and sentences, text learning based on short text analysis, etc. vocal analysis provides students with the entrance of resource query, resource retrieval and English short text analysis; In the system design stage, we have designed as many function entrances as possible for different users [9]. Users can

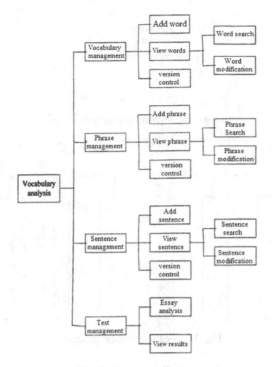

Fig. 4. Structure diagram

choose to use them according to their own needs, and customize unused user interfaces and function groups according to specific situations.

4 Design of Key Modules of English Teaching System Based on J2EE

The entry of phrase module and sentence module are the same, both of which belong to verbal analysis. The operation process is shown in Fig. 5:

The system adopts struts1 + Spring + Hibernate architecture, open source MySQL database system, Linux operating system, open source software for application server, and B/S structure for resin system. The architecture is presentation layer, business logic layer, persistence layer and resource layer in turn [10].

Below, Ill share a few tips for working with English and Japanese typetogether on the web which is shown in Fig. 6.

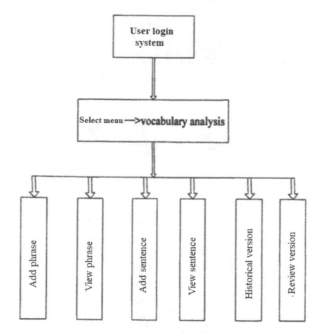

Fig. 5. System operation process

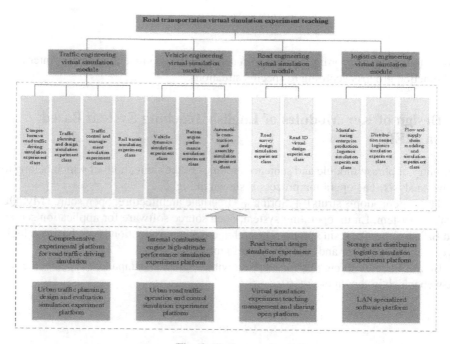

Fig. 6. Design result

5 Conclusion

With the rapid development of computer technology, network has become an important guarantee for social development. Taking the network as the link, quickly, efficiently and conveniently realize the transfer of knowledge, promote the teaching reform by modern means, and transform the traditional classroom teaching into a variety of learning methods, such as students' autonomous learning through the network at home and autonomous learning in school, which is the direction that educators should strive for. The network teaching platform based on J2EE technology is designed and developed by relying on the advantages of campus network. Through this platform, students can browse teaching contents, complete homework and participate in tests on the Internet without being limited by time, space and underground city. Teachers can also use this platform to release announcement information, release test questions, upload and download courseware, organize discussion, answer questions and other functions.

References

1. Huang, Y., Jin, X.: Innovative College English Teaching Modes Based on Big Data, Kuram ve Uygulamada Egitim Bilimleri (2018)
2. Huang, R.: A study on multimodal teaching mode for adult english learners under epidemic situation. Open J. Mod. Linguist. **21**, 476–489 (2020)
3. Dong, S.: Intelligent English teaching prediction system based on svm and heterogeneous multimodal target recognition. J. Intell. Fuzzy Syst. **35**, 2212–2225 (2020)
4. Xing, Y.: Strategies to improve the effectiveness of business english classroom teaching based on intelligent teaching system. In: 2020 12th International Conference On Measuring Technology and Mechatronics Automation (ICMTMA) (2020)
5. Zhang, L.: A study on trilingual teaching mode of English class in ethnic areas under the multimedia network environment. In: 2021 13th International Conference on Measuring Technology And Mechatronics Automation (ICMTMA) (2021)
6. Guo, X.: Design of interactive college english distance teaching system based on multimedia technology. In: 2021 International Conference on Education, Information Management and Service ScienCE (EIMSS) (2021)
7. Zhuomin Sun, M., Anbarasan, D., Kumar, P.: Design of online intelligent english teaching platform based on artificial intelligence techniques. Comput. Intell. **14**, 671–688 (2021). (IF: 3)
8. Wei, W., Lun, M., Yong-An, L., Qianqian, Q.: An analysis of AI technology assisted english teaching based on the noticing hypothesis. In: 2021 2nd International Conference on Artificial Intelligence and Education (ICAIE) (2021)
9. Wang, H.: Teaching strategies for improving English effectiveness in higher vocational colleges based on the present situation of English teaching (2021)
10. Miao, Y.: Online and offline mixed intelligent teaching assistant mode of English based on mobile information system. Mob. Inf. Syst. **44**, 133–146 (2021)

An Analysis of Hotel Management Business Strategy Research Under the Background of Tourism Boom Under the Correlation Algorithm

Yiqiong Zhang[1](✉) and Guohao Yu[2]

[1] Southwest Minzu University, Chengdu 610225, Sichuan, China
lianhui20210708@163.com
[2] Chongqing Wenli College, Chongqing 402160, China

Abstract. With the continuous improvement of the economy and people's living standard, people pay more and more attention to the enjoyment of life, and going out for tourism has become an important way of leisure and entertainment category. As an important part of the development of the tourism industry, hotels and the tourism industry interact and develop together. The economic benefits created by the tourism clientele account for a large part of the hotel business. In this regard, how to stand out from the fierce competition in the tourism boom is a problem that needs to be solved in the development of hotels. This paper analyzes the hotel management business strategy research under the background of tourism boom development under the association algorithm, and proposes the tourism hotel management business strategy based on the association rule algorithm.

Keywords: Tourism industry · Hotel management · Business strategy · Association algorithm

1 Introduction

Tourism first emerged in the UK when Thomas founded the Travelex Travel Agency in 1841, marking the birth of modern tourism, and in China it emerged in the early 20th century. Tourism is a comprehensive industry that provides tourism, food and beverage, accommodation, transportation, shopping and entertainment services to tourists through the use of tourism resources and tourism facilities. The tourism industry is a comprehensive industry that provides tourism, catering, accommodation, transportation, shopping and entertainment services to tourists through tourism resources and facilities. The hospitality industry is an organisational structure formed by the grouping together of units or individuals engaged in hotel operations. Its origins predate the tourism industry. The modern tourism industry is closely linked to the hotel industry, and the increasing number of hotels attached to tourist-oriented cities and tourist attractions has enhanced the

M. A. Jan and F. Khan (Eds.): BigIoT-EDU 2022, LNICST 465, pp. 46–52, 2023.
https://doi.org/10.1007/978-3-031-23950-2_6

comprehensive service level of the tourism industry, and both provide transport, sight-seeing, accommodation, catering, shopping and entertainment services for tourists, and share a common service target of tourists.

With the development of the economy, the development of the tourism industry has been further promoted, and people are enjoying the pleasures of tourism, while also greatly enriching their spiritual world. There are still many problems in the development of the tourism industry due to various factors. However, through the supervision and legislation of the relevant authorities, the tourism industry has maintained a positive trend [1]. The potential of the tourism industry is endless, and the income and demand at people's disposal is increasing, which has expanded the tourism market and made China a major tourist country. The country's support for the development of the hotel industry and the export of hotel talent has decided to provide a certain level of protection and talent for the development of hotels. The development of the hotel industry in China has continued to mature, and hotels are developing to a relatively high standard to provide users with certain services, so that customers can feel a more relaxed spiritual atmosphere. With the further development of the economy, hotels are also facing more challenges in the development process, which brings more difficulties to the specific development of hotels. The previous way of hotel management has not been able to well meet the current market development needs, and some hotels are constantly challenged in their development, and the economic benefits they can obtain are declining. The hotel management has been hampered by the unreasonable structure and relatively homogeneous services. The hotel faces strong competitors in the development, if the hotel does not keep up with the development of the times to make corresponding reforms and adjustments to their own development, and cannot really improve their own strength, it is difficult to obtain a place in the fierce competition in the market.

2 Association Rule Algorithm

In 1993, Agrawal et al. first proposed the problem of discovering the relevance of user purchase patterns from customer transaction databases, and proposed the Apriori algorithm based on frequent sets. Originally proposed in the context of supermarket data, its aim was to discover potential, implicit relationships between data. By analysing the relationships between different items purchased by customers in a transactional database, patterns of customer purchase behaviour were obtained. At present, association rules are not limited to transactional databases, but can also be used in relational databases and data warehouses, and with the popularity of the Internet, a large amount of Web data can also be mined using association rules [2].

2.1 Definition of Association Rules

Let $I = \{i_1, i_2, ..., i_m\}$ be the set of items, the elements of which are called items. Let D be the set of transactions T. A transaction T is a set of items and $T \subseteq I$. Each transaction is uniquely identified as $T \subseteq D$. Let X be a set of items in I. If $X \subseteq T$, then a transaction T is said to contain X. An association rule is an implication of the form $X \Rightarrow Y$, here $X \subseteq I$, $Y \subseteq I$, and $X \cap Y = \varphi$.

Definition 1. The support of an association rule is the ratio of the number of transactions containing X and Y to the number of all transactions in the set of transactions D, denoted $support(X \Rightarrow Y)$ i.e.

$$\sup port(X \Rightarrow Y) = \frac{\{T|X \cup Y \subseteq T, T \in D\}}{\{D\}} \tag{1}$$

Definition 2. The confidence of association rules, also known as confidence, refers to the ratio of the number of transactions containing X and Y to the number of transactions containing x, which is recorded as $confidence\ (X \Rightarrow Y)$

$$confidence(X \Rightarrow Y) = \frac{|\{T|X \cup Y \subseteq T, T \in D\}|}{|D|} \tag{2}$$

Definition 3. Frequent itemsets, also known as large itemsets, refer to the occurrence frequency of itemsets $\geq$ MinSup. The set of frequent K-itemsets is usually expressed as L_k, and all large itemsets can be expressed as: $L = \cup L_k$, where maxk is the length of the longest itemset.

2.2 Feature Association Rule Mining Framework

The visual description of the association feature mining framework is shown in Fig. 1. It is mainly divided into the following processes:

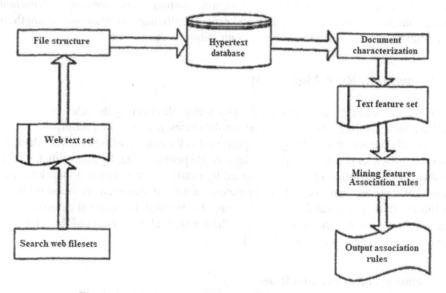

Fig. 1. Web text characteristic association rule mining frame

Next, we will make an in-depth discussion on the core module in the computing framework - the structure of HTML files, the characterization of files, and the mining of association rules.

(1) Collecting web file sets: you can dynamically obtain web files in the Internet through an information collection mechanism similar to WWW in search engines, or you can use the query mechanism of search engines to obtain relevant file sets;

(2) File structure: Semi-structured web file sets are formed into hypertext records with certain semantic structure and stored in the database;

(3) Document characterization: the text in hypertext database is processed in combination with the semantic attributes formed in the process of document structuring, and the feature set of the text is extracted;

(4) Mining file feature association rules: using association rule mining algorithm to obtain association rule set for file feature set;

(5) Output association rules: save the obtained association rules set, and obtain the association rules of interest to users after cutting with certain algorithms, which can be used for web knowledge discovery, topic learning, personalized design of WWW sites, etc.

3 Problems in Hotel Operation and Management

3.1 Unreasonable Structure and Lack of Effective Communication

The operation and development of the hotel is composed of different departments. Through the mutual cooperation and communication between these departments, we can better carry out various work. Some departments mainly include catering, safety and other relevant departments. These departments are set up to perform their respective duties for the normal operation of the hotel and provide more satisfactory services to customers. However, in the actual operation of the hotel, it can be found that the structure of the hotel is complex in the development. All departments only pay attention to their own business, lack communication, and even cumbersome business. There will also be shirking responsibility or comparison. There is a lack of effective communication between various departments. The work efficiency of various departments is relatively low and can not meet the needs of customers in a real sense, which will affect the image of the hotel to a certain extent and even lose customers [3]. Due to the confusion of the structure, the staff are not clear about their own responsibilities at work and shirk each other when there are problems, which is not conducive to the solution of the problems, resulting in the retention of the problems, which hinders the development of the hotel and is not conducive to the stable and healthy development of the hotel.

3.2 There is a Shortage of Professional Hotel Management Talents

Based on the current development situation of the hotel, the talent selection mechanism adopted by them needs to be further improved. At present, there are often unprofessional talents and even low quality in hotel management. The quality of the staff is generally low, and the hotel does not have high educational requirements for the staff. Even some hotels implement the family management mode in the development and use a large number of their own relatives. These members are often not directly trained in professional theories or skills and are not competent in practical work, so they can not meet the needs of customers, It has brought great losses to hotel operation and management.

3.3 Single Service Mode and Lack of Characteristics

At present, the hotel is facing more and more fierce competition in its development. The mode of hotel operation and management is relatively single, and the management mode adopted can not well meet the needs of customers. Whether the services provided by the hotel can meet the needs of customers will affect customers' final choice of the hotel to a certain extent, and will also affect the economic benefits obtained by the hotel itself. Due to the constraints of their own conditions, the services they can provide are relatively single, and all hotels are similar. This assimilation type of service can not well meet the needs of consumers. Once the novelty is over, the hotel will be replaced by other competitive hotels. At the same time, there is a current situation of mutual imitation in the development of the hotel, which can not provide corresponding services according to its own development characteristics. The existence of this service model leads to the fact that the hotel can not attract more customers because of its own advantages, which is unfavorable to the rapid development of the hotel itself.

4 Hotel Management Strategy Under the Background of Tourism Prosperity and Development Under the Correlation Algorithm

In the development of the hotel industry, we should recognize that the development of the tourism industry has brought great challenges to the development of the hotel industry, and the development of the tourism industry can also bring more economic benefits to the hotel. At the same time, the development of the tourism industry also makes the development of the hotel face more competition. In order to achieve a more healthy and sustainable development, the hotel industry should pay attention to the transformation of its own concept. Urge the hotel to cooperate with each other, innovate management methods, operate diversified, provide high-level services and attract more consumers [4].

4.1 Optimize the Management Structure and Unite and Cooperate

In the actual development, the hotel should constantly improve its own management department and structure, strengthen the communication between various departments, and realize the sharing of resources, so as to better promote the development of the hotel. In the future operation and management, the hotel should focus on strengthening the cooperation between wine and store departments. For different management structures and levels between hotels, clear rights and responsibilities should be achieved, and various problems caused by unclear positions should be avoided as far as possible. For example, all departments of the hotel should be able to clarify their responsibilities, so as to better meet the needs of customers. This requires all departments to communicate and cooperate with each other and exchange information, so as to ensure that all work can be implemented, so as to lay a solid foundation for the sustainable and good development of the hotel. Only when all departments cooperate with each other and communicate with each other, can we better promote the smooth implementation of all the work of the hotel.

4.2 Strengthen Cooperation and Improve the Level of Specialization

In the process of hotel development, we should realize that only by providing its own platform can we attract high-quality talents and attract more tourists through talent services. Therefore, hotel operators should improve the employment mechanism of talents in the development. In the development of the hotel, whether for senior management or grass-roots staff, we should pay attention to the selection of talents according to certain standards, and strengthen the cooperation between hotels. Provide more internship opportunities for professional students, improve the rules and regulations of the hotel's own development, and strengthen the salary. In this way, we can better protect the rights and interests of all aspects, provide better services for customers, and strengthen their service quality. Provide training opportunities and platforms for the majority of employees, learn relevant knowledge and more professional hotel service knowledge according to the development needs of employees, so as to provide more professional services for customers. You can invite experienced hotel management experts to exchange experience by means of "please come in and go out", or you can appoint employees to go out to study and incorporate more excellent experience into your own hotel management, so as to bring more economic and social benefits to your own hotel development.

4.3 Provide Diversified Services and Adopt Personalized Operation

With the continuous development of the tourism industry, the hotel industry is facing more and more competition in the development, which affects the sustainable and healthy development of the hotel. We should pay attention to adopting more personalized ways to strengthen our own development advantages, so as to provide more diversified services. The hotel's own occupancy rate will also affect the embodiment of the hotel's own characteristics to a certain extent, and whether it can provide users with more comprehensive services. Therefore, in the development of the hotel, the hotel can arrange the hotel according to its own hotel advantages, and also combine the local tourism characteristics. For example, it can provide delicious food, so that customers can have a more perfect check-in experience and provide local characteristic services. It can also provide some special services for customers and provide some private services according to customers' requirements. For example, it can send some small gifts or souvenirs so that customers can feel the warmth of their families in the hotel and like the hotel.

5 Conclusion

With the continuous development of the tourism industry, the important position of hotels is becoming more and more prominent. The further development of the tourism industry brings more opportunities to the development of the hotel industry. Due to the different needs of each customer, the hotel services will also be diversified. Therefore, it is necessary for the hotel to make corresponding adjustments according to the needs of customers in the development, but it should also be recognized that there are still many problems in the development of the hotel under the background of the current tourism prosperity. In the development of the hotel, the structure is complex. All departments of the hotel should perform their respective duties and pay more attention to the work of each department, so as to promote the enthusiasm of employees. There is a shortage of talents in the development of the hotel. At present, the education of grass-roots employees of the hotel is generally not high. Because the service mode adopted by the hotel is relatively single, it can not meet the needs of customers. Therefore, strengthen management and do a good job in the mutual connection between various departments, so as to promote the sharing of resources. In the process of development, the hotel should constantly seek relevant strategies according to the existing forms, so as to better promote the sustainable and healthy development of the hotel itself.

References

1. Youyong, Y., Jing, Y.: Research on Sanya hotel management strategy based on value chain theory. China Econ. Trade Guide (China) **12**, 129–130 (2019)
2. Zhihua, C., Xuesong, Y., Hui, L.: Research on parallel algorithms for mining association rules. Comput. Appl. Res. **19**(2), 9–11 (2002)
3. Nan, W.: Research on the management strategy of scenic hotels in the era of global tourism. Chinese Foreign Entrepreneurs **36**, 212–213 (2018)
4. Qun, S., Shengli, J.: Development of hotel industry under the background of optimization of tourism industrial structure -- Taking Jiangsu hotels as an example. Enterp. Econ. **32**(04), 96–99 (2013)

An Industrial Software Model Checking Method Based on Machine Learning and Its Application in Education

Ting Zhang[1,2] and Yong Wang[1,2(✉)]

[1] School of Artificial Intelligence, Wuhan Technology and Business University, Wuhan 430065, Hubei, China
zhangting@wtbu.edu.cn, 506532097@qq.com
[2] Institute of Information and Intelligent Engineering Applications, Wuhan Technology and Business University, Wuhan 430065, Hubei, China

Abstract. In the era of big data, the traditional industrial software model detection methods can not meet the actual needs in the massive data. This paper studies an industrial software system, which is widely used in many industrial fields. A comprehensive analysis of its behavior and correctness has practical needs and significance. At present, there are symbolic, combinatorial and statistical model detection methods to verify the correctness of the system interaction and random behavior. Because there are many variables in the detection system, it is easy to cause the state space explosion of verification; When using abstract technology, verification is incomplete. To solve the above problems, we focus on the processing of variables in the detection system.

Keywords: Machine learning · Software verification · Model detection

1 Introduction

With the continuous expansion of software scale, using traditional methods to eliminate errors in software system has become more and more difficult to meet the actual needs. We must pay attention to new software verification theories and methods. Among the many theories and methods proposed for this purpose, model detection is remarkable for its simplicity and high degree of automation. With great success in the field of hardware and protocol verification, model checking is gradually applied to software verification.

Detection system design is widely used in many industrial fields and is suitable for complex system development. The whole system is regarded as composed of a group of detection (modules) connected. Detection design has many advantages: detection reusability, designed detection can be used by other detection, reducing repeated development; Detection flexibility, modification, addition and deletion of detection will not affect other detection of the system; Detection abstraction. Detection only provides interfaces for interaction with other detection, and does not need to provide implementation details. In addition, the detection system has a clear structure and is easy to verify. The

M. A. Jan and F. Khan (Eds.): BigIoT-EDU 2022, LNICST 465, pp. 53–61, 2023.
https://doi.org/10.1007/978-3-031-23950-2_7

system has a short cycle from design and development to putting on the market. Detection system design has many advantages. However, designing a correct detection system that meets the requirements is full of challenges. Joseph Sifakis, winner of Turing prize, pointed out in his research work that the design of detection system needs rigorous detection design theory, detection model and auxiliary tools. At present, there are some model-based detection system design methods with strong description ability, and the models describing the detection system have formal semantics, such as BiP detection model. However, it is still very difficult to prove the correctness of the detection system. Whether in the system development and design stage or after completion, people can use testing to find out the defects of the system. Although testing can quickly and directly find out system errors, it is difficult to cover all possible operating states of the system. There are many operating states of the system, and the use test can only check a small part of them. Therefore, the test cannot guarantee the correctness of the system. Different from the test method, the formal verification method can cover all possible running states of the system.

2 Related Technologies

Ref [5] demonstrate a method for the reduction of testing effort in safety-critical software development using DO-178 guidance. The key objective of Ref [6] first, is to determine the potential local behaviors using sequential rule mining considering time constraint. Drawing from research traditions in mathematical logic, programming languages, hardware design, and theoretical computer science, model checking is now widely used for the verification of hardware and software in industry. The editors and authors of this handbook are among the world's leading researchers in this domain, and the 32 contributed chapters present a thorough view of the origin, theory, and application of model checking [7]. Theoretical research and experience show that when using conventional design approaches it is impossible to guarantee high confidence to those systems [8]. Ref [9] propose a description language for envisioned scenarios in the problem domain of consistency management, as well as a complementary description language for solution strategies in terms of method fragments and method patterns in the solution domain of Model-Driven Engineering (MDE). A watershed segmentation algorithm with an optimal marker is proposed [10]. Ref [11] propose a method for testing design models using EAST-ADL architecture mutations. Taking a whole plant steam pipeline as an example Ref [12] introduce the stress check criterion of pipeline in ASMEB31.3. Ref [13] present a novel method, using semantic web technologies, to model and validate complex scheduling constraints. Ref [14] propose a mutation-based framework for effective and efficient conformance checking between virtual/silicon device implementations and their specifications.

2.1 Overview of Machine Learning

At the online Amazon cloud technology China Summit on September 14, 2021, Swami subramasan, vice president of artificial intelligence and machine learning of Amazon cloud technology, talked to deep learning, an artificial intelligence education company

Al founder Wu Enda Anders, China n, discussed the future of machine learning and the basic skills that the next generation of computer researchers need to master [1].

Haoenda shared the skills of bringing machine learning from proof of concept to production on site, and quickly won the first project to obtain driving force, so as to ensure that senior managers responsible for developing and implementing machinery research strategies can fully educate the technology. You only need to quickly build the "initial components" of the first prototype system to understand what is possible. By recording the speed, acceleration and position of the working parts for many times, then establishing the data model and continuously optimizing the "training" model, and finally obtaining the best motion curve. Simply understand, machine learning is to establish a mathematical model through various algorithms, and then continuously use data to train the model to improve the accuracy of the model. Therefore, it can be summarized that the introduction of machine learning into industrial automation requires three steps: collecting industrial field data, establishing models and training models, and downloading them to practical applications. This link will be used for tools such as many products of our automation control (such as twincat3scope, twincat3mysql server, twincat3dataagent and twincat3analyticslogger of Beifu). These tools can use this tool to collect them into local database or cloud storage and display the data, so as to build the model and training in the next step. After model training, generate and export description files that can provide twincat3 and other mode operation environments: XML files or onnx files. When it comes to model building and model training, the last step is to load the model into an industrial computer or controller for operational calculation. Figure 1 shows the machine learning research model.

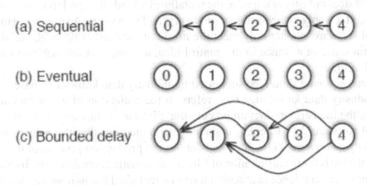

Fig. 1. Machine learning research model

The correct machine learning model should be based on the understanding of business problems, and data and machine learning algorithms must be applied to solve problems to build a machine learning model that can meet the needs of the project. It can make it easy to build and train machine learning models. To succeed in the construction of machine learning model, the most important thing is to be prepared to avoid mistakes in the early stage, and constantly find improvements and better ways to meet the business needs of the sustainable development of the organization.

Industrial software (English: industrial software) refers to the software applied in the industrial field, including system, application, middleware, embedded, etc. Generally speaking, industrial software is divided into programming language, system software, application software and middleware between the two. The system software provides the most basic functions for computer use, but it is not specific to a specific application field. Application software is just the opposite. Different application software provides different functions according to users and the fields they serve. Industrial software is generally divided into two types: embedded software and non embedded software. Embedded software is the acquisition, control, communication and other software embedded in the controller, communication and sensor devices. Non embedded software is the design, programming, process, monitoring, management and other software installed in the general-purpose computer or industrial control computer.

In particular, embedded software, which is applied in the fields of military electronics and industrial control, has high requirements for reliability, security and real-time, and must undergo strict inspection and evaluation. Special emphasis should also be placed on the design related software, such as CAD, CAE, etc. In addition to the nature of software, industrial software also has distinct industry characteristics. With the continuous development of the automation industry, through the continuous accumulation of industry knowledge, the industry application knowledge as a key element in the development of the automation industry has gradually become the main factor for enterprises to adjust the economic structure and change the mode of economic growth.

1. Industrial software is inseparable from process support
   The industrial control software in different industries serves different objects. The iron and steel industry is aimed at the metallurgical industry, and its control software is difficult to apply to the machinery industry, and vice versa. A set of good industrial control software can not only meet the needs of the current process, but also have a certain sense of advance in the control idea, and will not fall behind in a certain period of time.

2. Industrial software should be supported by industry data knowledge base
   The industry data knowledge base refers to the collection of experience accumulated in the industry production process that plays a supporting role in the industry control software. In particular, it should be pointed out that the collection of key knowledge, software, know-how and data in the production process of the industry is also the basis for the installation of China's automatic control system. Its main contents include: experience calculation formula, technical know-how, various accident handling experience and various operation experience, operation manual, technical specification, process model, algorithm parameters, coefficient and weight proportion distribution after various data are collected in the production process. It includes not only technical specifications, operation specifications, national standards, etc. in the form of documents, but also core software contents and solution tools such as empirical formulas and model algorithms. The development and production of industrial control software products for different industries are rising. The data knowledge base of various industries is becoming the core of industrial control software and the development and expansion of basic elements. This is also our advantage. Building a good industrial data knowledge base will turn industrial knowledge into the driving

force for the development of industrial control software, And promote the technical level of China's industrial control software to better complete the transformation from low-end to high-end.

2.2 Model Inspection

Probabilistic model detection can make qualitative and quantitative analysis of attributes on the stochastic system model, verify whether the probability of attributes meets the limited threshold, or calculate the probability of attributes to be verified. The attributes to be verified are expressed by probabilistic temporal logic. Specifically, the model detection logic pctl and pctl * 1 are used to express the probability attribute on the discrete-time Markov chain model, and can express whether the probability of random behavior is within the limited threshold. For example, "in a network protocol, the probability that information can finally be sent is greater than 0.9", or "95% of the probability that information transmission is completed within 10 ms", etc. Csli60l is the expression of probability attributes on continuous time Markov chains. It has an operator s that describes the stability probability of the system. For example, "after a long period of time, the probability that the message queue in the network is full is 0.5". In addition, probabilistic logic can express the desired properties of the system. The random component system is modeled as Markov reward model, and the system expectation to be verified can be described by pctl, pctl * or CSL. For example, "given the current probability distribution, the energy consumption in the network is in the interval [30MW, 50MW] for a given period of time". When the attributes are not satisfied, the probabilistic model detection method can not directly provide the counterexample leading to the result, and additional methods are needed to analyze the system counterexample [2].

Prism platform integrates probabilistic model detection and statistical model detection tools, which can conduct a more comprehensive probability analysis of modular (component) systems. In particular, an effective statistical model detection algorithm is used. Compared with SBIP verification tool, prism's statistical model detection algorithm is more efficient, and can verify all bounded temporal logic and some non bounded logic attributes. Andova et al. Extended pctl to describe the temporal logic on Markov reward model, and implemented an algorithm to verify it in prism. Prism tool uses modular language L64 to describe the system model. For component system, the description ability of the model is limited, and it is difficult to describe the behavior and interaction of complex component system.

3 An Industrial Software Model Detection Method Based on Machine Learning

Industrial software model checking is an effective method to alleviate the explosion of system verification state. It deduces the attributes satisfied by the whole complex component system from the attributes satisfied by each sub component. The combined model detection method based on invariants is to verify whether the system attributes (invariants) can be derived from the invariants calculated by each sub component. The effectiveness of industrial software verification depends on the system infrastructure or the attributes to be verified, or both. In the detection system, in addition to the behavior of each sub component, the interaction behavior between components should also be considered.

Machine learning "ml" is driving the explosive growth of artificial intelligence "Ai" applications to help software understand the uncertain and unpredictable real world. The main difference between machine learning and traditional computer software is that human developers have not written code to instruct the system how to distinguish between bananas and apples. In addition to machine learning, various methods are used to build aI systems, including evolutionary computing and other methods of expert systems, which is shown in Fig. 2.

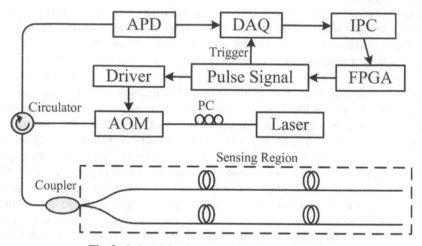

Fig. 2. Industrial software model detection method

However, from a practical point of view, machine learning is the research of improving algorithms through experience or data. Since the 1950s, the research on machine learning has played a leading role in the practical application of related disciplines, from the initial research on the methods based on neuron model and function proximity theory to the emergence of symbolic calculus rule learning and decision tree learning, and the subsequent introduction of concepts such as summary, interpretation and analogy in cognitive psychology. Programmers develop algorithms to guide computers in new tasks, which is the basis of the advanced digital world we see today [3]. The basic process of machine learning is to provide training data for learning algorithms. By using different training data, the same learning algorithm can generate different models. Non experts tend to use automl to automate as many pla steps as possible, and they can't maintain model performance only by manpower · the three advantages of automl 1 It also helps to avoid manual operation; Compared with traditional data analysis, data mining reveals the unknown relationship between data. The random detection model of industrial software is shown in Fig. 3 below.

Machine learning software uses data to train models. Among many statistical algorithms, the more popular ones are: simple Bayesian algorithm for emotion analysis, spam

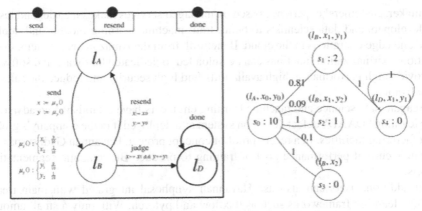

Fig. 3. Random detection model of industrial software

detection and recommendation, decision tree for result prediction; Multiple deterministic forests can be combined to improve the prediction of random forests; Logistic regression using binary classification "a or B"; AdaBoost, gas, bayuan, materials, leader and k-mease clustering reorganize data, such as market segmentation. Training in artificial intelligence and mechanical research models. However, converting data into order may be a time-consuming and detail oriented process, which may require manual processing. Model parameters are automatically learned by machine learning software from artificial intelligence input data in the training process, although users can manually change parameter values in the training process.

4   Machine Learning Improves the Model Detection Rate

From a horizontal perspective, from the free computing pool prepared for individual developers to the al model optimization tools required by large factory professionals, the corresponding releases are also available. Awsmaker canvas treats many steps of the machine learning model as interactive u to solve their business problems [4]. As a supplement to his machine learning toolkit, the head of the data science group of the application department said: Canvas enables us to share and collaborate with the data science team to help produce more machine learning models and ensure that the models meet quality standards and specifications.

This is a new type of example designed specifically for training machine learning models. With the example of Amazon ec2dl1, customers can optimize workloads such as natural language processing, object detection and classification, fraud testing, recommendation and personalization engine, intelligent document processing and business forecasting. In order to improve the prediction accuracy of the model, data scientists and machine learning engineers are building more and more complex models.

Developers and data scientists can also optimize the Gaudi accelerator from the reference model provided in the Havannah hackhub repository, including popular patterns for various applications, including image classification, object detection, natural language processing and recommendation systems. Accessing the D1 instance through Amazon sagemaker, customers' experience based on managed services makes it easier and faster for developers and data scientists to build, train machine learning models and deploy cloud and edge operations in the cloud. Benefiting from the Amazon unar system, many traditional virtualization functions can be unloaded to dedicated hardware and software to provide high performance, high availability and high security and reduce the sales of virtualization.

Seagate data science and machine learning engineers have established an advanced deep learning "DAAD" defect detection system and deployed it in the company's global manufacturing facilities. In a recent proof of concept project, Havannah Gadi surpassed Seagate's current performance goal of training to produce BL semantic segmentation models.

In addition, users can also use Havannah synphosal integrated with mainstream machine learning frameworks such as tlaxflow and pytorch. With only a small amount of code change, the current machine learning model based on GPU or CPU operation can be seamlessly migrated to D1 instance for training, which is shown in Fig. 4.

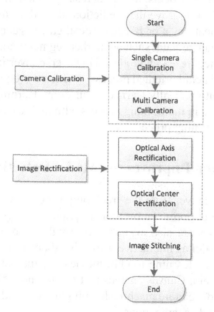

Fig. 4. Software flow chart using image proceed

5   Conclusion

With the deepening of the research on model checking technology and software formal verification technology, the software verification technology based on model checking will be gradually improved and become a necessary method to ensure software quality in the process of software development. This paper uses traditional methods to eliminate errors in software systems, which has become more and more difficult to meet the actual needs. We must pay attention to new software verification theories and methods. Among the many theories and methods proposed for this purpose, model detection is remarkable for its simplicity and high degree of automation. With great success in the field of hardware and protocol verification, model checking is gradually applied to software verification.

Acknowledgements. This work was supported by the Scientific Research Plan Guidance Project of Hubei Education Department (Project No. B2021310).

References

1. Deb, S.D., Jha, R.K., Jha, K., Tripathi, P.S.: A multi model ensemble based deep convolution neural network structure for detection ofcOVID19. Biomed. Signal Process. Control. **71**(Part), 103126 (2022)
2. Mohebbanaaz, Sai, Y.P., Rajani Kumari, L.V.: Cognitive assistant DeepNet model for detection of cardiac arrhythmia.Biomed. Signal Process. Control. **71**(Part), 103221 (2022)
3. Togacar, M., Muzoglu, N., Ergen, B., Yarman, B.S.B., Halefoglu, A.M.: Detection of COVID-19 findings by the local interpretable model-agnostic explanations method oftypes-based activations extracted from CNNs.Biomed. Signal Process. Control. **71**(Part), 103128 (2022)
4. Verma, S.S., Prasad, A., Kumar, A.: CovXmlc: high performance CoVID-19detection on X-ray images using Multi-Model classification. Biomed. Signal Process. Control. **71**(Part), 103272 (2022)
5. Sun, Y., et al.:Functional Requirements-Based Automated Testing For Avionics, ARXIV (2017)
6. Setiawan, F., Yahya, B.N.: Improved behavior model based on sequential rule mining. Appl. Soft Comput. (2018)
7. Clarke, E.M., Henzinger, T.A., Veith, H., Bloem, R.: Handbook of Model Checking (IF: 5) (2018)
8. Todorov, V., Boulanger, F., Taha, S.: Formal verification of automotive embedded software. In: 2018 IEEE/ACM 6TH International Fme Workshop on Formal Methods in Software Engineering (FORMALISE) (2018). (IF: 3)
9. Anjorin, A., Yigitbas, E., Leblebici, E., Schürr, A., Lauder, M., Witte, M.: Description languages for consistency management scenarios based on examples from the industry automation domain, ARXIV (2018). (IF: 3)
10. Zhang, H., Tang, Z., Xie, Y., Gao, X., Chen, Q.: A watershed segmentation algorithm based on an optimal marker for bubble size measurement. Measurement (2019). (IF: 3)
11. Enoiu, E.P., Seceleanu, C.: Model Testing of Complex Embedded Systems Using EAST-ADL and Energy-Aware Mutations (2020)
12. Pu, Z., Wang, J., Ren, B., Song, P., Zhao, F.: The Research on The Stress Analysis of Overhead Steam Pipeline (2020)
13. Soman, R.K., Molina-Solana, M., Whyte, J.K.: Linked-Data Based Constraint-Checking (LDCC) to Support Look-ahead Planning in Construction, AUTOMATION IN CONSTRUCTION (2020). (IF: 3)
14. Gu, H., Zhang, J., Chen, M., Wei, T., Lei, L., Xie, F.: Specification-driven conformance checking for virtual/silicon devices using mutation testing. IEEE Trans. Comput. (2021)

Design and Implementation of Learning Management System Based on User Behavior Dynamic Recommendation Algorithm

Chi Xiao-hua[✉]

Yantai Vocational College, Yantai 264670, Shandong, China
jinisi333118@126.com

Abstract. This paper studies the design and implementation of the learning management system of user behavior dynamic recommendation algorithm. With the rapid development of the Internet and the increasing number of information, the learning and thinking methods of college teachers and students have changed greatly, and the traditional education model has been unable to meet the requirements of teachers and students. In class, the teacher explains the knowledge step by step, and the teacher can't get the feedback from the students in time, which may cause the students to not understand the knowledge and feel great pressure. The existing resources can not be effectively shared, nor can they provide interactive learning. At the same time, it is impossible to provide personalized recommendations based on users' behavior. When more and more students join the classroom, their learning space is not only limited, but also can not meet the basic needs of personalized learning.

Learning management system is the product of the perfect combination of traditional education and the Internet. Through the existing classroom teaching means, teaching activities can transfer knowledge to students more conveniently and effectively. The system provides personalized services such as search, recommendation and resource reuse, which not only simplifies the workload of college teachers, but also provides the function of statistical analysis. Combined with the actual situation, the system uses a unique recommendation model to analyze the user's behavior, and then provides users with personalized recommendation content.

Keywords: Dynamic recommendation algorithm · Learning management · Data processing

1 Introduction

Network education is the modern expression of distance education. Distance education is a form of education in different places at the same time or at different times. With the rapid popularization of network, network education has been greatly developed in recent 20 years, so it is more and more widely used in modern education system. But at present,

M. A. Jan and F. Khan (Eds.): BigIoT-EDU 2022, LNICST 465, pp. 62–72, 2023.
https://doi.org/10.1007/978-3-031-23950-2_8

there are still many problems in online education. Although the development of network technology enables the sharing and autonomy of teaching resources at a low level (mainly through HTTP and HTML), it is far from enough for the complete sharing of resources. Such consequences are a large waste of teaching resources and repeated development of small workshops at a low level. Therefore, higher education press and our company jointly develop a learning and education platform for college students, and my group is responsible for developing the core system - online learning management system. Teaching is far from meeting the needs of the majority of learners inside and outside the school, and the network, as a rapidly developing resource, has become an important means to solve China's educational problems, which is favored by everyone. Therefore, there are still many basic theoretical problems to be further studied and discussed in the discipline of network education. Even so, network education is an application level discipline after all. With the continuous development of science and technology, more and more new technologies have been introduced into the field of education. They have played a great role in reform and further promoted the development of education. However, technology can not solve all problems, and the effective application of technology is the fundamental. Therefore, we should not only apply technology efficiently and reasonably, but also pay attention to the theoretical guidance in technology, actively explore the most valuable theory and constantly update and develop the original theory. The value of theory lies in the guidance to practice, which is not only reflected in the application level, but also consistent with the definition of the discipline characteristics of "application level" of network pedagogy, which is the characteristics and trend of the development of network education in China.

At present, the development of network education in China has great limitations, the function is not perfect, the application level is relatively low, and there are many aspects of application, but there is the problem of repeated construction of resources. On the surface, there are a lot of network knowledge, but there are few network knowledge really suitable for learning, and the level of these limited network resources is also uneven. Online education institutions design and produce their own curriculum resources, which are almost each set, resulting in a great waste of human and material resources. They can not learn from each other in the construction of curriculum resources, and there is a state of disorder. In fact, many resources should be shared instead of going their own way. For example, colleges and universities now offer popular majors, such as computer and economic management. Many courses are basically the same. It is not necessary for each school to develop its own resources, resulting in repeated construction of teaching resources and waste of network resources[1].

Online learning management system is the perfect combination of network and teaching work. It provides a good teaching experience between teachers and students. Through the current way of classroom learning, teaching activities can easily transfer knowledge and content to students. Various educational resources from different regions are stored in the database, and learning materials can be updated online in real time, which not only simplifies the workload of classroom teachers and provides the function of statistical analysis, but also students can provide resources, You can also obtain teaching resources and strengthen training through terminal equipment anytime and anywhere.

Students' knowledge teaching is one of the main tasks of the school. With the continuous reform of the university system, students' after-school management is becoming more and more complicated, and relevant education departments greatly promote smart classroom. Therefore, the research on learning management system based on user dynamic behavior recommendation is of great significance.

Visionlms and training treasure are learning management systems that can be searched on Baidu immediately [2]. It only aims at small-scale enterprise training, without considering a series of problems such as resource sharing, personalized learning and solving teachers' workload. In addition to the learning management system used by colleges and universities in China, the learning system on the Internet is mainly divided into two camps. The first is the question bank system platform, among which the ape question bank system, which provides users with personalized test paper generation and simulated examination based on big data, and the easy question bank system, which comprehensively evaluates users through the data of users' online practice, According to the historical data mining user information, teachers strengthen the contact with students according to the practice statistical data of students, which not only allows teachers to fully grasp the situation of students, but also provides assistance for teaching work. The second is the online course platform, such as MOOC (massive open online courses), which not only provides all the courses of coursera, udacity and EDX [3], the three major mainstream course providers, but also sinicizes many courses for the convenience of users. There are also a series of online course learning platforms such as Netease cloud classroom and Baidu education, which are well-known and leading learning and education platforms in China. However, there is no effective learning management system integrating question bank and online classroom education in China.

2 Related Work

2.1 Functional Requirements

According to the business analysis of higher education, the learning management system should meet the various needs of students' online learning and greatly facilitate students' online learning. From the perspective of function, the interface is required to be simple. The courseware in the system can be displayed on the home page to meet the query and demonstration viewing of non login users, and provide students with online course selection and purchase, It is convenient for students to ask questions online and teachers to answer questions online, and it is convenient for teachers to track students' learning online. After the system goes online, it can enable the students of the existing higher education press to realize online learning, attract more students to study on the online learning website of higher education, and attract new users for higher education [4].

In order to achieve the above purpose, the learning management system needs to carry out business planning, organically combine the characteristics of higher education and services that can be put forward with online teaching, and realize an online teaching system with complete functions and convenient learning for students. The business modules and sub modules provided by the above need are: courseware as the carrier of learning content, The function in this system is to carry and display content and encrypt and protect content. The courseware must realize the communication with the system interface, so that the system can provide various control information of the courseware, and the courseware can return the use information to the system. Offline courseware must be encrypted resources protected by the authorized authentication system. It must be able to effectively control the learning duration and validity period, and upload learning records at the same time. The learning time control of offline courseware is completed by the communication between offline courseware and authorized authentication platform [5]. The learning records of offline courseware are displayed in the system only when the offline courseware uploads the learning records through the interface, otherwise the system will not record these data.

Courseware is the carrier of course learning content. A course can have one or more courseware as its learning content. When users learn a courseware in the course, their learning time will be deducted from the allowable learning time of the courseware at the time of purchase. When the remaining class hours of the user's course are O Prevent users from entering the learning courseware again. When the validity period of the courseware reaches the limit, users are also prevented from entering the learning courseware again.

Only when the courseware communicates with the system can it make a corresponding decision on whether to continue learning. When the courseware communicates with the system, it is necessary to give information on whether to continue learning, and judge whether to prevent the courseware from running according to the information.

According to the above analysis, this chapter first needs to analyze the user behavior, then establish relevant models, collect the user behavior data and standardize the data. According to the extracted large amount of key information, LSA (late semantic analysis) argot analysis technology is used to reduce noise and matrix dimensionality, and K-means clustering algorithm is used to statistically cluster the user behavior [6], Thus, the problem of item classification is effectively solved, the error of recommendation is reduced, the use of computing resources is reduced, and the quality of recommendation is improved. Then, after the user's interest is obtained through the user's historical behavior data and its retrieved keywords, the user's interest is analyzed in a deeper level, so as to recommend textbook resources for them. Finally, the above recommendation processes are parallelized to improve the recommendation efficiency. Next, first analyze and model the user behavior.

2.2 Mongodb Database

Mongodb is a memory based document NoSQL (full name is "not only SQL") database. It is developed by 10gen company. It naturally supports distributed storage and is an open source database. It is written in Ch + language to provide users with methods with good performance and strong scalability. It has no fixed data structure format and is different from MySQL and Oracle traditional relational databases. Its data structure is similar to JSON and is called bson in mongodb database, so it can store complex data well. Its main features are: ① support document embedding; ② flexible structure without creating data structure in advance; ③ support multiple replication modes, providing redundancy and automatic failover; ④ good performance and fast speed, and its query speed is much faster than MySQL; ⑤ complete index support; ⑥ built-in gridfs, support mass storage; ⑦ self-contained distributed features, unique primary key, Directly configurable distributed

⑧ adopt efficient network protocol and high performance ⑨ third, rich support and active community, providing many optimization schemes.

Maven is based on the project object model (POM). For maven, the unique identification of a project is jointly determined by the organization unique identification (groupld), artifact ID and version number information. Each project has a packaging type, which can be jar, war, ear or POM. The type of generated package directly determines the type of project export. POM type is used for component multi module engineering. There are two relationships between projects: dependency and aggregation. It can well manage the interdependence and aggregation between projects, especially in the jar package version dependency [7].

Collaborative filtering recommendation algorithm is the so-called domain based algorithm. It mainly involves two types of algorithms, one is the algorithm for recommendation based on user information, and the other is the algorithm for recommendation based on item information. Its main features are as follows:

(1) Files in HDFS are segmented according to block, and the specific parameter DFS block. Size can be accessed through HDFS site Property in XML. If it is not configured manually, in Hadoop 2 The default size of the block in X is 128M, and the default size of the block in the old version is 64M.

(2) the HDFS distributed file system will provide a directory tree for the accessed client, so that the file can be accessed by using the address, such as: hdfs://master:9000/input/a.txt.

(3) Namenode node is mainly responsible for the management of abstract directory tree and block data (metadata). It is the main node of distributed file system cluster.

(4) The datanode node is responsible for the storage of massive data. The same block can store copies on different datanode nodes. The specific parameter is DFS Replication can be through HDFS site Configure the number of replicas according to the property in XML, which cannot exceed the number of cluster datanodes.

(5) HDFS distributed file system is suitable for large file storage, does not support file modification, and is more in line with a large number of read operations.

The specific architecture is shown in Fig. 1.

MapReduce is a distributed programming framework for data computing. Its core function is to integrate user-defined business logic and form a complete distributed computing system with its own components [8]. The frame composition is shown in Fig. 2.

2.3 Dynamic Recommendation Algorithm

The packet length of DES algorithm is 64 bit, and the key K is also 64 bit, but only 56 bit is valid, and the other 8 bits are parity bits. The algorithm mainly includes initial permutation, 16 rounds of iterative product transformation, inverse initial permutation and 16 sub key generation. A set of 64 bit plaintext is input from one end of the algorithm, and 64 bit ciphertext is output from the other end.

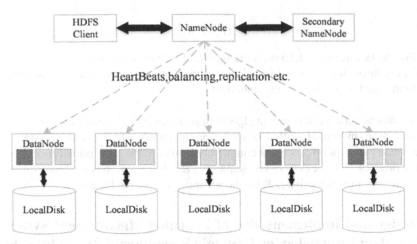

Fig. 1. HDFS architecture diagram

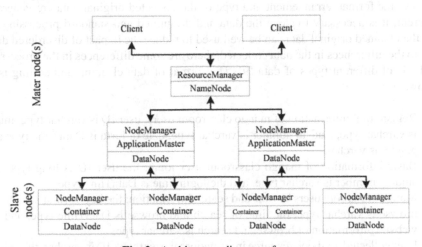

Fig. 2. Architecture diagram of yarn

A group of data to be encrypted must first be processed through the initial replacement IP, and through a series of operations, and then through the inverse replacement IP-1 of the initial replacement to give the encryption result.

(1) Initial replacement IP: first, transpose the 64 bit plaintext according to the initial replacement IP table.

(2) The 64 bit data output by the replacement is divided into left and right halves. The left half is called l0 and the right half is called R0, with 32 bits each.

(3) Calculate 16 iterations of the function. The encryption of R0 by key K1 is realized by encryption function f, and the result is 32-bit data

$$L_i = R_{i-1} \tag{1}$$

$$R_i = L_{i-1} \oplus f(R_{i-1}, K_i), i = 1, 2, ..., 16 \tag{2}$$

(4) For the last iteration, L16 is on the right and R16 is on the left.
(5) Then, through the inverse initial replacement of IP-1, the data is disordered and rearranged to produce 64 bit ciphertext.

Des adopts iterative structure in algorithm structure, which makes its structure compact and clear, and the algorithm is involution operation, which is easy to implement. Moreover, its decryption process is completely similar to the encryption process, except that the order of 16 cycles of pre key sequences K1, K2, ..., K16 is reversed, that is, the first cycle uses the 16th sub key K16, the second cycle uses K15, and so on.

3 Design and Implementation of Learning Management System Based on User Behavior Dynamic Recommendation Algorithm

Because the format, arrangement and type of the collected original data are generally different, it is necessary to clean the data and do unified and standard processing, so that the obtained original data can be well used to reduce the impact of disordered data. Due to the differences in the data collected, there are some differences in the processing methods of different types of data [9]. The format of data cleaning and sorting is as follows:

(1) Registration information of mango classroom users: user ID is varchar type, major is varchar type, student number is varchar type, date of birth is DataTime type and gender is varchar.
(2) Basic information of mango classroom user login: the user ID is long type, the student number is varchar type, and the login time is DataTime type.
(3) Mango classroom users browse and search information: the keyword of search and browse is varchar type, the time of search and browse is DataTime type, and the website information of browse and search is varchar type.
(4) User collected textbook resource information: the textbook ID is varchar, the collection time is DataTime type, the name of the collected textbook resource is varchar type, and the access address of the collected textbook resource is varchar type.
(5) Textbook resource information: textbook ID is varchar type, popularity is smallint type, textbook resource access address is varchar type, and textbook resource name is varchar type.

The above are some data format specifications in data cleaning and sorting, including numerical information, nominal data and binary metadata. It is necessary to clean up invalid data and standardize the format of effective data. The specific details are described below.

As the actual received data is incomplete, noisy and inconsistent due to the influence of the network and system, which seriously affects the results of the following recommended calculation, it is necessary to standardize the data, remove the noise and irrelevant data, convert the data into data suitable for storage and calculation, and reduce the dimension and compress the high-dimensional data [10]. The specific operation methods are as follows:

(1) Binary value conversion. For a series of standard values such as gender, Boolean value and location, it needs to be converted to a computable standardized value of 0/1, and the location can be converted to a zip code.
(2) Noise reduction. Through the numerical information calculated by the average value and standard deviation, the discrete and deviation points are excluded, making the calculation more accurate.
(3) Replacement of missing value and wrong value. Replace illegal characters such as null to avoid calculation errors.
(4) Cleaning and sorting of other data. The address information data maintains its original form, the invalid data is set to null, and the date needs to be processed in a unified format.

After the above data cleaning, sorting and conversion, the data initialization has been basically completed. DCI (abbreviation of comsysdata cleaning and integration software) data products independently developed by Kangsai Information Technology Co., Ltd. are used in the process of data cleaning, sorting and conversion.

In order to ensure the clear hierarchy and good expansibility and maintainability of the system, the system adopts hierarchical architecture design. The overall architecture is divided into UI user interface layer, application service layer, technical support layer, data resource layer and basic platform layer.

The user layer is the UI user interface layer. As the name suggests, its responsibility is to interact with users. With the help of browser, html is rendered into a user-friendly interface, and JavaScipt script language is used to complete the interaction with background information request. Among them, the interfaces for teachers include: registration login interface, course creation interface, online classroom interface, correcting and browsing test papers (homework) interface, pre class preparation interface, retrieval interface, etc. the interfaces for students include: registration login interface, classroom practice interface, online question answering interface, retrieval interface, recommendation interface, etc. The pages about teaching assistants include: registration login interface, course creation interface, online classroom interface, correcting and browsing test papers (homework) interface, pre class preparation interface, retrieval interface and other functional interfaces for auxiliary teachers [11]. The system administrator interface includes a list of resource management interfaces, such as textbook management interface, system message push interface, resource audit interface, etc.

Application service layer interface is mainly used to control business logic and provide services for UI user interface. It mainly includes the following functions: creating courses, preparing lessons, attending classes, experiments, reviewing assignments, course question bank, teaching summary, discussion area, adding courses, browsing documents, classroom answers, submitting experiments, completing assignments, uploading exercises, sharing resources, recommending resources, reviewing, reporting resources, resource management, resource retrieval, etc.

Technical support layer: use mature technology to build a system platform to provide service support, mainly including multimedia engine, report engine, search engine, teaching interaction, web crawler, data collection, data mining, data analysis, etc.

Basic platform: the hardware equipment mainly used in the system platform, mainly including MySQL database cluster, mongdb database cluster, web server cluster, distributed file system, cache server redis and other basic platform facilities.

Among them, I am responsible for the creation of courses, lesson preparation, class, course question bank, teaching summary, discussion area, adding courses, browsing documents, classroom answers, uploading exercises, sharing resources, recommending resources, reviewing and reporting resources, the realization of resource management functions, ffmpeg video conversion, webmagic web crawler The construction of open source multidimensional data platform saiku, the establishment of multidimensional database model and a series of technical applications such as recommendation module.

4   System Implementation

This function is mainly to extract the key information in the user's behavior log record, and use MapReduce in the big data framework to parallelize this function. First, create the preprocessmapper class and inherit the mapper class, override the map method, and then split the text file. Then send the standardized data to the preprocessreducer class. The preprocessreducer class summarizes mapper's results and connects them with ":", uses the user ID as the key and the behavior summary results as the value, and outputs them to the distributed file system. The specific code implementation of the preprocessmapper class is shown in Fig. 3:

```
map(uid, bookIds){
    for (bookid: bookIds) {
        context.write(bookid, uid);//
    }
}
```

Fig. 3. Preprocessmapper class specific code

It is mainly composed of application layer, service layer, data processing layer and database. The application layer is divided into foreground application interface and background application interface. The service layer is all business logic processing layers. The data processing service layer is divided into five parts: learning record processing service, general data processing service, other basic services, user authority management service and external interface service, The database consists of three data services: learning record database, core database and user database [12].

Before the establishment of the project, in the project planning stage, the project team made a comprehensive comparison between the development tools and the actual needs, and decided to adopt the combination of cocoon framework and java servlet language. Cocoon framework is a sub project of Apache, which can be seamlessly combined with java servlet. The system plans to query the database with java servlet for business processing, and finally provide cocoon with the required XML output data file. Cocoon organizes the front-end business processing according to the data file output by java servlet and formats it into the pages required by the foreground. In this way, the combination of cocoon and java servlet can make each functional component unitized, which is conducive to development, And later maintenance and upgrading. Cocoon is rarely used in China, and there is a lack of relevant documentation. However, the current technology can be well applied, but we need to explore and find a more effective combination scheme with servlet. Improve the overall performance of the website [13].

Developing projects with cocoon can greatly facilitate developers and is conducive to the healthy and stable progress of the project. The project design adopts the method of outputting XML format data files in the background and outputting static pages in XML format by foreground cocoon. In this way, a stable, efficient and portable background language is needed to support the generation of XML data files. It is the best choice to choose javaservlet as the underlying background development, because javaservlet and cocoon can be well combined. The pipeline in the learning management system is shown in Fig. 4 below.

```
<map:match pattern="*/*">
    <map:generate type="request-extend" />
    <map:transform src="getparameter.xslt" >
        <map:parameter name="file" value="{0}.xml" />
    </map:transform>
    <map:transform type="xinclude" />
    <map:transform src="pagexml2html.xsl" >
        <map:parameter name="basecontext" value="${basecontext}" />
        <map:parameter name="service" value="${service}" />
        <map:parameter name="sessionid" value="{session-attr:sessionid}" />
        <map:parameter name="currenttoken" value="{session-attr:token}" />
    </map:transform>
    <map:transform type="xinclude-extend" />
    <map:serialize type="html"/>
</map:match>
```

Fig. 4. Learn the pipeline code in the management system

5 Conclusion

This paper studies the design and implementation of the learning management system of user behavior dynamic recommendation algorithm. With the online operation of the online learning management system, the learning management system is a construction project based on the Internet. Combined with the actual situation, SSM (Spring +

springmvc + mybatis) framework is selected for the construction of the system, because it is a relatively mature framework at present. Spring is a lightweight control inversion and aspect oriented container framework. With the efficient operation of online learning management system, higher education press has made unique advantages in online education and further consolidated its position in the industry. More and more users have registered in the learning management system, studied in the system and purchased their favorite courseware. On the other hand, the online learning management system has increased the user viscosity of Higher Education Publishing House, making more and more users choose to study in Higher Education Publishing House. The purpose of learning management system is to improve the efficiency of teachers and students, enhance the interaction between teachers and students, strengthen the reuse of resources, and establish a good learning environment for teachers and students.

References

1. Wan, Z.: Google classroom: Malaysian University students' attitudes towards its use as learning management system. In: First International Conference on Science, Technology, Engineering and Industrial Revolution (ICSTEIR 2020) (2021)
2. Suriya, H.P., Zainudin, M., Yektiana, S.: Pedagogical competence of mathematics education lectures using LMS (Learning Management System) moodle in the era Covid-19. Jurnal Math Educator Nusantara Wahana Publikasi Karya Tulis Ilmiah di Bidang Pendidikan Matematika 7(1), 64–80 (2021)
3. Ardan, T., Zahra, D.F., Junaedi, F.R., et al.: Dokumentasi Software Testing Berstandar IEEE 829–2008 untuk Learning Management System Fakultas Ilmu Komputer Universitas Subang. Multinetics 6(2), 179–191 (2021)
4. Shanika, S., Amandi, D.: The student perspective on usability of learning management system at University of Sri Jayewardenepura. In: 18th Research Sessions Faculty of Management Studies and Commerce (FMSC) (2021)
5. Chen, J., Wang, B., Ouyang, Z., et al.: Dynamic clustering collaborative filtering recommendation algorithm based on double-layer network. Int. J. Mach. Learn. Cybern. 12(1), 1–17 (2021)
6. Chen, G., Zeng, F., Zhang, J., et al.: An adaptive trust model based on recommendation filtering algorithm for the Internet of Things systems. Comput. Netw. 190(15), 107952 (2021)
7. Garg, N., Ratnarajah, T.: Random-Mode Frank-Wolfe algorithm for tensor completion in wireless edge caching (2021)
8. Liu, M., Tu, Z., Xu, X., et al.: DySR: a dynamic representation learning and aligning based model for service bundle recommendation (2021)
9. Adzharuddin, N.: Learning management system (LMS) among university students: does it work? Int. J. e-Educ. e-Bus. e-Manage. e-Learn. 3, 248–252 (2013)
10. Popescu, E., Trigano, P., BadiCa, C.: Evaluation of a learning management system for adaptivity purposes. In: International Multi-conference on Computing in the Global Information Technology, p. 9. IEEE Computer Society (2007)
11. Lansari, A., Tubaishat, A., Al-Rawi, A.: Using a learning management system to foster independent learning in an outcome-based university: a gulf perspective. Issues Informing Sci. Inf. Technol. 7, 73 (2010)
12. Awang, N.B., Darus, M.: Evaluation of an open source learning management system: claroline. Procedia. Soc. Behav. Sci. 67, 416–426 (2012)
13. Arumugam, R., Yahya, D., Rozalina, K., et al.: Usage of learning management system (Moodle) among postgraduate students: UTAUT model. Asian Soc. Sci. 10(14), 186–192 (2014)

Design and Implementation of Oral Training System Based on Automatic Speech Evaluation

Zhengzhong Pan[✉]

Department of Foreign Languages, Jiangxi Teachers College, Yingtan 335000, Jiangxi, China
juanpan520.good@163.com

Abstract. With the development of human-computer interaction technology, autonomous learning using computer-aided language learning system (call) has become an important learning method for students' English learning. Oral learning only helps you on the road. As for the latter, it depends on yourself, And to this extent, adults are fully capable of summing up their own learning experience and methods, and counseling appears in the form of mutual communication. Aiming at the application of speech recognition technology in oral English training system, according to the characteristics of voiced pronunciation, each syllable must have voiced part and voiced pronunciation energy is large, an improvement of HMM Speech automatic segmentation algorithm is proposed; It is proposed to evaluate the quality of oral pronunciation from the three dimensions of correctness, rhythm and fluency, which better ensures the authority of the evaluation results, and makes the results of machine evaluation and expert evaluation have high likelihood. The research on speech signal and speech recognition is not only an important research content.

Keywords: Automatic language · Speech recognition · Oral training · System design

1 Introduction

As the most widely used language in the world, English has become an indispen.

The function of a few oral pronunciation learning software is relatively single, which can only carry out simple repeated operations such as pronunciation and reading, lack of effective evaluation and feedback, and the training effect is not ideal.

In the past two decades, the rapid development of computer technology, network technology and electronic information technology has provided a good opportunity for English teaching reform. It has become an inevitable development trend for colleges and universities to carry out English teaching reform with the help of computer-assisted language learning (call) system. The mature application of human-computer interaction technology and voice processing technology in call system makes the ways of language learning more diversified, and practitioners can learn in a virtual environment similar to the real environment. In social practice, the use of language includes listening, speaking,

M. A. Jan and F. Khan (Eds.): BigIoT-EDU 2022, LNICST 465, pp. 73–84, 2023.
https://doi.org/10.1007/978-3-031-23950-2_9

reading and writing, in which listening and speaking is the foundation of language. Call system has become the best way of oral learning. In the oral learning of call system, the evaluation of pronunciation quality is the most key technology. It uses the computer to evaluate the learners' oral pronunciation by using the voice processing technology to replace the evaluation of experts. Therefore, the evaluation result of computer is required to be accurate and can reach the level of expert evaluation. At present, many speech scoring mechanisms of call system are based on extracting the acoustic features of speech signal. This evaluation mechanism ignores some information hidden by the features of speech signal in other aspects. Therefore, the study of a better voice scoring mechanism to achieve a more accurate evaluation of the learners' oral pronunciation can better help the learners find the shortcomings of their oral pronunciation, better improve the efficiency of the learners' oral English learning and improve the effect of oral English learning.

Oral English is an important tool to realize communication and exchange between people, and oral English level is an important standard to measure conversational ability. With the implementation of the new curriculum reform, China's current English teaching pays more and more attention to the cultivation of communicative ability such as English listening and speaking, and more and more English learners pay more and more attention to their oral ability, Oral English teaching has become one of the important research fields of applied language.

However, as a non-native second language, oral English teaching is weak in English teaching. There are many factors that lead to the poor effect of students' oral English learning, which leads to a large number of primary and secondary school students and even college graduates in China who are still "dumb" who can only write but not speak after more than ten years of English learning. There are many factors, including teachers, There are also student factors. Under the traditional teaching conditions, the only place for communication training is the classroom or English corner. Oral English teaching can only be seen, read and mechanically imitated. Teachers usually only use blackboards and books to provide students with a real language communication environment. Most of the time, teachers are talking and students are listening. Teachers pay attention to the teaching of knowledge and ignore the cultivation of oral communication ability. There are few opportunities for students to speak. These boring "cramming" teaching methods, which are completely divorced from the context, let students speak for the sake of speaking, and do not mobilize students' enthusiasm for active participation in the real sense [1]. Therefore, it is impossible to effectively improve students' verbal communication ability. In addition, a series of tests such as the high school entrance examination and the college entrance examination make students blindly pursue their grades, while the proportion of English oral test scores is much less than that of written test, which makes students mistakenly think that reading and writing are more important than speaking. However, this violates the gradual law of learning language from listening, speaking, to reading and writing. Therefore, "dumb English" has become the primary problem to be solved urgently in China's current English teaching.

2 Related Work

2.1 Basic Principles of Speech Recognition

The general recognition process is divided into: speech signal preprocessing, feature parameter extraction, reference model training, pattern matching (recognition), rule judgment, and output recognition results (as shown in Fig. 1).

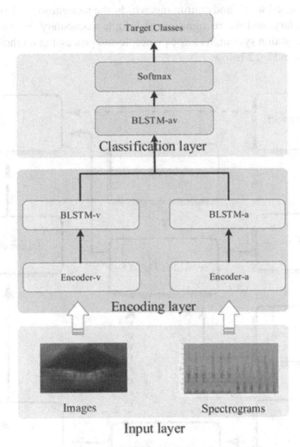

Fig. 1. Schematic diagram of speech recognition

Speech signal processing mainly includes the sampling of speech signal, anti aliasing filtering, the removal of the influence of individual pronunciation differences, and the influence of noise caused by environment and hardware equipment. At the same time, speech signal processing also involves the selection of speech recognition primitives and endpoint detection.

Speech signal feature extraction is mainly used to extract the acoustic parameters that reflect the essential features of speech, such as average energy, average zero crossing rate, formant, etc., for acoustic model processing. The extracted special parameters must meet the following requirements:

The language model includes a grammar network composed of speech recognition commands or a language model composed of statistical methods. For the input signal, language processing finds the word string that can output the signal with the maximum probability according to the acoustics, language model and expert knowledge (such as word formation rules, grammatical rules, semantic rules, etc.)[2].

According to the different applications in practice, the speech recognition system can be divided into: the recognition of specific people and non-specific people, the recognition of isolated words and continuous words, the recognition of small vocabulary and large vocabulary, and the recognition of infinite vocabulary. However, no matter what kind of recognition system, its basic principle and processing method are generally similar, as shown in Fig. 2 below.

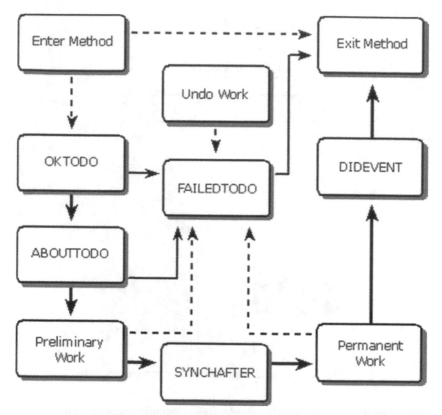

Fig. 2. Forward algorithm probability transition diagram

Pattern matching: match the unknown patterns with the existing model base one by one through the original set standards, so as to obtain the best matching.

Training of acoustic model: after processing the characteristic parameters according to certain standards, the model parameters that can represent the characteristics of these modes are extracted from a large number of known modes to form a template library.

In speech recognition, the main technologies applied to pattern matching and acoustic model training are: dynamic time warping (DTW), hidden Markov model (HMM), artificial neural network (ANN).

HMM is a parameter representation of the time-varying characteristics of language signals. The statistical characteristics of signals are described by two interrelated random processes [3]. The model parameters include HMM topology, state transition probability and a set of random functions describing the statistical characteristics of observation symbols.

The application of ANN in speech recognition system is a research hotspot at present. The network is essentially an adaptive nonlinear dynamic system, which simulates the basic principle of human brain neuron activity, and has the abilities of learning, memory, judgment, association, comparison, reasoning, generalization and so on.

Compared with HMM and ANN, DTW is an earlier pattern matching and model training technology. It successfully solves the problem of unequal time length in the comparison of speech signal characteristic parameter sequence by using dynamic programming method, and obtains good performance in isolated word speech recognition. However, because it is not suitable for continuous speech large vocabulary speech recognition system, it has been replaced by HMM and ANN.

2.2 Analog Signal Digitization

Speech recognition based on Hidden Markov model, on the one hand, uses the hidden state to correspond to the relatively stable pronunciation units in the acoustic layer, and describes the changes of pronunciation through state transition and state residence; On the other hand, the probability calculation model is introduced. The probability density function is used to calculate the output probability of speech feature parameters to HMM model. The recognition result is determined by finding the best state sequence of the function and taking the maximum a posteriori probability as the criterion.

The technical difficulty of speech recognition is how to carry out acoustic analysis, which includes preprocessing and feature extraction. Finally, the feature vector of speech signal in frame is obtained to prepare for HMM model modeling and training. Speech signal is a one-dimensional analog signal, and its amplitude changes continuously with time. Only after digital processing can the signal be analyzed by computer. That is, the digitization of speech signal is the premise of digital processing. The processing process of speech signal digitization includes sampling and quantization. After these two processes, the digital signal with discrete time and amplitude can be obtained.

Automatic speech segmentation algorithms have different classification methods: Based on ASR (automatic speech recognition) algorithm and boundary detection technology.

1) Based on boundary detection algorithm
This algorithm mainly adopts similar edge detection technology, uses some feature information with high resolution in time domain or frequency domain, and determines the boundary points according to a certain detection mechanism according to

its variation characteristics in time domain. The commonly used characteristic information includes short-time energy, zero crossing rate, etc. The algorithm is simple and fast, but the accuracy is poor[4].

2) ASR algorithm

At present, this kind of algorithm is the most mature and has the best application effect. The package mainly includes dynamic time warping (DTW) algorithm and hidden Markov model (HMM) algorithm. Such time-dependent processing means usually use a finite length window sequence {w (m)} to intercept a speech signal for analysis, and let the window to analyze the signal near a certain time. Its general formula is:

$$Q_n = \sum_{m=-\infty}^{x} T[x(m)]^* w(n-m) \qquad (1)$$

where $T[]$ represents a certain operation, and $[x(m)]^*$ is the input signal sequence, as shown in Fig. 3 below.

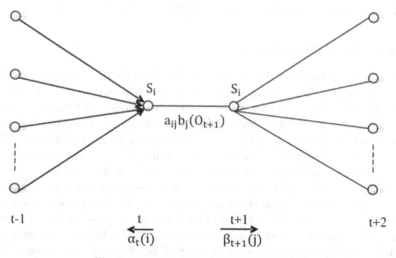

Fig. 3. Algorithm calculation training plan

2.3 Voice Endpoint Detection

HMM training method is one of the important factors affecting the effect of automatic segmentation. This is because based on the statistical method, how to select the appropriate training data and methods is the key to ensure the statistical processing method, which can truly reflect the characteristics of the training data and maximize the characteristics of the data to be processed. Common methods to improve performance include[5]:

1) HMM is trained by speech data after segment segmentation, which is also called restricted HMM.

Training and test results show that this method can greatly improve the segmentation accuracy; It separates the two by using the property that the convoluted components of the signal can be separated after proper homomorphic filtering (as shown in Fig. 4).

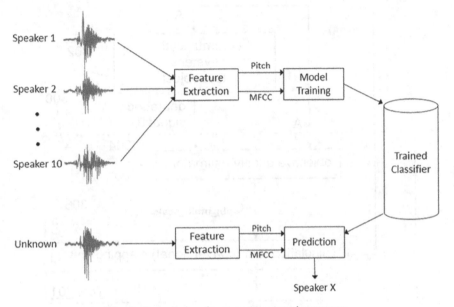

Fig. 4. Speech signal cepstrum processing process

2) In the actual segmentation of speaker speech, using speaker adaptation technology, such as maximum likelihood regression or maximum a posteriori probability method, using a small amount of adaptive data to establish speaker adaptation can also improve the segmentation accuracy.

Correct endpoint detection is the key of all automatic speech recognition systems.

The energy of voiced speech varies significantly with the time. Therefore, the energy of voiced speech is more obvious than that of voiced speech. For signal {x (n), short-time energy is defined as follows:

$$E_n = \sum_{m=-\infty}^{\infty} [X(n) \times w(n-m)]^2 \tag{2}$$

The meaning of short-time average zero crossing rate refers to the number of times that the signal of each frame passes through the zero value. For discrete speech signals, the short-time average zero crossing rate is essentially the number of symbol changes at the sampling point. As shown in Fig. 5 below, the framework of language signal processing system is shown.

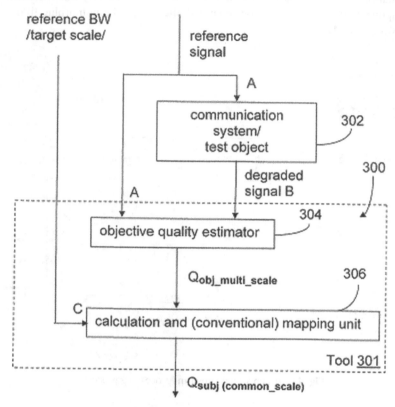

reference BW
/target scale/

reference
signal

A

communication system/ test object   302

degraded signal B   300

A

objective quality estimator   304

$Q_{obj\_multi\_scale}$ 306

C   calculation and (conventional) mapping unit

Tool 301

Q_{subj} (common_scale)

Fig. 5. Framework of speech signal processing system

In order to overcome this, it is found that the signal is the result of convolution between the excitation source and the channel frequency, and the "cepstrum feature" is established.

3   Design and Implementation of Oral training System Based on Automatic Speech Evaluation

Automatic speech evaluation, also known as automatic evaluation of pronunciation quality, refers to the technology that automatically evaluates the pronunciation level, detects errors and gives correction guidance through the machine [6]. It uses the computer to automatically evaluate the standard degree of the voice sent by the user, and its application in computer assisted language learning (call) system, It can help practitioners understand their deficiencies in pronunciation and promote practitioners to improve their pronunciation [7]. At present, automatic speech evaluation is mainly based on speech recognition, which uses the acoustic gap mapping between the practitioner's pronunciation and the standard pronunciation to obtain the practitioner's pronunciation. The complete speech evaluation research includes the establishment of standard pronunciation model, segmental prosody analysis of pronunciation and manual score mapping training.

In the aspect of oral evaluation based on oral learning, the following problems should be solved:

(1) How to better apply oral evaluation technology to oral learning and play a greater role. For example, analyze the special pronunciation of the practitioner, accurately detect the pronunciation problems of the practitioner, and put forward effective suggestions for improvement.

(2) How to ensure the accuracy of the evaluation results and make the machine evaluation results consistent with the expert evaluation results. This requires that we must conduct more in-depth research and development on all aspects of evaluation technology, including technical details, and effectively improve the evaluation algorithm.

(3) How to eliminate various factors (such as environmental noise, local voice, equipment abnormalities, etc.) that affect the oral evaluation technology, and ensure the accuracy of the evaluation by properly correcting and compensating the evaluation results..The speech recognition module is shown in Fig. 6:

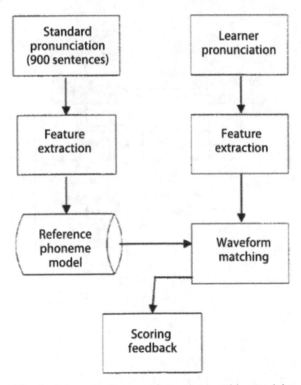

Fig. 6. Schematic diagram of speech recognition module

Basic process of automatic voice evaluation:

1) Pretreatment
   Acoustic features for speech recognition are extracted from speech signals. And analyzing the text to obtain the speech segmentation position, speech acoustic model, recognition network and other information required for speech recognition;
2) Speech recognition
   Pattern matching is carried out according to the language acoustic model to complete speech recognition, and the recognized phonemes and phoneme boundaries are output;
3) Extract scoring features:
   According to the recognition results, imitating the evaluation of experts, combined with the characteristics of text and acoustics, the scoring features that can be quantified to describe the integrity of content, fluency and standard of speech are extracted;
4) Calculated score:
   Use the trained speech model to segment the speech features (usually using vierbi algorithm), then calculate various pronunciation quality test degrees on the segments, and finally have a trained score mapping model to convert the pronunciation quality measure into an intuitive score. Figure 7 below shows speech model vs. speech features.

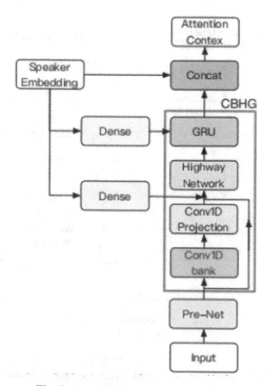

Fig. 7. Speech model vs. speech features

External function: realize visual window. Example sentence Library View: play according to the specified example sentences or learning strategies. Information view: display sentences and phonetics; Display monosyllabic score and correction; Display sentence prosody score and correction, and play correction. User management interface: display user records, study files, analyze fallible phonemes and common errors [8]. The system can recognize English learners with strong Chinese accent.

4 System Process

Speech evaluation is basically similar to speech recognition, but the ultimate purpose is different. Speech recognition is to search and compare the segmented units with the dictionary, and select the one with the greatest probability as the recognition result [9]; The evaluation does not need to give specific recognition results, but only calculate the similarity with the maximum recognition results internally.

Speech evaluation needs multi-dimensional comparison. The main comparison dimensions of the paper are: correctness, prosody and fluency: 1) Correctness: correctness has been introduced in detail in the speech recognition part. After segmentation, only.

The distance can be calculated according to the corresponding characteristic information, which is commonly used as Euclidean distance.

2) Fluency: in this paper, fluency defines the effective pronunciation duration. This definition is for simplicity.

The definition can be defined according to the accuracy and the duration of effective pronunciation unit in the follow-up study.

3) Prosody: prosody is an important measurement dimension. If the voice of the statement is gentle, the interrogative sentence is generally ascending. According to these characteristics, prosody can be characterized by pitch period.

For example: can I take your order?

Because it is difficult to accurately calculate the pitch period, and the calculated period position may not be corresponding, it is not easy to directly convert the distance into fraction [10].

5 Conclusion

The design and implementation of oral training system based on automatic speech evaluation studied in this paper. To evaluate the quality of oral English, the purpose of the system should be to provide the user with the most accurate information about his / her oral performance in order to improve this performance. In addition, it is important that such a system should be easy for users to use and understand. Automatic speech recognition (ASR) technology uses a computer to convert audio files into text. The ASR system uses an algorithm to recognize words or phrases from recorded sound samples. These systems can be used in voice mail transcription, dictation, document retrieval, call center automation and other applications.At the same time, by embedding automatic voice evaluation technology in the system, the system can timely and accurately feed back the results of practice after training, so that students can quickly find their weaknesses, and then supplement learning, so as to improve their oral English level.

Acknowledgements. "Speech Recognition Technology in College Oral English Teaching System" (NO. GJ213205), scientific and technological research project of Jiangxi Provincial Education Department.

References

1. Tripodi, D., Cosi, A., Fulco, D.: The Impact of Sport Training on Oral Health in Athletes. Dentistry J. **9**(5) (2021)
2. Rakhee, P., Claire, R., Gallagher, J.E.: Collaborating for oral health in support of vulnerable older people: co-production of oral health training in care homes. J. Public Health (2021)
3. Stengel, S., Merle, U., Peters-Klimm, F., et al.: Intersectoral online training and exchange during the COVID-19 pandemic in a district. ZFA. Zeitschrift fur Allgemeinmedizin **97**(6), 252–256 (2021)
4. Hsu, W.C., Hsieh, Y.P., Lan, S.J.: Home care aides' attitudes to training on oral health care. PLoS ONE **16**(4), e0249021 (2021)
5. Qiu, X., Chen, Y., Chen, H., et al.: Learning syntactic dense embedding with correlation graph for automatic readability assessment. In: Proceedings of the 59th Annual Meeting of the Association for Computational Linguistics and the 11th International Joint Conference on Natural Language Processing (Volume 1: Long Papers) (2021)
6. Tripathi, A., Bhosale, S., Kopparapu, S.K.: Automatic Speaker Independent Dysarthric Speech Intelligibility Assessment System. Comput. Speech Lang. (2021)
7. Ahmed, B., Konje, J.C.: Fetal lung maturity assessment: A historic perspective and Non – invasive assessment using an automatic quantitative ultrasound analysis (a potentially useful clinical tool). Europ. J. Obstetrics Gynecol. Reproductive Biol. (2021)
8. Liguori, P., Al-Hossami, E., Orbinato, V., et al.: EVIL: Exploiting Software via Natural Language (2021)
9. Pappagari, R., Cho, J., Joshi, S., et al.: Automatic detection and assessment of Alzheimer Disease using speech and language technologies in low-resource scenarios (2021)
10. Phipps, A.: Decolonising the languages curriculum: linguistic justice for linguistic ecologies (2021)

Design and Implementation of Student Physical Fitness Analysis System Based on Data Mining Technology

Chen Kun Zhang[✉]

Nanchang University College of Science and Technology, Nanchang 330001, Jiangxi, China
zck524065750@163.com

Abstract. The student physique analysis system is based on data mining technology. The main purpose of this project is to develop a system that can predict students' physical health level and provide them with appropriate guidance according to their needs, so that they can improve their health level. Data collected from students can be analyzed to determine their physical health level. In this project, we will use data mining technology to analyze data and develop a model, which can be used as the input of the final output. A model is a set of rules or algorithms used to predict results. This study provides students with opportunities to participate in various activities, such as games, sports and other activities related to their health. The application will help improve students' overall performance by providing sufficient information about their current health status and its impact on other aspects (such as academic, social life, etc.).so it is difficult to give scientific guidance to students through complicated data. Taking the physical test data of colleges and universities as an example, Through data statistics, according to the performance evaluation standard in the national physical exercise standard, this paper obtains five basic indexes: cardiopulmonary function, muscle strength, muscle endurance, softness and obesity. Using decision tree C4 5.

Keywords: Students' physical fitness · Data mining · Physical analysis · System design

1 Introduction

With the comprehensive construction of quality education, physical education in Colleges and universities has also set off an upsurge of educational reform. As early as the national college sports conference held in December 2006, it has been clearly emphasized that "to carry out quality education is not only to pay attention to students' achievement and moral education, but also to cultivate students' strong physique and healthy body and mind". According to the outline of healthy China 2030 plan issued by the CPC Central Committee and the State Council, the development goal of healthy China has been clearly pointed out [1]. In view of the declining trend of the physical health status of China's youth, the National People's Congress revised the sports law of the people's

© ICST Institute for Computer Sciences, Social Informatics and Telecommunications Engineering 2023
Published by Springer Nature Switzerland AG 2023. All Rights Reserved
M. A. Jan and F. Khan (Eds.): BigIoT-EDU 2022, LNICST 465, pp. 85–96, 2023.
https://doi.org/10.1007/978-3-031-23950-2_10

Republic of China twice in 2009 and 2016. Chapter III of the sports law of the people's Republic of China stipulates the status of school sports in talent training, the opening of physical education classes, extracurricular sports activities, sports venues and facilities, the opening of physical education classes Physical education teachers and students have made clear provisions on physical fitness monitoring [2]. Figure 1 below shows the system test and detection process.

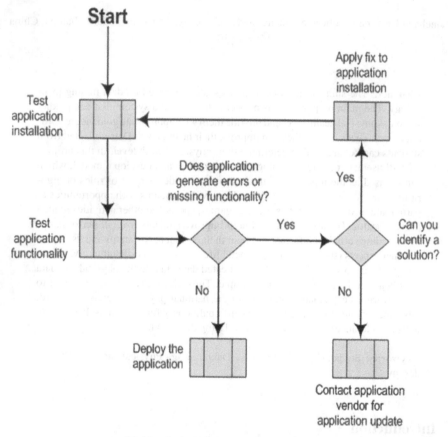

Fig. 1. System test and detection process

The State Council also clearly pointed out that "the physical health of China's youth is an important event related to national rejuvenation and national development. Governments at all levels, Party committees, university organizations and the whole society need to give comprehensive attention and support". However, the survey shows that when the state and society attach great importance to sports construction, there are many reasons for the decline of young people's physical health in China. One of the very important reasons is that young people in China do not cultivate good habits of physical exercise and do not use scientific methods for physical exercise [3].

2 Related work

2.1 Health System Analysis

A healthy constitution is the premise for everyone to carry out other activities. As for the definition of physique, there are different understandings and expressions in different countries. Chinese scholars believe that physique refers to "the quality of human life. A person's physique itself is a relatively stable feature of human form and body function under the comprehensive effect of innate acquisition and acquired learning". Therefore, on the basis of heredity, what level of physical fitness you want to achieve depends on the acquisition of the day after tomorrow [4].

Health means that a person is in good physical, mental and social condition. According to the explanation given by the World Health Organization, health not only refers to whether a person has disease or weakness, but also refers to a person's physical, psychological and social good state [5]. As shown in Fig. 2 below, the framework of healthy constitution analysis is shown.

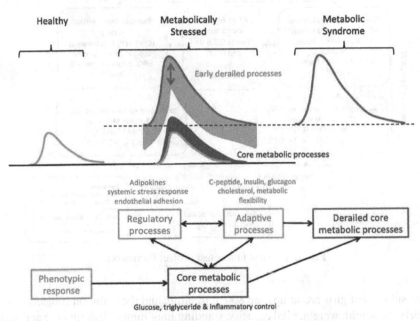

Fig. 2. Analysis framework of healthy constitution

A person's sports ability and physical condition are the main indicators to evaluate his constitution, but also the key to evaluate his health condition. Physical fitness is also called physical adaptability [6]. Exercise ability refers to the ability of the human body to complete special actions coordinated by muscles under the control of the brain. Physical fitness is closely related to sports ability. Figure 3 below shows the framework of the physical fitness test project.

According to the latest standards, there are eight subjects in the physical fitness test of college students. The unique subjects of boys are pull-up and 1000 m running, the

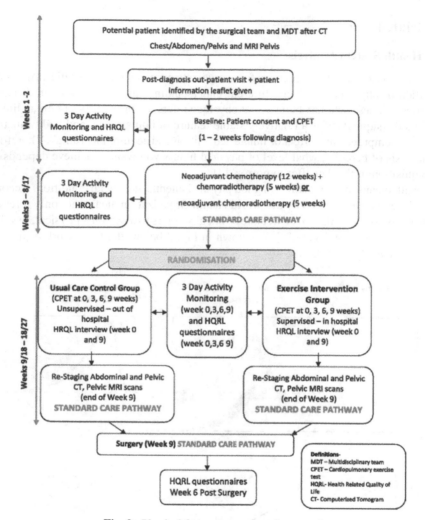

Fig. 3. Physical fitness test project framework

unique subjects of girls are sit ups and 800 m running, and the common subjects of boys and girls are height, weight, vital capacity, standing long jump, 50 m running and sitting posture forward bending. The scoring standard is to convert the scores of various data, remove the test omissions, untested and test free data, and the remaining effective data are statistically divided into four grades: excellent, good, pass and fail, of which the total score of 90 and above is excellent; A total score of 80 to 90 is good; a total score of 60 to 79 is pass; If the total score is less than 60, you will fail.

At present, there are many related researches on fitness testing in China, mainly including the research on the analysis of fitness test performance data and the research on fitness test equipment.

Data analysis and research focus on the following aspects: Research on the current situation of students' physique, research on the causes of students' physique decline, research on the distortion of test data and Research on students' exercise behavior.

The physical health of students is related to the future of the country, and all countries attach great importance to it [7].

Japanese research on physical fitness testing tends to integrate physical factors and living habits. Research by Fuyong et al. Shows that the physical quality and mental state of college students are correlated with exercise habits and sleep habits. Nakajima's research on the correlation between the body mass index and lifestyle factors of freshmen at Fukuoka University shows that the regularity of diet, sleep level, physical exercise, daily fatigue and so on affect the body mass index of students. These studies have provided effective help to promote the physical quality development of college students in Japan. However, the physical fitness test standards implemented in Japan are also very different from those in China, mainly because they refine the age groups and have optional items, such as endurance evaluation. Women can choose endurance running and 20 m round-trip running.

Although the research on physical fitness test abroad is more in-depth, the standards used for physical fitness test are different, and the research focus is also different.

2.2 Data Mining Tasks

At present, the university information management system accumulates all kinds of data every day, and there are more and more scenes of using big data technology for data analysis and mining. Common big data processing technologies include Hadoop ecosystem using MapReduce computing framework, impala providing fast interactive queries, and storm, a real-time stream processing framework with low latency. The data mining information task framework is shown in Fig. 4 below.

Compared with the above technologies, spark technology has advantages in the comprehensive utilization of resources everywhere. With the continuous development of spark, it has become a core library with spark core, including machine learning (mlib), spark streaming, instant query (spark SQL), graph computing (graphx) and other components. Compared with the MapReduce computing framework based on disk computing adopted by Hadoop, the computing speed of spark can reach more than 10 times that of MapReduce [8]. This is because spark is based on memory computing, while Hadoop is based on disk computing. Because spark computing framework uses memory for computing, coupled with its component sparkstreaming, spark has an obvious advantage in real-time stream processing.

The core abstraction of spark is elastic distributed data set, which is called RDD for short. RDD represents a data set that is read-only, partitioned, and provides a series of rich operation modes. Users can operate RDD through rich API commands, which are mainly divided into two types: transformation and action.

In data analysis, this paper uses sparksqli to establish a relational database, uses HDFS to store files, and uses spark computing framework to build a big data analysis platform.

On the other hand, data mining can also scientifically predict the development of things in the future, and then give full play to the maximum value of data.

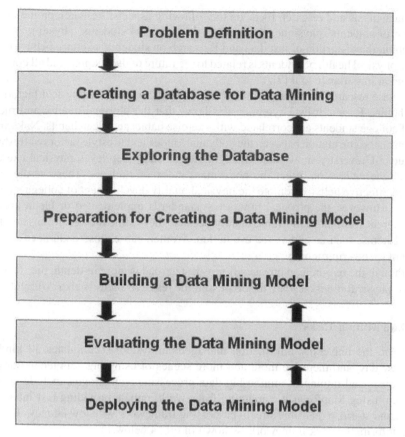

Fig. 4. Data mining information task framework

In the education industry, most studies are aimed at student achievement. Scholars explore the internal relationship between education data and student achievement through data mining technology. Promote the transformation of education mode and gradually change the traditional teaching management mode into a personalized teaching system.The prediction method is to extract the test data set from the original data, and then construct the prediction model to analyze and predict the data, so as to evaluate the knowledge information contained in the unknown data.

Cluster analysis is an unsupervised learning method, which classifies according to the specific characteristics of different individuals. Individuals clustered in the same category have high similarity, but there are differences between different categories. Common clustering analysis algorithms include k-means algorithm, hierarchical clustering algorithm and so on.

2.3 Data Mining Process

The details are as follows:

(1) Select data

  After determining the analysis objectives and objects, we need to analyze the data in our area to understand which data can support the business and which data can be used to solve problems. The goal at this stage is to select the appropriate data set and identify the data set most related to the object, so as to lay a good foundation for the follow-up work.

(2) Data cleaning

  After confirming the data set, the data needs to be preprocessed. At this stage, it may be found that there are missing data, duplicate values, outliers, etc. in the data set. The missing value generally depends on the degree of missing. If the missing part is less, it can be filled in by means of average value and so on; If there are many missing values, the attribute or this piece of data will be deleted directly.

The general data flow is shown in Fig. 5.

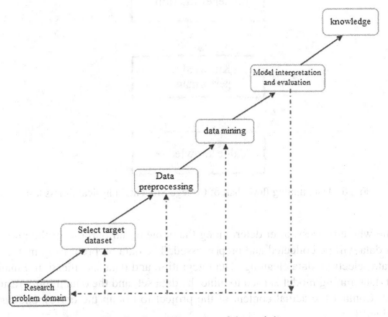

Fig. 5. General process of data mining

3 Application of Data Mining Technology in Students' Physical Fitness Analysis

3.1 Description of Physical Problems of College Students

For the above problems, data mining method can be adopted to analyze the sports test data of college students. The flow chart is shown in Fig. 6.

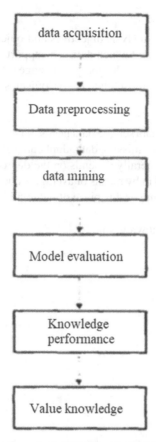

Fig. 6. Data mining flow chart of College Students' physical fitness test

In the whole process, after determining the content and purpose of the project, the relevant data will be collected and preprocessed. The data preprocessing includes four steps: data selection, data cleaning, data integration and data specification. Finally, the relevant data mining model is used to mine the data set, and the data mining results are obtained. Contact the actual content of the project to obtain the corresponding value knowledge[9].

3.2 Data Preprocessing

Data preprocessing is to select and clean up these data. Clean up some data without analytical value and select more appropriate data for experimental analysis, so as to improve the efficiency and accuracy of data mining. In addition, data integration, data standardization and data specification can reduce data redundancy and maintain data integrity, so as to improve the level of data mining.

In the physical fitness test data collection, affected by the measurement accuracy and error of the front-end data collection of the Internet of things and other objective factors, some data measurement will be inaccurate, or even seriously deviate from the normal situation, and then produce data outliers. The occurrence of outliers will not only affect the performance query work, but also reduce the reliability of the results if the original data is mined, and even the rules cannot be mined or the wrong rules can be mined. Therefore, it is necessary to screen the original data through outliers detection [10].

Physical health intervention measures refer to physical education teachers making sports training plans according to students' grades to help improve students' physical health test results. Due to the different training venues, time and environment of different subjects, this paper analyzes the importance of individual subjects for improving the overall evaluation results, provides suggestions for rapidly improving the physical fitness test results of college students, excavates the links between various subjects, and further verifies them through Pearson correlation coefficient. After getting the relevance between the subjects, when it is limited by the teaching time and teaching venue, and it is impossible to carry out special training for a subject, it can be trained for the subjects with strong relevance and low requirements for teaching venue and time, so as to improve the performance of the above-mentioned poor subjects, which is of great help to formulate physical education teaching plans and improve the efficiency of physical education teaching and performance improvement.

For distance measurement, ultrasonic distance measurement duration of the high level is the time from the transmission to the return of the ultrasonic. According to the time difference between the transmission and reception, the distance between the ultrasonic and the measured object can be calculated.

If the ultrasonic module probe is placed at a distance of 2.5 m from the ground when measuring height, and the distance between the probe measured by the ultrasonic module and the height measurement lifting platform is h, then h = (high level time x sound speed) /2, and then the height h = (250-h) can be obtained. Similarly, in the subjects of standing long jump and sitting forward bending, ultrasonic distance measurement module can also be used to measure students' grades.

3.3 Design of College Students' Physical Fitness Analysis System

In order to meet the use needs of the above administrators, teachers and students, the system design requirements are as follows:

(1) System permission requirements

The system operates as students, teachers and administrators. Therefore, according to the actual needs of the three types of users, it is necessary to distinguish the different permissions of the three users when operating the system. When a user logs in, he / she can identify the user's role through the user name and password. After passing the background verification, he / she can enter the system. This part corresponds to the corresponding permissions of his / her role.

(2) Analysis of students' functional needs

① Students can fill in the physical health self-assessment form in the system and input personal information through the "self-assessment form" system. After receiving students' personal information, the background will store it in the database and wait for calculation.

② Check the physical test results and evaluation results in the system. The system stores student physical test data and student evaluation data, which need to be converted into a more readable grade standard through corresponding calculation and evaluation standards. Enable students to have a clearer understanding of the results and get corresponding guidance and suggestions.

(3) Analysis of teachers' functional needs

① Check the physical test data and evaluation data of each student, and be able to add, delete, modify and check the data. ② Check the overall physical health analysis results of the whole school. By collecting the physical test information of the whole school students, we can show the physical health distribution map of the whole school students, so that teachers can better carry out physical education activities.

② Using data mining to mine students' data information and interpret the output value of the results of data mining analysis to make it more readable. Teachers can also give corresponding and targeted guidance to different students according to the mining analysis results.

(4) Analysis of administrator function requirements

① Cover all permissions of students and teachers.
② Modify the fields and evaluation system of the physical health self-assessment form, and the administrator can add, delete, modify and check the problems and options in the self-assessment form, and control the score of each option and the overall scoring standard.
③ Control the operation of data mining algorithm and the generation of results.

The technical architecture of the system is divided into three layers: presentation layer, business logic layer and data layer, as shown in Fig. 7.

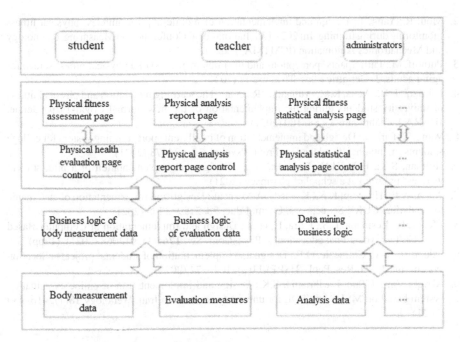

Fig. 7. Overall technical architecture of the system

4   Conclusion

The design and implementation of student physique analysis system based on data mining technology is to make a computerized system that can analyze student data to detect students' performance level, and teachers will use it to evaluate students. The main components of the project are data mining technology, artificial intelligence, database management system and Internet. The system aims to analyze the physical quality of middle school students. The system will be able to collect data from each student and then process it using data mining technology. The main purpose of this project is to create a database that can help us predict individual results based on individual performance in examinations. The database will also provide teachers, parents and students with useful information about their performance so that they can improve their skills accordingly, from the perspective of research methods, this paper only adopts the decision tree and association rule algorithm in data mining, and there are a variety of data mining algorithms that can study and analyze the project, so as to provide a more comprehensive basis and guidance for physical fitness analysis. Third, for the system function, it only involves body test data.

References

1. Zhu, L.: Design and implementation on physical fitness and health standards query system for college students. Syst. Autom. **21**, 223–234 (2018)

2. Mou, R., Yang, J.: Design and implementation of mobile app for athletes' physical fitness monitoring during training. In: 2021 13th International Conference on Measuring Technology and Mechatronics Automation (ICMTMA) (2021)
3. Puthoff, M.: Participants' perceptions and the implementation of a physical fitness screen for aging adults. J. Geriatric Phys. Therapy, 44 (2021)
4. Fahrizqi, E.B., Agus, R.M., Yuliandra, R., et al.: The learning motivation and physical fitness of university students during the implementation of the new normal Covid-19 pandemic. JUARA J. Olahraga 6(1), 88–100 (2021)
5. Wang, T., Park, J.: Design and implementation of intelligent sports training system for college students' mental health education. Front. Psychol. 12, 634978 (2021)
6. Holman, S.K., Folz, H.N., Ford, B., et al.: Design and implementation of a pilot student wellness program at a school of pharmacy (2021)
7. Allen, W.E., Hosbein, K.N., Kennedy, A.M., et al.: Design and Implementation of an Organic to Analytical CURE Sequence. J. Chem. Educ. 98, 2199–2208 (2021)
8. Efendi, R., Lesmana, L.S., Putra, F., et al.: Design and implementation of Computer Based Test (CBT) in vocational education. J. Phys. Conf. Ser. 1764(1), 012068 (2021). (12pp)
9. Ndubuisi, A.A., Chimezie, O.E.: Design and implementation of students' projects allocation system. Int. J. Sci. Res. Publ. (IJSRP) 11(6), 164–174 (2021)
10. AlAqbi, A., Al-Taie, R., Ibrahim, S.K.: Design and implementation of online examination system based on MSVS and SQL for university students in Iraq. Webology 18(1), 416–430 (2021)

An Intelligent Piano Teaching System and Method Based on a Cloud Platform

Sha Liu[✉]

Hubei Engineering University, XiaoGan 432000, HuBei, China
liushahua_123@163.com

Abstract. With the progressive development of the 'Internet+' trend and the elevation of artificial intelligence to a national strategy, the use of new Internet cloud technologies and hardware and software technologies such as computers to serve music dissemination and music education has become an inevitable trend. In this wave, a large number of software and hardware systems and new teaching platforms have emerged over the years for piano education, which is an important area of popular music education. In the whole platform of intelligent piano teaching, the main aspects include hardware construction methods, software design methods, music presentation forms, teaching methods, etc. Based on the currently available technologies and theories, different methods have different characteristics in the whole teaching. This paper is based on a study of intelligent piano teaching systems on a cloud platform, and in this regard hopes to make such approaches better for new models of music education and to provide references for the transformation of other music disciplines on the Internet.

Keywords: Intelligent piano · Teaching software · Implementation methods

1 Introduction

Today, as the East meets the West, the piano has found its way into millions of homes. Its beautiful tone and rich expressiveness are loved by the Chinese public. The art of performing the piano has developed to a relatively high level and the playing method has become more scientific. In recent years, there has been a proliferation of smart piano concepts and products, a form that has brought about some influence and changes in piano teaching, especially in this wave of new computer software, internet and electronic circuitry as the main means of implementation of the system, which has brought about changes in all aspects of piano teaching, from the structure of the instrument, to the content, to the teaching methods and practice methods. Regardless of the current results, at least this change represents an exploration of traditional music teaching models in a new way of thinking, and we have reason to believe that this exploration is bound to provide some basis for future musical development [1].

The research and development process of this new approach requires the participation of researchers from several fields, such as piano repair, piano performance, piano

M. A. Jan and F. Khan (Eds.): BigIoT-EDU 2022, LNICST 465, pp. 97–102, 2023.
https://doi.org/10.1007/978-3-031-23950-2_11

pedagogy, digital audio production, multimedia production and internet software development, so the current design of this type of approach is relatively complex and there is much room for improvement in the currently available implementations. This paper is based on a study of an intelligent piano teaching system on a cloud platform, and in this regard hopes to make this type of approach better for the new music education model, so that this new approach can be better and more appropriately applied to piano teaching.

2 The Current Situation of Piano Teaching

2.1 Students are Passive Learners and Rely Heavily on the Teacher to Teach Them

The piano teaching has not yet left the track of the teacher-apprentice system, one-to-one, hand-to-hand teaching, where knowledge is transmitted orally by the teacher, and the students' knowledge is largely limited by the teacher's level. Foreign education emphasises active learning on the basis of the student's own initiative. The professor plays a guiding role. Students seek advice from the teacher, who is not responsible for their learning. In our case, teachers have a high degree of responsibility and always want to make every student a qualified person.

2.2 The Emphasis is on the Transmission of Knowledge from the Teacher to the Neglect of Cultivated Knowledge

There are two sources of knowledge: one is the direct transmission from the teacher and the other is indirect learning through books. As the piano is a highly technical instrument, students have to spend a lot of time practising technique and mastering literature, which makes it particularly easy to neglect cultivated knowledge. It is therefore important to note that in our teaching we also focus on direct teaching and neglect to direct students to the books. It is very important to ask for advice from books, because they contain the experiences and lessons of those who have gone before us and can prevent us from taking a wrong turn. It is said that Cortol taught his students to hand in a piece of background material on the author and the work before learning a new piece, forcing them to do their studies. In foreign countries, the library is the base of study for students, but in our case, how much material of academic value lies asleep on the shelves for a long time and is rarely asked for, how much audio material is underused, and some students rarely even listen to concerts other than piano [2]. The Japanese have progressed rapidly because they have done a lot of translation and research, and information flows. Now Taiwan and Hong Kong are also ahead of us in academic research. Our students' weaknesses in musical performance are inseparable from their poor knowledge and poor musicianship.

2.3 Theoretical Education About the Basic Concepts and Fundamentals of Piano Playing Should be Emphasized in Teaching

We have to repeat the same words in almost every lesson (e.g. relaxation, natural weight, tone, pedal, rhythm, etc.), and teachers are indeed very tired, but many students have been learning piano for years, but they still haven't figured out what playing piano is all about. The reason for this is that the specific instruction and perceptual understanding in teaching does not rise to a rational level and some basic concepts are not yet established in the student's head, so they often learn blindly and lack awareness, and their learning efficiency will not be high. Therefore, I wonder what kind of foundation we should give to our students in the process of learning the piano, just technical training and learning a lot of piano literature? No. Rather, it should be a study of various teaching materials to establish the basic concepts of the art of piano playing, to acquire some basic knowledge of the rules, to develop a scientific approach to learning and to train practical working skills. The foundation should be interpreted in a broad sense, including playing skills, learning methods and musical understanding. In the case of vocal issues, the concept of sound is closely linked to the method of playing and touching the keys. Compared with the best international players, there is still a considerable gap between our voicing, which is hard, does not travel far, does not have a large range of forces, does not have many variations in levels, and is not beautiful enough. The reason for this is that in our training we have placed more emphasis on the solidity of the sound and the granularity of the fingers, so that there is not enough variety in the touch of the keys and very little training in legato Jegeropp etc. The first thing to do is to have an imagination for the beauty of the sound in order to find the right way to play it. The theory of relaxation and control, the use of natural weight, is not new to us, but in practice there are still many problems that affect the penetration and softness of the sound. Music is an art of sound, and in order to play with charm, one must work hard on the sound, which is one of the major trends in the world. It is therefore important that students are given the correct concept of the beautiful voice and the playing methods associated with it. Many students never understand that, in the final analysis, the support and control of the fingertips is the most important thing in terms of relaxation.

3 Teaching Software Implementation of Intelligent Piano Based on Cloud Platform

3.1 About the Music Score

The first thing to be solved in a cloud-based intelligent piano teaching software system is the display of the score and the accompanying synchronous playback, etc. In this case we first need a digital score made by computer music edition technology, and then develop the corresponding analysis and reproduction technology based on such a score, in order to basically meet the teaching needs of intelligent pianos.

Since the 1980s, with the development of the personal computer, the traditional computer music notation was gradually replaced by computer music notation, especially with software such as Sibelius, MuseScore and Finale, which made it possible to enter complex scores into the software and to display and play them instantly, and to extract scores, etc. In addition, open-source libraries such as LilyPond, which follows the GNU protocol, support the input of scores as text. Other libraries such as Vexflow (Java Scrip library), Verovio (JavaScript and Python library), Guido Engine (C++ library) etc. also have their own unique features. This score system is also closely related to the related music evaluation systems, music reproduction, and score display systems, which have been a research challenge for a long time, especially for complex scores [3].

While all of the above-mentioned software and tools can be used as platforms for the production of digital scores, the most common and suitable common interchange format for scores is MusicXML, an open XML-based music notation file format for music interchange and music distribution.MusicXML aims to create a common general Western music notation format. Compared to MIDI, MusicXML allows for the recording of richer information such as music notation, as shown in Fig. 1. This is why MusicXML has been considered in recent years to be one of the most popular common formats for the exchange of content. Although other common file formats are being developed, standards and formats that allow musicians to easily exchange music on the Internet, MusicXML is still the most respected format.

Fig. 1. MusicXML score and message correspondence diagram

3.2 About Playback

Unlike traditional scores, digital scores have the advantage that they can be played back, synchronising the accompaniment of the piece or the sound of other voices while the score is being played. The playback speed can also be adjusted according to the teaching scenario. This makes it necessary to use the relevant technical means to play the score. There are also two ways of playing the score and the accompaniment, mainly through MIDI and audio playback.

This is due to the different operating systems and platforms (computers or mobile devices). There are also differences in performance. The MIDI playback method is firstly due to the size of the MIDI file, which allows for significant savings in storage space or data traffic. Secondly, because of the ease of editing MIDI files, it is possible to change their speed without compromising on sound quality. However, as we all know, MIDI files are not audible per se and we need to prepare the appropriate software sound source to work with them, but the methods and problems encountered in implementing audio playback vary from platform to platform, operating system to operating system and programming language to programming language, making it somewhat more difficult for the programmer.

The advantage of using audio for playback is that you don't have to provide a source, and you can also use real instrument recordings in the production of the music, which in theory gives a better reproduction and acoustic quality. Usually the audio will be in the usual wav, mp3 etc. formats and will take up much more space or traffic than a MIDI file. In addition, the sound quality is significantly reduced when the audio is subjected to some variable speed, and there is a delay in playback in some operating systems and programs, which does not facilitate synchronisation of display and playback.

3.3   On Error Correction and Scoring Mechanisms

The ultimate point of intelligent piano teaching system is the ability to automatically correct and score errors according to the input of real-time playing signals and digital music information.

The three elements of sound, including pitch, intensity and timbre, together with time, make up the four elements, which are synchronised to the position of the keys, the strength of the keys, the timing of their press and the timing of their lift. As the tone is mainly influenced by the material and construction of the piano itself, it is largely ignored in the evaluation process of intelligent pianos, and the core points become the above four. The start time, point and lift point of the keys are used to calculate the time value of each note, while the rhythm of the player is judged by the time point of the key presses, and the position of the buttons determines the pitch accuracy of the playing. In summary, the main points of judgement in an intelligent piano are accuracy, intensity, rhythm and timing. Accuracy can be judged in four categories: left-handed unison and left-handed chord, right-handed unison and right-handed chord, but in practice these can be combined into two categories, unison and polyphony, as the system does not distinguish between left- and right-handed presses [4].

At the same time, from another point of view the judging mechanism can be divided into three cases: missed notes, multiple notes and misplayed notes. In all three cases, it is theoretically necessary to first obtain the correct pitch and number of tones to be played at the current point in time from the digital score, and at the same time to obtain the pitch and number of tones being played through the hardware system of the intelligent piano, and to compare this information, firstly, according to the number, whether the current situation is one of missed tones or multiple tones or neither missed tones nor multiple tones, and then to compare again whether there are tones played incorrectly. The next step is to compare whether there is a misplay.

Rhythmic and temporal judgements are also useful in assisting with the accuracy of music playing. For example, a common algorithm for evaluating performance accuracy is as follows: if the current weight of the note is set to w, the current tempo is Tempo, and the current time value of the note is d, then the current tempo weight of the note = current tempo/current time value of the note, i.e. $w = 60/Tempo/d$;

We then set the note score to a, the actual time point in the performance of the note is T, and the standard note should be played at ST; then the score of the note = |actual time point - standard time point|*note current rhythm weighting.

The final score is the sum of the note scores divided by the total number of notes. If the total number of notes is S, then the formula for the final note accuracy C is as follows (the subscript of the symbol is the note number):

$$C = \frac{1}{S} \times \sum_{n=1}^{\infty} (|T_n - ST_n| * 60/Tempo/d_n) \tag{1}$$

In the overall assessment of the performance, the assessment of pitch accuracy is relatively logical and should be the most heavily weighted item in the overall assessment criteria, with rhythm and timing only being given a small weighting. Figure 2 is an example of the final display of data and markers such as correct errors:

Fig. 2. Example of a score judging page in an APP

4 Conclusion

In the midst of the global technological revolution of the Internet, the traditional musical instrument industry is moving towards intelligence. The result will be a further lowering of the barriers to learning musical instruments and the creation of new segments or completely new fields. Based on the technology currently available, there are limitations to the problems that intelligent pianos can solve, and we need to properly understand the impact that intelligent pianos can bring, neither ignoring their role nor exaggerating it. At this stage, we need to respect the laws of piano teaching and let this approach work together with teachers to improve teaching efficiency.

References

1. Liu, X.: On the innovative teaching implementation of progressive piano performance training. Northern Music 2017(06) (2017)
2. Li, N.: Structural characteristics of electronic piano and piano teaching. Electri. Transmiss. 2019(12) (2019)
3. Kang, J.: Combining piano teaching with modern technology--analysis of the superiority of teaching digital piano group lessons. Electron. Test 2013(24) (2013)
4. Han, S.: The "Industrial Revolution" of piano teaching: an introduction to digital piano teaching system and digital piano group classes. Music Time and Space. 2013(10) (2013)

Analysis and Prediction of CET4 Based on Data Mining

Haiyan Liu[✉]

Xi'an Siyuan University, Xi'an 710038, Shaanxi Province, China
tangyijie3@163.com

Abstract. CET4 analysis and prediction based on data mining is a technology that uses data mining technology to analyze system performance. It can be used as an effective tool to predict the future performance of any system or application. The main goal of this technology is to identify the weaknesses in the system in order to improve it, so as to obtain better results and efficiency. This technology helps improve the productivity of employees and improves their efficiency by identifying areas where they need more training or improvement. Based on the analysis and prediction of CET-4 scores based on data mining, this paper analyzes many factors affecting CET-4 based on multiple linear regression algorithm. According to the idea of data mining, historical data are collected and transformed appropriately, and many factors affecting CET-4 are analyzed by using statistical analysis technology. It is concluded that the linear regression relationship between CET-4 and its influencing factors has a high degree of fitting, which can be used to predict CET-4, and has a great guiding role and use value for students' learning and school teaching management.

Keywords: Data mining · CET-4 · Performance analysis

1 Introduction

In the 20th century, with the increasing updating of database technology, the of database management system has been widely popularized, and the data is growing rapidly., human beings can exchange a large number of data information and work together on the network at different places and at different times. Therefore, what we are facing now is not limited to the huge database information gathered by our departments, units and the whole industry, but a large amount of information knowledge. On the surface, most of the data are chaotic and have no rules to follow. In fact, behind these soaring data are many valuable information. At present, ordinary database systems can basically achieve the functions of effective data query, input and preliminary statistics. However, they can not find a certain relationship from the data, so they can not predict the future development direction according to the current analysis methods [1]. There is a lack of means to mine the valuable, resulting in the phenomenon of "data expansion and lack of knowledge". Behind a large amount of data, there is a large amount of information

M. A. Jan and F. Khan (Eds.): BigIoT-EDU 2022, LNICST 465, pp. 103–113, 2023.
https://doi.org/10.1007/978-3-031-23950-2_12

helpful to human development. If these data can not be well transformed into useful knowledge, assuming that there is no correct means, human beings begin to face the ocean of information, but there is nothing to do. Therefore, people began to consider how to mine effective knowledge from massive information, deal with it more deeply, and improve the utilization rate of knowledge. Facing the challenge of massive data to human beings, people first discover knowledge in databases, and then to its core technology - data mining, which naturally appears, develops rapidly and shows strong vitality [2].

Today's society is in the process of internationalization, globalization, cultural diversity and rapid and vigorous. Among them, the rapid development of educational informatization and the sharp strengthening of the attention of talents and manpower, how to use and make use of science and technology to find favorable information from a large number of cumbersome data, so as to improve the existing teaching methods and strategies to help students improve their grades, which provides a reference basis for educational reform [3]. It is very beneficial to apply data mining technology to the field of education, mine and analyze the data of students' grades, provide important decision-making basis for educational work, and use the results to serve teachers and students and make them carry out more effective teaching activities.

In the constitution of the Teaching Steering Committee, it is pointed out that we should adhere to the "people-oriented", promote the "four returns" and comprehensively improve the talent training ability of colleges and universities [4]. CET-4 is to assess students' Comprehensive English ability and make scientific prediction. These data can not be used only for query or simple statistics. Combined with my major and work, this paper uses the method of statistical analysis to find out the relevant factors affecting the passing of CET-4, and find out some factors affecting whether college students pass CET-4, so as to provide practical and effective suggestions and measures to help students learn English well and use English well, At the same time, it is of great practical significance to improve teaching quality and teaching methods for teachers [5].

In the notice of the, reasonably improve the academic challenge, increase the difficulty strictly enforce the examination discipline, strictly control the exit of graduation, and resolutely cancel the "clear examination" system. It can be concluded that if college students want to graduate smoothly, they need to learn the required courses well [6]. Otherwise, if some courses fail to pass the exam, they will face the risk of not graduating without "clear examination". Therefore, it is very necessary to identify which courses have a great impact on students' graduation, and provide early warning to students with poor grades and the risk of re studying or dropping out of school as soon as possible to help students graduate smoothly, and assist the school management department to formulate effective management methods to help students. Through the students' scores in the first four semesters during the school period to predict the students' graduation, obtain the distribution of students' scores, analyze the students' scores in various subjects through methods, classify and analyze the students' graduation, and establish relevant prediction models. It is of great practical perfect the problems existing in the existing teaching.

2 Related Work

2.1 Overview of Data Mining

Data mining is a process of extracting hidden, unknown but potentially useful information and knowledge from a large number of incomplete, noisy, fuzzy and random data by using various analysis methods and technologies. In other words, data is extracted from a database called knowledge retrieval (KDD). Data mining is an interdisciplinary subject integrating artificial intelligence, database technology, model recognition, machine learning, statistics and data visualization. At present, it is widely used in finance, retail, insurance, medicine, communication, electronics, aviation and other fields. One of the most common standards in the industry is the cross industry data extraction process. According to this standard, the process of data mining is divided into six stages: 1) understanding the operation, 2) understanding the data, 3) preparing the data, 4) modeling, 5) evaluation and 6) deployment. Modeling must be based on different business scenarios, namely [7].

2.2 Data Mining Steps

The ultimate purpose of data mining is application-oriented. Only through application can we reflect its value and promote the development of data mining. The successful application of data mining in various fields has attracted more and more attention. Its main applications are divided into two categories: analyzing the hidden laws of data and practical support in decision-making. For example, cheating inspection, background analysis, competitive sports skills, risk analysis and management, customer relationship management (CRM), web analysis based on data mining and target market for consumption are being applied. In addition, some new fields have emerged, such as stream data mining and DNA and biological data analysis [9].

Among various applications, the application of knowledge mining (KDD) in database has become the core of data mining. Because data mining, the data of data mining basically comes from the database, development direction. The basic steps of database knowledge mining are shown in Fig. 1 below.

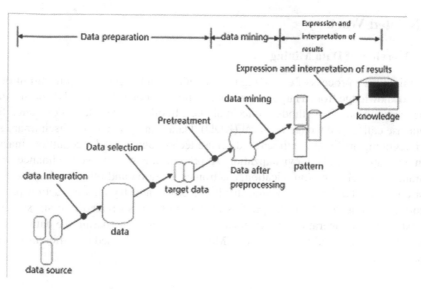

Fig. 1. Basic steps of knowledge mining

To carry out data mining, we must know the basic steps of data mining. The first step is to understand the application fields of data mining, including relevant knowledge and application objectives, so as to know which knowledge or patterns you are interested in, and only after understanding relevant knowledge can you reasonably process; The second step is to select data - data transformation; The third step is to select the function of data mining and the algorithm of data mining. This step is the key step of data mining, which determines the performance and effect of data mining; The fourth step is to find the model of interest, eliminate the misleading model, evaluate the model and express knowledge; Finally, use the excavated knowledge.

is shown in Fig. 2. Its bottom layer, that is, the object of data mining, that is, the source of data. There are many types of databases, but the most perfect development in technology is relational database, and the related tools are also the most, so relational database is the most used in data mining. The upper layer of the database, which is responsible for data storage, query, update, transaction processing and other related functions. It is responsible for transforming the data mining engine on the server into the data mining engine on the server. After data mining obtains the pattern of interest, it is to evaluate the pattern. It is responsible for comparing with the knowledge base to see whether the pattern meets the conditions [8]. This process is determined by the upper layer of the data mining engine, that is, the pattern evaluation layer. Finally, the interested patterns should be presented to users in a way that users can understand.

2.3 Factor Analysis of CET-4

Although colleges and universities have abolished the linkage between CET4 scores and degree certificates, this does not mean that CET4 scores are no longer important. CET-4 score is an important index to measure a student's English level. It can reflect

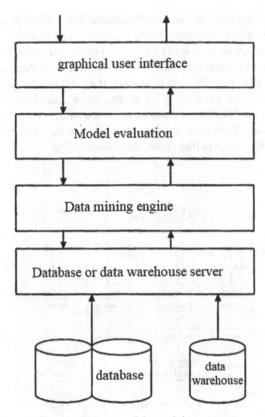

Fig. 2. Structure of data mining system

a student's comprehensive English level. In addition, the passing rate of CET-4 can also reflect the level. The content and form of English test also have certain guidance for College English teaching. Colleges to CET-4 achievement test. It can be seen that factors affecting the achievement of CET4. Therefore, in this chapter, this paper will take the relevant information of college students, the scores of four college English tests and CET-4 as the research data, and study and analyze the relationship and closeness between students' CET-4 passing and various factors [10].

2.4 Data Preparation

In order to analyze the factors related to CET-4 scores, this paper collects the relevant information of students from three colleges of a university. The information includes the following contents: gender, major, place of origin, entrance English scores, college entrance examination scores, four positive College English test scores during the school period, and CET-4 scores (including listening, writing and reading scores) during the four semesters during the school period. There are a total of 2821 pieces of data, each of which has the following characteristics: gender, major, college, place of origin, admission

English, college entrance examination results, course No. 1, English score 1, course No. 2, English score 2, semester, listening, writing, reading and grades.

In terms of data adoption, data sorting is carried out based on the particularity of data. On the one hand, some students pass CET-4 for the first time. Although these students have not completed all college English courses, if they still use the future English scores to analyze and predict the passed CET-4 scores when analyzing the data, it will be unreliable and unreasonable; On the other hand, some students may need to take CET-4 for many times to pass. Therefore, the data of students who repeatedly take CET-4 are regarded as independent data in this paper. As shown in Fig. 3.

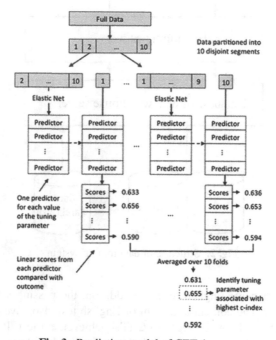

Fig. 3. Prediction model of CET-4 scores

2.5 Data Preprocessing

The original data set collected often contains some incomplete and noisy data. Such as abnormal value and missing value. In addition, the data set may contain some data that is not suitable, data sets need to be preprocessed such as data cleaning and data transformation. The specific data preprocessing is as follows:

First, use python programming to make a simple statistical analysis of the data to see which features contain missing values and abnormal values. The results are as follows:

As shown in Fig. 4 above, students' "entrance English scores" and "college entrance examination scores" have missing values. After calculation, the proportion of missing values in the total data is 2.37% and 2.06% respectively. Through further inspection, 118 of them are of grade 2013 and 5 of them are of grade 2014. Considering that "entrance English score" may have a strong correlation with CET4 score, and in order not to cause data imbalance, this paper temporarily retains the two characteristics of "entrance English score" and "college entrance examination score". It can also be found in the above table that the lowest score of "college entrance examination score" is 329, which is significantly lower than 400. Since the colleges and universities studied in this paper are provincial key colleges and universities, their enrollment scores should not be lower than the provincial key score line. It can be seen that the college entrance examination scores below 400 should be abnormal data. After checking the abnormal data, it is found that the students corresponding to the data are from Jiangsu Province and Shanghai. Through verification, the total scores of the college entrance examination scores of these two provinces and cities in that year are 480 and 600 respectively, which is different from the full score of 750 in other cities. In order to keep the data consistent, this paper needs to convert the student scores of Jiangsu Province and Shanghai.

count	2763	2754	2821	2821	2821	2821	2821	2821	2821
mean	67.06207021	533.2377563	72.69266218	69.09961007	3.064870613	143.153492	132.2860688	149.471464	424.911024
std	20.14536335	28.04436905	13.98852795	12.11898765	0.907245984	23.5255598	17.60689886	27.77197522	54.2560866
min	0	329	14	0	2	0	0	0	238
25%	59	520	63	62	2	127	121	131	389
50%	70	536.09212	77	68	3	142	132	151	424
75%	80.5	549.108115	83	77	4	157	144	170	460
max	109	601	99	99	4	220	200	223	616

Fig. 4. Statistical information table.

The specific calculation formula is as follows:

Jiangsu students' scores after processing = college entrance examination scores × 750 ÷ 480.

Shanghai students' scores after processing = college entrance examination scores × 750 ÷ 600.

In order to better understand the correlation between the adopted data and CET4, as well as the importance of each feature. From the perspective of correlation, this paper calculates the correlation coefficient of each data feature, as shown in Fig. 5:

Because the Pearson correlation coefficient between "college entrance examination scores" and CET-4 scores is only 0 081, so it is considered that there is basically no inevitable connection between CET-4 and college entrance examination scores. This conclusion is inconsistent with Zheng Lidan's conclusion that college entrance examination scores determine students' CET-4 scores. The Pearson correlation coefficient between entrance English score and CET4 score is 0.39, and there is a weak correlation between them. This feature is retained in this paper for better analysis and prediction. The correlation coefficient between reading and CET-4 is 0.84, which shows that there is a great relationship between CET-4 and reading score, that is, reading comprehension has a great impact on whether students can pass CET-4. The correlation coefficient between "English score 2" and CET4 is 0.62, which is higher than that between "English score 1" and CET4 58. This is consistent with the inference of this paper. College English

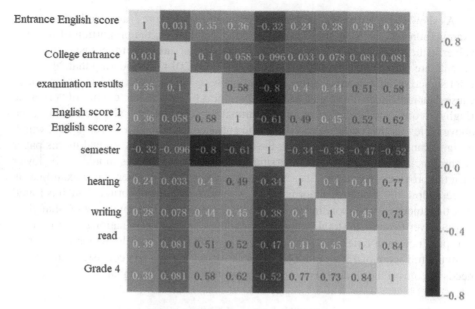

Fig. 5. Pearson correlation coefficient

scores that are longer away from CET-4 have less impact on CET-4 scores. In order to accurately understand the relationship between each factor and CET-4, the relationship between each factor and CET-4 will be analyzed one by one. The correlation between "semester" and CET-4 is -0.52, indicating that there is a strong negative correlation between "semester" and CET-4. It can be seen from this that the higher the "semester", the worse the grade of CET-4. That is to say, the later the students take CET-4, the less likely they are to pass CET-4.

3   Analysis and Prediction of CET4 Based on Data Mining

When using k-nearest neighbor algorithm for prediction classification, it is necessary to determine the appropriate number of nearest neighbors K and select important features. In order to make the classification accuracy higher and the classification performance more stable, this paper uses an iterative method to select k and important features. Firstly, take all features as input variables to determine the nearest neighbor number k of several, then reduce the features successively under the condition that the K value remains unchanged, select important features according to the standard of prediction effect, and finally take the important features as input variables to determine the appropriate K value.

Using python programming, the curves of accuracy, accuracy, recall and F - value in the above 8 cases are obtained. The accuracy reflects the ability of the classification model (algorithm) to correctly classify and predict, including predicting positive cases as positive cases and negative cases as negative cases. The accuracy rate reflects the ability of how many of the predicted positive cases are real positive cases, while the recall rate reflects the ability of how many of the positive cases can be correctly classified and predicted.

As shown in Fig. 6, the accuracy in eight modes increases with K-shaped amplification. $K \geq 11$, the accuracy is basically stable under all working conditions With the increase of potassium content, some changes have taken place, but the change is very small, usually no more than 2%. Case 1 has the largest input property, but the prediction accuracy is not the highest in terms of display accuracy. Although the input property is very small, the average accuracy of Sect. 11 prediction can be $\leq K \leq 29$, and the variation range is relatively small. In the accuracy chart and inverse modulus chart, the variation range of each curve is larger than that of the accuracy chart and f chart, indicating that the number and nature of the recent K have a great impact on the prediction accuracy and callback rate. In these eight cases, the precision, recall coefficient and F value of condition 8 are not the highest, but the precision, recall coefficient and F value of condition 8 are relatively high. As for the purpose of this prediction, I want to predict students' grades in College English. Finally, considering the importance of indicators to the prediction of College English test results, only three characteristics of English entry, English 1 and English 2, are selected.

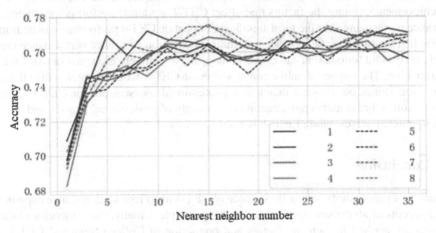

Fig. 6. Accuracy chart

Considering that the relevant scores have been standardized, and the distance between samples is less than 3, this paper selects Gaussian function as the function of weight. The specific steps of realizing weighted k-nearest neighbor classification are as follows:

(1) Initialize the value of K;
(2) Loading data;
(3) Calculate the Euclidean distance between the samples to be classified and the training data;
(4) Sort the distance values in ascending order;
(5) Extract the first k distances D1, D2,..., DK from the sorted array;
(6) Using Gaussian function, the voting weights W1, W2,..., WN of the first k distances are calculated;

(7)   Win the sample type corresponding to the initial distance K, and calculate the total weight of each category
(8)   Go back to the results of the plan.

In order to predict the results of CET-4 more accurately, the data are processed in advance, the classified variables are converted into factors, and the quantitative variables are standardized. Then select the input prediction function and nearest neighbor K according to various indicators. The nearest neighbor classification model of K is established Finally, a K-Neighborhood subclass weighted model is established to accelerate the classification of CET4 results.

English scores have the greatest influence on CET-4 scores and play a decisive role. The teaching effect is not ideal simply according to the quality of English performance, because there are many reasons for the quality of English performance. For example, some students have a good foundation, but do not study after enrollment, resulting in poor English performance and CET-4 can not pass; Some students can't keep up with the teaching progress because of their poor foundation. Although they study hard, their English grades are still not very good, and they can't pass CET-4. This paper lists English achievement as a reference attribute and studies the influence of other factors on CET-4 achievement. Among the factors that affect CET-4 academic performance, students' entrance performance has the most significant impact on CET-4 performance in addition to English performance factors, because students with good entrance performance have a relatively solid foundation, can actively study, and a relatively high pass rate of CET-4 examination. The impact of public course scores on CET-4 scores is weaker than that of admission scores, but stronger than that of professional course scores on CET-4 scores. The reason is that students pay attention to the study of professional courses and invest less in public courses, while English is a public course.

4   Conclusion

Firstly, this paper points out the importance of CET-4 to college students, then expounds the concepts of algorithm, and focuses on the principle. Finally, some theories of data mining are applied influencing factors and prediction of College Students' CET-4. It has clear conditioning, in-depth analysis and close to reality, which has certain reference value and guiding significance. The main features are: (2) the data comes from the accumulation of many years of work, which is true and effective; (2) It can skillfully transform and process individual field data, making the analysis more illustrative and universal; (3) The analysis and prediction of CET-4 has certain practical value for students, teachers and teaching managers. Of course, not all the influencing factors are taken into account, such as students' family situation and English teachers' teaching situation, which leads to a certain gap between the predicted and actual results of very few students. In the future actual prediction, the influencing factors should be taken into account as much as possible to reduce the error. However, the model will also become relatively complex at that time.

References

1. Wang, S.H., Ji-Rong, L.V., Feng, B.: Analysis and prediction of performance of CET4 based on data mining. Comput. Knowl. Technol. (2014)
2. Wang, H.: Analysis and prediction of cet4 scores based on data mining algorithm. Complexity **2021**(12), 1–11 (2021)
3. Liang, S.W.: Research and analysis of the accuracy of listening question of cet4 based on the multi-media environment
4. Qiao, Q.S., Wang, H.T., Wang, Z.Y., et al.: CET4 passing rate analysis based on fuzzy decision tree induction and active learning. In: International Conference on Machine Learning & Cybernetics. IEEE (2011)
5. Reflection of the Reform in CET4 writing based on language testing theory. 2015(8), 2 (2015)
6. Xin, Z., Shuang, G., Yu, S.: A study on Post-CET4 college English teaching model based on intercultural communication
7. Zhang, S.Z., Shang, L.L., Lu, X., et al.: The analysis and discussion of CET4 scores based on data statistics. J. Jiamusi Vocational Institute (2017)
8. Paterva Evolution Data Mining for the Google Generation. https://www.facebook.com/Symantec
9. The Effects of MI Theoy-based Learning Strategies on Vocational College Students' CET4 Vocabulary Learning
10. Yan, X.U., Zheng, D.F.: Based on CET4 and CET6 new topic of the listening comprehension ability training. Sci. Technol. Vis. (2017)

Analysis of the Rational Use of Context Construction in College English Teaching Based on Association Rules Mining Algorithm

Chuanwei Zhang[✉]

Ganzhou Teachers College, Ganzhou 341000, Jiangxi, China
zcwteacher@163.com

Abstract. In our country's education, in order to help more students have a strong interest in learning, teaching methods are various and colorful. Among them, the teaching method of situational teaching is to take students as the main body, through some specific scenes, students can participate in it, learn more knowledge, and situational teaching is more conducive to developing students' vision, Mobilize the enthusiasm of students. In order to improve the level and efficiency of College English teaching, the paper designs the analysis of the rational application of context construction in College English Teaching under the association rule mining algorithm. Through the analysis of the connotation of situational teaching, this paper studies the application of situational teaching in College English teaching, so as to better arouse students' interest in English.

Keywords: Association rules · College English teaching · Situation construction · Mining algorithm

1 Introduction

In our country, the basic courses for students are constantly undergoing comprehensive reform. With the increasing competitiveness of our country in the world market, English has also been attached great importance to by us. English teaching is of great significance in education [1]. We need to improve the English teaching system, create new English teaching methods, and promote students to better accept and learn English knowledge. In the traditional English teaching mode, English teachers explain English knowledge to students. The atmosphere in the classroom is relatively low. In the face of too rigid grammar knowledge, students' interest in learning English can not be stimulated. The proposal of situational teaching can fully mobilize students' enthusiasm in the classroom and clarify students' dominant position in the classroom, Try to make students learn more English in specific situations. The application of situational teaching in College English teaching is in line with the requirements of the new curriculum reform in China, and helps students learn happily.

M. A. Jan and F. Khan (Eds.): BigIoT-EDU 2022, LNICST 465, pp. 114–119, 2023.
https://doi.org/10.1007/978-3-031-23950-2_13

2 Application of Association Rules Mining Algorithm

2.1 Data Mining Process Design

The process of data mining is: to confirm the data types to be mined, to transform and clean the data in the database, to mine the data according to the accurate data types through association rules mining algorithm, to analyze and evaluate the mining results after mining, and to show them to users through the client. The detailed process of data mining is shown in Fig. 1.

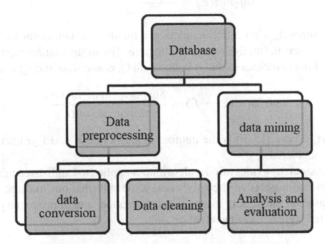

Fig. 1. The process of College English data mining

In the application of association rules mining algorithm in College English teaching, the first task of this method is to build a suitable teaching situation. In the process of constructing the situation, we need to follow the basic principles mentioned above, not only fit the teaching content, but also have some fun. Not only that, but also need to do a good job in the screening of situational materials. To choose materials that meet the cognitive level of college students, it is neither too simple nor too difficult. Then the material and teaching content are combined and transformed into specific teaching situation, which can be applied to teaching activities. Moreover, according to the different aspects of situation introduction, we can construct the situation from the aspects of introduction, teaching and divergence [2].

2.2 Algorithm Design of Association Rule Mining

1) Association Rules Mining Algorithm

Generally, the basic idea of Apriori can be divided into two sub problems.

① Discovery of frequent itemsets. All frequent itemsets with minimum support are searched according to the minimum support given by users. The frequent itemsets searched may have inclusion relation. Generally, only the frequent large itemsets not included in other frequent itemsets are searched, This kind of frequent large itemsets is the basis of generating association rules.

The generation of association rules. Based on the minimum confidence given by users, the association rules whose confidence is greater than or equal to the minimum confidence are found from the maximum frequent item day set.

Suppose that the set B of English teaching situation contains the above constraint association rules, then in the constraint Q. The support (E) of project set under E is as follows:

$$Support(E) = \frac{Support\_count(E)}{m} \quad (1)$$

where: m and support_ Count (E) indicates the number of data (total events) and the number of e-item sets in English teaching situations. B% of the management in the set B of English teaching situations includes both e with Q. constraints and Q; F of constraint.

$$confidence(E \rightarrow F) = \frac{Support\_count(E \cup F)}{Support\_count(E)} \quad (2)$$

where: support_ Count (EUF) is the number of times that E and f project sets appear together in management.

The above association rules mining algorithm is applied to English teaching situation, which can mine all aspects of the user's education information, manage the relevant information based on the mining association information, and improve the performance of the system in English teaching situation.

3   The Application of Context Teaching in College English Learning Under Association Rules

3.1   Construction of Cooperative Teaching System

In English classroom, the students break the dull atmosphere in the classroom through situational teaching. In the set situation, the students can communicate with each other through mutual cooperation and communication, carry out dialogue or scenario reproduction, fully mobilize the enthusiasm of students to learn English, make students learn English knowledge happily in an easy environment, and cultivate their own learning ability, It can make students have a strong interest in English, improve their oral English, and deeply understand and digest the English knowledge or grammar deduced in class. As a new form of education, situational teaching is more conducive to strengthening the students' team cooperation ability, increasing the mutual communication between students, making them face difficulties, solve problems and improve together. In addition to improving students' English learning ability, it also fosters the team spirit of students and improves the comprehensive quality of students [3].

3.2 Design Teaching Process from Students' Interests

How can we help students to accomplish heavy tasks? It is necessary for teachers to design professional, practical and interesting situations from the interest of students, help students to establish their determination to learn English well, and drive the enthusiasm of students to learn English. In order to reduce the pressure on students to learn English, they can better help students improve their learning results and complete the learning tasks easily. Teaching activities are the interaction between teachers and students. Situational Cognition is an effective way for students to solve the difficulties in general knowledge. This requires teachers to understand students deeply, stimulate students' desire for knowledge and guide them to participate in learning projects actively.

3.3 Democratic and Harmonious Atmosphere is the Foundation of Situational Teaching

In context teaching, teachers and students need to have a democratic and harmonious atmosphere in the classroom. Teachers actively guide students to participate in the set situation. Students should also actively cooperate with teachers to complete the learning tasks, effectively communicate and communicate with students in situational teaching. Students can improve their oral ability by learning English knowledge better in the context, Teachers need to find out the problems that students encounter in learning and correct them in time, so that teachers and students can improve in situational teaching, and better cultivate the emotion between teachers and students.

3.4 General Connection of Concern

Paying attention to the universal connection of things, connecting things, events and characters in different fields can often achieve better results. The common connection between things can be put forward to carry out comparative teaching on similar topics, deepen the theme, and study relevance analogy, not limited to a point, diffuse thinking, deepen discussion level, expand the discussion scope, which is conducive to the development of students' intelligence and improve the discussion effect. In this way, the development of students' potential ability and dialectical relationship between things can effectively improve students' learning methods, and make series and depth of familiar and interesting topics, so that students can master the English content they have learned more and more deeply.

4 The Significance of Situational Teaching in College English

4.1 Situational Teaching Opens a New Chapter for College English Classroom Teaching

Situational teaching has really created a new situation for College English classroom teaching, which has fully played the students' subjective initiative, and thus created an active atmosphere of English classroom. Situational teaching fully shows the main position of students, fully displays the students' unique personality, helps students alleviate the huge pressure in the learning process, creates a harmonious and cheerful learning environment for students, and truly realizes that students' needs and interests can arouse students' enthusiasm for learning English and communicate with teachers better, Thus, the heavy English teaching content can not only improve their learning results, but also gain strong satisfaction and self-confidence in the relaxed learning environment. Through the new teaching method of situational teaching, the teaching effect and teaching quality can be improved.

4.2 Practical Application of Situation Teaching to Realize Knowledge

Situational teaching helps to transfer knowledge from one situation to another, and to realize the practical application of knowledge. The purpose of English Teaching in Colleges and universities is to cultivate students' comprehensive application ability, especially English listening and speaking ability, and to enhance their independent learning ability and comprehensive cultural literacy. It is no longer an isolated and monotonous process to make learning a real application of the knowledge learned in life, to achieve the application of learning, so that students can truly realize the use of learning, in a variety of language environment, deepen the practical application of cultural knowledge, which is conducive to the improvement of comprehensive quality and practical ability.

4.3 Situational Teaching Stimulates Students' Interest in Learning and Meets Their Learning Needs

With the development of economic globalization, the application of English in practical work has been paid more and more attention. Therefore, students need to learn English well during the school. However, in English classroom, teachers explain various English knowledge and grammar, which can not drive students' enthusiasm for learning English, nor train their oral and practical application ability, which creates a relatively boring classroom atmosphere for English classroom, which leads to some students unable to focus on English learning, and English performance is getting worse and worse [4], Finally, the students lose their confidence in learning English well. The application of situational teaching in College English teaching provides a relaxed and Harmonious English classroom for students and teachers. While mobilizing students to actively participate in the set situation, the students' oral English ability and practical application ability are constantly improved, so that students can truly master English as a foreign language. In addition, the construction of the cooperation system also promotes the harmonious relationship between students, and realizes common progress. Meanwhile, learning to cooperate with teams is the spirit that students must have in the society and get positive exercise in the context teaching.

5   Conclusion

In the teaching of College English, the use of association rule mining algorithm can play a good role in the situation construction. Therefore, for English teachers, we should recognize the basic principles of situational construction method, combine with the teaching practice, create and introduce the situation, make it fully penetrate into English classroom, improve teaching effect and strengthen students' English literacy.

References

1. Liping, L., Xinyou, Z., Xiaolu, N., et al.: Review of parallel association rule mining algorithm based on spark. Comput. Eng. Appl. **55**(9), 1–9 (2019)
2. Dongmei, S.: An empirical study of situational approach in high school English Grammar Teaching. East China Normal University, Shanghai (2012)
3. Haili, Z.: Exploration of situational english teaching in junior middle school. New Educ. (6) (2010)
4. Qingshan, L.: Exploration of college english vocabulary teaching based on humanistic context construction. Youth **12**, 115–116 (2015)

Application and Implementation of Education Management System Based on Cloud Storage

Xia Lu[✉]

Wuhan University of Engineering Science, Wuhan 430200, Hubei, China
`xialu_2009@126.com`

Abstract. This paper studies the research and design of education management system based on cloud storage. Cloud storage is a storage strategy that gathers a large number of different types of storage devices in the network through application software to work together and jointly provide data storage services through cluster applications, distributed file systems and other functions. In the research on massive data storage of university education management system, we deeply study cloud storage technology, compare various data layout algorithms, and propose an improved data layout algorithm combined with consistent hash algorithm, improved consistent hash algorithm and sieve algorithm, so as to improve data access efficiency and meet the requirements of dynamic scalability of storage space of cloud storage platform, At the same time, a local duplicate data deletion algorithm according to the characteristics of teaching data is proposed to reduce the data redundancy. Information construction in Colleges and universities is the key factor to realize modern education. In the process of information construction in Colleges and universities, due to the similarity of teaching data, there are a lot of duplicate data between the education management systems independently built by colleges and universities, resulting in a great waste of storage resources, and the teaching data is growing exponentially, which brings great storage pressure to the traditional data center.

Keywords: Cloud storage · Teaching data · Management system

1 Introduction

Education management is to use teaching management measures to guide teachers to achieve teaching objectives through administrative departments and administrative mechanisms. Management measures, objects and personnel constitute three elements of educational management, each of which plays its own role in management. In the actual implementation process, although the education management has achieved remarkable results, there are still many problems. Therefore, under the new situation, the education management of colleges and universities should establish correct objectives, formulate and improve management measures. This paper will discuss the current situation and mechanism innovation of efficient management under the new situation, in order to improve the level of educational management in Colleges and universities.

© ICST Institute for Computer Sciences, Social Informatics and Telecommunications Engineering 2023
Published by Springer Nature Switzerland AG 2023. All Rights Reserved
M. A. Jan and F. Khan (Eds.): BigIoT-EDU 2022, LNICST 465, pp. 120–130, 2023.
https://doi.org/10.1007/978-3-031-23950-2_14

The management concept and content are relatively old, which seriously affects its efficiency. At present, most colleges and universities in China follow the education management system in the period of planned economy. Although they have experienced many reforms, this education system has been deeply rooted, and the reform has not fundamentally changed it. Therefore, the management concept of colleges and universities in China is ten times old. The content of the existing rules and regulations is relatively old, which has been unable to play its due role, resulting in the low effect of management. Therefore, the politicization of the management mode has been inconsistent with modern higher education, the management concept of management staff has not changed with the reform of education, and there is a lack of educational thought of "people-oriented" and "student-oriented". The backward management concept and outdated content will directly lead to the low efficiency of teaching management, and then affect the teaching effect. The means of education management are relatively single, and the management system is relatively backward [1]. At present, China's colleges and universities still use the management method of experience teaching, so the means of education management is very single and the method is very old. They pay too much attention to the standardization and institutionalization of work, which can not meet the needs of social development. Moreover, at this stage, the means of educational management are lack of scientificity, and all the work is completed by manual management. It can be said that the educational management of colleges and universities in China has not kept pace with the progress of science and technology. The market competition in today's society requires the transformation of talents. The original education management system can no longer guarantee the cultivation of excellent and cutting-edge talents. Therefore, the education management model needs to be further reformed. In the process of reform, we should pay attention to people-oriented and the dominant position of students in the process of education. 1.3 the level of education management is low and lack of scientificity. At present, although China's colleges and universities have increased a lot of human, physical and financial resources in the work of educational management, they have not achieved corresponding results. With the continuous reform of education, the school running system is also constantly improving and perfecting, and the function of educational management is also changing, constantly tending to service and guidance. At this stage, in order to better realize educational management, we must cultivate more capable educational management groups to get out of the misunderstanding of "management for management" and further promote or even achieve the goal of "management for no management". However, the educational management of colleges and universities in China is lack of scientificity. Many management systems are only superficial forms and can not play any role, so that the educational management can not meet the requirements of the new era.

Innovate the educational management mode of colleges and universities. At present, the educational management mode of colleges and universities in China is relatively backward, which can not meet the requirements of talent training in today's society. With the continuous reform of education and teaching ethics, its management concept is also constantly improving. In order to make education management better serve the training of talents, we must draw lessons from successful and excellent management modes at home and abroad, extract the essence and remove the dross [2]. Only by constantly improving and improving in this way can we find the most suitable management mode for our colleges and universities and better cultivate talents who meet the needs of modernization. In the construction of management system, we must strengthen the management system and guiding function. Therefore, the reform of education management system should be weakened on the basis of retaining the original functions. The purpose of weakening is to better highlight that education management is to serve students. When guiding the innovative education concept, we should pay attention to the personalized development of students, implement the "people-oriented" student view, teach students according to their aptitude, and create a learning environment of independent learning, equality and freedom for students [3].

In the past two years, cloud computing technology has developed rapidly. Its core idea 3 is to provide software, platform and it equipment resources in the form of services. The goal is to integrate a large number of cheap physical computing resources with low performance into a powerful computer system with high computing power, large storage capacity and powerful functions, so as to provide a unified service interface. Users can pay for software, platform or underlying hardware equipment according to their actual needs.

2 Related Work

2.1 University Education Management System Architecture Based on Cloud Storage

Cloud storage is a flexible concept. It is an extension and expansion of the concept of cloud computing. It refers to a technology that allocates storage resources in the network on demand. Similarly, it also refers to a technical idea of integrating storage resources through software to work together. This idea has absolute advantages for making full use of computing resources and storage resources. The cloud storage platform can process tens of millions or even billions of information in a few seconds to achieve the same powerful network service as the "supercomputer". The cloud storage model is shown in Fig. 1.

Compared with traditional storage, cloud storage has the following three advantages:

1. Storage management can be automated and intelligent. All storage resources are integrated, and customers see a single storage space.
2. It has the function of automatic allocation of storage space through virtualization, and can improve the efficiency of storage space re allocation.
3. Cloud storage can achieve scale effect and elastic expansion, reduce operating costs and avoid resource waste.

Compared with traditional storage, cloud storage has less transmission speed than traditional storage (this feature may change with the commercial use of 5g), but it is relatively more intelligent and can access video data more intelligently. Moreover, cloud storage also has advantages in cost and can achieve the purpose of storage through low-cost operation and maintenance [4].

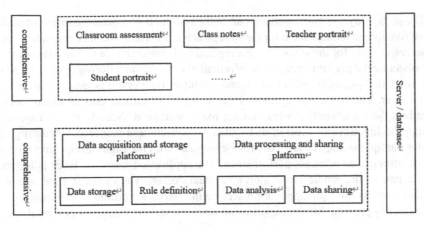

Fig. 1. Cloud storage model

The university management integrated query system based on cloud storage architecture is mainly based on the idea of cloud storage, combined with the basic architecture of cloud storage and the actual situation of the query system, to achieve the following system objectives:

(1) Distributed storage based on cloud computing does not use database, and files are stored with high compression ratio. Plan during system implementation use the idea of distributed storage to support the reuse and heterogeneity of pcserver, blade machine, minicomputer and other machines; Support management and processing of dynamic scaling and dynamic expansion, and realize application level disaster recovery at the same time. In this way, it can not only reduce investment, but also adopt data storage with high compression ratio to save storage space.

(2) Diversity of management support. The system will eventually support bill data storage and query.

(3) High speed query. The first construction goal of the system is to use the idea of search engine and memory index grouping mechanism to improve the system performance.

It is required to achieve high-speed concurrent query and provide quasi real-time query, so as to improve the real-time experience of users.

(4) Unified query platform. Through a unified and centralized data storage platform, it can meet the needs of comprehensive information storage, management and query of each subsystem in the boss system.

Provide a unified and centralized management platform for colleges and universities, with the goal of comprehensively supporting and meeting the needs of customers' management and comprehensive inquiry, and provide high-quality services [5].

The comprehensive query system of college education management based on cloud storage architecture includes all four layers of general cloud storage architecture model, namely storage layer, basic management layer, application interface layer and access layer.

The storage layer is the most basic part of the system. It specifically carries out unified read-write storage management for the storage devices in the system. At the same time, it is also responsible for the status monitoring and fault maintenance of hardware devices, and collecting the performance status information of the system during operation. At the same time, the file organization and management of the system is also the main work of this layer. The basic management layer is the most critical part of cloud storage. It realizes the collaborative work among many storage devices in the storage layer through the functions of cluster, distributed file system and resource scheduling, and enables multiple storage devices to provide services with the same service interface and provide stronger data access performance. The application interface layer is the most flexible part of the whole cloud storage system design. The cloud storage operation unit can develop multiple application service interfaces according to different service types, flexibly provide different application services, and provide more powerful system management, query and monitoring services for other personnel who use the university education management query interface for application development and design. The access layer will enable any college education management user to access the system through this layer. At the same time, the system also provides many different access methods, such as facilitating the call of different access methods.

Data server node: this type of server node includes functional modules such as data storage management, data writing, data extraction, data copy replication, heart-beat detection, status report, etc.; The data storage management module is used for the management of the file system of the data server. The data writing module receives the writing request from the outside and cooperates with the index management module to write the data [6]. The data extraction module receives the external request and reads the relevant consumption information for feedback. The heartbeat detection is used to send the heartbeat information to the central control server, Indicates that the data server is still alive and can provide services. If the heartbeat signal is not sent to the central control server within the set threshold time, it will be recorded that the data server has been down. Status reports are used in conjunction with heartbeat detection.

2.2 System Technology

Ajax technology is the abbreviation of asynchronous JavaScript and XML. It is a web development technology for creating interactive web applications. It was first proposed by James Garrett. The Ajax method is a collection of all technologies that can be used in the browser through JavaScript scripts.

Ajax technology is not a new technology, but a combination of four existing different technologies. Ajax actually follows the request/sever network response mode. Therefore, the basic process of this framework is: object initialization → send related requests - > server data reception → server data return → client data reception → modify the page content of the client. But this process is asynchronous.

(1) Capture events for a page

When the data or content of the page in the browser is changed and the user clicks the submit button, the corresponding event will be triggered. For example, < ASP: button id = "btnok" runat = "server" text = "submit" onclick = "btnok_click"

> < / ASP: button >, when the mouse clicks, the corresponding btnok will be triggered_ Click event.

(2) XMLHttpRequest to initialize

After capturing the user's event, if communication with the server is involved, we need to instantiate XMLHttpRequest [7]. At this time, we need to note that different browser types or versions have different ways to instantiate them. For example, we should fully consider the implementation of various types of ActiveX controls in the form of Mozilla browser. Therefore, we should fully consider the implementation of various types of ActiveX controls in the form of Mozilla browser.

(3) Send request to server

After instantiating the relevant XMLHttpRequest, we need to specify the corresponding response processing function, that is, the callback function after the server responds, so that we can send an HTTP application request to the server.

(4) Receive the return information from the server

After sending the request to the server, we need to check the status of the XMLHttpRequest object through the corresponding processing function. When the status shows that all the information returned by the server has been accepted, we also need to judge whether the corresponding returned status code is correct, so as to judge whether the returned data is correct.

(5) Update the current page status.

Through the received data, XMLHttpRequest will be processed in the following two ways: some unstructured data information will be used as strings, and some structured data information will be used as XML documents.

3 Research and Design of Education Management System Based on Cloud Storage

This paper studies the design of education management system. Due to the limitations of higher education teaching means, the traditional teaching mode can not better meet the deeper learning requirements of students. The scientific application of employment oriented teaching mode can well mobilize the learning enthusiasm of college students, give scientific play to their subjective initiative, and promote the realization of College Students' knowledge, ability and quality objectives. According to the training objectives of higher education, scientifically evaluate the comprehensive quality of students, so that most students can have healthy psychology and good morality, and become talents needed by the country and society. Cloud storage is a network online storage mode, that is, data is stored on multiple virtual servers usually hosted by a third party rather than exclusive servers. Hosting companies operate large data centers. People who need data storage and hosting meet the needs of data storage by purchasing or renting storage space from them. According to the needs of customers, data center operators prepare storage virtualization resources at the back end and provide them in the form of storage pool, so that customers can use this storage resource pool to store files or objects by themselves [8]. In fact, these resources may be distributed on many server hosts. At the same time, we should make college students have a strong interest in the learning knowledge and research methods of this major, so as to cultivate their innovative thinking and realize college students' vision and pursuit of a better life. The task of education management in Colleges and universities is arduous. We need to fully mobilize human resources inside and outside the school. We should make concerted efforts to carry out education management, always adhere to the management principle of "scientific education, full education and comprehensive education", create a people-oriented education atmosphere, and build the connotation of leadership style, teachers' teaching style and students' study style, The development and construction of various forms of campus culture can promote the healthy development of college students, and the rich and colorful class culture and dormitory culture can improve the aesthetic taste of college students and enrich the cultural connotation of college students.

As a core component of cloud computing, cloud storage undertakes the task of data storage and information collection at the bottom of data. It is the foundation of the whole cloud platform and cloud services. Compared with traditional storage devices, its definition can not be simply understood as a single hardware device. This device can also be understood as a system. This system is generally composed of hardware environments such as server, storage, network and related software.

The concept of cloud storage is similar to cloud computing. It refers to a system in which a large number of different types of storage devices in the network work together through application software through the functions of cluster application, grid technology or distributed file system, so as to jointly provide data storage and business access functions, ensure the security of data and save storage space. In short, cloud storage is an emerging solution to put storage resources on the cloud for people to access. Users can connect to the cloud through any networked device at any time and anywhere to access data conveniently.

Storage layer: it is the foundation of cloud storage university education management system [9]. The university education management system of cloud storage relies on the storage layer to interconnect different storage devices to form a service-oriented distributed storage system. Above the physical storage device is a unified storage device management layer, which realizes the functions of logical virtualization management, status monitoring and maintenance of physical storage devices.

Management and scheduling layer: it is the core of cloud storage university education management system. The main function is to deploy distributed file system or establish and organize storage resource objects on the storage resources provided by the storage layer, segment the user data, and store the segmented data to specific storage resources in the form of multiple copies or redundant erasure codes according to the set protection strategy. At the same time, in this layer, read-write load balancing scheduling, business scheduling and data reconstruction and recovery after the failure of nodes or storage resources will be carried out among nodes, so as to always provide high-performance and highly available access services. However, in the specific implementation, the function of this layer may also be moved up, located between the access interface layer and the application service layer, or even directly embedded into the application service layer, which is closely combined with business applications to form a college education management system with business dedicated cloud storage.

Access interface layer: This is a freely extensible structure layer oriented to user requirements. In general, various interfaces can be opened and various services can be provided according to specific conditions and needs.

User access layer: On any machine connected to the Internet, as long as the user is authorized, he can enter the cloud stored college education management system platform system through this layer, carry out the allowable authorization operation on the cloud stored college education management system, and enjoy various services brought by the cloud stored college education management system.

With the deepening of educational modernization, the amount of data in educational management system shows an exponential growth, which brings severe challenges to the traditional data center. The most direct way to store massive data is to increase the number of storage devices in the data center. However, simply relying on the addition of storage devices to solve the storage problems caused by the explosive growth of data will greatly increase the storage cost of colleges and universities. Moreover, due to the poor dynamic scalability of traditional systems, the large increase of storage devices will bring great challenges to the maintenance and upgrading of relevant systems. Facing the explosive growth of data, how to realize the efficient storage of this part of data is an urgent problem to be solved in Colleges and universities [10]. Through the analysis and research of various data layout algorithms in cloud storage technology, an improved data layout algorithm is proposed to meet the requirements of fairness and adaptability at the same time; In addition, according to the characteristics of college teaching data, a local duplicate data deletion algorithm based on the characteristics of teaching data is proposed to minimize the data redundancy and reduce the pressure of network bandwidth, so as to reduce the storage pressure of massive data on the traditional data center and the complexity of system upgrading and maintenance in the future.

The introduction of large virtual nodes solves the unsolved fairness requirements of consistent hash algorithm. In addition, because the consistent hash algorithm is adopted in the set, it can well meet the requirements of self adaptability. Moreover, because the storage nodes are classified according to the weight, the allocation of intervals and large virtual nodes are for the classified set, the number of intervals and virtual nodes is greatly reduced, which effectively avoids the problems of excessive storage overhead caused by the introduction of a large number of virtual nodes in the improved consistent hash algorithm.

4   System Implementation

Although students' awareness of autonomy has been improved when they enter colleges and universities from middle school, with the increasingly fierce employment competition, college students' desire for self-expression and self promotion ability have become the demand for college students' professional ability and quality in the future. Excellent student cadres in school are the priority indicators of many employers. The self-education, self-management, self-service and other activities that college students participate in during their stay in school are of great significance to train their management ability, improve their teamwork ability, enhance their strong will and cultivate their noble ideological quality. Therefore, we should give scientific play to the functions of student organizations such as the Communist Youth League, student unions and classes, and establish a practical model of students' self-education and self-management.

The construction of digital campus has achieved initial results in major colleges and universities. The use of network, multimedia and other high-tech means for auxiliary teaching or online teaching has been gradually carried out. Analyzing the current daily teaching process of major colleges and universities, we can find that although the campus network has been built, the actual utilization rate of each teaching system is not high, and the auxiliary function for daily teaching work is not complete. For example, there are two common teaching activities, teaching courseware sharing between teachers and students and online submission of students' classroom homework. At present, there are mainly three ways: one is to copy teachers' teaching courseware through USB flash disk, that is, students use USB flash disk to copy teachers' teaching courseware in spare time such as recess; The second is to share teaching resources by sending e-mail by teachers, that is, teachers uniformly set and publish a shared mailbox, and student users in a specific class use password to share teaching resources and submit classroom homework by logging in to this shared mailbox; The third is to use FTP server.

College teaching data are mostly stored in the local education management system in the form of electronic data. In this storage mode, once the education management system suffers a disaster, it will paralyze the school teaching system and affect the normal progress of education and teaching activities.

In view of the above problems, through the research and summary of university resource sharing methods, this paper puts forward the sharing strategy based on university resource space and role; Secondly, through the research and analysis of the current backup strategies of the existing education management system, a resource level backup strategy based on the characteristics of teaching data is proposed [11]. Combined with the distribution characteristics of the underlying equipment, a data redundancy strategy is proposed to further improve the security of education data.

The public resource sharing area provides a shared pool for all users in Colleges and universities, and allocates a large storage space in the actual cloud storage space to store public resources for all users in Colleges and universities. The storage area is open to all teachers and students in the school. All roles are automatically bound to the space and assigned corresponding permissions.

The class resource sharing area is oriented to the class groups in the actual teaching process. It allocates storage space for all classes in the school to store the data shared within each class. Each space is only open to the internal members of the class. Users are automatically bound to the corresponding class resource sharing area according to the actual class division of the school, and only have the relevant permissions of their class resource sharing area.

The course resource sharing area is oriented to the course classes in the actual teaching process. Storage space is allocated for all courses to store the data shared by each course class. Each space is only open to the students who choose the course and the teachers who set up the course. All student users are automatically bound to the corresponding course resource sharing area according to the opening course selection results, and only have the relevant permissions of the resource sharing area.

External interface: the system provides storage, reading and deletion interfaces for developers at the upper layer. Developers can call the interface provided by the platform to complete the storage, reading, modification and deletion of data. The main implementation interfaces include:

1. Performput (string nativepath) / / storage interface. The parameter is the local storage path; 2. Performget (string nativepath, string remoteobjectname) / / read interface. The parameters are the data storage path and the ID of the read data;

3. Performmodify (string objectname) / / modify the data interface. The parameter is the ID of the modified data;

4. Performdelete (string objectname) / / delete the data interface. The parameter is the ID of the deleted data.

Back end storage device group: the back-end storage device group is composed of a large number of cheap PCs with different performance and a large capacity server[12]. The improved data layout algorithm is proposed to connect all storage nodes into a ring to form a large virtual storage pool to provide unified storage services. As shown in Fig. 2 below, some codes of data storage development are shown.

```
>> function [C,L,L1,1]=lagran1(X,Y)
m=length(X);L=ones(m,m);
for k=1:m
    V=1;
    for i=1:m
    if k~=i
        V=conv(V,poly(X(i)))/(X(k)-X(i));
    end
end
L1(k,:)=V;1(k,:)=poly2sym(V)
end
C=Y*L1;L=Y*1;x=[0.4,0.5,0.6,0.7,0.8];
y=[ -0.756291,-0.443147,-0.150826,0.133325,0.416856];
[c,L,L1,1]=lagran1(x,y)
```

Fig. 2. Data storage development part code

5   Conclusion

This paper studies the research and design of education management system based on cloud storage. The teaching content management module is mainly designed to improve the flexibility of the system. The administrator can change the teaching content of the system by adding, deleting and modifying the teaching content. Research and propose solutions to the problem of massive data storage. The cloud storage technology and data deduplication technology are deeply studied respectively to better meet the performance requirements of fairness and adaptability in the data layout algorithm at the same time. The improved data layout algorithm avoids the disadvantage of the lack of fairness consideration of the consistent hash algorithm, solves the problem of poor adaptability of sieve algorithm, effectively reduces the number of virtual nodes introduced in the improved consistent hash algorithm, and reduces the storage overhead and algorithm complexity. According to the characteristics of teaching data in Colleges and universities, a local duplicate data deletion algorithm is proposed to greatly reduce the redundancy of teaching data and storage overhead.

References

1. Ahn, B.: Construction of video management system based on remote education. Int. J. Innov. Technol. Explor. Eng. **10**(7), 91–94 (2021)
2. Djuraevna, A.Z.: Formation of student management activities in the higher education management system. Psychology (Savannah, Ga.) 58(2), 1494–1499 (2021)
3. Zakarija, I., Skoir, Z., Ubrini, K.: Human resources management system for Higher Education institutions (2021)
4. Sokhom, W., Mekruksavanich, S.: A cooperative education management system using technology acceptance model. In: 2021 Joint International Conference on Digital Arts, Media and Technology with ECTI Northern Section Conference on Electrical, Electronics, Computer and Telecommunication Engineering (2021)
5. Kanagamani, V., Karuppiah, M.: Zero knowledge based data deduplication using in-line Block Matching protocol for secure cloud storage. Turk. J. Electr. Eng. Comput. Sci. **29**(4), 2067–2083 (2021)
6. Al-Qora'N, L.F.: Social RE-PBL: an approach for teaching requirements engineering using PBL, SNSs, and cloud storages and file-sharing services. Int. J. Inf. Educ. Technol. **11**(7), 342–347 (2021)
7. Chaudhari, S., Swain, G.: Efficient and secure group based collusion resistant public auditing scheme for cloud storage. Int. J. Adv. Comput. Sci. Appl. 12(3) (2021)
8. Ming, Y., He, B., Wang, C.: Efficient revocable multi-authority attribute-based encryption for cloud storage. IEEE Access, PP(99), 1–1 (2021)
9. Yin, C., Zhang, J.: The study of benefit evaluation model and management system on education equipment (2012)
10. Wicander, G.: Mobile supported e-Government systems: analysis of the education management information system (EMIS) in Tanzania. Karlstad University (2011)
11. Juan, R.: Personalized service model system design of college education management system based on web data mining. Computer Study (2010)
12. Guan, Q., Tian, T.: Historical review of development of chinese management system for physical education. Journal of Shanxi Datong University

Application of Big Data in Comprehensive Management and Service of Sports Training System Under the Background of Informatization

Jian Zhang(✉)

Nanchang Institute of Technology, Nanchang 330044, Jiangxi, China
Zhugewolong88@163.com

Abstract. With the development of computer technology and network technology, we have taken the step of information construction. In just a few years, we have carried out systematic preparations for information technology, such as preparing to build a fully automated office system and educational administration management system. However, there are still major defects in physical education and teaching. There is no operable software at all. Physical education teachers are facing a huge workload during the annual physical education test period. Therefore, this paper combs and analyzes the big data precipitated in the process of sports comprehensive management and service, and finds that the rational use of big data resources makes sports management decisions more scientific and effective, and sports services more reasonable and humanized, so as to realize the transformation and upgrading of sports education management and service work.

Keywords: Physical training · Promotion of information technology · Big data · Integrated management and services

1 Introduction

With the development and application of computer network technology and the prevalence of modern high-tech education supporting facilities, a variety of network information management system software have been widely used in Colleges and universities. According to the disadvantages of physical education in Colleges and universities, build the corresponding data information system, and make full use of high-tech data mining technology, To achieve fully automated processing and a huge sports data information analysis system, so that students can query their grades more easily, and teachers can analyze and count the data more conveniently. The advantage of this system equipment is not only that it can efficiently, accurately and accurately find all kinds of results, but also classify and summarize the results ranking and screening work. The most important thing is that it can formulate different training plans according to students with different physical qualities, track and evaluate students' health status at any time. In this way,

© ICST Institute for Computer Sciences, Social Informatics and Telecommunications Engineering 2023
Published by Springer Nature Switzerland AG 2023. All Rights Reserved
M. A. Jan and F. Khan (Eds.): BigIoT-EDU 2022, LNICST 465, pp. 131–139, 2023.
https://doi.org/10.1007/978-3-031-23950-2_15

Students can know their physical condition like the back of their hand, improve their love for sports, and really integrate cultural education and physical education.

Nowadays, many colleges and universities have begun to explore and study the system software one after another [1]. Data mining technology is used in the current teaching and education management system, and students' physical fitness is obviously enhanced, which greatly improves the teaching management level of the school. Here, the author boldly puts forward the scheme of student sports performance assessment management system based on the current problems in Colleges and universities. The purpose is to use the system to solve various problems faced by colleges and universities in physical education, so as to help students have enthusiasm for physical exercise and make students have excellent physique, So as to ensure the teaching quality and teaching effect of the school.

Sports training system refers to a comprehensive examination and observation of the body of people engaged in sports training through medical and biological means, to evaluate their level and state, and to provide basis for scientific training. It is an important means to ensure the normal training and achieve good results. In order to improve the competitive level of athletes, athletes should undertake high-intensity and high-volume training, which requires the use of medical and biological means and technologies to monitor athletes. Timely understand the changes of athletes' physical functions and their adaptation to training. Only in this way can we ensure that athletes can give full play to their potential without causing sports diseases and affecting training. It includes the following aspects:

1. Athlete self supervision

Mainly through the athletes' self-monitoring table, the athletes themselves record the changes of some physical indicators, timely find some of their own problems, and remind the coaches to pay attention.

2. Physical examination

Including the examination and evaluation of athletes' body shape and function. Establish the basis of athlete evaluation model.

3. Diagnosis of sports diseases

Mainly for the diagnosis, first aid, treatment and rehabilitation of some diseases caused by exercise.

4. Supervision of athletes' physical function

This is an important component of medical supervision. An accurate evaluation of athletes can help coaches accurately understand the situation of athletes and reasonably arrange training. At the same time, athletes should know their own situation and adjust in time to ensure a good level of function.

5. Reasonable fatigue elimination measures

Eliminating exercise-induced fatigue is an important component of medical supervision. Ensure that the athletes are in good physical and functional condition, and ensure the athletes' training level.

6. Reasonable nutrition measures

Reasonable nutrition measures can ensure and improve the athletes' functional level.

2 Research Status at Home and Abroad

The concept of big data was first proposed by Mai Qingxi, a world-famous consulting company. It generally refers to the massive data generated in the era of information explosion. Through the processing and analysis of these massive data, we can filter or mine some valuable information. This information can effectively analyze the causes of problems, improve work efficiency, improve scientific decision-making, correctly predict the future, understand the laws of things, and provide the direction of solution and decision-making basis. By searching academic resource websites, relative to the research and Discussion on the application of big data in the fields of Ideological and political education and library management, the relevant research in College Physical Education and teaching mainly focuses on three aspects. First, the era of big data will have multiple effects on physical education and teaching. Zhang Hui's research shows that big data has the characteristics of large volume, complexity and value, which makes people reach an unprecedented height in the analysis, understanding and application of data, and all industries and fields are facing great impacts and challenges. Through the analysis of the concept of big data, this paper reveals its impact on college physical education teachers, college students and college physical education teaching, and analyzes and considers the preparations that the physical education industry should make when facing the huge value released by massive data. Second, big data is applied to the comprehensive reform of physical education, especially the management of physical education and teaching. For example, Zhou Xi and Liu Huijing made a countermeasure analysis in the research on comprehensive reform of School Physical Education - from the perspective of big data and innovation of physical education in Colleges and universities. Zhang Wenhua's research analyzed the impact of big data on "teaching" and "learning" of physical education from the perspective of information, Find the challenges and development prospects in physical education. Third, the theoretical discussion of big data in physical education teaching [2]. For example, Liu officials and Liu Huaijin put forward in the article that through the analysis and processing of the data in physical education teaching, we can find the value that can be used, reveal the essence behind its teaching phenomenon and explore the law of physical education teaching, the training system is shown in Fig. 1.

From the analysis of existing literature, the research on big data in physical education management and service is still relatively weak. On the one hand, most of the existing research focuses on the theoretical level and possibility, and lacks specific research on the process and practice of big data in physical education management and service; On the other hand, there is little empirical research on College Physical Education under the condition of big data environment in the previous research, which can not deeply mine, systematically integrate and locate the big data resources precipitated in physical education teaching. Moreover, although some studies have systematically analyzed the application of big data in physical education, there are still great limitations. They have not been deeply into the system to reveal the relationship between physical education teaching, physical supervision, extracurricular exercise, the second classroom, sports training of high-level sports teams and other factors. The research on the application of big data in college physical education is still blank. With the wide popularization and in-depth application of big data concepts and technologies, and with the rapid promotion of physical education reform, there will be more and better research on big data in

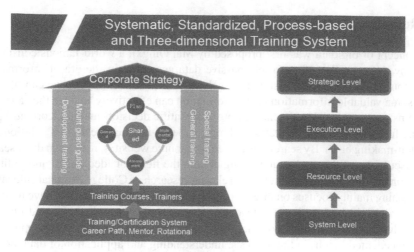

Fig. 1. Systematic training system

the field of physical education in Colleges and universities. Because practice does not stop, there will be new development in theory, and big data will penetrate all aspects of physical education in the future. Therefore, Exploring the specific application of big data in college physical education management and service has become an important topic.

3   Data Flow Analysis of Sports Training System

Because data is mobile in the process of operation and processing, data flow analysis is to analyze these flowing data. On the whole, the content to be analyzed is all data information.

In order to successfully complete the data analysis, there are two contents that need special attention: (1) data flow direction. It is the first condition to solve some data problems; (2) What changes have been made in the data flow process, and write down these changes in time. The purpose of data flow analysis is to find out the difficulties and vulnerabilities in data flow, such as flow interruption, numerical difference, etc. these difficulties and vulnerabilities should be clearly exposed during analysis and handled one by one.

The biomaster job analysis evaluation and exercise training system is the first integrated job in China. It is a comprehensive rehabilitation function diagnosis and treatment equipment integrating virtual reality, interactive training and rehabilitation evaluation. Through advanced wireless human body sensor technology and virtual reality technology, biomaster can record human joint activity and three-dimensional kinematic parameters in real time, and formulate personalized situational interactive training programs for patients, so as to improve patients' limb motor function and cognitive level. It is a comprehensive rehabilitation evaluation and sports training equipment. The biomaster hardware is mainly composed of advanced wireless human body sensing equipment.

Through the rehabilitation evaluation and training of different joints or trunk, it can collect spatial three-dimensional kinematic information in real time to accurately reflect the kinematic characteristics of the patient's joints or spine. Biomaster software: the biomaster software includes three modules: virtual reality, interactive training and rehabilitation evaluation. Through the collection of three-dimensional kinematic data, accurately evaluate the patient's joint activity, and carry out targeted personalized situational interactive training through the biofeedback technology of visual or auditory signals.

After analyzing the data flow, record the analysis results, and visually display the data flow direction through the data flow diagram. Developers develop corresponding software based on the flow information of these data. Three layer flow diagram is the most common data flow diagram description method. It can intuitively present the whole situation of data flow to developers [3]. The three-layer flow diagram has top, zero and one layer. The top level is for the flow of the entire data. Focus on the performance of edge data information: the zero layer is the refinement of the top layer, which describes the flow of data in the operation of functional modules in detail: the first layer, as the final functional module, is the smallest unit that can be realized. Figure 1 is the top-level data flow diagram of the system.

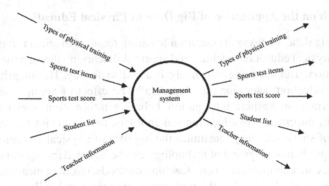

Fig. 2. Event level data flow chart of sports team performance Puli

4   Research on the Application of Big Data in Sports Comprehensive Management and Service

All links of sports management and service work can constitute the basic elements of big data. It is necessary to form a system and mechanism to ensure the collection, sorting and analysis of various data and their authenticity and integrity, accept big data thinking with a positive attitude, establish a public platform and operation mechanism for big data of sports management and service, and realize data sharing inside and outside the school, Barrier free experience the changes brought by big data, formulate the long-term plan of big data education application, and realize the transformation and upgrading of physical education management and service. Promote the deep integration of modern information technology and education and teaching, and accelerate the reform of education and teaching.

4.1 Practical Research on Big Data in Physical Education Management

Big data makes the physical education management process digital and intelligent, realizes the real-time mobile management of teachers' teaching and students' learning, and improves the authenticity and effectiveness of teaching evaluation and the effective value of feedback application; When big data is applied to venue management, it can collect real-time data on the use of venues and students' extracurricular activities, so as to scientifically set the allocation, use and construction management of venue resources. In order to achieve integration, cross-border, foundation and breakthrough of big data in sports comprehensive management and service, we need to make full use of the existing education information technology and realize the leapfrog deployment of technical resources related to big data application through advanced cloud computing and virtualization technology.

$$Vis(p) = 1 - \frac{1}{1+e^{(\text{Con}-\text{Con}(p)/k_2)}}$$
$$Dis(p) = \frac{1}{1+e^{(\bar{S}-S(p)/k_1)}}, \tag{1}$$

4.2 Research on the Application of Big Data in Physical Education

The role of "big data" in physical education teaching requires the final reform and optimization of physical education teaching and sports skill learning through the procedures of data collection, data screening, data analysis and data display. The integrity and accuracy of data collection determine the "big data" The effect of application, including the basic information, learning information, behavior information, social information and sports skill information of education stakeholders, that is, the internal and external environment of sports learning, constitutes the big data of physical education The real-time data and prediction judgment of technology can be adjusted and optimized in sports item selection, curriculum arrangement, teaching methods, teaching means and teaching evaluation, and gradually develop the traditional, empirical and collective teaching to a more scientific, visual and personalized education. "Big data" Applied physical education teaching is through the record of physical education learning process and track, through learning analysis (that is, it mainly involves the research and application of learning analysis, behavior analysis and prediction analysis), establish a learning model to judge students' sports learning effect and sports behavior trend. The application of big data technology can convert physical characteristics, learning materials, practice times, action standards, learning methods and learning effects into data. Students can correctly understand the action standards, adjust the practice frequency, understand their own advantages and disadvantages in sports skill learning, and change them in time Correct and wrong actions to realize students' self-directed learning [4]. The digitization of the whole teaching process enables teachers to fully understand students, provide personalized sports skill training programs for students with different physical and personality characteristics according to their learning data, better achieve the combination of collective guidance and individual guidance, enhance students' interest in learning, and then turn sports interest into sports Habit, make personalized physical education possible and lay the foundation for lifelong physical education.

The application of big data in physical education classroom is separated from the classroom, and learning resources become richer and easier to obtain. The online and offline open teaching mode makes the physical education classroom more a place for summary, communication and display, and bid farewell to the era of only one physical education class per week. By comprehensively and accurately mastering and analyzing the current situation of students' physical quality, analyze students' interest and love in sports Good and strong points, develop courses, teaching methods and training methods aimed at students' physical quality and characteristics, implement teaching according to their aptitude and comprehensively promote students' physical health; enrich and expand physical education teaching mode, change physical education teaching design, change students' learning methods through teaching design, meet students' personalized learning needs, and effectively promote teaching and learners' knowledge competition To improve the effective teaching and learning of physical education.

4.3 Practical Research on the Promotion of Students' Physical Health by Big Data

Through the collection of physical fitness test data organized by the Ministry of education every year, the conversion and storage of data are realized according to the reasoning rules, and the database is established, which can accurately analyze the current situation of students' physical fitness to improve the pertinence and effectiveness of education. Big data records the changes of students' movement trajectory and physical fitness, solves the problem of collecting students' physical fitness data every year, and can calculate the number of movements in real time According to and physical data, through analysis, it provides students with Sports Prescriptions of different gender, age and sports habits, provides students with real-time data comparison, improves the effect of sports prescriptions, improves students' Sports confidence, and helps teachers to comprehensively guide and evaluate students' sports skills and physical quality.

4.4 Research on the Application of Big Data in Competitive Sports of School Sports Teams

Through the big data of sports world campus app running, wechat sports, keep and other sports software in students' extracurricular exercise, we can understand students' exercise time, exercise frequency, exercise content and other information, so as to provide more scientific exercise methods, means and forms, and improve students' enthusiasm to participate in physical exercise. Through data analysis, activity project development can effectively guide students Extracurricular physical exercise, scientifically guiding students to exercise, plays a role in improving students' Sports literacy, effectively improving students' Participation Effect in physical exercise and enhancing their physique Figs. 2 and 3.

$$Coe(p) = Dis(p) \cdot Vis(p).$$

Rely on big data technology to realize the material selection, training means, technical analysis, running track, state diagnosis and pre competition information collection

Fig. 3.   The traning programs system in the paper

in the field of competitive sports of college sports teams, so as to scientifically guide students in training; coaches give targeted guidance to athletes' technology and scientifically train athletes' professional quality; analyze athletes' competitive state through training big data To predict the competitive state of athletes in a certain period, so as to provide a scientific basis for coaches to formulate training plans. The test indicators are shown in Fig. 4.

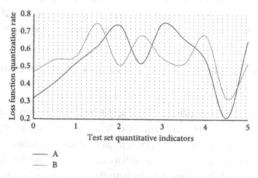

Fig. 4.   Test set indicators

5   Conclusion

China attaches great importance to the construction of statistical informatization. The construction of statistical informatization has been carried out since the 1980s. From the earliest computer application, through the application of statistical information system and the application of Internet technology. From the simplest stand-alone data processing system to the current online reporting comprehensive data processing platform, statistical informatization technology has developed rapidly and has been developed so far It is beginning to take shape. We should reasonably mine, systematically integrate and locate a large number of data resources precipitated in the process of sports comprehensive management and service, make rational use of the methods and means of big data processing and analysis, and make full use of the accurate and timely information provided by big data, so as to make sports management decisions more scientific and effective, make sports services more reasonable and more human, so as to realize sports education management And service transformation and upgrading.

References

1. Hui, Z.: On the impact and challenge of big data on college physical education. Contemporary Sports Sci. Technol. 5(26), 224–225 (2015)
2. Xi, Z., Huijing, L.: Research on comprehensive reform of school physical education -- from the perspective of big data and innovation of physical education in Colleges and universities. The 10th National Physical Education Science Conference 2015 (2015)
3. Wenhua, Z.: Impact of big data on physical education. J. Guiyang Univ.: Natural Sci. Edition 9(2), 47–51 (2014)
4. Tu, T.: Thoughts and enlightenment of school physical education reform in China in the era of Xiangyu grand data. J. Nanjing Institute Phys. Educ.: Soc. Sci. Edition 8, 91–94 (2016)
5. Niu, K., Chen, Y., Shen, J.: Dual-channel night vision image restoration method based on deep learning. Computer Applications, vol. 41, no. 6, p. 10, 2021.View at: Google Scholar
6. Tan, Y., Fan, S., Infrared thermal image recognition method for substation equipment based on image enhancement and deep learning. Chinese J. Electr. Eng. 41(23), 8 (2021). View at: Google Scholar
7. Fu, Z., Wang, F., Sun, X.: Research on image steganography method based on deep learning. J. Comput. 43(9), 17 (2020). View at: Google Scholar
8. Ren, X., Chen, G., Cao, J.: mage retrieval method based on deep learning features. Comput. Eng. Design 39(2), 8 (2018). View at: Google Scholar
9. Xu, S.L., Chen, S.: Image classification method based on deep learning. Appl. Electr. Technol. 44 (6), 4, (2018). View at: Google Scholar
10. Z. Wang, Y. Wang, and W. Song, "Leaf image segmentation algorithm based on deep learning," Forest Engineering, vol. 35, no. 1, p. 5, 2019.View at: Google Scholar
11. Pan, J.: Research progress of image deblurring method based on deep learning. Comput. Sci. 48(3), 5 (2021). View at: Google Scholar
12. Zhang, Z., Zhang, Z., Hu, Q.: Research on multi-product coal image classification method based on deep learning. Coal Sci. Technol. 49(9), 7 (2021). View at: Google Scholar
13. Luo, J., Jiang, S., Shen, S.: Deep learning and intelligent detection of apparent diseases of underwater piles and piers based on sonar imaging. Chinese J. Civil Eng. 54(7), 11, (2021). View at: Google Scholar
14. Shen, K., Shi, Y., Wang, H.: Multimodal visibility deep learning model for visible light-far infrared images. J. Comput. Aided Design Graph. 33(6), p. 8 (2021). View at: Publisher Site | Google Scholar

Application of Big Data Informatization in Public Utilities Response

Yang Liu[✉]

Lanzhou Resources and Environment Voc-Tech University Lanzhou, Gansu 730021, China
lixdong@lzre.edu.cn

Abstract. With the advancement of China's market-oriented reform, the response of public utilities is developing towards diversification and normalization. The new environment has higher and higher requirements for the reliability and accuracy of public utilities response, and there is an urgent need for perfect technical support. Neural network algorithm can accurately identify the complex external environment and make the optimal decision, which can meet the relevant requirements of public utilities response. Based on this, the application of neural network algorithm technology in public utilities response is studied and discussed in this paper. Firstly, this paper combs the development process and research status of neural network algorithm, and analyzes the research status and future development needs of public utilities response problem. On this basis, the feasibility and method of applying neural network algorithm to public utility response business are discussed, which provides a reference for the of public utility response.

Keywords: Neural network algorithm · Public utilities · Demand response

1 Introduction

The construction of a socialist harmonious society must focus on solving the most concerned, direct and realistic interests of the people, and strive to develop social undertakings. Public utilities are the core content of social undertakings. The so-called public utilities are a general term for all industries that produce intangible economic value through collective selection and collective arrangement. It mainly includes three parts: social public welfare undertakings, public utilities and public resource protection. Its essence lies in its sociality. Public utilities not only include social public welfare undertakings under China's planned system, that is, the five commonly used "science, education, culture, health and sports" industries and social welfare and social relief industries, but also include new social public welfare undertakings such as environmental resource protection, greening, social security, social security and employment services and community services under the market system, as well as public utilities such as roads, transportation Protection and operation of industries such as shipping, water supply, power supply and gas supply and public resources such as forests, water sources, mountains and parks. To build a harmonious society jointly built and enjoyed by all the people, we must vigorously develop public utilities and build a public service-oriented system with Chinese characteristics [1].

M. A. Jan and F. Khan (Eds.): BigIoT-EDU 2022, LNICST 465, pp. 140–148, 2023.
https://doi.org/10.1007/978-3-031-23950-2_16

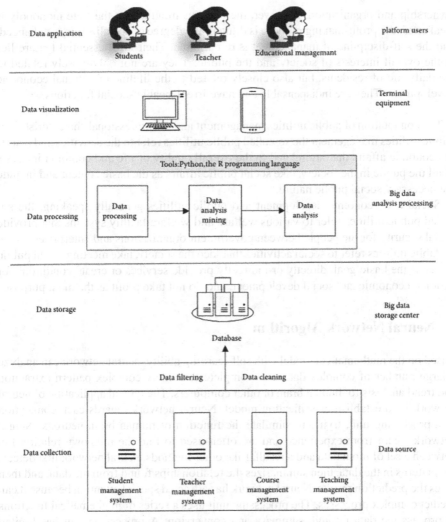

Fig. 1. The public information platform

Utilities face the continuous challenge of consistently meeting the demand for electricity. Facilities for power generation are usually well suited to supplying a constant amount of electricity. However, consumers' demand for electricity is often the opposite, because the total electricity demand changes significantly in the process of delay. One or more 'peak' demand times or periods in which the daily change leads to the greatest demand for utility companies, and the 'non peak' demand times or periods in which the demand for utility companies decreases. Therefore, this paper studies the application of neural network algorithm in public utility response problem Fig. 1.

From the perspective of China's reality and future reform trends, departments such as culture, education, social security, urban water supply, environmental protection and meteorology, and urban transportation are playing their own roles in different forms of ownership and organization. However, the obvious trend is that the state monopoly is weakened, the profit-making purpose is diluted, the degree of socialization is enhanced, and the self-discipline of management is remarkable. Their most essential feature lies in the overall interests of society and the public. They are not only closely related to the daily life of residents, but also closely related to the lifeline of national economic development. They are indispensable and have irreplaceable special functions.

1. The connotation of public utilities management and the professional characteristics of public utilities management the so-called public utilities refer to the activities and results of economic affairs that are related to the overall quality of life and common interests of all the public in the society, take social public affairs as the basic content and include the necessary social public nature.

2. Social and economic development and public utilities generally speaking, the so-called public utilities refer to various welfare and welfare facility systems that provide social security for the people between government organizations and enterprises.

3. Public utilities refer to social activities that face the society, take meeting social public needs as the basic goal, directly or indirectly provide services or create conditions for national economic and social development, and do not take profit as the main purpose.

2 Neural Network Algorithm

Based on the mathematical model with self-learning ability, neural network can analyze a large number of complex data, and complete extremely complex pattern extraction and trend analysis for human brain or other computers. The typical application of neural network is to establish classification model. Neural network regards each connection as a processing unit, trying to simulate the function of human brain neurons. Neural networks learn from experience and are often used to find the unknown relationship between a set of input data and a result. Like other methods, neural network first detects the patterns in the data, then summarizes the relationships found from the data, and then gives the prediction results. Neural network has attracted special attention because it can predict complex processes. The processing unit uses a series of mathematical functions to process the data through summary and conversion. A processing unit has limited functions, but after several processing units are connected to form a system, an intelligent model can be created. Processing units can be interconnected in many different ways. In order to more accurately fit the data for which the model needs to be established, they can be trained several times or even ten million times. The processing unit shall be connected with the input/output unit. The training of neural network is repeated according to the historical sample data. In the process of network training, the connection strength (i.e. weight) between input unit and output unit needs to be modified. The strength of a connection increases or decreases according to its importance to producing a result. The connection strength depends on the weight given to it in the process of repeated training. In the training process, a mathematical method called learning rules is used to adjust the weight. When the output results are consistent with the known results at the specified accuracy level, or meet other end criteria, the network training will not be carried out. In order to predict the outcome variables of each sample, a network should try various schemes.

$$\begin{cases} E(t)\dot{x}_k(t) = f(t, x_k(t)) + B(t)u_k(t) + d_k(t) \\ \qquad\qquad y_k(t) = C(t)x_k(t) \end{cases} \tag{1}$$

Among various neural network models, the feedforward neural network model is more applied and studied, as shown in Fig. 2 [2]. The feedforward neural network model is trained. Back propagation (BP) algorithm is a typical learning algorithm for feedforward network.

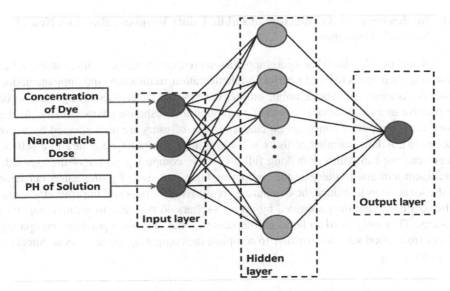

Fig. 2. Neural network model

The biggest advantage of neural network is that it can accurately predict complex problems. However, the neural network method also has some disadvantages:

First, although neural networks are useful in prediction, they are difficult to understand. However, the new neural network tools in the market have been significantly improved.

Second, neural networks are vulnerable to over training. If the neural network with strong learning function is trained with a small amount of data supporting this function, at the beginning, as we hope, the network learns the general trend in the data, but then the network continues to learn the very specific features in the training data, which is not what we want. Such networks lack generalization ability because they remember the training data. Today's commercial neural network has effectively solved this problem. The public information platform flow chart is shown in Fig. 3.

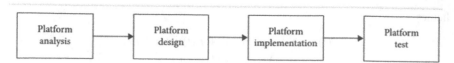

Fig. 3. The public information platform flow chart

3 Implementation Architecture of Public Utilities Response Based on Neural Network Algorithm

3.1 Implementation Architecture of Public Utility Response Based on Neural Network Algorithm

Neural network algorithm has a good application prospect in public utilities response, but how to apply it needs to build a perfect implementation architecture and implementation process. As mentioned above, public utilities have the characteristics of large number of responsive users and variable power consumption and response characteristics. At the same time, the power consumption characteristics of users are also affected by many factors [3]. A large number of users will bring huge computing pressure to e-sellers. Therefore, we can consider making full use of the computing power of the user side intelligent terminal to delegate the computing tasks perceived by single user behavior to the local, so as to reduce the computing pressure of e-sellers and improve efficiency. After collecting the data uploaded by users, e-sellers do not need to set up computing devices. They only need to build a computing model, and then purchase computing power from cloud service providers to complete the computing process. Its architecture is shown in Fig. 4.

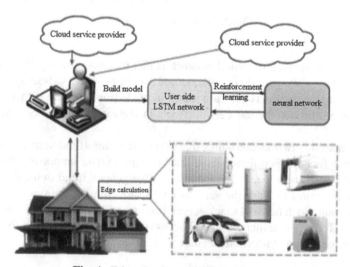

Fig. 4. Edge cloud computing architecture

On the user side, the local public utility response terminal collects the power consumption of users with different loads, establishes an LSTM network to perceive and deduce the power consumption behavior of different loads, and then when receiving the incentive signal from the incoming self-sale e-commerce, deduces the user's different responses and their response probability according to the incentive signal and external environment, and uploads them to the cloud. In the cloud, e-commerce sellers learn and integrate the power consumption behavior and response characteristics of user groups according to the response information fed back by users and combined with the real-time external environment, and select the optimal decision through the method of neural network algorithm, which is shown in Fig. 5 [4].

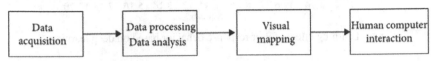

Fig. 5. System platform process.

3.2 User Virtual Response Network Based on LSTM:

The neural network algorithm trains the deep Q network by "trial and error" in the environment, and then selects the optimal strategy. In order to build a complete "trial and error" environment, it is necessary to establish a virtual environment that can simulate user response behavior to support algorithm training. According to the characteristics of users' actual response behavior and the characteristics of deep learning algorithm, a user virtual response network based on LSTM can be constructed on the user side with the support of edge intelligent devices on the user side.

The accuracy of user virtual response network for user behavior prediction will have a great impact on the training of neural network algorithm parameters, and then affect the comprehensive decision-making of e-commerce sellers. In order to verify the prediction accuracy of user virtual response network based on LSTM network, this paper preliminarily verifies the prediction accuracy of LSTM network based on the existing empirical formula. At present, some literatures have simplified the modeling of the response behavior of public utilities in response to users, and most of them use a quadratic function to approximate the user benefit function [5–7].

The existing empirical formula of user response is similar to the actual response of users to verify the learning effect of LSTM network on user response behavior. Where, a and β The normal distribution random value with 0.2 as the variance, considering that the response characteristics of users will change due to the change of environment in different periods, a and β The expected centers of normal distribution are different [8–10].

Figure 6 is a schematic diagram of the results of learning a user's response behavior using the LSTM network and then predicting its response behavior. In the figure, the response behavior of users in the next 20 public utilities response services is predicted (20 public utilities response services are distributed in different periods, and users receive

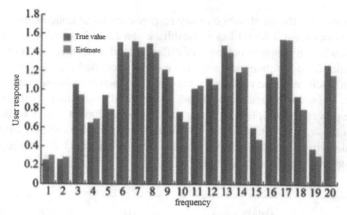

Fig. 6. Learning effect of user response behavior based on deep learning

different degrees of incentive). It can be seen that the prediction accuracy of user virtual response network based on LSTM network is high [11], and the response behavior of users can be simulated more accurately. At the same time, in the simulation process, set the training times to 200 times, and the model training time of ordinary laptop is less than 2 min. After the model training, the prediction time of the model is less than 1 s, so that the user's edge computing equipment can support the optimization of the depth model, It also shows that the user response virtual environment based on LSTM can

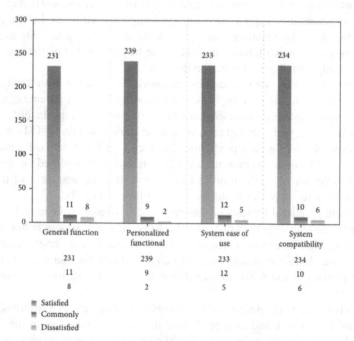

Fig. 7. The system platform testing simulation analysis result

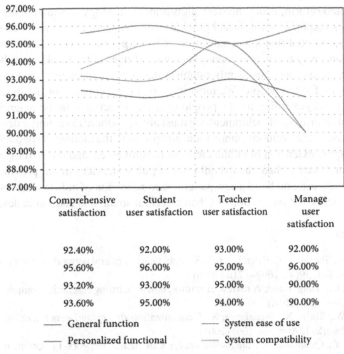

Comprehensive satisfaction	Student user satisfaction	Teacher user satisfaction	Manage user satisfaction
92.40%	92.00%	93.00%	92.00%
95.60%	96.00%	95.00%	96.00%
93.20%	93.00%	95.00%	90.00%
93.60%	95.00%	94.00%	90.00%

—— General function   —— System ease of use

—— Personalized functional   —— System compatibility

Fig. 8. Survey results of public information platform satisfaction

provide a more reliable external virtual "trial and error" environment for neural network algorithm [12–14].

The system platform testing simulation analysis is as follows which is shown in Figs. 7 and 8:

4 Conclusion

Neural network algorithm has strong information recognition and decision-making ability. With the rapid development in recent years, it has been successfully applied in many fields. With the progress of China's power market-oriented reform, the public utility response business also began to develop towards diversification and accuracy. There is an urgent need for a perfect user information identification and incentive decision-making system, and the neural network algorithm can meet this requirement. Therefore, this paper combs the development process of neural network algorithm, constructs the system architecture of neural network algorithm participating in public utility response business, and discusses the implementation process of neural network algorithm in detail. This paper only makes a rough analysis of the application and development of neural network algorithm in the field of public utility response, and the more in-depth detailed design needs to be modified and improved in the actual business development process. With the development of neural network algorithm technology and the promotion of market-oriented reform, neural network algorithm technology is bound to integrate into public utilities response business and provide strong support for business development.

It can be predicted that the equalization of basic public services in urban and rural areas has a long way to go, and cannot be achieved overnight. Looking at the gap and looking to the future, we must firmly establish the concept of caring for the people and seeking benefits for the people. We must implement the concept of building the party for the public and governing for the people in practical actions. In the magnificent new round of rural reform and development, we must always adhere to scientific development, constantly promote institutional innovation, and promote the inclination of public finance to rural areas, the extension of public facilities to rural areas, and the coverage of public services to rural areas, Make the overall level of public services in our province into the forefront of the west, and build a new pattern of equalization of public services for urban and rural residents and integration of urban and rural social and economic development.

References

1. Licheng, J., Shuyuan, Y., Fang, L., et al.: Seventy years of neural network: review and prospect. J. Comput. Sci. 39(8), 1697–1716 (2016)
2. Xuesong, C.: Yang Yimin A review of reinforcement learning research. Comput. Appl. Res. 27(8), 2834–2838 (2010)
3. Haikun, W., Sixin, X., Wenzhong, S.: Generalization theory and generalization method of neural network. J. Automat. (06) (2001)
4. Xinghui, Y., Quantong, L.: diagnostic analysis of neural network in nonlinear dynamics. Microcomput. Inf. 01, 179–180 (2009)
5. Paul, A., Jeyaraj, R.: Internet of things: a primer. Hum. Behav. Emerg. Technol. 1(1), 7–47 (2019). View at: Publisher Site I Google Scholar
6. Jeyaraj, R., Pugalendhi, G., Paul, A.: Big Data with Hadoop MapReduce: A Classroom Approach. Apple Academic Press, Cambridge (2020)
7. He, X., Tang, W., Liu, J., Yang, B., Wang, S.: Research on educational data mining based on big data. In: Liu, S., Sun, G., Fu, W. (eds.) eLEOT 2020. LNICSSITE, vol. 340, pp. 265–278. Springer, Cham (2020). https://doi.org/10.1007/978-3-030-63955-6_23
8. Huang, Y., Zhao, C., Zhao, G.: Intelligent technology for educational process mining: research framework, current situation and trend. E-education. Research, 41(8), 49–57 (2020). View at: Google Scholar
9. Xing, W., Wadholm, R., Petakovic, E., Goggins, S.: Group learning assessment: developing a theory-informed analytics. J. Educ. Technol. Soc. 18(2), 110–128 (2015). View at: Google Scholar
10. Liu, C., Xie, L., Han, Y., Wei, D., Yuan, X.: AutoCaption: an approach to generate natural language description from visualization automatically. In: 2020 IEEE Pacific Visualization Symposium (PacificVis), pp. 191–195, Orlando, USA, (2020).View at: Google Scholar
11. Yafeng, Z.H.E.N.G., Yaning, Z.H.A.O., Xue, B.A.I., Qian, F.U.: Survey of big data visualization in education. J. Front. Comput. Sci. Technol. 15(3), 403 (2021). View at: Google Scholar
12. Mikalef, P., Boura, M., Lekakos, G., Krogstie, J.: Big data analytics and firm performance: findings from a mixed-method approach. J. Bus. Res. 98, 261–276 (2019). View at: Publisher Site I Google Scholar
13. Tang, Z.: On study of application of big data and cloud computing technology in smart campus. IOP Conf. Ser.: Earth Environ Sci. 100(1), 012026 (2017). View at: Google Scholar
14. Cheng, S.L., Xie, K.: Why college students procrastinate in online courses: a self-regulated learning perspective. Internet Higher Educ., 50, 100807 (2021). View at: Google Scholar

Application of Classification Mining Technology Based on Decision Tree in Student Resource Management

Hongting Li[✉]

Wenhua College, Wuhan 430074, China
lhh1028@163.com

Abstract. This paper discusses mining method based on decision tree in student resource management. With the increase of college enrollment, the number of students is also increasing. Oral teaching management produces a lot of data every day, and the existing teaching management system is becoming more and more problematic. With the wide application of database management system, the ability of data collection has been greatly improved and a large amount of data has been accumulated. Behind these data are very important and valuable information. The establishment of data mining technology is to analyze these data at a higher level and obtain the potential information of future operation and life. Data mining is a process of extracting hidden, unknown but potentially useful information and knowledge from a large number of incomplete, noisy, fuzzy and random fact data. How to transform these data information into knowledge representation, reasonably use these information to serve teaching management, scientifically guide teaching and improve teaching management level is an urgent topic for us to study. Data mining technology is a feasible and effective method to solve this problem.

Keywords: Decision tree · Excavation technology · Student resource management

1 Introduction

At present, teaching resources show a large number, many types and miscellaneous forms. It is a problem to be solved to realize the effective organization and management of these resources, enable teachers to quickly search and browse the required information in enable teachers to publish courseware conveniently and quickly.

In addition, the school-based resource management system mainly serves for school education and teaching, so as to improve teaching efficiency and promote the all-round development of students [1]. Therefore, the system is also required to realize certain user interaction and become teachers to communicate.

The school-based resource management system is to facilitate the administrator to manage the teaching resources. Running the application software can be used with

M. A. Jan and F. Khan (Eds.): BigIoT-EDU 2022, LNICST 465, pp. 149–160, 2023.
https://doi.org/10.1007/978-3-031-23950-2_17

less system cost. When it is put into operation, it can save a lot of human and material resources for the school's teaching resource management. The benefit brought by the system is far greater than the development cost of the system software, which is convenient, effective and simple.

After careful analysis, the designed interface of the school-based resource management system is concise and clear, taking into account some habits of people when using as much as possible, making the operation simple. After each operation, it will respond to the user, with flexible and reliable data reading, complete functions and easy use.

Data extraction methods have obvious advantages in analyzing large amounts of data. Analysis methods based on data extraction have been widely used in finance, insurance, telecommunications and other major industries. With the development of data mining technology and the expansion of its application scope, some university scholars began to study university data mining technology in the field of teaching management. For example, using relevant rules to study the hierarchical structure of relevant professional courses and the relationship between CET-6 management and CET-4 management, the research results have made an important contribution to improving the level of school education management.

The application of data collection technology in family education started late. In particular, the data mining technology used by students for data analysis and processing is rarely reported in the literature. The traditional student management and analysis methods generally only include data backup, retrieval, statistics and sorting [2]. Examination management data contains a lot of useful information. If it is not used, it is easy to waste data. At present, the number of students in a university is as few as thousands or as many as tens of thousands, and the examination management data can easily reach millions or even tens of millions, which makes the traditional management analysis methods more difficult to meet the needs of evaluation.

As the support of decision-making process, data extraction is a detailed data analysis method. It will be very useful to apply data extraction technology to management evaluation. We can comprehensively analyze the internal relationship between audit management. For example, data collection tools can answer similar questions, such as "factors affecting student management", which cannot be answered by traditional evaluation methods.

At present, digital campus has become an important goal of school information development in China. In the process of digital campus construction, a lot of information has been accumulated, and the amount of data in the database is increasing. If we still use simple statistical methods, it is obvious that we cannot find the connection between data and rules. Data extraction methods can obtain useful information from these massive data. In order to solve this problem, data mining technology came into being [3].

Data mining method is used to analyze and deal with students' learning, get students' evaluation results, and correct students' bad behavior in time. Give full play to the examination effect, comprehensively evaluate the teaching quality, timely feed back the teaching results, and communicate the teaching information.

2   Related Work

2.1   Decision Tree Algorithm

Decision tree is a data classification algorithm based on predictive variables As a prediction model, decision tree draws the conclusion of target variables through the analysis of prediction variables. The decision tree is constructed in the same way as the flow chart. All internal nodes are test attributes, and all nodes are test results. One advantage of decision trees is that they are relatively simple and easy to describe. To create a decision tree, select an input variable (target and multiple presets), and then create a backlight in the detector until a valid structure is created. The decision tree consists of nodes, roots, leaves (sometimes called terminal nodes) and branches. Figure 1 below shows the decision tree flowchart structure.

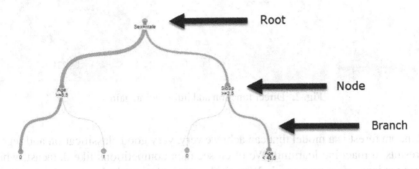

Fig. 1. Decision tree flowchart structure

Classification is a very important data extraction method According to the adopted classification model, data classification methods mainly include decision tree generalization, Bayesian classification and Bayesian network, Decision tree classification algorithm is one of the most widely used algorithms in generalized reasoning [4].

Each node defines the attributes it represents. On the basis of the decision results, different branches of input nodes and leaf nodes represent the classification results.

The top of the node is the root and the end is the leaf. The whole paper is used to predict the output of Y variables in the classification section The internal (non terminal) node specifies the decision point of the data partition. Branches are the results of each test (node).

Decision trees can be used for classification or digital data. If you want to predict which variables will be classified, create a classification tree. If the target variable is continuous, a regression tree is created, but it is different in some aspects. The most obvious is the partition definition (the variable threshold of the segmented data).

There are many algorithms to build decision trees. Here we only discuss two kinds:

1. Classification and regression tree - use Gini index (classification) as the measure.
2. ID3 (iterative dichotomizer 3) - use the direct function and information gain as the measurement, as shown in Fig. 2 below.

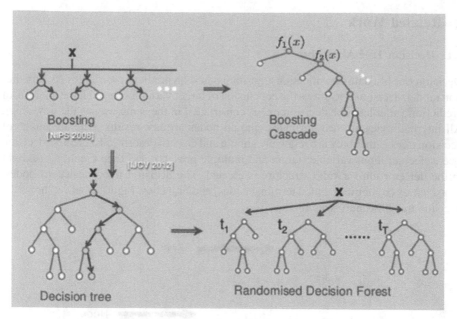

Fig. 2. Direct function and information gain

Random forest is a model that can achieve very, very good classification and regression results in machine learning. We often see data competitions like datacast, which also use random forest very much. We can also get better results by directly classifying or regressing random forests.

2.2 Data Mining Processing

The data source used for data mining must be real and large, and may be incomplete and include some interfering data items. The discovered information and knowledge must be interesting and useful to users. Generally speaking, the result of data mining is not required to be completely accurate knowledge, but to find a general trend.

Data mining can be simply understood as the process of discovering useful knowledge through the operation of a large amount of data.

The knowledge discovery of data mining is not to discover universal truth, to discover theorems and pure mathematical formulas, nor to prove machine theorems. In fact, has specific preconditions and constraints, faces specific fields, and can be easily understood by users [5]. It is best to express the discovered results in natural language. Figure 3 is an example of several common correlations.

Data mining can not only establish descriptive (retrospective) models from historical data, but also establish predictive models, which provides a powerful solution tool for us to extract useful information from large-scale databases. Data mining knowledge. The knowledge obtained through data mining is "explicit", which can not only be understood, but also easy to store and apply. Therefore, it has been widely valued as soon as it appears [6]. A large number of different situations of known results can be stored in the computer,

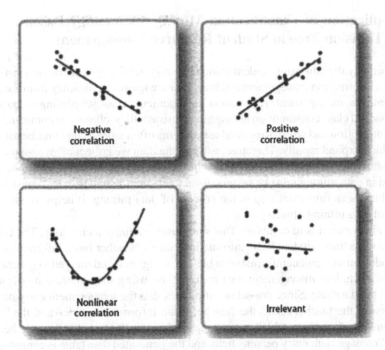

Fig. 3. Examples of dependencies

and then the data mining tools can search for gold from these information, extract the information that can produce the model, and express the model in a way that is easy to understand, such as graph, table, formula and so on.

Data mining is a young interdisciplinary field. It integrates the theories and technologies. It is the result of the evolution of information technology.

A typical data collection system consists of the following parts:

1. Database and data warehouse. A database, data warehouse, or other repository is a database or database, data warehouse, spreadsheet, or other type of repository. Data processing and synthesis.

2. Data retrieval machine is the most important part of data extraction system. It includes functional modules such as symptom, correlation, classification, cluster analysis, evolution and variance analysis.

3. Using models to estimate and measure interest rates is helpful to design data acquisition modules, with the focus on extracting more meaningful models.

4. Graphical interface is the bridge between users and data retrieval system It allows users to interact with the system, define queries or tasks related to data extraction, and provide information that helps to find the focus, which depends on the intermediate data retrieval results of data retrieval.

3 Application of Classification Mining Technology Based on Decision Tree in Student Resource Management

The especially the education student management system, helps the training institutions to realize information management and improve management efficiency from the aspects of student file management, registration management, class scheduling management, class hour and class consumption management, growth files, classroom comments, home school interaction and so on. Real database systems often store a large number of diverse data, which expand rapidly. Therefore, usually, the data we collect often contain a lot of noise data, and even some incomplete and inconsistent data. Therefore, the data objects involved in data mining must be preprocessed to ensure the integrity and consistency of data, which is an important step in the process of data mining. It helps to improve the quality of data mining objects.

Data integration is to combine. This study uses database technology. The collected database table files "student basic information table", "teacher basic information table" and "student management information table" are integrated and merged to generate "initial table of student management data analysis" by using the connection operation of tables in the database. Since our school stipulates that the management entry person of the course is the teacher itself, the "teacher basic information table" and the "student management information table" are connected through the "teacher job number" field and the "management entry person" field, and the generated data table is connected with the "student basic information table" through the "student number" field. The "initial table of student management data analysis" generated after this connection includes the following fields: student number, student name, major, province of origin, enrollment management, job number, teacher name, teacher gender, teacher title, educational level, course code, daily management, examination management, comprehensive management, management input person, remarks and other attributes, The number of records is 1157 lines. As shown in Fig. 4 below.

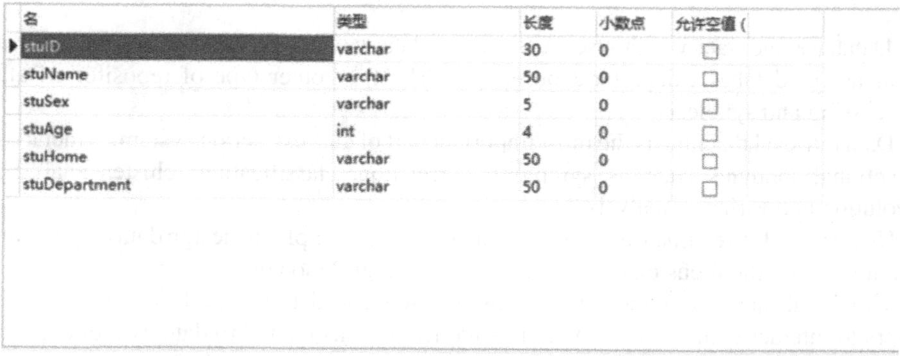

名	类型	长度	小数点	允许空值 (
▶ stuID	varchar	30	0	☐
stuName	varchar	50	0	☐
stuSex	varchar	5	0	☐
stuAge	int	4	0	☐
stuHome	varchar	50	0	☐
stuDepartment	varchar	50	0	☐

Fig. 4. Design data sheet

The "initial table of student management data analysis" includes many attributes, such as student number, student name, student gender, major, student source Province, enrollment management, job number, teacher name, teacher gender, teacher title, educational level, course code, daily management, examination management, comprehensive management, management entry person, remarks and so on. In the actual data classification process, we can only select some attributes as classification objects [7]. Therefore, we need to analyze and summarize the attributes in the table, remove the attributes that have nothing to do with the analysis of management data or have poor correlation, and select the attribute values related to management data as the research object. In order to facilitate the establishment of the decision tree model, this paper selects the three attributes of "student gender, peacetime management and teacher title" which are closely related to the management attributes as the basis for establishing classification decision tree model, and generates the "student management data mining table".

1. Determine the object and goal of data classification. The objects of data classification often need to be clearly defined according to the actual situation of data mining database. Due to the unpredictability of data classification results. In addition, is very important for the establishment of data classification objects and even the generation of the whole classification results.

2. Data collection. Data acquisition covers a wide range and has a variety of ways. For example, we can collect student achievement data and teachers' basic information data; We can obtain data from some existing databases, or collect and summarize data through questionnaires. In short, data acquisition is a time-consuming and laborious work.

3. Data preprocessing. This stage usually includes four links: data cleaning, data integration, data transformation and data summarization. The purpose of data processing is to ensure the integrity and consistency of data in the database.

4. The final result of data mining is to establish a classification model. First, according to the test objectives, formulate appropriate data extraction methods, such as the classification method used in this work. Secondly, like C45 decision tree algorithm, we should design a classification mining algorithm according to the actual location of the test data set, classify the student performance data, and finally establish a "student decision tree model".

5. Formulate classification rules. This will make the classification rules of mining results consistent with the previous data classification. This means rules for extracting symbols from visual classification models. It is worth noting that the decision tree generated in advance is often pruned before generating the classification rules, otherwise the classification rules may be meaningless or inconsistent with the objective law due to the over training of the decision tree by the classification algorithm [8].

6. Application of knowledge. The so-called knowledge here is the classification rules generated in the previous link. For the application of classification rules, we can not only directly apply them to daily teaching activities, but also predict new data. For example, this paper makes full use of the knowledge generated by the experimental results, obtains the conclusions and methods to guide the teaching, and systematically realizes the data prediction function.

4 System Design

Because the construction of educational resources has the characteristics of regional universality, technological complexity and cultural diversity, it is difficult to share a large number of educational resources and communicate with different educational systems. The key to solve this problem lies in the standardization of educational information. At present, many countries and regions in the world have established organizations specializing in the standardization of educational information, and formulated a series of educational information standards, involving learner related, content related, data and metadata, management systems and application software. Among them, the metadata standard of educational resources is the basis for effectively describing educational information resources and realizing resource discovery and exchange.

To realize the co construction and sharing of educational resources and build a distributed and shared educational resource management system is an active project all over the world. Metadata with good interoperability and based on resource discovery and retrieval is the basis and key to effectively realize the description, retrieval and utilization of these resources. The co construction and sharing of educational resources have been carried out in countries all over the world. The United States is one of the countries with the most abundant educational resources in the world. The U.S. government, universities and non-governmental organizations have invested a lot of funds and research forces in the construction and use of network resources. Among them, representative ones are Eric (American Educational Resource Information Center), free (Federal quality educational resources), Ohio link (Ohio Library and information network) and Ceres (Educational Resource Center project), etc. In the United States, it is very common for schools to jointly build and share educational resources, such as the MIT open courseware project, which has attracted the attention of many countries and universities around the world.

The overall design includes the following key designs: the design of computer configuration, the design of system module structure, database and various files. When we carry out this task, we need to separate all parts of the software, and design different modules carefully to make it have its own functions. Software decomposition is also called divide and conquer [9]. First separate the functions of the software, and then integrate each module to make them a whole. This design should be based on the following principles as far as possible;

1. Practical: designed according to the actual needs;
2. Easy maintenance: adopt a good model for design, so that the system can be easily maintained in the later stage, so that the school does not need to invest too much money;
3. Convenient operation: the designed system needs to be convenient for users according to the situation of the school, and can not make the operation of the designed products troublesome and wasteful;
4. Safety: the designed products are closely related to the privacy of students, so the safety factor must be particularly high;
5. Reasonable function: the system we designed must ensure that each function can be used by users, so we need to make the system both beautiful and practical when designing;

6. Design time: we should not only ensure the quality of the system, but also ensure that it can be developed within a reasonable time.

SSM is a combination of three frameworks (Spring + spring MVC + mybatis). The framework is a relationship mapping and a solution of reusable software architecture. SSM is an efficient development framework commonly used at present. Because I have done practical training before, the teacher can directly design a similar system with only Maven. Relatively speaking, SSM seems to use more frameworks, but in the design process, the development efficiency of SSM is really very efficient. The logic of the background is not as complex as maven, so I learned the SSM framework to design the system, as shown in Fig. 5. The design works are relatively simple and can be used as a basic reference.

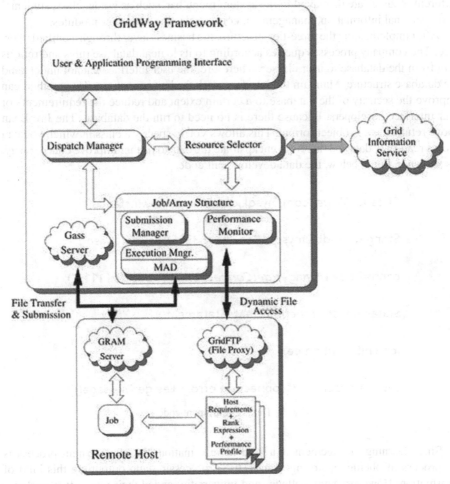

Fig. 5. Student resource management system

Integrating the three, SSM uses spring MVC as the controller of hierarchical management. Springloc is responsible for managing component resources, and spring AOP is responsible for aspect programming management. Mybatis acts as the database access persistence layer, realizes the data interaction between Dao in spring and data control system, and is responsible for database transaction management. SSM framework is suitable for building various large-scale application systems, which can be applied to school educational administration system management, student dormitory management, enterprise management, government department management and so on [10].

Analyze the system function and performance requirements to realize that different user systems have different operation permissions. After the user types of login system are generally divided into student users and administrator users, enrich the management content of student information, and set modules on the system page to display the diversified information of students. After distinguishing user types in the login interface, different modules are displayed in the system menu bar, such as grade, class, students' basic personal information, management, course selection and other modules.

After implementing the three-tier structure, the business layer through a unified interface. The company processes queries according to its logical database rules and returns data from the database to user classes. Therefore, the user interface cannot understand the database structure. Maintain the interface with the business phase. This method can improve the security of the database to a certain extent and reduce the requirements of user interface developers. Because there is no need to run the database. The JavaBean above returns data in object format. This allows you to specify a class in which you can access read-only data and therefore encapsulate the data to further improve data security. As shown in Fig. 6 below, the data development code.

```
Class.forName("com.mysql.jdbc.Driver").newInstance();

String url="jdbc:mysql://localhost:3306/xscj_database";

conn=DriverManager.getConnection(url,"root","111111");

Statement stmt = conn.createStatement();

}catch(Exception ee){

System.out.println("connect db error:"+ee.getMessage());
```

Fig. 6. Data development code

Since learning management is a kind of information, the management process is the process of obtaining, storing, transmitting, processing and outputting this kind of information. However, many colleges and universities ended their work after marking, management publishing, reporting, classified registration and storage, without in-depth analysis from a large number of management and mining information conducive to teaching work, Taking these as the end of the work is a waste of teaching information resources [11]. The reason can be attributed to the tedious work, scattered data, traditional manual operation, high labor intensity and low efficiency, which is not convenient for query, classification and summary, and can not provide all kinds of information in time and accurately. The traditional student learning management analysis is nothing more than to get the mean, variance, difference significance test, reliability and so on. It is often considered based on the teaching itself. These need further analysis to draw a conclusion for education managers to make corresponding decisions, but these information can not be obtained by using the traditional student management analysis methods, real reasons affecting students' learning management, we can formulate corresponding measures to improve the quality. The studying management is to find out the factors affecting the regularity of management change through the disclosure of the law, and on this basis, "suit the remedy to the case" [12]. At the same time, restrain negative factors on students and guide them to study actively and develop healthily. Processing of large-scale data. It can extract the useful information hidden behind the data. It is being used in more and more fields and has achieved good results. It is very beneficial. It can find examination management and various factors through the comprehensive analysis of relevant data. For example, through the analysis of student related data, data mining tools can answer similar questions such as "which factors may have an impact on student management", This is not available in traditional evaluation methods.

5   Conclusion

With the valuable information emerges from a large number of data collected by data mining technology. At present, data extraction technology has been widely used in biomedicine, financial data analysis, e-commerce, telecommunications and other fields. At the same time, there are few examples of successful application of data extraction technology in university education system. In view of the general trend of educational informatization, data mining technology is used to obtain the information of educational activities, so as to lay a foundation for teachers' educational activities in the future, improve teaching methods and improve the quality of education. This paper analyzes the design of student information management system. The design of the system includes the overall design and creation of the database and the data table structure. It describes the company.

References

1. Letina, A., Dikovic, M.: Student teachers' classroom management orientations and their beliefs on effective teaching behaviour, sodobna pedagogika. J. Contemp. Educ. Res. 72(138), 128–143 (2021)
2. Thamrin, R.M., Andriani, R.: Design web-based registration and data management of student thesis information system. SISFOTENIKA 11(1), 101 (2021)
3. Liu, Z., Cai, Y.: Construction management of student affairs center guided by the student-based idea: taking the business school of beijing institute of technology zhuhai institute as an example. In: 1st International Conference on Education: Current Issues and Digital Technologies (ICECIDT 2021) (2021)

4. Mao, L., Zhang, W.: Analysis of entrepreneurship education in colleges and based on improved decision tree algorithm and fuzzy mathematics. J. Intell. Fuzzy Syst. **40**(2), 2095–2107 (2021)
5. Dinesh, T.: Higher classification of fake political news using decision tree algorithm over naive bayes algorithm. Revista Gestão Inovação e Tecnologias **11**(2), 1084–1096 (2021)
6. Hardiani, T.: Comparison of Naive Bayes Method, K-NN (K-Nearest Neighbor) and Decision Tree for Predicting the Graduation of 'Aisyiyah University Students of Yogyakarta. Int. J. Health Sci. Technol. **2**(1) (2021)
7. Arigi, A.M., Park, G., Kim, J.: An approach to analyze diagnosis errors in advanced main control room operations using the cause-based decision tree method. Energies 14 (2021)
8. Rahmawati, A., Yan, R., Riana, D.: Deteksi defect coffee pada citra tunggal green beans menggunakan metode ensamble decision tree. Technol. Commun. **20**(2), 198–209 (2021)
9. Djordjevic, D., Cockalo, D., Bogetic, S., et al.: Predicting entrepreneurial intentions among the youth in serbia with a classification decision tree model with the QUEST algorithm. Mathematics 9 (2021)
10. Gatwood, J., Hohmeier, K., Kocak, M., et al.: Acceptance of productivity software as a course management and collaboration tool among student pharmacists. Currents in Pharmacy Teach. Learn. **13**(4) (2021)
11. Boomars, R., et al.: Optimizing airway management and ventilation during prehospital advanced life support in out-of-hospital cardiac arrest: a narrative review. Best Practice Res. Clin. Anaesthesiol. **35**(1), 67–82 (2021)
12. Scott, A.T., Dpm, C., Dpm, T., et al.: Review of achilles tendon reattachment using double-row knotted and knotless techniques in the management of insertional achilles tendinopathy (2021)

Application of Computer Intelligent Proofreading System in English Phrase Translation

Huang Jing(✉)

Wuhan Technology and Business University, Wuhan 430065, Hubei, China
20071208017@wtbu.edu.cn

Abstract. This paper studies the application of computer proofreading system in English word translation. The technology is closely related to the development of computer technology, structural theory, linguistics and other fields. With the improvement of computing power and explosive availability of multilingual information resources, from early dictionaries to regular dictionary translation combined with language knowledge, and then to statistical machine translation based on thesaurus. Machine translation technology has begun to come out of the ivory tower and provide real-time translation services for simple users. We notice that the English translation proofreading system of grammar and sentence patterns is an important problem of correct proofreading, and the intelligent proofreading system based on the improved word translation model can not solve the inconsistency problem. Through the establishment of semantic text and word combination conversion algorithm to simulate the syntactic part. Through semantic feature analysis and word combination, optimize the automatic translation algorithm, load the translation algorithm, and design the automatic translation system software based on the embedded environment. Therefore, cross compiler and multi-threaded word translation are used to design the translation system automatically. The development process of software module mainly includes system application, network translation, customer, translation organization and management, online translation interaction and other modular structures. Finally, the design system is verified. The verification results show that the system can meet the requirements of users for horizontal demarcation and improve the efficiency of demarcation.

Keywords: Intelligent proofreading system · Translation of English phrases · System development

1 Introduction

After entering the 21st century, with the rapid development, science and technology are becoming more and more frequent, and the amount of information is increasing sharply, which has greatly deepened people's understanding and demand for language, knowledge and intelligence. All words that may be misunderstood as "machine" as the

© ICST Institute for Computer Sciences, Social Informatics and Telecommunications Engineering 2023
Published by Springer Nature Switzerland AG 2023. All Rights Reserved
M. A. Jan and F. Khan (Eds.): BigIoT-EDU 2022, LNICST 465, pp. 161–171, 2023.
https://doi.org/10.1007/978-3-031-23950-2_18

subject has "intelligence" are problematic from the perspective of science and technology and pragmatics. "Machine intelligence", "machine learning", "Machine Cognition", "machine..." These words, as well as "man-machine symbiosis", "man-machine integration", "man-machine..." These specious words should have been avoided in the strict sense of science and technology. Although there are many "conventional" word usages in human society, it should only be "conventional" based on "agreement". If we understand and use these easily misunderstood words from their literal meaning, or even use them as the description of scientific research objects, I'm afraid they will not produce original research results and will only lead the research direction astray, which scholars should try to avoid. Using these words to name courses and even majors will only mislead people's children.

The so-called "artificial intelligence", human beings and their intelligence, should always be the first! Taking "artificial intelligence" as a technical means, human beings creatively discover, predict, recognize, summarize, abstract, calculate and construct all kinds of things in the social activities of understanding and transforming nature, so as to gradually and continuously improve the intelligence level of human beings, which is the correct direction of the progress of human society. No matter in scientific research, technological development, engineering practice, or in social communication, information exchange and daily life, excessively blindly believing in and relying on "machine intelligence" will inevitably lead to the overall degradation of the "human intelligence" of the dependent! In fact, such degradation phenomenon has been recognized and warned by some sober scholars in the world. Because it is beyond the purpose of this paper, it will not be repeated here.

In contradiction, the language barrier is becoming more and more serious. Relying solely on manual translation of massive data is not only inefficient, but also very expensive.

In essence, machine translation is the process of automatic transformation from one language to another. From the 1980s to 1990s, rule-based methods occupied the mainstream. Machine translation translated the source language through the grammatical rules designed by linguists, and achieved some results. Since the early 1990s, the acquisition of various bilingual corpora has become relatively easy. With the continuous improvement of computer processing ability, the implementation of statistical methods in technology and resources has become possible. During this period, various corpus based statistical machine translation methods have flourished, which greatly improves the translation system. Even in some specific fields, the quality of to a certain extent [1]. However, the current technologies and methods can not make the machine truly simulate the human translation process, let alone reach the level of human translation. However, the challenge and the demand of serving the public continue to inspire research institutions and researchers all over the world to devote themselves to the research and application of machine translation.

English is used to expressing complex concepts in long sentences, while Chinese is different. It often uses a number of short sentences for hierarchical narration. Therefore, when translating from English to Chinese, we should pay special attention to the differences between English and Chinese, and decompose the long sentences in English into short sentences in Chinese. In the process of translating long English sentences, the following methods are summarized.

Firstly, when the content narrative level of English long sentences is basically consistent with that of Chinese, they can be translated into Chinese according to the hierarchical order of the original English, so as to make the translation basically consistent with the original English. Secondly, the expression order of some long sentences in English is different or even completely opposite to that in Chinese. At this time, translation must start from the back of the original text. In Chinese, attributive modifiers and adverbial modifiers often precede the modified ones.

In addition, there are mainly methods for English translation. In other words, when translating a long English sentence into Chinese, modifier phrases will be added before the elements of English are incorporated into the text in the usual Chinese order. But the decorative elements should not be too long. Otherwise, it will cause delay and contradiction [2].

Sometimes in English long sentences, the relationship between the subject or the subject sentence and the modifier is not very close. In translation, the clauses or phrases of long sentences can be transformed into sentences and described separately according to the habit of using short sentences in Chinese. In order to make the meaning coherent, it is sometimes necessary to add words appropriately, that is, to translate the whole English long sentence into several independent sentences by dividing the whole into parts, with the order basically unchanged and coherence.

The so-called word alignment refers to automatically extracting the corresponding relationship between words from bilingual parallel corpus. Figure 1 shows an example of word alignment of English and French sentence pairs. At present, most statistical machine translation systems use IBM model and hidden Markov model (HMM) for word alignment, but both models have a limitation on word alignment, that is, a source language word can only correspond to one target language word at most. Therefore, the word alignment generated by IBM model is usually also called asymmetric word alignment.

Fig. 1. Examples of word alignment in English and French sentence pairs

2 Related Work

2.1 Computer Intelligent Proofreading System

The advent of the big data era has brought the explosion of text information, and all kinds of traditional text analysis and processing work have begun to be replaced by computers. The larger the amount of text data, the more errors it contains. It is particularly important to correct the errors in the text through proofreading. Traditional proofreading mainly relies on manual work, which can find and correct errors in the text. Manual proofreading has low efficiency, high intensity and long cycle. Obviously, it can not meet the needs of the rapid growth of the text. Intelligent proofreading system came into being under this background. With the development of machine learning and natural language processing technology, it is possible to use algorithm model to solve the problem of text proofreading. The research and development of intelligent proofreading system has greatly reduced the workload of proofreaders and made the previous heavy work mode simple, easy and efficient [3]. As shown in Fig. 2. Starting from the technical problems encountered in proofreading, this paper will lead readers to understand the technical methods of proofreading in the industry, as well as the technical principles and practical experience of cognitive intelligence laboratory in algorithm proofreading.

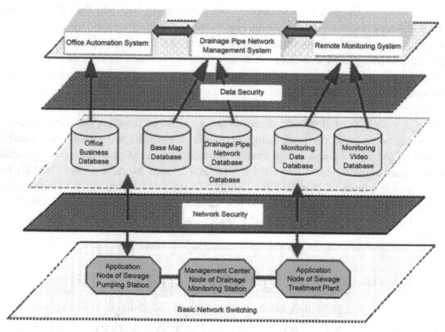

Fig. 2. Computer intelligent proofreading system

Automatic text proofreading is one of the main application fields of natural language processing, and it is also a research problem. The difficulties are mainly reflected in:

1. The distribution of true error samples is unknown. This problem is very different from other natural language processing problems or pattern recognition problems. Other natural language processing tasks have objective correspondence, that is, the model obtains the answer by identifying fixed patterns. However, in text proofreading, correct sentences and words are found from wrong sentences or words, and there is no objective correspondence. It can only be said that different proofreaders will get different answers,

and the final judgment of the answer is related to the cultural level and knowledge structure of proofreaders. Because it is "wrong" to find "right", a correct word may produce different wrong words due to different user input habits. In the error sample data set in the online real production environment, the distribution law from wrong words to right words will change at any time, which challenges the machine learning based on the independent distribution hypothesis.

2. A wide range of fields. Since the company's business serves all walks of life, the input text encountered in proofreading contains proper nouns in various fields, and a large number of professional knowledge dictionaries are needed to correct the input errors of input users from different industries [4]. In addition, in different professional fields, the character distribution of corpus varies greatly, so it is difficult to find the distribution balance of input training corpus when training the model, that is, how much corpus from different sources should be input into the model for training.

3. High performance requirements. It is embodied in recall rate, accuracy rate and model reasoning speed. Recall rate is the main evaluation basis for the performance of the proofreading system. It is used to describe how many errors in the real errors can be found by the algorithm. Accuracy is an important guarantee of good customer experience. Imagine a system with low accuracy and false positives throughout, which will greatly affect users' feelings and reduce users' efficiency. Fast model reasoning is an important requirement for the system to serve customers. If the speed of model proofreading is slow, the experience will be particularly poor for users who use proofreading services online.

2.2 Translation of English Phrases

Due to the differences in expression methods and habits between Chinese and English, translators are required to skillfully deal with the corresponding details and adjust the order of Chinese and English words in time. In general, when translating, the corresponding positions of Attributives and Adverbials must be adjusted to complete the translation.

For example, in Chinese, we usually use "she is cooking in the kitchen." To describe the action of the subject. However, in English, "she is cooking in the kitchen." To express the action of the subject [5]. The position of the adverbial of the two sentences has changed and transformed, which can meet the expression of the corresponding language and greatly improve the fluency of the sentence.

In English, if the position of the sentence attribute is a word, the word is usually placed before the modified word. In Chinese, this usage is the same. However, if postposition occurs in English, the translator needs to precede the attribute in the process of translation, so as to ensure the fluency of Chinese sentences and improve the quality and level of translation.

If it is necessary to translate more Chinese nouns into the front of the sentence, it can still be adjusted according to the English language. For example:

They have a lot of thing dificult to do.
他们有很多困难的问题需要解决。

In the process of translating English sentences, we should adjust the translation order according to the expression habits of Chinese, ensure the complete translation of the meaning of the article according to the corresponding principles and the context of the article, and ensure the smoothness of the translated sentences, so as to improve the quality and level of English translation. In the process of adjusting and transforming the English word order, we should first translate according to the logical relationship of the sentence itself, and then adopt relevant translation skills, so as to meet the requirements of English translation.

Adjust according to the time sequence. In the translation between English and Chinese, the usage of the two is slightly different in terms of time order, so we need to understand this difference in translation, and we can translate according to the corresponding language habits to better meet the characteristics of the corresponding language. For example, in English, sentences describing time can usually be placed before or after the subject. However, when expressing in Chinese, it needs to be described according to the specific time and order of the action.

3 Application of Computer Intelligent Proofreading System in English Phrase Translation

At present, the research of statistical machine translation is developing in a diversified direction. A variety of knowledge sources and methods have been introduced into the research of statistical machine translation, such as language features, syntactic structure features, semantic features, word network, semantic network, etc., which has greatly promoted the research and development of statistical machine translation, and has basically met the application requirements in some specific fields. Basic realization: ordering + translation = decoder. Based on rules or statistical methods. In the middle process, there are a variety of smoothing and disambiguation methods, as shown in Fig. 3 below.

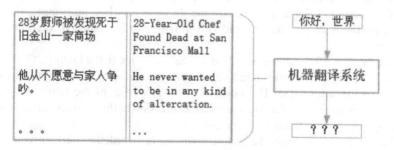

Fig. 3. Organize the sentence structure of the translation

An intelligent English automatic translation system platform is constructed, which is mainly composed of phrase translation combination based translation system, hierarchical phrase translation combination based translation system and syntax based translation system [6]. We mainly design the platform from two aspects: automation and modularization.

Optimization implementation: for phrase based statistical translation. They have certain advantages in ambiguity elimination, local sorting and decoding efficiency, reduce the complexity faced by the machine translation system and show good model robustness. They are often used as the baseline of statistical machine translation system research.

Automation mainly means to minimize manual intervention. The operations from corpus preprocessing to model training, from test set input to translation result generation, from system initialization to automatic parameter adjustment are completely completed by computer; Modularization means that the translation system is an extremely complex and systematic process from front-end corpus processing to back-end translation result generation. At the same time, due to the different implementation and construction principles of multiple translation engines, there will be different requirements and representations in different operation stages. The technical route is shown in Fig. 4.

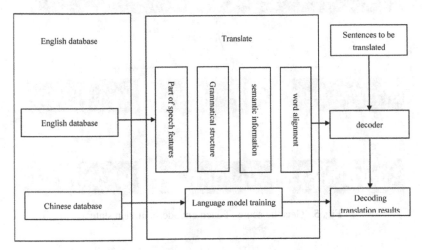

Fig. 4. Technical route of translation system

Section 5 below fig shows how one can effectively allocate limited attention resources when browsing images. The red area indicates that the visual system pays more attention to the target [7]. Of course, in the above cases, you can see the face, title and first sentence of the article.

In essence, the attention mechanism in deep learning is similar to the mechanism of human selective visual observation. The main purpose is to select important information from various sources for the purpose of this task.

The translation quality evaluation of machine translation system is an important factor to promote the rapid development of statistical, especially the development of automatic evaluation technology is the direct driving force of statistical machine translation methods. For the evaluation methods of translation quality, the current evaluation standards can be divided into two kinds [8]. One is subjective evaluation, that is, according to the given reference translation, the system translation results are scored manually, mainly including two indicators: Fluency and fidelity; Another method is automatic evaluation, that is to score the translation results according to a certain mathematical model. Similarly, the goal of automatic evaluation method is to achieve a balance between fluency and loyalty.

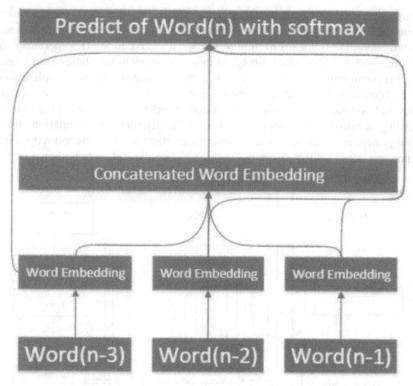

Fig. 5. Gets the score of each encoder's hidden state

At the stage of model reasoning, the mainstream autoregressive translation models are predicted by step. Each step requires the state of the previous, several or all artificial neurons. Every operation of transformer's decoder requires a lot of repeated calculations in the previous state.

Keep part of the calculated state, and make tradeoff in memory overhead and calculation overhead to realize acceleration.

Tensor2tensior gives the original open source implementation of Google's official transformer. Among them, the reasoning cache acceleration of vanilla transformer follows the above idea and obtains nearly twice the speed of long sentence reasoning. The calculation formula is shown in (1).

$$BLEU = BP \times exp\left(\sum_{n=1}^{N} w_n log p_n\right) \tag{1}$$

where PN is the proportion of the number of n-grams appearing in the reference translation to the total number of n-grams in the candidate translation, $w_n = 1/N$, which means taking the geometric average of n-gram, and N is the maximum n-ary syntax order (generally 4). BP is the length penalty factor to punish the short translation. The calculation formula is shown in (2).

$$BP = \begin{cases} 1 & c > r \\ e^{(1-r/c)}, & c \leq r \end{cases} \tag{2}$$

where, R is the length of the effective reference translation in the test corpus, which can be defined as three lengths: the length of the shortest reference translation, the length of the reference translation closest to the sentence length of the system candidate translation, the length of the longest reference translation, and C is the length of the system candidate translation [9].

Using the intermediate results generated by the attention mechanism of the translation model, a set of auxiliary pointer network is designed to realize the placeholder translation engine. After the key information is classified and replaced according to the part of speech, the translation obtained by the input model greatly reduces the missing translation and wrong translation rate of this kind of information.

With the continuous maturity of the technical framework, how to make more efficient use of resources has become a new challenge in academia and industry, including low resource learning, high concurrency or real-time model design, multilingual large-scale system establishment and so on. At the same time, the rapid iteration of machine translation technology has also triggered and driven more thinking and research, including the support of upstream models, the expansion of downstream applications, the integration of a priori common sense or domain knowledge, etc. a series of methodologies have continuously promoted the accelerated landing and improvement of artificial intelligence in natural language processing tasks.

4 Simulation Analysis

After the failure of rule-based system, new translation methods have been developed. They are not based on grammatical rules, but on probabilistic and statistical models.

The establishment of statistical translation system requires a lot of training data. Among them, the same text is translated into at least two languages. This kind of double translation text is called parallel material library [10]. Similarly, scientists in the 18th century found an Egyptian Hieroglyph from Greece on the 9th monument in losetta. The same pattern is also engraved on the stone tablets of Greece, ancient Egypt and folk characters. By comparing the contents of different language versions, modern archaeologists have the opportunity to explain the meaning and structure of Egyptian hieroglyphs that disappeared more than a thousand years ago. Today, it is an important milestone in the study of ancient Egyptian history. Computers can use parallel corpora to predict how texts are translated from one language to another.

Fortunately, there are many translators in the world. For example, the European Parliament has translated its agenda into 21 languages. Therefore, researchers will use these data to establish a translation system, as shown in Fig. 6 below.

The English automatic translation system is designed into two parts: algorithm and software. The design of the system software adopts the modules of dictionary information processing and dictionary program automatic control based on embedded environment.

English	Spanish
Resumption of the session	Reanudación del periodo de sesiones
I declare resumed the session of the European Parliament adjourned on Friday 17 December 1999, and I would like once again to wish you a happy new year in the hope that you enjoyed a pleasant festive period.	Declaro reanudado el periodo de sesiones del Parlamento Europeo, interrumpido el viernes 17 de diciembre pasado, y reitero a Sus Señorias mi deseo de que hayan tenido unas buenas vacaciones.

Fig. 6. The translation system a large amount of training data

In order to extract the information that reflects the characteristics of the system information distribution rules, the type of information integration and intelligent scheduling is selected to realize the intelligent management and scheduling of the system. An automatic translation system is designed based on embedded ARM system, and the system network component interface is designed by TinyOS The information management system software is compiled in the Linux kernel, which improves the intelligent level of system management.

Establish your own language translation system. There is a presentation that can be translated between English and French. But not cowards and people with limited budgets. This is still a new technology with limited resources. Even with advanced computers equipped with modern video cards, it may take a month to learn language translation.

In addition, the rapid development of translation technology from sequence language to sequence language is difficult to achieve [11]. Many innovations (such as increasing attention and context monitoring) have significantly improved translation results, but they are innovative, not Wikipedia. If you want to switch from one sequence to another, you need to update it as technology advances.

The system network node interface based on TinyOS is optimized in application hierarchy, operation layer and data layer. In the design stage, the combined information is transmitted through the base station, the information is transmitted through the sensor node, and the high-speed a/d converter is converted into a vector for digital conversion. For this, the intelligent management function software of the automatic translation system is developed.

Current scope of application of machine translation: people who do not understand the source language want to know about the contents of some less professional information, such as e-mail, instant chat information, and some technical documents with high text repetition rate [12].

Idealized development after machine translation: through the continuous expansion and optimization of corpus, the development of search and capture technology and the expansion of the scope of statistical objects, in order to obtain the corresponding entry pairs with higher statistical probability and improve the accuracy of translation.

5 Conclusion

The core of the algorithm is to optimize the English automatic translation algorithm from the perspective of English translation combination. Cross compilation and program loading are used to load the algorithm into the information processing module of the system. On the basis of software development, the development of English automatic translation platform based on the combination of word and translation is promoted. Researching and establishing an automatic English translation automation platform based on the combination of words and translation can further improve the intelligence and automation level of English translation. At present, machine translation methods are mainly statistical methods, and word based translation is the most mature of statistical methods, as the main component of statistical translation. In recent years, grammar based statistical machine translation has gradually become a hot topic in statistical machine translation research. The system design includes software design and machine translation algorithm By combining semantic feature analysis with word translation and optimizing automatic translation algorithm, the software design based on embedded automatic translation environment is realized.

References

1. Zhang, J., Luan, H., Sun, M., et al.: Neural machine translation with explicit phrase alignment. IEEE/ACM Trans. Audio Speech Lang. Process. **99**, 1 (2021)
2. Xl, A., Hy, B.: Parataxis or hypotaxis? Choices of taxis in Chinese–English translation. Lingua **251**, 103026 (2021)
3. Hidalgo-Ternero, C.M.: Google Translate vs. DeepL: analysing neural machine translation performance under the challenge of phraseological variation. MonTi Monografías de Traducción e Interpretación **32**, 154–177 (2021)
4. Ding, L., Wang, L., Liu, X., et al.: Progressive multi-granularity training for non-autoregressive translation **21**, (2021)
5. Min, J.: Research on the application of computer intelligent proofreading system in college English teaching. J. Phys: Conf. Ser. **1915**(3), 032078 (2021)
6. Guo, X., Zhu, Y., Zhang, J., et al.: Intelligent pointer meter interconnection solution for data collection in farmlands. Comput. Electron. Agricult. **182**(13), 105985 (2021)
7. Jamshidifarsani, H., Garbaya, S., Lim, T., et al.: Intelligent games for learning and the remediation of Dyslexia: using automaticity principles. IEEE Syst. Man Cybern. Mag. **7**(1), 15–24 (2021)
8. Gao, J., Guo, Z.: Application of text proofreading system based on artificial intelligence. In: Atiquzzaman, M., Yen, N., Zheng, Xu. (eds.) Big Data Analytics for Cyber-Physical System in Smart City: BDCPS 2020, 28-29 December 2020, Shanghai, China, pp. 722–727. Springer Singapore, Singapore (2021). https://doi.org/10.1007/978-981-33-4572-0_104
9. Zhu, W., Tan, C., Xu, Q., et al.: Heterogeneous identity trust management method based on risk assessment. J. Intell. Fuzzy Syst. **11**, 1–14 (2021)
10. Jansen, P.: Darmok and Jalad at Tanagra: a dataset and model for English-to-Tamarian translation (2021)
11. Lin, Z., Song, X., Guo, J., et al.: Peer feedback in translation training: a Quasi-experiment in an advanced Chinese–English translation course. Front. Psychol. **12**, 631898 (2021)
12. Peng, X.: Thinking path schema of English translation for Chinese classics: an empirical study on translation schema in translation courses. Engl. Lang. Teach. **14**(2), 56 (2021)

Application of Data Analysis Technology in Physical Education Teaching

Lin Wang[✉]

Kunming College of Arts and Sciences, Kunming 650000, Yunnan, China
wl707488932@163.com

Abstract. Learning situation analysis is not only the basic link of teaching activities, but also one of the basic ways to improve effective teaching. However, only on the premise of ensuring the effectiveness of learning situation analysis can we improve the effectiveness of teaching. Compared with other teaching, physical education teaching has more urgent needs and stricter requirements for learning situation analysis. Therefore, this paper uses data analysis technology to elaborate what teachers should pay attention to and how to do when doing learning situation analysis of physical education teaching from the current situation of learning situation analysis of physical education teaching, the mode of learning situation analysis of physical education teaching and the method of learning situation analysis of physical education teaching, In order to provide theoretical guidance for physical education teaching practice.

Keywords: Sports · Data analysis technology · Teaching · Academic situation analysis

1 Introduction

At this stage, there is a gap between theory and practice in academic situation analysis. At present, the analysis of learning situation in China is mostly the product of teachers' "taking it for granted", which is the result of teachers' conjecture about students' learning situation according to their experience rather than scientific analysis. On the one hand, teachers have preliminarily understood that learning situation analysis is the basis and premise of teaching design. On the other hand, teachers may not apply learning situation analysis to actual teaching, or the value of learning situation analysis can not be brought into play due to improper application. Its specific performance is as follows: (1) teachers have not applied physical situation analysis to teaching. At this time, learning situation analysis is only a formalism. Teachers do not bring it into daily teaching. Learning situation analysis, which is just "talking on paper", must not play a common role, resulting in the separation between learning situation analysis and actual teaching activities. (2) Teachers' understanding of learning situation analysis is not deep. Teachers' understanding of learning situation analysis determines the role of learning situation analysis. If teachers lack a deep understanding of learning situation analysis, they can

M. A. Jan and F. Khan (Eds.): BigIoT-EDU 2022, LNICST 465, pp. 172–178, 2023.
https://doi.org/10.1007/978-3-031-23950-2_19

not apply learning situation analysis to teaching design, and naturally can not fully play the role of learning situation analysis. (3) The way of learning situation analysis is too single. Teachers themselves have carried out learning situation analysis, but most of them have the color of empiricism. It is teachers' subjective conjecture on a single dimension of learning situation through many years of teaching experience without scientific basis [1]. At this time, learning situation analysis can not help teachers improve teaching quality, but will increase teachers' workload and see no good teaching effect. Even if teachers know the importance of learning situation analysis, they are unable to change the embarrassing situation that learning situation analysis has become a "chicken rib".

2 Big Data Analysis Technology

2.1 The Role of Big Data Analysis and Mining Technology and Decision-Making

In data mining, we extract valuable data in a large amount of data in the shortest time, and apply the information technology to industry development. Most of them are large data analysis drilling techniques, and the concrete industry combines algorithms in the data analysis process. Combining genetic algorithms in the biosphere helps ensure data mining speed, accuracy and integrity. During the course of data mining, we continue to analyze large data in the process of digging data under high data backgrounds, combining high performance computing, machine learning, artificial intelligence, model recognition, statistics, data visualization, database technology and expert systems, and It is possible to form a complete system, to put emphasis on optimization, and to make the measures more accurate. You can understand the demand well. Currently, each industry uses data mining as the main data analysis method. Technology such as classification, optimization, identification and prediction in data mining plays an important role in many industries.

With the development and application of large data technology, there are major changes in the various fields of society such as finance, medical care, telecommunications, education, and so on, there are large amounts of data every day, social uncertainty factors, and the processing of data types become more complicated. After applying computer technology, there are still significant limitations on traditional processing methods and problem solving. Now, data mining technology effectively resolves large data problems and becomes the "king of data". Data drilling technology also faces great opportunities and challenges. The application of data mining algorithm greatly improves data analysis ability and can effectively deal with actual problems [2].

2.2 Big Data Analysis and Application Status

Big data analysis and application platform mainly includes five key processing steps: selecting platform operating system, building Hadoop cluster, data integration and preprocessing, data storage, data mining and analysis, which further improves the efficiency of big data application.

(1) Select the platform operating system. In the process of big data analysis and processing, it faces many data resources. In order to improve the organization and

management efficiency of these data resources, it is necessary to use the matching operating system to realize the priority access and hot data storage of big data as much as possible, manage the physical storage space of big data, and realize the scheduling and allocation of resources. Common operating systems include Red-Hat. CentOS or Debian, which can be used as the operating tools of the underlying platform, have strong scalability and can support data processing. The platform operating system can also realize the virtualization function according to the, so as to expand the physical storage space of the system, share CPU and improve the utilization of communication bandwidth.

(2) Build Hadoop cluster. Hadoop is a software platform that can run big data processing software. The core technology is MapReduce, which can form a cluster of a large number of computers to realize massive data distributed computing. Hadoop has attracted many commercial companies to develop and design, and has built various open source components, including sqoop, HBase. And spark. Hadoop includes many constituent elements. The lowest constituent element is Hadoop Di distributed file system (HDFS), which can maintain all storage node files in the Hadoop cluster platform. The upper layer of HDFS is a MapReduce engine, which includes two constituent components, jobtrackers and tasktrackers. Hadoop can be used to realize data processing and operation, Further meet the distributed data operation.

(3) Data integration and preprocessing. There are many resources for big data integration, such as file logs, relational data, object data, etc. These have both structural and non structural data. Therefore, preprocessing is required when integrating the data together, so that the service bus can be used for communication transmission and improve the consistency and reliability of the data. Data preprocessing can use tools such as impala. Sparksql and hivesql.

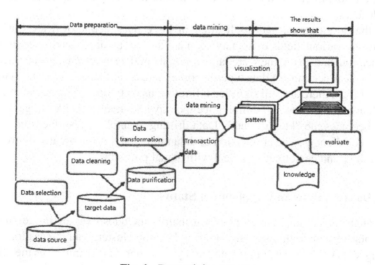

Fig. 1. Data mining process

(4) Data mining and analysis. There are many resources for big data storage. These resources are usually disordered and messy. Although certain organization principles are adopted, people's use of data is also very complex. Therefore, the introduction of data mining and analysis function can improve the timeliness of data utilization and shorten the data processing time. Artificial intelligence technology is introduced into data mining and analysis, such as BP neural network, Bayesian algorithm, support vector machine and K-means algorithm. The data mining process is shown in Fig. 1.

3 Analysis of Learning Situation in Physical Education Teaching

3.1 Necessity of Situation Analysis in Physical Education Teaching

Physical education is a special course. It is an organized, purposeful and conscious social activity with physical exercise as the basic means and the purpose of improving health and physique. Physical education has two levels: first, physical exercise, the body needs to bear a certain exercise load, which is essentially different from other disciplines; Second, physical education includes the relevant theories of physical education and basic health care knowledge supporting its practical activities. While physical exercise, we also need to learn and master relevant theories. It can be seen that physical education is a complex subject, and there are more uncertain factors in the teaching process [3]. Therefore, its demand for learning situation analysis is more urgent and strict.

3.2 Types of Emotional Analysis in Physical Education Teaching

Learning situation analysis provides the basis for teaching content, teaching design and later teaching evaluation, and needs to be related to subsequent teaching activities. According to the different objects of learning situation analysis, it can be divided into two types: the analysis of students' situation and the analysis of students' learning situation. The former has a larger scope than the latter and is generally used for learning situation analysis in the semester or academic year. The latter has a smaller scope and mainly refers to the factors directly related to the learning process, including learning starting point, learning state and learning results. According to the different time periods of learning situation analysis, it can be divided into learning situation analysis before the semester or academic year, learning situation analysis of a unit and learning situation analysis of a class/a knowledge point. The learning situation analysis of the semester or academic year is the basis for teachers to select teaching contents. To a certain extent, it determines the contents that students need to learn in this learning period, which should be carried out before the teaching objectives and textbook analysis of this learning period, while the learning situation analysis of a unit, a class or a knowledge point should be arranged after the textbook analysis and combined with the conclusion of textbook analysis, It is mainly used as a reference for the selection of teaching methods.

3.3   Mode of Situation Analysis in Physical Education Teaching

Physical education teaching design has its systematicness. Physical education teaching design starts from the overall function of physical education teaching system. In terms of working procedures, it is often not to complete one step first and then start the next step, but constantly complement each other, and fully consider all factors to produce the overall effect and achieve the most optimization of physical education teaching effect. Therefore, physical education teaching design is a whole, which needs to be designed closely around the established objectives, so as to achieve the consistency of objectives, process and evaluation. When analyzing students' learning situation, the whole process of teaching should be regarded as a whole, and the analysis of learning situation should run through the whole process. Therefore, some teachers analyze the learning situation of the whole teaching process through the model before, during and after class, so as to ensure the effectiveness of teaching.

Pre class learning situation analysis is a problem that teachers should first consider and can not avoid in learning situation analysis. It mainly includes students' learning starting point and pre class preparation. The starting point of students' learning is the degree of students' pre mastery of the learning content of the course, including the degree of cognition of the course content, the basis of mastering the skills and the attitude towards the learning of the course. The pre class preparation state is aimed at what kind of preparation the students have made for the course, what their learning motivation is and the development degree of their own cognitive level. The analysis of learning starting point is directly related to the teaching content, and students' pre class preparation affects teachers' choice of teaching materials and methods [4].

The analysis mode before, during and after class is also the concrete embodiment of teaching evaluation. Teachers design the evaluation scheme before class, implement the evaluation scheme in the teaching process, evaluate the results after class, analyze and report the evaluation results, and finally deal with the evaluation results. For the teaching design of daily class, teachers can directly modify and adjust the teaching scheme according to the analysis of evaluation results, so as to serve the next teaching. Therefore, it can be considered that the three analysis dimensions before, during and after class are interrelated and interdependent to form a whole, and none of them is indispensable. The relationship between pre class, in class and after class analysis modes can be shown in Fig. 2.

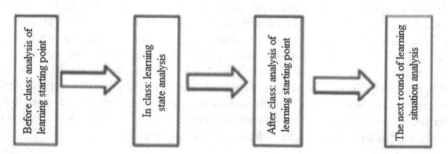

Fig. 2. Relationship diagram of learning situation analysis model

4   Methods of Learning Situation Analysis

After selecting the object and determining the analysis content, we will start the investigation. Common survey methods include observation, conversation and interview, questionnaire survey, etc. Combined with relevant literature, this paper briefly discusses how to carry out learning situation analysis in physical education teaching.

(1) Observation method. This is the most direct and simple method, especially physical education. It is a course that pays attention to practical application ability. Only through direct observation can we accurately grasp students' learning and other situations. Teachers can observe the analysis object in class or students' extracurricular activities.

(2) Interview method. Conversation is a direct and positive contact with the analysis object to ask about the subject's learning experience. The interview was conducted from the human hand side of the contact people around the analysis subject. Both methods have their limitations. The conversation method will be affected by the age and cognitive level of the interviewees, especially the junior students, who can not make an objective and accurate judgment on themselves. The selected objects are usually other teachers or their parents, and they can only make a general description, especially parents, whose description may be more personal subjective thoughts.

(3) Questionnaire survey method. Most of them are used to investigate students' sports theoretical knowledge or their interests, generally for senior students. The problem with the questionnaire survey is that some students may not be able to describe the theoretical principle of a sports skill in words, but they can show this skill. On the contrary, some students can understand the principle, but they can't master this skill in classroom practice. Therefore, the survey method should not adopt a single one, but multiple combination, mutual supplement and comprehensive analysis.

(4) Establish students' Sports portfolio, that is, material analysis. Portfolio evaluation is no longer a new thing in the field of education. This method can also be used in physical education teaching to establish students' Sports portfolio for analysis. Some researchers suggest that students should complete their own sports portfolio and design their own personalized portfolio cover with sports color. Students' sports performance evaluation form, photos of students' sports activities, award-winning certificates of various sports, teachers' words, their own sports perception, collected sports materials, etc. can be put in the archive bag. All sports related materials can be put in the room. Using these materials, teachers can have a more comprehensive understanding of students. When analyzing the learning situation, these are powerful empirical materials, and the teaching design can be targeted.

5   Conclusion

Learning situation analysis is the analysis of students' situation. Learning situation analysis is for students' learning. Learning situation analysis in physical education can be carried out from the aspects of knowledge and skills, process and methods, emotion and so on. The object of analysis can be all or sampling. Every class in the teaching process should be analyzed to grasp the situation of students, improve the effectiveness of teaching activities and promote the development of students.

References

1. Ying, C.: Using effective learning situation analysis to improve work efficiency. China Educ. Technol. Equipment **4**, 59–62 (2011)
2. Peifen, Z., Songjie, Q.: Let learning situation analysis run through the whole process of teaching. Sports Teach. Friends **1**, 4–5 (2011)
3. Zhangfa, Y.: How to do well in learning situation analysis. Guizhou Educ. **16**, 26–27 (2010)
4. Haiping, Z.: Learning situation analysis, how to get out of the practical dilemma. Phys. Educ. **2**, 22–24 (2008)

Design and Implementation of Teaching Assessment System in Higher Vocational Colleges Based on Association Rule Algorithm

Yunhua Liu(✉)

Marxist Institute, Hunan Communication Polytechnic, Changsha 410132, Hunan, China
hnjymy01@163.com

Abstract. The systematic assessment of teachers' classroom work is to adjust teachers' behavior, improve classroom quality, and then manage them well. This paper expounds the problems existing in the assessment of Higher Vocational Colleges in China; Taking the teaching management of higher vocational colleges as the background and teaching assessment as the research object, this paper discusses the design and implementation method of teaching assessment system under the environment of data warehouse. This paper attempts to build a decision support system for teaching management in Universities under the environment of data warehouse, which can first promote the improvement of teachers' personal teaching level, and then improve the overall teaching quality of the school. This paper discusses the design and implementation of teaching assessment system in Higher Vocational Colleges Based on association rule algorithm. In connection with the present condition and development requirements of assessment, and further combine their own situation, design a practical teaching assessment system with the participation of students, teachers, supervisors, educational administration managers, branch (workstation) teaching managers and experts, which can comprehensively and objectively evaluate the teaching situation of teachers, So as to promote the improvement of teaching quality.

Keywords: Teaching assessment · Association rule algorithm · Higher vocational colleges · System design

1 Introduction

For a long time, the whole society has a keen expectation for universities to cultivate high-quality talents, which makes universities regard improving teaching quality as the core work of universities. In recent years, with the continuous expansion of enrollment scale of universities in China, there have been a series of practical problems faced by universities, such as the decline of assessment quality [1]. Establishing a scientific teaching assessment system and assessment methods is an important means to strengthen the teaching management level and improve the teaching quality. Therefore, teaching assessment has always been an important part of teaching management in Universities.

© ICST Institute for Computer Sciences, Social Informatics and Telecommunications Engineering 2023
Published by Springer Nature Switzerland AG 2023. All Rights Reserved
M. A. Jan and F. Khan (Eds.): BigIoT-EDU 2022, LNICST 465, pp. 179–189, 2023.
https://doi.org/10.1007/978-3-031-23950-2_20

At current, our universities in China have carried out many exploration and research work in establishing and improving the teaching assessment system, and formed a variety of assessment models. Some universities use the method of filling in the teaching quality assessment card to collect data, and then the educational administration department makes statistics to determine the teacher's teaching quality assessment grade. In addition, most universities have realized the networking of teaching assessment with the help of campus network. Teaching assessment plays a role in supervising, monitoring and promoting teaching work [2]. However, there are also some problems that can not be ignored in the current teaching assessment:

(1) Ignoring the fundamental purpose of teaching assessment is to improve teachers' teaching professional level. Most university managers only link the assessment results with professional title promotion and teaching awards, but the role of teaching assessment in promoting the improvement of teachers' professional skills and teaching level has not been brought into full play.

(2) Ignoring the diversity of assessment objects, without comprehensive consideration of the characteristics of students, teachers and courses, the assessment calculation method is single, the formation method of assessment results is simple and lack of scientificity. Generally, the average score or standard deviation is simply obtained, and other implicit factors are not fully considered in the statistical process. It can not explain which factors the score is related to, but only reflect some aspects of teaching work [3]. Therefore, some teachers doubt the reliability and validity of the assessment and resist the teachers' teaching assessment.

(3) The accumulated teaching assessment data can not be used effectively for a long time. The traditional query and statistical methods deal with these valuable data, and can not predict the future development trend according to the existing data. In addition, due to the dynamics of the teaching process, some data are inconsistent. For example, the change of student status (grade repetition, professional transfer, etc.) and the change of teachers' professional title will affect the data analysis results due to the different data analysis time [4].

(4) Teaching assessment is a long-term work. At present, the teaching assessment work of most universities, from the assessment index system to the assessment work mode and process, is unchanged once established. It remains the same for several years, which is very unfavorable to the assessment work itself.

With the deepening of educational informatization construction in Universities, universities have gradually realized the importance of teaching assessment, and hope to apply modern information technology means to make teaching assessment apply to the teaching decision-making process of the school, so that teaching assessment can really improve the teaching level and give full play to its due efficiency [5]. Facing a large number of assessment indicators and a large number of data, how to separate and extract useful information from these data to provide support for scientific decision-making is an important research topic.

Nowadays, the important problems faced by the teaching quality assessment system in higher vocational colleges are the lack of application of modern scientific and technological methods and means, and the imperfect control mechanism and assessment feedback [6]. The association rule algorithm in data mining technology can not only assist in the construction of teaching assessment system, but also realize the knowledge mining of teaching assessment data, Therefore, the design and implementation of teaching quality assessment system in Higher Vocational Colleges Based on association rule algorithm will be an important trend of educational science research, and has great practical significance.

2 Related Work

2.1 Data Mining

Data mining is a process of obtaining correct, novel, potential application value and ultimately understandable patterns from a large amount of data.The knowledge extracted from data mining should be expressed in many forms, such as concept, law, pattern, constraint, visualization and so on.

Data mining is produced by the development of information technology and the joint action of many factors. It is demand driven. Different from the previous complex data analysis methods, data mining is a kind of deep-seated data analysis methods. It is deep inside the data, and its special place is the ability to establish predictive models.

Data mining is an interdisciplinary subject involving a wide range. It brings together many technologies, such as database, mathematical statistics, artificial intelligence, visualization, parallel computing and so on. The powerful function of data mining is that it can automatically (or a small amount of manual intervention) find potential information patterns in a large amount of data, predict trends, and help enterprises build new ideas of operation and marketing [7]; Through data analysis, those seemingly unrelated things are actually related; Let users have more options to analyze and understand data, and let the data tell us more things.

There are many methods of data mining, among which the typical ones are association analysis, sequential pattern analysis, cluster analysis and so on. Different data mining methods have different application ranges, and the comprehensive application in reality can often achieve good results.

Cluster analysis: it is a method of studying "birds of a feather flock together". It is a branch of multivariate analysis. At present, it has been widely used in the research fields of geology, psychology, biology, economy, image recognition, meteorology and so on. Cluster analysis is to determine the affinity relationship of samples by mathematical methods according to the attributes and characteristics of samples, and classify them naturally and objectively according to their affinity, so as to obtain a reasonable classification system [8]. There are many mature clustering analysis methods, such as system clustering method, dynamic clustering method, fuzzy clustering method and so on.

2.2 Association Rule Mining Technology

Association rules were originally proposed for market basket analysis. The development of bar code technology enables retail institutions to collect and store a large number of sales records. Through the analysis of the accumulated sales data, the sales information of various commodities can be obtained. A large number of shopping basket data is an important basis and basis for marketing activities and business decisions. Through the data mining of shopping basket, we can find the relationship between different goods put into the "shopping basket", so as to know the shopping habits of customers, make more reasonable orders of various goods, and then reasonably control the inventory of various goods. In addition, according to the relevant conditions of various commodity sales, the sales relevance of commodities can be analyzed, so that the basket analysis and combination management of commodities can be carried out, which is more conducive to commodity sales.

(1) Basic concepts of association rules

Suppose L1, L2, L3 Is an item, l = {L1, L2, L3..... Is a collection of items. There is a transaction database C = {D1, D2, D3, D4.....}, Each transaction in the database DL $\in$ L, D2 $\in$ L, D3 $\in$ l Let a $\in$ L, B $\in$ L, and a $\cap$ B = φ, The implication of a $\rightarrow$ B is the association rule on database C, the probability p (a $\cup$ b) is the support of association rule a $\rightarrow$ B in database C, which is recorded as support (AB), and the conditional probability p (B | a) is the confidence of association rule a $\rightarrow$ B in database C, which is recorded as confidence (AB). If the minimum support and minimum confidence of association rule a $\rightarrow$ B meet the values set by the user, a can be called frequent itemset.

(2) Types of association rules

Association rules can be classified based on a variety of principles. For example, they can be classified based on the categories of variables processed in the rules, including Boolean and numerical types. The value processed by Boolean association rule is 0 or 1, which is convenient to explain the relationship between sub itemset A and sub itemset B in transaction set. Numerical association rules can be combined with multi-dimensional or multi-layer association rules to process numerical fields, dynamically segment them, or directly process the original data. Of course, numerical association rules can also contain category variables [9].

2.3 Common Algorithms of Association Rules

(1) Apriori algorithm

Apriori algorithm is a classic algorithm in association rule algorithm. Many scholars have improved and innovated Apriori algorithm in the future. The breadth first search strategy is applied in the algorithm. The steps to find all frequent itemsets are as follows: first, count all item sets with length of 1 to get frequent itemset K1, and then find out according to frequent itemset K1 In this way, the loop stops when a new frequent itemset cannot be found. The most important part of Apriori algorithm is to find frequent itemsets.

We agree as follows:

Each item in the transaction database is represented by < itemid, itemname >, in which itemid is used to identify the corresponding transaction in the transaction database, and itemname is used to identify the corresponding item name in the transaction database. Use size to identify the number of items in each item set in the transaction database; Lset is used to identify the item set with length L; LM is used to identify lset with minimum support, and LC is used to identify lset with the largest possible item set. The length of the initial item set is 1, so that the maximum length of the item set generated by the algorithm is 1. When looking for frequent itemsets in a loop, when the loop goes to step m, the first step is to use a specific function. We name it ITSC, generate the candidate itemset LC with the maximum itemset LM-1 generated in step M-1, and then calculate the support of the candidate itemset LC. Support is identified by lcsupp. The minimum support is identified by minisupp.

(2) FP growth algorithm

Apriori algorithm generates candidate item sets and then checks whether they are frequent. FP growth algorithm abandons the method of generating candidate sets by Apriori algorithm and uses the method of growing frequent sets (FP trees) to organize data. When searching the database, FP growth algorithm constructs the path of FP Tree to correspond to each transaction in the transaction database. Because the transactions in the database may have the same items, the path in FP Tree may also be repeated [10–14]. In this way, the effect of compressing information can be achieved through FP Tree. Because reading data from memory in the computer is much faster than reading from external memory, this can speed up the processing speed. FP growth algorithm includes two steps: one is to construct frequent pattern tree FP Tree, and the other is to call FP growth algorithm for frequent itemset mining.

(3) Partition algorithm [15–18]

The two algorithms described above are realized by scanning the database many times to find all the frequent item sets. If we reduce the scanning times of the database, we can not only reduce the 1 / 0 cost of the system, but also reduce a lot of computing costs.

Savasere proposed the partition algorithm in 1995. Its main concept is extended from Apriori algorithm. It is similar to Apriori algorithm in searching frequent itemsets and mining association rules. However, when mining association rules, Apriori algorithm will spend more time on the search of database, which is a great burden. In view of the shortcomings of Apriori algorithm, partition algorithm adopts the method of partitioning on the database to be mined, obtains all possible itemsets through the partitioned candidate itemsets, and calculates their support [19, 20].

The execution sequence of partition algorithm is as follows: firstly, the transaction database to be mined is divided into thousands of regions, and then these partitions are put into the memory of the computer for calling at any time. The algorithm is executed for each partition to generate the candidate set, and then the candidate item set of each partition is combined to calculate its support. If the support meets the requirements of the user, Is the frequent itemset you are looking for. The advantage of partition algorithm is that it only needs to retrieve the transaction database twice, which can greatly reduce the I / O overhead. However, there are also some problems: the partition algorithm can generate too many frequent itemsets for each partition after partition, When retrieving the transaction database for the second time, the time and storage space overhead of merging the frequent itemsets generated by each partition is too large. Another disadvantage of partition algorithm is that the amount of computation will increase compared with Apriori algorithm. Moreover, the frequent itemsets generated by each partition may be repeated. In addition, the threshold of each partition needs to be adjusted after partitioning, which will also increase the candidate itemsets. In this way, additional expenses must be added for screening.

3   College Teaching Assessment System

3.1   The Role of College Teaching Assessment in Teaching Management

Curriculum assessment refers to the value judgment of curriculum content and process. Teaching assessment is to make a comprehensive investigation and value judgment on the overall or partial teaching system by using practical assessment methods and means according to a certain teaching purpose and teaching principle, and teaching assessment involves the assessment of teachers' classroom teaching quality.

Teaching assessment is an educational activity to judge the value of teachers' teaching process and results according to education and teaching objectives. It is based on the effective collection of data. Teaching assessment is an important link in educational activities (as shown in Fig. 1); It is also an effective means of teaching management and a research direction of education and teaching management.

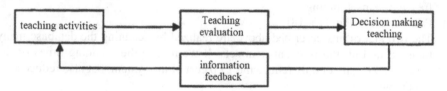

Fig. 1. Assessment block diagram

Teaching assessment plays an important role in the improvement of education and teaching quality. Teaching assessment is an important part of teaching monitoring. Improving the quality of education and teaching is also the core goal of teaching assessment:

(1)   Teaching assessment is the basis of teaching monitoring management decision-making. Through the effective assessment of teaching activities, we can get a lot of information about the evaluated objects. After scientific and reasonable statistical analysis, we can find out the shortcomings in education and teaching work, clarify the improvement direction of teaching work, and provide a reliable basis for the decision-making of education and teaching work.

(2)   Teaching assessment plays a guiding role. In the process of teaching assessment, the assessment index system and assessment results have a certain tendency. For example, in the assessment index system, the weight distribution of each index and the interpretation of the assessment results have pre value judgment, which plays a guiding role in some links or components of education and teaching.

3.2   Overall Design Objectives

The teaching assessment system is to meet the actual needs of the TV university system. Through the assessment of students, teachers, supervisors, educational administrators, branch (workstation) teaching managers and experts, it can timely understand the actual situation of teachers' teaching quality and provide scientific basis for improving teaching quality. The system has the characteristics of low cost, simple operation, high efficiency, easy maintenance and expansion. The flow chart of teaching assessment is shown in Fig. 2.

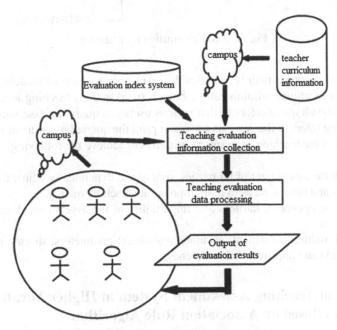

Fig. 2. Flow chart of teaching assessment

The system mainly includes six parts: system management, basic information management, assessment management, result management, result query and result printing. Among them, system management refers to user management. Users here include students, teachers, supervisors, educational administration managers, branch (workstation) teaching managers, experts, system administrators, etc. Basic information management mainly includes: basic information management of students, basic information management of courses, basic information management of teachers, basic information management of supervision, basic information management of educational administrators, basic information management of branch school (workstation) teaching administrators, etc. As shown in Fig. 3 below.

Assessment management mainly includes: student assessment management, teacher assessment management, supervision assessment management, educational administration management personnel assessment management, branch (workstation) teaching management personnel assessment management, expert assessment management,

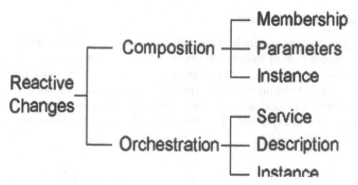

Fig. 3. Basic information management

etc. Result management mainly includes the result management of students, teachers, supervisors, educational administrators, branch (workstation) teaching administrators and experts. Result query refers to that various users can query the assessment results. Result printing refers to that various users can print the queried assessment results.

The goal of the teaching assessment system is to achieve the following:

(1) Through the assessment of all parties, timely and dynamically adjust the teaching methods and modes, so as to help improve the teaching quality.
(2) Ensure the openness, fairness and impartiality of the assessment through online assessment.
(3) Through online assessment, accurate assessment parameters, shorten the assessment cycle and improve work efficiency.

4   Design of Teaching Assessment System in Higher Vocational Colleges Based on Association Rule Algorithm

4.1   System architecture

In order to facilitate user access, the system adopts the three-tier structure of B/S model of web application. The three-tier (B/s) structure is formed by adding "web and application server" to the traditional two-tier (C/s) structure model. Its advantage is that the client only needs a browser to browse. Because the web requires to respond to the requirements of users, the network throughput should be large, the response speed should be fast, and the network stability should be good. Based on B/s, the three-tier architecture consists of presentation layer, business logic layer and data access layer. The architecture of the system is shown in Fig. 4.

4.2   System Function Structure

Developing any form of dynamic web system should follow the steps shown in Fig. 5.

The teaching assessment system developed in this paper also follows the same steps. Firstly, according to the requirements of different users, design functional modules,

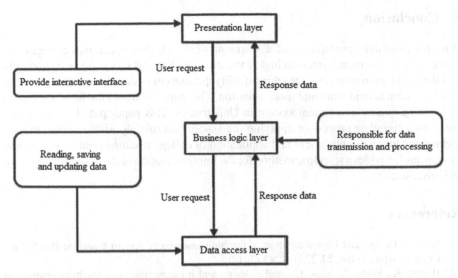

Fig. 4. System architecture diagram

layout the whole web page according to the functional modules, and each web page completes relatively centralized and independent functions. At the same time, consider the directness and convenience of user operation, and deal with the core contents such as the location and operation mode of different objects. Then, according to the design, write the corresponding script. It involves page development tools, dynamic page interaction technology, database selection and design and other important processes. Finally, test the system, debug each functional module, and complete the whole design and development process.

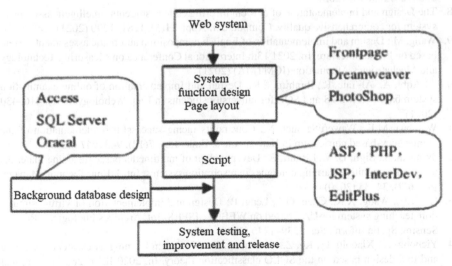

Fig. 5. Functional structure diagram of Web system

5 Conclusion

With the extensive development of assessment work in higher vocational colleges, the research on Assessment System in higher vocational colleges is more and more in-depth, and the application research of teaching quality assessment system based on association rule algorithm is paid more and more attention. This paper analyzes the implementation of teaching quality assessment system in Universities, This paper puts forward a new idea and a complete process of applying the association rule algorithm in data mining technology to the establishment and application of college teaching quality assessment system, and provides a scientific method for the implementation of the assessment system in Universities.

References

1. Sun, Z.: Design and implementation of teaching assessment system based on B/S Model. Comput. Appl. Softw. **23**, 2231–2243 (2012)
2. Huang, K., Wang, J., Xian, L., et al.: Design and implementation of teaching assessment system based on B/S. J. Chongqing Jiaotong Univ. (Natural Science) **45**, 1248–1256 (2012)
3. Design and Implementation of Teaching Assessment System Based on PHP+Apache+MySQL. **000**(015), 3456–3458 (2013)
4. Guo, J.: Design and Implementation of Automatic Assessment System in College English Writing Teaching Based on ASP.Net, pp. 1622–1626 (2021)
5. Tian, F., Zhu, Y., Li, Y.: Design and Implementation of Dance Teaching System Based on Unity3D. In: 2021 6th International Conference on Intelligent Computing and Signal Processing (ICSP) (2021)
6. Lin, H., Wei, Y.: Design and implementation of college English multimedia aided teaching resources. Int. J. Electr. Eng. Educ. **24**, 1131–1145, 002072092098351 (2021)
7. Cheng, L., Niu, W.C., Zhao, X.G., et al.: Design and implementation of college physics teaching platform based on virtual experiment scene. Int. J. Electr. Eng. Educ. **52**, 3348–3359, 002072092098468 (2021)
8. The Design and implementation of new engineering college students' intelligent assessment system for comprehensive quality. Comput. Sci. Appl. **11**(5), 1281–1290 (2021)
9. Wang, M.: Design and implementation of English composition automatic assessment system based on B/S architecture. In: 2021 13th International Conference on Measuring Technology and Mechatronics Automation (ICMTMA) (2021)
10. Al-Aqbi, A., Al-Taie, R., Ibrahim, S.K.: Design and Implementation of online examination system based on MSVS and SQL for university students in Iraq. Webology **18**(1), 416–430 (2021)
11. Wambua, M.E., WaweruSamuel, N.: Constraints facing successful implementation of the competency-based curriculum in Kenya. Am. J. Educ. Res. **7**(12), 943–947 (2019)
12. Ningsih, S., Sigit, D. V., Lisanti, E.: Devepopment of multimedia based teaching materials to increase cognitive learning outcomes in respiration systems. Int. J. Eng. Technol. Manage. Res. **6**(7), 34–35 (2020)
13. He, Y.R., Wang, X.R., Chen, Q.J., Leng, P.: Design and implementation of virtual simulation teaching system for UAV based on WEBGL. ISPRS- Int. Archives Photogram. Remote Sensing Spatia Inform. Sci. 1239–1246 (2020)
14. Yichong, Z., Xiaoniu, L., Ke, Z., Chunhong, L.: Classroom learning assessment: modeling and tool design based on the SOLO classification theory. In: 2020 IEEE 2nd International Conference on Computer Science and Educational Informatization (CSEI) 2020

15. Liu, X., Dong, F., Tang, W., Yu, Z., Liu, X., Huang, M.: Reform and Implementation of Technical English Course for Brewing Engineering Undergraduates Based on STEAM Theory. Sheng Wu Gong Cheng Xue Bao = Chinese J. Biotechnol. **42**, 1128–1139 (2020)

16. Sun, Z., Anbarasan, M., Praveen Kumar, D.: Design of Online Intelligent English Teaching Platform Based on Artificial Intelligence Techniques. Comput. Intell. **37**(2), (2021). (IF: 3)

17. Xiang, H.: Design and function of teaching incentive mechanism of university teachers under the background of Big Data. In: 2021 International Conference on Internet, Education and Information Technology (IEIT), 2021

18. Wu, S.: Exploration and practice of the curriculum reform of real estate appraisal based on OBE education concept. In: 2nd International Conference on Computers, Information Processing And Advanced Education (2021)

19. Zhang, Q.: An Automatic Assessment Method for Spoken English Based on Multimodal Feature Fusion, Wireless Commun. Mobile Comput. **2021** (2021)

20. Said, R. R., Jamil, H.: The Analysis of Implementation and Scoring for KSSM Oral Assessment Among The Lower Secondary Teachers. Int. J. Acad. Res. Progress. Educ. Develop. (2021)

Application of Data Mining Algorithm in Value Engineering in the Selection of Highway Engineering Design Scheme

Mingjiao Sun[✉] and Jun Yang

Wuhan Huaxia University of Technology, Wuhan 430223, China
sunmingjiao_02@163.com

Abstract. The paper analyzes and compares the rationality, scientificity and engineering value of highway engineering design scheme by combining technology and economy with value engineering, considering and analyzing two factors of function and cost. Through the calculation flow and algorithm, taking the multi scheme design comparison of Expressway isolation facilities as an example, the paper elaborates the algorithm and application of value engineering in highway engineering design scheme selection.

Keywords: Value engineering · Highway engineering · Design scheme

1 Introduction

According to the national capital construction procedure, the feasibility study stage of the project feasibility study project can be carried out after the project proposal is approved. On the basis of the road network status for the regional social and economic development, the necessary economic rationality of the project construction shall be fully investigated, evaluated, predicted and necessary investigation The feasibility of technology implementation possibility puts forward comprehensive research and demonstration results to determine whether the project is approved or not. Because highway engineering has the characteristics of large-scale, complex and complex capital consumption, long-term use after long-term operation, the feasibility study of the project is particularly important. Its quality is related to whether it can provide scientific basis for investment decision-making and whether to guarantee the project to play an investment effect and the choice of construction projects is a particularly important link in the engineering [1].

Highway engineering design mainly considers two factors: function and cost to meet the driving demand. However, no matter how attentive the designer is, due to the influence of time, cost, experience, habit and other factors, unnecessary or unnecessary functions and costs may still exist in the design scheme. If the function design of highway engineering is too high and complete, it will inevitably lead to the increase of cost, and the part of users who exceed the necessary functions do not need it, which will cause the excess of functions; On the contrary, it will cause the function insufficiency. Because

M. A. Jan and F. Khan (Eds.): BigIoT-EDU 2022, LNICST 465, pp. 190–196, 2023.
https://doi.org/10.1007/978-3-031-23950-2_21

highway construction cost is concentrated in short term (2-4a) and reflected in cost, it is easy to be recognized by people. However, the operating cost of service life (decades) is often many times of construction cost, but it is easy to be ignored due to scattered expenditure. This paper uses value analysis technology to control the function cost, and compares and selects the multi design scheme comprehensively, and selects the most reasonable scheme.

2 Concept and Principle of Value Engineering

2.1 Concept

The so-called value engineering refers to the functional analysis of products or services through collective wisdom and organized activities, so as to achieve the necessary functions of products or services reliably with the lowest total cost (life cycle cost), so as to improve the value of products or services. The main idea of value engineering is to improve the value of the object by analyzing the function and cost of the selected research object. The value here refers to the proportion between expense and acquisition, expressed in mathematical proportion as follows:

Value = total function/total cost.

where: the total function refers to the function of use;

Total cost = production cost + use cost.

As a method of technology economy analysis, value engineering has achieved the close combination of technology and economy. In addition, the unique feature of value engineering is that it pays attention to and improves the value of products, pays attention to the work in design stage, and takes function analysis as its own unique analysis method. Because value engineering expands the scope of cost control and involves the cost of life cycle of the project, it is necessary to analyze and study the rationality, scientificity and engineering value of the technical economy of engineering design carefully, explore the possibility of improvement in each construction stage, analyze the relationship between function and cost, and improve the value coefficient of the project; At the same time, the unnecessary functions in engineering design are found and eliminated through value analysis, so as to reduce cost and investment [2].

2.2 Principle

Only when the total production cost and the use cost are the minimum, the product value can reach the maximum and the better economic benefits can be obtained. The relationship between product function and cost is shown in Fig. 1.

In the figure: C_1 is the production cost. With the increase of product function, the production cost will rise; C_2 is the use cost. With the increase of product functions, users can use it easily, and the use cost will decrease; $C = C_1 + C_2$, which refers to the life cycle cost of the product. When the function is P_0, C reaches the lowest point.

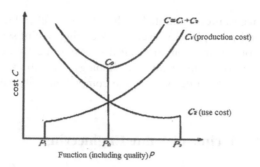

Fig. 1. The relationship between product function and cost

At this time, the value of the product is the highest. When the function is P_1, although the production cost of the product is relatively low, the function of the product is also less, which can not meet the needs of users, resulting in the use cost of C_2 is too high. When the function is P_2, the production cost of the product is too high, which leads to the increase of the product price and the inability of consumers to bear, which will also affect the efficiency.

The purpose of value engineering is to eliminate redundant functions, so that the total function can be reduced to the level required by users. At the same time, the cost can also be reduced to C_0. For highway engineering, the unification of function and cost should be achieved when the scheme is compared and selected, and the minimum investment should be used to meet the use function. The project cost in the construction period is the production cost, while the investment in the operation period is the use cost. If the road grade standard is set too high, the investment in the construction period will be large, that is, the production cost will be high. Although the road use function standard is high and the large and medium-sized maintenance cost is low, it is difficult for investors to raise funds in the construction period under the condition of tight funds. If it is a toll road, the toll standard will be relatively high, which is hard for road users to bear and the overall benefit is not good; If the grade and standard are set too low, the investment in the construction period will be less, that is, the production cost will be lower, the use cost such as large and medium-sized maintenance cost will be increased, the road user cost (such as the increase of fuel consumption due to low grade, the increase of accident rate, etc.) will also be increased, and the overall benefit will not be good. By using the principle of value engineering to compare and select schemes, the cost of the selected scheme can be the lowest and the functional requirements can be met [3].

3   Calculation Flow and Algorithm

3.1   Calculation Process

There are three indexes in the formula of value analysis. In order to get the value V, we must first calculate the function coefficient F and cost coefficient C. The calculation process is shown in Fig. 2.

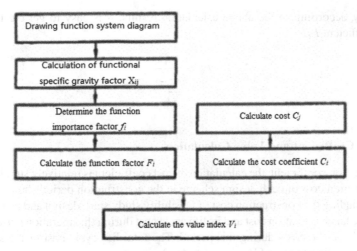

Fig. 2. V_i calculation process

3.2 Function Coefficient Algorithm

The core of value analysis is function analysis. Obviously, f in the formula; It is the key index of the formula, and its determination is complicated. The determination method usually adopts the forced scoring method. Firstly, according to the function of each function in the analysis object, the proportion of each function in the analysis object is calculated. Usually, the 0–10 forced scoring method is used to obtain a function proportion factor matrix

$$x_{ij} = \begin{pmatrix} x_{11} & x_{12} & \dots & x_{1n} \\ x_{21} & x_{22} & \dots & x_{2n} \\ \dots & \dots & \dots & \dots \\ x_{m1} & x_{m2} & \dots & x_{mn} \end{pmatrix} \tag{1}$$

Then compare each function in pairs, using the 0–4 compulsory scoring method for comparison, the score grades are divided as follows: F_1 is more important than F_2, F_1 gets 4 points, F_2 gets 0 points; F_1 is more important than F_2, F_1 gets 3 points, F_2 gets 1 point; F_1 is equally important than F_2, F_1 gets 2 points, F_2 gets 2 points; F_1 is less important than F_2, F_1 gets 1 point, F_2 gets 3 points; F_1 is far less important than F_2. F_1 scores 0 and F_2 scores 4.

The column matrix of $\sum\limits_{i,j=1}^{n} Y_{ij}$ is obtained by summing each row of the matrix

$$\sum_{i,j=1}^{n} Y_{ij} = \begin{pmatrix} \sum\limits_{j=1}^{n} Y_{1j} \\ \dots \\ \dots \\ \sum\limits_{j=1}^{n} Y_{nj} \end{pmatrix} \tag{2}$$

Finally, according to the above calculation results, it is easy to get the functional index coefficient F_i:

$$F_i = \frac{f_i}{\sum\limits_{i=1}^{n} F_i} \tag{3}$$

3.3 Cost Coefficient and Value Calculation

For the function coefficient, the calculation of cost coefficient is relatively simple. Firstly, the construction cost of each design scheme in the construction period should be determined, including the construction cost of feasibility study start, design and construction; The maintenance operation cost and its life cycle cost during the operation period should also include all the costs during this period. The total life cycle cost of the scheme is obtained by adding the two [4].

$$C_j = C_{j1} + C_{j2} \tag{4}$$

Finally, divide the function coefficient by the cost coefficient to get the value

$$V_i = \frac{F_i}{C_j} \tag{5}$$

4 Design Scheme Comparison and Application

Expressway is a fully enclosed belt type civil engineering project. There are many traffic safety facilities along the highway, among which the isolation facilities (usually as a part project) have the largest investment. The unit price of various forms of isolation facilities varies greatly. Therefore, the isolation facilities with different quality index requirements for different highway sections can reasonably and effectively control the cost. In different road sections, isolation facilities have different quality indicators. For example, in sparsely populated embankment, isolation facilities usually only serve to isolate animals and people; The road section near the urban entrance and exit has higher requirements for aesthetics and certain sound insulation function. The following case is the use of value analysis technology to compare and select the isolation facilities design scheme of the sparsely populated general section of expressway.

(1) Draw the functional system diagram.

According to the characteristics of highway isolation facilities, the functional objectives are determined and the functional system chart is drawn. Obviously, the main quality requirements of customers for highway isolation facilities include isolation effect, sound insulation effect, durability, function, structure, beauty, convenience, etc.

(2) Calculate the functional specific gravity factor.
     According to the role of the above functions in the divisional project (the original data is provided by the technical department), the proportion of various functions in the divisional project is calculated. In this case, 0–10 compulsory scoring method is adopted, that is, the score is based on the degree that each comparison scheme meets various quality indicators, and the full score is 10 points.
(3) Determine the functional importance coefficient.
     Function importance coefficient, also known as function evaluation coefficient or function index, is expressed by F, which is the proportion of each function of the evaluation object in the overall function. This case uses 0–4 mandatory scoring method.
(4) Calculate the cost factor.
     According to the relevant information and budget cost, the cost coefficient of each divisional project is calculated.
          Cost coefficient = the sum of LCC of each alternative/LCC of each alternative. The calculated data are shown in Table 1.

Table 1. Cost factor calculation table

Comparison scheme	Construction cost	Maintenance cost	Life cycle	Cost coefficient
Barbed wire wall	80	160	240	0.1765
Barrier	140	140	280	0.2059
Reinforced concrete isolation wall	300	40	340	0.2500
Reinforced concrete art wall	400	100	500	0.3676
total	-	-	1360	1.0000

Through the above analysis, the barbed wire fence wall is the most suitable design scheme for the isolation facilities in the sparsely populated highway section. It basically meets the basic requirements of road users for the isolation facilities in this section, such as stable structure, convenient maintenance, isolation and durability. Compared with other schemes, it reduces the redundant functional requirements such as sound insulation and beauty, thus reducing the unnecessary cost of redundant functions.

5 Conclusion

As a mature management method, value engineering has been widely used in engineering construction in many countries. It can be used for scheme comparison, scheme optimization and many other aspects. The emphasis of value engineering should be in the stage of product research and design. For highway engineering, the application of value engineering can optimize the scheme in the project feasibility study stage, so as to improve the investment efficiency.

References

1. Wei, P.: Value engineering and design scheme optimization (2), Huazhong building (1997)
2. Yisheng, L.: Basic Theory and Relevant Regulations of Project Cost Management. China Planning Press, Beijing (2003)
3. Huaiyu, S.: Practical Value Engineering Course. Machinery Industry Press, Beijing (1999)
4. Mengxi.: The application of value engineering in real estate development enterprises. China real estate (1998)

Application of Network Curriculum Platform Based on Cloud Computing in Physical Education Teaching

Jian Zhang[✉]

Nanchang Institute of Technology, Nanchang 330044, Jiangxi, China
Zhugewolong88@163.com

Abstract. With the rapid development of information courses, there are problems in the construction of educational resources, such as huge total resources, serious alienation of resource structure and weak sharing and application. Students are often lost of teaching resources. In order to use cloud computing technology to build a network curriculum resource sharing platform, which can realize the physical education, suitable for college students' cooperative learning and achieve better physical education teaching results.

Keywords: Cloud computing · Network courses · Resource sharing · Physical education

1 Introduction

With the construction of a series of network courses such as excellent courses, excellent resource sharing courses and excellent video open courses widely carried out by the Ministry of education, various colleges and universities have widely carried out and built various forms of network courses, which provides a very good platform for students' autonomous learning. However, with the in-depth development of online courses, there are also problems such as repeated construction of curriculum resources in Colleges and universities, low utilization rate and difficult sharing of structural alienation, which hinder the development of educational modernization and are difficult to meet the increasing needs of students for online self-help learning. Based on the above problems, it is of great significance to build a fully open online course resource sharing platform [1].

Cloud computing technology has the characteristics of low cost, high efficiency and can deal with massive resources. It is very suitable to be used as the sharing platform of network curriculum resources. The cloud platform can realize the effective construction and management of massive teaching resources. The realization of platform functions is placed in the cloud, which is conducive to give full play to the work efficiency of programmers and facilitate the use of users. In addition, cloud computing can minimize the cost of educational institutions to purchase equipment and independently develop

M. A. Jan and F. Khan (Eds.): BigIoT-EDU 2022, LNICST 465, pp. 197–205, 2023.
https://doi.org/10.1007/978-3-031-23950-2_22

systems [2]. Cloud computing has the characteristics of distribution, collaborative work, co construction and sharing. It is very suitable for students' personalized learning, independent inquiry learning, team cooperative learning and innovative practical learning, which are in line with the development of modern educational learning methods.

Sports has existed since ancient times, but it can develop rapidly only under the conditions of modern society. For nearly half a century, information technology based on Microelectronics has developed rapidly. The application of many new and advanced technologies, new technologies, new materials, new energy and biotechnology has brought mankind from the industrial society to the so-called "third direction" of the information society. This fundamental change has accelerated the development of social productive forces and the pace of working life [3]. On the one hand, it has brought more benefits and convenience to mankind, extended leisure time, greatly improved living conditions and lifestyle, and continuously improved the quality of life. On the other hand, due to the improvement of mechanization, electrification, automation and intelligence, as well as the tension in the workplace and home environment, the threat to health is becoming increasingly obvious. In the 1970s, the institutions of the United Nations Educational, scientific and cultural organization called for the provision of modern education for teachers to meet the needs and needs of society. "Good health, high morality, rich scientific and cultural knowledge." The level of physical education was recognized as one of the most important standards of "triple" training for the first time. This has greatly improved the important role of physical education in the education system and attracted the attention of sports. In addition, a series of reviews and reforms have been carried out on the content, teaching materials and teaching methods of physical education [4]. These include Japan's "sports for fun", the inclusion of sports textbooks into sports textbooks, research group teaching methods, etc. At a new starting point, we should improve the internal relationship between sports and personality shaping, guide physical education, promote physical and mental harmony and improve simple movement skills.

2 Related Work

2.1 Overview of Cloud Computing

It is a supercomputing mode. In the remote data service center, a large number of computers and servers are connected into a computer cloud, which can integrate computing, parallel computing and grid computing in the form of services Storage and video are provided to users by certain means, such as computers, notebooks, mobile phones, etc. [5]. Its computing power can be circulated as commodities, which is convenient to use and cheap. It is like the centralized power supply mode of power plants. From the above definition of cloud computing, we can get two meanings of cloud computing, that is, the infrastructure of building applications and cloud computing applications based on it.

The architecture of cloud computing is very large. Through the analysis of the existing cloud computing system, it can be regarded as a set of services. The basic architecture of cloud computing is shown in Fig. 1.

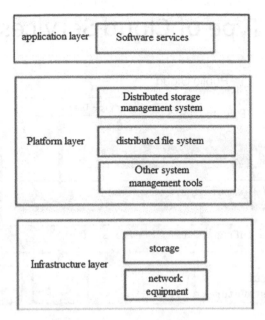

Fig. 1. Basic architecture of cloud computing

2.2 Shared Learning Mode Based on Cloud Computing

The traditional learning mode has not adapted to the rapid. The shared. This model makes full use of resource sharing and interactive communication to realize collaborative learning, reflect students' personalized development needs, and ensure learning activities that can effectively achieve teaching objectives. Cloud computing provides a platform support for collaborative learning [6]. Under this platform, students can easily share files, software, teaching content and other resources, and support online editing, user evaluation and learning resource sharing [7]. As shown in Fig. 2.

The shared learning mode based on cloud computing has the following typical characteristics:

(1) High efficiency and economy. Cloud computing technology can greatly reduce the cost of network course construction in Colleges and universities, especially the investment and maintenance cost of hardware equipment, and there is no need to arrange professionals to be responsible for maintenance. The software and hardware equipment of cloud computing are provided by a professional third party, which can ensure the efficient operation of the system. Therefore, cloud computing technology with high efficiency and low cost has obvious cost advantages.

(2) Collaboration and sharing. With the support of cloud computing technology, teacher users can cooperate to complete the development and construction of resources, and student users can also carry out distance cooperative learning. All users can share their high-quality resources on the cloud platform. The idea of cloud computing co construction and sharing of high-quality resources [8].

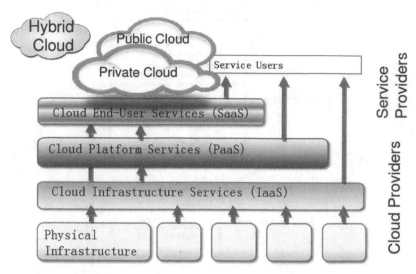

Fig. 2. Shared learning mode based on cloud computing

(3) Convenience and flexibility. Convenient operation. Users can use the high-quality resources and services provided by cloud computing without understanding the working principle and operation mechanism of cloud computing. Only a computer or smart phone that can connect to the Internet can obtain all the resources on the platform and enjoy various services provided by the platform.

(4) Energy saving and environmental protection. At present, the whole society is advocating energy conservation and environmental protection. The shared learning mode based on cloud computing has low requirements for equipment configuration and does not need the support of high energy consuming server equipment. It can not only help energy conservation and emission reduction, but also save costs. Users can enjoy the services brought by cloud computing only by terminal devices that can access the Internet.

3   Design and Implementation of Physical Education Resource Sharing Platform Based on Cloud Computing

3.1 Design Idea

The theoretical research and technical practice of foreign online course platforms are very rich. A considerable number of platforms adhere to the concept of open source software, open source code to users free of charge and absorb users to participate in the development of final products. After research and testing, the better ones are Sakai and blackboard in the United States, Moodle in Australia, bodington in the United Kingdom, atutor in Canada, and web CT, virtual-u, learning space, etc., which are called network teaching platforms. These platforms belong to the third generation of online course design products, in addition to providing learners with teaching materials through web pages, relevant educational network connections, and asynchronous two-way communication through e-mail, electronic bulletin boards, online exercises and measurements; It also realizes the function of synchronous two-way communication through online conversation room, teleconference, video conference or muds (Moos) system. Take Moodle in Australia for example, in moodle The official website of www.org has registered 171 countries and 21830 sites using the platform, including 3130 in the United States, 477 in Australia, 128 in Chinese Mainland, 305 in Taiwan, 46 in Hong Kong, 47 in Singapore and 240 in Japan. From this data, we can see the development of educational informatization application around the world, and it is enough to make us feel that there is a long way to go [9].

Based on the shared learning mode of cloud computing, puts forward the way of collaboration and sharing, the wisdom of users, makes teaching resources under the cloud platform, and develops a teaching resource sharing platform based on cloud computing under the guidance of this idea. The specific design ideas are as follows: first, the platform resources should be highly open and shared. Teachers and students can fully share and exchange, and jointly build and share curriculum resources. Secondly, the platform should fully reflect the service and efficiency. The platform must reflect the powerful resource management and service advantages of cloud computing and provide users with convenient, fast and efficient services. Finally, the platform should be able to support collaborative learning. At present, students like communication and interaction and are difficult to complete tasks alone. Therefore, the platform must provide interactive functions to facilitate the interaction between students, teachers and teaching resources, and run collaborative learning through the whole sharing platform.

The subject of physical education is students The effect of sports should be shown in students Students are highly malleable Every idea and link of physical education teaching directly affects the growth of students. The correct education for students lies not only in the fluidity of lateral muscles and muscle lines, but also in the healthy development of bones and organs.

The comprehensive sports system embodies the regularity and integrity of sports development.

Consistency: it shows the "consistency" of students' physical development and the "consistency" of main organ development.

3.2 Architecture of Physical Education Resource Sharing Platform Based on Cloud Computing

Combined with the characteristics of B/S structure and cloud computing, this paper constructs the architecture of physical education resource sharing. The characteristic of B/S (Browser/Server Architecture) structure is to make full use of the browser to facilitate users' operation and hand over cumbersome application programs, data calculation and task processing to the server. However, with the expansion of resource scale, it brings heavy pressure to the server, especially it is difficult to realize a large number of user interaction. Therefore, it is very necessary for us to build a physical combined with advanced cloud computing technology. As shown in Fig. 3, the platform is composed of presentation layer, the user uses the terminal device to send access request information to the cloud computing service pool through the browser [10]. The business layer is responsible for handling the business application logic of various teaching resource sharing platforms. The data layer is responsible for the unified storage and maintenance of data. The log and Statistics Center is responsible for data statistics, and distributed services run through the whole business layer and data layer.

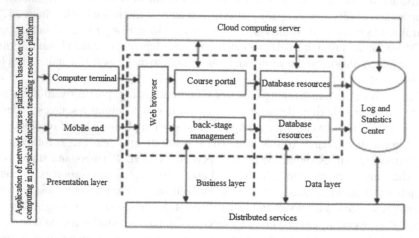

Fig. 3. Architecture of physical education resource sharing platform based on Cloud Computing

4   Application of Network Course in Physical Education

4.1   Pay Equal Attention to the Design of Teaching Content and Teaching Environment, and Give Full Play to the Potential of Teaching Resources

At present, in the process of making network courses, producers often invest more energy in the selection and design of teaching related contents, but do not consider enough in teaching design such as teaching situation, teaching organization and so on. Therefore, we cannot make full use of educational resources in the teaching process. Constructivists believe that knowledge is not obtained through teachers' education, but in a specific social and cultural environment, with the help of others, including teachers and learning partners. In the creative learning environment, curriculum design should not only consider the analysis of curriculum objectives, but also create an environment conducive to students' self-esteem, which is one of the important contents of curriculum design.Learning in the network environment requires learners to construct meaning more autonomously, so the creation of situation is particularly important. Online courses not only provide materials, but also cultivate students' ability of autonomous learning, affect students to become their own "teachers", change me to learn, so as to improve learning efficiency to a certain extent. At present, most online courses still emphasize "teaching", it emphasizes the teaching of knowledge, starts knowledge teaching as soon as you enter, and does not give a certain situational guidance. Some online courses are simple presentation of text teaching materials or teachers' speeches. Some courses are empty, do not make a unified plan for the whole course according to the teaching objectives, do not set up simulated real learning situations for learners, and lack some problems for learners to solve Practical problems can not fully reflect learners' initiative.

We should be good at making use of the attraction contained in sports activities, and multiply and enlarge this attraction through reasonable teaching organization. And the independent liberation of personality, so as to make interpersonal relations loose and harmonious, so that students can freely, carefree, and unknowingly obtain the healthy development of body and mind in a relaxed and lively environment and in a happy and cheerful mood.

The unity of physical and mental fitness in physical education teaching is reflected in three aspects:

First of all, when choosing sports textbooks, we should not only pay attention to the positive impact of these textbooks on students' physical conditions, different sports skills and different physical qualities, but also pay attention to the impact of these textbooks on students' psychology. We should work hard from the perspectives of psychology, aesthetics and sociology to make students have a good experience. When I finish the story, I can't help feeling the joy and joy of harmony, breathing, trend and success.

Second, the should focus on overcoming the continuous integration mode that reflects the sports lifestyle, so that students' activities are more free, happy and rich, so as to achieve the purpose of physical and mental harmony, both inside and outside.

In addition, we should also pay attention to changing students' physical exertion and mentality. In physical education and physical education, students engage in sports at the same time In the process of repeated exercise and rest, the changes of students' physiological functions have common regularity. In practice, physiological function began to change and the level of physiological function began to improve. To a certain extent, students' physiological functions change with the difference of waveform exercise and rest. Therefore, students' psychological activities (mainly thinking, emotion, attention and will) also have tendentiousness. The changing law of this form of physical and mental stress reflects the obvious rhythmic and harmonious physical and mental education.

Therefore, in the process of network curriculum construction, we should set up the curriculum from the social needs, and take people's self realization as the core of curriculum design: highlight the emotional basis of the curriculum, root the educational content and methods in the emotional soil, and emphasize the unity of emotional education and cognitive education; pay attention to the individuation of the curriculum, give full play to the main participation role of students and the educational function of the society; emphasize the diversity of the curriculum There are formal academic courses, social practice courses, self awakening courses and self-development courses; it emphasizes that teaching must start from the needs of learners, emphasize the importance of situational creation and collaborative learning, and put the learning goal on learners' problem-solving ability.

4.2 Give Full Play to the Autonomy of Participants and Enrich Learning Resources

Autonomous learning is a major feature of online education. Learners realize the separation of time and space of learning activities through autonomous learning. At present, online courses only reflect learners' own learning in autonomous learning, and do not provide them with all kinds of resources conducive to autonomous learning. Due to the wide range of network users, teachers may not be able to predict the original cognitive structure of online learners Structure and level. For a course, it is impossible to be encyclopedic, so we can only focus on the teaching of this course. In this way, it is difficult for learners who do not know much about the field, especially for some highly professional disciplines, who need an electronic library of relevant knowledge. For all learners, in When they want to check their learning effect, they need to provide a large number of relevant cases in the course, so that they can reconstruct their knowledge in the process of solving cases. However, most of the current network teaching systems do not fully support this aspect, which is not conducive to the full embodiment of learners' learning efficiency.

Therefore, we can learn from the popular and mature model on the Internet, regard the course users as builders at the same time, and take the resources and feelings sorted and accumulated by learners in the learning process as the related resources of the course, as shown in Fig. 4. This not only provides learners with a private space to preserve their learning experience, but also can be converted into course resources through certain technical means Realize the growth of experience system and enrich the content of relevant courses.

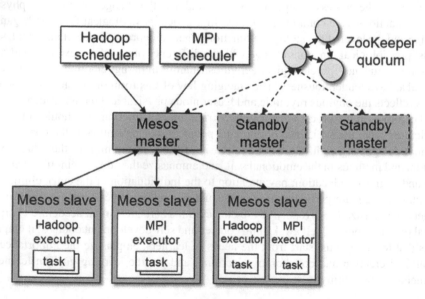

Fig. 4. Resource sharing mode of online course platform

5   Conclusion

The is very rapid. Information technology, and cloud computing is an emerging and revolutionary concept. Cloud computing will change our physical education teaching mode. The network-based teaching method has separated teaching and learning activities in time and space. However, Its application is still in the exploratory stage. So far, there is no unified standard and implementation method of cloud computing. It is a long-term project to apply cloud computing to the construction of network course resource database. However, we believe that, it will construction of network course resource database.

References

1. Shaoli, Z., Xiaoqi, Z., Hui, Z.: Construction and mechanism research of education big data information platform based on resource sharing. Modern Intell. **12**, 90–95 (2017)
2. Huaping, L., Peng, X., Xiaoming, H.: Construction of high-quality teaching resource sharing platform in Higher Vocational Colleges Based on cloud computing. J. Anhui Electron. Inform. Vocational Tech. College **4**, 56–60 (2016)
3. Yang, G.: On the diversification of higher vocational physical education teaching mode under the information environment. Sci. Technol. Inform. **15**(30), 164–165 (2017)
4. Feng, S.: Research and construction on the integration of information technology and higher vocational physical education curriculum teaching. Agricult. Staff **19**, 138 (2017)
5. Ma, Y.: Low-light image enhancement method based on deep learning. Inform. Technol. **45**(1), 5, (2021) View at: Google Scholar
6. Xu, F., Cheng, K., Zhang, J.: Pedestrian re-identification based on the combination of deep learning and attribute learning. Data Collection Process. **33**(4), 7 (2018). View at: Publisher Site | Google Scholar
7. Liu, W., Wen, B., Gao, S.: Research on intelligent image processing based on deep learning. Autom. Instrument. **4**(8), 2020. View at: Google Scholar
8. Zheng, X., Sun, X., Lv, J.: Behavior recognition based on deep learning and intelligent planning. Chin. J. Electron. **47**(8), 8 (2019). View at: Google Scholar
9. Liu, D., Jia, J., Zhao, Y., Qian, Y.: A review of image denoising methods based on deep learning. Comput. Eng. Appl. **57**(7), 13, (2021). View at: Google Scholar
10. Song, L., Shi, L., Wang, P.: Intelligent fault diagnosis method based on dynamic statistical filtering and deep learning. J. Instrument. **8**(7), 2019. View at: Google Scholar
11. Chang, H., Gou, J., Li, X.: Application of faster R-CNN in industrial CT image defect detection. Chin. J. Image and Graph. **23**(7), 11 (2018). View at: Google Scholar
12. Tao, C., Wang, Y., Chen, M.: Hyperspectral image classification with multilayer local perception convolutional neural networks. J. Sichuan Univ. Natural Sci. Edition, **57**(1), 10 (2020). View at: Google Scholar
13. Lu, L., Meng, P.: Recognition of common traffic warning signs in China based on fully convolutional neural network. J. Changchun Univ. Sci. Technol.: Natural Science Edition, **43**(2), 8 (2020). View at: Google Scholar
14. Zhong, F., Yang, B.: A novel deep learning-based single image rain removal method. Comput. Sci. **45**(11), 283–287 (2018). View at: Google Scholar

Application of Data Mining in Psychological Education of College Students in Private Independent Colleges

Lingying Yan[✉]

College of Arts and Sciences Kunming, Kunming 650000, Yunnan, China
15887225894@163.com

Abstract. With the development of information technology, the means of collecting, storing and managing data are becoming more and more perfect. Data mining came into being. For private independent colleges and universities, psychological education has always been a very key problem. With the increasing social pressure and the changes of the times, college students have more or less certain psychological health problems, and the psychological problems of college students are becoming more and more serious. Therefore, it is very necessary to carry out psychological health education for college students in private independent colleges and universities, Let college students correctly face their own development and existing problems, and establish a good attitude, which will also be of great help to college students entering the society in the future. Therefore, this paper will analyze the problems of data mining in the psychological education of college students in private independent colleges, and provide some solutions for reference only.

Keywords: Data mining · Private independent colleges and universities · Psychological education · Guide

1 Introduction

With the change of the times and environment, college students in private independent colleges are greatly affected by various external factors, and college students will have some psychological cognitive deviations and go from face to face to negative psychological path because of their more or less problems, which has a great impact on the healthy and all-round development of College Students. However, most students in Colleges and universities have to contact the society for work. Therefore, it is very important to carry out appropriate psychological education for college students, which is not only conducive to building a harmonious campus, but also the key to promoting social civilization. In the new era, to carry out psychological education for college students, we should first recognize the existing problems of psychological education, and then take scientific countermeasures.

M. A. Jan and F. Khan (Eds.): BigIoT-EDU 2022, LNICST 465, pp. 206–215, 2023.
https://doi.org/10.1007/978-3-031-23950-2_23

Due to the lack of identity with private colleges, private college students often exaggerate the differences between themselves and public college students, lose confidence in themselves, have no vision for the future, and fall into a state of depression all day. Therefore, the mental health of private college students directly affects the overall mental health level of college students in China. In order to adapt to the current balanced development of higher education and improve the quality of private higher education, private colleges and universities must pay attention to the mental health education of college students, cultivate their good mental quality and ensure the stable development of their mental health.

College students in private independent colleges are in the stage of transition from adolescence to adulthood, that is, youth. As a special social group, college students' individual physiological development is close to maturity, and their individual psychological development is moving towards maturity, showing unique psychological development characteristics different from both children and adults.

The intellectual development of college students in private independent colleges is in the golden age and reaches its peak. Observation, memory and imagination have been greatly improved, the independence and flexibility of thinking have been significantly enhanced, and the breadth and profundity of thinking have also been greatly developed. Specifically [1]:

1) White control ability is weak, but emotion is obviously rich. Most college students can think and act rationally and try to adjust their impulses, but many college students are often deeply distressed by their weak self-control, feel that they are often easily disturbed by internal emotions and external environment, can't do what they want to do, and it's difficult to control strong emotions.

2) Increased decisiveness but lack of perseverance. Youth is a key period for the development of self-consciousness. During this period, the development of College Students' self-consciousness is in a period of differentiation, contradiction and unity, which is manifested in the differentiation of self-consciousness and the contradiction of self-consciousness.

3) Intellectually developed, but lack of identification ability. The abstract logical thinking ability of this age group occupies a dominant position, active thinking, quick response, good at independent thinking, dare to innovate and have a tenacious exploration spirit. But after all, they lack social practice, their thoughts are divorced from reality, and sometimes they tend to go to extremes, showing a certain degree of one sidedness, superficiality and blindness.

Private colleges and universities refer to the schools or educational institutions that implement higher academic education or higher non academic education, which are run by enterprises and institutions, social organizations, other social organizations and individual citizens, using non-state financial education funds and in accordance with the establishment standards of colleges and universities formulated by the state and the Municipal Education administrative departments. After three decades of rapid development, the quality and quantity of private higher education in China have made considerable progress. By June, 2013, the number of private colleges and universities in China was close to 1000, with more than 2.8 million students, accounting for more than 40%

of the total number of colleges and universities in China. Over the past 30 years, private colleges and universities have absorbed high-quality students at multiple levels, directly increased the proportion of citizen higher education, trained and delivered a large number of qualified practical talents for various industries in society, become an important part of China's higher education system, and improve China's higher education level. Compared with ordinary colleges and universities, private colleges and universities have their particularity in many aspects. The running funds of private colleges and universities mainly rely on self raised funds. In addition to part of the source of tuition fees, they also rely on multilateral forces such as enterprises, social organizations and personal investment. In this case, it generally comes from the investment of social forces such as tuition fees, social groups and individuals. As far as China is concerned, the general tuition fees can provide about 80% of the expenses of private colleges and universities. Due to the huge economic pressure, the charging standard of private colleges and universities is generally about twice that of ordinary colleges and universities. Take Zhengzhou Shengda Economic and Trade Management College as an example. In 2013, the tuition fees of college students were basically 12000 yuan. In addition to various food, accommodation and miscellaneous expenses, the total cost for a Zhengzhou Shengda Economic and trade management college undergraduate student to complete his four-year study was nearly 60000 yuan. This is a very heavy educational investment for most families with average income. For some poor families, they generally need to borrow money to study, This has also increased the psychological pressure on students in private colleges and universities such as Zhengzhou Shengda Economic and trade management college. In addition, due to the relatively weak learning foundation of private college students and the new content of their professional courses, a considerable number of students can not find appropriate learning methods, and some students relax their learning because of the relatively loose learning environment, resulting in poor performance; At the same time, some students in order to reduce the economic burden, in the school field work study, not only delayed learning, but also increased the pressure on learning. Generally speaking, college students admitted to private colleges often choose to attend private colleges because their college entrance examination scores are not ideal. Therefore, many private college students are full of a sense of inferiority and loss.

2   Related Technologies

2.1   Concept of Data Mining Amount

Data mining is a high-level technology in business intelligence applications. It is a process of extracting hidden, unknown but potentially useful information and knowledge from a large number of incomplete, noisy, fuzzy and random data. 1. Using data mining, users can more easily find the laws of data, and users can use these laws to predict some data in line with the characteristics.

The information obtained by data mining should have three characteristics: first unknown, effective and practical. First unknown means that the information obtained by data mining should be the information that can not be obtained by intuition or general technical methods. The more unexpected the residence is, the more valuable it may be. A typical example in this regard is that a chain store found an amazing connection between children's diapers and beer through data mining. The purpose of data mining is to be effective and practical.

Let s be the total number of training set samples, there are m classes of $C_i (i = 1, 2, 3, \ldots, m)$ samples, and S is class C_i The number of samples in is calculated as follows:

$$I(s_1, s_2, \ldots, s_a) = -\sum_{i=1}^{m} p_i \log_2(p_i) \tag{1}$$

$$E(X) = \sum_{J=1}^{Y} \frac{S_{1J} + \ldots + S_{MJ}}{S} J(S_{1J}, \ldots, S_{MJ}) \tag{2}$$

$$I(S_{1J}, \ldots, S_{MJ}) = -\sum_{i=1}^{m} p_{ij} \log_2(p_{ij}) \tag{3}$$

$$A(X) = Gain(X)/I(s_1, s_2, \ldots, s_n) \tag{4}$$

There are many analysis methods of data mining [2]. There are different analysis methods for different purposes. The more common analysis methods are as follows: classification, prediction, correlation grouping, live association rules, clustering, valuation, description and visualization, complex data type mining, including text data mining. Web data mining, graphics and image data mining, video and audio data mining.

2.2 Data Mining Process

The process of data mining generally consists of three main stages: data preparation, mining operation, result expression and interpretation. The discovery of knowledge can be described as the repeated process of these three stages.

(1) Data preparation
   This stage can be further divided into three sub steps: data integration, data selection and data preprocessing. Data integration combines the data in the multi file and multi database running environment, solves the semantic fuzziness, handles the omission in the data and cleans the invalid data. The purpose of data selection is to identify the data set to be analyzed, narrow the processing range and improve the quality of data mining. Preprocessing is to overcome the limitations of current data mining tools.
(2) Data mining
   The key points of practical analysis in this stage are: first decide how to generate hypotheses, whether to let the data mining system generate hypotheses for users, or whether users put forward hypotheses about the knowledge that may be contained in the database. The former is called discovery data mining; The latter is called validation data mining. Then select the appropriate tools to explore knowledge, and finally confirm it.

(3) Expression and interpretation of results

Analyze the extracted information according to the needs of users, select effective information, and transfer it through decision support tools. Therefore, the task of this step is not only to express the results (for example, using the information visualization method), but also to filter the information. If the user is not satisfied, it is necessary to repeat the above data mining. The task of this step is not only to express the results (for example, using the information visualization method), but also to filter the information, If the user is not satisfied, the above data mining process needs to be repeated.

2.3   Problems in College Students' Psychological Education

(1) Insufficient attention to mental health education

Many people are biased against psychological education and think that most of the people who receive psychological education are people with psychological diseases. Therefore, many people are not very willing to receive psychological guidance in mental health education. Moreover, many college students have less understanding of psychological education, which has a great relationship with the publicity of the school. The school does not pay enough attention to psychological education and lacks effective publicity channels, resulting in the low understanding of college students about the relevant knowledge of psychological education. There are also relatively independent colleges that pay more attention to college students' mental health education, teachers and schools pay more attention to mental health education, and students deal with their own psychological problems and study mental health better [3].

(2) School mental health education is relatively scarce

Relevant surveys show that many independent colleges have implemented the mental health education mechanism for college students, but it is still in the primary stage. The core content of mental health education and the significant problems such as the difference between educational content and reality have not been solved. The specific contents and are all based on the traditional educational mechanism as a reference. They are not innovative and lack of content. They can not adapt to the cultural and psychological needs of the diversified era; Ideological education is mainly reflected in the surface of psychological education, and the deeper content of mental health education is not understood enough. Therefore, the mental health education thought carried out by schools should be advanced and profound. It is very important to strengthen the deep and perfect people in all aspects.

(3) Defects in family education

Many college students are the only child in the family, and many parents spoil their children. Most of them are spoiled. These children generally have no social exercise and have less independent life experience. Generally, such people are grumpy, and most of them are in a rebellious period. They don't know how to get along and communicate with others. When they get along with others, many are prone to contradictions, and they won't take the initiative to solve the conflicts with others. In addition, there are many and complex emotional disputes among college students, which is also a loophole in college students' mental health education. Psychological education can not correctly guide students. What rational methods should be taken to solve their own emotional problems, do not know how to correctly solve the problems existing in the learning process, and are at a loss for the problems in daily life.

3 Application Analysis of Data Mining in Psychological Education of College Students in Private Independent Colleges

Using data mining technology to analyze the psychological status and characteristics of college students in private independent colleges, college teachers should carry out timely psychological education on the premise of abiding by the principles of psychological education, and strive to make them mentally healthy. Can affirm their own ability, can cope with general life pressure, good mental state, effective learning, and can contribute to the collective and society [4].

(1) Carry out various activities to disseminate psychological knowledge
   For different grades and types of students, carry out lectures with different contents, such as "Freshmen's psychological adaptation", "re understanding themselves" and "how to correctly deal with interpersonal relations" for freshmen; Give lectures on learning psychology and love psychology for sophomores; Junior students give lectures on career counseling; Senior students will give lectures on employment counseling and career direction. At the same time, various media in the school. For example, television, film and radio play a subtle role in affecting the healthy growth of college students. Make full use of these media to widely publicize the relationship between mental health and talent. Arouse college students' conscious requirements for optimizing psychological quality and improving mental health level, and create a good cultural atmosphere in which everyone cares about psychological quality and attaches importance to mental health [5–7].

(2) Treat different situations separately
   The working object of psychological education is people. People are different, and no one method can solve everyone's problems. Therefore, counselors must respect individual differences and treat them individually in psychological education. This includes age differences, gender differences, personality differences, growth background differences and so on.

(3) Help students adapt to the new environment
   From middle school to university, it is a new world for every freshman. Great changes have taken place in both living environment and learning methods, both self goals and social expectations. Whether they can adapt to the new university life as soon as possible under this environmental change is directly related to whether college students can have a good start in the road of growth and whether they can spend the University era effectively and successfully. Therefore, after freshmen study, counselors should help students adapt to the new environment, shorten the adaptation period required for psychological transformation, form a positive attitude, and lay a good foundation for the growth of the whole university stage. In addition, there are obvious individual differences in the extent and degree of

freshmen adapting to the environment, so counselors should pay more attention to students with fluctuating psychological emotions, pay more attention to them, communicate and talk with them, and improve their mental health level [8–11].

4 Conclusion

The application analysis of data mining in the psychological education of college students in private independent colleges and universities studied in this paper is that mental health education is an important content in college students' ideological education, and the education needs strong publicity and constantly improving the educational mechanism, so as to imperceptibly affect the psychological development of students. To carry out mental health education for college students, we should fully combine with the ideas of the times, establish an effective educational mechanism according to the educational objectives and the characteristics of students' development, and actively absorb western advanced technology and ideas, which is also the key to the innovation of College Students' mental health education. While effectively learning from western culture and realizing the combination of Chinese and foreign cultures, we should also pay attention to practical problems, Pay attention to the inheritance and innovation of the essence of traditional culture, deeply affect the psychology of college students, and enable college students to establish a good attitude towards life and affairs and develop healthily.

At present, there are still backward ideas, which limit the school running thought of private colleges to the single training mode of teaching professional knowledge and skills, define qualified talents as mastering a certain knowledge or technology, ignore the fundamental significance of private higher education as education itself, and fail to see the importance of improving personality quality to the healthy growth of students. Under the guidance of this educational ideology, private colleges and universities have not paid due attention to mental health education, and the discipline construction has stagnated, Become -i "1 the dispensable vase major cannot play its important role in the talent training system. Zhengzhou Shengda Economic and trade management college has always attached importance to students' moral education and started from many aspects of students' Ideological and political education. However, with the development of society and the expansion of the college scale, like other private colleges and universities, college students have exposed more and more psychological problems, which has affected their normal study and life. University Health is a group, and individual mental health affects the stability of the group. Under the social conditions of popularization of higher education and fierce competition in the employment market, excellent psychological quality is an essential professional quality for excellent talents to base themselves on the society and develop for a long time. It puts forward practical requirements for private higher education to realize quality education. This requires students to attach great importance to students' mental health education, make them independent from ideological and political work, cultivate and develop independently, and serve college students.

According to the characteristics of private colleges and universities, there are certain limitations and obstacles in the development of mental health education, which is undeniable for private colleges and universities. However, since they know the problem, they should spare no effort to eliminate various adverse factors, establish a special mental health education department, allocate special mental health education staffing and funds, hire full-time and part-time mental health education staff, and from the perspective of their own team building, Find problems and gaps, and strive to make the mental health work of college students develop stably and vigorously [13–17]. Set up various psychological courses and lectures, set up professional psychological counseling institutions, improve the psychological crisis intervention system, and make full preparations to deal with various psychological problems and psychological crisis events that may occur to students [18–20].

Based on the opportunities and challenges of the classified management reform to the private compulsory education schools in the new era, this study constructs the institutional framework of teacher incentive in private compulsory education schools. Based on the incentive status, satisfaction and demand of private teachers, starting from the three types of teacher incentive systems of life security, humanistic care and career development and the three dimensions of their subordinates according to the institutional framework, this paper analyzes and discusses the problems existing in the incentive and the causes of the problems. Finally, based on the incentive problems and demand of teachers in private compulsory education schools, it puts forward corresponding system improvement strategies. The research is summarized as follows: firstly, the life security incentive system of private compulsory education schools is the basic system of teacher incentive, which determines the bottom limit of teacher incentive, that is, the life security incentive in place can prevent teachers from negative dissatisfaction, on the contrary, it will severely dampen teachers' work enthusiasm. In the life security incentive system, salary performance is the basic incentive, welfare treatment is the key incentive, and health management is the fundamental incentive. All incentive subjects should spare no effort to protect teachers' basic rights, safeguard teachers' legitimate rights and interests, improve teachers' welfare benefits, reduce pressure and burden for teachers, and ensure teachers' basic living needs. Secondly, the humanistic care incentive system of private compulsory education schools is an important system of teacher incentive. It determines the internal fundamental motivation of teacher incentive. It is one of the most easily ignored but influential factors. In recent years, it has gradually attracted people's attention. In the incentive system of humanistic care, interpersonal communication is the basic incentive, work identity is the internal incentive, and cultural atmosphere is the implicit incentive. Each incentive subject should carry forward the humanistic spirit of "humanistic care", pay attention to the internal needs of teachers, pay attention to the inner world of teachers, respect and care for teachers, and make teachers an enviable profession.

Thirdly, the career development incentive system of private compulsory education schools is the key system of teacher incentive. It determines the promotion space of teacher incentive. It is one of the factors most needed by teachers and most valued by the state. It affects the quality of school education and teaching. In the career development incentive system, promotion evaluation and employment is the basic incentive, scientific research and training is the important incentive, and the display platform is the additional incentive. Each incentive subject should reasonably improve the promotion, evaluation and employment system of teachers, improve the teacher training system, open up the channels of the teacher display platform, and promote the equal opportunities of private teachers in career development. Finally, the three factors in the framework of the teacher incentive system of private compulsory education schools, namely, life security, humanistic care and career development, are interrelated, inseparable, linked and progressive. Life guarantee is the material guarantee of teachers' motivation, humanistic care is the emotional support of teachers' motivation, and career development is the spiritual pursuit of teachers' motivation; Life security is the prospect, humanistic care is the foundation, and career development is the ultimate destination. Therefore, for the teacher incentive system of private compulsory education schools, it might as well be a teacher incentive system framework worth trying. In the process of investigation, interview and understanding, it is found that some private primary and secondary schools are not satisfactory, but it is also found that private primary and secondary schools that have done very well in all aspects, which shows that private education can be made into high-quality education. It is hoped that excellent private schools can share their experience and achievements for other private schools. It is hoped that the development of private education in our country will be better and better.

Acknowledgements. Yunnan Provincial Education Department of the sixth batch of university science and technology innovation team project construction "Yunnan Province university wisdom tourism science and technology innovation team".

References

1. Hu, N., Yang, J., Joo, S.W., Banerjee, A.N., Qian, S.: Cell electrofusion in microfluidic devices a review. Sens. Actuators B Chem. **178**, 63–85 (2013)
2. Dimova, R., Bezlyepkina, N., Jordö, M.D., et al.: Vesicles in electric fields: some novel aspects of membrane behavior. Soft Matter **5**(17), 3201–3212 (2009)
3. Leary, T., Yeganeh, M., Maldarelli, C.: Microfluidic study of the electrocoalescence of aqueous droplets in crude oil. ACS Omega **5**(13), 7348–7360 (2020)
4. Mhatre, S., et al.: Electrostatic phase separation: a review. Chem. Eng. Res. Des. **96**, 177–195 (2015)
5. Seifert, T., Sowade, E., Roscher, F., Wiemer, M., Gessner, T., Baumann, R.R.: Additive manufacturing technologies compared: morphology of deposits of silver ink using inkjet and aerosol jet printing. Ind. Eng. Chem. Res. **54**(2), 769–779 (2015)
6. Nguyen, V.D., Byun, D.: Mechanism of electrohydrodynamic printing based on ac voltage without a nozzle electrode. Appl. Phys. Lett. **94**(17), 173509 (2009). https://doi.org/10.1063/1.3126957
7. Rozynek, Z., Mikkelsen, A., Dommersnes, P., Fossum, J.O.: Electroformation of Janus and patchy capsules. Nat. Commun. **5**(1), 3945 (2014)
8. Sun, X.-T., Yang, C.-G., Xu, Z.-R.: Controlled production of size-tunable Janus droplets for submicron particle synthesis using an electrospray microfluidic chip. RSC Adv. **6**(15), 12042–12047 (2016). https://doi.org/10.1039/C5RA24531A
9. Jia, Y., Ren, Y., Liu, W., et al.: Electrocoalescence of paired droplets encapsulated in double-emulsion drops. Lab Chip **16**(22), 4313–4318 (2016)
10. Song, R., Abbasi, M.S., Lee, J.: Fabrication of 3D printed modular microfluidic system for generating and manipulating complex emulsion droplets. Microfluid. Nanofluid. **23**(7), 1–11 (2019). https://doi.org/10.1007/s10404-019-2258-2

11. Less, S., Vilagines, R.: The electrocoalescers' technology: advances, strengths and limitations for crude oil separation. J. Petrol. Sci. Eng. **81**, 57–63 (2012)
12. Yang, D., Ghadiri, M., Sun, Y., He, L., Luo, X., Lü, Y.: Critical electric field strength for partial coalescence of droplets on oil-water interface under DC electric field. Chem. Eng. Res. Des. **136**, 83–93 (2018)
13. Taylor, G.I.: Disintegration of water drops in an electric field. Proc. R. Soc. Lond. A: Math. Phys. Sci. **280**(1382), 383–397 (1964)
14. Taylor, G.I.: Studies in electrohydrodynamics I The circulation produced in a drop by electrical field. Proc. R. Soc. Lond. A: Math. Phys. Sci. **291**(1425), 159–166 (1966)
15. Torza, S., Cox, R.G., Mason, S.G.: Electrohydrodynamic deformation and bursts of liquid drops. Phil. Trans. R. Soc. Lond. A **269**(1198), 295–319 (1971)
16. Abbasi, M.S., Song, R., Kim, H., Lee, J.: Multimodal breakup of a double emulsion droplet under an electric field. Soft Matter **15**(10), 2292–2300 (2019)
17. Ajayi, O.: A note on Taylor's electrohydrodynamic theory. Proc. R. Soc. Lond. A **364**(1719), 499–507 (1978)
18. Bentenitis, N., Krause, S.: Droplet deformation in dc electric fields: the extended leaky dielectric model. Langmuir **21**(14), 6194–6209 (2005)
19. Zholkovskij, E.K., Masliyah, J.H., Czarnecki, J.: An electrokinetic model of drop deformation in an electric field. J. Fluid Mech. **472**, 1–27 (2002)
20. Latham, J., Roxburgh, I.W.: Disintegration of pairs of water drops in an electric field. IEEE Trans. Ind. Appl. **295**(1440), 84–97 (1966)

Application of Quaternion Instructional Design Mode in Higher Education Based on Personalized Algorithm

Hua Zhong[✉]

Gold Campus, Gannan Medical University, Ganzhou 341000, Jiangxi, China
zhonghua2021111@163.com

Abstract. Based on personalized algorithm, the application of quaternion instructional design mode in higher education is studied, and it is stipulated that teachers should choose the corresponding best teaching method before teaching all the target content. Data mining and personalized recommendation service content. This method is suitable for the tasks with less close relationship between various objectives, but the teaching effect is poor when teaching complex professional tasks that need to integrate knowledge, skills and attitudes and coordinate different skills. For the latter, it is more appropriate to design teaching centered on the overall and practical tasks. This paper introduces the task-based four element teaching design mode, and discusses the problems and future development of the implementation of Task-based education program.

Keywords: Personalized algorithm · Four element teaching design · Integrated learning

1 Introduction

The continuous development and innovation of society and technology put forward high requirements for the field of education. In order to cope with the growing trend of globalization, multidisciplinary and mobility, as well as the complexity of current and future work, we attach great importance to the quality and efficiency of education and training at all levels (European Union, 2009–2018). In order to prepare learners for the growing job market, education programs must provide them with a broad knowledge and skills base, so that they can flexibly use this knowledge and skills when dealing with new tasks in daily practice. More and more people begin to call for the choice of educational content based on ability and result. Since the 1990s, the balance of educational methods has shifted from "goal-based instructional design method" to "Task-based Method", in order to better solve the problem of learning complex cognitive skills and professional ability [1].

In order to solve the problem of fragmentation and segmentation caused by goal-based teaching, the task-based approach focuses on real problems or professional tasks, so as to better connect the learning environment with the work scene and cultivate the

M. A. Jan and F. Khan (Eds.): BigIoT-EDU 2022, LNICST 465, pp. 216–224, 2023.
https://doi.org/10.1007/978-3-031-23950-2_24

necessary skills. The educational program advocated by this method includes the learning task sequence based on real professional tasks. The task-based teaching mode includes "cognitive apprenticeship", "fine processing theory", "primary teaching principle" and "Task-based four element teaching design mode". In medical education, communication training, technical training, information solution processing and teacher training, the number of documents related to the application of the 4C/ID model is increasing, which proves that the model has a strong research foundation and popularity. The ten steps of the 4C/ID model provide guidance for analyzing real-life tasks to discover different types of knowledge and skills needed in daily practice (cognitive task analysis). At the same time, the model also has a blueprint for education program design, which consists of learning tasks, related knowledge, support procedures, and special exercises.

Since the release of the national vocational education reform implementation plan (20 articles on Vocational Education) in 2019, the country has raised the vocational education teaching reform to an unprecedented height from the central to local levels. At the beginning of this year, Shandong Province and the Ministry of Education jointly issued the opinions on the construction of a highland for the innovative development of Vocational Education jointly built by ministries and provinces, vigorously developing the reform of vocational education, innovating the development plan of vocational education, deepening the integration of production and education, improving the closeness between students' professional learning and industry development, and vigorously cultivating skilled, professional and compound talents required by the new era and new economic transformation.

In the new era, new demands have been raised. In particular, the impact of the epidemic on education at all levels in the country in the first half of 2020 has increased the panoramic online teaching function and strengthened the development needs of the new model hybrid teaching. At present, various online cloud teaching data collection mechanisms and platforms are used, and various online classes and conference software are prepared for online live teaching, The academic ideas and viewpoints of the online online and offline two-way teaching theory have played a certain enlightening role. Innovating online teaching methods and building a "four element" mixed teaching model are conducive to the practical ability of higher vocational college students, bringing the new online and offline teaching model closer to learning practice, and improving the weight of online teaching in mixed teaching, Strengthen the review of offline courses and look forward to the learning results of online teaching, which can better improve the teaching research for the purpose of mixed teaching goals. The contents of "four elements" are as follows:

(1) Highlight unitary timeliness

As artificial intelligence and global networking become more and more mature, more and more network interactions become indispensable. Their immediacy, simplification and convenience can solve many problems existing in offline real-life teaching. Especially in the epidemic period, timely and effective teaching contact has made irreplaceable contributions to not delaying teaching because the network has become real and reliable. It is hard to imagine that without the network, What will happen to students at home without online teaching during the epidemic.

(2) Strengthening unitary practicality

Classroom teaching is limited by space and time. Teachers should have the concept of paying equal attention to time and efficiency. To a large extent, teachers' teaching preparation (writing teaching plans, teaching plans and other teaching arrangements), implementation of classroom teaching, after-school evaluation strategies and so on. Changing the effectiveness of teaching implementation methods and using limited time and space to carry out efficient online teaching undoubtedly play an important role in improving the efficiency of offline classroom teaching, Of course, online teaching students' study seriousness and self-discipline ability have certain management defects due to network reasons. Paying attention to practical operation and making good use of online detection are conducive to the practical operation level of students in higher vocational colleges.

(3) Strengthen the unitary pertinence

Strengthen online teaching to make up for the new advantages of traditional classroom teaching, comprehensively analyze the shortcomings of online teaching, especially the research on the integration of the two, improve the collaborative development of online and offline teaching, and enhance the learning awareness, reflection awareness and research awareness of teachers and students, so as to improve the quality of school education and teaching, and make a breakthrough in teaching methods.

(4) Focus on unitary effectiveness

In order to develop the advantages of mixed teaching in long-term education and teaching, the extreme whole line teaching during the epidemic period is taken as a research model, and a set of long-term effective and effective mixed teaching achievements are formed through personal experience and extensive research, which can be more purposefully applied to the improvement of teaching quality.

Based on the experience gained from online teaching during the epidemic period, combined with personal teaching summary and the opinions of other teachers, and according to the characteristics of Higher Vocational Majors, the "four element" new hybrid teaching mode can effectively integrate online teaching into hybrid teaching, focusing on cultivating students to use online teaching platforms, flexibly manipulate learning software, and be flexible, convenient, entertaining, powerful Many advantages of online teaching with a strong sense of picture further strengthen students' autonomous learning and understanding ability, strengthen the response and digestion steps of online learning and problem-solving in offline teaching, take online learning as the guidance of offline teaching content, and offline classroom has become an auxiliary scene for face-to-face communication between teachers and students in Online learning.

2 Quaternion Teaching Based on a Personalized Recommendation Algorithm

Highlight the advantages of hybrid teaching combining online and offline teaching, especially the use of various excellent online learning and communication platforms, carriers and software used during the epidemic, which has been recognized by many teachers.

According to the author's collection and summary, there are mainly the following online video software that can meet the application of the "quaternion" mixed teaching mode at present. They are:

(1) Tencent classroom

The professional online education platform launched by Tencent has gathered a large number of high-quality educational institutions and famous teachers, and set up many excellent online learning courses, such as vocational training, TOEFL IELTS, oral English, primary and secondary education, to create a classroom for teachers' online teaching and students' timely interactive learning.

Operating steps: first, the teacher must install Tencent classroom express version on the computer, and students install Tencent classroom on the computer or mobile phone (students can click the link sent by the teacher to listen to the class, but the function is less than the installed client). Secondly, the teacher runs Tencent class on the computer, shares the QR code or a link to the students, and the students scan the code or click the link to enter the class and listen to the class.

Software features: 1. The teacher can switch the shared desktop window, the open PPT, the video to be played and the camera in the computer. The camera can be embedded in the PPT image or the corner of the shared desktop to form a picture in picture. 2. The teacher can control the students' hand raising and voice connection. 3. There is an answer board on the teacher's side. When there are questions such as selection and judgment in the courseware, students can interact with each other through the answer board sent by the teacher. The current version can generate playback video (downloadable).

(2) Tencent Conference

It is an audio and video conference product under Tencent cloud. It has the functions of 300 people online conference, one key access of the whole platform, intelligent audio and video noise reduction, beauty, background virtualization, locking conference, screen watermark, etc. The software provides real-time shared screens and supports online document collaboration. From January 24, the conference coordination capability of 300 people will be open to users free of charge until the end of the epidemic. At present, the international version application has been developed and launched.

Operating steps: teachers and students must install Tencent Conference on computer or mobile phone, book the conference, set the conference code, and students can enter the conference through the conference code to participate in learning.

Software features: 1. Teachers' computers and mobile phones can initiate meetings. 2. Teachers and students can open video and voice communication, and anyone can share their own desktop. 3. Teachers can switch between running various teaching software on the computer, and can also switch to the open video and music window at any time, so that video and music will not be subject to any restrictions on inserting courseware to play, and the sound transmission is clear and smooth without delay. 4. Teachers and students can open the text exchange area for text exchange. 5. In case of any interference during the live broadcast, the meeting initiator can set all staff to mute.

2.1 Data Mining

Data mining refers to the process of extracting valuable information and knowledge from numerous, incomplete, unclear and real-time generated four element teaching data, which is contained in the middle, unknown in advance, but related to each other. It is the core of knowledge discovery in database. Specifically to this paper, we mainly use the log mining in Web usage mining technology to provide personalized services, so as to complete the design of four element teaching method.

2.2 Personalized Teaching System

Personalized recommendation service refers to recommending information that users are interested in according to the characteristics of users' interests. After entering the personalized network teaching system constructed in this study, students input their basic information and learning information into the learning platform. Each student browses different pages in the process of learning. The generated browsing sequences can reflect the progress, levels and interests of students, and these browsing sequences are transferred to the personalized recommendation module. The learning platform stores all the access history of students in the user log of the server, because the web log mining module is embedded in the system, all the user log data is preprocessed in the module, and then the web access transaction database is obtained. Then, the personalized recommendation algorithm is used to mine the web access transaction database, and the frequent itemsets are generated and stored in the learning resource knowledge base built by the system. Next, the browsing sequence of students is extracted by the personalized recommendation module. Through the analysis of the confidence and support of association rules, the matching frequent patterns are found in the learning resource knowledge base. Finally, we recommend the last item of the association rules to the students. Figure 1 shows the implementation process of the improved Apriori like algorithm.

After preprocessing the data in the system, we can analyze the personalized recommendation algorithm of the obtained data. Here, we mainly use the improved Apriori algorithm to get the frequent item set and association rule pattern. If there is some regularity between the values of two or more data items, it is called Association. Association rules of these data items can be established. Generally, the two thresholds of "support" and "confidence" are used to eliminate the useless association rules. Among them, for the four element teaching method has recommended the appropriate education program [2].

The four element instructional design model aims to help instructional designers develop educational programs for teaching comprehensive or professional abilities. It describes the four elements of various educational programs: learning tasks, relevant knowledge and abilities, support procedures and special exercises (see Fig. 2).

In the teaching system based on personalized algorithm, firstly, the registration information, access content, path and other data of students are collected from the web log document on the server side to get the transaction database. Using the improved Apriori algorithm, using the intermediate results of frequent itemsets counting process, the invalid transactions are deleted continuously in each scan to complete the filtering of

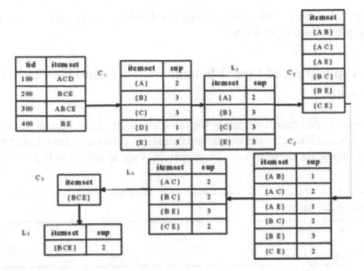

Fig. 1. Implementation process of improved Apriori like algorithm

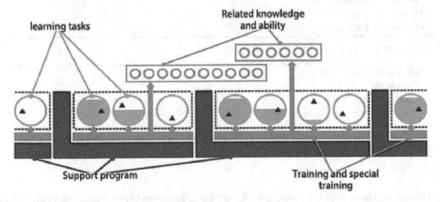

Fig. 2. Four elements

transaction database, and the frequent itemsets and association rules accessed by users are obtained, which corresponds to the quaternion teaching method.

The blended learning module introduces the learning tasks proposed in the course and the learning tasks to be completed in the workplace during the internship. Students usually go to the discussion area to communicate with other students or teachers before they submit their homework. This is a group of frequently visited pages. The designer of the website should mark the links of the above two pages with distinguishable colors in the eye-catching part of the submitted page, so as to speed up the query.

Most of the students will browse the related content of slide making while learning the operation of document typesetting. In the original website, there is no link between the two pages. After browsing the first page of association rules, students must go back to the course selection page to browse the second page of association rules, which causes unnecessary delay in time. So website designers should add hyperlinks between the two pages to improve learning efficiency.

3   The Application of Four Element Instructional Design in Higher Education

When designing educational programs with four elements, activities can be divided into five categories [3]. Four element instructional design has formed many design principles based on evidence for each activity. These activities are as shown in Fig. 3:

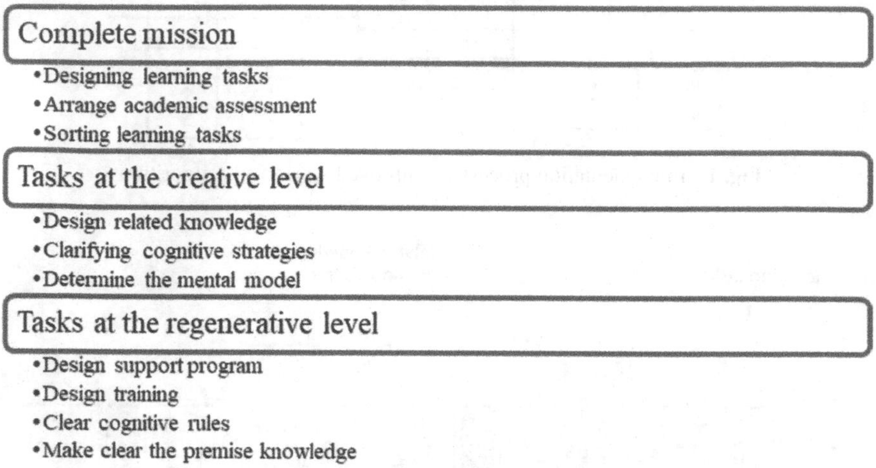

Complete mission
- Designing learning tasks
- Arrange academic assessment
- Sorting learning tasks

Tasks at the creative level
- Design related knowledge
- Clarifying cognitive strategies
- Determine the mental model

Tasks at the regenerative level
- Design support program
- Design training
- Clear cognitive rules
- Make clear the premise knowledge

Fig. 3. Five groups of activities in four element instructional design

1. Design learning tasks. Learning tasks are usually based on real tasks in professional or daily life. Design principles involve realistic level fidelity, variability, support and guidance. The types of learning tasks include common learning tasks (i.e. independent learning tasks, learners must find solutions), complete learning tasks (learners must supplement some of the given solutions) and sample learning tasks (learners must learn the given solutions).
2. Arrange academic assessment. Learners need to get feedback when they complete the learning task, that is, the evaluation of their academic performance. Academic goals are based on skill levels, and describe the standards (requirements, values and attitudes) learners must meet for different aspects of their studies. The assessment tool contains a scoring rubric for all of these criteria.
3. Sorting learning tasks. Learning tasks are gradually changing from simple to complex, which can be sorted by either complete task or partial task. If teachers can evaluate the progress of learners, they can establish personalized learning trajectory or provide learners with the best choice of learning tasks.

4. Design related knowledge. Relevant knowledge and ability can help learners to complete the creative level of learning tasks, and provide them with domain model (for the development of psychological schema), systematic problem-solving methods (for the development of cognitive strategies) and cognitive feedback. Sometimes, teachers need to deeply analyze the psychological schema and cognitive strategies they want to obtain.

5. Design support procedures and special exercises. The support program tells learners how to complete the learning task at the regenerative level, and provides them with "instructions for use" (for the development of cognitive rules) and corrective feedback. Sometimes, teachers need to deeply analyze the cognitive rules and prerequisite knowledge they want to acquire. When the selected regenerative level tasks need to reach a full proficiency level, special drills can be designed.

4 Teaching Tasks

Colleges and universities should list the main principles of designing learning tasks. First of all, professional or daily tasks should be the starting point of learning task design. This kind of real-life task is usually composed of knowledge, skills and attitudes to help learners develop comprehensive or professional abilities.

Secondly, learning tasks are usually completed by learners in simulated task environment or real task environment. In order to provide a safe learning environment and prevent novice learners from dealing with too many irrelevant details, learners can first try in a low fidelity (such as written cases, role play) environment, then transition to a high fidelity (computer simulation, high fidelity simulation) environment, and finally provide practical tasks in the workplace.

Thirdly, it is essential that learning tasks in education programs should be different in all dimensions, because real-life tasks are also different, and learning tasks must represent the tasks that professionals encounter in the real world. The surface features that do not affect the way to complete the task and the structural features that affect the way to complete the task should reflect a certain degree of variation [4].

Fourthly, learners should be fully supported and guided at the beginning of learning tasks. Support should be embedded in the task and related to the use of "example learning task" or "case learning task", "completion learning task", "free goal problem", "reverse learning task" and "imitation learning task". Guidance should be "added" to the task and related to the guidance provided by the teacher or the guidance questions in the worksheet. Following the systematic problem-solving approach, guidance can help learners use effective cognitive strategies.

Finally, each complexity of the learning task should have a "scaffolding" process, which means that as learners acquire more professional knowledge, support and guidance will gradually reduce until they can complete the learning task independently without any support and guidance. Then, learners may complete the task with a higher level of complexity, and the scaffolding process starts from scratch, thus forming serrated support and guidance in the whole education program.

5 Conclusion

In a word, the current and future development of the job market requires that education programs can cultivate lifelong learners, who must have the knowledge, skills and attitudes to cope with the complex tasks familiar and unfamiliar in their fields.

The formation of a new quaternion hybrid teaching mode can more effectively integrate online teaching into hybrid teaching, maximize the effectiveness of online teaching, form an online teaching as the main force, cultivate students' online use of teaching platforms and flexible control of learning software, and further strengthen students' autonomous learning and understanding ability through flexible, convenient, entertaining, powerful and powerful online teaching advantages, Strengthen the response and digestion steps of online learning and problem-solving in offline teaching, take online learning as the guidance of offline teaching content, and make offline classroom an auxiliary scene for face-to-face communication between teachers and students in online learning. In words, it must be called network content and practical operation process, and take offline classroom teaching as an auxiliary field for improving learning and exchanging experiences in higher vocational colleges, Form truly practical and effective mixed teaching achievements.

The "four element" hybrid teaching is very suitable for the training needs of innovative, practical and applied talents in higher vocational colleges. Under the classroom teaching mode of the mixed teaching concept, teaching activities extend from 45 min in the classroom to form an integrated learning process of "pre class, in class and after class". By using the methods of course playback and online live communication, students' learning, thinking, communication and practical operation can be greatly improved.

References

1. Jing, F.: Current situation and countermeasures of personalized employment guidance in Colleges and universities. J. Qiqihar Teachers Coll. **1**, 26–27 (2015)
2. Yanhong, D.: Countermeasures for personalized employment guidance in colleges and universities: based on the investigation of the current situation of employment guidance in colleges and universities in guangdong province. Employment of College Students in China **4**, 44–47 (2012)
3. Qin, Q., Qian, L.: Current situation and reform plan of personalized employment guidance in Colleges and universities. Employment of College Students in China (2), 33–35.32 (2012)
4. Gandhi, O.P., Chen, J.-Y.: Numerical dosimetry at power-line frequencies using anatomically based models. Bioelectromagnetics **13**(S1), 43–60 (1992). https://doi.org/10.1002/bem.225 0130706

Application of Data Mining Technology Based on Weka in Student Management

Yang Li[✉]

Wenhua College, Wuhan 430074, Hubei, China
liyang3713@dingtalk.com

Abstract. This paper studies the application of data mining technology based on Weka in student management. As an open data mining platform, Weka collects a large number of machine learning algorithms that can undertake the task of data mining, including data preprocessing, classification, regression, clustering, association rules and visualization on the new interactive interface. Student work is the central work of the school, and student management is the top priority of school management. Reflecting on the management of school students, I personally believe that the following aspects still need to be further strengthened: conduct in-depth research on the decision tree analysis method in data mining technology, deeply analyze the environment and resources of the school, correctly evaluate their own level, make their own value orientation, and put C4 The algorithm is applied in student management, constructs the student psychological state model based on student personal information, and obtains some relevant laws. Make the educational behavior complete the rational leap, form the correct teaching management thought, and lay the foundation for quality education to a higher level. Practice has proved that this method improves the efficiency and quality of students' work, and provides a scientific reference for students' management and guidance system.

Keywords: Weka software · Data mining technology · Student management

1 Introduction

Data mining technology through in-depth analysis of information to find out the potential relationship and law between data. Data mining technology is applied to student management. Through the analysis of student data, the hidden internal relationship between students' school performance and various factors is discovered, so as to predict students' behavior and guide students' management.

Quality education is the main melody of current education. School is a place to educate people and a place to cultivate people. To make quality education effective, we must also carry out effective student management. Only effective student management can ensure the smooth progress of quality education. Advanced teaching and student management is to meet the requirements of society and the need of education and training multi-standard talents.

© ICST Institute for Computer Sciences, Social Informatics and Telecommunications Engineering 2023
Published by Springer Nature Switzerland AG 2023. All Rights Reserved
M. A. Jan and F. Khan (Eds.): BigIoT-EDU 2022, LNICST 465, pp. 225–235, 2023.
https://doi.org/10.1007/978-3-031-23950-2_25

Society is a colorful group. It needs talents of various types, specifications, levels and characteristics. The arrival of knowledge economy has put forward new requirements for education. It requires that education is not only a comprehensive education, but also to realize the unity of scientific education and humanistic education, general education and training, and realize the coordination of knowledge, ability, morality and emotion. While paying attention to cultivating the creativity of the educatee, it also needs to cultivate his coordination ability and cooperation consciousness with the surrounding world; Moreover, education is required to be creative, diverse, open and personalized. As a student manager of a school, we must stand at the commanding height of the times, focus on the 21st century, deeply analyze the environment and resources of the school, correctly evaluate our own level, and make our own value orientation, so as to outline a viable development strategy and basic goal in line with our own reality, so as to make a rational leap in educational behavior, Form a correct teaching and student management thought and lay a foundation for quality education to a higher level. Rationality is the crystallization of wisdom and the embodiment of rationality. The management of teaching students must pay attention to rational innovation. Student management should be good at active learning and lead a group of teachers who are good at learning. Student management should master advanced ideas in continuous learning experience, change educational ideas in learning, establish a correct outlook on education by learning from the experience of various schools at all levels, and obtain a fresh outlook on Teaching in the training, teaching and research and teaching activities with teachers.

Only by adhering to long-term learning can student management skillfully combine practical experience with theoretical wisdom, and create new methods, new languages, new ideas and new experience with school characteristics. Teaching and student management should be emotional. Convince people with reason and move people with emotion [1]. The ingenious combination of reason and emotion can achieve good results. Pay attention to the close relationship between schools and society. Under the background of today's market economy, student management needs innovation and communication with people from all walks of life. In the process of communication, we should adhere to the two principles of being conducive to the development of the school and abiding by laws and regulations. Correctly handle the relationship with the superior leaders, correct the relationship between the superior and the subordinate, learn the way of transposition thinking, learn to be good at expressing opinions, and obtain the help of the superior leaders and the support of the subordinate colleagues. Make student management get twice the result with half the effort.

School based student management is the trend of contemporary school student management reform. Due to the long-term constraints of the "external control" school student management system, student schools generally lack the tradition and practical experience of school-based student management, and the institutionalized operation of school-based student management still needs a gradual realization process.

With the advent of knowledge economy and information age, social competition is becoming increasingly fierce, and parents pay more and more attention to their children's education. They not only require schools to improve the quality of education, but also have a growing desire and voice to participate in school student management. With the development of community education, school student managers gradually realize that school and community are closely related. The survival and development of schools must rely on, base on and serve the community. All these not only exercise the school-based student management ability of school student managers, but also enhance the subject consciousness of all sectors of society to participate in school-based student management [2]. The innovative concept of teaching and student management will bring new vitality to the cause of education. With the continuous reform of the teaching system in Colleges and universities in recent years, especially the development and deepening of the credit system and course selection system, the daily management of students is becoming more and more heavy and complex. In the daily management of students, there is a lot of work to count the information of students in all aspects, such as student status, achievement, award evaluation, dormitory, teaching and employment, etc. Although the functions of querying and processing the information of students' growth can not be realized efficiently according to the existing information of people and rules, it is impossible to find and process the information of students' growth.

Student education is the key basic education stage of life. Education and teaching management is an important part of student management, which marks the comprehensive strength and school running level of the school. Efficient education and teaching management is a powerful guarantee for students' good teaching quality. Teaching management refers to the management of both teachers and students according to the requirements of social development and the development characteristics of students [3]. The purpose of teaching management is to coordinate the relationship between teachers and students in teaching practice and achieve good teaching effect. At present, the rapid development of economy and culture has promoted the development of all walks of life. With the proposal of comprehensive quality education and the implementation of the new curriculum reform, teaching ideas and teaching methods have changed. It is of great practical significance to explore the effective strategy of student education and teaching management.

2 Related Work

2.1 Weka Software

Weka is one of the platforms of data mining. Weka integrates many algorithms, which are mainly used in data mining, such as face recognition, text recognition, genetic engineering and so on. Different algorithms have different effects [4]. The main developer of Weka is from Waikato University in New Zealand. It is a free, non-commercial, open source machine learning and data mining software based on Java environment. Figure 1 below shows the Weka software interface.

Weka can preprocess, classify, cluster, association rules, attribute selection and visualization of data. Weka's source code is written in Java. All its jar packages can also be imported into Java projects and directly call APIs. Weka can be opened Xls file (Excel file) can be connected to the database (MySQL database is connected here). Weka data format: ARFF (attribute relation file format) file is shown in Fig. 2 below.

There are four commonly used test options: used as training set, used as test set, cross test (10 times cross test by default), and proportional segmentation (dividing the data

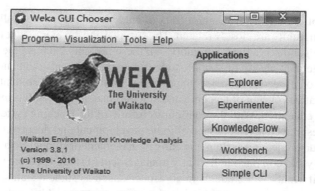

Fig. 1. Weka software interface

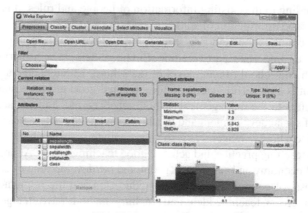

Fig. 2. Weka data format

set into training set and test set according to a certain proportion). In addition, there are some options for classifier output, such as evaluation index, choosing to output classifier code in Java language, etc. [5].

All the current classification results are displayed in the result list. Right click a result in the list and some options will appear, such as visualizetree (graphical decision tree), visualize classifier errors (the classification results are represented in a scatter diagram, the correct classification instances are represented as small crosses, and the wrong classification instances are represented as small hollow squares), as well as some other options. Open the explorer interface, click the preprocessing tab, import the nominal weather data set (weather. ARFF), enter the classification tab, select j48 classifier, test options, select as the training set, the decision tree will be generated, and the relevant output will be output in the classifieroutput. Select test options again, select as the test set strategy, then find output predictions in more options, and select plain text to output the test situation.

2.2   Data Mining Principle

Data is the most valuable commercial capital and the prerequisite of data mining. Valuable information sources can be found in enterprises and have a wide range of boundaries. For example: internal and external data sources, both structured and unstructured.

Internal data sources (such as databases, reports and spreadsheets) store a large amount of data. External databases and various Internet resources are also excellent ways to obtain business value. They can be combined with internal resources to better insight into the problems being studied.

The quality of data is the key to effective data mining. Without proper data, even if the best data mining experts are employed, it is impossible to obtain any valuable knowledge. The most important data quality requirements are:

Relevance - whether the data is applicable to the current problem;
Validity - whether the data follows the current environmental laws;
Integrity - noisy data or missing data are two major factors affecting data integrity;
Consistency - Information Island is the main reason for data inconsistency. This problem can be solved by using integrated information system · display visualization; Portals, aggregation applications, dashboards, charts, spreadsheets, etc.;
Trust - use reliable data sources to effectively process subjective data;
Timeliness - minimizes the time delay between data collection and data processing.

In short, data mining is to extract or "mine" knowledge from a large amount of data. Data mining should be more correctly named "mining knowledge from data". Excavation is a very vivid term, which captures the characteristics of the process of finding a small amount of gold bullion from a large number of unprocessed materials [6].

Data mining is the application of a series of technologies to extract information and knowledge of interest from large databases or data warehouses. These knowledge or information are implicit, unknown in advance and potentially useful. The extracted knowledge is expressed in the form of concepts, rules, laws, patterns and so on. It can also be said that data mining is a kind of deep-seated data analysis.

Data mining, also known as data mining and data mining, is to extract rules (or patterns) that can be interpreted as knowledge from massive data according to the established business objectives, including association rules, feature rules, distinction rules, classification rules, summary rules, deviation rules, clustering rules, etc. Most of them are based on data mining, test and learning. The methods corresponding to these technologies are often confusing to both novices and experienced data analysts [7].

It can be considered that the data mining method mainly consists of three parts: model representation, model evaluation and search. Model representation is a language used to describe patterns that can be found. If this representation is too limited, no amount of time and examples can produce an accurate model for the data. It is important for a data analyst to fully grasp the representative assumptions that may be implied in a particular method. Similarly, it is also very important for an algorithm designer to clearly express what representative assumptions a specific algorithm can make. Note that with the enhancement of the model representation ability, the risk of over fitting of the model to the training data also increases, resulting in the reduction of its prediction accuracy of unknown data.

2.3 Student Management

With the continuous promotion of the new curriculum reform, we now attach great importance to the subject status of students, and the content of student management is the main student management resource, which has a decisive impact on students' education and student management. Therefore, teachers must reasonably arrange the content of student management. In the process of student management, according to students' learning foundation and students' cognitive ability, Arrange the corresponding learning plan, and also consider the acceptance of students, so that teachers can present some student management contents in a more specific way in the process of student management, such as using multimedia to present some knowledge in the form of pictures, pictures and videos, which can deepen students' learning impression and enhance students' school efficiency [8], In addition, the self-management ability of students in this stage is relatively poor. In the process of explaining the student management content, teachers must make some student management content live, so as to stimulate students' learning initiative and enthusiasm, so as to improve students' learning efficiency and continuously enhance students' abilities in all aspects.

The improvement of students' management quality is not achieved overnight, which requires the cooperation and common development of all forces. According to the experience of the effectiveness of student management in education summarized previously, to improve the quality of student management, we must require the whole society, the whole school, teachers, parents and students to actively cooperate in the process of daily student management, give full play to their strengths in improving the quality of student management and complement each other's weaknesses [9], And then give full play to the advantages of each party. The responsibility of head teachers is more arduous. As a bridge connecting schools and family students, we should give full play to our responsibilities and urge all parties to jointly improve the quality of student management. In daily learning, it is needless to say that it is important to urge students to be individual. In the educational work, we should also timely feed back the problems encountered in the process of educational student management to the school superiors, so as to make a specific analysis of specific problems, and it is best to put forward suggestions or solutions. After all, the head teacher is the direct receiver of the problems, and can better understand the seriousness of the problems, so as to lay the foundation for the school to feed back the problems in time. For students' family learning environment, we should also be diligent in communication and work with parents to help their children grow and develop.

3   Application of Data Mining Technology Based on Weka in Student Management

Most college student management workers show a certain weak awareness of informatization in the specific work process, that is, they do not understand the development trend of informatization and the relationship between informatization and student management. Affected by many factors, some colleges and universities began to practice student management informatization, but the practice only stayed in the primary stage, did not make in-depth attempts and exploration, and the informatization effect was weak.

Student management is a relatively complex work, which is long-term and systematic. The practice process is accompanied by a large amount of data. Through observation and analysis, these data have the characteristics of low degree of structure. They are mainly composed of unstructured data and semi-structured data. Unstructured data mainly includes text, video, documents and pictures, Semi structured data mainly involves e-mail, resource database and reports. However, there are still some deficiencies in mining and processing, and no in-depth analysis and exploration has been made, which has affected the degree of data structure to a great extent. A member variable uses an array of member variables to save the corresponding data [10]. All contents depend on the operation of the class object, and the data saved in each management class object is different.

The difference at present is for better reusability. Like the later data, it is for the unity of data. The powerful function of Weka software provides a platform for us to deeply study student information. Based on the existing student information data, we preprocess the data, then analyze and make decisions on the processed data through Weka software, and finally display the data and laws in the form of tables and graphics, and finally build a perfect student management and guidance system (see Fig. 3).

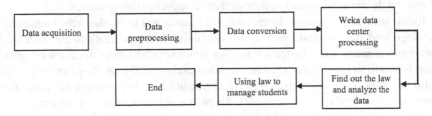

Fig. 3. Student guidance management system

First, use big data thinking in the student course selection system. Due to the relatively large distribution of majors in Colleges and universities, there are more professional courses and elective courses involved, so as to truly provide high-quality curriculum for students. We should make full use of big data thinking in course selection to meet the needs of different students for different courses, so as to promote the all-round development of students. In order to make the effective connection between colleges and students, students can understand the majors, curriculum and advantageous courses of colleges and universities. At the same time, colleges and universities can understand the specific needs of students and really provide targeted courses for students, which requires the use of big data for analysis, induction and summary, so as to provide students with courses with professional characteristics and meet their own development needs in combination with teaching tasks. Therefore, in order to ensure that students can really choose appropriate and professional courses in the course selection process, a big data analysis system should be established to collect, summarize and summarize the data of each course, so as to understand the development of the course and students' satisfaction with the course. By using big data thinking to make the school curriculum meet the development needs of students and adapt to the all-round development of students. For example, students choosing courses is like watching movies on video websites. Once the video websites provide several movies for each person and others are watching them, this behavior belongs to the cooperative screening of big data. In the curriculum and course selection settings of colleges and universities, we can make full use of this big data thinking.

Second, use big data thinking to carry out academic early warning for students. In order to truly cultivate excellent talents, colleges and universities must accurately grasp the learning situation of students. Only when students complete the curriculum and pass the examination of relevant courses can they obtain the graduation certificate and degree certificate [11]. At the same time, students should also know whether they have met the graduation standards in the process of learning, which requires the use of big data thinking for academic early warning. Academic early warning system can not only let students grasp their academic completion, but also let students understand the gap between themselves and graduation requirements. At present, many colleges and universities have adopted the management mode of academic early warning. Therefore, in order to improve the actual effect of academic early warning management, we must use the thinking of big data to innovate and optimize the efficiency of the current early warning management. By using the relevant data of big data, students can grasp their academic status in time. And it is conducive to help students find their own shortcomings and constantly improve, so as to improve their comprehensive quality.

Today, with the continuous development of science and technology, the management of college students has developed in the direction of informatization, but affected by many factors, many work systems have low timeliness and have not been integrated, which is bound to lead to the lag of information exchange, that is, they can only rely on a third party for information exchange; Data transmission is no exception. It needs the support of e-mail and other attachments. Therefore, it can be seen that the transmission efficiency is low. At this stage, the role of student management is becoming more and more obvious, involving many departments. These system barriers greatly increase the difficulty of data audit. During data transmission, counselors need to play the role of system relay identity. It should be noted that the effectiveness of data transmission is closely related to the amount of data requests and information types. Generally speaking, The information category is cumbersome or has large-scale data requests, the timeliness of data transmission is low, and the workload of counselors is increased.

College student management is a relatively complex work, involving many aspects, and different contents correspond to different departments. In other words, each department needs to undertake different work, and student information also needs to be classified in combination with reality, that is, each department stores and manages student information based on classification. For example, educational administration information should be stored in the school education department Logistics information should be stored in the logistics department, etc. Due to the lack of good communication and interaction between departments, the mobility of student information is not strong. If you want to use the student information in charge of other departments, you need to submit an application. You can use the required information only after obtaining the review and permission of the head of the Department [12]. The coordination efficiency is generally low. With the continuous progress and development of science and technology, some colleges and universities have gradually realized the importance of student management informatization and began to try student information management. However, affected by the language factors developed by developers, various subsystems are difficult to integrate and operate, reflecting a certain degree of independence. Whether it is data export, data format processing or data import, they are relatively closed, It is prone to errors, which affects the collaborative efficiency.

There is a certain neglect of data integration. The information involved in student management is mostly dynamic information, such as students' classroom performance, students' original information, etc. whether from the perspective of type or structure, these data have a certain complexity and are related to many departments. Compared with other data, grass-roots data has certain particularity, which is inconsistent with the required form. Errors are easy to occur in the process of data collection, which increases the difficulty of data collection; Affected by useless data or data format characteristics, the data summary results will also change to some extent, and the accuracy needs to be improved.

4 Simulation Analysis

Decision tree is a tree structure that can automatically classify data. It is the knowledge representation of tree structure and can be directly transformed into decision rules. It can be regarded as the prediction model of a tree. The root node of the tree is the whole data set space. Each sub node is a splitting problem. It is a test of a single variable, The test divides the data set space into two or more blocks, and each leaf node is a data partition with classification. Decision tree can also be interpreted as a special form of rule set, which is characterized by the hierarchical organization of rules. Decision tree algorithm is mainly used to learn the learning method with discrete variables as attribute types. Continuous variables must be discretized to be learned.

Student management system, as its name implies, is an information system that manages and analyzes all kinds of information of students [13]. It can effectively support the decision-making and control of educational administrators, as well as the use and control of information by students themselves. Student management is different from the general management information system. It is the specific application of management information system in the field of student management. However, student management can learn from the theory, method and development process of management information system and apply it to specific practice. Different from the management information system, student management has its own important characteristics:

College student management is a very specific and detailed work. All links are inter-related. It not only has a large workload, but also is very complex and involves a wide range. For example, in the process of student status management, performance management and curriculum setting, it is necessary to repeat the operation of a large number of forms and make accurate statistics on these forms. Moreover, with the expansion of the scale of colleges and universities, there are more and more students in Colleges and universities, followed by a large amount of student information and a large number of data statistics. The cumulative information of each student is also amazing, which brings great pressure to the student information management of colleges and universities.

Load the CPU data set in the preprocessing tab, select the linearregression classifier in the classification tab, and select the 10 fold cross test. By default, click start to generate the regression equation and test results, as shown in Fig. 4 below.

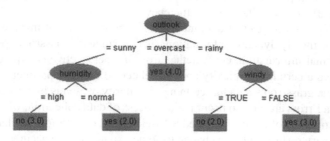

Fig. 4. Data set decision tree

Student management system (hereinafter referred to as the system) is a powerful tool for educational information management. It can comprehensively manage students' academic performance, behavior performance, semester comprehensive evaluation, excellence and awards in the whole process from enrollment to graduation. After data accumulation, a large amount of data is collected [14]. In order to find the valuable information hidden behind such a large amount of data, data mining technology is applied to the system to form a data mining subsystem. It mainly analyzes the student information and draws a scientific and reasonable conclusion. As shown in Fig. 5 below, the operation results of student management using Weka are shown.

```
=== Cross-validation ===
=== Summary ===

Correlation coefficient                0.9012
Mean absolute error                   41.0886
Root mean squared error               69.556
Relative absolute error               42.6943 %
Root relative squared error           43.2421 %
Total Number of Instances             209
```

Fig. 5. Weka operation results

5 Conclusion

This paper studies the application of data mining technology based on Weka in student management. Using Weka software, this paper applies the decision tree algorithm to the analysis of student information management system, selects representative data indicators, and tests the sample data. University managers can use the test results to analyze the management of colleges and universities and student information, and use data analysis to mine valuable information from behind the data, so as to better manage students. The research significance of this paper is to transform student management information into effective, orderly, regular and decision-making knowledge and promote the construction of campus digitization.

References

1. Abdullahi, K., Kadir, A.: Social justice issues in education and management of student development in Nigeria. Contemp. Educ. Res. J. **11**(3), 78–91 (2021)
2. Han, X: Design of counselor student management system based on competency model. In: 2021 13th International Conference on Measuring Technology and Mechatronics Automation (ICMTMA) (2021)
3. Razak, F., et al.: Investigating the linkage between service quality and satisfaction in context of student management system: an evidence from Malaysia. J. Phys: Conf. Ser. **1793**(1), 012033 (2021)
4. Fata, M., et al.: Curriculum development management in increasing student excellence research context (Multisite Study at MTsN 1 Trenggalek and MTsN 2 Trenggalek) (2021)
5. Damayanti, D.: Perbandingan akurasi software rapidminer dan weka menggunakan algoritma K-Nearest Neighbor (K-NN) (2021)
6. Geyik, B., Erensoy, K., Kocyigit, E.: Detection of phishing websites from URLs by using classification techniques on WEKA. In: 2021 6th International Conference on Inventive Computation Technologies (ICICT) (2021)
7. Ahmed, A., et al.: An approach to detect cyber attack on server-side application by using data mining techniques and evolutionary algorithms (2021)
8. Wiweka, N.A., Mahadewi, L., Suwatra, I.: Pengembangan multimedia flashcard bilingual terhadap mata pelajaran bahasa bali kelas I SD (2021)
9. Suman, Mittal, M.P.: A comparative performance analysis of classification algorithms using weka tool of data mining techniques (2021)
10. Dnler, Z.B., Ahn, C.B.: WEKA ortamn kullanarak derin renme ile kimlik hrsz web sitelerinin tahmini. Eur. J. Sci. Technol. (2021)
11. Jalal, A.A., Ali, B.H.: Text documents clustering using data mining techniques. Int. J. Electr. Comput. Eng. **11**(1), 664–670 (2021)
12. Akyürek, M.B.: Time management skills of university students. Yuksekogretim Dergisi **11**(1), 139–147 (2021)
13. Moon, M., Oh, E.G., Baek, W., Kim, Y.M.: Effects of nurse-led pain management interventions for patients with total knee/hip replacement. Pain Manag. Nurs. **22**(2), 111–120 (2021). https://doi.org/10.1016/j.pmn.2020.11.005
14. Efthymiou, L., Zarifis, A.: Modeling students' voice for enhanced quality in online management education. Int. J. Manag. Educ. **19**(2), 100464 (2021)

Application of Decision Tree Algorithm in Teaching Quality Analysis of Physical Education

Chengliang Zhang[✉] and Hui Yang

Qujing Medical College, Qujing 655000, Yunnan, China
1605857401@qq.com

Abstract. Learning situation analysis is not only the basic link of teaching activities, but also one of the basic ways to improve effective teaching. However, only on the premise of ensuring the effectiveness of learning situation analysis can we improve the effectiveness of teaching. Compared with other teaching, physical education teaching has more urgent needs and stricter requirements for learning situation analysis. Therefore, this paper uses data analysis technology to elaborate what teachers should pay attention to and how to do when doing learning situation analysis of physical education teaching from the current situation of learning situation analysis of physical education teaching, the mode of learning situation analysis of physical education teaching and the method of learning situation analysis of physical education teaching, In order to provide theoretical guidance for physical education teaching practice.

Keywords: Sports · Data analysis technology · Teaching · Academic situation analysis

1 Introduction

At this stage, there is a gap between theory and practice in academic situation analysis. At present, the analysis of learning situation in China is mostly the product of teachers' "taking it for granted", which is the result of teachers' conjecture about students' learning situation according to their experience rather than scientific analysis. On the one hand, teachers have preliminarily understood that learning situation analysis is the basis and premise of teaching design. On the other hand, teachers may not apply learning situation analysis to actual teaching, or the value of learning situation analysis can not be brought into play due to improper application. Its specific performance is as follows: (1) teachers have not applied physical situation analysis to teaching. At this time, learning situation analysis is only a formalism. Teachers do not bring it into daily teaching. Learning situation analysis, which is just "talking on paper", must not play a common role, resulting in the separation between learning situation analysis and actual teaching

© ICST Institute for Computer Sciences, Social Informatics and Telecommunications Engineering 2023
Published by Springer Nature Switzerland AG 2023. All Rights Reserved
M. A. Jan and F. Khan (Eds.): BigIoT-EDU 2022, LNICST 465, pp. 236–242, 2023.
https://doi.org/10.1007/978-3-031-23950-2_26

activities. (2) Teachers' understanding of learning situation analysis is not deep. Teachers' understanding of learning situation analysis determines the role of learning situation analysis. If teachers lack a deep understanding of learning situation analysis, they can not apply learning situation analysis to teaching design, and naturally can not fully play the role of learning situation analysis. (3) The way of learning situation analysis is too single. Teachers themselves have carried out learning situation analysis, but most of them have the color of empiricism. It is teachers' subjective conjecture on a single dimension of learning situation through many years of teaching experience without scientific basis [1]. At this time, learning situation analysis can not help teachers improve teaching quality, but will increase teachers' workload and see no good teaching effect. Even if teachers know the importance of learning situation analysis, they are unable to change the embarrassing situation that learning situation analysis has become a "chicken rib".

2 Big Data Analysis Technology

2.1 The Role of Big Data Analysis and Mining Technology and Decision-Making

In data mining, we extract valuable data in a large amount of data in the shortest time, and apply the information technology to industry development. Most of them are large data analysis drilling techniques, and the concrete industry combines algorithms in the data analysis process. Combining genetic algorithms in the biosphere helps ensure data mining speed, accuracy and integrity. During the course of data mining, we continue to analyze large data in the process of digging data under high data backgrounds, combining high performance computing, machine learning, artificial intelligence, model recognition, statistics, data visualization, database technology and expert systems, and It is possible to form a complete system, to put emphasis on optimization, and to make the measures more accurate. You can understand the demand well. Currently, each industry uses data mining as the main data analysis method. Technology such as classification, optimization, identification and prediction in data mining plays an important role in many industries.

With the development and application of large data technology, there are major changes in the various fields of society such as finance, medical care, telecommunications, education, and so on, there are large amounts of data every day, social uncertainty factors, and the processing of data types become more complicated. After applying computer technology, there are still significant limitations on traditional processing methods and problem solving. Now, data mining technology effectively resolves large data problems and becomes the "king of data". Data drilling technology also faces great opportunities and challenges. The application of data mining algorithm greatly improves data analysis ability and can effectively deal with actual problems [2].

2.2 Big Data Analysis and Application Status

Big data analysis and application platform mainly includes five key processing steps: selecting platform operating system, building Hadoop cluster, data integration and preprocessing, data storage, data mining and analysis, which further improves the efficiency of big data application.

(1) Select the platform operating system. In the process of big data analysis and processing, it faces many data resources. In order to improve the organization and management efficiency of these data resources, it is necessary to use the matching operating system to realize the priority access and hot data storage of big data as much as possible, manage the physical storage space of big data, and realize the scheduling and allocation of resources. Common operating systems include Red-Hat. CentOS or Debian, which can be used as the operating tools of the underlying platform, have strong scalability and can support data processing. The platform operating system can also realize the virtualization function according to the, so as to expand the physical storage space of the system, share CPU and improve the utilization of communication bandwidth.

(2) Build Hadoop cluster. Hadoop is a software platform that can run big data processing software. The core technology is MapReduce, which can form a cluster of a large number of computers to realize massive data distributed computing. Hadoop has attracted many commercial companies to develop and design, and has built various open source components, including sqoop, HBase. And spark. Hadoop includes many constituent elements. The lowest constituent element is Hadoop Di distributed file system (HDFS), which can maintain all storage node files in the Hadoop cluster platform. The upper layer of HDFS is a MapReduce engine, which includes two constituent components, jobtrackers and tasktrackers. Hadoop can be used to realize data processing and operation, Further meet the distributed data operation.

(3) Data integration and preprocessing. There are many resources for big data integration, such as file logs, relational data, object data, etc. These have both structural and non structural data. Therefore, preprocessing is required when integrating the data together, so that the service bus can be used for communication transmission and improve the consistency and reliability of the data. Data preprocessing can use tools such as impala. Sparksql and hivesql.

(4) Data mining and analysis. There are many resources for big data storage. These resources are usually disordered and messy. Although certain organization principles are adopted, people's use of data is also very complex. Therefore, the introduction of data mining and analysis function can improve the timeliness of data utilization and shorten the data processing time. Artificial intelligence technology is introduced into data mining and analysis, such as BP neural network, Bayesian algorithm, support vector machine and K-means algorithm. The data mining process is shown in Fig. 1.

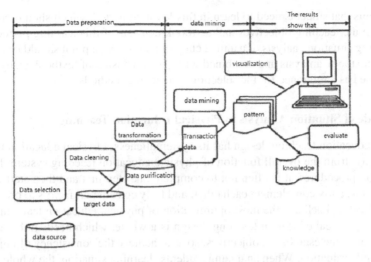

Fig. 1. Data mining process

3 Analysis of Learning Situation in Physical Education Teaching

3.1 Necessity of Situation Analysis in Physical Education Teaching

Physical education is a special course. It is an organized, purposeful and conscious social activity with physical exercise as the basic means and the purpose of improving health and physique. Physical education has two levels: first, physical exercise, the body needs to bear a certain exercise load, which is essentially different from other disciplines; Second, physical education includes the relevant theories of physical education and basic health care knowledge supporting its practical activities. While physical exercise, we also need to learn and master relevant theories. It can be seen that physical education is a complex subject, and there are more uncertain factors in the teaching process [3]. Therefore, its demand for learning situation analysis is more urgent and strict.

3.2 Types of Emotional Analysis in Physical Education Teaching

Learning situation analysis provides the basis for teaching content, teaching design and later teaching evaluation, and needs to be related to subsequent teaching activities. According to the different objects of learning situation analysis, it can be divided into two types: the analysis of students' situation and the analysis of students' learning situation. The former has a larger scope than the latter and is generally used for learning situation analysis in the semester or academic year. The latter has a smaller scope and mainly refers to the factors directly related to the learning process, including learning starting point, learning state and learning results. According to the different time periods of learning situation analysis, it can be divided into learning situation analysis before the semester or academic year, learning situation analysis of a unit and learning situation analysis of a class/a knowledge point. The learning situation analysis of the semester or academic year is the basis for teachers to select teaching contents. To a certain extent, it determines the contents that students need to learn in this learning period, which should be carried out before the teaching objectives and textbook analysis of this learning period, while the learning situation analysis of a unit, a class or a knowledge point should be arranged after the textbook analysis and combined with the conclusion of textbook analysis, It is mainly used as a reference for the selection of teaching methods.

3.3   Mode of Situation Analysis in Physical Education Teaching

Physical education teaching design has its systematicness. Physical education teaching design starts from the overall function of physical education teaching system. In terms of working procedures, it is often not to complete one step first and then start the next step, but constantly complement each other, and fully consider all factors to produce the overall effect and achieve the most optimization of physical education teaching effect. Therefore, physical education teaching design is a whole, which needs to be designed closely around the established objectives, so as to achieve the consistency of objectives, process and evaluation. When analyzing students' learning situation, the whole process of teaching should be regarded as a whole, and the analysis of learning situation should run through the whole process. Therefore, some teachers analyze the learning situation of the whole teaching process through the model before, during and after class, so as to ensure the effectiveness of teaching.

Pre class learning situation analysis is a problem that teachers should first consider and can not avoid in learning situation analysis. It mainly includes students' learning starting point and pre class preparation. The starting point of students' learning is the degree of students' pre mastery of the learning content of the course, including the degree of cognition of the course content, the basis of mastering the skills and the attitude towards the learning of the course. The pre class preparation state is aimed at what kind of preparation the students have made for the course, what their learning motivation is and the development degree of their own cognitive level. The analysis of learning starting point is directly related to the teaching content, and students' pre class preparation affects teachers' choice of teaching materials and methods [4].

The analysis mode before, during and after class is also the concrete embodiment of teaching evaluation. Teachers design the evaluation scheme before class, implement the evaluation scheme in the teaching process, evaluate the results after class, analyze and report the evaluation results, and finally deal with the evaluation results. For the teaching design of daily class, teachers can directly modify and adjust the teaching scheme according to the analysis of evaluation results, so as to serve the next teaching. Therefore, it can be considered that the three analysis dimensions before, during and after class are interrelated and interdependent to form a whole, and none of them is indispensable. The relationship between pre class, in class and after class analysis modes can be shown in Fig. 2.

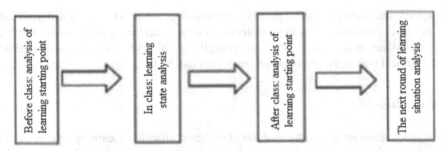

Fig. 2. Relationship diagram of learning situation analysis model

4 Methods of Learning Situation Analysis

After selecting the object and determining the analysis content, we will start the investigation. Common survey methods include observation, conversation and interview, questionnaire survey, etc. Combined with relevant literature, this paper briefly discusses how to carry out learning situation analysis in physical education teaching.

(1) Observation method. This is the most direct and simple method, especially physical education. It is a course that pays attention to practical application ability. Only through direct observation can we accurately grasp students' learning and other situations. Teachers can observe the analysis object in class or students' extracurricular activities.

(2) Interview method. Conversation is a direct and positive contact with the analysis object to ask about the subject's learning experience. The interview was conducted from the human hand side of the contact people around the analysis subject. Both methods have their limitations. The conversation method will be affected by the age and cognitive level of the interviewees, especially the junior students, who can not make an objective and accurate judgment on themselves. The selected objects are usually other teachers or their parents, and they can only make a general description, especially parents, whose description may be more personal subjective thoughts.

(3) Questionnaire survey method. Most of them are used to investigate students' sports theoretical knowledge or their interests, generally for senior students. The problem with the questionnaire survey is that some students may not be able to describe the theoretical principle of a sports skill in words, but they can show this skill. On the contrary, some students can understand the principle, but they can't master this skill in classroom practice. Therefore, the survey method should not adopt a single one, but multiple combination, mutual supplement and comprehensive analysis.

(4) Establish students' Sports portfolio, that is, material analysis. Portfolio evaluation is no longer a new thing in the field of education. This method can also be used in physical education teaching to establish students' Sports portfolio for analysis. Some researchers suggest that students should complete their own sports portfolio and design their own personalized portfolio cover with sports color. Students' sports performance evaluation form, photos of students' sports activities, award-winning certificates of various sports, teachers' words, their own sports perception, collected

sports materials, etc. can be put in the archive bag. All sports related materials can be put in the room. Using these materials, teachers can have a more comprehensive understanding of students. When analyzing the learning situation, these are powerful empirical materials, and the teaching design can be targeted.

5 Conclusion

Learning situation analysis is the analysis of students' situation. Learning situation analysis is for students' learning. Learning situation analysis in physical education can be carried out from the aspects of knowledge and skills, process and methods, emotion and so on. The object of analysis can be all or sampling. Every class in the teaching process should be analyzed to grasp the situation of students, improve the effectiveness of teaching activities and promote the development of students.

References

1. Ying, C.: Using effective learning situation analysis to improve work efficiency. China Educ. Technol. Equip. **4**, 59–62 (2011)
2. Peifen, Z., Songjie, Q.: Let learning situation analysis run through the whole process of teaching. Sports Teach. Friends **1**, 4–5 (2011)
3. Zhangfa, Y.: How to do well in learning situation analysis. Guizhou Educ. **16**, 26–27 (2010)
4. Haiping, Z.: Learning situation analysis, how to get out of the practical dilemma. Phys. Educ. **2**, 22–24 (2008)

Application of Environmental Isotopes to Study the Origin and Recharge Mechanism of Geothermal Water

Yuanhao Zhang[1]([⊠]) and Jiacheng Dong[2]

[1] University of Chinese Academy of Sciences, Beijing 100049, China
zhangyuanhao20@mails.ucas.ac.cn
[2] China University of Geosciences (Beijing), Beijing 100084, China
2005200001@cugb.edu.cn

Abstract. To study the recharge mechanism of groundwater, it is necessary to determine the source of recharge water, the location of recharge area, recharge period, recharge channel and recharge rate. The study of groundwater recharge by using environmental isotopes is based on the change of isotopic composition of water with space and time. On the one hand, the isotopic composition is not affected by physical and chemical processes and remains basically unchanged during the migration from the heat source to the sampling point. Therefore, it is suitable for labeling or tracer; On the other hand, they are very sensitive to temperature change, water rock interaction, steam emission, mixed dilution of water from different sources and surface evaporation. Therefore, they are suitable as geological indicators of these processes.

Keywords: Environmental isotopes · Geothermal water · Origin and supply mechanism

1 Introduction

Most of the heat energy in the geothermal system is stored in the rock mass, but the heat energy transmission is not only through heat conduction, but also mainly through the convective circulation of water (liquid water and steam). Therefore, geothermal water is the main object of geothermal field exploration and development. In recent 30 years, the scale of geothermal water exploitation and drilling depth in China are increasing day by day, which requires scientific evaluation of geothermal water resources. One of the important topics is to establish a geothermal water mathematical model or simulation model in line with the actual conditions of geothermal field. Therefore, it is necessary to establish and correct the scientific theory and means of the model.

Since the early 1960s, the International Atomic Energy Agency began to operate the global atmospheric precipitation monitoring network (GNIP), which promoted the birth of isotopic hydrology and provided theories and methods for studying the natural water

M. A. Jan and F. Khan (Eds.): BigIoT-EDU 2022, LNICST 465, pp. 243–248, 2023.
https://doi.org/10.1007/978-3-031-23950-2_27

cycle and evaluating the age of groundwater from the nuclear level. China has also operated the China atmospheric precipitation isotope monitoring network (CNIP) since 1985 to study the temporal and spatial distribution and environmental effects of atmospheric precipitation in China (Wang Dongsheng, 1993), which provides background data and basic theory for the application of environmental isotopes in all scientific fields related to natural water in China [1].

Therefore, environmental isotopes have been increasingly applied in the exploration and development of geothermal water in China. A series of studies have been carried out on the origin, recharge and chronology of geothermal water, and an attempt has been made to correct the conceptual model of geothermal water by using environmental isotopes (Wang et al., 2001). The study of geothermal water recharge mechanism and chronology is the basis of applying environmental isotopes to correct the conceptual model of geothermal water. This paper focuses on the theory, method and latest progress of the application of environmental isotopes in the study of geothermal water recharge mechanism.

2 Related Work

2.1 Origin of Geothermal Water

The origin of geothermal water can be atmospheric precipitation, river water, lake water, etc., collectively referred to as "atmospheric water"; it can be water buried in the formation, such as formation water, syngenetic water, etc., collectively referred to as "sealed water" At first, it was thought that magma was the common origin of heat, water and solute. Later, geothermal water was found by comparing the isotopic composition of geothermal water and regional atmospheric precipitation δ The H value tends to be close to the local atmospheric water (Craig, 1963), indicating that the geothermal water mainly originates from the atmospheric water, because the surrounding rock is usually poor in hydrogen, and the geothermal water is very weak during its migration from the heat source to the sampling point δ It is inconvenient to keep the H value basically. At the same time, it is found that the ^{18}O value of geothermal water is greater than that of local atmospheric water in varying degrees. The experiment shows that this is the relationship between water and surrounding rock under high temperature conditions δ ^{18}O values are usually about + 10%) as a result of isotopic exchange. The increase of ^{18}O values of many geothermal waters relative to local atmospheric precipitation is increasing δ The D-^{18}O diagram shows a nearly parallel drift, which indicates that there is little composition of geothermal water from magma with uniform isotopic composition. Of course, the possibility of magmatic water participating in atmospheric water recycling is not ruled out [2].

Through the comparative study of hydrogen and oxygen isotopes of atmospheric precipitation and geothermal water, China's geothermal water is divided into cyclic geothermal water and sealed geothermal water. Cyclic geothermal water occurs in the deep aquifer outside the fold system and large artesian basin, which is mainly controlled by hydrostatic pressure and geostatic pressure. Cyclic geothermal water has isotopic composition and hydrogeochemistry similar to modern atmospheric precipitation

Genetic coefficient, geothermal water points are distributed along the global atmospheric drawdown line, as shown in Fig. 1.

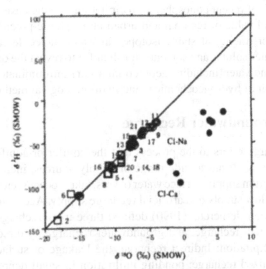

Fig. 1. Hydrogen oxygen isotopic composition diagram of geothermal water and atmospheric precipitation

2.2 Application Principle of Environmental Isotopes

The so-called environmental isotopes refer to those stable isotopes and radioisotopes that exist in the environment and whose concentration is not controlled by the researcher during the research project, which are different from those manually put in quantitatively under the control of the researcher.

In recent 40 years, environmental isotopes have been applied to large geothermal fields in the world. At present, they have become a common means of geothermal development. Among them, the application of stable isotopes has two aspects: on the one hand, the isotopes of some elements, such as the stable isotope atmosphere of hydrogen, due to the lack of hydrogen in the surrounding rock, the migration of deuterium from the heat source to the sampling point is not affected by physical and chemical processes, and the concentration remains basically unchanged, which is suitable for marking or tracing the origin of water molecules; On the other hand, the isotopes of some elements, such as oxygen isotope ^{18}O, are very sensitive to temperature change, water rock interaction, steam emission, mixing and dilution of water from different sources, and surface evaporation due to the oxygen enrichment of surrounding rock [3]. It is suitable to be used as a geological indicator of these processes.

In the hydrological cycle, when the physical state of water (gaseous liquid solid) changes, the fractionation intensity of the isosteric cords of hydrogen and oxygen in water molecules is inversely proportional to the ambient temperature, which is related to factors such as latitude, elevation and season. Therefore, the mass number difference of stable isotopes of hydrogen and oxygen in water molecules can be used to mark the formation environment of water. Tritium and 'C are the most commonly used radioisotopes in geothermal investigation. They can be used to determine the age of geothermal water or to find out the share of recent atmospheric precipitation. On the basis of monitoring the isotopic background value of regional and urban atmospheric precipitation, combined with the labeling or tracing of stable isotopes in water molecules and the timing of radioisotopes in water solutes and solvents, it is helpful to reveal the origin and recharge mechanism of groundwater (including geothermal water) and eliminate the multi solution of single application of hydrogeochemical and hydrogeological methods.

3   Study on Groundwater Recharge

Groundwater recharge refers to the process that the aquifer or aquifer system obtains water from the outside. It has a wide range of supply sources, including atmospheric precipitation infiltration supply, surface water (rivers, lakes, oceans, etc.), irrigation water return supply, overflow supply and artificial recharge supply. According to the recharge source of groundwater, lerneretal (1990) defined three main recharge mechanisms, as shown in Fig. 2: direct recharge, and groundwater recharge by direct infiltration in a large range of precipitation; Indirect recharge: the leakage of surface water supplies groundwater; Localized recharge: ponding infiltration in small depressions, and three recharge mechanisms can exist at the same time. These three recharge mechanisms recharge groundwater through the downward infiltration of precipitation into the soil, and the infiltration of precipitation into the soil and through the soil matrix is a complex process.

Generally speaking, there are two main infiltration modes after precipitation enters the soil: piston flow and preferential flow. In the piston flow, the soil water moves in the form of stratification, and the new water discharges the old water in the form of horizontal push from top to bottom, so that the soil water is pushed down. In the preferential flow, the new water may bypass the old water existing in the soil matrix through shortcuts (such as vertical cracks, megaspores, rotten plant roots and earthworm holes), so as to migrate faster to the deeper soil layer. Among the three recharge mechanisms, these two different water infiltration modes can exist at the same time, and the differences of infiltration modes can be reflected from the properties of soil water. For example, two different infiltration types will produce different soil water isotope profile distribution characteristics, and then the infiltration type can be determined, that is, the infiltration mode of water in soil can be determined.

Mastering the groundwater recharge mechanism can provide basic information for water resources management. Therefore, since the mid-1980s, the international hydrogeological community has paid attention to the quantitative study of groundwater recharge, and the study of groundwater recharge has entered the peak. The methods of quantitative research on groundwater recharge have gradually become richer, and the application of methods has changed from one method to multiple methods. However, different research methods have their applicability and limitations. It is very important to select appropriate methods, especially for areas with thick unsaturated or water storage, the hydrological process is very complex, and the selection of groundwater recharge research methods is very key.

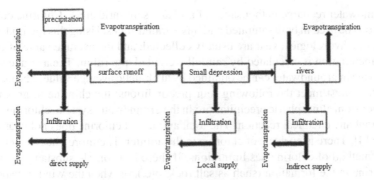

Fig. 2. Groundwater recharge mechanism

4   Application of Environmental Tracer in Groundwater Recharge

(1) Hydrogen and oxygen stable isotope
Environmental isotopes widely exist in various water bodies in nature. In the process of conversion between different water bodies, isotopes have different contents in different water bodies due to their fractionation effect. Using the difference of isotopic contents, we can study the mutual transformation formula and amount of different water bodies. The change of stable isotopic composition in nature is very small, so it is generally used internationally δ Value to represent the isotopic content. δ Value refers to the thousandth difference between the stable isotope ratio (R) in the sample and the isotope ratio of standard water sample, i.e.:

$$\delta = \frac{R_{sample} - R_{reference}}{R_{reference}} \times 1000\% \tag{1}$$

When δ ^{18}O and δ When D is positive, it means that the sample is enriched with ^{18}O and D than smow standard (standard average seawater); When it is negative, it indicates that the two isotopes in the sample are poorer than those in smow standard. For different water bodies δ ^{18}O and δ The difference and correlation of D value can reveal the source of precipitation water vapor, the way of precipitation supplying groundwater, the way of soil water transport and the transformation relationship of different water bodies.

(2) Conservation of chlorine
The conservation of chlorine was proposed by briksson and khunakasem in 1969. It was originally used to study the groundwater recharge in the coastal plain of Israel. The basic principle is that the chlorine element of rainfall and groundwater is conserved. After measuring the chlorine element content of rainfall and groundwater, the recharge of groundwater can be calculated. Namely:

$$\overline{P} \times \overline{C}_p = \overline{R}_t \times \overline{C}_{gw} \tag{2}$$

Chloride mass balance (CMB) can directly obtain the rate of direct infiltration recharge of precipitation at spatial points. It is the main method for the study of groundwater recharge in thousands of arid and semi-arid areas. Chlorine conservation can be used in both saturated and unsaturated zones. Using this method, rainfall data of a hydrological year are usually collected, and the average value of chlorine in precipitation is calculated by rainfall weighted algorithm. The average value of chlorine in groundwater can be obtained by arithmetic average value. The use of this method must meet the following four preconditions: the chlorine in groundwater comes from atmospheric precipitation; In the groundwater system, chlorine is stable without any chemical reaction; The total amount of chlorine does not change with time [4]; There is no cycle of chlorine in the aquifer. Therefore, the mass conservation method of chlorine has limitations. If there is a soluble substance containing chlorine in the formation (such as salt rock, etc.), or when the wind transports the salt from another system to the study area, the chlorine conservation method is not applicable. Soil chloride ion sampling shall be conducted in areas with little impact of human activities as far as possible to avoid the impact of human input of chloride ions (such as non irrigated wasteland). When there is human input of chloride ions (such as irrigation), the chloride ions input from irrigation must be taken into account in the chloride ion mass balance to improve the accuracy of evaluation.

5   Conclusion

On the basis of monitoring the isotopic background value of regional atmospheric precipitation, combined with the labeling or tracing of stable isotopes in water molecules and the timing of radioisotopes in water solutes and solvents, it is helpful to reveal the origin and recharge mechanism of groundwater (including geothermal water) and eliminate the multi solution of single application of hydrogeochemical and hydrogeological methods. Taking deuterium as the main marker of the origin of geothermal water, through the comparative study of environmental isotopes and hydrogeochemistry between geothermal water and atmospheric water, magmatic water or formation water in North China Plain, it is found that cyclic geothermal water has isotopic composition and hydrogeochemical genetic coefficient similar to modern atmospheric precipitation, indicating that it mainly originates from atmospheric water, Chronological studies show that circulating geothermal water is usually not supplied by modern times, and its main supply period is the cold and wet period of late Pleistocene, while sealed geothermal water is ancient water with an age of hundreds of millions of years, and its origin is related to the dehydration of gypsum or the dehydration and exhaust of upper mantle.

References

1. Wang, D.: Stable isotope study on the origin of yellow and black halides in Sichuan Basin. Hydrogeology and engineering geology, (total 106), 21–24 (1989)
2. Liping, C., Wenzhao, L.: Soil water stable isotope characteristics of several typical land use types in the Loess Plateau. J. Appl. Ecol. 23(3), 651–658 (2012)
3. Dongsheng, W., Jinglan, W.: Basic types and genetic characteristics of geothermal water in China. Quatern. Res. 2, 139–146 (1996)
4. Nan, L.A.N.: Analysis on countermeasures for sustainable utilization of groundwater resources in China. China environmental protection industry 2008(7), 38–42 (2008)

Application of Flipped Classroom Teaching Mode Based on Ant Colony Algorithm in Higher Vocational Java Course

Ru Zhang$^{(\boxtimes)}$

Xi'an Mingde Institute of Technology, Xi'an 710014, Shaanxi, China
zhangru06s@163.com

Abstract. Under the Internet plus era, information technology has become an effective choice for classroom teaching innovation. Among them, flipped classroom, as a new teaching means and teaching mode, can not only change the traditional teaching links, but also make teachers change from their previous role to the guide of students' learning, and effectively highlight the dominant position of students. The application of flipped classroom teaching mode is also conducive to stimulate students' learning enthusiasm, effectively let students participate in teaching interaction, and create a good personalized learning environment for students. Therefore, based on the application of flipped classroom teaching mode under ant colony algorithm in Higher Vocational Java curriculum, this paper solves the problems existing in previous Java curriculum teaching, introduces a variety of teaching means and teaching resources through flipped classroom, highlights students' personalized learning needs in Java curriculum teaching, gives full play to the advantages of traditional classroom, and further improves students' enthusiasm for curriculum learning, Realize the innovative teaching of java course with students as the main body.

Keywords: Flipping classroom · Ant colony Java courses · Teaching strategy

1 Introduction

Today's society is an information age, with the rapid development of science and technology. The competition of national comprehensive national strength is mainly reflected in the competition of talent quality. Education is the key to cultivating talents. Receiving continuing education and lifelong education will be necessary for everyone in future life. Education is developing in the direction of popularization, lifelong and networking, which requires a wide coverage of education, multi-mode and all-round service [1]. The goal of future education development should ensure that anyone, anytime and anywhere can receive a good education. The imbalance of regional economic development in China leads to the imbalance of knowledge development. Excellent teachers are concentrated in cities, rural teachers and teaching resources are poor, and the gap between urban and rural education levels is gradually increasing. Therefore, under such

© ICST Institute for Computer Sciences, Social Informatics and Telecommunications Engineering 2023
Published by Springer Nature Switzerland AG 2023. All Rights Reserved
M. A. Jan and F. Khan (Eds.): BigIoT-EDU 2022, LNICST 465, pp. 249–260, 2023.
https://doi.org/10.1007/978-3-031-23950-2_28

a background, it is urgent to adopt a new technical means to make full use of various resources, strengthen the popularization of education, narrow the gap between urban and rural areas, and build a lifelong learning environment [2]. Network teaching provides a solution to the above contradiction. Although online education resources are rich, they are intermingled, disorderly, inconvenient to use and difficult to manage and maintain. So, how to build excellent teaching resources, ensure their quality, make them give full play to the advantages of network sharing, and carry out the exploration and Research on the standardization of teaching resources construction of modern network learning is very necessary [3].

For the learning of java course, the capacity of the course is large, and the students' knowledge level varies greatly. Relying on several face-to-face counseling courses alone, it is impossible for students to understand and learn thoroughly. The time for teaching discussion by using face-to-face counseling courses is even limited. Our students are all over the north and south of the motherland, but under this heuristic teaching mode, this discussion and communication is essential. The best choice to solve this demand is to use network teaching. Figure 1 below shows the Java structure function diagram.

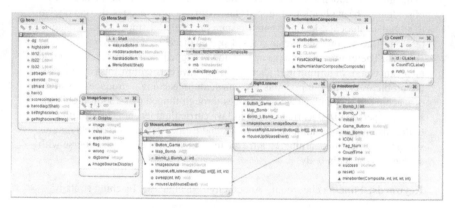

Fig. 1. Java structure function diagram

In short, it is our primary task to network the classroom teaching content and provide online communication function [4]. Moreover, teachers can independently manage and control the networked teaching and communication platform, and there is no need for system administrators. And the teaching system should be adjusted according to the classroom teaching situation at any time. At the same time, teachers play the role of system administrator and can fully control the whole system platform. Java course teaching based on flipped classroom teaching mode aims to ban the traditional teacher centered teaching mode, make rational use of learning ways inside and outside class, open up a new learning platform for students with the help of wechat and the Internet, and carry out java course teaching flexibly [5]. The application of flipped classroom teaching mode in java course teaching can use the existing network platform to design new teaching links, further improve students' practical ability and innovation ability, stimulate students' learning initiative, solve students' learning problems in classroom teaching, and give full play to the advantages of traditional classroom through students' learning and interaction before and after class, Exercise students' ability of communication and independent thinking [6]. Taking the tank war of java course teaching as an example, this paper discusses how to apply the flipping teaching mode to java course teaching, explore how to give full play to the advantages of flipping classroom teaching, and solve the problems existing in Java programming. According to the characteristics of java course, the application of flipped classroom teaching mode based on Ant Colony Algorithm in Higher Vocational java course.

2 Ant Colony Algorithm

With the continuous expansion of the field of intelligent computing, swarm intelligence algorithms for solving optimization problems are pouring in, among which the most common are ant colony algorithm (ACO), particle swarm optimization algorithm (PSO), firefly algorithm (FA) and bat algorithm (BA). This kind of algorithm provides a better method to solve NP hard problem. Its design principle comes from the imitation of biological behavior in nature. Ant colony algorithm, as the earliest proposed bionic algorithm, has been concerned by experts and scholars. In recent years, many scholars have conducted in-depth research on ant colony algorithm, applied it to various fields, and successfully solved many NP hard problems [7]. Based on the improvement of ant colony algorithm, this paper uses it to optimize the flipped classroom teaching mode in order to achieve the expected effect.

2.1 Basic Ant Colony Algorithm

Ant colony optimization (ACO) was first proposed by Italian scholar Marco Dorigo in 1991. It is a bionic algorithm inspired by ant foraging process. The researchers found that ants will release a hormone called pheromone on the path, which will gradually volatilize over time. Later ants can feel the existence of pheromone, find a path with high pheromone concentration, move forward and release a certain amount of pheromone at the same time. There will be more and more pheromones on the selected path, and the ants will gather on the same path, The positive feedback mechanism is formed. The ant selects the next city that is not visited according to the probability formula (1) and adds it to the tabu list.

$$p_{ij}^k(t) = \begin{cases} \dfrac{\tau_{ij}^\alpha(t)\eta_{ij}^\beta}{\sum\limits_{j \in N_j^k} \tau_{ij}^\alpha(t)\eta_{ij}^\beta} \\ 0 \end{cases} \tag{1}$$

The basic ant colony algorithm flow is shown in Fig. 2.

Although ant colony algorithm has been produced for more than 20 years, it still lacks the necessary theoretical framework, and most of them just rely on empirical experiments. Most of the understanding of the working mechanism of ant colony algorithm starts from quasi ecological scheduling, and the algorithm lacks mathematical model and analysis description. The following describes the theoretical research progress of ant colony algorithm in recent years from three aspects:

(1) Research on convergence of algorithm
Many domestic scholars have also made in-depth research on the convergence of ant colony algorithm. Zhang Feijun and others proposed an encounter ant algorithm. A complete travel path is completed by two encounter ants, which improves the running speed of the algorithm and expands the search space of understanding; Yang Yanqing et al. fixed the maximum and minimum of pheromone, which effectively avoided the difference of pheromone on the path; Mhuang et al. Introduced the 3-opt switching strategy for the vehicle routing problem, and the initial planning path has been further optimized; Zhang Qi et al. Adjusted and improved the local heuristic function of the algorithm for the path planning problem of mobile robot, introduced cross operation and adjusted the parameter values at the same time; Jiang Kunlin and others proposed a new city selection strategy based on roulette, and combined with the method of ending the task in advance to reduce the running time of the algorithm; Zhu Haodong improved the algorithm by selecting the next node transfer rule, which effectively improved the probability of selecting the optimal path; Hu Wei combines ant colony algorithm with tabu search algorithm to improve the local search ability of ant colony algorithm [8].

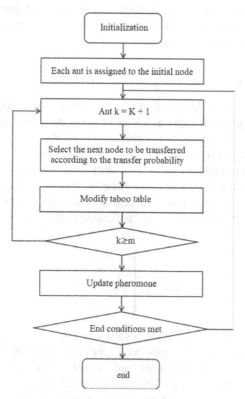

Fig. 2. Basic ant colony algorithm process

(2) Research on the relationship between algorithm and other optimization algorithms
The research of ant colony algorithm is not limited to the algorithm itself. With the rise of intelligent optimization algorithm, the combination of ant colony algorithm and other intelligent optimization algorithms to form a hybrid intelligent algorithm has become a research hotspot. For example, Gao Wei and others used ant colony algorithm in geotechnical engineering for the first time. In order to improve the solution accuracy, they combined immune algorithm with continuous ant colony algorithm to form immune continuous ant colony algorithm, which successfully overcome the shortcomings of analysis method; Zhang Yongheng et al. Proposed the solution of boundary layer differential equation based on particle swarm optimization algorithm and ant colony algorithm, and analyzed and compared with other optimization algorithms, which shows that it is feasible to combine the two algorithms to solve the differential equation; Zlochin et al. Applied a model-based search algorithm framework to ant colony optimization algorithm, explored the methods of two algorithms to update parameter model, and used these two methods to guide ant colony algorithm to update pheromone.

2.2 Ant Colony Optimization Algorithm

The basic ant colony algorithm has some defects in the selection of optimal path and convergence speed. In the following, a new improved method is proposed for the initial pheromone distribution and pheromone volatilization factor. Firstly, the initial pheromone is reset according to the global path, so that the algorithm does not search the pheromone path blindly in the early stage, so as to speed up the convergence speed of the algorithm; Then, the pheromone is volatilized twice to improve the accuracy and later convergence ability of the algorithm.

(1) Improvement of initial pheromone
In the basic ant colony algorithm, let the number of ants be m and the number of cities be n, The amount of pheromone at the beginning is m/C'', where C is the length of the path constructed by the nearest neighbor method. In the initial stage of the algorithm, when the pheromone concentration is small, the ability of ants to detect pheromones is relatively weak. It takes a period of exploration to find a relatively optimal path. In this process, it takes a lot of time and reduces the convergence speed of the algorithm. In order to improve this situation, consider The path distance resets the distribution of the initial pheromone to make the algorithm search in a direction to overcome the blindness of the search. The initial pheromone is improved as follows:

$$\tau_{ij}(0) = \begin{cases} \min(d_{ij})/d_{ij}, i \neq j \\ 0, otherwise \end{cases} \tag{2}$$

(2) Improvement of pheromone volatilization factor
In the basic ant colony algorithm, pheromone updating is only to update the pheromone on the better path. However, the sub path of the optimal path is not always the shortest path, and there may be a longer path, which will lead to the ant

choosing the wrong path from the beginning and missing the optimal path. In order to solve this defect, the path contribution is introduced. In the optimal path, the sub path whose contribution to the overall path is greater than the path contribution threshold is found.

In the basic ant colony algorithm, the pheromone volatilization factor is a certain value. Because the poor solution obtained in each iteration is not helpful to the final result, if the pheromone volatilization is relatively slow on the poor path, the more pheromones left will affect the speed of the algorithm to find the optimal solution. Therefore, it is necessary to appropriately slow down the pheromone volatilization of the better path, Accelerate the volatilization speed of pheromone on the poor path, so consider secondary volatilization for the pheromone after secondary updating of pheromone, so that the secondary volatilization coefficient is inversely proportional to the square of iteration times.

3   Basic Concepts of Flipped Classroom Teaching Mode

3.1   The Concept of Flipped Classroom Teaching Mode

Flipped classroom is translated from "flipped classroom". Domestic scholars have given different definitions of flipped classroom teaching mode from different angles. Zhang Yueguo and Zhang Yujiang (2012) of Chongqing Jukui middle school, combined with their own flipped classroom teaching experience, believe that flipped classroom is a means to increase the interaction and personalized learning time between students and teachers; It is an environment in which students are responsible for their own learning; It is a classroom in which all students study actively; It is to enable all students to get personalized education; Flipped classroom is not synonymous with online video. In addition to teaching video, there should also be face-to-face interaction time; Instead of replacing teachers with videos [9].

Zhang Jinlei, Wang Ying, Zhang Baohui and others (2012) analyzed the teaching structure and believed that the traditional classroom generally includes two stages: classroom knowledge transfer and after-school knowledge internalization, while the flipped classroom is "pre class knowledge transfer and classroom knowledge internalization", emphasizing the reversal of the teaching structure. In addition, Zhong Xiaoliu, song Shuqiang, Jiao Lizhen and others (2013) started with learning resources and information technology application, and believed that flipped classroom teaching is that in the information environment, course teachers provide learning resources in the form of teaching video, and students complete the viewing and learning of teaching video and other learning resources before class, It is a new teaching mode that teachers and students complete homework answer and interactive communication in class [10].

Whether emphasizing the reversal of teaching structure or focusing on the application of learning resources and information technology, we should reverse the core of the classroom, reverse the teaching structure, and promote the internalization of knowledge and the achievement of teaching objectives. Based on the above scholars' understanding of flipped classroom, the author believes that flipped classroom model is supported by information technology. Teachers provide teaching micro video, audio, animation, courseware, exercises and other learning resources. Students use these resources for independent learning before class to complete the teaching of knowledge; Classroom teachers carry out learning activities such as doubt solving, cooperative exploration and interactive communication according to the problems existing in students' learning process and some difficult contents, so as to complete the internalization of knowledge and achieve teaching objectives.

3.2 Theoretical Basis of Flipped Classroom Teaching Model

(1) Constructivist learning theory

Constructivism theory rose in the 1990s. Its main representatives include J. Piaget, Bruner and vogotsky. Constructivist learning theory holds that knowledge is not imparted by teachers, but obtained by learners through meaning construction with the help of others (including teachers and learning partners) in a given situation, that is, social and cultural background. "Context", "construction", "caring", "competence" and "community" constitute the basic elements of constructivist learning theory. Meaning construction is the ultimate goal of the whole learning process. Its essential content is student-centered, emphasizing students' active exploration, discovery and construction of knowledge.

Flipped classroom teaching pays attention to the active construction of knowledge, which is in line with the learning concept of constructivism. In flipped classroom teaching, teachers not only provide learners with rich learning resources and individualized guidance, but also act as organizers, guides and learning promoters. At the same time, under the guidance of teachers, students establish a learning community, complete the internalization of knowledge through group cooperative learning and teacher-student interaction, and finally achieve the learning goal. In the whole teaching process, the acquisition of knowledge is the result of learners' active construction. At the same time, flipped classroom emphasizes that the classroom environment should be conducive to students' independent construction of knowledge and cooperative learning. Rich high-quality resources can provide learners with a support for the construction of knowledge meaning.

(2) Master learning theory

Mastering learning theory is a teaching idea put forward by American educational psychologist bloom. Bloom believes that 90% of All the students can master the teaching materials and get a pass grade or above. Any teacher can help all students learn well, help "stupid" students learn like smart students, and help "slow" students learn like "fast" students; Help "mentally retarded" students learn like talented students; The key is that teachers teach students in accordance with their aptitude and give different types of students enough learning time. "Its core content mainly includes two points:

① Teaching for mastery; Bloom believes that the vast majority of students in the class can reach the mastery level, and believes that all students can develop; In mastering learning, teachers must establish a correct view of students. The difference of students' learning ability is man-made, accidental and formed by the day after tomorrow. Flipping the classroom reverses the teaching structure.

Teachers have more time to care for students and provide individualized guidance to students with different learning foundations, so that the vast majority of students can master the teaching content.

② Learning for mastery; Bloom believes that every student is seeking recognition of his own value and needs to see himself as competent for learning. However, students often fail and will cause students to doubt their learning ability. Therefore, they should be guided to seek trust and competence in the experience of classroom learning activities. Bloom stressed that if the classroom can not give students more opportunities for success, they refuse to learn not only in class but also outside class. Flipped classroom teaching encourages teachers to use incentive evaluation mechanism, timely feedback, learning resource support and other strategies to stimulate students' self-confidence, help students obtain more successful experience and enjoy the joy of learning; At the same time, it is also necessary to learn for students to master and normalize the diagnostic examination before class. The effect of autonomous learning before class is related to the internalization of classroom knowledge, and then affects the overall teaching effect.

(3) Blended learning theory

Blended learning is a concept put forward by the field of educational technology. Professor he Kekang believes that blended learning basically includes three meanings: (1) the integration of traditional learning and online learning; (2) The combination of various media and tools in e-learning learning environment; (3) Combination of various teaching methods and learning techniques; In other words, in the design and implementation of the teaching system, we should not only give play to the leading role of teachers in guiding, enlightening and monitoring the teaching process, but also fully reflect the initiative, enthusiasm and creativity of students as the main body of the learning process. We should not only pay attention to the cultivation of innovative spirit and ability, but also pay attention to the teaching and mastery of systematic scientific knowledge, We should also pay attention to the design of learning environment and autonomous learning strategies, and try to use information technology to create an ideal teaching environment for learners, so as to realize the requirements of autonomous exploration, multiple interaction, cooperative learning, resource sharing and so on.

Therefore, in order to give better play to the dual role of "teacher leading and student main body", flipped teaching practice should pay attention to the flexibility of teaching methods and multimedia technology in the mixed learning environment, and adopt the methods of independent inquiry and cooperative learning to guide learners to participate in learning activities and actively construct knowledge; At the same time, it also emphasizes that learners need to communicate with each other, share experience, promote learners' active learning, innovate boldly, and cultivate students' innovative spirit and ability.

4   Application of Flipped Classroom Teaching Mode Based on Ant Colony Algorithm in Higher Vocational Java Course

The application of flipped classroom teaching mode in java course teaching should not only turn over the traditional learning process and allow students to complete independent learning of knowledge points and concepts outside class, but also redesign the course teaching content, reasonably arrange teaching links according to students' learning needs, and introduce classroom discussion, group communication, teacher Q & A and other methods into course teaching, Achieve better teaching effect, realize the new teaching structure of internalizing knowledge in the classroom and learning knowledge outside the classroom, so as to improve the effectiveness of students' learning.

4.1   Provide Students with Pre Class Learning Resource Support

Taking the tank war project as an example, when sharing learning resources before class, teachers must first develop corresponding video resources for students, consolidate and analyze knowledge points through the explanation of knowledge points and cases, so that students can complete independent learning before class. In the flipped classroom teaching mode, teachers should record and screen videos and learning resources before class, so as to sort out the learning resources needed for students' Preview. At present, students' favorite course learning resources are videos, reference learning and teaching courseware. They like to obtain resources, read and preview on the platform of wechat and QQ. Therefore, teachers should screen and re record corresponding micro videos and online learning videos on the Internet before teaching. They will share these resources to QQ learning group or WeChat official account homepage, which is convenient for students to subscribe and download, and confirm the learning trend of students through subscription and downloading.

4.2   Creating a Personalized Learning Environment for Students in Classroom Teaching

In classroom teaching, teachers should first analyze the teaching environment, take theory and practice as the basic teaching route, equip students with corresponding multimedia equipment and computers, provide LAN and Internet services, and distribute experimental contents and theoretical materials to students, as shown in Fig. 3. Because the tank project training involves many pilot courses, such as programming, advanced programming and database application. Before teaching, teachers should also analyze the students' previous learning subjects, let the students with good basic ability serve as the team leader, then share the micro video of tank war programming to the learning group, and share the corresponding enterprise software projects with the students, so as to start the design of experimental projects and theoretical knowledge exploration. The task driven teaching method carries out classroom practice teaching, completes knowledge teaching with the flipped classroom teaching mode, selects program driven tasks with moderate difficulty in the stage of comprehensive application and practical exercise, and studies in groups. Guide students to design tank war products and integrate app to further improve students' information screening and programming ability.

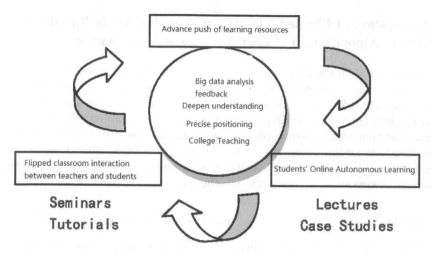

Fig. 3. Flipped classroom teaching mode

4.3 The Three Links of Theory, Practice and Experiment are Coordinated and Unified

Including the control program of tank war, which can integrate theory and practice. Teachers should guide students to complete the review of relevant pilot courses such as single chip microcomputer, analog electronics, digital electronics and communication before class, and some auxiliary teaching materials, through the project description, students' experimental guidance and program code, etc., Let students master some basic java knowledge before the design of tank war project, promote students to learn with problems after class, design a series of questions based on the characteristics of tank war project, guide students to complete independent learning and preview after class, and introduce the thinking results and sleepiness into the classroom, and study in groups through joint discussion in class, Develop students' learning career, complete problem analysis and discussion, and promote students to participate in teaching. In experimental teaching, teachers can also take some hardware design of tank war as practical training tasks, promote students to show their previous hardware works to students while learning programming design, and promote learning interaction through experimental internalization of knowledge, so as to strengthen students' practical ability.

Java's security checking mechanism stifles errors in many programs. In addition, the Java language also has many features to ensure the stability and robustness of the program (strong typing mechanism, exception handling, automatic garbage collection, etc.), which effectively reduces errors and makes the Java application more robust. Java is usually used in the network environment. Therefore, Java provides a security mechanism to prevent malicious code attacks, which can improve the security of the system. Java platform independence is realized by Java virtual machine. Java software can run normally in any computer environment without the constraints of computer hardware and operating system. There is no built-in multithreading mechanism in C++ language, so the multithreading function of the operating system must be called for multithreading programming, while Java language provides multithreading support. Multithreading mechanism enables applications to execute multiple tasks in parallel at the same time. This mechanism enables programs to have better interaction and real-time.

5 Conclusion

Flipped classroom teaching mode can make rational use of existing teaching resources, change traditional teaching links, highlight students' personalized learning needs in teaching, build the classroom into a new platform for understanding, practice and exercise, carry out professional teaching around classroom teaching and pre class students' learning, and improve the efficiency of classroom teaching. Compared with the traditional teacher centered classroom teaching mode, flipped classroom not only subverts the traditional teaching links, but also changes the role of teachers and students. Students in flipped classroom teaching are the main body of learning and the leader of the classroom. Teachers are the organizers and guides of the classroom, and teachers and students are in an equal interactive position. Teachers teach according to students' problems and development, providing students with more independent thinking and knowledge strengthening practice time, so as to effectively improve the effect of classroom teaching. Based on the problems existing in the current java course teaching, in order to guide students to study more rationally, it is necessary to realize the common improvement of knowledge, ability and literacy. The application of flipped classroom in java course teaching must highlight students' learning needs and strengthen students' practical training, so as to strengthen the learning effect and ensure that students can realize the internalization of knowledge and Consciously carry out extracurricular learning.

Acknowledgements. Educational Reform Project of Xi'an Mingde Institute of Technology (Project No.: JG2021YB01).

References

1. Shuang, L.I., et al.: Application of flipped classroom teaching mode taking osmotic pressure of dilute solutions as example. China Health Industry (2016)
2. Zhang, X.H., et al.: Application of flipped classroom teaching mode in college english teaching. Heilongjiang Researches on Higher Education (2016)
3. Wu, Y.: Application of flipped classroom teaching mode in the teaching of electronic information specialty in colleges and universities. Science and Technology & Innovation (2015)
4. Yang, Y.U., Liang, H.Q.: Research on the construction and application of flipped classroom teaching mode based on mobile learning platform. Education Modernization (2018)
5. Application of Flipped Classroom Teaching Mode to One of the Lectures of Automation for Students of the Training Program of Outstanding Talents for. (2017)
6. Zhang, F.: Research on the Application of Flipped Classroom Teaching Mode Based on Network in College Physical Education. J. Books Proceedings, 0
7. Sun, Q.X.: The Application of Flipped Classroom Mode in College English Teaching Based on MOOCs **10**(6), 4 (2020)

8. Zheng, L.: Application Research on "Flipped Classroom" Teaching Mode in Colleges and Universities (2016)
9. Li, C.: A study on the application of flipped classroom teaching mode in college english teaching. In: Proceedings of the 4th International Conference on Humanities Science, Management and Education Technology (HSMET 2019) (2019)
10. Feng, Y., et al.: Research on the Application of Flipped Classroom Teaching Mode in "Fruit and Vegetable Processing". Education Teaching Forum (2019)

Application of Fuzzy c-Means Clustering Algorithm in Consumer Psychology

Sun Shufen[(⊠)]

Shanghai Urban Construction Vocational College, No. 2080 Nanting Road, Fengxian District,
Shanghai 201415, China
rainheart0528@163.com

Abstract. In order to increase the sales share, mobile phone manufacturers must understand the needs of consumers. The traditional c-means analysis method is sensitive to distance, and the shortcomings of the traditional method can be overcome with the help of fuzzy control theory. In this paper, 200 college students are randomly selected to conduct a questionnaire survey on the six factors affecting the purchase of smart phones, and the data are analyzed by using the improved fuzzy c-means clustering. The results show that the function, appearance and brand of mobile phones have an impact on the purchase of mobile phones. The results are helpful for mobile phone manufacturers to understand users' consumption psychology and improve product competitiveness.

Keywords: Consumer psychology · Mobile phone · Fuzzy clustering · C mean

1 Introduction

As an independent subject, consumer psychology belongs to a branch of general psychology. It refers to the psychological activities that consumers implement, adjust and control their own consumption and purchase behavior according to their own consumption demand and consumption ability under the influence of the overall social economic level and consumption environment. Psychological activity is the reflection process of people's brain to objective things or external stimuli. Consumers' choices, preferences and consumption habits are dominated by psychological activities. This kind of psychological activity can usually be reflected in consumer behavior [1]. Sellers and designers also understand and master consumers' psychological status through observation, analysis and speculation, and meet consumers' psychological needs through a series of promotional activities or changing business methods. On the contrary, sellers and designers can also guide consumers' consumption psychology to a reasonable consumption mode and promote market prosperity in a reasonable and legal way [2].

With the rapid development of China's economy, people's living standards are getting higher and higher, and the use of mobile phones has become very popular. Users have more choices in choosing different brands, systems, styles and functions. However, due to a variety of choices, sales manufacturers are facing unprecedented pressure. How

M. A. Jan and F. Khan (Eds.): BigIoT-EDU 2022, LNICST 465, pp. 261–272, 2023.
https://doi.org/10.1007/978-3-031-23950-2_29

to stand out in the competition and strive for market share is particularly important. To solve these problems, this paper takes the popular touch-screen smart phone in the market as an example to study the user's consumption psychology, understand the user's needs, carry out cluster analysis, and find out the influencing factors of the user's product selection, so as to understand the reasons why they are unwilling to buy, and then make improvement. After improvement, stimulate the user's purchase intention and expand the sales scale of the company's products.

2 Related Work

2.1 Basic Concepts

Consumer psychology is an important branch of psychology. It studies the psychological phenomena and behavior laws of consumers in consumer activities. It is one of the main research fields of business psychology to study the behavior laws of consumers in purchasing and using goods and services.

Consumer psychology holds that any kind of consumer activity is the result of the joint influence of consumer psychology and consumer behavior. Consumer psychology refers to people's subjective thinking as consumers; Consumer behavior is observed from the perspective of market circulation. People's consumer activities are not general mechanical activities. It is a behavioral impulse at a certain time. This behavioral impulse has different changes under the influence of certain consumer environment and psychological factors. Generally speaking, people's consumption psychology can be divided into the following two kinds: first, it is dominated by people's physiological factors and belongs to the instinctive consumption psychology in the natural state; 2. Social consumption psychology caused by socio-economic and consumption environmental factors. These two consumer psychology are interdependent and influence each other [3]. As the basis of human survival and development, instinctive consumption psychology is the natural expression and reflection of people's psychological activities, while social consumption psychology is a psychological activity higher than instinctive consumption psychology on the premise of specific social, political, economic and cultural elements [4].

The research on consumer psychology can be traced back to psychology. As a very classic theoretical model, Maslow's hierarchy of needs theory is not only an important theory to explain personality, but also an important theory to explain motivation. It reflects the common law of human behavior and psychological activities to a certain extent. Psychologist Maslow divides human needs into five different levels: physiological needs, security needs, social needs, respect needs and self realization needs. (as shown in Fig. 1) the demand hierarchy theory is a theoretical system based on people's needs, exploring people's incentive mechanism and studying people's behavior. Its basic view is that people's needs continue to develop from low level to high level [5]. The demand hierarchy of most people in a country is directly related to the country's scientific and Technological Development and people's cultural quality. Generally speaking, people's needs will develop to a higher level after meeting one level [6].

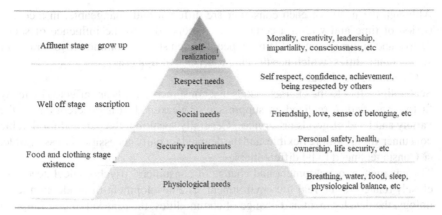

Fig. 1. Maslow's demand theory

2.2 Modern Consumer Demand Analysis

(1) Characteristics of consumer demand

Consumer needs mainly refers to a kind of psychological activity, which will strongly promote consumers to achieve their goals and meet their needs. It is the most common internal reason to promote consumers to carry out various consumption behaviors, It is a psychological tendency before consumption behavior "Need is the motivation and starting point of the purchase process. Without people's needs, all goods will lose their significance of existence. However, in the actual process, the performance of consumers' needs is very complex. It is affected by both consumers' own characteristics and various external factors [7]. Therefore, it is necessary to analyze the characteristics of consumers' needs before analyzing consumer demand OK, I understand. Its main features are as follows:

① Consumers need to show diversity

Due to the different income level, education level, occupation, personality, age, nationality and living habits of each consumer, they will naturally have a variety of hobbies and interests, so consumers' demand for goods and services is also very different. This difference is reflected in the diversity of consumer demand.

② Consumers need to be developmental

With the development of society, the psychological needs of consumers will continue to be intensified and promoted. One need will be met, and another demand will be generated. When the needs of the old generation are met, the new generation will have higher needs, and move forward again and again. The unlimited development of consumers' needs for goods interacts with the development of science and technology, which has become an important driving force for the development of human society. The development trend of consumption needs always develops from low-level to high-level, and from simple to complex.

③ Consumers need to be full of characteristics of the times

Although the needs of each consumer are different and changeable, in a certain period of time and within a certain social scope, due to the influence of social factors and environment at that time, people often show a common love for one or some commodities, which has the characteristics of that era.

④ Consumers need scalability

Scalability refers to the characteristics that consumers' needs are affected by many factors, satisfied or realized, or suppressed or weakened. It is different due to the variety and level of goods or services. Generally speaking, the demand for durable consumer goods is more flexible, and the demand for daily necessities is less flexible.

⑤ Consumers need to be differentiable

The emergence, development and change of consumers' psychological needs are closely related to the real life environment. The development of production technology, the development and change of commodities, the renewal of consumption concept, the change of social fashion, the change of working environment, the edification of culture and art, and the induction of packaging and advertising may change the needs of consumers.

(2) Emotional consumption needs

According to Maslow's hierarchy theory of human needs, according to its importance, human needs are divided into five kinds: physiological needs, security needs, belonging and love needs, self-esteem needs and self realization needs. They are interrelated and gradually arranged into a hierarchy from low to high. Then, on the basis of Maslow's hierarchy of needs theory, aldev, a professor at Yale University, further classified human needs into three categories: survival needs (physiological and security needs), relationship needs (social and respect needs), and personal growth needs (self-esteem and self realization needs). From these two sets of theories, we show that human needs are a process from low-level material needs to high-level spiritual needs. Only when all the needs are met in succession will there be the need for self realization at the highest level.

Western marketing theory divides consumer demand development into two stages:

The first stage is the era of quantitative consumption, which is due to the limitations and lack of social productivity, socio-economic conditions and material resources. In the early stage of entering the commodity economy, people's demand for consumer goods only stayed on the necessities of life. In this consumption period, social consumer goods only meet people's most basic survival needs and are in a low consumption state of survivability [8]. The quality of goods in this period is often ignored.

The second stage is the era of qualitative consumption. During this - period, people's income level and self-awareness have improved, and the corresponding consumption demand has also changed. Consumption should not only meet the needs of survival, but also meet the needs of life and self affirmation. Therefore, people gradually began to pay attention to the quality of consumption, not only at the material level, but also in the direction of high quality, diversification and differentiation. This stage belongs to the era of perceptual consumption. When people enter the information society, their pace of life is accelerating day by day. Consumers' demand for goods is more expressed as emotional satisfaction and desire, and pay attention to spiritual pleasure, personality realization and other demand tendencies. Therefore, we find that the transformation of consumer demand is consistent with the essence of human needs, which also rises from material needs to emotional needs.

2.3 Analysis of Consumers' Purchase Motivation

(1) Analysis on the characteristics of consumers' purchase motivation
In psychology, motivation refers to the psychological motivation that triggers and maintains individual behavior and leads to certain goals. Consumer motivation is generated on the basis of consumer needs. It is the direct cause and driving force to trigger consumer consumption behavior. Consumer motivation behaviorizes consumer needs. Usually, consumers choose and consume specific commodity types according to their own motivation [9]. The generation of consumers' purchase motivation is the result of the interaction of a series of complex factors and presents many characteristics. The analysis of modern consumers' purchase motivation needs to be based on the grasp of consumers' purchase motivation. The characteristics of its consumer motivation are:

① Conflict: because consumers will be exposed to a wide variety of goods in the selection process before purchase, it will produce two or more motives, which will cause psychological contradictions. Its concrete manifestation is that several contradictory consumption motives struggle with each other, and the result of the struggle will determine how to buy goods and what kind of goods to buy. In real life, the situation of motivation contradiction is very complex, including double tendency conflict, double avoidance conflict, avoidance conflict, multiple conflict and so on.

② Fuzziness: when consumers buy goods, they often have many different purchase motives. Some of these motives are clearly recognized by consumers, while others are potential consciousness that consumers do not feel. Whether they are aware or not, they are intertwined and jointly affect consumers' purchase behavior.

③ Induceability: in the process of selecting goods, consumers' original motivation may be transferred due to external stimulation and inducement. In other words, in the purchase process, consumption will be stimulated by various commodities and affected by the shopping environment, and its original motivation status can be changed.

(2) Emotional purchase motivation is the dominant motivation of modern consumption
Because purchase motivation is the direct driving force of consumption behavior. No one's actions happen for no reason, and any activities they engage in are caused by certain motives. Similarly, most of consumers' purchase behavior is the result of the joint action of multiple motives. Among them, the strongest and most stable motivation of consumers is the dominant motivation of purchase. Under the same other factors, the purchase behavior is consistent with the dominant motivation. Consumers' purchase motivation is complex, changeable and multi-level. In the research of consumer psychology, purchase motivation is divided into physiological purchase motivation and psychological purchase motivation.

① Physiological purchase motivation refers to the needs of consumers to maintain and continue life organisms
Students' purchase motivation. Physiological factors are the root of consumers' physiological purchase motivation. In order to continue their life, consumers must seek food, clothing and safety, be able to organize families and reproduce, as well as enhance their physique and intelligence. All these needs must be met through various commodities. The motivation to buy these commodities is based on physiological needs. With the development of society, modern people's physiological needs have been greatly met and began to pursue emotional satisfaction. Correspondingly, in the modern society, there are fewer and fewer Purchase Motives driven by purely physiological needs, Physiological purchase motivation is often mixed with other non physiological purchase motivation. The degree of mixing is generally closely related to the consumption level. The higher the consumption level, the higher the degree of mixing.

② Psychological purchase motivation refers to the purchase motivation caused by the change of consumers' psychological activities. People's psychological activities are divided into perceptual psychological activities and rational psychological activities. Consumers' psychological purchase motivation is also divided into perceptual purchase motivation and rational purchase motivation. Emotional purchase motivation can be divided into emotional motivation and emotional motivation due to the different degree of emotional stability. Emotional motivation is people's purchase motivation with impulse, improvisation and instability; The purchase motivation with relatively stable morality, taste and aesthetics is emotional motivation. Like people's psychological activities, emotional motivation and emotional motivation also have an interactive relationship. Emotional motivation opportunities are affected by emotional motivation, but more depend on people's rational consumption concept and consumption demand. Rational consumption motivation comes from the analysis and comparison of product quality, price, purpose, style and variety on the basis of consumption demand. Consumers with rational consumption motivation have certain requirements and standards for the price, service and practicability of goods [10]. This standard is based on the rational cognition of goods. Compared with emotional purchase motivation, rational purchase opportunity is more objective, practical and detailed. The price of the product will affect the type of consumers' purchase motivation. For example, the consumption of one yuan candy is easy to trigger emotional purchase motivation, and the consumption of 10000 yuan computer is more likely to trigger rational purchase motivation. Due to the different income of consumers, the purchase of the same commodity will also be different.

Generally speaking, with the continuous improvement of living standards and demand levels, compared with consumers' psychological needs and physiological needs, their psychological needs play a more important role in purchase motivation and purchase behavior. Psychological consumption motivation has gradually become the leading motivation of modern consumption, as shown in Fig. 2. The demand concept of consumers is not only to obtain more material products and products themselves, but also to consider the symbol of goods. In short, consumers pay more attention to the satisfaction of personality, spiritual pleasure, comfort and superiority through consumption [11]. Therefore, in store design, we should pay attention to the psychological feelings of consumers.

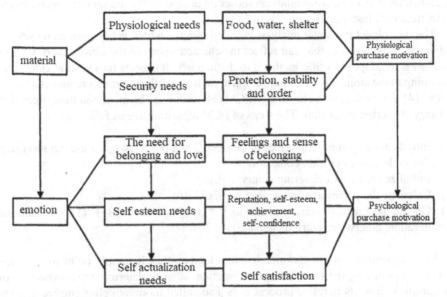

Fig. 2. Conversion between consumer needs and purchase motivation

3 Classification Algorithm

3.1 Overview of Fuzzy Clustering Algorithm

Traditional cluster analysis is a kind of hard partition, which strictly divides each object to be identified into a certain class, and only belongs to this class, with the nature of "either or". However, in real life, due to the complexity of things, the boundary between clustering objects is often not very clear, especially in humanities, such as social science, economic management, regional planning, pedagogy, etc. this ambiguity is more prominent in some disciplines here. Since the first mock exam of fuzzy set theory was established by Professor Chad in 1965, because of his success in dealing with the uncertainty and fuzziness of a wide range of problems, he has been more and more popular in dealing with the complexity and complexity of systems, and to some extent, to make up for the deficiency of classical mathematics and mathematical mathematics. L.A. Zadeh has been increasingly popular [12].

The first mock exam provides a powerful tool for analyzing soft partition, and brings new vitality to the classical clustering analysis. In 1973, dunnl first proposed the first fuzzy C-means (FCM) clustering algorithm, which is an extension of the hard c-means

(HCM) clustering algorithm proposed by ball and Hall. Because fuzzy clustering obtains the uncertainty degree of the sample belonging to each category, that is, it establishes the uncertainty description of the sample for the category, which can more objectively reflect the real world and describe the unclear objects, so as to make the actual clustering results more reasonable [13]. Especially when the classical cluster analysis meets the obstacle of coincidence, fuzzy cluster analysis shows its unique skills and quickly becomes the mainstream of cluster analysis.

The data object in cluster analysis is called sample, which is represented by several indicators or parameters that can reflect the characteristics of the object itself. Cluster analysis is to adopt scientific methods to distinguish all objects into several categories according to the similarity between samples, such as similarity in nature and character-istics [14]. Fuzzy c-means clustering (FCM) algorithm is the most common algorithm in fuzzy clustering algorithm. The steps of FCM algorithm are as follows:

(1) Initialization: given the number of clusters C and $0 \leq C \leq n$, set the iteration stop threshold ε, Set iteration counter B = 0;
(2) Initialize the fuzzy clustering center V (0);
(3) Calculate the partition membership matrix U (0);
(4) Update the fuzzy clustering center to V *, if $\mid V (b) - V (B + 1) \mid \leq \varepsilon$, End the iteration, otherwise return to step (2).

FCM algorithm obtains the membership degree of each sample point to the class center by optimizing the fuzzy objective function, so as to determine the ownership of the sample points. Its iterative process uses a so-called mountain climbing technology to find the optimal solution.

3.2 Fuzzy c-Means Algorithm

The traditional dynamic clustering method divides m samples into C categories respec-tively, so that the mean value of each sample and its category is the minimum sum of squares of error, i.e.

$$(t) \leq ce^{at} + \int_0^t e^{a(t-\tau)} mi(\tau) y\tau \tag{1}$$

Minimum, where m is the sample mean of class I, $y \in \tau$ Is all samples divided into class I. The method to minimize the result is the C-means method. In the C-means algorithm, there are many methods to calculate the discrimination between samples, such as calculating the similarity between two samples or the distance between samples. In this paper, the hard partition is changed into fuzzy partition, that is, fuzzy c-means method.

The iterative method is the fuzzy c-means algorithm. The specific steps of the algorithm are as follows:

① Set the number of clusters C and parameter B;
② Initialize each cluster center m;
③ Repeatedly calculate the membership function and update various clustering centers until the membership value of each sample is stable.

When the algorithm converges, each membership value is obtained, and finally the fuzzy clustering division is completed.

3.3 Improved Fuzzy c-Means Clustering Algorithm

Assuming that M is a fuzzy relation on universe u, if M can satisfy the conditions: m (a, b) = 1 and m (a, b) = m (B, a), then we call m a fuzzy similarity relation on u, and m (a, b) represents the similarity between elements a and B in U. When u includes many elements, i.e. u = {U1, U2,..., UN}, the fuzzy similarity relationship of M can be expressed as fuzzy matrix M = [mij] m × N, mij is the membership function. In the established fuzzy matrix, the elements on the diagonal are the similarity between themselves, so the value is 1 and meets mij = Mji. The matrix satisfying such conditions is called fuzzy similarity matrix.

For example, let one person give it to five strangers ($\mu 1$, $\mu 2$, $\mu 3$, $\mu 4$, $\mu 5$) The similarity degree between is scored, and the scoring results are as follows:

$$||\Delta x_{k+1}(t)|| \leq k_f \int_0^t ||\Delta x_{k+1}(t)||d\tau + m_1 \int_0^t ||\Delta u_k(\tau)||d\tau + m_2||x_d(t)|| + m_3||x_{k-1}(t)||$$

(2)

In the formula, the elements on the diagonal represent their similarity with themselves, so the value is 1. The larger the value of the element in the matrix, the higher the degree of similarity between two people. The smaller the value, the lower the degree of similarity.

4 Specific Case Analysis Based on Fuzzy Clustering

The factors affecting consumers' purchase psychology and behavior include internal conditions and external conditions. The internal conditions include consumers' psychological activity process, consumers' personality psychological characteristics, consumers' psychological activities in the purchase process and psychological factors affecting consumers' behavior; The external conditions include the influence of social environment on consumption psychology, the influence of consumer groups on consumption psychology, the influence of consumption situation on consumption psychology, the influence of commodity factors on consumption psychology, the influence of shopping environment on consumption psychology, and the influence of marketing communication on consumption psychology. Under the influence of these two conditions, in the general purchase process, people's psychological activities mostly go through three stages: cognitive process, emotional process and will process:

① Cognitive process: from the perspective of consumer psychology, consumers' overall first feeling initially obtained from factors such as commodity, store image design and internal design is the cognitive process, which is the premise of purchase behavior;

② Emotional process: on this basis, different customer groups will have unique experiences or attitudes towards the items sold by the store, forming an emotional process;

③ Will process: the behavior that consumers decide whether to consume is the will process.

Based on the open-ended questionnaire, a questionnaire on purchasing smart phones was compiled, and a random sampling survey was conducted on 200 students in normal college. Subjects were asked to understand the mobile phone functions that affect their purchase intention (μ 1), speed (μ 2), appearance (μ3), screen size (μ 4), price (μ 5), mobile phone brand (μ 6) And other 6 attributes, using the 10 level scoring method, the weight of 1–10 in turn indicates that they don't care very much - they care very much and other 10 different degrees, which are scored by the subjects. Fuzzy clustering method is used for classification, as shown in Fig. 3.

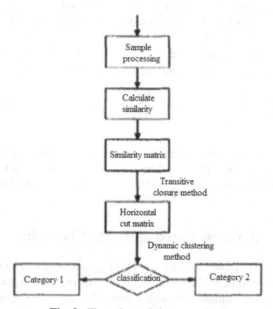

Fig. 3. Flow chart of cluster analysis

The mutual information method is used to calculate the chance that any two attributes affect the purchase intention at the same time, and the similarity is obtained.

Then take different thresholds λ Classify the samples, such as:

① λ = At 0.85{μ 1, μ 3} The classification shows that the appearance and function of mobile phones play a major role in consumers' purchase psychology.

② λ = At 0.82{μ 1, μ 3, μ 6} It belongs to the first category, and the rest belong to the first category, indicating that the function, appearance and brand of mobile phones play a major role in consumers' purchase psychology Through many experiments, choosing a reasonable threshold plays a very important role in analyzing the factors affecting consumers' purchase determination.

5 Conclusion

Maslow put forward the "five levels theory of human needs", he said: "generally, only after meeting the low-level needs, the high-level needs will gradually appear." Nowadays, with the improvement of living standards, people's requirements for their quality of life are gradually transitioning from simple life products to products that provide spiritual needs. When shopping, many consumers do not buy in a simple sense or just to meet their own living needs. They will also buy their own satisfactory products and services in combination with their own actual situation and consumption habits. This study classifies the samples through the improved fuzzy c-means theory, obtains the ideal classification effect, reflects the influence of some factors on consumers' purchase psychology, and provides a reference for enterprises in the production of products.

References

1. Wu, W., Yin, B.: Personalized recommendation algorithm based on consumer psychology of local group purchase e-commerce users. J. Intelli. Fuzzy Sys. **37**(5), 5973–5981 (2019)
2. Kühbauch, G.W.: A new algorithm for automatic Rumex obtusifolius detection in digital images using colour and texture features and the influence of image resolution. Precision Agriculture (2007)
3. Canellidis, V., Giannatsis, J., Dedoussis, V.: Genetic-algorithm-based multi-objective optimization of the build orientation in stereolithography. Int. J. Adv. Manuf. Technol. **50**(1–4), 419 (2010)
4. Luo, L., et al.: Curve fitting using a genetic algorithm for the X-ray fluorescence measurement of lead in bone. J. Radioanal. Nucl. Chem. **269**(2), 325–329 (2006)
5. Fischer, B., Modersitzki, J.: A Super Fast Registration Algorithm. Springer, Berlin Heidelberg (2001)
6. Millán, S., et al.: An Algorithm to Calculate the Expected Value of an Ongoing User Session. Springer Berlin Heidelberg (2005)
7. Kong, Y.T., et al.: Cricothyrotomy training increases adherence to the ASA difficult airway algorithm in a simulated crisis: a randomized controlled trial. Canadian Journal of Anesthesia/Journal canadien d'anesthésie (2015)
8. Pandian, P.P., et al.: Secondary population implementation in multi-objective evolutionary algorithm for scheduling of FMS. Int. J. Adv. Manuf. Technol. **57**(9–12), 1143 (2011)
9. Cinaroglu, S.: Comparison of Fuzzy C-Means and K-Means Clustering Performance: An Application on Household Budget Survey Data (2021)
10. Singh, S., Srivastava, S.: Kernel fuzzy C- means clustering with teaching learning based optimization algorithm (TLBO-KFCM). J. Intelli. Fuzzy Sys. **1**, 1–9 (2021)
11. Kuo, R.J., Lin, J.Y., Nguyen, T.: An application of sine cosine algorithm-based fuzzy possibilistic c-ordered means algorithm to cluster analysis. Soft. Comput. **25**(11), 1–16 (2021)

12. López-Oriona, N., et al.: Quantile-based fuzzy C-means clustering of multivariate time series: Robust techniques (2021)
13. Tokat, S., et al.: Fuzzy C-means clustering-based key performance indicator design for warehouse loading operations. J. King Saud Univ. Comp. Info. Sci. (2021)
14. Saxena, S., Kumari, N., Pattnaik, S.: Brain Tumour Segmentation in FLAIR MRI using sliding window texture feature extraction followed by fuzzy C-Means clustering. Int. J. Healthc. Info. Sys. Info. (IJHISI), 16 (2021)

Application of Game Equilibrium Theory and Algorithm in Modern Talent Training Model

Kaijie Kang[✉]

Lanzhou Vocational University of Resources and Environment, Lanzhou 730070, Gansu, China
kang7585@126.com

Abstract. With the advent of the information society in the 21st century, colleges and universities, as the training base of various senior talents required by the society, are facing new challenges and development opportunities, and shoulder the important task of how to cultivate comprehensive talents with all-round quality to meet the needs of the information society. To accomplish this historical mission, colleges and universities are required to constantly update and change their ideas in educational consciousness, teaching content, educational technology means and training objectives in order to adapt to the rapid development of information society. Provide scientific and quantitative methods for the training mode of talents. Taking employment as the guidance, this paper analyzes the game between talent training and social demand, and establishes the game model of talent training mode for the well-off group; Finally, the solution algorithm of the model is developed by using the equilibrium theory of game theory. Under the limited conditions of school training and social needs, food and clothing employees will randomly choose the training mode of the minimum value of learning consumption function; The game mode of P*, which ensures the lowest level of income for both sides of the well-off society. Through the example of the algorithm and the analysis of the results of the game model, it shows that the model and the solution algorithm are scientific, feasible and effective, which can be used as a reference for the cultivation of all kinds of talents.

Keywords: Game theory · Personnel training · Nash equilibrium

1 Introduction

In recent years, through continuous development and reform, higher education has greatly improved in quality and scale, and has made great contributions to the rapid, healthy and sustainable development of China's economy and society. However, at present, China is in a period of rapid development, social and economic development and transformation, new opportunities and challenges emerge one after another, and the international situation is also changing. As the cradle of talent training, higher education is facing new problems and challenges with each passing day. Under the new situation, China's international status is gradually improving externally, and China's interaction and exchanges with other countries in the world are more frequent [1]. It is urgent for

© ICST Institute for Computer Sciences, Social Informatics and Telecommunications Engineering 2023
Published by Springer Nature Switzerland AG 2023. All Rights Reserved
M. A. Jan and F. Khan (Eds.): BigIoT-EDU 2022, LNICST 465, pp. 273–285, 2023.
https://doi.org/10.1007/978-3-031-23950-2_30

the talents trained by colleges and universities to have international and open thinking: internally, the resource consuming economic development mode that has driven China's rapid economic growth in the past three decades is no longer applicable, Human capital will become the supporting point of China's economic development in the future. There is an urgent need for talents trained in Colleges and universities to have innovative thinking and creative ability; At the same time, the sustainable development of our society and the construction of spiritual civilization also urgently need the talents trained by colleges and universities to have high quality and good moral and civilization consciousness.

The key to creating an innovative country is to have innovative talents. Only by taking innovative talents as intellectual support and talent guarantee can we achieve the strategic goal of creating an innovative country. The cultivation of innovative talents has a long history both in theory and practice, and developed countries have made remarkable achievements in this regard [2]. It has really become an ideological trend in China since the end of the 20th century. It can be said that the cultivation of innovative talents in Colleges and universities is a new topic. The research on the cultivation of innovative talents involves multi-disciplinary knowledge. In addition to pedagogy, it also needs the theoretical support of psychology, management and other disciplines. In recent years, although some colleges and universities in China have made different attempts in the theoretical and practical circles of innovative education, their theoretical research is still quite weak, there is no unified theoretical system, and the practice is not very systematic. Therefore, taking the cultivation of innovative talents as the research topic has important theoretical significance and practical value. Everything is composed of elements. The state of elements is the influencing factor, and so is the cultivation of innovative talents.

Higher education shoulders the important mission of cultivating high-quality professionals and top-notch innovative talents. Improving the quality of talent training in Colleges and universities is not only the need of the development law of higher education itself, but also the need of running higher education to the satisfaction of the people and improving students' employability and entrepreneurial ability, but also the need of building an innovative country and building a socialist harmonious society [3]. With the continuous reform of the teaching system in Colleges and universities, the strategic core of the development of colleges and universities is more people-oriented and pays more attention to the all-round cultivation of students. The evaluation of students' training quality can help university managers find out the gap between the actual education situation and the educational objectives, and find the direction of teaching reform and the development of colleges and universities.

With the improvement of China's comprehensive national strength, the requirements of society for talents are also advancing day by day. It is not only required that the talents trained by colleges and universities have solid professional basic knowledge, but also hoped that the people trained by colleges and universities can have various abilities, such as good innovation ability and communication ability. Through the evaluation of various abilities of talents, the goal of all-round development can be established, Promote the multi-dimensional development of college students and improve the overall quality.

In order to meet the needs of the society and the changes of the employment market, more and more colleges and universities have diversified the talent training mode, that is, innovative, applied and ordinary training coexist. Unfortunately, most of these reforms and explorations are based on social statistical data and qualitative research, and there are no quantitative results. From a quantitative point of view, guided by employment and according to the social demand for innovative, applied and ordinary talents, this paper gives the game analysis of talent training in Colleges and universities, establishes the game model of well-off employment training, and obtains the Nash equilibrium solution of the model through the algorithm[4]. I hope it can provide some reasonable suggestions and useful reference for colleges and universities and college students.

2 Related Work

2.1 Modern Talent Training

There have been many literatures on the research of talent training mode in Colleges and universities. Up to the present stage, the talent training mode in Colleges and universities has attracted extensive attention from the educational and academic circles. Hundreds of papers with the title of "talent training mode" have been published in various academic journals, and many research works on talent training mode have also been published. Of course, scholars have many different understandings on the connotation of talent training mode. Analyzing and studying the connotation of these definitions is the basis of studying and optimizing the talent training mode in Colleges and universities [5]. This paper summarizes the definition of talent training mode in chronological order.

As society develops to different stages, the mode of talent training is changing, and our definition of the concept of "talent training mode" is also different. In 1994, the reform plan of teaching content and curriculum system of higher education for the 21st century proposed that the talent training mode is the talent quality and training mode of the future society. In 1998, "opinions on deepening educational reform and cultivating high-quality talents to meet the needs of the 21st century", the Ministry of education defined "talent training mode" as: students build the structure of knowledge, ability and quality under the cultivation of schools, and the way to realize this structure ". After entering the 21st century, Zhou Yuanqing, Vice Minister of the Ministry of education, expressed the talent training mode as: "it is the talent training goal, training specification and training mode". The so-called talent training mode is actually the sum of the process of implementing talent education through certain teaching content and management system under the guidance of educational thought and educational theory, under the guidance of talent training objectives and talent training specifications.

Driven by the reform of teaching content and curriculum system, the reform of talent training mode has ushered in an upsurge [6]. Therefore, the educational circles gradually regard the theoretical research of talent training mode as the focus. In 1994, Liu Junming and others defined the concept of talent training mode for the first time in their book on the essentials of university education environment, and pointed out that "talent training mode is a teaching and education mode conceived or selected to achieve a certain training goal under the conditions of certain software such as teaching staff and hardware such as teaching infrastructure". It is considered that the elements involved in the talent training model include "educational approaches, teaching means, curriculum system, teaching methods, teaching organization forms and so on". In order to implement the training objectives, we must grasp the core elements of talent training. The curriculum system is the core of talent training, and other elements are to make the curriculum system scientific and effective [7].

Talent training mode refers to the training content and requirements, training specifications, training school system and methods.

Talent training mode refers to the organization of many elements of training objectives, education system, training plan and teaching process under the guidance of certain educational thought.

Talent training mode refers to a certain standard operation mode and composition style of the training process under the guidance of certain educational theory and educational thought and under the traction of training objectives and training specifications.

The essence of talent training mode lies in talent training objectives, training specifications and basic training methods. It is the unity of educational concept and education process, and the unity of training objectives and operating procedures. It has many constituent elements, and the main constituent elements are educational purpose, educational content and educational methods.

The talent training mode of colleges and universities refers to a certain standard construction style and operation mode of the training process adopted to achieve the training objectives under the guidance of certain educational ideas and educational theories.

The talent training mode in Colleges and universities is the product of the organic combination of educational concepts, training objectives, training specifications and training methods. It involves many educational and teaching links, such as specialty setting, curriculum design, teaching management and quality monitoring.

2.2 Analysis on Talent Training and Social Demand in Colleges and Universities

With the rapid development of science and technology, China, as the largest developing country in the world, in order to meet the needs of the development of socialist market economy and various opportunities and challenges after China's accession to the WTO We must give priority to accelerating scientific and technological progress and innovation in order to maintain sustained and healthy economic and social development, which is an important decision in line with the current law of economic and social development [8].

The decision of the CPC Central Committee and the State Council on deepening educational reform and comprehensively promoting quality education points out that quality education should focus on cultivating students' innovative spirit and practical ability. The process of implementing quality education It is the process of constantly innovating educational concepts and models and cultivating innovative talents. Now we must be soberly aware that the social talent competition is not only the competition of talent quantity and structure. And it is the competition of talent's innovative spirit and creative ability. It is the competition of innovative talents. Although China has made rapid development in the fields of economy, social development, science and technology since the reform and opening up However, there are still some contradictions and problems to be solved in many fields. The development of society is inseparable from the cultivation of talents. College education must actively adjust the talent training mode to meet the requirements of social development [9]. The talents cultivated in

Colleges and universities should not only master basic scientific knowledge, but also have high-quality talents with all-round development such as good character, interpersonal communication ability, social adaptability and independent innovation ability. Talent training in Colleges and universities must be guided by social needs and guided by the scientific outlook on development in the process of talent training. Correctly grasp the basic law of the development of talent education in Colleges and universities, respond to the practical needs of economic and social development, and under the environment of market economy. Every college student is constantly facing employment, layoffs and job changes. Therefore, it is urgent to cultivate college students' adaptability, learning ability, ability to unite and cooperate with others, ability to face setbacks and ability to grasp opportunities. College talent training urgently needs to adjust the training mode according to social needs.

In recent years, the number of college graduates in China has increased rapidly. The employment problem of college students has increasingly aroused widespread concern in the society. Influenced by traditional ideas for a long time, China's higher education adopts the training mode of professional talent education in the talent training mode of colleges and universities, pays attention to the division of disciplines, systematically teaches professional knowledge, and emphasizes the use of discipline education to train talents, resulting in the dislocation between talent training in many colleges and universities and social needs:

(1) The structure of talent training specialty and social demand in Colleges and universities is misplaced. With the progress of science and technology, the social industrial structure is constantly adjusted. The social demand for college graduates is also changing, but the talent training in Colleges and universities is difficult to respond immediately to the social demand [10]. The professional construction of colleges and universities needs to be adjusted according to the social needs for a long time. The existing professional structure of colleges and universities can not be coordinated with the social industrial structure and its adjustment and change in time. Failed to create a mechanism to actively adjust the specialty setting of colleges and universities according to social needs The specialty of talent training in Colleges and universities can not be adjusted according to the needs of the social market, and the existing specialty division in Colleges and universities is too detailed. The trained talents have relatively poor social adaptability. Compared with social needs, the specialty setting lags behind.

(2) The imbalance between talent training in Colleges and universities and social demand structure. One of the typical manifestations of the imbalance between the results of talent training in Colleges and universities and social demand is that it is difficult for college graduates to obtain employment, and many college graduates are unemployed. However, there is a shortage of talents in many sectors of society. It is difficult to recruit qualified talents. First, it is because of the slowdown of global economic growth. The relative demand for jobs is insufficient, and many enterprises have correspondingly reduced some jobs; Second, some college students have high goals but low hands. Employment expectations are high, especially for the environment, work intensity and treatment of employment and work units. Some college

students do not go to non-state-owned enterprises, foreign enterprises and government departments, but their demand for talents is limited. There is a shortage of talents in relatively backward areas in the central and western regions, and no one can use them; Third, the talent training in Colleges and universities can not effectively meet the market demand. With the rapid development of science and technology and the corresponding adjustment of industrial structure, some popular majors in Colleges and universities used to be. Including English, computer, accounting and other majors, the number of unemployed graduates is the largest; Fourth, many colleges and universities are now keen to build comprehensive universities and do not fully consider the construction characteristics of the University, resulting in repeated construction of majors, waste of materials and training of too many talents of the same category. As a result, the supply of talents exceeds the demand, while some so-called unpopular majors gradually disappear; Fifth, the cultivation of talents in Colleges and universities does not pay enough attention to the comprehensive quality and ability of college students. As a result, college students can not adapt to the changes of market demand after graduation. For example, the society needs comprehensive talents who understand technology, have experience and have management ability, but few colleges and universities can cultivate talents who can meet the needs of the society.

(3) The talent training mechanism of colleges and universities is misplaced with social needs. At present, there is a phenomenon of disconnection and dislocation between the talent training mechanism of colleges and universities and the social needs. It is common that the quality and ability of college graduates do not meet the requirements of most enterprises. The specialty setting, enrollment and talent training methods of colleges and universities are mainly implemented according to the provisions of the education management department, which does not proceed from the actual situation of social development and talent demand, resulting in unreasonable specialty setting, In addition, the curriculum is also divorced from reality, which seriously despises the cultivation of College Students' social practice ability. Many practical courses are mere formality and have not been seriously implemented according to the curriculum training objectives; In the process of talent training in some colleges and universities, too much emphasis is placed on meeting social needs. When formulating the training plan, we should pay attention to vocational training for college students, put skill training in the first place and train students as working tools, ignoring other qualities that college students must have as social people. Students are only processed as products. The students cultivated have poor comprehensive quality and lack creativity, which is difficult to meet the needs of the society.

3 Application of Game Equilibrium Theory and Algorithm in Modern Talent Training

3.1 Summary of Game Theory

Game theory, English name game theory, is to study the decision-making when the behavior of decision-makers interact directly and the equilibrium of this kind of decision-making. In other words, when a subject, such as the choice of a person or an enterprise, is affected by the choice of others (other enterprises), and in turn affects the decision-making and equilibrium of others (other enterprises). So in this sense, game theory is also called "game theory". It is a theory that uses rigorous mathematical models to solve the conflict of interests in reality. Because conflict, cooperation, competition and other behaviors are common phenomena in reality, Bo Ben theory can be applied in many fields, such as military field, economic field, political diplomacy and so on. The difference between game theory and conventional optimal decision-making theory lies in: the participants in game theory have conflicts of interests; Participants should make their own optimization decisions and try to maximize their personal interests; There is interaction between everyone's decision and others, that is, others' decision will affect someone, and someone's decision will also affect others; In Bo Zi theory, it is generally assumed that the individuals involved in decision-making are "rational", so as to carry out rational logical thinking. To specify or define a game, it is necessary to set the following contents:

(1) Participants in the game. That is, in the defined research, which individuals or organizations make independent decisions and bear the results independently. For us, organizations should make unified decisions, take unified actions and bear the results in the game. No matter how large an organization is, even one country or even the United Nations composed of many countries can be a participant in the research.

(2) Game information. Information is very important for the meaning and role of game participants. The amount of information will directly affect the accuracy of decision-making, which is related to the success or failure of the whole game. Experienced bobun participants collect as much game information as possible, so as to take the initiative in making decisions.

(3) A collection of all behaviors or strategies that a player can choose. That is to specify the methods, practices or the level and quantity of economic activities that each game player can choose when making decisions (at the same time or successively, one or more times). In different games, the number of strategies or behaviors that can be selected by the players is very different. Even in the same game, the optional strategies or behaviors of different players are often different, sometimes there are only a limited number or even one, and sometimes there may be many or even infinite kinds.

(4) The order of the game. In various decision-making activities in reality, when there are multiple independent decision-makers to make decisions, sometimes these penetrating parties must make choices at the same time, because this can ensure fairness and rationality. Many times, the decision-making of each game party must be

divided in order, and in some games, each game party has to make more than one decision-making choice, which is inevitable to have an order problem. Therefore, the order of a game must be specified. Different orders must be different, even if other aspects are the same.

(5) The benefits of the game side. Corresponding to each group of possible decision-making choices of each blogger, there is a result representing the gains and losses of each player under the strategy combination. Since we can only judge and analyze the result of boben by comparing the quantity, the result of the game we study must be quantity itself or at least can be quantified as quantity The decision-making problem whose result cannot be quantified as quantity cannot be studied in game theory. We call the quantitative values of various possible results in boben as the benefits of each player in the game under the corresponding circumstances. Stipulate that a game must stipulate the benefits. Income, namely income, profit, loss, quantitative utility, social utility and economic welfare, can be positive or negative. It is worth noting that although the benefits of each game party under various circumstances exist objectively, this does not mean that all game parties fully understand the benefits of each party. In many games, there are always situations in which some game parties cannot understand the benefits of other Bo Ben parties.

In the game g = {S1,..., Sn; U1,..., UN}, for example, in a strategy combination (S1,..., Sn) composed of one strategy of each player in each game, the strategy Si of player I in any game is the best strategy for the strategy combination of other players (S1,..., SI − 1, Si, Si + 1,..., Sn)

$$U_i(S_1, ..., S_{i-1}, S_i, S_{i+1}, ...S_n) \geq U_i(S_1, ..., S_{i-1}, S_{ij}, S_{i+1}, ...S_n) \tag{1}$$

3.2 Game Model of Employment Oriented College Students' Training Model

At present, the high level of employment of college students coexists with the phenomenon of employment difficulties. Different graduates have different requirements, so they can be divided into food and clothing type and well-off type. For graduates who have enough to eat and wear, because they only need to have a job, they usually choose the training mode with the least learning consumption at random regardless of income; For well-off graduates, this paper will establish a game model for college students to choose the training mode under the limitation of the above game results between the cultivation of college talents and social needs.

Now establish a game model with the level of social effort and the probability of students' choice of training mode as the decision variables.

(1) There are two people in the model, college students and society;
(2) The strategy of "college students" in the game is three-dimensional vector (B, P2, 1-p1-p2), and the strategy set is [0,1] × [0,1] × [0,1], the strategy of the player's "society" is a one-dimensional vector E, and the strategy set is [0,1];
(3) The benefit function of "society" in the bureau is

$$f(p_1, p_2, e) = \alpha(e)(\sum_{i=1}^{3} U_i y_i^*) - r(p_1, p_2, e) \tag{2}$$

4   How to Solve the Dislocation Between Talent Training in Colleges and Universities and Social Needs

How to meet the needs of society is a systematic project. It involves the government, universities and society. Positive and effective measures should be taken to reduce the dislocation between talent training in Colleges and universities and social needs. We should pay attention to the all-round and whole process training and education of students in school, not only to the content of classroom teaching. Moreover, we should pay attention to the overall planning and coordination of practical teaching links and extracurricular educational activities, pay more attention to the cultivation of students' interpersonal skills and other aspects, and pay attention to the improvement of students' comprehensive quality and ability.

Pay attention to the changes of the external environment of colleges and universities. The influence of social consumption hot spots and policy orientation on talent training the change of social demand has a direct impact on the employment of college graduates. The rise and fall of the industry directly determines the survival of majors in Colleges and universities. College education decision-makers must fully consider social changes and formulate education policies. In today's society, we are facing fierce international competition This competition has penetrated into the fields of economy, society, science and technology, culture, national defense and other aspects, which is closely related to our life. The essence of these competitions is the competition for talents. We should put the cultivation of talents in Colleges and universities in an important strategic position Colleges and universities should shoulder the important task of training and transporting excellent talents with international competitiveness to the country. Social development is inseparable from innovation The cultivation of talents in Colleges and universities should meet the needs of social development, focus on the cultivation of innovative talents, and not only pay attention to the learning of talents' knowledge. More attention should be paid to the cultivation of talents' personality. The cultivation of talents in Colleges and universities should cultivate more new talents with innovative consciousness, innovative thinking, innovative ability and innovative personality In this way, we can cultivate talents who can meet the needs of rapid social development.

Colleges and universities should establish a new talent training model to meet social needs and meet people's own development is the fundamental goal of talent training in Colleges and universities in China. It is also the fundamental driving force for the reform of talent training mode in Colleges and universities in China. Compared with the international community, China attaches too much importance to academic qualifications, takes academic qualifications as the value orientation of education, and ignores the cultivation of talent ability. It is necessary to change the traditional colleges and universities, which attach importance to enrollment, neglect training, ignore social needs and students' Employment Tendency, from the perspective of lifelong education Education is only one stage of learning Ability is an important standard to measure a person's lifelong learning achievement, and the cultivation of talent ability in Colleges and universities is the ultimate goal of cultivating talents in Colleges and universities. Therefore, colleges and universities should boldly reform the current teaching mode and education and teaching concept. Use new educational means to optimize the combination of educational resources, effectively combine discipline system knowledge, talent science, psychology, practical operation and other links, help students establish innovative consciousness, creative thinking and innovative ability, and cultivate excellent talents with comprehensive ability who can meet the needs of society.

From the evolution and development process of modern university concept, we can see that the core content of modern university concept is to cultivate complete people with broad and profound knowledge, good personal cultivation and the ability to serve the society. Using this concept to guide our educational practice, we must correctly deal with the following relations when designing the talent training mode of modern universities.

(1) "General knowledge" and "specialty" go hand in hand

Newman pointed out in the preface of his ideal of University: "university is a place to impart universal knowledge." "This training process is called liberal education. This kind of education is not for a specific or accidental purpose, not for a specific occupation or profession, nor for research or science, but for intelligence. It is to enable intelligence to perceive its appropriate object, and for the highest culture." He added: "University training is a means to achieve a great and ordinary purpose. It aims to improve the ideological style of the society, improve the intellectual cultivation of the public, purify the national interest, provide real principles for the enthusiasm of the public, provide precise goals for the aspirations of the public, expand the ideological content of the times, keep this thought in a sober state, promote the application of political power and It's the refinement of personal life. "The above discussion points out the purpose of university education, with special emphasis on the importance of university general education.

In today's society, science and technology are developing rapidly. The situation that everyone is only fixed in a certain field or major for life is gradually broken. Therefore, we must improve the basic quality and career conversion ability of future talents in order to make them invincible under complex and rapidly changing working conditions. At the same time, with the rapid development of science and technology, there has been a trend of both high differentiation and high integration among disciplines, dominated by integration and integration. On the one hand, some existing and relatively independent basic disciplines are forming a huge system including many branch disciplines, with more and more specialized knowledge and more detailed categories; On the other hand, the trend of scientific integration is becoming more and more obvious. Many disciplines have lost their original strict boundaries. The growth points of new science and technology, major breakthroughs in theory and major inventions in technology are increasingly emerging among different disciplines, in the infiltration and transfer between different disciplines, and the organic relationship between disciplines is becoming stronger and stronger. Not only has the connection between science and engineering, humanities and Social Sciences strengthened in their own fields, but also the penetration and combination between natural sciences, humanities and social sciences are becoming closer and closer. More and more subjects can be solved only when natural sciences, humanities and Social Sciences work together. The new century puts forward higher requirements for talents. It requires talents in modern society not only to be proficient in the knowledge of a specific discipline, but also to have a deep understanding of natural science, humanities and social sciences. Only in this way can such talents better adapt to and serve the society. Strengthening general education does not require students to master all fields of human knowledge. The essence of general knowledge lies in the emphasis on "knowledge" and "communication", that is, the universality of knowledge and wisdom, and the incoming wisdom and its control over human wisdom. Today, people attach importance to making one's higher education reach a certain degree of unity, obtain a unified world outlook and form a rational habit. Therefore, general education should not only guide students to receive good professional knowledge training, but also make them have intellectual skills and good thinking habits. As shown in Fig. 1.

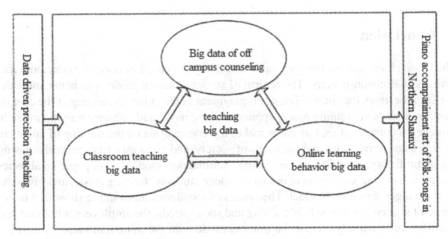

Fig. 1. Big data talent training mode

(2) Pay equal attention to knowledge, ability and quality

In the 21st century, science and technology are advancing by leaps and bounds, and the structure and content of knowledge are changing with each passing day. The information revolution and the development of information technology will further expand people's creativity; The development of life science and bioengineering technology has brought new gospel to human beings to control themselves and improve their health level and quality of life; The development of nano science and technology will bring the revolution of materials and manufacturing industry; Major changes and breakthroughs will be made in natural sciences such as new energy, new resources and new materials. Therefore, talents in the new century must adapt to the competition and cooperation of economic globalization and international science and technology, and pay equal attention to knowledge, ability and quality.

Talents in the new century should have a wide range of knowledge and a solid foundation. They must have a new knowledge structure, master new learning and scientific working methods, and grasp the frontier of scientific and Technological

Development and the constantly updated social needs. In line with this, we must change educational ideas, renew educational concepts, promote educational reform, strive to liberate from traditional educational concepts, re understand the functions, missions and roles of future universities, actively adapt to the requirements of economic, social, scientific and technological development, adjust professional structure, and reform teaching contents and Curriculum system, We should reform educational methods and means, change the past tendency of too narrow professional scope, too many course hours and too heavy burden, broaden professional orientation and enhance adaptability. We should change the old concept that teachers impart knowledge one way, students learn passively, and take the test score as the only standard to measure the quality of education, develop people's wisdom, learn scientific knowledge, cultivate scientific spirit and master scientific methods.

5 Conclusion

The research on student training mode has always been a hot issue for educators and University decision-makers. The reform of student training mode is to better meet the needs of the times for talents. Taking employment as the guidance, aiming at the coexistence of innovative training mode, applied training mode and ordinary training mode in Colleges and universities, this paper makes a game analysis on the training of talents in Colleges and universities and the needs of society, and gives quantitative results. Using the game theory, equilibrium theory and optimization method, this paper establishes the game model of employment oriented college students' training mode, and gives the solution algorithm of the model. The results of the algorithm example show that under the limited conditions of school training and social needs, the employees with food and clothing will randomly choose the training mode with the minimum value of learning consumption function; The choice of training mode for well-off workers and the level of social efforts have reached a balance at the point, which changes with different values.

Acknowledgements. 1. Research project of Lanzhou Vocational And Technical University of Resources and Environment: "Research on Supply Chain Financial Business Risk Control and Talent Training Practice of Logistics Enterprises in Lanzhou New Area" (Topic No.: Y2021D-02).

2. University Innovation Fund Project of Education Department of Gansu Province "Lanzhou Noodle Shop" International Talent Promotion Project Based on the background of "Symphony Silk Road" (Topic No.: 2020B-317).

References

1. Zhang, Q.: Application of game theory non-cooperative equilibrium method in construction project management informationizatio. J. Intell. Fuzzy Syst. **9**, 1–11 (2021)
2. Fakhari-Kisomi, B., Erden, L., Ebner, A.D., Ritter, J.A.: Equilibrium theory analysis of pressure equalization steps in pressure swing adsorption. Ind. Eng. Chem. Res. **60**(27), 9928–9939 (2021)
3. Sarkar, S., Un, I.W., Sivan, Y., Dubi, Y.: Theory of non-equilibrium hot carriers in direct band-gap semiconductors under continuous illumination. New J. Phys. **24**, 053008 (2022)

4. Lalli, L.: A Criticism of Hayek's General Equilibrium Theory (2021)
5. Vakulchyk, I., Kovalev, V.M., Savenko, I.G.: Nonequilibrium theory of the photoinduced valley Hall effect. Phys. Rev. B **103**, 035434 (2021)
6. Nukpezah, J.A.: Punctuated equilibrium theory and enhancement of local government investment pool innovation. Int. J. Public Sect. Perform. Manage. **7**(2), 217 (2021)
7. Gao, J., AdjeiArthur, B., Sifah, E.B., Xia, H., Xia, Q.: Supply chain equilibrium on a game theory-incentivized blockchain network. J. Ind. Inform. Integr. **26**, 100288 (2021)
8. Saydaliev, H.B., Urazova, A., Tolybay, B.: Time inconsistency, inflation expectation and economic growth: application of game theory. Adv. Interdisc. Sci. **1**, 1–14 (2021)
9. Jain, N., Mittal, S.: Bayesian nash equilibrium based gaming model for eco-safe driving. J. King Saud Univ. – Comput. Inform. Sci. **34**, 7482–7493 (2022)
10. Gomes, G.D.O., Bolmont, E., Blanco-Cuaresma, S.: On the influence of equilibrium tides on transit-timing variations of close-in super-Earths. I. Application to single-planet systems and the case of K2–265 b. Planets Planet. Syst. **651**, A23 (2021)

Application of ID3 Algorithm in College Students' Mental Health Education

Jie Hou[⊠]

College of General Aviation, Jingchu University of Technology, Jingmen 448000, China
houjie8445@163.com

Abstract. This paper studies the application of ID3 algorithm in college students' mental health education. ID3 algorithm is a classical decision tree data mining algorithm for data classification and analysis, which is widely used. College Students' mental health and school mental health education have once again become a hot spot in the society. In order to make the mental health education in Colleges and universities embark on the road of healthy development, the first and basic thing is to have a clear understanding of the existing model of mental health education in Colleges and universities, and establish a new model of mental health education suitable for yourself on this basis. In this way, it is conducive to the practical and effective development of all aspects of mental health education. The ID3 algorithm is applied to the evaluation system of College Students' mental health education. By establishing the decision tree model of the attribute of the teaching quality of mental health education, the mental health education is classified according to the teaching quality, and the incentive effect is formed through affirmation or negation, so as to promote the improvement of the teaching quality of mental health education and the development of education and teaching.

Keywords: ID3 algorithm · Mental health education · Data processing

1 Introduction

Colleges and universities undertake many functions such as scientific research, talent education and training, cultural communication and exchange. It is an important foundation and guarantee for social development. The occupation of mental health in Colleges and universities has the characteristics of comprehensiveness, creativity and competitiveness. Therefore, how to make full use of the database Data mining and other technologies provide more effective support for the evaluation and management of mental health teaching quality, which has important theoretical research and application value.

It is necessary for college students to take the course of mental health. First of all, as college students, we are just coming of age. Although the appearance of college students looks very mature, in fact, their hearts have not reached the appearance of maturity. As the saying goes: you just look mature. Then, the university is equivalent to a small society. College students who have just entered the society may not adapt to the university life that is inconsistent with the learning and life mode of junior and senior high school

M. A. Jan and F. Khan (Eds.): BigIoT-EDU 2022, LNICST 465, pp. 286–297, 2023.
https://doi.org/10.1007/978-3-031-23950-2_31

[1]. The university is not a place that only tells you about your academic achievements, but a place that allows you to develop comprehensively. In high school, as long as you study hard and get good grades, you can get the likes of teachers and classmates and get scholarships, but not in college. Therefore, some students can't adapt to the rhythm and mode of college life after entering the University for several months. Secondly, in many key universities, every year, more or less, students end their precious lives because they are too stressed to find someone to talk to (they are likely to suffer from depression). In fact, this is the psychological pressure is too great, leading to their psychology began to become unhealthy. And now the psychological pressure of college students comes from all aspects, so now many universities hold psychological drama competitions every year in order to make students strengthen their awareness of mental health.

In fact, mental health and physical health are equally important to people. Physical health, mental health is not healthy, sooner or later will be stuffy out of the disease, but mental health is beneficial to physical health (mainly good mentality).

Strengthening college students' mental health education is not only an important way to improve college students' psychological quality, promote their healthy growth and cultivate all-round socialist builders and successors, but also one of the important tasks to strengthen and improve college students' Ideological and political education. As a college student, we should understand the meaning and standards of mental health, study the characteristics and influencing factors of College Students' mental development, clarify the theories and principles of College Students' mental health, and grasp the materials and methods of College Students' mental health education [2]. People with mental health should have relatively correct cognition, good emotions, strong will and healthy personality psychology.

When dealing with the new environment, there will be all kinds of emotions, such as irritability, depression, depression, etc. when dealing with problems that cannot be solved by yourself, don't bear alone, let alone dig into the horns, be enterprising, take the initiative to adjust your psychology and understand how to adapt to the environment; We should correctly deal with setbacks and hardships in life; We should learn to change the way of learning, make learning simple and pleasant, and then determine a realistic goal; Know what you know and know what you don't know. Stop without knowing, and act with knowing. We should learn to understand everything in reality from the heart, and be at ease once, so as to make ourselves have strong adaptability.

As early as the late 1970s and early 1980s, machine learning researcher J. Ross Quinlan developed the decision tree algorithm (iterative dichotomy). It can be used as a classification algorithm in the form of rule-free induction or prediction tree. Among many classification methods in the field of data mining, decision tree classification method has been welcomed for its advantages of high speed, high precision, intuitive and easy to understand and simple generation mode.

This paper applies the decision tree algorithm to the evaluation system of mental health teaching quality in Colleges and universities, constructs the decision tree of related attributes of mental health teaching quality, classifies mental health according to the level of teaching quality, and forms an incentive effect through affirmation or negation, so as to promote the improvement of mental health teaching quality and the development of education and teaching.

2 Related Work

2.1 ID3 Algorithm Principle

Decision tree is a machine learning model, which is very intuitive and easy to understand, and is closely combined with data structure. Our learning threshold is also very low, which is much simpler than those models that are prone to a pile of formulas.

In fact, we often use decision trees in our lives, but we don't find them ourselves. The essence of decision tree is a bunch of if else combinations. For example, we go to a small stall to buy watermelon. How do the fruit vendors do it? Pick up the watermelon, roll it around, take a look, and then stretch out your hand to pat it. You will know whether the watermelon is sweet or not. We remove the factors related to these actions and extract the core essence [3]. Basically, there are three:

1. The color on the surface of watermelon is often sweet if it is bright The sound of watermelon beating is crisp and often sweet. 3 Whether there are melons and vines in watermelon, those with vines are often sweet.

These three are obviously not equal, because the sound of beating is the most important, perhaps followed by the surface color, and finally melons and vines. So when we choose, we must first listen to the sound, then look at the melons and vines, and finally look at the color. We abstract the logic and organize it into a tree structure, so it becomes a decision tree.

The word "information entropy" is very puzzling. Its original English text is information entropy, which is actually equally difficult to understand. Because entropy itself is a concept in physics and thermodynamics, which is used to measure the non-uniformity of object dispersion. In other words, the larger the line, the greater the degree of dispersion of the object, which can be simply understood as the more scattered. For example, if we overturn a box of sorted table tennis balls in the room, the table tennis balls inside will obviously be scattered to all parts of the room [4]. This scattered process can be understood as the process of direct increase.

Information line has the same meaning, which is used to measure the disorder of a piece of information. The larger the number, the more disorganized the information. Otherwise, the more conditioned the information is. Information is derived from the famous information science masterpiece "information theory", whose author is the famous Shannon. But this word is not original by Shannon. It is said that it was taken by Feng Neumann, the father of computer. The meaning of his name is also very simple, because everyone doesn't understand what this word means.

We have explained this concept in detail when we introduced cross line before. Let's briefly review it. For an event x, assuming that its probability of occurrence is p (x), the amount of information of the event itself is:

$$I(X) = -\log_2 P(X) \tag{1}$$

Then the meaning of information entropy is actually the expectation of the amount of information, that is, multiplying the amount of information by its probability:

$$H(X) = -P(X)\log_2 P(X) \tag{2}$$

Similarly, suppose we have a data set in which there are k samples, and the proportion of each type of sample is p(k), then if we regard this proportion as probability, we can write the information of the whole set:

$$H(D) = -\sum_{i=1}^{K} P(K) \log_2(P(K)) \tag{3}$$

According to the definition of information entropy, we can know that if the data becomes pure, the information entropy should be reduced. The more you reduce, the better the effect of segmentation. So we found a way to measure the segmentation effect, which is information gain. According to the definition of information gain, we can easily figure out the whole process of decision tree establishment. Every time we select the segmentation feature, we will traverse all the features. Each value of the feature corresponds to a subtree. We find the feature with the largest gain after segmentation by calculating the information gain [5]. After the upper structure is created, continue to build the tree in the form of recursion until the data set after segmentation becomes pure or all features are used.

This algorithm is called ID3 algorithm, which is also the most basic construction algorithm of decision tree. Here is a small detail. According to the definition of ID3 algorithm, each segmentation selects the feature rather than the value of the feature. And each value of the feature selected as the segmentation feature will establish a subtree, that is, each feature will appear only once in the decision tree. Because after one use, all values of this feature will be used up. But expand the dict to get the tree structure in Fig. 1 below:

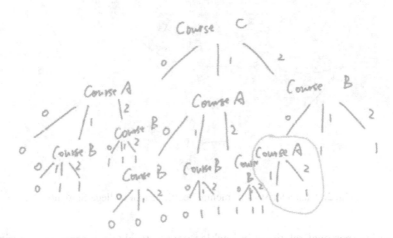

Fig. 1. Dict expanded decision tree structure

In the decision tree algorithm, the classification weight of the root node is the highest and decreases successively downward; Selecting the feature with the strongest classification ability as the root node can greatly improve the classification efficiency. The classification ability of each feature is quantified by information gain. The greater the feature information gain, the stronger the classification ability, that is, calculate the information gain of each feature point in the data set. The feature point with the largest information gain is used as the root node of the decision tree and recurs downward in turn.

2.2 Students' Mental Health

Mental health is an important guarantee for college students to master cultural and scientific knowledge. With a good attitude, they can not only achieve good learning results, but also benefit their lifelong development. College students should achieve mental health, strive for physical and mental health, be able to read relevant psychological counseling books, carry out psychological counseling if necessary, carry out regular physical exercise, have a good time, enhance their psychological quality, and meet the challenge with good psychological quality [6]. Figure 2 below shows the characteristics of College Students' mental health data.

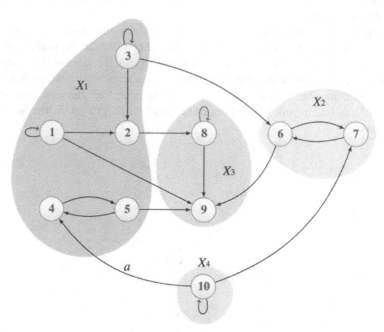

Fig. 2. Characteristics of mental health data of College Students

Good interpersonal relationship enables people to obtain a sense of security and belonging, give people spiritual pleasure and satisfaction, and promote physical and mental health; Bad interpersonal relationships make people feel depressed and nervous, bear loneliness and loneliness, and hurt their physical and mental health. Therefore, we college students should cultivate good communication skills. We should adhere to harmonious interpersonal relations, be willing to communicate with others, and be able to live in harmony with others with an attitude of understanding, tolerance, friendship, trust and respect. Through interpersonal communication, we should recognize the social responsibilities of college students and cultivate the habit of abiding by discipline and social ethics. Enhance the ability of psychological adaptation, be able to work together and cooperate with others, adhere to a coordinated relationship with groups, and ensure the healthy psychological development of college students.

Love has become a common phenomenon among modern college students. College students must establish a correct outlook on love. In love, we should follow: take love as the foundation, take noble interests as the driving force for the development of love, respect each other's choices, freedom, rights and personality in love, abide by their duties, be loyal and single-minded, and treat each other sincerely. We should take understanding as the premise, dedication as the material and being loved as the result. College students should avoid the negative impact of love, learn to use the skills of love, learn to clarify emotional values, make love decisions, pay attention to love communication, and perform the duty of love.

Psychology is the subjective response of organisms to the objective material world. Psychological phenomena include psychological process and personality. Human psychological activities will have a process from occurrence to development and then to disappearance. Psychology is also the function of our human brain and the subjective reflection of our human brain on the objective material world. People's psychology includes psychological process and personality psychological characteristics [7]. The process of psychological development is an active process, not what we think of as a passive process. So what is mental health and what are the standards of our college students' mental health? In a broad sense, mental health is an efficient, satisfactory and sustainable mental state. In a narrow sense, mental health refers to the process of people's basic psychological activities, which has content integrity and coordination, that is, from recognition to emotion, then to will, behavior and personality integrity and coordination, so that people can adapt to the society and keep pace with the society. A healthy person should have normal intelligence, be able to control emotions, be emotionally stable, have a strong will, be normal, adapt well, have good self-awareness and interpersonal relationships, and have a healthy personality. Some people think that psychological problems are physiological diseases when they have not been exposed to the discipline of psychology. In fact, psychological problems are not different from physiological diseases. Psychological problems are a series of problems caused by people's internal mental factors, precisely a series of problems caused by the control system of the central nervous system of the brain. It will indirectly change people's character, world outlook and emotion, so, Psychological problems also have a great impact. We should pay attention to psychological problems. In case of psychological problems, please consult a psychologist more often, so as to make our new youth grow healthily.

3   Student Mental Health Data Processing

The influence of parental rearing patterns on children's psychological and behavioral development and health can not be ignored. A survey of 165 freshmen to junior students in the branch of Medical College of Zhengzhou Railway Vocational College shows that the parental rearing style has a direct impact on the mental health of children and adolescents.

Intimacy, care and consideration make children form personality characteristics such as enthusiasm, self-confidence, self-esteem, independence, perseverance and positive emotion, which promotes the development of mental health. Exclusion and negation make children form the psychology of humiliation, inferiority, self sin, helplessness, caution, indecision, fear of being rejected, don't know what love is, and don't know how to be loved. Parents' excessive intervention in the way of education makes children form personality characteristics such as lack of self-confidence, excessive self-control and excessive dependence. The harsh educational methods make parents feel inferior, helpless and insecure. Severe punishment is especially easy to lose children's self-esteem and produce anxiety and obsessive-compulsive symptoms.

Using the clinical symptom Checklist-90 (SCL-90) and self-made family information questionnaire, 5090 freshmen of grade 2020 in a university in Chengdu were investigated. The results showed that family structure had a significant impact on the overall level of mental health and the three factor scores of interpersonal sensitivity, depression and psychosis. In terms of student communication, students from sojourning families are more sensitive than students from other families [8]. There are more students from single parent families and their overall mental health is poor. College students from single families have serious psychological barriers, such as depression, loneliness, inferiority complex and rebellious psychology. Due to the imperfect family structure, children often lose the possibility of communicating with their parents, and can only get partial care compared with children in ordinary families; Their hearts will be covered, prone to sensitivity and inferiority.

A harmonious family atmosphere can make children happy physically and mentally, reduce psychological pressure, and is conducive to the healthy development of body and mind. In disharmonious families, quarrel, doting, indifference and domestic violence do harm to people's physical and mental health in varying degrees, especially the two family atmospheres of doting and violence.

The survey found that the mental health level of students with financial difficulties was significantly lower than that of students with financial difficulties. The lower the income, the lower the mental health level of college students; Most of the students from poor families come from rural areas. They are under great economic and psychological pressure. Most poor college students are unable to change the current situation for a time due to financial constraints, limited vision and lack of communication ability. They are prone to sensitivity, inferiority complex, depression, anxiety, interpersonal tension and other characteristics. At the same time, college students living in affluent families and poor students will also have more mental health problems.

Over fitting means that the model performs very well in the training data set, but the data outside the training data set can not fit the data well. It may be that the number of samples is too small, and the attributes of the samples cannot replace all the overall data [9]. Therefore, even if the samples can be well distinguished, the data outside the samples may not be well distinguished.

Decision tree algorithm is easy to understand and interpretable. It is a very common and excellent machine learning algorithm, which can be classified or regressed. Now many of the best integration models are also based on decision trees. Therefore, the series of decision tree algorithms can not be bypassed by machine learning. It requires very systematic and profound learning and understanding.

In information theory, the greater the information gain of an attribute, the stronger the ability of the attribute to reduce the entropy of the sample. In other words, determining this attribute will make the system more stable and orderly (the smaller the entropy, the more stable the system is), and the higher the purity of the partition.

No matter how many features a data set has, only one feature can be selected each time the data set is divided. Then which feature is selected as the reference attribute for division for the first time to classify the data faster?

The answer must be the feature with the best classification ability, but the question comes, how to judge which feature has the best classification ability? A more perceptual concept can be introduced, that is, purity. The purer after splitting, the better. There are three common methods to measure purity. Different measurement methods may lead to different splitting [10].

ID3 algorithm: iterative dichotomizer 3, the third generation of iterative binary tree, is the first proposed decision tree algorithm, which uses information gain as the splitting criterion.

4   Application of ID3 Algorithm in College Students' Mental Health Education

Modern college students are active, eager for knowledge, pursuing progress, enterprising, ambitious, and able to integrate their personal ideals and aspirations with national rejuvenation The great cause of national prosperity has become the mainstream of College Students' psychological development. However, with the advent of knowledge economy and information society, great changes have taken place in people's ideas and lifestyles. Science and technology are changing with each passing day. With the intensification of social competition, college students are facing great psychological pressure in the period of "psychological weaning". College students are increasing day by day because of the extreme psychological problems. According to the relevant survey of the Ministry of education, 20.33% to 25.63% of the students in school have varying degrees of psychological problems, psychological problems and psychological problems.

There are two parts of the data from the school's educational administration system and the performance management system (one part is the data from the school's examination and the other part is the performance management system); The other part is the questionnaire of students, including the mastery of College Students' mental health course before learning, learning interest, learning attitude, learning habits, theoretical learning effect, computer learning effect and computer time after class. A total of 321 samples were collected. Data preprocessing can ensure the data set quality of data mining. The method of data preprocessing includes data cleaning, data reduction and data transformation. In the student survey data, some data items are not filled in, resulting in the invalidity of the questionnaire. Among the scores of College Students' mental health courses derived from the educational administration management system, there are two kinds of special data. One is the students who have been retaken. Their poor completion of various teaching tasks usually leads to the poor scores of College Students' mental health courses; The other is the absence or delay of a small number of students due to illness, taking various examinations and other special reasons. The final score of College Students' mental health course is 0. This kind of data will be deleted. There are many attributes in the collected data, but not every attribute is closely related to the task of data mining. Data reduction can obtain a smaller attribute set than the original data, and the new attribute set does not affect the results of data mining. First, convert the usual score and total evaluation score of College Students' mental health course scores into characters. The conversion rules are as follows: 80–100 are represented by a, 60–79 by B and 0–59 by C. Secondly, delete the student number and name attributes irrelevant to data mining.

Calculate the information gain [11]. Taking "College Students' interest in mental health courses" as an example, the calculation of information gain is as follows: the first step is to calculate the subset information entropy divided by attribute values.

Attribute "College Students' interest in mental health courses" = "a", of the 31 samples, 28 samples with a total rating of "yes" and 3 samples with a total rating of "no".

IS11,S12) = I(28,3) == 0.4586.

Attribute "College Students' interest in mental health courses" = "B", I (S21, S22) = 0.2602.

Attribute "College Students' interest in mental health courses" = "C", 1s31, S32) = 0.4395.

Attribute "College Students' interest in mental health courses" = "d", 1s41, S42) = 0.

Calculation information expectation:

$$\max \sum_{I} \left[U^I(X^I) - C^I(X^I) \right] \tag{4}$$

E (College Students' interest in mental health courses) = S11, S12 + I (S21, S22) + I (S31, S32) + I (S41, S42) = 0.3315.

Calculate information gain:

$$O_v = \sum_{u \in N[v]} w_{u,v} x_u \tag{5}$$

Gain (College Students' interest in mental health courses = I (S1, S2) – e college students' interest in mental health courses) = 0.3982–0.3315 = 0.0667 step 5: determine the root node of the decision tree. According to the principle of ID3 algorithm and the above calculation results, the test attribute is "usual score". Each attribute value corresponds to a branch, and other attributes are also divided and constructed in this way [12].

The sixth step is to further divide the branch nodes according to the above method. In order to prevent the training data from over fitting and delete the leaf nodes with low probability, the post pruning is used to prune the generated decision tree to form the final decision tree, as shown in Fig. 3.

Students' identification with the school is an important indicator to evaluate a school's management level and education level, and improving college students' identification

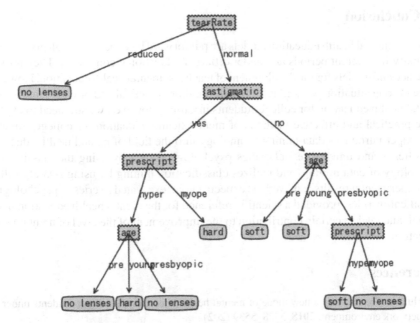

Fig. 3. Final decision tree of mental health education

with the school through mental health education is also one of the ways. First, the school should improve the relationship with students, strengthen interaction and pay attention to students' learning, life and psychological state [13]. For example, a long-term activity of "President and Secretary listen to me" carried out by a university in Guizhou allows students to fully express their needs for the school and implement the reform, which solves the problems that may arise in students' life and study, At the same time, it strengthens students' participation and sense of belonging. Second, colleges and universities should strengthen the linkage mechanism between Counselors and student work offices, pay attention to the psychological state of each student, and once problems are found, they should jointly solve them in time according to the specific situation of students. For example, when counselors find that students are frustrated in love and start to get tired of learning, they need to link with the student office to seek the advice of psychological counselors and give corresponding psychological counseling, Provide targeted help to students. Third, some students from rural areas are prone to inferiority complex in the face of many students with superior urban conditions due to family conditions [14]. However, we should not pay too much attention, otherwise it will be counterproductive, which requires the school to carry out some inspirational lectures or publicity, establish examples of excellent character and learning, recognize the aura on ourselves through the comparative effect, and establish the life idea of "struggling life is valuable", so as to gradually eliminate the psychological state of inferiority and improve the sense of recognition and belonging to the school.

5 Conclusion

Different mental health education models are put forward by experts through practice and summary in different periods and under different educational conditions. They provide guidance and models for the development of teachers' mental health education. However, in the current situation, we still need to explore more practical and effective methods of mental health education for college students in China. However, we still need to explore more practical and effective methods of mental health education for college students. This paper introduces data mining technology into the field of mental health education in Colleges and universities, classifies psychological data by using the classification technology of data mining, and realizes classification mining by using ID3 algorithm. The experimental results achieved the expected goal, excavated a series of psychological classification rules, provided a scientific reference for the mental health education in our school, and made a certain contribution to the improvement of the level of mental health education.

References

1. Hu, N.: Constructing a new mode of mental health education for college students under the network environment. **2018**, 5528–5539 (2021)
2. Xie, W.: Big data analysis on the management content of college students' mental health education. In: 2021 13th International Conference on Measuring Technology and Mechatronics Automation (ICMTMA) (2021)
3. Pottinger, A.M., Passard, N., Gordon Stair, A.: Using faith-based organisations to promote mental health education to underserved populations in Jamaica. Health Educ. J. **80**(5), 461–471 (2021)
4. Liu, Q., Liao, X.: Research on university mental health education based on computer big data statistical analysis. In: 2021 2nd International Conference on Big Data and Informatization Education (ICBDIE) (2021)
5. Javed Mehedi Shamrat, F.M., Ranjan, R., Hasib, K.M., Yadav, A., Siddique, A.H.: Performance evaluation among ID3, C4.5, and CART decision tree algorithm. In: Ranganathan, G., Bestak, R., Palanisamy, R., Rocha, Á. (eds.) Pervasive Computing and Social Networking. Lecture Notes in Networks and Systems, vol. 317. Springer, Singapore (2022)
6. Arlis, S., Defit, S.: Machine learning algorithms for predicting the spread of Covid19 in Indonesia. TEM J. **10**(2), 970–974 (2021)
7. Li, P., Zhou, Y.: An analysis of english listening and speaking teaching mode based on ID3 algorithm. In: Xu, Z., Parizi, R.M., Loyola-González, O., Zhang, X. (eds.) CSIA 2021. AISC, vol. 1343, pp. 773–777. Springer, Cham (2021). https://doi.org/10.1007/978-3-030-69999-4_107
8. Kuang, Y.: Innovative development of combination of digital media technology and virtual reality technology. In: Zheng, X., Parizi, R.M., Loyola-González, O., Zhang, X. (eds.) Cyber Security Intelligence and Analytics: 2021 International Conference on Cyber Security Intelligence and Analytics (CSIA2021), vol. 2, pp. 210–216. Springer International Publishing, Cham (2021). https://doi.org/10.1007/978-3-030-69999-4_28
9. Gu, Z., He, C.: Application of fuzzy decision tree algorithm based on mobile computing in sports fitness member management. Wirel. Commun. Mob. Comput. **2021**(6), 1–10 (2021)
10. Singh, G., Sharma, S.: Impact of digital transformation of education system on the mental health of students. In: Innovative Teaching Practices for Education Par Excellence in Online Era (2021)

11. Scholarworks, S., Shulski, A.: How to reduce mental health crises by improving training and education for law enforcement first responders (2021)
12. Deshpande, D., Mhatre, C.K.: A study of impact of online education on mental health and academic performance of children of project affected people studying at undergraduate level in Navi Mumbai. Revista Gestão Inovação e Tecnologias **11**(4), 3866–3875 (2021)
13. Stegenga, S.M., Sinclair, J., Knowles, C., Storie, S.O., Seeley, J.R.: Lived experiences of mental health in higher education: a comparative analysis of determinants to supports and services. Am. J. Orthopsychiatry **91**(6), 738–750 (2021). https://doi.org/10.1037/ort0000575
14. Bynum, W.E., Sukhera, J.: Perfectionism, power, and process: what we must address to dismantle mental health stigma in medical education. Acad. Med. **96**(5), 621–623 (2021)

Application of Random Simulation Algorithm in Practical Teaching of Public Physical Education in Colleges and Universities

Xianglie Tan[✉]

Guangdong University of Business and Technology, Guangzhou 526020, China
tan382495303@163.com

Abstract. This paper studies the application of random simulation algorithm in the practical teaching of Public Physical Education in Colleges and universities. When the current national physical education gives new goals and requirements to college physical education, the limitations and one sidedness of the old teaching mode and method appear. In the simulation part of public physical education practice teaching, the quantitative scoring method in public physical education practice teaching and comprehensive evaluation method is used as the simulation basis. When determining the range of public physical education practice teaching and historical public physical education practice teaching data, according to the degree of detail of the historical data they have, A fuzzy cluster analysis method based on fuzzy equivalence matrix is proposed to classify the unknown, and pay attention to the unity and standardization of teaching form, structure, content, method, examination and evaluation. The distribution function of public physical education practice teaching is obtained through statistical analysis and test of historical data, and the random number of this public physical education practice teaching is generated by computer. According to the specific bid evaluation methods and scoring rules in the teaching documents, a public physical education practice teaching interval or public physical education practice teaching value with high scores in public physical education.

Keywords: Random simulation algorithm · Public sports · Practical teaching

1 Introduction

Nowadays, the administrative system of rest education in China is the Ministry of Physical Education (Teaching and Research Office), and the main task of the Ministry of Physical Education (Office) is to complete physical education. Colleges and universities in China does not have a special system to manage theoretical teaching. Many teachers believe that theory accounts for less class hours and there is no need to engage in special management. College students have received physical education in primary and secondary schools for more than ten years. It can be said that they have a certain foundation in sports technical skills, but their theoretical knowledge is extremely poor. Sports not

M. A. Jan and F. Khan (Eds.): BigIoT-EDU 2022, LNICST 465, pp. 298–309, 2023.
https://doi.org/10.1007/978-3-031-23950-2_32

only shoulder the task of physical exercise, but also promote the healthy development of College Students' body and mind through sports [1]. Sports has produced a large number of human body movement laws around sports practice, and these laws are the theoretical basis for guiding physical development. Therefore, the sports department should set up a special theoretical teaching and research department. The director of the teaching and research department should pay attention to the management work, strengthen the construction of theoretical teaching materials and teaching aids, reasonably allocate theoretical teaching personnel.

Physical exercise is the main characteristic of physical education, so the teaching of technical skills should occupy an important position and a large proportion in the highest stage for students to receive education in school, so this section of technical skills teaching should have a certain depth and difficulty. This depth and difficulty should not be reflected in the high level of technology and skills that he has acquired, but in the fact that they should have certain biomechanical knowledge to understand the formation principle of sports technology skills and certain sports physiology knowledge to understand sports technology The role of the formation process of skills on the development of human body and learning how to measure and evaluate yourself in the process of sports to obtain the ability of scientific exercise. In short, physical education in Colleges and universities should make full use of the guiding role of physical education theoretical knowledge in physical education practice, so that students can truly "know why" in the process of learning technical skills Practical teaching of Public Physical Education in Colleges and universities is an effective way to learn sports theoretical knowledge and master sports skills [2]. It is an important means to enhance students' physique, improve students' physical health and improve students' physical quality. With the implementation of a series of measures to deepen the reform of college education system in China, the reform of public physical education practice teaching in Colleges and universities from concept, content to method and means has begun to be beneficial exploration.

Physical education is the main form of school physical education. This is a targeted, organized and organized learning process, which meets certain learning standards and courses. Bilateral activities include training of teachers and students. Listening, observation, learning and evaluation are the most common teaching and research activities. This is of great significance to change PE Teachers' teaching skills, improve their skills, improve teaching quality, develop teaching research, teaching reform and quality education.

This paper studies the application of random simulation algorithm in public physical education practice teaching in Colleges and universities. The development of modern science and technology puts forward new requirements for physical education teaching mode. Under this new requirement, the random simulation algorithm assisted teaching, which is different from the traditional teaching mode, will become the trend of physical education teaching reform. Random simulation algorithm technology involved in physical education teaching process is bound to affect physical education teaching mode Put forward new requirements in teaching methods and teaching design [3]. As a teaching leader, physical education teachers should fully realize the importance of random simulation algorithm technology, and reasonably carry out teaching design according to the cognitive characteristics of students, in order to improve the quality of physical education teaching and cultivate students with comprehensive quality. Therefore, physical education teaching should take the initiative to seize the opportunity.

2 Related work

2.1 Stochastic Simulation Algorithm

Simulation, also known as simulation, is a technology that imitates the research object by other means.

Stochastic simulation, also known as Monte Carlo simulation, statistical test or random sampling, is to sample according to the distribution characteristics of random variables to simulate the occurrence of real systems, so as to calculate the asymptotic statistical estimation of random variables. Its theoretical basis is to use sample parameters (sample mean and sample variance) to estimate the overall parameters. With the development of computer science and the in-depth study of simulation theory, random simulation method has been widely used in engineering [4]. The purpose of system simulation is to provide decision-making basis for the final public sports, that is, to select a certain public sports interval or several public sports in order to achieve the optimal goal – medium The bidding probability is the highest and the expected profit is the best. As shown in Fig. 1.

$$\lim_{k \to \infty} y_k(t) = y_d(t) \tag{1}$$

The main advantage of applying stochastic simulation is that it can make quantitative analysis of the problems to be solved by the system quickly and economically. However, this method also has its own inherent disadvantages: stochastic simulation is only a numerical calculation method, which does not have the optimization function. Each simulation can only get a workable solution, but not a general solution. If you want to get the optimal solution or satisfactory solution, Through multiple simulations, it has the weakness of enumeration method, and its simulation results are not as accurate as those obtained by analytical method.

$$e_j = -k \sum_{i=1}^{n} f_{ij} \ln f_{ij} \tag{2}$$

How to accurately determine the distribution type of random variables according to the mastered data is not a simple thing. It needs to be inferred with the help of certain methods. The commonly used methods in teaching are histogram method and probability diagram method.

The evolutionary algorithm only needs to calculate the value of the objective function, and the requirements for the nature of the optimization problem itself are very low. Unlike the mathematical optimization algorithm, it often depends on a lot of conditions, such as whether it is convex optimization, whether the objective function is differentiable, whether the derivative of the objective function is lipschitzcontinuity, and so on. For example, the design of the vehicle dynamics model mentioned above is constrained by the fluid partial differential equation. At this time, you don't know whether

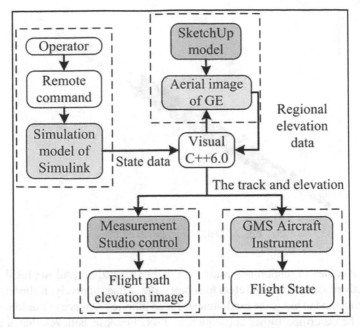

Fig. 1. Principle of random simulation algorithm

the objective function is convex, differentiable or not. This is the biggest advantage of evolutionary algorithm over mathematical optimization algorithm [5]. In fact, it is also a disadvantage of evolutionary algorithm, Because the problem independent nature works well for all problems, it often means that we do not make full use of the characteristics of different problems to further accelerate and optimize the algorithm (there is a philosophical dialectic that advantages often lead to disadvantages). In this way, the rules and regulations of mathematical optimization algorithm actually delimit the scope of application of mathematical optimization algorithm. If it is out of this scope, we don't know whether it is easy to use or not, but within this scope, mathematical optimization can give a basic theoretical guarantee. Evolutionary computation methods based on some specific combinatorial optimization structures have actually introduced more information about the problem itself. This is why evolutionary computation can compare with traditional mathematical optimization in some combinatorial optimization problems. Figure 2 below shows the data used to generate the regression model.

For the optimization problem with determined problem structure, when there is sufficient information about the optimization problem to use, mathematical optimization generally has advantages, such as linear programming, quadratic programming, convex optimization and so on. On the contrary, evolutionary algorithms may have advantages. For some problems that can not be completely solved by mathematical optimization, such as NP hard problem, evolutionary algorithm also has great application prospects. More use of the structure of specific problems to design specific evolutionary computing algorithms is bound to improve the ability of evolutionary computing.

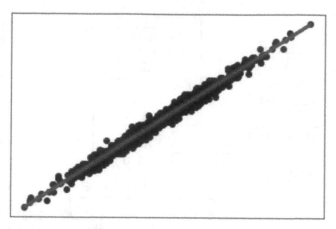

Fig. 2. Data of regression model

When it comes to randomness, this is probably a puzzling philosophical problem. What exactly random behavior refers to is best defined quantitatively. Kolmogorov once proposed a method to judge the randomness: for an infinite sequence of random numbers, it can not be described by its subsequence. J. N. Franklin believes that a sequence is random if it has the properties of each infinite sequence obtained by independent sampling from a uniformly distributed random variable. These definitions are not very precise and sometimes even lead to contradictions [6]. It can be seen how cautious mathematicians are when talking about this problem.

Random number generator is just an algorithm to generate random numbers that conform to a specific distribution. These so-called random number sequences are actually periodic.

There are a large number of random number generators, but finding a good, easy to transplant and industrial standard random number generator is a difficult goal. The standard method of generating non-uniform distribution is to generate uniformly distributed random numbers first, and then convert them into specific distributed random numbers.

2.2 Practical Teaching of Public Physical Education

On the origin of sports practical training, what is modern sports practical training, and the concept of sports practical training. In order to carry out reasonable physical practice training in public physical education teaching in Colleges and universities, we must first solve these problems.

Sports practice training originated in the Second World War. In World War II, the allied fleet was repeatedly attacked by German Nazi submarines. Few sailors survived after the ship sank, which greatly reduced the effective strength of the Allied forces. After detailed investigation and research, the Allies found that most of these sailors who could survive were sailors with good psychological quality. They saved themselves with tenacious will to life. Then, "Success does not depend on physical fitness, but on The concept of "is well known by people. After continuous evolution, physical practice training has gradually become a popular training form for modern people. It is characterized by cultivating people's comprehensive quality, improving personality and returning to nature. The traditional training methods of unique creativity and personalized words have been preserved. This advanced training method was introduced in China in the 1990s, and physical practice training has become popular in China It has become a fashion. Carrying out physical practice training in public physical education in Colleges and universities has become an important means to create a pioneering physical education teaching model.

The object and content of sports practice training have realized continuous innovation. The group receiving sports practice training and the employees of the company Students and other groups. The training objectives were expanded accordingly. The previous training objectives were mainly physical fitness and survival training. In order to meet the needs of modern life, the training objectives were extended to personality training, personal will training, management training and team spirit training [7]. In sports practice training, participants can exercise their will, realize the perfection of personality and effectively cultivate team spirit.

The so-called sports practice training refers to the scientific design of special facilities and environment, through the form of outdoor activities to enable participants to obtain the corresponding emotional experience. In the activities, cultivate the spirit of self defeating and enterprising, the consciousness of motivating others and good team consciousness. At present, China's sports practice training projects mainly include barrel rolling, trestle bridge and water floating Soft ladder, balance beam, etc. It can be said that the forms of sports practical training are becoming more and more diversified.

In the traditional sports teaching, students' interest is not greatly reduced. In the teaching process, many courses are too old. Although China's colleges and universities continue to improve the classroom teaching courses, the subjects set up in the teaching process are still relatively old traditional courses such as football and basketball. With the development of China's economy, students have enough opportunities to contact these sports after class. In this way, students are no longer satisfied with shallow teaching in class. The introduction of sports practice training in public sports can effectively promote the improvement of classroom teaching mode. It is favored by students with novel teaching ideas and teaching forms, and the classroom teaching effect is remarkable.

In physical training, students' comprehensive quality can be effectively improved. College sports practice training is mainly divided into personal quality training and team training. In personal quality training, individuals should complete the corresponding training items as required within the specified time. In this tense and stimulating process, students' psychological quality and physical quality have been improved. Moreover, due to the requirements of time, students will give up some items [8]. Students learn to give up appropriately in this process, which is of great significance to some blind and confident students. In team training, students should form corresponding training teams according to requirements. In team training, the student union establishes a good team consciousness and forms a healthy team culture. In order to complete the team project, team members must trust each other and actively communicate and communicate. Since then, the team consciousness of students has been improved. Most of the current college students in China are only children and do not form team consciousness in life, which is inconsistent with the current situation of emphasizing team consciousness in modern society.

3 Application of Random Simulation Algorithm in Practical Teaching of Public Physical Education in Colleges and Universities

To carry out outward bound training in public sports teaching in Colleges and universities. The content selection of Outward Bound training is particularly important. Generally speaking, the forms of Outward Bound training are relatively flexible and diverse, and the operation is simple. According to the form of Public Physical Education in Colleges and universities, outward bound training can be divided into large and small classes. In small classes with relatively short class hours, it is mainly to cultivate students' personal quality. The selection of training items should also start from cultivating students' personal quality [9]. In random simulation, the simulation number n is the first parameter to be determined. The simulation times are directly related to the calculation accuracy. Theoretically, the greater the number of simulations n, the smaller the error caused by replacing probability with frequency or expectation with mean, and the higher the accuracy. However, blindly increasing the number of simulations will undoubtedly increase the running time of the program, and after the simulation reaches a certain number of times, the accuracy changes little with the increase of the number of times. The calculation method of simulation times n of random variables under given confidence and error conditions is introduced below.

In order to obtain the expectation of random variables, the public physical education teaching is simulated, and the sample mean value is used to replace the overall expectation. The error can be expressed as:

$$\|\Delta x_{k+1}(t)\|_\lambda \leq m_1 \frac{1 - e^{(b-\lambda)t}}{b - \lambda} \tag{3}$$

The overall distribution is unknown, and the number of simulation times IV of public physical education teaching is determined;

When the distribution type of the simulated best public physical education sample value is unknown and the sample is large, the central limit theorem is used to estimate the error:

$$e_{k+1}(t) = C(t)\Delta x_{k+1}(t) \tag{4}$$

Public physical education teaching data plays a decisive role in the process of selecting the type of probability distribution. Different public physical education teaching actually has different probability distribution. Generally, the distribution of public physical education teaching has the following characteristics:

(1) There is a distribution interval (a, b), in which public physical education teaching always takes a finite positive value;
(2) In the interval (a, b), the density curve of public physical education teaching shows a single peak continuous distribution;
(3) The distribution of different public physical education teaching may be positive, negative and symmetrical.

It should be pointed out that the psychological characteristics of students are different. When designing the training content, we should comprehensively test the students' personality. For example, students with insufficient balance can strengthen the training of balance beam, and students with weak willpower can carry out roller ball training in a short time. The major course is mainly to cultivate students' team consciousness, so the selection of training items should focus on cultivating students' team consciousness. For example, two person kangaroo jump is a relatively difficult training project, but it requires a high sense of cooperation between the two [10]. In order to win, students should actively cooperate and make use of their own advantages to make up for the disadvantages of their peers, so that the students' sense of cooperation can be improved. In some colleges and universities with better conditions, the network wall can also be used for training. The main form is: the students combine by themselves, and each group of six people will complete the climbing of the net wall within the specified time. The members of the group shall not fall. If one falls, they will be disqualified from the competition, but the team members are allowed to rescue. The group with shorter time is the victory group, and the team consciousness of students climbing the net wall can be established, And formed a good habit of helping each other.

In the past, if the exact distribution of a variable is not known, it is generally assumed that the variable obeys the normal distribution, mainly because it satisfies the central limit theorem, that is, and the normal distribution is the limit distribution of many statistics. At the same time, many data processing methods with excellent statistical characteristics in theory are derived. However, the normal distribution is an unbounded distribution with symmetrical tail, which is not in line with the basic characteristics that the actual public physical education teaching intervals are bounded and non negative, and the public physical education teaching is not always a symmetrical distribution or a typical distribution, but mostly a close distribution. In view of this, this paper adopts multi parameter statistical distribution when simulating public physical education teaching β Distribution, and different values can be taken continuously through its parameters to represent various actual distributions and statistical characteristics of public physical education teaching, which may be closer to the actual situation than assuming that public physical education teaching obeys a typical distribution, and β The distribution has many advantages as follows.

Take different values through parameters (R, n), β (, n) can be a smooth continuous distribution with symmetry or asymmetry, single peak or single valley, increasing or decreasing, and can approach various typical distributions such as normal, triangular, trapezoidal, elliptical, uniform, anti sinusoidal, exponential, right angle, Rayleigh, etc. [11]. In addition, it can also approximate t distribution, F distribution, lognormal distribution, absolute normal distribution, truncated normal distribution, non central Rayleigh distribution, etc., as well as more complex distribution between them. so β The distribution has polymorphism that can approximate various actual distributions.

At the same time, β The distribution also has certain theoretical analysis characteristics.

Anyway, β The distribution has the characteristics of boundedness and polymorphism, which can not only be analyzed theoretically, but also convenient for practical calculation β It is feasible to generate the random number of public physical education teaching by distribution, which provides a convenient method for constructing different distribution forms of public physical education teaching.

4 Practical Teaching Model of Public Physical Education

Any mathematical model is based on certain assumptions. As an analytical modeling tool, stochastic simulation needs to follow certain rules in the modeling process of determining the best public physical education teaching interval.

Data preprocessing is mainly carried out through data cleaning, integration, selection, transformation, concept layer and so on. The main purpose of data processing is to delete 28 completed questionnaires and 25 unverified student health data. Data integration includes analyzing the basic information of students and the data elements in the questionnaire in the form of data sets. At the level of a = 0.05, 8 of the 32 statistically significant variables are selected from the analysis, and a random simulation algorithm model of the influence of public physical education factors in Colles and universities is established.

$$W_j = d_i / \sum_{j=1}^{m} d_j \tag{5}$$

$$P_{loss} = 1 - \frac{1 - p_0}{p} = \frac{p_0 + p - 1}{p} = \sum_{n=1}^{N} P_K \tag{6}$$

Participating in sports competitions helps to improve students' local skills. Compared with traditional educational institutions, the sports environment is relatively strange and complex, which may lead to complex changes in students' psychology [12]. Complex psychological changes will not only produce positive effects and emotional reactions, but also lead to negative effects and emotional reactions. In sports competitions, contestants must overcome the impact of environmental changes, maintain a stable state of mind through positive self-regulation, and achieve better results in the field of competition. As the number of students participating in sports competitions increases, their ability to participate in drama competitions also improves.

Second, the influencing factors include "preference level" and "teacher qualification level". Students have different degrees of love for sports, and their grades in public physical education classes are also different. Basically, students who like sports do better than students who don't like sports. Therefore, in the process of community sports practice teaching, we should cultivate students' interest in sports and enhance students' learning motivation. Teachers' technical level is also related to students' academic achievements in community sports. Under the guidance of high-quality teachers, students' academic performance in sports is high.

In addition, the diversity of teachers' teaching means, the class hours of public physical education courses and students' physical quality are also closely related to students' performance of public physical education courses. Teachers use more teaching methods in the practical teaching of public physical education, and students' performance in public physical education is better. With the increase of class hours of public physical education courses, the opportunities for students to practice sports action technology are increased, and the students' performance in public physical education courses is also better. Students have good physical quality and master the basic movements of sports quickly [13].

Because of the different influencing factors, the teaching strategies of public physical education will also change. However, this change is not groundless, but there are certain laws. As long as we can find this internal law, we can make full use of it to guide public physical education teaching.

Because public physical education teaching is affected by many factors, public physical education teaching should be a function of these factors. Public physical education teaching decision-making can be understood as an optimization problem under constraints. Linear programming is a method to solve the optimization problem under constraints. Here, it can be assumed that the objective function p (final public physical education teaching) is linear, And has one or more constraints. Based on this, this paper puts forward the following public physical education teaching model. In order to facilitate the analysis of problems, it can be expressed by the following formula:

$$d_{k+1}(t) = f(t, x_d(t)) - f(t, x_{k+1}(t)) \tag{7}$$

The internal structure of random algorithm public physical education practice teaching model generator, such as fence structure and the distribution of hyperplane points, is also very important. There are specific detection methods for different generators [14]. Spectrum test is the most used in structure detection. Spectrum test is based on the maximum distance between adjacent parallel hyperplanes. The greater the distance, the worse the generator. As shown in Fig. 3 below:

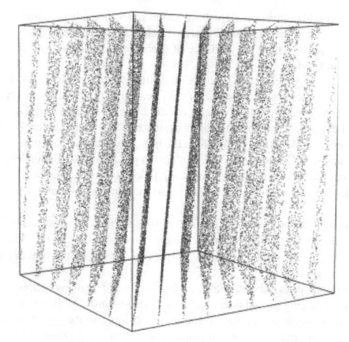

Fig. 3. Internal structure of random algorithm public physical education practice teaching model generator

In other words, the stochastic simulation model of the impact of university public physical education is the most important factor of the "number of participants" of decision-making institutions, followed by "preferences" and "teacher qualification level". These have highlighted the important aspects that affect the teaching practice of Public Physical Education in Colleges and universities.

5 Conclusion

This paper studies the application of random simulation algorithm in the teaching practice of Public Physical Education in Colleges and universities, and gives the similar data of public physical education that simulates public physical education. On the basis of various models and statistical data, public physical education standards have been formulated, and public physical education institutions have been established. According to the specific evaluation rules stipulated in the evaluation method, the full coverage of public physical education has been achieved. Contestants can regularly participate in public sports activities to increase educational opportunities. Data mining is a process of automatically searching a large number of complex data sets by computer, and extracting hidden and previously unknown potential value information, rules and knowledge from high-quality, heterogeneous data and random data. Different from traditional statistical data analysis, the main feature of data extraction method is to obtain unknown, effective and useful information, rules and knowledge through data extraction method without clear assumptions. The introduction of data extraction methods in college physical education teaching research has injected new impetus into the development of college physical education.

References

1. González-Peo, A., Franco, E., Coterón, J.: Do observed teaching behaviors relate to students' engagement in physical education? Int. J. Env. Res. Public Health **18**(5), 2234 (2021)
2. Yang, Z.: Advantages of computer information technology in physical education teaching practice. In: Zheng, X., Parizi, R.M., Loyola-González, O., Zhang, X. (eds.) Cyber Security Intelligence and Analytics: 2021 International Conference on Cyber Security Intelligence and Analytics (CSIA2021), vol. 2, pp. 688–695. Springer International Publishing, Cham (2021). https://doi.org/10.1007/978-3-030-69999-4_94
3. Miller, J., Kai, J., Kunert, W., Axt, S.: Evaluation of different teaching methods for providing practical skills in general surgery during the current pandemic situation. In: Conference: 138. Deutscher Chirurgen Kongress – DCK 2021. DigitalAt, Mainz, Germany (2021)
4. Aksovi, N., et al.: Teaching methods in teaching physical education. Comput. Comput. **14**, 2214–2226 (2021)
5. Tang, S., Jiang, M., Abbassi, R., Jerbi, H., Iatifi, M.: A cost-oriented resource scheduling of a solar-powered microgrid by using the hybrid crow and pattern search algorithm. J. Clean. Prod. **3**, 127853 (2021)
6. Liu, G.X., Qin, Q., Zhang, Q.H.: Linear array synthesis for wireless power transmission based on brain storm optimization algorithm. Int. J. Antennas Propag. **2021**(7), 1–8 (2021)
7. Settar, A., Fatmi, N.I., Mohammed, B.: Quasi-maximum likelihood estimation of the component-GARCH model using the stochastic approximation algorithm with application to the S&P 500. Math. Model. Comput. **8**, 379–390 (2021)
8. Al-Abri, S., Mishra, V., Khan, A.: A bio-inspired localization-free stochastic coverage algorithm with verified reachability. Bioinspir. Biomim. **16**(5), 056009 (2021)
9. Florio, A.M., Hartl, R.F., Minner, S., Salazar-González, J.-J.: A branch-and-price algorithm for the vehicle routing problem with stochastic demands and probabilistic duration constraints. Transport. Sci. **55**(1), 122–138 (2021). https://doi.org/10.1287/trsc.2020.1002
10. Xu, Y., Meng, R., Zhao, X.: Research on a gas concentration prediction algorithm based on stacking. Sensors **21**(5), 1597 (2021)
11. Montero-Carretero, C., Cervelló, E.: Teaching styles in physical education: a new approach to predicting resilience and bullying. Int. J. Env. Res. Publ. Health **17**(1), 76 (2019). https://doi.org/10.3390/ijerph17010076
12. Landa, B.H.: Kinesiological educational technology in academic physical education. Teoriia i Praktika Fizicheskoĭ Kul'tury **3**, 8 (2021)
13. Pearrubia-Lozano, C., Lizalde-Gil, M.: Perception of the usefulness of augmented reality in physical education teachers initial training. In: International Academic Conference on Teaching, Learning and E-learning 2020 in Venice (2020)
14. Chróinín, D.N., Coulter, M., Parker, M.: "We took pictures": children's meaning-making in physical education. J. Teach. Phys. Educ. **39**(2), 216–226 (2020)

Application of Intelligent Fuzzy Decision Tree Algorithm in English Translation Education

Bing Chen$^{(\boxtimes)}$

Chengdu Polytechnic, Chengdu 610000, Sichuan, China
applechen123@126.com

Abstract. Fuzziness is the basic characteristic and conventional phenomenon of the real world. As a language describing the objective world, it is bound to have fuzziness. Fuzziness, as one of the basic characteristics of language, widely exists in any language in the world and frequently appears in people's daily communication and literary works. It can express infinite meaning with limited language means. The accurate use of fuzzy language can enhance the flexibility of language and improve the expression effect of language. Fuzzy language is used at all levels of language use, resulting in a humorous, funny and vivid language charm. Although fuzziness is common to all languages, due to different life and cultural backgrounds, English and Chinese have great differences in Fuzziness and fuzzy beauty. These differences have brought many challenges and difficulties to translation.

Keywords: Fuzziness · English translation · Decision tree algorithm

1 Introduction

Fuzzy information is a common phenomenon in natural language, which mainly includes lexical fuzziness and semantic fuzziness. Lexical vagueness includes time words, age words, color words, temperature words, taste words, etc. because the boundary of the meaning it refers to is difficult to be clearly defined, it forms fuzzy information. For example, there is generally no clear definition of how old "young people" refer to. Semantic vagueness can also be reflected in some words used in sentences, such as I wonder, I propose, it is estimated, it sees, which can mean subjective speculation or reporting others' views; A bit, adequately, approximately, around and other words can adjust the degree of authenticity or scope of change of discourse [1].

With the development of information processing technology, a large number of intelligent translation software continue to appear. Machine translation gradually replaces manual translation and becomes an important role in English translation in the future. The accuracy and adaptability of machine translation become an important topic in the research of translation software in the future. The optimization of machine translation is based on semantic selection and feature extraction. By extracting the text semantic

© ICST Institute for Computer Sciences, Social Informatics and Telecommunications Engineering 2023
Published by Springer Nature Switzerland AG 2023. All Rights Reserved
M. A. Jan and F. Khan (Eds.): BigIoT-EDU 2022, LNICST 465, pp. 310–315, 2023.
https://doi.org/10.1007/978-3-031-23950-2_33

information features of English context, combined with intelligent analysis and semantic information retrieval technology, ontology mapping and adaptive adjoint tracking of semantic information are realized, and English intelligent translation is realized combined with pattern recognition method, The research on fuzzy semantic selection technology in English semantic machine translation is of great significance in optimizing machine translation software design and improving translation accuracy and artificial intelligence. The traditional methods mainly include topic tree feature matching method, support vector machine algorithm, particle swarm optimization evolution method, etc. language evaluation set model construction and feature combination matching are carried out for the semantic features of English translation to improve the accuracy of translation, and some research results have been achieved. However, the traditional methods have some problems, such as weak suppression ability of context interference, easy coupling interference and so on.

2   Overview of Relevant Technologies

2.1   Overview of Fuzziness

Classical logic is a binary logic that satisfies the law of contradiction and exclusion, that is, it can only be judged according to binary logic such as "yes and no", "right and wrong", "0 and 1", and there is no middle zone. However, as the main body of understanding the world and transforming the objective world, the reflection of human brain on natural phenomena is usually vague. This fuzziness is reflected in that it is not a clear and accurate reflection of "either this or that". It more reflects the uncertainty between the attributes of things and the attribute division caused by the transition of differences, which makes the concept unclear and appears "this or that" and "seems to be rather than". In 1965, Professor L.A. Zadeh of the University of California published a famous paper, in which he first put forward an important concept to express the fuzziness of things: membership function, which broke through Cantor's classical set theory at the end of the 19th century and laid the foundation of fuzzy theory. It not only broadens the classical mathematics, but also builds a bridge between man and machine in theory, making the intelligence of machine possible [2].

Definition: fuzziness refers to the indistinct extension of the concept of things in the objective world, and the same and different attribution of things to the concept.

$$U = \{u_1, u_2, \ldots u_n\} \tag{1}$$

$$V = \{v_1, v_2, \ldots v_m\} \tag{2}$$

$$A = \{a_1, a_2, \ldots a_n\} \tag{3}$$

$$R_i = \{r_{i1}, r_{i2}, \ldots r_{in}\} \tag{4}$$

2.2 Decision Tree Algorithm

As a common classification algorithm in data mining, decision tree algorithm has been widely used in many fields. It has many advantages, such as small amount of calculation, convenient rule acquisition, high classification accuracy and so on. From the initial CLS algorithm to today's various decision tree classification algorithms, the representative ones are ID3, C4.5 algorithm and so on. The following is a brief description of these common decision tree classification algorithms.

1) ID3 Decision Tree Algorithm

ID3 decision tree algorithm, which mainly aims at the problem of selecting attributes during the construction of decision tree. It is the most influential and classic algorithm in decision tree. ID3 decision tree algorithm takes information theory as the theoretical basis, measures the criteria of attribute selection through information entropy and information gain in information theory, and realizes the best selection of candidate attributes. The algorithm calculates the information gain of each candidate attribute, and then selects the candidate attribute that can maximize the information gain as the test attribute to construct the node of the decision tree, so as to construct the decision tree.

ID3 decision tree algorithm has clear theory and simple algorithm structure by using information gain in attribute selection, but ID3 algorithm depends on attributes with a large number of attribute values when calculating information gain, and ID3 algorithm is sensitive to noise and can not deal with continuous attributes well.

$$\text{SplitInfo}(A) = -\sum_{i=1}^{m} \frac{|S_j|}{|S|} \times \log_2 \frac{|S_j|}{|S|} \tag{5}$$

2) C4.5 Decision Tree Algorithm

Aiming at some shortcomings of ID3 algorithm, C4.5 decision tree algorithm uses information gain rate to select the best candidate attribute as the test attribute, which can eliminate the dependence of ID3 algorithm on multivalued attributes, and C4.5 algorithm can have good processing effect on continuous attributes and can process incomplete data sets.

Due to the complexity of fuzziness itself, it is difficult to fit with a unified form of function in practice. At present, the selection and establishment methods of membership function mainly include fuzzy based method, comparative ranking method, expert evaluation method and so on. As shown in Fig. 1, triangular membership function diagram.

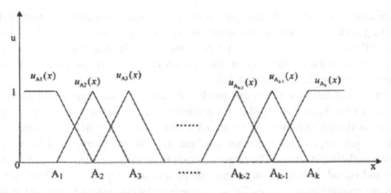

Fig. 1. Triangular membership function graph

3 Application of Intelligent Fuzzy Decision Tree Algorithm in English Translation

Nida also pointed out: "although absolute communication between people is impossible, highly effective communication between people is still possible regardless of the same language region or between different language regions, because people's ideas, physical reactions, cultural experiences and the ability to adjust other people's behavior are similar."

The expression of the target language (or target language) is the ultimate goal of translation. Expression is to reproduce the ideological content and style of the original text to the greatest extent, reproduce the attitude, feelings and writing techniques of the original author, and conform to the expression habits of the target language. Understanding is an extremely complex process with some fuzziness; Expression is not easy, so we need to use various translation skills in order to make the translation conform to the expression habits of the target language.

Proper use of vague language in target language expression can not only improve the accuracy of language expression, but also make language expression euphemistic, implicit and appropriate. To a certain extent, appropriateness in language use is as important as accuracy. We can also say that appropriateness itself is communicative accuracy. To achieve this - point, in the process of expression, we need to comprehensively consider the commonness and individuality in the expression of the source language and the target language, the differences in the understanding of the source language and the target language, the mutual social and cultural background and differences embodied in the source language and the target language, and so on [3].

Language fuzziness has been especially favored by writers since ancient times. Therefore, in the treasure house of Chinese literature and English literature, literary fuzziness is a common means for writers to describe characters, scenery and character. For example, Song Yu's words used to describe beauty in the lustful Fu of dengtuzi are very popular because of the fuzziness of his language: "an increase of one cent is too long, and a decrease of one cent is too short. The powder is too white, and Shi Zhu is too red." after talking for a long time, I don't know how long, how short, how white and how red it is, but it is very vivid and thought-provoking. The expression of the target language should reproduce the thoughts, feelings, attitudes, positions, rhetorical devices and writing style of the source language author as "equivalent" as much as possible, but also reflect the social, cultural and contemporary characteristics contained in the source language to the greatest extent, and conform to the expression habits of the target language, so as to make a good translation.

Machine translation systems can be divided into different types according to different standards. According to the use environment of machine translation systems, machine translation systems can be divided into three categories: low-end machine translation systems, custom high-end machine translation systems and Internet-based machine translation systems. The target customers of low-end machine translation systems are individuals, while the target customers of custom high-end machine translation systems are companies and bases The machine translation system based on the Internet is a machine translation system used through the Internet.

Fuzziness of lexical data in English Translation

For continuous data, the commonly used discrete methods are: equidistant segmentation method, which divides the English translation data into n equidistant parts, and the equidistant parts have the same distance, but this method has a great impact on the collection of outliers and can not deal with inclined data well; equifrequency segmentation method, by dividing the data into equal parts, each equal part has the same amount of data, this algorithm It has good scalability and is suitable for data classification; the histogram method divides the data into thousands of buckets and represents each bucket with the average value or sum in the bucket; the cluster analysis method is based on "the maximum similarity within the class and the minimum similarity between classes" This paper uses the cluster center point to represent the objects contained in this class. This method is very effective and meets many actual data conditions.

4 Processing of Fuzzy Information in English Translation

Literal translation is the most common method to deal with fuzzy information in business translation, that is, using the fuzziness of one language to translate the fuzziness of another language, so as to retain the fuzzy information and realize the equivalence of fuzzy information [4].

The transformation syntax can be used for parsing, that is, the parser. Although the interpretation relationship expressed by transformation grammar simplifies the processing of subsequent stages, transformation rules are designed for deep structure, and it is very complex to use transformation rules to deal with surface structure. In short, there are at least three basic problems:

(1) For a given sentence, it can generate a set of syntactic trees. This set of syntax trees should include all surface trees to which the transformation syntax should be assigned;

(2) For a given tree that does not belong to the base, determine the transformation rules that can be used to generate the tree;

(3) You can judge the conversion rules one by one. If the result is the current tree, this rule will not be executed.

If we deal with these problems in the most direct way, we may have to try many wrong methods. Of course, for the first question, you can use context free syntax to generate transformation syntax. Syntax can be assigned to all surface trees of a sentence, and its number may be large. This syntax is also called overlapping syntax.

5   Conclusion

In the field of professional translation, machine translation technology is being used more and more widely. Therefore, we should change our ideas, improve the teaching conditions of machine translation, strengthen training, improve the level of teachers in machine translation, accumulate strength and compile relevant teaching materials. In addition, we should also cooperate closely with translation companies or enterprises to create conditions for machine translation teaching, actively carry out research and practice in this field and cultivate high professional quality, Talents who master various editing skills and word processing technology, and can use various translation software and modern technology to complete translation tasks quickly and efficiently, so as to serve social development and economic construction.

Acknowledgements. "Big Data Application Research Center for Higher vocational foreign language Education" (19kypt06), a scientific research platform project of Chengdu Polytechnic.

References

1. Jiangtao, L.: At present, the gap of translation talents in China is as high as 90%. World Educ. Inform. **4**, 5 (2006)
2. Yining, Y.: Translation technology and the cultivation of technical translation talents in China. Chin. Sci. Technol. Trans. **2**, 51–54 (2005)
3. Zhang, Y.: Computer aided translation. Shanghai Science and Technology Translation (1) (2002)
4. Murray, L.V.L.: Computer aided translation technology and translation teaching. Foreign Lang. Circ. **2007** (3), 37 (2007)

Application of Intelligent Water Conservancy Information System in Agricultural Water-Saving Irrigation

Yi Li[✉]

Lanzhou Resources and Environment Voc-Tech University, Lanzhou 730021, Gansu, China
hxy201106@163.com

Abstract. Water conservancy project is not only the infrastructure of national economic development, but also an important factor related to the coordinated development of social natural environment, economic environment and cultural environment. Especially with the continuous emergence of Internet information technology and Internet of things technology, a variety of advanced technologies and sensing test instruments are used to monitor regional water environment, flood disaster and agricultural irrigation, and build an information monitoring system for water quality and water regime covering regional water systems, which can realize the modern and intelligent management of agricultural water-saving irrigation.

Keywords: Intelligent water conservancy · Agricultural water-saving irrigation · Information system

1 Introduction

Although with the acceleration of national development and the improvement of industrialization speed, it has gradually become an industrialized country. But generally speaking, China is still a large agricultural country and a large agricultural irrigation country. Water is crucial to agriculture. However, there are great contradictions in the utilization of water resources in China: on the one hand, water resources are very scarce, on the other hand, the waste of agricultural water is serious. First of all, the broad masses of farmers have a weak awareness of water resources. Farmers generally believe that water is inexhaustible, and the idea of not using it for nothing is serious. Secondly, irrigation water is unscientific. China's traditional agricultural farming methods for thousands of years have a great impact on farmers, resulting in serious waste of agricultural water, which is reflected in the low water use coefficient of agricultural irrigation [1]. At present, the national average is only 0.4–0.45. In many places, the irrigation water consumption even exceeds 20 times or even higher than the national water quota. According to the current utilization rate of agricultural water, it can be simply estimated that at present, China's irrigation area is 820 million mu, of which the area of canal irrigation accounts for about 75% and the area of well irrigation accounts for about 25%. Even if calculated

M. A. Jan and F. Khan (Eds.): BigIoT-EDU 2022, LNICST 465, pp. 316–325, 2023.
https://doi.org/10.1007/978-3-031-23950-2_34

according to the utilization rate of 0.45, more than 180 billion cubic meters of water may be lost due to leakage or evaporation loss in the process of water transmission every year [2]. Thirdly, water management is extensive. Many irrigation areas do not have good water metering devices, and they lack a more accurate grasp of the water demand of the irrigation area in a certain period. Water discharge irrigation has great randomness and blindness. In addition, from the perspective of irrigation facilities, some reservoirs have no main canals and rely on river channels for water delivery; In many irrigation areas, only trunk and branch canals have been built. The canal system below the branch canal is not perfect, the matching rate is low, and the aging of the project leads to great loss of irrigation water. Therefore, it is difficult to meet the current needs of agricultural water in China, whether from the perspective of water awareness, the scientificity of agricultural water and the matching rate of agricultural water projects [3].

At present, the main problems faced by the construction and development of water conservancy projects in China have changed from the treatment of natural floods and sudden water conditions in the past to the supervision of water resources, ecological environment and water conservancy projects. Facing the general trend of the rapid development of Internet information technology, all regions have water The benefit department should make use of the Internet of things technology to make all-round parameter detection, data information acquisition and data integration analysis on the existing surface water height, underground water regime and water quality, as well as the seepage situation during the construction and operation of water conservancy projects, and put forward suggestions on the construction of intelligent water conservancy overall structure, so as to provide support for the management of water conservancy information monitoring personnel [4].

With the rapid development of computer technology, Internet of things technology has also accelerated the pace of development. Backward agriculture can also be transformed through advanced technology, and Internet of things technology can quickly solve the water shortage problem of China, a large agricultural country. Therefore, the importance of Internet of things technology in water-saving irrigation is self-evident. The popularization of intelligent irrigation control can effectively use the limited water resources, and is of great help to the production of crops. On the premise of less destruction of ecological resources, it greatly reduces the survival cost, and enables us to get better, cheaper and higher quality food. The modern intelligent irrigation system has many advantages over traditional irrigation methods: for example, it can irrigate part of the day in the dark, for example, it can reasonably control the water pan, for example, it can very well control the time. This is a very beneficial technology for Ningxia, which lacks water resources. If we make full use of the intelligent water-saving irrigation system under the Internet of things technology, it will greatly solve the big problem of water shortage in Ningxia [5].

With the accelerated development of modern agriculture, some agricultural facilities and equipment are constantly updated. Green intelligence from the perspective of the country's future development needs, the use of solar energy, wind energy and other green energy is the development trend of our country. The popularity of green energy is increasing, and it is widely used in agriculture, such as the installation of solar energy technology on insect repellent lamps, and the use of wind for water-saving irrigation.

With the deepening of green energy conservation, its application conditions are more convenient. For example, it is not affected by weather and climate, and it saves water and energy. This paper is mainly based on green energy In addition, the remote intelligent irrigation system is integrated with uwp technology, wireless communication network GPRS and computer technology. Such a system can make information more timely, more convenient for management, save a lot of manpower, establish a more scientific detection process, and provide convenience for life [6]. The research and development of remote intelligent control irrigation system through uwp technology makes use of cross platform information sharing between different platforms, eliminating information islands and facilitating information sharing, which is now known as cloud platform. In this system, the information sharing between different devices is realized, which ensures the maximum performance advantage of the irrigation system. At the same time, it is also applicable to the latest Microsoft system.

2   Intelligent Water Conservancy Information System

2.1   Overview of Intelligent Water Conservancy Information System

China is a large agricultural country, and its water consumption is often greater than that of other countries. With the increasing lack of water resources, all countries need to find effective ways to save a lot of water. Among many methods, sprinkler irrigation and micro irrigation technology can solve this problem very well. In recent years, water-saving irrigation technology in China has developed rapidly, and great breakthroughs and progress have been made in spray and drip irrigation technology, and a lot of valuable practical experience has been accumulated. Therefore, the spray drip irrigation technology is widely used in our country, and has achieved good results.

With the extensive development of computer technology in our country, more and more enterprises have implemented the transformation of management mode from people-oriented to computer-controlled. However, at this stage, China's management level is relatively backward compared with developed countries. At present, in the field of water-saving irrigation, China is still in the traditional artificial irrigation mode or the way of manually controlling irrigation, which has not yet reached the integrated control mode. Even if there is intelligent agriculture or intelligent control system, it is also a small-scale and small-scale controlled irrigation. However, the real large-scale cluster deployment in the form of Internet of things using computer control is still rare [7]. China has carried out extensive research on water-saving irrigation, such as Lai Heyuan fully exploring the role of GPS measurement and GIS technology in the survey, design and construction of efficient water-saving irrigation projects; The water management information system of Shijin Irrigation Area Based on WebGIS designed by Yang Ming; Ji Jianwei, The automatic control system of paddy field irrigation based on PLC designed by Deng Weiwei et al. "; the vegetable greenhouse automatic irrigation system based on single chip microcomputer designed by Ju Yongsheng and Li Xingkai. At present, the system is put into use in most parts of China, and has the best effect in Dalian and Beijing, and has achieved certain social and economic benefits; like the Institute of agricultural mechanization, Tianjin Institute of water conservancy science has independently developed the greenhouse drip irrigation and fertilization intelligent control system. In general, my knowledge of precision irrigation technology It is equivalent to the initial stage of advanced countries [8]. There are too few research knowledge about the whole digital agriculture and smart agriculture, the simulation technology is not advanced enough, and the research problems are not thorough enough.

Intelligent water conservancy information system is to install a variety of sensors, sensors and other hardware equipment to the reservoir outlet, water source and radioactive source area, and then generally connect these physical hardware equipment with the help of Internet of things software technology, so as to form the collection, transmission and analysis of multivariate data information in the Internet of things network. At present, the network communication technology used in intelligent water conservancy information system mainly includes GPRS CDMA. 4G and other communication technologies, as well as Internet of things technologies such as cloud computing, big data server and water conservancy monitoring software platform. By using a variety of Internet of things sensing technologies to more quickly perceive the real-time indicators of the regional water conservancy system, we can comprehensively monitor the rise of surface water, underground water regime, water environment pollution, sudden flood disasters, etc., and formulate patrol management, disaster command and emergency management plans on this basis.

In the intelligent water conservancy information system, there are usually hydrological telemetry terminal, water level gauge and open channel flowmeter Rainfall profile, water pressure sensor, conductivity sensor, temperature sensor, water turbidity sensor, radio frequency identification sensor and other equipment automatically collect information about water conservancy project operation and hydrological changes, which can help the management department grasp the transmitted hydrological data in a timely and comprehensive manner [9]. Then, the monitoring center and network software service platform of the water resources bureau will carry out distributed calculation and storage of the collected hydrological data information, and provide users with web page access, information acquisition and download services according to their personal needs, so as to complete the more intelligent management of water conservancy information and water conservancy problems in key areas.

2.2 Construction Strategy of Intelligent Water Conservancy Information System in a Region

Since the 1980s, a certain area has established a large number of water conservancy projects with important functions with the management objectives of water resources monitoring, flood control and drought relief. According to the investigation and statistics by using the water conservancy information system, a certain area is surrounded by large and small rivers and lakes, with more than 4000 water and rain monitoring points, 3 data acquisition center stations and more than 300 soil moisture stations.

A water conservancy electronic map with a ratio of 1:250000 has been built in an area. The map will reflect the real-time rain and water conditions, as well as the development of historical hydrology, flood and drought prevention, and can monitor the existing water conditions, moisture and water resources pollution. For the monitoring and early warning of hydrological monitoring, agricultural irrigation, water and soil conservation, flood control and drought relief of small and medium-sized rivers, a variety of sensor monitoring equipment will be used to carry out systematic data monitoring in different water conservancy areas through the communication network connected by the backbone network, combined with the business monitoring needs of water resources pollution, surface hydrology, water level height, groundwater change, open channel irrigation flow, water disaster and so on Statistical analysis and storage, and transmitted to the government intranet and unit business network of the Provincial Department of water resources to ensure that the water conservancy project can be built, used well and used for a long time.

To effectively allocate water resources, we need to integrate limited water resources, and the development of modern technology provides us with a very good solution, the Internet of things. The Internet of things will solve the difficult problems of water conservancy informatization, such as the low degree of monitoring automation and insufficient transmission network coverage, and will be more and more widely used in the hot issues of water conservancy informatization, such as flood and drought warning, water ecological monitoring, water conservancy facilities monitoring, water resources scheduling and so on. At present, most parts of China do not have such awareness, which leads to a large-scale waste of energy and resources. The older generation of engineers do not understand the combination of the Internet and engineering. In fact, if we can use modern technology and traditional irrigation technology, we can produce the greatest effect. In this way, on the basis of saving money, labor and energy, On the other hand, it is also a kind of awareness of environmental protection. Therefore, in view of the rise of the Internet of things, we should not rule it out, but should accept its advantages, and then apply it to agriculture and water conservancy in combination with China's national conditions.

Through the application of Internet of things technology, the difficult problems of water conservancy informatization, such as low degree of monitoring automation and insufficient transmission network coverage, have been well solved, which greatly reduces the administrative cost, improves the work efficiency, and has remarkable benefits. The era of Internet of things is an era of high information development. Everything common around us can be connected with the Internet. The water conservancy project is the key to government affairs and the livelihood of the people. Reasonable combination of Internet of things technology can improve efficiency within a certain range, so as to effectively plan limited resources. While the water conservancy business is developing rapidly with the help of IOT technology, we can also further expand and extend it. For example, through IOT technology, we can automatically connect the supervision and governance of exploration, construction, safety, environmental protection, police and water conservancy industry, and realize the seamless link of information through IOT, so as to form intelligent big data and bring the development of water conservancy into a new stage of development.

3 Composition of Farmland Water Conservancy Information System

3.1 Underground Water Regime Monitoring System

The underground water regime monitoring system uses modern communication, computer, digital network and electronic technology to realize the remote automatic measurement and reporting of dynamic information (water regime) of water resources. The system is divided into subsystems such as water regime detection, signal transmission, data transmission and analysis and processing. It has the characteristics of high scientific and technological content, high precision, strong stability and timeliness. It realizes the unmanned collection and automatic measurement and reporting of groundwater monitoring data, and improves the work efficiency and office automation level, At the same time, it is also convenient for water administrative departments and earthquake monitoring and management departments to timely and accurately grasp the real-time situation of water resources, so as to provide a reliable scientific basis for water resources allocation and earthquake prediction. The application of the system makes the city's water resources management and monitoring step into a fast, accurate and efficient track, which will produce huge economic and social benefits [10]. The groundwater regime monitoring system relies on GPRS network, and the staff can view the groundwater regime data in the monitoring center.

The monitoring management software of the monitoring center can realize remote data collection and remote monitoring. All monitored data enter the database and generate various reports and curves. The underground water regime monitoring system consists of four parts: monitoring center, communication network, intelligent liquid level transmitter and solar power supply scheme.

3.2 Video Monitoring System

The video monitoring system consists of local monitoring system and video service system. The local monitoring system is mainly composed of camera PTZ decoder (it is composed of PTZ lens control, video encoder and other equipment to complete the collection, processing and transmission of video information on the project site, accept the monitoring and control instructions of remote users, and execute the control of camera lens and PTZ to obtain image information from different angles, different directions and different effects. The video service system is mainly composed of video management server, data management server and media It is composed of server, video client and other equipment and relevant software to complete the functions of video information reception, processing, storage, deployment, on-demand and playback. At the same time, it manages the users of video client to meet the video monitoring needs of users in different regions, different levels and different monitoring requirements.

3.3 Meteorological Monitoring System

The mobile automatic weather station adopts integrated design and is a multi-element automatic weather station specially developed and produced for microclimate observation, mobile weather observation post, short-term scientific investigation, seasonal ecological monitoring, etc. It can measure conventional meteorological elements such as wind direction, wind speed, temperature and humidity, air pressure, rainfall, solar radiation, solar ultraviolet, soil temperature and humidity, and automatically calculate and store wind cold index, et transpiration evaporation and temperature / humidity / light / wind index according to the aerodynamic method in micro meteorology. This kind of meteorological station has become the most comprehensive microclimate observation station for measuring meteorological elements in China. The structure of the terminal controller is shown in Fig. 1.

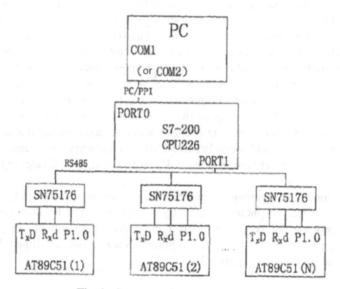

Fig. 1. Structure of terminal controller

3.4 Greenhouse Intelligent Irrigation Management System

The greenhouse precision irrigation system takes the root layer soil moisture as the control index, controls the root layer soil moisture according to different growth stages of crops, and determines the irrigation time and irrigation quota. The whole irrigation control system is composed of upper computer software system, regional control cabinet, shunt controller, transmitter and data acquisition terminal, which is organically combined with the water supply system to realize intelligent control. Transmitter (soil moisture transmitter, flow transmitter, etc.) will monitor the irrigation status in real time. When the soil moisture in the irrigation area reaches the preset lower limit, the solenoid valve can be opened automatically. When the monitored soil moisture content and liquid level reach the preset irrigation quota, the solenoid valve can be closed automatically. The solenoid valve of the whole irrigation area can also be scheduled to work in turn according to the time period. Irrigation can also be controlled manually Irrigation and collection of soil moisture. The whole system can coordinate the work, implement rotation irrigation, fully improve the efficiency of irrigation water, save water and electricity, reduce labor intensity and reduce labor input cost.

4   Specific Application of Intelligent Water Conservancy Information System in Agricultural Water-Saving Irrigation

4.1   Application in Pollution Monitoring of Water Environment and Resources

In the process of water quality monitoring of the water resources monitoring system, water departments in different regions often use the water turbidity sensor of the water resources measurement and control terminal to obtain the amount of water resources from rivers, lakes or reservoirs. With the water conservancy monitoring software platform as the center, the water intake flow, pump / valve status and equipment power supply are automatically controlled, and the measurement of water intake is remotely controlled. For example, there are a large number of lakes in Hubei, Hunan and other areas. For the monitoring of lake water quality and water environment pollution, multiple water intake points in a certain area are often determined first, and then the wireless network communication network, water intake equipment and intelligent detection software are used to monitor the acidity, alkalinity, pH value, solids, chlorides, nitrogen and phosphorus pollutants, sulfur compounds and heavy metals of the water environment. After detecting that a variety of water pollution indicators exceed the standard, corresponding management measures shall be taken to control them.

4.2   Application in Surface Hydrology and Water Level Height Monitoring

There are many large and small rivers and lakes in different regions of China. The main purpose of dams built on rivers and lakes is to adjust the height of water level and control the change of water temperature. Then, in the face of flood disaster, a variety of sensing equipment are used for timely early warning, so as to reduce the loss of personnel, economic property and so on. For example, the water conservancy department needs to monitor the river water level, flow velocity, flow and rainfall change in unit time in real time, automatically alarm the monitored abnormal data, and automatically open the drainage and drainage ports by the dam body. Through the coordinated operation between different modules in the system, it is convenient for the staff to timely adjust the monitoring plan and the treatment plan of flood disasters, The implementation flow of the system topology is shown in Fig. 2.

It can be seen from Fig. 1 that the pressure type 1 float water level gauge and ultrasonic / Radar water level gauge are mainly used to obtain the data information of multiple hydrological monitoring points, including important areas and locations prone to flood disasters, and then collect the multivariate data through the hydrological telemetry terminal. Then by using GPRS CDMA. 4G and other communication technologies will transmit the received hydrological monitoring data resources to the water conservancy monitoring software platform, which will make processing and decision-making of surface hydrology and water level height.

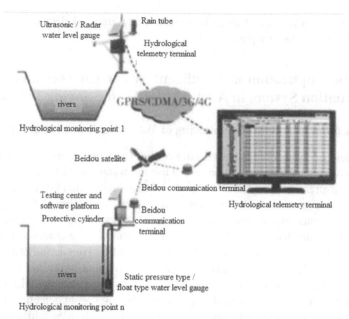

Fig. 2. Topology flow chart of hydrology and water level height monitoring system

The irrigation area module is mainly divided into three parts: irrigation area information, irrigation volume and equipment control. The interference of abnormal physiological functions of plants caused by water shortage is called water stress. Yang Yanfen, Du Taisheng and other examples have done relevant research on the change of soil moisture content during the growth of different crops. Through a large number of data research and summary, they found that the change law of crop water demand depends on the soil moisture content. Crops can grow healthily only when the moisture content in the soil is not lower than the value of water required by crops. Therefore, it is particularly important to master soil moisture content and crop water demand threshold.

Irrigation area information: it mainly displays the soil humidity and soil temperature in real time according to the soil humidity sensor and temperature sensor, displays the basic information of the irrigation area, analyzes the content of soil nitrogen, phosphorus and potassium in real time, and the soil temperature and humidity sensor. Through the computer display screen, it can intuitively display the temperature and humidity and solar sunshine of the test field in China, so as to facilitate the continuous understanding of observers or staff. Then take corresponding measures according to different changes. For example, selecting irrigation area 1 can add and delete temperature and humidity sensors and nitrogen, phosphorus and potassium sensors. Secondly, it can display the current soil temperature, humidity and the status of nitrogen, phosphorus and potassium in real time. The significance of this function lies in the unlimited addition of sensors.

Irrigation volume: mainly for irrigation volume, duration and periodic operation, it can automatically control the upper limit and lower limit of soil humidity. It can set the upper limit and lower limit of soil humidity according to different crops and local soil conditions, the time to start irrigation and the date of circulation. Note: when the upper limit and lower limit of soil humidity are set to 0, it means that the solenoid valve is manually controlled, The significance of this function is that it can achieve regular and quota irrigation according to different crops.

5   Conclusion

Using the intelligent information interaction technology of the Internet of things, this paper puts forward a complete construction scheme of water conservancy information system, and forms a water conservancy business service module with perfect functions around the monitoring directions of water environment pollution, surface hydrology or water level height, groundwater level or water temperature change, open channel irrigation water level and flow, which can solve the information problem of the development of regional water conservancy industry.

References

1. Li, X., Zhang, S., Wu, H., et al.: Research and application of reservoir safety monitoring system for intelligent water conservancy. IOP Conf. Ser. Mater. Sci. Eng. **794**, 012004 (2020)
2. Li, F., Li, X., Zhang, H.: Understanding and thinking of intelligent water conservancy in China under the background of informatization. IOP Conf. Ser. Earth Environ. Sci. **643**(1), 012102 (2021)
3. Li, Y.W., Cao, K.: Establishment and application of intelligent city building information model based on BP neural network model. Comput. Commun. **153**, 382–389 (2020)
4. Wu, W.: Application of agricultural intelligent irrigation system based on internet of things technology. Journal of Agricultural Mechanization Research (2020)
5. Chen, S., Ning, Z., Lin, W., et al.: Application of intelligent blood temperature and humidity monitoring system in blood station. Nat. Sci. **14**(5), 7 (2022)
6. Kurdi, M.Z.: Text complexity classification based on linguistic information: application to intelligent tutoring of ESL (2020)
7. Wang, P.: Application of intelligent manufacturing technology in the field of ship design and manufacturing. J. Phys. Conf. Ser. **2074**(1), 012075 (2021)
8. Bian, L., Zhang, J., Cui, Q., et al.: Research on the realization and application of intelligent IoT platform for electrical equipment under industrial internet. J. Phys. Conf. Ser. **1982**(1), 012078 (2021)
9. Nie, G., Xu, Y.: Research on the application of intelligent technology in low voltage electric automation control system. J. Phys. Conf. Ser. **1865**(2), 022072 (2021)
10. Li, Q., Chen, Y.: Application of intelligent nursing information system in emergency nursing management. Journal of Healthcare Engineering (2021)

Application of Machine Learning Algorithm in Marketing Education

Qianyu Wang[✉]

SiChuan TOP IT Vocational Institute, Chengdu 611743, Sichuan, China
wqy81803@163.com

Abstract. The scientific and technological revolution of mankind has overturned the cognition of hawkers who only knew how to set up stalls more than a decade ago. At this stage, the transformation from simple business relations to complex online transactions not only highlights the development of science and technology and the progress of the times, but also indirectly reflects the changes in marketing methods and tools. In the field of marketing at home and abroad, database marketing, as a cost-effective marketing method, has attracted more and more attention in recent years as a "novice" salesperson in the sales market. However, as a forecaster of unpredictable market or neutron electronics, database marketing is completed through a simple data analysis, which is used in specific practice. Therefore, this paper is based on the application of machine learning algorithm in the field of marketing.

Keywords: Machine learning algorithm · Marketing management

1 Introduction

In this article, we will understand the application of machine learning algorithm in marketing education. In this article, we will understand the application of machine learning algorithm in marketing education. Machine learning is a process that involves using algorithms to train data sets to perform tasks such as pattern recognition and prediction. Training data sets are usually provided by analysts or researchers who collect them through surveys or other means. Once the algorithm is trained on a large enough sample, it can be used to accurately predict the new data set without human intervention. This allows machine learning algorithms to deal with real-world problems.

Since the 1990s, database marketing, a unique marketing method to adapt to the modern information society, has been used by enterprises. However, at this stage, consumers have many access platforms and diverse fields. Although reaching a large number of goods, they also. At the same time, businesses locate target consumers to face the increasing business [1]. The establishment of database marketing strategy is shown in Fig. 1 below.

The business of many e-commerce platform stores has been diluted due to too many products of the same type. If you want to gain an advantage in the increasing market

M. A. Jan and F. Khan (Eds.): BigIoT-EDU 2022, LNICST 465, pp. 326–335, 2023.
https://doi.org/10.1007/978-3-031-23950-2_35

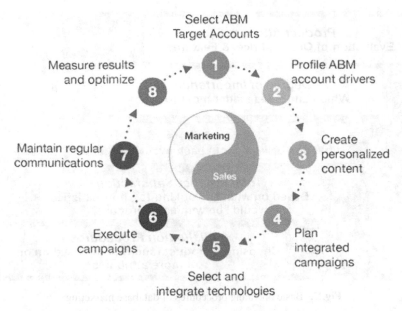

Fig. 1. Establishment of database marketing strategy

competition, an important way is that e-commerce stores accurately identify intended buyers in a large consumer group, so as to improve the marketing efficiency of stores. Based on the idea of database marketing, the customer purchase prediction model is finally constructed, and the database marketing countermeasures are further put forward [2].

2 Related Work

2.1 Basic Procedures of Database Marketing

Database marketing can not only provide comprehensive quality control and management, but also develop a new marketing model based on information technology, which has reached a new level in the current practice and verification. With the improvement of database marketing, it is widely used in business services, order services, big data marketing, non-profit organizations and even industrial production finance. Database marketing can which requires reasonable macro control and thoughtful marketing plan. In order to quantitative, more accurate in classification and positioning, and it is an effective marketing plan. Should establish trust and "intimate relationship" with consumers [3]. This reveal the human-machine relationship, Establish an artificial core, evaluate the rights of consumers and sellers. As shown in Fig. 2, the basic procedures of database marketing can generally be summarized as follows:

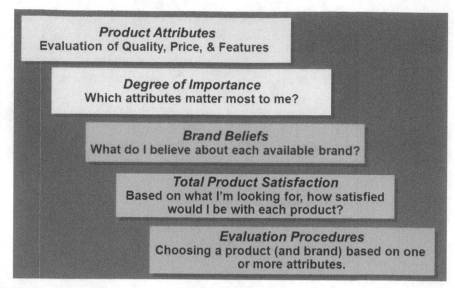

Fig. 2. Basic operating procedures of database marketing

2.2 Overview of Machine Learning Algorithms

Machine learning is a method of self-learning and self-improvement and optimizing performance from a large amount of existing data. Machine learning classification algorithm is mainly divided into two processes: model establishment and classification. Firstly, the classification algorithm is selected, and a classification model is obtained by training the model parameters through the training data set, and then the trained model is used to label the unknown sample data to be tested. Machine learning mainly includes unsupervised classification and supervised classification.

Unsupervised classification is mainly used for clustering, that is, without knowing the classification of the training data set, automatically find rules from the data set to establish clusters. The mark each cluster to form a category.

$$y_j = \sum_1^n w_{ij} - \theta_j \tag{1}$$

$$h_{w,b} = f(W^T x) = f(\sum_{i=1}^3 w_i x_i + b) \tag{2}$$

Classification is to mark the cluster and category of the data by calculating the marked clusters. Some scholars have classified clustering algorithms, which are mainly divided into five clustering algorithms based on division, hierarchy, density, network and model. At clustering methods mainly include k-means algorithm, DBSCAN algorithm and so on. The typical k-means method is based on "birds of a feather flock together" "First, then calculate the similarity distance between the remaining samples and the K cluster centers and classify them as the nearest cluster center, and finally recalculate the average value of all samples in the K cluster as the new cluster center. This process iterates repeatedly until the objective function converges or reaches a certain value Threshold, usually including Manhattan distance, Minkowski distance and Euclidean distance, among which Euclidean distance is the most commonly used distance.

Supervised classification mainly constructs a classification model through training data sets to classify unknown data into known categories [4]. Commonly used supervised classification algorithms mainly include, naive Bayes and ANN. Among them, SVM was proposed by Cortes & Vapnik in his book in 1995. It realizes the principle of SRM (structural risk minimization), has strong generalization ability, and introduces kernel mapping. Compared with traditional statistical methods, SVM not only overcomes the requirements for a large number of samples, but also overcomes the problems of dimension disaster and local minima. Therefore, it is used in processing such as text classification, face recognition It has good performance on complex problems such as biological information processing. The framework is shown in Fig. 3 below.

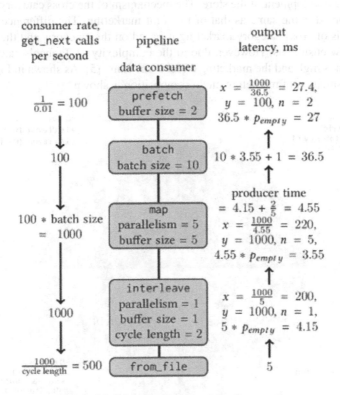

Fig. 3. Machine learning algorithm framework

3 Current Situation of Marketing Mode Composition

With Taobao gaining a firm foothold in the market and the gradual decline of the real economy, more and more businesses choose to enter Taobao, resulting in increasingly fierce competition in online marketing. In the face of complex competitive environment, they continue to introduce newer and more comprehensive marketing methods, including link, cross category marketing, contact recruitment, similar groups Competitive products and cross platform marketing.

At present, crowd marketing is the most efficient. At first, this marketing method came from the marketing example of Wal Mart, a world-famous brand. They put diapers and beer together on the shelf, which greatly increased the sales of diapers and beer. The reason is that Wal Mart has made good use of big data technology and successfully found the potential connection between "diapers" and "beer". Apply this idea and use historical data to calculate the relationship between various commodities in the store. On the one hand, bundle the most closely related commodities. On the other hand, there is no bundling sales, and sales are increased by pushing different materials closely linked. Since this marketing method is always aimed at regular customers, even though the marketing efficiency and precision are high, it now seems that it has certain limitations on the future development of the store. The mechanism of the cross category marketing method adopted is the same as that of the joint marketing. The difference is that the joint analysis of cross category marketing is based on the category, and the marketing object is new customers. However, due to the complexity of Taobao's categories, the analysis cost is high and the marketing effect is the same [5]. As shown in Fig. 4 below, the current situation of marketing mode composition is shown.

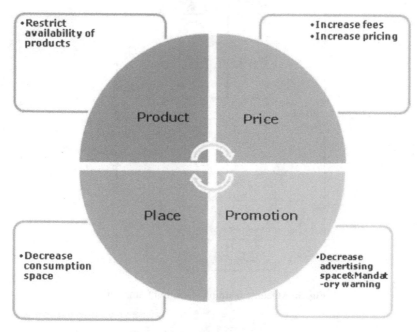

Fig. 4. Current situation of marketing mode composition

The purchase conversion rate of contact recruitment marketing method is very low, and the marketing effect is the worst. The main reason for choosing operation for a long time is that the object of marketing in this way is new customers, which can expand publicity to a certain extent and improve brand penetration, so as to lay a certain foundation for subsequent purchase transformation. Similar people are also called enlarged people, which is to extract the characteristics of the buying people and find people with the same characteristics. The magnification is too small and the number of crowd packages is small. In the delivery process, the impact of bidding mode will lead to obstacles in the delivery of crowd packages. If the magnification is too large, the similarity between the looking group and the buying group is low, which will dilute the marketing effect. The "predatory" marketing method of competitive products is only used as an auxiliary means because of its high cost and difficult predatory[6]. Cross the diversification and diversification, which provides enterprises with favorable marketing platforms. However, from the perspective of the current overall social media marketing and form, the cognition and practice of social media marketing are still in its infancy, and the marketing effects brought by short video media, live media, industry information media and tool media are not significant.

4   Database Marketing Idea Based on Machine Learning Algorithm

The beginning of the big data era has triggered a revolution in database marketing to a certain extent. In database marketing, significant changes have taken place in data display and statistical methods, but also as [7] functional database marketing according to the development. On the other hand, in the broader data context, the data format has the characteristics, diverse data models and so on. First of all, with the popularity of the Internet, the amount of information is growing rapidly. Second, visual and information can be transformed multimedia means. The idea of database marketing is shown in Fig. 5 below.

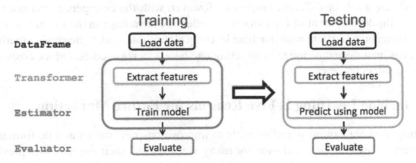

Fig. 5. Database marketing thought

Not all data is useful. Information overload makes it difficult to retrieve and store data. On the under the generalized data background is often a prediction algorithm. In traditional database marketing, several descriptive statistical methods described from different angles are used. The most common is sales channel analysis. After interacting with the flagship store "horse racing", we bought it through other channels. After interacting with other channels, we will buy from the flagship store of the Jockey Club and other channels. Therefore, according to the results of comparative analysis, whether to invest in the relevant costs of plundering resources from other sources can be decided. The relevant data is only the behavior, which is small and easy to access [8]. The flagship store "horse racing" generates a lot of data every day. If we continue to use this simple analysis and operation method, the beginning of "10000 vision" will be accompanied by the initial effects of big data, high cost and dilution. At present, technologies compatible with computer clusters are used in big data processing Machine learning with an effective cloud computing intelligent grid and prediction algorithm can quickly and knowledge from a large amount of data.

Due to the complexity of data format, the diversity of data structure and the limitations of data marketing methods, the integration of machine learning algorithm and database marketing came into being. First, machine learning algorithms must be applied to the field of database marketing. On the other hand, the data of marketing database has many forms. Traditional statistical methods only allow the analysis of digital data, and the difficulties of text, audio and video data processing restrict the development of database marketing. On the other hand, machine learning algorithm is the "only" method of data analysis. Through the targeted separation and organization of information, machine learning can study the potential information that users can use or obtain. These functions make database marketing easier, which can not only attract new consumers, establish long-term relationships with consumers, but also improve their value. Therefore, database marketing can more effectively cooperate with the trend of modern e-commerce era. The foundation of marketing needs the support of machine learning algorithm. Secondly, improving database marketing requires comprehensive machine training In fact, database marketing has only two purposes. In other words, hire new customers by changing contacts, cross platform flows, cross species predation, and analyzing competitive products. Frequent customer transactions are designed to maintain customer relationships, calculate repurchase cycles and repurchase rules [9]. Different methods are used for different purposes. However, with the emergence, can not fully adapt to the development of lynx stores. In order to e advantage in the market, marketing will combine big data with machine learning algorithms, update marketing methods and ideas, introduce customized marketing databases, increase costs, reduce costs, and improve sales efficiency.

5   Machine Learning is Five Reasons for Future Marketing

Leading stars are exploring online tools to improve business trends and performance. Of course, they can visit and monitor many websites and their content. Obviously, I found the advertisement of the same company on the Internet by time on the front of the book. What is more surprising is how Facebook integrates search practices and online activities to improve the integrity and standardization of advertising activities. Figure 6 below shows the complete foundation of database marketing.

Which provides opportunities for automatic learning and experience improvement in the system (uncertain programming). Machine learning focuses on developing computer programs to access, analyze, and learn data.

In addition to products such as Siri and Amazon [10]. This applies not only to Google, Facebook, Microsoft and other companies, who believe that our R & D budget is huge

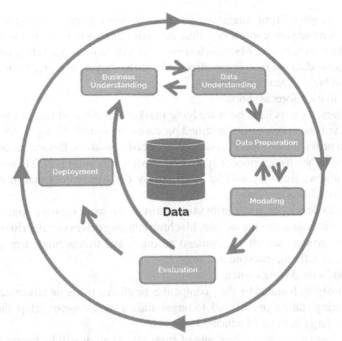

Fig. 6. Database marketing Integrity framework

on the whole. In fact, machine training can help most of the more than 500 enterprises operate more effectively and earn more money.

There are five reasons why enterprises need to implement machine learning and marketing strategies in scale.

A. It brings "real time" to life

For years, marketers have been bragging about the phrase "real time", but it was not until machine learning appeared on the scene that it really became possible. No previous system is close to the response level provided by machine learning. Consumers view quotation changes by minute based on the almost unlimited data created by their behavior for machine processing. The repositioning of Facebook ads is just one example. The time of visiting the website is not long, so you can place advertisements on the agenda [11].

CEO adyton lafargenesis said, "machine learning and other modern technologies have opened up new possibilities for smarter marketing budgets." In the future, the company will provide enterprises with machine learning solutions and other services. "With the help of these new technologies, enterprises can analyze a large amount of data in real time around the clock, deeply understand and manage big data, and obtain strong operational advice, which is the basis of current online business."

B. Eliminate the biggest enemy of marketing

Effective marketing can attract audiences and bring changes. The problem is that marketing wastes this very simple problem. Due to the lack of more effective strategies, marketing activities have also begun. Whether on or outside the network, sports is essentially for sowing and germination.

You can imagine. Your marketing job mainly depends on who you want to see. People who browse your content or online advertisements say they are most interested in your products or services. Machine learning can reduce most marketing mistakes. By using behavioral data, marketers can effectively attract buyers and greatly improve their ability to turn buyers into customers.

C. Open the market forecast portal

For many years, experts have been studying market and demand forecasting. In many cases, the plan is based on a trend oriented procurement model. Using AI for marketing purposes can provide more specific content for decision makers. Before customers know what they need, they have a good way to deliver what they want [12]. These efforts will basically continue. But they will be informed by the data, rather than making blind suggestions to selfless consumers.

The famous developer kevincarrol said, "most of the work we have done in machine learning is carried out under the surface. Machine learning drives our algorithm to predict demand, rank product search, recommend products and transactions, arrange product promotion, detect fraud, translate and so on"

D. It helps build marketing content

Writers use insights handled by their companies or clients to create advertisements and e-mail marketing campaigns that talk to target audiences. However, adopt the catch-up method and a large number of educated guesses.

Machine learning narrows the range of supports. Then, it will be better: it provides a practical means of emotional analysis so that marketers know what to say and how listeners react [13]. The effect of emotional analysis has been exposed on twitter, and marketers can monitor social chat to understand the resonance with specific target audiences. Brand experts and writers can immediately adjust advertisements in response to comments and trend responses. This brings the right information to the surface.

E. It lowers costs

At present, the world is almost completely online, and machine learning can solve the biggest marketing problem. The charge is always close to the highest.

Machine learning reduces marketing costs. Because there are far fewer people who need help. Most customers can book articles, online advertisements and other materials through automatic e-mail and social media, and the price can be updated at any time, so the communication cost has also decreased significantly [14].

The accuracy of machine learning can also be used to produce and sell offline materials. Therefore, marketing can find the right amount and adopt the most effective method to reduce the excessive expenditure related to overproduction.

6 Conclusion

Machine learning is a set of algorithms that can be used to solve problems. The algorithm learns from the data and uses the knowledge obtained to predict the new data. Machine learning algorithms are based on statistical models, which are mathematical descriptions of how variables in data sets change together or over time. These models are trained by applying them to many examples of the same data set and similar data sets with different characteristics. Once these models are trained, they can make accurate predictions of invisible data when new inputs are given (for example, if we use our model to predict customer churn after observing the churn rate of previous customers). Therefore, this paper studies the application of machine learning algorithm in the field of marketing. Deeply understand the database marketing means algorithm to lay the the construction of models.

References

1. Chang, L., Jie, Y., Feiyue, G., et al.: Forecasting the market with machine learning algorithms: an application of NMC-BERT-LSTM-DQN-X algorithm in quantitative trading. In: ACM Transactions on Knowledge Discovery from Data (TKDD) (2022)
2. Xu, J., Deng, X., Yan, F.: Application of machine learning algorithm in Anesthesia. Zhongguo yi xue ke xue yuan xue bao. Acta Academiae Medicinae Sinicae **42**(5), 696–701 (2020)
3. Pan, X.: Application of machine learning algorithm in human resource recommendation: from tradition machine learning algorithm to AutoML. In: 5th International Conference on Social Sciences and Economic Development (ICSSED 2020) (2020)
4. Liu, Y., Yang, S.: Application of decision tree-based classification algorithm on content marketing. J. Math. **2022**, 6469054 (2022)
5. Liu, T., Li, Z., Tang, Y., et al.: The application of the machine learning method in electromyographic data. IEEE Access **PP**(99), 1 (2020)
6. Range, D., David, D., Kovalsky, S.Z., et al.: Application of a machine learning algorithm to predict malignancy in thyroid cytopathology. Cancer Cytopathology (2020)
7. Melchiorre, J., Bertetto, A.M., Marano, G.C.: Application of a machine learning algorithm for the structural optimization of circular arches with different cross-sections, vol. 9, no. 5, p. 12 (2021)
8. Qi, G., Chen, Z., Zhao, H., et al.: Construction and application of machine learning model in network intrusion detection. J. Phys. Conf. Ser. **1883**(1), 012001 (2021)
9. Huang, W.H.: Performance evaluation and application of computation based low-cost homogeneous machine learning model algorithm for image classification. In: ICBDM 2020: 2020 International Conference on Big Data in Management (2020)
10. Zhao, S.: Application of machine learning in understanding the irradiation damage mechanism of high-entropy materials (2021)
11. Zhang, J., Feng, Q., Zhang, X., et al.: A machine learning approach for accurate modeling of CO_2-brine interfacial tension with application in identifying the optimum sequestration depth in saline aquifers. Energy & Fuels XXXX(XXX), 0c00846 (2020)
12. Meharie, M.G., Mengesha, W.J., Gariy, Z.A., et al.: Application of stacking ensemble machine learning algorithm in predicting the cost of highway construction projects. Engineering Construction & Architectural Management, 2021, ahead-of-print (ahead-of-print)
13. Lv, Y., Kong, J.: Application of collaborative filtering recommendation algorithm in pharmacy system. J. Phys. Conf. Ser. **1865**(4), 042113 (2021)
14. Pothuganti, K.: Overview on principal component analysis algorithm in machine learning. Int. Res. J. Sci. Technol. **2020**, 2582–5208 (2020)

Design and Implementation of Dynamic Grouping Algorithm Based on Sports Track

Wangwei Jia[✉]

China.India-China Yoga College, Yunnan Minzu University (International Tai Chi College),
Yunnan 650504, China
jiawangwei2021@163.com

Abstract. Track and field is the "mother of sports" and the basis of all kinds of sports. In the commonly used games management software, the grouping and lane division of sports track events mostly adopt fixed eight lanes, and the AR arrangement algorithm is fixed, which has some defects. The traditional manual arrangement has low operation efficiency, low accuracy, heavy copying task and heavy workload, which requires a lot of human and material resources. The arrangement of order book by computer makes the tedious organization and arrangement work completed manually realized through simple operation, and makes the organization and management of sports meeting simple, efficient and flexible. In this paper, a dynamic grouping algorithm is proposed, the design idea of the algorithm is discussed in detail, and the order arrangement is realized by computer, so as to realize the cumbersome organization and arrangement manually through simple operation, simplify the organization and management of the game, and be efficient and flexible. Using the dynamic grouping algorithm proposed in this paper, the sports track events can be grouped flexibly and quickly, which makes up for the deficiency of the existing sports meeting management software to a certain extent.

Keywords: Sports track · Dynamic grouping algorithm · Layout

1 Introduction

The arrangement of campus track and field games is a very cumbersome work. The traditional manual arrangement has low operation efficiency, low accuracy, heavy copying task and heavy workload, which requires a lot of human and material resources. The arrangement of order book by computer makes the tedious organization and arrangement work completed manually realized through simple operation, and makes the organization and management of sports meeting simple, efficient and flexible.

Through physical exercise, students hone their will quality, cultivate their awareness of rules and stimulate patriotism. As a leading school in the region, Yizheng experimental primary school strives to build a complete campus physical education curriculum, including spring track and field games, autumn fun games, winter Triathlon exercises and headmaster's Cup Basketball Games. Students not only cultivate their physical skills,

M. A. Jan and F. Khan (Eds.): BigIoT-EDU 2022, LNICST 465, pp. 336–346, 2023.
https://doi.org/10.1007/978-3-031-23950-2_36

but also establish the spirit of daring to fight. In the past few years, our teachers and students have carried forward the spirit of hard work and innovation, and made gratifying achievements in campus construction, educational characteristics and education and teaching. We must not only have the courage to learn, but also make new breakthroughs in moral, intellectual, sports and aesthetics, especially sports. Sports is a strength competition, sports is a wisdom competition, sports is a beautiful display, and sports is an ideal flight. I believe that through the efforts of teachers and students, this track and field games will be safe, orderly, healthy and wonderful!

At present, among the various software related to sports meeting management, for the problem of grouping and lane separation of sports track sprint events, eight lanes are fixed, and the lanes of athletes are arranged in the order of athletes' registration. This arrangement method sometimes leads to the situation that there are only one or two athletes in the last group and eight athletes in other groups, or the situation that multiple athletes of a certain college and department compete in the same group, or a certain college and department always compete in a fixed track. In long-distance track and field events, circle recording has always been a difficult point for referees. Whether amateur or national professional competition, due to the error of circle recording, it has had an irreparable impact on the competition. In recent years, some professionals have actively studied the circle recording of track and field middle and long-distance running, race walking and other projects, put forward some new circle recording methods and developed some new equipment, but the feasibility and universality of its application can not meet the needs of various similar projects. With the rapid development of modern science and technology, using computer technology to improve the work efficiency of referees is an effective method. Therefore, it is of great value and practical significance to develop an application program suitable for long-distance track circle recording and dynamic scoring. In college physical education, there are many sports factors related to track events, such as explosive force and speed related to sprint, endurance related to medium and long distance running, etc. the sports ability of track events is directly related to the teaching effect of other events [1]. From the current situation of the implementation of public sports in Colleges and universities, track and field events have basically disappeared, and some college track and field fields are basically idle. In view of the irreplaceable role of track and field in human health, many experts and scholars continue to call for the return of track and field. Therefore, this paper proposes a dynamic grouping algorithm not limited by the number of tracks, which can effectively solve the problems existing in the grouping and lane separation of sports track events.

2 Related Work

2.1 Research Background and Significance

With the increasing strength of China's economic strength, the status of a big country is becoming more and more obvious. To a certain extent, the results of sports events are the embodiment of a country's comprehensive strength, and the analysis of the results of sports events is of great significance, mainly reflected in the following aspects:

1) Analyze the position of China's event results in the international stage, so as to provide basis and effect analysis for the formulation of national sports related policies and strategies;

2) Analyze the achievements and change laws of advantageous projects in China, and be able to analyze them in combination with the changes of relevant policies and strategies, so as to provide basis and effect analysis for various reform schemes in the field of sports;

3) The analysis of the relationship between the performance of the event and the basic quality of athletes (age, height, weight, etc.), as well as the differences in the performance of different sports, will provide a basis for the selection of athletes and scientific training;

4) The higher and stronger sports spirit in the competition is an embodiment of the spirit of self-improvement of the Chinese nation. Building a knowledge base corresponding to the results and automatically answering common questions based on the knowledge base is conducive to the popularization of science about the existing sports results and the publicity of sports "Heroes" and "models".

In addition, with the increasing maturity of Internet technology, the openness of results is getting better and better. All kinds of event organizers and associations have created relevant websites, and all kinds of event results can be published in time, which makes it easier to obtain all kinds of event results and enriches the application scenarios of these data. Statistical analysis based on big data and prediction of possible future situations have become the focus of attention.

Track and field has been a major gold medalist in various comprehensive events over the years. Even everyone agrees that "those who win track and field win the world", so countries pay special attention to it. China's dazzling achievements in middle and long-distance running events, the dominance of throwing events such as shot put and discus, the birth of Liu Xiang's flying man, the recent rise of men's long jump and high jump, and the emergence of Su Bingtian and Xie Zhenye in men's sprint events have raised people's enthusiasm for track and field events. In this context, the scientific use of various data has become the key, and building an intelligent information management platform for track and field events has become one of the core tasks at this stage.

2.2 Dynamic Grouping Algorithm

Packet classification is an important part of QoS mechanism. The so-called packet classification refers to grouping packets into different categories according to some information in the packet header, so that different packets may get different services [2]. The TOS (type of service) domain of IP packets in the original IPv4 protocol is an example of packet classification. However, because the TOS domain has never been really used, the role of packet classification can not be reflected. However, packet classification plays a great role in the DiffServ Model of IETF. DiffServ Model redefines the header of P packet, as shown in Fig. 1 below.

The DiffServ Model redefines the TOS domain of the IP packet header in IPv4, which is renamed DS domain (differentiated service field). As shown in Fig. 1, the first six bits of the DS domain are called DSCP (differentiated service code point), and the

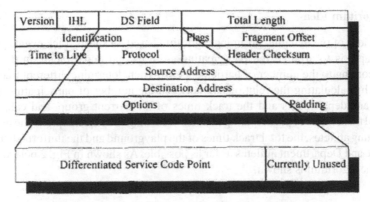

Fig. 1. Definition of DS domain in DiffServ Model

last two bits are not used. In the DiffServ Model, when a group enters the edge of the track, it must first be classified, and its classification results are encoded and recorded with DSCP. The subsequent sports event group selects the PHB of the group according to the DSCP value of the group [3]. This is actually a traffic aggregation, so that a large number of flows are clustered into a small number of classes according to their different business properties.

The so-called packet scheduling means that when a packet needs to be sent, the sports event group selects an appropriate packet from several different queues to forward according to a certain algorithm. FIFO (first in first out) queue is the simplest example. In this queue, sports event groups always forward packets in the order of arrival. The order of packet departure in other algorithms may be different from the order of packet arrival.

Traditional sports event groups always use FIFO to forward packets, but this method has several disadvantages [4]: 1 Streams cannot be isolated from each other, and the behavior of one stream may affect other streams; 2. Unable to provide track guarantee for convection; 3. Delay guarantee cannot be provided for convection; 4. Improper flow will lead to a sharp rise in data loss rate; 5. Unable to treat all flows fairly. Therefore, it is necessary to use other algorithms to improve.

By using appropriate packet scheduling algorithm, the sports event group can ensure the requirements of packet track, delay, delay jitter, loss rate and so on. The application can make an appointment for the required resources first, and then use the track after obtaining the guarantee, so as to ensure the QoS requirements of the application.

Of course, the use of complex scheduling algorithms in sports event groups also has to pay a certain price. Complex scheduling calculation and transmission will bring additional delay to packets, which requires that the complexity of the algorithm should be considered when designing the algorithm, and hardware can be used to implement it if necessary,

2.3 Algorithm Idea

The core idea of the dynamic grouping algorithm based on sports track events proposed in this paper is to arrange the participating colleges and departments in descending order according to the number of participants [5]. Then determine different track filling methods by calculating the relationship between the number of participating athletes' colleges and departments and the track times of the current group, and calculate the group and track times of participating athletes according to the principle of the number of participating athletes, the total track times of the playground and the uniform distribution of college and Department athletes as far as possible. As shown in Fig. 2 below, the idea flow of the algorithm is shown.

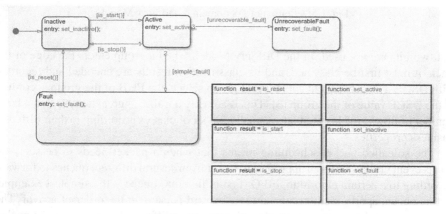

Fig. 2. Algorithm thought flow

Different from the traditional way out, the track link weight used by QoS is not only the number of hops, but can include multiple parameters such as track connection, delay, current load and so on. These parameters can be either statically specified or obtained through dynamic measurement network. There are many ways to use these parameters as the basis for route selection. You can either set the weight for each parameter and calculate the weight of a single track, or use multiple track tables in the sports event group to make the group have multiple tracks to choose when forwarding is needed.

The use of QoS based tracks will also introduce new problems. When the sports event group finds a path with light load through the QoS track, it will direct the service flow to the path, so as to change the current network load [6]. After a period of time, it may be found that the load of the original heavily loaded path has decreased, so the traffic flow will be directed back to the original path. If the rate of traffic switching back and forth on different tracks is too fast, it will lead to network oscillation, which will produce too much unnecessary additional overhead and is not conducive to the utilization of network resources. In addition, QoS track protocols and algorithms are complex, which will increase the amount of track information transmitted between sports event groups and increase the computational overhead of sports event groups. These factors should be taken into account when using QoS track.

3 Design and Implementation of Dynamic Grouping Algorithm Based on Sports Track

3.1 Design of Dynamic Grouping Algorithm Based on Motion Trajectory

In the information management of large-scale sports events, personnel management is very important. Personnel management includes the management of athletes, referees, Venue Managers and volunteers. The application of dynamic grouping technology in sports event information management is to realize the collection and storage of personnel data information. The information management of all kinds of personnel is very necessary, such as the management of audience information, which is convenient for the audience to register information and enter the stadium, which is conducive to maintaining the good order of the event; Athletes' information is the main basis and basis of schedule arrangement, especially in large-scale sports events. This is because large-scale sports events involve more venues and a large amount of information, which needs to be applied to dynamic grouping technology to deal with huge data. Based on the dynamic grouping technology, the personnel information is collected and saved. The information changes can be centrally managed or authorized distributed in each venue. The database of the competition venue maintains data communication with the central database through the network, and always keeps synchronization, so as to ensure the accuracy and consistency of personnel information. For example, in the 2002 World Cup, the world's largest voice and data fusion network was built and adopted for the first time in the event, and it was the first time to connect the infinite LAN to the sports competition. Insert a wireless network card into the laptop to cover the LAN in the sports competition venues. The media can use the network to broadcast sports events timely and effectively, and use the network for personnel management. Its personnel include athletes, referees, Venue Managers and volunteers. In personnel management, the registration and change of personnel basic information are carried out. The information registration of athletes needs to be carried out according to the competition arrangement of sports events. In large-scale sports events, multiple venues are involved. Therefore, it is necessary to accurately record personnel information. The application of dynamic grouping technology in personnel information management can make personnel information management more efficient and conducive to the process of sports events.

For any large-scale event, ensuring public safety is the top priority. As a link of network information security, personnel information collection is the key to ensure public security. Among the complex and numerous information resources, dynamic grouping provides the best choice for solving the integration and management of information resources. For example, it is very important to establish intelligent video monitoring and command and control solutions, implement the general basic standards of network information security, and improve the ability of dynamic grouping system to resist network attacks to ensure the safety of events, The Charter of trust signed at the Munich Security Conference in 2018 also reflects the importance of network information security. China should also speed up the establishment of general standards for network security of sports events, so that dynamic grouping can provide great guarantee for sports event information management in a standardized system.

In the DGA algorithm model, the device with packet forwarding function is called network element, which is characterized by two error values C and D. Where, C is the maximum packet length of a single stream, D is equal to L/C, l is the length of the maximum packet in all packets passing through the network element, and C is the capacity of the network element, that is, the total track. These two values represent the deviation of network elements from the ideal flow model.

$$P_{loss} = 1 - \frac{1 - p_0}{p} = \frac{p_0 + p - 1}{p} = \sum_{n=1}^{N} P_K \tag{1}$$

$$Sim_1(d_i, d_{1j}) = \frac{\sum_{k=1}^{M} W_{ik} \times W_{1ik}}{\sqrt{\sum_{k=1}^{M} W_{ik}^2} \cdot \sqrt{\sum_{k=1}^{M} W_{1jk}^2}} \tag{2}$$

According to the basic idea of DGA algorithm, we use c# language and office Net component 3 ^ designs and implements the automatic generation module of track events according to sub item grouping list in the order book management system of the sports meeting. Its specific functions include: inserting the pre-set format of the track sub item grouping list of each college and department, obtaining the information of athletes participating in each track event, filling athletes into their due groups and passes according to the track event grouping and lane separation rules, and filling the results into the track sub item grouping list of each college and department.

Yes In DiffServ Model, sports event groups are divided into two categories: edge router and core router, and their functions are obviously different [7]. The boundary sports event group should control the business flow injected into the event service, and its work includes: admission control should be carried out according to the SLA agreed in advance between the event service provider and the athlete; Shaping the injected business flow; Aggregation of microfluidics; Mark each group with DSCP, etc. After passing through the boundary sports event group, the business flow is divided into a few QoS classes for the core sports event group of the event service. The core sports event group is located inside the event service and is responsible for different processing of packets belonging to different QoS classes. These embedding methods are called PHB, and the DSCP domain in the packet is used to select PHB.

IETF does not specify what PHB must be realized by sports event groups, and the corresponding relationship between DSCP and PHB is not fixed in the whole network [8]. The subnet that provides a specific PHB service set and specifies the corresponding relationship between DSCP and PHB is called DS domain. Generally, the event services of different event service providers belong to different DS domains. When the group leaves one DS domain and enters another DS domain, it is often necessary to re label the DSCP, which is the work to be completed by the sports event groups located between different DS domains. Because the sports event group is the exit of the group leaving the DS domain, it is called the export sports event group, which is different from the entry sports event group when the group enters the event service.

After completing various preparations before the competition, enter the basic information of the participants (such as the participating unit, name, number, etc.) into the "participant registration form". Then install the program on the computer for recording the competition referee, double-click the program icon to run the application. When the competition starts, click the "start" button on the menu bar, and the program starts to record the competition start time. Whenever an athlete arrives at the recording desk, the operator records the athlete's number, and the program instantly displays the dynamic ranking and relevant information of the athlete.

3.2 Analysis of Simulation Results

The dynamic interaction between the classes and their methods involved in the business model of the automatic generation module of track event grouping list.

The business model of the automatic generation module of track event grouping list mainly involves four user-defined classes [9]:

(1) The wordmethods class is responsible for calling word components to realize the formatted output of word documents.
(2) The wordmanager class is responsible for calling wordmethodlibrary The D11 component can realize the formatted output of the itemized grouping list of track events of each college and department.
(3) Eventorderitem class is responsible for storing the grouping information items of track events. It has four attributes: trackno, PlayerNo, playername and dept-name. These are the contents involved in the track sub grouping list of colleges and departments.
(4) Eventorderlist class encapsulates the DGA algorithm to realize the grouping and lane separation of athletes.

As shown in Fig. 3 below, it is easy to understand from bottom to top from the code: we directly start from the bottom, the simplest and the smallest problem scale, f (1) and f (2), until we push to the answer we want, f (n). This is the idea of dynamic programming. This is why dynamic programming generally breaks away from recursion, but completes the calculation by cyclic iteration [10].

Depending on the solution of the subproblem, the top-down of the slow band memo is also self-determined down, but the results of the subproblem can be saved and used to avoid repeated calculation, fast bottom-up, and directly start from the bottom, the simplest, and the smallest problem scale until the desired calculation results are obtained.

```
int countMethods(int n){
    if(n==1||n==2)
        return n;
    int f[n];
    f[0]=0;
    f[1]=1;
    f[2]=2;
    for(int i=1;i<n;i++){
        f[i+2]=f[i+1]+f[i];
        if(i+2==n)
            return f[i+2];
    }
}
```

Fig. 3. Dynamic grouping calculation code

4   Application of Dynamic Grouping in Sports Event Management

Sports events are inseparable from competition venues and venues. The venue style of sports events is an important condition for the development of sports events. The application of dynamic grouping makes the stadium information construction of sports events more rapid. At the same time, the state has also given a lot of support and help in the information construction of stadiums and gymnasiums. In China, there are more than 10 high-level comprehensive training venues. In recent years, China has held many large-scale sports events. In practice, it is found that the awareness of comprehensive fitness is helpful to improve the level of competitive sports in China [11]. The construction of sports venues is also continuously enhanced. Internet technologies such as cloud computing technology, triple play technology, dynamic grouping technology, mobile Internet technology and new flat panel display technology are continuously integrated into the construction of stadiums and gymnasiums, and are committed to building intelligent stadiums and gymnasiums. Judging from the current situation of sports venues construction in China, the construction of smart venues is still in the primary stage, in terms of technology and application conditions There is still a lot of room for improvement [12].

With the development of the Internet, information technology has penetrated into various fields. The combination of the Internet and sports has given birth to a new sports development model. China has given great support to the development of sports industry, and China's sports industry has also made great development and progress in recent years. As the basis of carrying the development of sports industry, the construction, improvement and development of stadiums and gymnasiums play a very important role in promoting the whole industry. With the emergence, development and industrialization of new generation information technology such as dynamic grouping and cloud computing, Internet plus sports has been constantly innovating, and the combination of sports venues and the Internet has become more and more closely linked, and the "smart venues" have emerged. "Smart venues" refers to the use of intelligent information technology in the initial stage of stadium construction and operation of sports events, and its integration into the actual operation of stadiums and gymnasiums [13]. It is a new type of stadiums and gymnasiums, and its development is based on dynamic grouping. In the future sports events, the application of smart venues should be very extensive, which is also the trend of the construction and development of sports venues. "Smart venues" can alleviate the problem of insufficient supply of stadiums and gymnasiums, improve the informatization of venue resources, improve the utilization rate of venue resources, and help the development of sports industry and sports undertakings. Under the background of dynamic grouping technology, the new "smart venues" have the following characteristics:

(1) The construction concept of "smart venues" always abides by "people-oriented". In the construction and operation of "smart venues", we always put people's needs first, take the market as the center, provide high-quality and diversified services for athletes and spectators, and constantly strengthen the strength of sports venues.
(2) "Smart venue" is an intelligent venue construction. The facilities and equipment inside the smart venue adopt dynamic grouping technology to make it more intelligent and provide more convenient conditions for various sports events. Through dynamic grouping technology, it collects and processes data to facilitate the needs of spectators and athletes, and uses big data analysis to continuously improve the venue construction and future development direction.
(3) "Smart venues" are characterized by "decentralization". Under the background of dynamic grouping technology, each point is a node in the connection of everyone, objects and characters. Any one point may become a central point. This central point is temporary and not permanent. In the construction of "smart venues", give full play to the brand effect, carry out publicity and promotion through the network, and achieve the purpose of obtaining good benefits.
(4) The characteristics of "sustainable development" of "smart venues". Inside the "smart venue", all intelligent equipment can be recycled, which needs regular maintenance, repair and renewal, and a professional talent team is established to achieve a higher combination of social and economic benefits [14].

When sports events are held in stadiums, a large number of people will gather, so it will involve safety issues. In the construction of smart venues, dynamic grouping technology needs to be applied to security. The non dead corner monitoring field of the exhibition hall, access control system, security system, fire control system, garage management, lighting control, air quality monitoring and monitoring of important items (valves, switches and gateways) are closely related to the basic safe operation of the exhibition hall. Using dynamic grouping technology, The whole exhibition hall will realize the construction of "hub" security of information center in the field of security.

5   Conclusion

In view of some disadvantages of sports event grouping and lane separation in the current sports meeting management software, this paper puts forward a dynamic grouping algorithm not limited by the number of lanes, and applies it to the order book management information system of campus track and field games, realizes the automatic arrangement of the order book of campus track and field games, and greatly improves the work efficiency of sports meeting managers. Practice has proved that the rationality of DGA algorithm for grouping and lane separation of participating athletes is higher than that of traditional eight Lane grouping algorithm, which makes up for the deficiency of current sports meeting management software to a certain extent.

References

1. Yu, H., Sharma, A., Sharma, P.: Adaptive strategy for sports video moving target detection and tracking technology based on mean shift algorithm. Int. J. Syst. Assur. Eng. Manag. 2021, 1–11 (2021). https://doi.org/10.1007/s13198-021-01128-5
2. Guo, Y.: Moving target localization in sports image sequence based on optimized particle filter hybrid tracking algorithm. Complexity **2021**(7), 1–11 (2021)
3. Niu, Z.: A lightweight two-stream fusion deep neural network based on resnet model for sports motion image recognition. Sens. Imag. **22**(1), 26 (2021). https://doi.org/10.1007/s11 220-021-00350-6
4. Liu, Y., Wang, X.: Mean shift fusion color histogram algorithm for nonrigid complex target tracking in sports video. Complexity **2021**, 5569637 (2021)
5. Biscarat, C., Caillou, S., Rougier, C., et al.: Towards a realistic track reconstruction algorithm based on graph neural networks for the HL-LHC (2021)
6. Bai, Y., Zheng, H., Zhou, J., et al.: A lane extraction algorithm based on fuzzy set. Math. Probl. Eng. **2021**(3), 1–6 (2021)
7. Sun, Y., He, Y.: Using big data-based neural network parallel optimization algorithm in sports fatigue warning. Comput. Intell. Neurosci. **2021**(3), 1–9 (2021)
8. Briat, C., Zechner, C., Khammash, M.: Design of a synthetic integral feedback circuit: dynamic analysis and DNA implementation. arXiv e-prints (2021)
9. Tyagi, A., Pandian, K., Khan, S.: Design and implementation of lightweight dynamic elliptic curve cryptography using schoof's algorithm. In: International Conference on Computing Science, Communication and Security (COMS2) (2021)
10. Tataria, H., Bengtsson, E.L., Edfors, O., et al.: 27.5–29.5 GHz switched array sounder for dynamic channel characterization: design, implementation and measurements (2021)
11. Iraola, E., Nougués, J.M., Sedano, L., et al.: Dynamic simulation tools for isotopic separation system modeling and design. Fusion Eng. Des. **169**, 112452 (2021)
12. Yang, S.J., Xiao, N., Li, J.Z., et al.: A remote management system for control and surveillance of echinococcosis: design and implementation based on internet of things. Infect. Dis. Poverty **10**(2), 2 (2021)
13. Gu, H., Jin, C., Yuan, H., et al.: Design and implementation of attitude and heading reference system with extended kalman filter based on mems multi-sensor fusion. Int. J. Uncertain. Fuzziness Knowl Syst. **29**(Supp01), 157–180 (2021)
14. Dall, C., Li, S.W., Nieh, J.: Optimizing the design and implementation of the Linux ARM hypervisor optimizing the design and implementation of the Linux ARM hypervisor (2021)

Application of Montage Thinking in Computer Sketch Painting

Minghua Hu[✉]

Software Engineering Institute of Guangzhou, Guangzhou 510990, Guangdong, China
h2m0451@163.com

Abstract. In the current field of painting, the formation of "montage thinking" has greatly affected the creation of painting and used by artists. This way of thinking connects artists, paintings and audiences as a "bridge". "Montage thinking", a divided, discrete and jumping secret way of thinking, provides artists with richer means of expression, more styles for works, and a wider perceptual space for the audience. Due to my own creative needs, when studying the painting creation using this kind of thinking mode, the author found that the past research has not systematically summarized the relationship between "montage thinking" and computer sketch painting creation.

Keywords: Montage thinking · Computer · Sketch painting

1 Introduction

Some scholars believe that painting with montage attribute has existed since ancient times. At that time, people began to use the of painting to record their own behavior in caves in a fragmented way. But it is only a painting with montage attribute style, which can not explain the emergence and use of "montage thinking", because the function of painting itself is only a tool for recording. As Eisenstein and other film theorists introduced this concept into film, montage theory gradually formed. With the continuous study of montage theory by later generations of theorists, montage also began to affect other art forms except film, even daily life itself. Gradually, "montage" changed from a technique to a way of thinking, that is, "montage thinking". In terms of seeking the diversity of painting creation, the application of "montage thinking" plays a great role.

The word "montage" first appeared in film theory. It is the most familiar technical technique of film lens and film editing [1]. As the name suggests, "montage thinking" is a unique thinking mode derived from the development of "montage" theory to a certain stage. It is a creative thinking based on the integration of human visual, auditory and perceptual forms. Taking the application and presentation of "montage thinking" in computer sketch painting as the research object, this paper explores and summarizes how "montage thinking" is presented through the artist's sketch painting concept. "Montage thinking" has always existed in art. It has always been a "bridge" to connect artists, works and audiences. In painting creation, this divided, discrete and leaping secret way

M. A. Jan and F. Khan (Eds.): BigIoT-EDU 2022, LNICST 465, pp. 347–352, 2023.
https://doi.org/10.1007/978-3-031-23950-2_37

of thinking provides artists with richer means of expression, more forms for works, and a wider perception space for the audience.

2 Montage Thinking

2.1 Concept of Montage Thinking

The word montage originated from montage in French. It was originally an architectural term. It originally meant assembly and composition. Later, it was introduced into the film field by artists, and its meaning has been greatly expanded. In the film, montage refers to the combination and connection of different scene segments according to the needs of the film theme and content, so as to achieve the effects of film plot interleaving, rhythm transformation, emotional expression and metaphorical symbols. Montage techniques, including contrast, metaphor and repetition, are used in the film to mobilize the audience's emotions and stimulate their imagination with pictures and music, so as to achieve the artistic realm of immersive.

Kurishov, a famous director of the former Soviet Union, applied a large number of experiments in film editing to summarize the kurishov effect, making montage a standard to measure the height of film aesthetics. Kurishov effect can stimulate the audience's imagination, associate and interpret the information transmitted by the film images according to their own experience, and produce new feelings. Kurishov effect further improved and developed montage technique. Since then, Eisenstein and other artists have arranged and combined the lens language according to the needs of conception and plot, enriched the techniques of montage, and then developed comparative montage, continuous montage and metaphorical montage, and interpreted the aesthetic characteristics and artistic effects of montage with their own film art practice.

Based on the deep psychological foundation of human beings, montage is not only an important artistic means of film, but also an artistic way of thinking. Montage thinking extends from the film field to other art fields [2]. Montage thinking can exist in different art fields. It decomposes and reorganizes the inherent space-time relations, order rules and structural logic in the objective world, breaks the daily logical relations and space-time characteristics, and produces suspense, contrast, metaphor, rhythm, etc., It deeply and vividly shows the internal relationship between things, so that people can obtain a new and strong emotional experience different from the real world. This kind of thinking exists in architecture, painting, film, design, literature and other art fields, and has become a widely used way of artistic creation.

2.2 Characteristics of Montage Thinking

Use montage thinking to deconstruct and reorganize the visual elements of the picture, explain the internal vitality and ideological connotation of things, so as to convey the photographer's subjective emotion and express the creator's subjective thought, so as to make the viewer obtain new perception and experience. It mainly has the characteristics of space-time combination, picture continuity, application universality and emotional experience. The combination of time and space is the most remarkable feature of montage thinking. The objective real world has the space-time characteristics of linear development. Montage thinking can deconstruct and combine time and space, break the order of linear development of space-time in the real world, and reorganize with specific personalized logic. Mr. Deng zhufei, a famous scholar, believes that the extremely important characteristic of montage thinking is its temporal and spatial structure, which is the key point different from other artistic thinking. The space-time in the objective world is extended and developed according to the linear relationship. Montage thinking can intercept several different components from the space-time structure and meaningfully combine them according to the corresponding order according to a certain logical relationship, so as to refine, deepen and focus life and produce a new impression. In the face of this new space-time combination, the audience is connected with their own existing experience. The interweaving and collision of new and old experience produce a new psychological shock and visual feeling.

Picture continuity is also an important feature of montage thinking. Picture continuity urges the individual and the whole in the picture to seek unity in contradiction. Each component element of montage thinking will work. After appreciating each element, the viewer will integrate these elements into a "continuous space-time" whole to produce a new sum of visual elements [3]. The visual effect can not be produced by a single element, which is jointly built by the creator and the audience in consciousness. When Eisenstein mentioned montage thinking in his works, he pointed out that "this law that the individual enters people's consciousness and emotion through the whole and the whole through the image is montage thinking.

3 Application of Montage Thinking in Computer Sketch Painting

With the development of social science and technology, the industry of visual design creation and production with computer as the main tool has formed. Internationally, the use of computer related technology for visual design creation is called CG. Computer art design has created new modeling language and expression, and also promoted the reform of art design method itself. Computer art designers can not only operate Computer artists who work as software must have solid art skills, high creative appreciation ability and profound artistic professional quality. The perfect combination of computer art production process and novel design creativity is the real computer art design.

3.1 Continuous Montage

Continuous montage is a rhythmic and continuous narrative along a single plot clue and according to the logical order of events. We know that the problem of art is first of all the problem of observation, and the purpose of the ability training of accurate description is to guide students to develop the habit of overall observation, train students' visual sensitivity, and enhance their ability to receive and process visual information, so as to achieve In the effective expression of visual information. Continuous montage and design sketch training can effectively cultivate students' keen feeling ability, observation ability and the ability of reproducing things. Continuous montage narrative is natural and smooth, simple and smooth, and has a strong sense of plainness and directness. However, due to its lack of space-time and scene transformation, it can not stimulate students' multiple thinking and creativity, so it is more suitable for It is used in the initial training of design sketch.

3.2 Contrast Montage

Contrast montage's comparative description in similar literature, that is, through the strong contrast between the lens or scene in content (such as pain and pleasure, life and death) or form (such as the size of the scene, the temperature of the color, etc.), produce conflicting effects, so as to express the Creator's moral or strengthen the content and thought.

The contrast montage technique in the design sketch training is mainly manifested in the structural arrangement of the picture space of artistic works, which we call "picture composition". The structural arrangement of the picture space of artistic works changes its picture size structure and object material according to the formal beauty laws such as contrast, proportion and rhythm, resulting in a comparative picture structure with clear graphic style and rhythm.

3.3 Metaphorical Montage

Metaphorical montage is an implicit and vivid expression of the creator's moral through the analogy of the lens or scene. This technique often highlights some similar characteristics between different things to arouse the audience's Association, understand the creator's moral and appreciate the emotional color of the event, as shown in Fig. 1, "This work is not only a question about the act of close reading, but also a question about the concept of reproduction. In this context, although the painting is concrete, it is by no means reproduced, let alone realistic, because the painter depicts an unreal scene that cannot be captured in real life."

Metaphorical montage is mainly manifested in image modeling training in design sketch training, which is through the combination of objective realism and subjective abstraction. Express the creator's understanding of the morphological structure and space of natural objects, so as to make the works more interesting, artistic conception and profound. For example, when we draw the shape of a girl, we compare the "shape" of a girl with the "shape" of a flower When they are painted together, girls and flowers are no longer girls and flowers in the original sense, because flowers and girls have a common feature: freshness and beauty [4]. This common feature makes the painting more vivid and thought-provoking. If we draw butterflies dancing on the picture, it will add more interest to the imagination of the picture. This kind of painting in the same picture The surface completes the expression of heterogeneous images, meets the needs of visual image "metaphor", and is a common montage way of thinking in design sketch training.

4   Computer Aided Drawing

Another important change brought about by the increasing popularity of computer graphics aided design is the reform of teaching forms and teaching methods. Multimedia teaching has become an inevitable way. Compared with the traditional teaching form

Fig. 1. Pleasure of text

of one-way indoctrination, the more intuitive and open multimedia teaching is obviously more suitable for the teaching and expression of modern design theories and concepts. Multimedia teaching also makes network teaching Learning becomes a possibility. Through the Internet (Internet), a broader space is opened for students. Through this space medium, students can obtain knowledge and resources synchronized with the world. At the same time, students' homework can also be transmitted through the network, so that students' evaluation coordinates of themselves can be expanded from a narrow group to a broader world.

The rapid development of computer graphics aided design in the field of design education in China may arouse people's interest in the principles of computer graphics design. Two to three years is only a short moment for the development of the long history of world civilization. People have experienced thousands of years from the use of bamboo slips to Cai Lun's paper making; from Cai Lun's paper making to Biyi's movable type printing Brush people have experienced hundreds of years; the input of hard pen culture has a history of nearly a hundred years; with the development of modern high technology, the promotion and application of computer graphics design technology in China is only a few years, which is really a very surprising thing. Why can computer graphics design replace traditional manual skills so quickly? Answer this question The problem may require more professional theory and more lengthy length, which is beyond the essence of this paper. However, if we compare the traditional manual skills with computer graphics design, we can at least explain some problems from the surface sense. We can compare the method of manually drawing indoor and architectural renderings with that of using computer graphics software A simple comparison is made between the method of fruit drawing. For example, for repeated objects and elements, computer graphics design is obviously different from manual drawing. Using the copy or array function of computer graphics software obviously improves the efficiency than manual repeated drawing.

Perspective (especially complex three-point perspective) It is the most difficult to draw the effect picture by hand, while in computer graphics design, the setting of the camera makes the complex perspective very simple. You can get your satisfactory composition by arbitrarily adjusting the position and angle of view of the camera. Compared with the hand-painted watercolor, gouache or spray painting technology, computer graphics design can achieve a more realistic visual effect.

Using the material editor of computer graphics design software, you can make all kinds of materials you need; through the setting and deployment of lights, you can get vivid light and shadow effects; when all this is set, open the rendering command, and the computer will automatically render the image. As for the final scene matching work, the method of manual pasting often leaves obvious manual effects Traces, and the use of computer image software for seamless overall processing of the effect drawing can make the work achieve better results. Of course, some people may miss the charm of hand-painted works, but the rich and vivid effects created by the special effects techniques of computer graphic design (such as fire, light, smoke, etc.) are incomparable to the manual drawing techniques.

5 Conclusion

The mutual penetration and integration among art categories is the trend of art development. Montage thinking provides an effective reference for the innovation of design sketch teaching, enriching and developing the expression language of design sketch. If sketch creators can deeply understand all kinds of montage expression methods, combine all kinds of montage thinking and apply them to design sketch creation, it will be better To achieve the training purpose of "from sketch to design".

Acknowledgements. 2019 Guangdong Higher Education Teaching Reform Project "Research on Design Sketch Teaching under montage thinking mode".

References

1. Deng, Z.: Introduction to film montage. China Radio and Television Press (1998)
2. Nicholas, S.: Modern art concept. Translated by Hou Hanru. Sichuan Art Publishing House (1988)
3. Yin, R.: A brief analysis of the artistic characteristics of the soviet montage film school. Popular Literature and Art (2013)
4. Cao Shifeng's Thoughts on "from" outside "to" inside "-- an analysis of the teaching reform of computer art design specialty. Journal of Wuchang Institute of Technology, February (2012)

Application of Network Course Platform Based on Cloud Computing in Physical Education

Jianbin Zhang(✉)

Basic Courses Department, JiangXi Technical College Of Manufacturing, Nanchang 330095, Jiangxi, China
762842609@qq.com

Abstract. On the basis of traditional teaching, through the combination and application of current network technology, we can finally break through the restrictions of space and time in the traditional classroom. This is the so-called network course teaching, which can meet the needs of modern education more effectively. With the continuous development of network course teaching, it has attracted the attention of many scholars, and the research on network course teaching has become more and more extensive and in-depth. Nevertheless, there are some problems in the process of the continuous development of network course teaching, and the introduction of cloud computing in network course teaching can effectively improve these problems. This paper introduces the application of network course platform based on cloud computing in physical education teaching for your reference.

Keywords: Cloud computing · Network course platform · Physical education

1 Introduction

For the specific situation of the current development of university education in China, physical education, as a formal discipline, plays a vital role in students' university life. In the teaching process of physical education in universities, It is mainly taught to students by combining theoretical knowledge with social practical experience "Among them, the theoretical knowledge mainly includes the relevant knowledge of physical education major and some expanded common sense. However, the integrity and reliability of these physical education knowledge are not so optimistic. In addition, sometimes the students can not master and skillfully apply them. In this regard, it has brought great difficulties and obstacles to the teachers in the process of school physical education teaching. Many teachers have been Try to find a way to solve this problem, but no better solution has been found. This problem has been perplexing the workers of physical education teaching.

The development of the Internet is changing our study and life. Applying network technology to college physical education classroom can not only enrich teaching means and intuitively show teaching content, but also improve students' learning interest and expand students' knowledge. Of course, everything has two sides, and network teaching also has some disadvantages [1]. Teachers and students need to work hard and make

M. A. Jan and F. Khan (Eds.): BigIoT-EDU 2022, LNICST 465, pp. 353–363, 2023.
https://doi.org/10.1007/978-3-031-23950-2_38

full use of the convenience brought by science and technology, so as to promote the development of physical education and teaching in Colleges and universities. This paper expounds the advantages and disadvantages of sports network teaching, analyzes the current situation of Sports Network Teaching in Colleges and universities, and puts forward improvement measures, hoping to promote the development of Sports Network Teaching in Colleges and universities.

The advantages of college physical education network teaching are mainly reflected in: first, compared with traditional multimedia teaching, network physical education teaching not only displays rich pictures and materials, but also has an activity communication platform. Teachers and students and students can interact and communicate and feed back teaching information in time. Second, network physical education can solve the contradiction between physical education teaching content and teaching hours [2]. Through sports network teaching, teachers can put the contents that are not talked about in class or can be self-taught through the network on the network platform, and students can use their spare time to study on the platform, which will expand students' learning of theoretical knowledge and improve the quality of outdoor classroom teaching. Third, sports network teaching can expand teaching content and improve teaching methods. The rapid development of science and technology and the times sometimes make us unimaginable. In particular, some professional knowledge and industry development trends, through the network, teachers can transfer the latest knowledge and dynamics through the network, so that the teaching content can keep up with the development of the times and disciplines.

Physical quality education is the basis and premise of comprehensive quality education. When carrying out physical education courses, colleges and universities must pay attention to the effective application of sunshine sports and lifelong sports ideas and thinking, constantly innovate and reform college physical education teaching strategies and methods, and promote the effective improvement of the effect and quality of college physical education. Physical education teachers in Colleges and universities must emancipate their minds, keep pace with the times, expand physical education with modern teaching thinking and ideas, fully tap and make use of mobile network technology resources to enrich the form and content of physical education in Colleges and universities, broaden the path of physical education in Colleges and universities, and provide good conditions for the better development of physical education in Colleges and universities [3]. At the same time, when carrying out physical education, colleges and universities should also comprehensively analyze the current situation and characteristics of the application of mobile network technology, master the specific problems of mobile internet teaching, and put forward practical solutions and countermeasures, so as to promote the effective improvement of the quality of physical education teaching in Colleges and universities.

With the advent of the Internet age, China's education is also undergoing reform and innovation. In order to promote the development of education, a new network teaching method is gradually rising, and schools also begin to carry out digital education. In order to adapt to the trend, many schools have established network teaching platforms and implemented online teaching. Relying on cloud computing technology and aiming at building a global integrated distance education mutual aid platform, the world university city provides conditions and possibilities for the new reform of education and teaching in the application-oriented information age. "Cloud platform" and "cloud space" are the sharp tools provided by the world university city for a new education and teaching revolution. It is the carrier and tool platform for the reform of teaching and learning methods in the information age Windows and ties, "The premise of" cloud space "teaching is the construction and continuous improvement of teachers' and students' personal" cloud space ", and the full development and excavation of the function of" cloud space "[4]. Physical education" cloud space " It is a powerful supplement to physical education in the information age. Compared with traditional teaching methods, online teaching can make use of rich network resources and greatly improve the quality of teaching. Some schools also build online physical education teaching platforms through network construction, including physical education theory education and learning progress assessment, which adapt to the trend of modern informatization, which not only improves the quality of teaching, Improve students' interest in physical education and have the best of both worlds. The establishment of sports network education platform can make students understand the significance of learning sports, establish the concept of sports and exercise, and cultivate a good living habit, which is of great significance.

2 Related Work

2.1 Cloud Computing

"Cloud computing" is a mode of increasing the use and delivery of Internet-based related services. It usually involves providing dynamic, scalable and often virtualized resources through the Internet, and providing a set of abstract, virtualized, dynamically scalable and manageable computing resource capacity, storage capacity A large-scale distributed computing aggregate of platforms and services. Computing technology has the advantages of high stability, rapid deployment, dynamic capacity expansion and on-demand services.

In popular understanding, the "cloud" of "cloud computing" is the resources existing on the server cluster on the Internet. The local computer only needs to send a demand information through the Internet, and thousands of computers at the far end will provide you with the required resources and return them to the local computer [5].

The "World University City" jointly developed by Huaxia high tech Industry Innovation Award Office, the Institute of campus card standardization of the education management information center of the Ministry of education and Beijing Hetian Yuxiang Internet Technology Co., Ltd. is a cloud service relying on "cloud computing" technology.

Cloud hosting, or personal space, is called personal homepage. It relies on cloud computing technology, relying on cloud platform, distributing personal electronic ID number according to personal effective identity information, and distributing the real learning space based on real name according to the electronic ID number. "Cloud space" has powerful The resource reserve function of personal space based on cloud computing technology is essentially - a powerful and massive information reserve. It has broken through the limitation of information reserve of traditional paper media and even a single information terminal, and provides unlimited possibility, reality and convenience for the storage of personal information (resources). The schematic diagram of the design concept of "cloud space" in physical education is shown in Fig. 1.

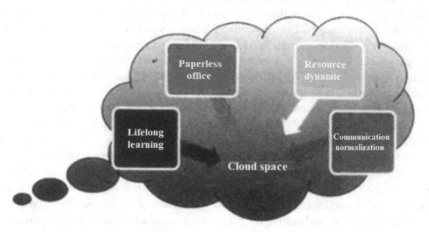

Fig. 1. Schematic diagram of design concept of "cloud space" in Physical Education

2.2 Advantages of Cloud Computing

(1) Cloud computing can improve the management efficiency of existing devices
Cloud computing can improve the management efficiency of existing equipment, which is mainly reflected in the following aspects: first, with the deepening of the integration content of cloud computing system and the aging and elimination of traditional manual management mode, cloud computing completely subverts the original management mode; Secondly, cloud computing can realize system resource allocation through VMware view manager; In addition, with the deepening of the integration content of cloud computing system and the aging and elimination of traditional manual management mode, compared with the traditional mode, cloud computing makes the management mode more simplified, so as to realize the unified management of the entrance.
(2) Cloud computing can improve the fault tolerance of existing devices
Similarly, in the traditional IT architecture model, high availability supports business systems. VMware view manager usually realizes fault tolerance through high availability mechanism. Compared with the hyper V Management Platform in Microsoft's Windows Server 2008, VMware view manager realizes fault tolerance, which is really completed at the virtual machine level. With the same level of fault tolerance, the price will be much smaller [6]. Or, for the same price, the cloud layer of fault-tolerant infrastructure can be higher. The development history of cloud computing is shown in Fig. 2 below.

2.3 Problems in Physical Education Teaching

At present, the main problems in the development of sports informatization in China are as follows:

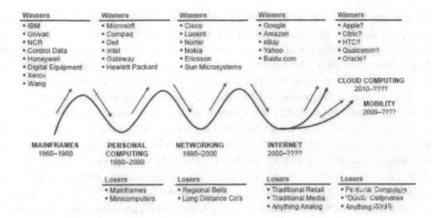

Fig. 2. Development history of cloud computing

1. The sports information resources with multiple subjects and multiple structures are too scattered, and there is a lack of ways and platforms for the efficient integration of massive information resources. If the data format is not unified and the data quality is uneven, it is impossible to develop deeper value.

2. The content of sports information public service platform is not open enough, the development means are insufficient, the interoperability is not strong, and the update is not timely. The process of sports informatization lags far behind the development level of modern sports industry, and a large amount of competition information can not be pushed to interested audiences.

"Smart sports" is a new form of sports informatization and a further expansion and promotion of digital sports. It comprehensively uses information technologies such as cloud computing, Internet of things, cloud computing, big data, intelligent perception and social network [7]. It has the characteristics of wide coverage, collaborative operation, intelligent processing and sustainable innovation. These characteristics effectively solve the development problems of the sports industry Build a new service system and service model in the way of "smart sports" to meet the needs of different groups. High efficiency and low-cost intelligent services enable sports participants to carry out efficient and coordinated operation and promote the all-round development of sports.

Generally speaking, when smart sports is completed, the operation of sports industry will be automated; At the same time, the service quality has also doubled. For example, intelligent sports facilities will be unattended and equipped with self-service Bracelet taking machines. After authentication through QR code, face recognition and other methods, you can get the bracelet, and then use the same method to return it; During the movement, relying on the automatic data collection of the control system, the management personnel can timely adjust the site temperature, humidity and other indicators to ensure the comfort during the movement. The light control system can intelligently adjust the lighting; People can also complete a series of operations online, such as online booking, credit payment, appointment, event registration and fee AA.

At present, China is in an important period of promoting the strategy of building a strong sports country, and the state strongly supports the development of digital sports industries such as intelligent sports equipment, "cloud computing + sports" and smart stadiums. However, from the current situation of sports development in China, there is still a certain gap between the sports level of China and developed countries such as the United States, Germany and the United Kingdom, Some high and new sports technologies are still mastered by foreign enterprises, and there are relatively few cases of integration of science and technology and sports in China, which urgently needs the support of the government [8]; At the same time, taking advantage of the favorable opportunity of national support for the development of smart sports, the sports industry needs to strengthen scientific research and innovation, and actively explore new business forms, new products and new models of the integration of sports and "cloud computing + ", so as to promote the improvement of China's sports level and contribute to a powerful sports country.

3   Overall Planning of Sports Online Education Platform

3.1   Advantages of Online Education Platform

Physical education network course is the sum of the teaching contents and teaching activities of a subject through the network. It includes two parts: the teaching content organized according to certain teaching objectives and teaching strategies and the supporting environment of network teaching. Compared with traditional classroom teaching, physical education online course has obvious advantages. It is not limited by time and space[9]. At the same time, it also provides students with a personalized learning environment. Today, with the rapid development of information technology, if we can make full use of the advantages of sports network curriculum and apply sports network curriculum platform to build a new teaching model of sports curriculum, it will solve the problems encountered in the current curriculum teaching to a great extent.

Blended learning (also known as blended learning) is a teaching method that combines the advantages of traditional learning methods with the advantages of e-learning (i.e. digital or network learning). Mixed learning mode enables teachers' teaching work to be implemented in the classroom and network, and network learning has become a natural extension of classroom learning [10]. After constructing the mixed learning model, teachers must organically integrate the classroom teaching content and network teaching content. The key points and core contents of the course are explained in detail in classroom teaching; Some details that cannot be taught and easy to understand due to the time limit of classroom teaching and knowledge points not involved in the exam, such as string, array, generalized table, etc., are put into the sports online course, which is left for students to study in their spare time according to their own situation. Teachers can also use the sports network curriculum to show students the horizontal and vertical links of various knowledge points, the links and differences between chapters, help students sort out the curriculum content, clarify its internal links, and promote students' learning and grasp of knowledge.

Cluster technology can be defined as follows: a group of independent servers are represented as a single system in the network and managed in a single system mode. This single system provides high reliable services for user workstations.

The purpose of cluster technology is to improve system performance, reduce cost, improve scale scalability and enhance reliability Common clusters include high-performance science cluster, load balancing cluster and high availability cluster. They are often mixed and crossed. Therefore, the classification of cluster categories is a relative concept [11]. The load balancing cluster can share the load (usually including application processing load and network traffic load) equally in the computer cluster as much as possible. Such a system is very suitable for providing services to a large number of users using the same group of applications. Each node of the cluster can bear a certain load and realize the dynamic distribution of load among nodes, To achieve load balancing Since the most urgent problem to be solved in the construction of sports network curriculum platform is how to realize system load balancing, load balancing cluster is selected here.

(1) Liberalized teaching methods

Network teaching is more convenient for teachers. Teachers can choose their own teaching mode arbitrarily, and the teaching methods are rich and diverse. Teachers can let students know more about physical education through online teaching resources, and gradually solve the shortcomings of closed teaching in the past. Students can improve their autonomous learning through the teaching platform without learning in a limited time.

(2) Diversified teaching contents

Network teaching can better show the sports content, including some difficult and difficult movements, which can make students understand and learn well, which can not be done in traditional sports teaching. Traditional physical education teaching is teachers' action explanation. Some actions can not be displayed at all, but can only be imagined by the students themselves. In this way, the learning efficiency is not high. The rise of network physical education teaching has solved this problem well, and can make students learn physical education better.

3.2 System Architecture

In order to prevent the disclosure of relevant important information in the school website, the physical education teaching system of colleges and universities will use HTTPS protocol, which is an HTTP channel to protect the security of the school website. The channel consists of many layers, of which the most basic layer is SSL. SSL is an important content of physical education in Colleges and universities.

Conformity of requirements: correctness and completeness [12]; Functional and non functional requirements; Overall performance (memory management, database organization and content, non database information, task parallelism, network multiplayer operation, key algorithms, impact of interfaces with network, hardware and other systems on performance); Operation manageability: it is convenient to control system operation, monitor system status and handle errors; Simplicity of communication between modules; Different from maintainability; Compatibility with other system interfaces; Compatibility and performance with network and hardware; System security; System reliability; Business process adjustability; Adjustability of business information; Ease of use; Consistency of framework style.

Development manageability: it is convenient for personnel division of labor (module independence, load balance of development work, schedule optimization, prevention of the impact of personnel turnover on Development), configuration management, rationality and moderate complexity of size; Maintainability: different from operation manageability; Scalability: upgrade, capacity expansion and expansion performance of the system scheme; Portability: different client and server; Compliance with requirements (consideration of the organizational structure of the source code).

It is actually an identification mark, which is mainly used to transmit some important data. Its main functions are:

(1) Authenticate users and accurately send data to specific devices;

(2) Encrypt the important data to be transmitted to avoid intermediate loss.

Under the college teaching network platform, we need to choose the appropriate architecture to promote the smooth operation of the platform. Users can find the required relevant data through the browser, and some data can be realized through a specific browser. The main reason for choosing this structure is that it can enable students or teachers to find the information they need in time, focus on relevant things, save teachers a lot of time and improve teachers' work efficiency. The system structure is mainly composed of six parts. The first part is the operating system, which is the most basic part and an important part. It mainly adopts the windows serve 2003 system, which can ensure the reliability of the system; The second part is the database system layer [13]. By giving full play to the functions of Windows NT and continuously improving the stability and configuration of the system structure, the relevant information and subject settings of students can be more detailed and reasonable; The third part is the IIS server, through which students can collect all kinds of data and information. The fourth part is the application service layer, in which the school physical education system mainly uses technical means for the exchange and use of information and data; The fifth part is the network interaction layer, which mainly includes other websites related to China Mobile and China computer network; The sixth part is the user client, which is mainly open to students and teachers. Users can exchange and use relevant data by using this function.

The system structure of the school is shown in Fig. 3.

4 Functional Modules of Sports Online Education Platform

From the perspective of function, the college physical education network education platform is composed of multiple modules, mainly including user management module, network course management module, question bank maintenance and management module, real-time examination module, paper evaluation and review module, system management module and user health information collection and analysis module [14]. The algorithm structure of physical education platform is shown in Fig. 4 below.

(1) User management

The management of users mainly depends on different permissions. The permissions of system administrators are relatively large, which maintains the stable operation of the

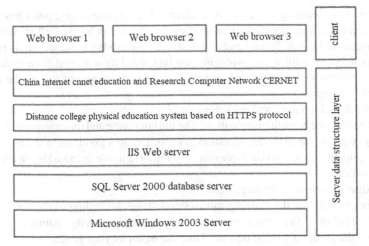

Fig. 3. System structure of College Physical Education Network Education Platform

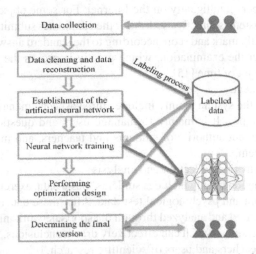

Fig. 4. Algorithm structure of physical education platform

system; Teachers mainly manage students' learning process and teaching stage planning; Students have only basic authority to manage the progress and knowledge of teachers.

(2) Network course management

Network course is a novel teaching method. Compared with the previous media, network course has the characteristics of dynamic information and interaction. Network course management is mainly introduced from five aspects. 1) The progress of online courses is completely completed according to the customization of students' teaching teachers, and the corresponding knowledge points are introduced for learning according to the normal progress; 2) The use of multimedia in teaching increases the interest of teaching and improves the learning efficiency of students; 3) Each knowledge point has a link. If you are interested, you can click to understand it, which can be used effectively.

Stimulate students to listen carefully and improve students' attention; 4) It is fully interactive during teaching, and problems can be solved through real-time dialogue and message. The establishment of this system plays a very important role in the progress of students' learning.

(3) Item bank maintenance and management

Question bank is the basis of examination. The maintenance and management of question bank plays a great role in the examination system. Doing a good job in the maintenance and management of question bank plays a very important role in the addition and change of test questions.

(4) Real time examination management

The teacher will divide the learning into several stages according to the process of the content in the class. After each stage, the corresponding knowledge points will be tested online, and the students will be online_ Take the exam as your grade.

(5) Marking review

The function of the open examination system is relatively powerful. It can directly mark and evaluate the papers intelligently on the Internet. For some objective questions, the open examination system is directly used. After the candidates submit the answer results, the system will directly mark and score according to the standard answers, and the results can be obtained after the examination, which greatly improves the work efficiency of teachers and saves a lot of time [15].

(6) System management.

The management of the system mainly includes three aspects: managing users, permissions and question types; It is mainly to manage users and question types, maintain the use and management authority of students and teachers, and maintain the normal operation of the system.

(7) User health information collection and analysis

Users' health information mainly includes students' basic data, exercise habits and interests, physical test data and psychological test data. After these data are collected, these information can be sorted and analyzed through the sports network information platform of colleges and universities, which can effectively draw conclusions. These conclusions play a great role in teachers and users of scientific research.

5   Conclusion

With the vigorous development of multimedia network technology, traditional school education is facing new opportunities and challenges. This challenge is not only reflected in the reform of teaching mode, means, curriculum and materials, but also in the reform of teaching thought and teaching concept. Reforming teaching methods and means, renewing teaching concepts and carrying out network education have become the requirements of the times. It can be concluded from the above that the establishment of a perfect college sports network information platform plays a great role. By using cloud computing technology, we can orderly sort out the health information, health information guidance, sports theory teaching and assessment information of student users, and effectively improve the proportion of sports theory knowledge in Colleges and universities, Meet the needs of College Students' targeted learning of physical education theoretical knowledge and classroom practice, and cultivate students' comprehensive ability, so as to achieve the purpose of reforming the college physical education curriculum system.

References

1. Zhou, J., Wei, Z., Jia, F., et al.: Course ideological and political teaching platform based on the fusion of multiple data and information in an intelligent environment. J. Sensors **2021**(9), 1–10 (2021)
2. Li, D.: Research on teaching design of colleges mathematics micro-course based on the perspective of network teaching platform. J. Phys. Conf. Ser. **1915**(2), 022078 (2021)
3. Wang, J.: Design of online teaching platform for printing color course based on visualization technology (2021)
4. Gan, L., Wang, D., Wang, C., et al.: Design and implementation of multimedia teaching platform for situational teaching of music appreciation course based on virtual reality. Int. J. Electr. Eng. Educ. **2021**, 002072092098609 (2021)
5. Yang, H., Zhang, X., Fang, G., et al.: Design of signal and system virtual teaching course platform based on LabVIEW. MATEC Web Conf. **336**, 05006 (2021)
6. Lei, R.: Remote intelligent teaching platform of automobile experiment course based on agent. In: 2021 6th International Conference on Smart Grid and Electrical Automation (ICSGEA) (2021)
7. Wu, Q.F.: Design of online teaching platform for accounting informatization course based on cloud computing (2021)
8. Wu, L.: An action research on comprehensive English course construction based on Foreign language network teaching platform (2021)
9. Luo, M., Li, Z.: Design of online teaching system for financial management course based on cloud platform (2021)
10. Ahmed, A., Hanan, A.A., Basma, N.M.: The impact of inverse learning style in learning teaching skills for third-year students' faculty of physical education and sports sciences - Diyala University. Psychol. (Savannah, Ga.) **58**(2), 1241–1248 (2021)
11. Yaqoob, L.R.: Professional competencies are an indicator of the objective selection of specialization in physical education from the viewpoint of teachers nominated for specialist supervision (2021)
12. Blegur, J., Tlonaen, Z.A., Lumba, A., et al.: The importance of self-esteem to students learning responsibilities and group learning commitment of physical education students. JETL (J. Educ. Teach. Learn.) **6**(1), 53 (2021)
13. Bakonu, T., Iri, V.: Describing the competence perception levels of physical education and sports teachers in integrative practices: Kirehir province example. Int. Educ. Stud. **14**(2), 21–33 (2021)
14. Ricci, J.M., Currie, K.D., Astorino, T.A., et al.: Efficacy of a fitness and skill-based high-intensity interval training program In elementary school physical education: 697. Med. Sci. Sports Exercise **53**(8S), 236–236 (2021)
15. Chen, Z.: Application of large-scale cognitive social networks based on cooperative transmission mechanisms in exploration of flipped classroom teaching strategy. Complexity **2021**(11), 1–11 (2021)

Design and Development of CAI Courseware for Basketball Teaching of Physical Education Specialty

W. T. Chen[✉]

Department of Physical Education, Nanchang Institute of Technology, Nanchang 330099, China
tat1982@sina.com

Abstract. Computer aided instruction (CAI) information technology is an important part of subject curriculum integration, and multimedia courseware is the main means to realize CAI. At present, multimedia courseware is gradually becoming an indispensable tool for teachers' teaching and students' learning. Like podium and blackboard, it has become the infrastructure of college teaching. Through the development of Basketball Teaching CAI Courseware for physical education specialty, this paper discusses the development of Basketball Teaching CAI courseware. Combine the traditional basketball teaching methods with computer-aided teaching technology to improve the teaching effect of basketball technology course. Through teaching experiments and expert evaluation, the practical value and popularization value of the development of CAI Courseware for basketball players' special physical quality training are verified.

Keywords: Basketball teaching · CAI courseware · Courseware design

1 Introduction

With the rapid development of modern education, multimedia CAI technology has become the commanding point and breakthrough in the reform from exam oriented education to quality education. It is also a strategic measure to improve teaching quality, expand teaching scale and establish a new education and teaching system. Multimedia teaching has become the basic direction of teaching reform in Colleges and universities in China. It will become an inevitable trend of teaching reform in the new century and will play an increasingly important role in the implementation of quality education.

At present, most physical education colleges and departments still focus on Teachers' oral instruction in the teaching of sports technology theory. The teaching contents such as technical actions and tactical forms are basically demonstrated to students by some simple teaching media such as chalk, blackboard and teaching wall chart. Because teachers are restricted by objective conditions such as age, gender, physical quality and teaching environment, it is difficult for teachers to demonstrate technical actions and tactical changes for students in the teaching process. The transmission of teaching information between teachers and students is mainly Abstract professional terms. It is

M. A. Jan and F. Khan (Eds.): BigIoT-EDU 2022, LNICST 465, pp. 364–375, 2023.
https://doi.org/10.1007/978-3-031-23950-2_39

difficult for students to correspond this theory with sports technology practice, It is difficult for students to establish correct technical movements and technical and tactical modes according to teachers' explanations [1]. Using multimedia CAI Courseware for auxiliary teaching has important practical significance for improving students' learning interest, promoting the formation and improvement of students' sports skills, expanding students' professional knowledge, improving teaching methods, highlighting teaching priorities and teaching difficulties.

The application of multimedia technology in basketball teaching is conducive to the reform of the concept and form of basketball textbook compilation; It is conducive to the reform of basketball courseware teaching system plan and teaching management mode; It is conducive to give full play to students' initiative and improve their interest in learning; It is conducive to students' better acquisition of knowledge: it is conducive to enriching learning content; It is conducive to facing all students and developing personality; It is conducive to better preservation of data. As shown in Fig. 1 below, multimedia basketball physical education teaching is in progress.

Fig. 1. Multimedia basketball physical education

For a long time, the teaching of basketball course for Physical Education Majors in Colleges and universities has followed the missionary mode of explanation, demonstration, practice, correction and re practice. This teaching model is conducive to teachers' teaching, but ignores the individual differences of students, limits the exertion of students' subjective initiative, and makes the classroom learning atmosphere dull. With the improvement of social requirements for talent training in Colleges and universities, we should reform teaching accordingly to meet the social needs for talent training.

Based on cooperative learning theory, this study explores new methods of basketball teaching. By consulting relevant materials, this paper studies the current situation of basketball teaching, cooperative learning theory and basketball teaching theory of Physical Education Specialty in Colleges and universities. Design and implement the basketball teaching experiment of cooperative learning. After research and analysis, the following conclusions are finally drawn:

1. The application of cooperative learning in basketball teaching is feasible and can significantly improve students' basketball skills.
2. Cooperative learning has greatly improved students' learning enthusiasm, and students have changed from passive learning to active learning.
3. Cooperative learning recognizes the differences among students, and sets corresponding learning objectives according to students' specific conditions in teaching practice, so that students can achieve learning objectives within their own ability.
4. Cooperative learning helps students understand the rules of basketball, stimulate their interest in learning, and pave the way for students' further learning.

The introduction of cooperative learning theory into the teaching of basketball course of physical education major in Colleges and universities has changed the single teaching form of teachers' explanation, demonstration and correction of errors in the past classroom, and students' observation and imitation practice [2]. A fair and democratic learning atmosphere has been formed in the classroom, which reflects the leading role of teachers and the dominant position of students, and forms a gratifying situation of teacher-student interaction and student-student interaction. The new curriculum standard of primary and secondary school physical education and health requires primary and secondary school students to learn cooperative learning. As the future primary and secondary school physical education teachers, the students of physical education colleges and departments should naturally learn the methods and Strategies of cooperative learning to prepare for becoming a qualified primary and secondary school physical education teacher.

2   Design of CAI Courseware

2.1   Theoretical Basis of CAI Courseware Design

Modern information technology, characterized by multimedia, networking and intelligence, is having a profound impact and transformation on the traditional curriculum concept, curriculum content, curriculum implementation and curriculum resources. It is to integrate information technology as a tool into the organic whole of the subject curriculum and become an integral part of the curriculum, so as to make all kinds of teaching resources, teaching elements and teaching links integrate with each other through the arrangement and combination of information technology tools, so as to achieve the overall optimization.

CAI courseware is essentially a kind of computer application software. Its development process and method have many similarities with general software engineering, and have many commonalities in the development of general multimedia projects. However, because CAI courseware is a kind of teaching software, its purpose is to enable learners to complete the effective learning of teaching content through the operation of courseware. Therefore, it is different from other types of multimedia application software in many factors such as content selection, structure organization, control strategy and interaction characteristics, so its development and implementation method has some uniqueness.

(1) Behaviorism learning theory and CAI courseware design. There are also different research frameworks and explanations of learning in the school of behaviorism theory, but they all have an important common feature: they think that learning is the connection between stimulus and response. Regard the external environment as a stimulus and the accompanying organic behavior as a response. Therefore, the research object turns to the external expression of psychological activities - "behavior", and holds that psychology is a science of behavior. Therefore, the theory of this kind of faction is called behaviorism theory.

(2) Cognitive learning theory and CAI courseware design. In the design of CAI courseware, people begin to pay attention to the internal psychological process of learners, and begin to study and emphasize the psychological characteristics and cognitive laws of learners; Learning is no longer regarded as a passive adaptive response to external stimuli; Instead, learning is regarded as a selective information processing process that learners actively make on the information provided by the current external stimuli by using their original cognitive structure according to their own attitudes, needs, interests and hobbies [3]. The famous scholar who applied cognitive learning theory to CAI in this period was Anderson. In the early 1980s, he proposed an adaptive control of thought (ACT) based on cognitive learning theory. This method emphasizes the control process of advanced thinking and tries to reveal the control mechanism and control principles of thinking orientation and thinking transfer. Anderson applied this method to build a cognitive student model, In order to realize the automatic tracking and control of students' thinking process of solving geometric problems, and achieve great success.

2.2 Basic Principles of CAI Courseware Design

At present, the biggest contradiction in the teaching of domestic colleges and universities is the contradiction between curriculum content and class hours, that is, more courses, more content and less class hours allocated. Now this contradiction is more prominent. For example: in the past, 102 class hours were allocated for the classical part and the modern part of the course of automatic control theory; Now, according to the new teaching plan, the second part - the total allocated class hours is only 72 class hours.

The teaching content remains basically unchanged, but the class hours are greatly reduced, which is very common in Colleges and universities. On the premise of ensuring teaching quality and not increasing teaching hours, to solve this increasingly prominent contradiction is to use basketball sports multimedia teaching technology to assist teaching. Practice has proved that using basketball sports multimedia teaching technology to assist teaching can save nearly one-third of class hours compared with traditional teaching methods. As long as teachers carefully prepare, reasonably arrange the content and highlight the key points when making multimedia teaching manuscripts of basketball physical education, students can fully accept them. The use of basketball sports multimedia teaching technology to assist teaching will make teaching more lively, students' interest in learning will be improved, they will pay more attention to the teaching content, and the learning efficiency will be improved.

Teachers don't have to waste time on writing blackboards and drawing pictures in class. The saved time can explain more contents and demonstrate more examples; It can even leave some time for students to do classroom exercises, digest the contents of classroom learning, enhance students' memory of learning contents, and solve some difficulties that are easy to cause students' questions [4]. The effect is very obvious. Students don't have to take too many notes, because teachers can easily put E-teaching manuscripts in a mailbox. Teachers tell students the email address and password. Students can enter the mailbox for review and review at any time. If necessary, they can also easily download them for students' further study.

In addition, students can also put their questions in learning and their opinions on Teachers' teaching in the form of e-mail. Teachers can choose the form of answer according to the universality of questions, and make appropriate reflection and correction on their opinions on teaching. This will increase the interaction between teachers and students, which is undoubtedly beneficial to teaching and learning. Teachers should stand at the forefront of the use of advanced technology and apply computer basketball sports multimedia teaching technology in teaching, which can not only improve the efficiency of teaching work, but also improve teachers' computer application skills, and inspire students, which will inevitably enhance students' confidence and determination in the application of computer Basketball Sports Multimedia teaching technology.

(1) Scientific and educational.

Any multimedia CAI courseware must first follow this principle. It requires designers to design multimedia CAI courseware according to the course content and students' physical and mental characteristics [5]. The specific requirements are that there should be no mistakes in knowledge, skills and professional terms in the courseware: the depth and breadth of the content covered should be appropriate; The order of appearance should be logical; The nouns used should be consistent; Words and pictures shall be readable; The difficulty should be moderate; Fully, appropriately and timely reflect the teaching content; It should be suitable for students' educational background; To be able to arouse students' interest in learning, etc. These requirements should be considered first as the designer of CAI courseware.

(2) Interaction and diversity.

Interaction and diversity are reflected in Multimedia CAI courseware. We should make full use of the function of human-computer interaction, constantly help and encourage students to learn, give students broad thinking space and give full play to their creativity. This principle requires CAI to provide learning evaluation function; Be able to record students' learning situation from time to time; Be able to make appropriate judgments on students' answers and have the ability to correct them; Be able to have diversified passion and encouragement: consider students' various solutions as much as possible; It can provide students with a broad thinking space, etc.

(3) Structure and integrity.

A good courseware structure is very beneficial to the designer's design and user's operation. In the design, we should consider that the courseware is mainly divided into several parts, what branches each part has, and how to connect between parts. A courseware is generally divided into three sections: courseware title, courseware content and courseware tail. Among them, the courseware content can be divided into review part, new teaching part and consolidation practice part according to the teaching process. The courseware content can also be divided into three parts: text, picture and animation according to the material type of the courseware. Each part of the courseware content maintains both independence and connection, which is very prominent in Chinese courseware.

3 Design of CAI Courseware for Basketball Teaching of Physical Education Specialty

3.1 Overall Design of Courseware

The participation of basketball sports multimedia teaching technology determines that the new classroom teaching mode is interactive and full participation. The use of basketball sports multimedia teaching technology can make all students actively participate all the time, solve the disadvantages of "Rao Xing psychology" (that is, only one person is asked at a time in traditional teaching) and "loss psychology" (some students who actively speak do not have the opportunity to answer) and maintain strong learning momentum. Enable students to obtain pleasant and successful emotional experience in continuous participation, so as to cultivate and improve their participation quality [6]. Feedback information can let teachers know whether students are in the best thinking state, adjust classroom strategies in time, and ensure the realization of teaching objectives. The feedback here refers to the timely feedback in classroom teaching. Students' thinking state, classroom participation atmosphere and emotional performance after learning new knowledge are the "barometer" of our classroom teaching feedback, which can be mastered by teachers in time through the participation of basketball sports multimedia teaching technology teaching. This is precisely the biggest weakness of traditional teaching.

(1) The guiding ideology of courseware design. Courseware should be the summary of teachers' many years of teaching experience and the product of the integration of teaching theory, educational psychological theory and computer technology. When using courseware, students should have the feeling of face-to-face teaching in class, guide students and teachers to think logically at the same time, and the key and difficult knowledge of teaching should be explained with dynamic graphics or dynamic surfaces However, graphics or animation should not dominate, but should strive to be concise, clear and smooth [7].

(2) Courseware teaching objectives Through the application of courseware in teaching or students' self-study, provide students with an interactive learning environment combining vividness and intuition, make full use of the functions of images, graphics, animation, audio and video in the courseware, make them establish correct

basketball technical and tactical concepts, master basketball technology and tactical cooperation methods and essentials, and master basketball technology and tactics in theory, Improve students' learning efficiency and interest Broaden students' knowledge and enable students to systematically master the relevant knowledge of the project.

(3) Courseware teaching content The main contents of this courseware include: overview, basketball technology, basketball tactics, group competition, physical quality, sports injury and common knowledge Q &amp. As shown in Fig. 2 below, CAI courseware basketball teaching is one hand shoulder shooting in place.

Fig. 2. CAI courseware basketball teaching in-situ one hand shoulder shooting

3.2 Courseware Making

Passing and receiving the ball is the basic technical action in basketball. It can be divided into in-situ passing and receiving, passing and receiving between marching, passing and receiving with both hands in front of the chest, single hand passing and receiving, etc. Among them, both hands chest front pass and catch is the most basic pass and catch action., Generally use both hands in front of the chest to pass at medium and close range. Two handed chest passing is the basis of passing technology, which has the characteristics of high accuracy, easy control and easy change. The action of passing and receiving the ball is divided into "passing" and "receiving". The purpose of passing the ball is to make the other party receive the ball better and smoothly [8]. Action Essentials: hold the ball in front of your chest with both hands, naturally separate your fingers, hold it on both sides of the ball backward, bend your knees and open it back and forth. When passing the ball, the center of gravity of the two legs moves forward, the two arms extend forward, the wrists turn upward, press down with the thumb, and the middle and index fingers pull the ball out in coordination. The technical essentials of catching the ball are that the two arms extend forward to meet the ball, the fingers are naturally separated, the two mother fingers form an eight character line, and the two hands are hemispherical. When the hand touches the ball, the two arms lead back to buffer and hold the ball in front of the chest.

The production process of courseware is shown in Fig. 3.

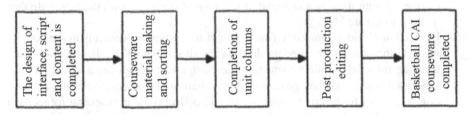

Fig. 3. Making process of basketball CAI courseware

(1) Script design of courseware. The script design of courseware is a very important part of courseware from design to finished product. The script design quality of courseware is directly related to the effect of CAI courseware. The script card design is mainly based on the content of text manuscript, and forms the teaching ideas, teaching strategies, selection of teaching media and information presentation in the courseware into each page It includes text, image, graphics, image, sound, music and other specific contents and their presentation forms in the page Script design is highly professional, and the design process must be detailed and accurate [9].

(2) Production of text materials There are three main characters in the courseware: ordinary static characters, animated characters and artistic characters. The three characters are mainly composed of Word2000 and Dreamweaver Flash and cool3d3 0 and other software. In the production process, different forms should be adopted according to different contents and themes, and strive to make the interface elegant and friendly.

(3) Image making The pictures, photos and graphics in the courseware are collectively referred to as images This part mainly comes from three sources: one is to scan photos and graphics through a scanner to generate image files, and then use Photoshop 5 0 and impactbalm; Second, for some other software or graphics and images downloaded from the Internet, capture the screen through PrintScreen and put them into the picture clipboard for processing and saving for standby; Third, capture some representative pictures in VCD and other videos through vidieosnip, save them as image files, and then apply them to courseware.

(4) Animation material production The animation material in this courseware is mainly the demonstration of basketball tactics Technical action demonstration is mainly realized through different video conversion Flash software is selected for animation production, focusing on the field background and complete tactical demonstration. An ideal flash animation model is made mainly according to the basketball tactical cooperation method and cooperation roadmap.

(5) Production of audio material Various sounds in the courseware come from three aspects: ① the explanation sound recorded according to the text manuscript; ② As background music; ③ Sound collected from VCD The sound of explanation must be accurate, with clear enunciation and reasonable rhythm. For MIDI selection of background music, four combinations should be highlighted, that is, the combination with the content of the interface; Combined with the color of the interface; Combined with the text and sound of this page; Combined with the action rhythm in the courseware [10].

(6) Production of video materials This is one of the important contents in the courseware. In the process of video production, we should select excellent audio-visual teaching materials, collect them into the computer through the acquisition card snazzi software, and then process and edit them with vidieoedor. In the acquisition, according to different needs, we should collect them into several forms such as sound, silent, slow action and constant speed action, and organize athletes and students to learn about some important teaching methods Typical errors, etc. shall be recorded with video equipment, collected and processed for standby.

(7) The overall production of courseware After the text, image, image, animation, audio, video and other materials are prepared, the overall preparation of the courseware is mainly based on the script card and courseware structure.

(8) Organize and pack the courseware After making the courseware as a whole, package the courseware after debugging, evaluation and modification When packing, all kinds of fonts and players are hit into the courseware, and then burned into a CD This courseware can be run with disk on computer.

4   CAI Courseware Teaching

4.1   Dynamic Display of Details and In-Depth Observation

Cai's rich and colorful audio-visual effects can enhance the intuition and vividness of teaching. Using cail can stimulate students' vision and hearing at the same time, highlight the key points and difficulties, and improve the efficiency of understanding and memory. For example, there are many key and difficult points in chemistry teaching, which are difficult for students to master through traditional teaching means, such as explanation, comparison, wall chart, demonstration and so on. CAI has great expressive power [11]. It is not limited by time and space, micro and macro. It leads students' vision to all fields at all times, at home and abroad, from micro to macro, and can reproduce all kinds of things, phenomena, scenes and processes in concrete images. In the courseware basketball physical education teaching, because the content is abstract, boring and difficult, the demonstration with general model can not give students movement, and it is easy to cause concept ambiguity. However, the balance of basketball layup, catch and running is clearly simulated by using the two-dimensional and three-dimensional image and animation functions of the computer, so that students have an intuitive feeling, It can understand the essence and characteristics of more scientifically and accurately, and achieve the effect that other teaching methods cannot or are difficult to achieve. Cai plays the role of turning difficulties into easy ones, highlighting key points and breaking through difficulties in teaching.

In nature, the speed of basketball achievement effect varies greatly. The most ideal observation can be realized with the help of CAI. The process is completed instantly, which is difficult to observe and judge [12]. Cal can display the pictures taken by the high-speed camera at normal speed, prolong its observation time and show the details in the reaction process. For other extremely slow technical actions, such as one handed shoulder shot during walking and two handed chest shot in situ, it is difficult to observe the process due to the long reaction cycle. The three-dimensional animation of CAI is used to simulate its process, compress the long change process to minutes and seconds, and vividly show the reaction process that is difficult to observe, so as to effectively remedy the deficiency of traditional teaching methods.

4.2 The Role of CAI Courseware in Basketball Teaching

(1) It is conducive to stimulate students' learning enthusiasm. As the saying goes, interest is the best teacher. Only by making students interested in this sport can we better stimulate students' enthusiasm for autonomous learning. Using CAI teaching mode and adopting more scientific and advanced teaching means and diversified teaching methods, students' attention can be better focused on classroom teaching and enhance the cohesion and appeal of the classroom, so as to stimulate students' autonomy in knowledge learning and make students more active in the process of learning, So that the efficiency and quality of classroom teaching can be essentially improved. A good technical action courseware through beautiful pictures Concise and clear images are very attractive and instructive to students [13].

(2) It is helpful to establish the correct concept of action. Using CAI teaching system, students can form a more profound concept of action in their mind by watching pictures, videos and sound from various aspects and angles. When they do the action again, students will have a more correct template to refer to and learn from, and the slow play, decomposition and other functions of HCAI teaching system are the effects that teachers can't achieve in classroom demonstration at ordinary times.

(3) It is conducive to highlight the teaching key points, break through the teaching difficulties and improve the teaching quality. The key and difficult points in the teaching process are the difficult points when teachers teach. The use of Multimedia CAI technology can strengthen the key points, make students pay more attention to the key learning, and analyze the difficult points more carefully, which is conducive to students' better research and mastery. Adding CAI teaching mode can effectively alleviate the problems of heavy teaching tasks and less class hours, and save teaching time, so that teachers can have more time to pay attention to students' practice and guide students' specific exercises [14]. Using multimedia technology to assist teaching can greatly increase classroom address, increase information density, improve teaching efficiency and enrich classroom content. Using the storage and network functions of the computer, teachers can display all kinds of information, pictures and sounds related to the teaching content of this class in the classroom, such as teaching courseware, video tape and CD, so as to help students master more content outside the textbook or the cutting-edge knowledge and latest technology of this subject. On the one hand, it enables students to master computer technology and comply with the trend of the information age [15]; On the other hand, it has

increased professional and technical knowledge, enriched amateur cultural life and broadened vision Promote the development of students' knowledge and ability, and help to improve the quality of education.

5 Conclusion

In short, the application of basketball CAI courseware not only solves the problem of tight and unsystematic teaching time of basic knowledge and theory in basketball course, but also improves the problem of non intuitive explanation of technology and tactics in theory part and the unity and standardization of technical actions in practice course. The application and development of multi-media teaching not only involves the reform of teaching methods and teaching means, It also affects the development of teaching mode and teaching theory. The use of multimedia technology teaching is the direction of physical education teaching reform in the future. College basketball teaching should try to use CAI technology for teaching when conditions permit, so that it can supplement the shortcomings of traditional teaching methods, so as to improve the teaching quality and really be popularized and applied in practice.

References

1. Song, S., Yao, L.: Research on multi-objective optimal image recognition and aerobics teaching system based on footprint image[J]. Personal Ubiquitous Comput. **25**(3), 1–10 (2021)
2. Chen, B., Kuang, L., He, W.: Framework Design and Material Processing of Gymnastics Teaching Network Courseware (2020)
3. José, P., Srini, C., Moat, J.B., et al.: Pallium Canada's Curriculum Development Model: A Framework to Support Large-Scale Courseware Development and Deployment[J]. J. Palliative Med. 2020 **23**(6), 759–766 (2020)
4. Septiani, A.: Development of interactive multimedia learning courseware to strengthen students' character[J]. Europ. J. Educ. Res. **9**(3), 1267–1279 (2020)
5. Essel, H.B., Osei-Poku, P., Tachie-Menson, A., et al.: Self-Paced Interactive Multimedia Courseware: A Learning Support Resource for Enhancing Electronic Theses and Dissertations Development[J]. J. Educ. Prac. **7**(2(2016)), 1–11 (2021)
6. Chen, W. , Wang, F.: Practical application of wireless communication network multimedia courseware in college basketball teaching[J]. EURASIP J. Wireless Commun. Netw. **1**, 1–21 (2021)
7. Wei, H.: Analysis on the application of network information technology in college public sports basketball teaching[J]. J. Phys: Conf. Ser. **1915**(4), 122–135 (2021)
8. Wang, Q., Wang, X.: Application research of computer simulation in basketball teaching[C] In: 2021 13th International Conference on Measuring Technology and Mechatronics Automation (ICMTMA) (2021)
9. Thomas, B.R., Gumaer, C., Charlop, M.H.:Teaching basketball shooting skills to children with autism spectrum disorder. J. Dev. Phys. Disabil. **34**, 113–125 (2022)https://doi.org/10.1007/s10882-021-09792-y
10. Liu, S.: Practical research on constructing college basketball curriculum with the concept of health first[J]. J. Higher Educ. Res. **2**(5), 4410–4423 (2021)

11. Li, C.: Design of basketball network teaching information system based on web. In: Sugumaran, V., Xu, Z., Zhou, H. (eds) Application of Intelligent Systems in Multi-modal Information Analytics. MMIA 2021. In: Advances in Intelligent Systems and Computing, vol 1385. Springer, Cham.2021 https://doi.org/10.1007/978-3-030-74814-2_92

12. Juditya, S., Zakaria, D.A., Hardi, V. J., et al.: Digital Material Teaching: Learning Model and Learning Outcomes of Basketball[J]. J. Educ. Sci. Technol. (EST) 7(2), 134–140 (2021)

13. Gamero, M.G., García-Ceberino, J.M., Ibáez, S.J., et al.: Analysis of Declarative and Procedural Knowledge According to Teaching Method and Experience in School Basketball[J]. Sustainability 13(11), 6012 (2021)

14. Liu, Ew.: Networked teaching system of college basketball course based on virtual reality. In: Fu, W., Xu, Y., Wang, S.H., Zhang, Y. (eds) Multimedia Technology and Enhanced Learning. ICMTEL 2021. Lecture Notes of the Institute for Computer Sciences, Social Informatics and Telecommunications Engineering, vol 388. Springer, Cham (2021)https://doi.org/10.1007/978-3-030-82565-2_16

15. González-Espinosa, S., García-Rubio, J., Feu, S., et al.: Learning basketball using direct instruction and tactical game approach methodologies[J]. Children, 2021, 8(5) 342 (2021)

Deep Learning in the Context of Big Data: The Theoretical Basis of Undergraduate Education Reform

Lianjuan Wei[✉]

Guangxi Police College, Nanning 530028, China
lianjuan0607@163.com

Abstract. With the rapid development of new information technology such as big data, cloud computing, artificial intelligence and so on, the process from industrial society to information society has been accelerated. With the uncertainty of knowledge, the value demands of undergraduate education have changed substantially. How to promote deep learning and cultivate students' deep learning is an important direction of current educational reform and development. Deep learning is an understanding learning with the characteristics of critical understanding, promotion of knowledge construction, and emphasis on transfer and application. It is an inevitable choice for the current undergraduate education reform to accurately understand the theoretical basis of deep learning, deeply excavate the value implication of deep learning, and devote ourselves to promoting the concrete practice of deep learning.

Keywords: Deep learning · Theoretical basis · Value implication · Practice orientation

1 Introduction

With the application and development of computer science and artificial intelligence, the transformation from industrial society to information society has been accelerated, and the whole society has entered the "Internet era ". The Internet has brought people more abundant and convenient information resources, which can fully mobilize the enthusiasm, initiative and even creativity of learners, which has a strong impact on undergraduate education and has caused the overall change of teaching and learning methods in the field of education and teaching. Under the background of core accomplishment, the value appeal of undergraduate education has undergone profound changes, emphasizing the subjective role of middle school students in the process of education, paying attention to the generative nature of educational content, advocating the cultivation of students' creative thinking and paying attention to the individuality of educational value. Deep learning is the expectation, choice and orientation of teaching methods in the era of core literacy. [1] As a symbol of the change of new educational concept and learning style, deep learning has become the common concern of undergraduate education reform and development.

M. A. Jan and F. Khan (Eds.): BigIoT-EDU 2022, LNICST 465, pp. 376–384, 2023.
https://doi.org/10.1007/978-3-031-23950-2_40

2   The Orientation of Undergraduate Education Reform and Development: The Theoretical Basis of Deep Learning

The research of deep learning mainly focuses on three aspects: learning style theory, learning process theory and learning result theory, which also represent different stages of deep learning development.

A way of learning to say. As early as the 1950s, Bloom thought that "learning is divided into deep and deep levels", and divided the teaching objectives into six levels: knowledge, understanding, application, analysis, synthesis and evaluation. This view contains the idea of deep learning. [2] The essential difference in learning: results and processes, Ference Marton(marton) and Roger Saljo(salcho), in 1976, first proposed deep learning, which is based on Bloom's principle of hierarchical division of cognitive dimensions. The concept of deep learning and shallow learning is clearly put forward for simple memory and non-critical knowledge. Deep learning here is generally understood as deep learning in the field of education. Some scholars believe that deep learning is a kind of advanced or proactive learning method of cognitive processing of knowledge, and the corresponding shallow learning is a low-level cognitive processing method (Biggs,1999) Professor Li thickening of Shanghai normal University first mentioned the theory and research results of deep learning abroad, and analyzed the essence of deep learning. "Deep learning is based on understanding learning, learners can critically learn new ideas and facts, and integrate them into the original cognitive structure, and can connect with many ideas, And can transfer the existing knowledge to the new situation, make the decision and solve the problem learning" [3].

The second learning process says. Some scholars believe that the core idea of deep learning is that learners should be good at grasping the internal relationship of knowledge in the process of learning (Osama bin Laden 1988); The National Research Council of the United States defines deep learning as the process by which individuals apply learning knowledge from one situation to another, that is, transfer. [4] Some scholars point out that deep learning is to enable students to really understand the learning content and store knowledge in memory for a long time, so that students can use what they have learned to solve new problems in different situations. [5] Some scholars also believe that deep learning needs to link real-world, meaningful, problem-oriented learning tasks, and teachers need to design such a learning environment to support the occurrence of deep learning [6].

Three learning results say. William and Flora, USA. Hewlett defines deep learning as: deep learning is the ability of students to be competent for work and civic life in the 21st century. These abilities enable students to master and understand subject knowledge flexibly and apply it to solve problems in class and future work. It mainly includes the basic ability of mastering core subject knowledge, critical thinking and complex problem solving, team writing, effective communication, learning to learn, learning perseverance [7].

3   Taking Student Development as the Center: The Value Implication of Deep Learning

(1)   Characterization of deep learning.

Deep learning and shallow learning permeate each other. Deep learning is a transition from simple and mechanical learning to meaningful and inquiry innovative learning based on shallow learning. In order to better distinguish deep learning from shallow learning and understand the characteristics of deep learning more clearly, it is necessary to compare them.

Comparative projects	Deep learning	Shallow learning
Presentation	Look critically at new ideas and knowledge and think deeply	Simple reproduction, mechanical memory,superficial understanding
Level of thinking	Higher-order thinking	Low-level thinking
Learning status	To analyze, identify and evaluate new knowledge and new problems using original knowledge and experience	Simple learning, lack of reflection
Learning content	The content itself and the learning process (cognitive strategies and metacognitive strategies)	Content of pure subject knowledge
Knowledge systems	Promote the integration of multidisciplinary knowledge and the connection between old and new knowledge to deepen the understanding of complex concepts and deep knowledge	Focusing only on knowledge itself and thinking of knowledge as an isolated, disconnected unit for memory and acceptance can not well promote understanding and long-term retention of knowledge and information
Learning objectives	Use your knowledge to analyze and solve problems creatively	Staying at the cognitive level of "understanding and knowing" can not promote the development of learners' higher knowledge and ability
Learning outcomes	High level, high quality	Low level, low quality

Through the comparison between deep learning and shallow learning and the analysis of the concept connotation of deep learning, we can conclude that the characteristics of deep learning are mainly manifested in the following aspects:

1. Deep learning pays attention to critical understanding. Deep learning is that learners, based on their own interests and learning needs, emphasize that learners accept new knowledge and information critically, and require learners to maintain a questioning and critical attitude towards all kinds of new things. Look at new things critically and think

deeply to promote the development of learners' innovative spirit and critical thinking. In contrast, shallow learning is for learners to accept new ideas and knowledge through mechanical memory, simple replication learning, driven by external tasks.

2. Deep learning promotes the construction and reflection of knowledge. Facing the information age of uncertain knowledge, the students trained in school education should not only have knowledge, but also learn to think and reflect, reorganize and integrate new knowledge and old knowledge, realize the adaptation and assimilation of knowledge, construct a new knowledge framework, and analyze, identify and evaluate the newly constructed knowledge to promote the development of high-level abilities such as critical thinking and cooperative innovation. Learners should not only transfer and apply their own knowledge in new situations, but also master how to better transform knowledge to solve practical problems. Deep learning emphasizes the process of cultivating learners' critical and innovative thinking, guiding learners to learn effectively and putting their knowledge into application.

3. Deep learning is devoted to the transfer and application of knowledge. Deep learning requires learners to "learn from one another" and "learn to use ", and transfer the new knowledge to new situations to solve complex problems in reality. If knowledge transfer can not be applied to real-life problem-solving, then such knowledge is only the product of originalism and dogmatism, which is not conducive to learners using principle knowledge to analyze problems and creatively solve all kinds of "complications ". Therefore, the transfer and application of knowledge is the starting point and focus of deep learning research and the main melody of undergraduate curriculum reform.

4. Deep learning develops higher-order thinking, which is mainly embodied in problem-solving, critical and creative thinking, and belongs to the category of deep learning. Deep learning focuses on the understanding and application of knowledge on the basis of shallow learning. At the cognitive level of "application, analysis, evaluation and creation", it cultivates students' problem-solving, critical and creative higher-order thinking activities. College students' innovation and entrepreneurship training program is an important practical way to cultivate students' independent thinking, practical ability and stimulate students' interest in innovation and entrepreneurship. It is an important means of the current undergraduate education reform to construct the education mechanism of "promoting education by competition, promoting reform by competition, and promoting innovation and entrepreneurship by competition" and to improve students' innovation and entrepreneurship ability. Innovation and entrepreneurship are meaningful activities carried out by using higher-order thinking, and the application and development of higher-order thinking are the key to the realization of deep learning, as well as the core characteristics of deep learning.

(2) Deep learning is the value demand of undergraduate education reform.

1. Undergraduate education promotes critical and creative thinking.

The Outline of the National Plan for Medium - and Long-term Education Reform and Development (2010–2020) emphasizes "what kind of people to train", which is consistent with the concept of deep learning, that is, we train talents not only to master knowledge, but also to use the knowledge to solve complex problems through thinking, with the spirit of criticism and innovation.With the rapid development of cloud computing, artificial intelligence and other information science, various fields have also caused profound changes. The direction of applied undergraduate education reform is mainly reflected in: requiring students to have a reasonable knowledge structure, master the general methods of scientific work, be able to correctly judge and solve practical problems, have the ability and habit of lifelong learning, and be able to adapt and be competent in changeable professional fields. The teaching of undergraduate education knowledge should not only develop to the depth of discipline, but also pay attention to the horizontal relationship between disciplines. At the same time, undergraduate education should pay attention to cultivating students' scientific thinking ability, creative ability, innovative spirit and entrepreneurial spirit[8]And the biggest difficulty that undergraduate education faces is how to cultivate students' innovative ability and interdisciplinary high-order thinking ability to deal with complex problems. The social life is complex and changeable, the new generation of students are facing a more complex environment, which must fully realize the importance of students' inquiry and innovative learning. The important significance of cultivating students' ability to adapt to the environment of future change and development and innovation and creativity.

2. Undergraduate education returns to whole-person education, emphasizing interdisciplinary interaction and integration of knowledge.

At present, the establishment of undergraduate education specialty in colleges and universities in our country is classified according to the subject category, and the division of specialty affects the connection of knowledge between disciplines. Strengthening professional ownership and knowledge specialization hinders the integration of knowledge across disciplines. The interdisciplinary cross-specialties keep up with the great social trend of the era of technology integration and knowledge integration, and train talents who meet the needs of social development with rich cultural knowledge and strong innovative thinking. Return to the whole person education is the value pursuit of the undergraduate education reform. The value goal of the whole person education is mainly reflected in: promoting the all-round development of human beings, is the harmony and unity of human body and mind, emotion, intelligence, spiritual potential, creativity and so on.

3. Undergraduate education pays attention to the subjectivity of educational process and promotes learners' meaningful learning.

The Ministry of Education, in response to a reporter's question on "Opinions on Deepening the Reform of Undergraduate Education and Teaching and Improving the Quality of Personnel Training in an All-round Way ", pointed out:" Adhere to student centres, combine strict management with careful care, increase the proportion of total credits and courses, increase the proportion of students' time to study independently, explore the establishment of student management models such as college system, guide students to read more, think deeply, ask questions and practice diligently, and stimulate students' learning potential and interest" [9] This shows that the reform of undergraduate education attaches importance to the internal experience of the main body of education, so the undergraduate education based on deep learning should pay attention to the subjectivity of the educational process, take students as the center, dig into the contents of teaching materials, coordinate and balance the proportion of knowledge and uncertain knowledge, make the content flexible, encourage learners to actively learn, connect isolated knowledge elements, guide students to integrate knowledge storage in memory in a situational way, and promote learners to carry out meaningful knowledge construction and personality development.

4. Pay attention to the generative content of education and emphasize the transfer and application of knowledge.

Wu Libao, a scholar, put forward:" The content of undergraduate education is generative, which regards education as the process of active participation of educational subjects, and is a manifestation of students' creativity. Through the joint creation and active construction of teachers and students, we can understand the significance and value of educational content, generate new learning experience and expand educational content " [10]. It can be seen that only the knowledge obtained through careful consideration, in-depth inquiry and knowledge application has the use value and is the essence of learning. Deep learning requires learners pay more attention to the initiative in a complex technical information environment to study and think critically, through deep understand complex concepts, depth of processing information, depth of knowledge inner link, take the initiative to construct the personalized knowledge system, the depth of the high-order thinking ability and skills and effective migration to solve complex problems in real life.

Deep learning promotes active, critical and innovative meaningful learning and requires learners to pay more attention to active learning and critical thinking in a complex technological information environment. The idea of deep learning provides a strong explanation and active and effective guidance for the reform of undergraduate education.

4 Pointing to the Reform of Undergraduate Education: Practice Direction of Deep Learning

At the National Conference on Undergraduate Education in Colleges and Universities in 2018, we put forward "taking this as the basis ", pushing forward" four returns ", emphasizing that "talent training is the basis and undergraduate education is the root ". The holding of undergraduate education conference is the focus on the quality of undergraduate education and the "booster" of the paradigm reform of undergraduate education ". The new idea and new strategy of undergraduate education determine the direction of undergraduate education development. Deep learning, as a new learning paradigm, promotes the development of undergraduate education reform in teaching strategies.

(1) The transformation of the educational concept into a "student-centered" and the construction of a learning-centered university.

The teacher's "teaching" and the student's "learning" are a kind of integrated relationship, and the learners' real deep learning is carried out under the premise of the teacher's deep guidance. For a long time, under the influence of examination-oriented education, the traditional teaching method of "spoon-feeding" is used in classroom teaching in colleges and universities. This kind of "quick-impact" classroom only pays attention to the memory of knowledge fragments, which leads to "dull thought" and dispels the cultivation of knowledge education and classroom teaching. At present, the reform of undergraduate teaching mostly appears the rough allocation of teaching time and the simple flipping of teaching procedure, and even regards knowledge as a symbol for surface learning. According to Egan," There are three basic criteria for'learning depth', that is, the full breadth, depth and relevance of knowledge learning ".[11] The quality of undergraduate education depends on whether educational resources can effectively promote the development of learners and adapt to the needs of social development. As the main body of teaching activities, learners' learning quality is an important index of undergraduate education quality. While deep learning embodies the representation of initiative, situational, interactive, critical, innovative, and so on. Learners' deep learning ability is the embodiment of high quality learning.

(2) The transformation of educational content to "integrated education" to deepen whole-person education.

The fundamental purpose of undergraduate education is to cultivate students into people with social responsibility. From another point of view, undergraduate education is a kind of intrinsic value pursuit that transcends the value of tools. It is a kind of cultural activity that faces the main body of life, cares for the inner experience, attaches importance to the dynamic generation, and promotes the common development of teachers and students. Undergraduate education is the key period of the formation of the three views of young students. High quality undergraduate education plays an important role in building a powerful country of human resources. Therefore, the reform of undergraduate education should return to the goal of all-person education. The whole-person education emphasizes the all-round development of human beings, which not only requires learners to learn knowledge, but also to accept correct values, so as to inspire learners to learn from one another and learn to use it in order to meet the needs of social development. In the face of uncertain knowledge, pointing to deep learning is an important choice for undergraduate education reform. On the one hand, the undergraduate education of "pointing to deep learning" should develop to the depth of the subject, but also pay attention to the horizontal relationship between the subjects. On the other hand, learners should master the core knowledge of the subject, understand the process of learning, grasp the essence of the subject, form positive internal learning motivation, advanced social emotion, positive attitude, correct values, and become independent, critical, creative and cooperative learners. The integration of interdisciplinary knowledge of undergraduate education is mainly the integration of curriculum content, which is reflected in the curriculum. Only by breaking the barriers between majors and disciplines and forming an interdisciplinary learning model can students extensively dabble in different subject areas, broaden their basic knowledge, form a variety of thinking models, and promote the all-round development of students.

(3) The transition of students' learning to "innovative learning" promotes meaningful learning by learners.

With the deepening and development of learning subject and artificial intelligence, the research on teaching and learning has changed from the relationship between teaching and learning to the study of paying attention to the learning process. Professor Guo Yuanxiang pointed out: at present, the direction of international teaching reform is to transcend the surface learning of symbolic knowledge, pay attention to deep learning, and pursue the personal significance of public knowledge. It can be seen that undergraduate education needs to transcend the simple transfer of knowledge, face the needs of talents for social development, integrate social responsibility, and cultivate learners' critical thinking and innovative ability. The concept of deep learning is highly compatible with the innovative learning of undergraduate education. The reform of undergraduate education pays more attention to the life itself, stimulates learners' thinking and improves learners' innovative ability in concrete practice. The process of learners' innovative learning is not their individual independent knowledge construction, but the process of equal dialogue and meaning construction between teachers and students, which effectively promotes learners to produce meaningful learning. Deep learning is not a result but a process" [12]"In this process, from the perspective, it can coordinate, integrate, and apply much knowledge" [13]Learning through dialogue, innovative learning, reflective thinking, promote meaningful learning is the breakthrough point of undergraduate education reform.

Deep learning is a kind of dialogue, understanding and reflective learning, which emphasizes reflective learning and critical thinking, pursues the extension of the intrinsic value of knowledge, and it has become an indisputable fact for learners to carry out deep learning. The cultivation of deep learning ability plays an important role in the reform and development of college students and even the whole higher education. In the future research and practice, under the premise of grasping the concept connotation, characteristics and objectives of deep learning, combining the national conditions and cultural characteristics of our country, we should carry out the undergraduate education reform pointing to deep learning, and explore the path of deep learning which is more effective and more suitable for the national conditions.

References

1. Liang, Z.: Where is the "depth" of deep teaching? – from knowledge structure to Knowledge application. Curr. Teach. Mater. Law Instruct. **07**, 34–39 (2019)
2. Guo, Y.: On In-depth teaching: origin, foundation and concept. Educ. Res. Exp. **32**, 2217–2229 (2017)
3. He, L., Li, J.: Promoting students' deep learning. Mod. Teach. **10**, 156–168 (2005)
4. National Research Council Panel: Education for Life and Work:Developing transferable knowledge and skills in the 21st century. National Academy Press, Washington, DC (2012)
5. Bransford, J., Brown, A., Cocking, R.: How People Learn: Brain, Mind. Experience and School. National Academy Press, Washington, DC, 65 (2000)
6. Wenbo, C.A.I., et al.: Development of undergraduate education in Chinese universities: policy evolution and value orientation. Mod. Educ. Sci. **64**, 1454–1468 (2019)

7. William and Flora Hewlett Foundation: Deeper learning competencies [DB/OL]. MP: WFHF (2016)
8. Ministry of Education Outline of the National Medium - and Long-term Plan for Education Reform and Development (2010–2020)
9. Wu, L.: Experience and inspiration of undergraduate education reform of research universities in the United States under the "Learning Paradigm". Mod. Univ. Educ. **38**, 285–301
10. Dewey, J.: How We Think: A Restatement of the Relation of Reflective Thingking to the Educative Process. D.C. Dewey & Company, Boston (1933)
11. Egan, K.: Learning The Depth: A Simple Innovation That Can Transform Schooling. Ontario, The Althouse Press, London (2010)

Decision Support System Model of Education Management Based on Cloud Storage Technology

Jianxiang Wang(✉)

Urban Vocational College of Sichuan, Chengdu 610101, Sichuan, China
scy2022@126.com

Abstract. This paper theoretically expounds the concept of cloud storage technology, and demonstrates the core application of cloud storage technology in educational management decision support system. Model management is not only the focus of decision support system research, but also the key to the practicability and success of decision support system. Flexible and practical model management is of great significance to assist decision-makers to understand complex practical problems, select appropriate models and improve the effectiveness of decision-making.

Keywords: Cloud storage technology · Education management · Decision support system · System model

1 Introduction

With the rapid development of the information age, the outside world has brought us more and more big information. A large amount of information not only brings convenience to people, but also brings a lot of trouble: too much information is difficult to digest, true and false information is difficult to identify, information security is difficult to ensure, and information format is difficult to unify. In the vast ocean of information, how can we not be submerged by information and find useful information in time? Therefore, this paper studies the model of education management decision support system based on cloud storage technology.

Due to the different application fields and research methods of decision support system, the structure of decision support system has many forms. The structure of decision support system based on model base and knowledge base and combined with expert system is called intelligent decision support system [1]. The decision support system based on data warehouse, online analytical processing and data mining is called the new decision support system. The integrated decision support system formed by integrating the above two decision support systems is a new development direction of decision support system. In order to better realize the purpose of auxiliary decision-making, data warehouse still needs the support of model. Model base system is an important part of

M. A. Jan and F. Khan (Eds.): BigIoT-EDU 2022, LNICST 465, pp. 385–393, 2023.
https://doi.org/10.1007/978-3-031-23950-2_41

decision support system. The quality of model determines the performance of decision support system. Conclusion cloud storage technology and establishing a reasonable and effective decision model can enable the decision support system to make effective decisions when dealing with semi-structured and unstructured decision problems, which is of great significance to help decision makers understand decision problems and implement decision schemes. The cloud storage technology is shown in Fig. 1.

The concept of "cloud" was first born on the Internet. With its development, cloud technology has been applied in all walks of life. "Cloud" is a metaphor. It is usually the back end, which is difficult to see. It makes people feel nihilistic, so it is called "cloud".

The construction of safe city and smart city promotes the application of security cloud storage technology. Smart city puts forward that one of its major requirements is to link and share video storage data with each other. For example, in the case of crime tracking, public security, transportation, civil industries and other multi-range storage data can be shared, and this sharing has the characteristics of cloud storage; Traditional storage technology can not meet the needs of social development, so the application of cloud storage in the field of security becomes inevitable.

At present, several safe cities in China have made attempts. In the future, with the help of the large-scale application of smart cities, we will gather people's strength to promote the improvement of relevant application standards. We believe that we can promote the application of cloud storage in the security field faster.

In terms of current application requirements, some industry users, such as oil, coal, gold, etc., need to aggregate all data for analysis and processing. This demand can create a private cloud; Some users want to build the whole monitoring system, but they don't want to spend too much energy. They also hope that all the data of the whole city can be shared and can be linked in time in case of accidents. This can adopt the common cloud method. If these application modes are widely used, it will have a significant impact on the traditional security engineering companies and integrators.

In the future, through cloud storage, more and more IT industry technologies and concepts will be introduced into security, and the traditional security will encounter more and more challenges. Some insiders even predict that the security industry will gradually be assimilated by it. There are still restrictions on the promotion of cloud storage technology in the security field. As the main branch of the security field, video surveillance consumes a lot of broadband data.

From the "cloud" of the Internet to the "cloud" of the security field, "cloud security" can be described as an exotic product. However, in the current market with diversified security storage technologies, cloud storage technology still stays in the demand and concept hype. It will be a long way to go if it really needs to be applied in a large area and occupy a place in the market. However, with the construction of smart cities and the investment in the construction of the Internet of things, it can be predicted that the future application of cloud storage technology in the security field will have a better prospect.

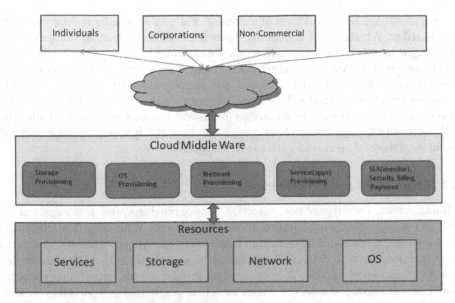

Fig. 1. The cloud storage technology

2   Cloud Storage Technology

2.1   Overview of Cloud Storage

Cloud computing not only represents an important development direction of information and communication technology and information service provision in the future, but also can effectively reduce energy consumption, which is in line with the overall development trend of green and energy saving. In 2010, the Chinese government decided to carry out the pilot demonstration work of innovative development of cloud computing services in Beijing, Shanghai, Hangzhou, Shenzhen, Guangdong and Wuxi, Jiangsu, so as to promote the construction and development of China's cloud computing industry. China's telecom operators also attach great importance to the development of cloud computing [2–4]. The three telecom operators have put forward their own cloud computing development strategies. Cloud computing technology developed rapidly in 2010: IBM integrated resources and launched comprehensive cloud computing solutions such as a new cloud service provider platform; Intel released cloud builder plan; Huawei released cloud development strategy and solutions; Cisco demonstrated the urban cloud platform based on the overall scheme of virtual computing environment Alliance (VCE) [5–8].

Cloud storage is a new concept extended and developed from the concept of cloud computing. It refers to a system that gathers a large number of different types of storage devices in the network through application software to work together and jointly provide data storage and business access functions through cluster applications, grid technology or distributed file system. Fundamentally speaking, cloud storage is a practical service, which can provide many users with a shared storage pool accessed through the network [9].

Cloud storage is an ideal form of expansion and may eventually replace internally archived data. Whether in the high-performance and high-cost side of the storage field, or in the high-capacity and low-cost side, the choice of storage technology will become more and more abundant. And the benefits of cloud storage are impressive. Cloud storage can provide almost unlimited scalability and a "pay as you go" model, which is particularly attractive for lower level and archive storage. From a physical point of view, the cloud is remote, allowing enterprises to obtain data for disaster recovery protection off-site [10–12]. As an outsourcing service, cloud storage can also simplify storage management and avoid the trouble of maintaining storage infrastructure.

2.2   Characteristics of Cloud Storage

Cloud storage is a new type of storage service. Service providers provide storage capacity and data storage services to customers through the network. At the same time, customers do not know the specific implementation details and underlying mechanism. Compared with traditional storage devices, cloud storage is not only a hardware, but a complex system composed of network devices, storage devices, servers, application software, public access interfaces, access networks, and client programs. Each part takes the storage device as the core and provides data storage and business access services through application software. All devices in the cloud storage system are completely transparent to users. Users only need to connect to the cloud through the network to access data. Users who need storage services no longer need to establish their own data center, but only need to apply for storage services from SSP (storage service provider), thus saving expensive software and hardware infrastructure investment. Compared with traditional centralized data storage solutions, efficient clustered cloud storage systems have the advantages of easy capacity expansion (including bandwidth), lower cost, safer data, uninterrupted service and so on [13–15].

As a popular emerging market, "cloud storage" has blossomed everywhere in China in just a few years. We can see that the "cloud" we need includes chu115, Jinshan online disk, Tencent transit, Xunlei online disk, baidu online disk, and cloud storage on many brands of smart phones or online TVs. This is an attractive big cake with broad prospects. Many businesses want to get a piece of it.

In addition to the rapid development of domestic cloud storage business, what is more unexpected is the enthusiasm of domestic users. The 2012–2016 China Network Storage Market Research and future development trend report shows that by the first quarter of 2012, the number of registered users of a large SSP in China had exceeded 3million, and the number of registered users of other SSPs was also comparable. However, compared with nearly 500million domestic Internet users, these figures still have a huge space for development. You know, the number of customers of Dropbox in the United States in the first three years was less than one million, but now it has far exceeded five million.

The domestic cloud industry is still in its infancy. The development of the market is not mature enough and faces many challenges. Although there are only a few foreign SSPs with great influence, their customers and businesses are relatively stable. Businesses can make up their minds to carry out various long-term businesses stably. However, the domestic cloud storage market has just started. The development stage of stability and mutual trust between customers and SSP has not yet entered. The market is not mature enough. There are still many unstable conditions in the business of customers and ssp.

3 Education Management Decision Support System Model Based on Cloud Storage Technology

3.1 Technical Architecture of Decision Support System

Using cloud services to improve decision support services is mainly based on the following decision analysis characteristics:

(1) From the dynamic nature of decision support. In the cloud manufacturing system, the demand of tasks is the comprehensive demand for various manufacturing resources and capabilities. At the same time, manufacturing tasks have a wide range of applications, the demand is dynamic, random and large-scale. Therefore, the service system performing these complex decision-making tasks should also have corresponding complexity and dynamics. Decision support services need to use distributed information environment, including end users and loosely coupled knowledge sources. Its problem-oriented and demand driven problem processing method is similar to cloud services.

(2) From the knowledge of decision support. Cloud service belongs to web service. It is a semantic rich web service obtained by uniformly embedding, encapsulating and virtualizing resources, information and knowledge through the Internet and other media in the cloud manufacturing platform. The acquisition, reasoning and integration of knowledge are the basis of decision support system. The completeness and accuracy of knowledge will directly affect the quality of decision-making. Therefore, with the help of rich semantic services in cloud manufacturing system, the problem of data inconsistency in decision support system can be effectively solved.

(3) From the systematicness of decision support. Cloud manufacturing virtualizes and serves all kinds of software and hardware manufacturing resources and manufacturing capabilities, carries out unified and centralized management and operation, realizes intelligent, win-win, universal and efficient sharing and collaboration, and provides safe, reliable, high-quality and cheap services that can be obtained at any time and used on demand for the product manufacturing process through the network. Decision support system also needs to virtualize design knowledge and information resources by using virtualization technology. In the process of realizing the transparent mapping of virtual resources, it weakens the physical dependence between resources at different levels, so as to realize the purpose of dynamic allocation and use of resources in virtual environment.

Based on the above considerations and referring to the traditional tripartite architecture of Web services, the author puts forward the technical architecture of decision support system based on cloud services. As shown in Fig. 1, the whole technical architecture consists of Requirements Driven Architecture (RDA), service - oriented architecture

(SOA), decision management architecture (DMA) It is composed of cloud infrastructure and semantic web, which jointly realize the decision-making ability of the system (See Fig. 2).

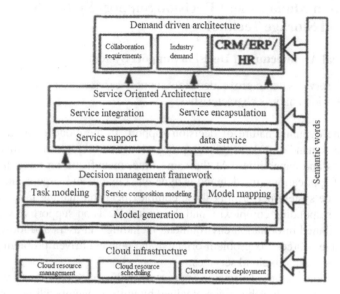

Fig. 2. Technical architecture of decision support system based on cloud service

Users access the system through the web access interface. In, RDA is at the core of the technical architecture of the whole decision support system the top layer, including collaboration requirements, industry requirements and CRM/ERP requirements, completes the transformation process of decision model construction with the help of service integration in the lower SOA; As an application construction method, SOA ensures that the services in cloud infrastructure can be developed and combined quickly to realize the non functional requirements in cloud services. Through a series of cloud service architecture operation such as service integration, service encapsulation and service support, it ensures that the infrastructure can meet various needs of applications; DMA provides runtime decision service support, including decision task modeling, decision service composition modeling, mapping from decision task model to decision service model, model generation and so on; Cloud infrastructure provides the relevant software and hardware environment under the cloud service platform to automatically deploy the standard SOA operating environment, including cloud resource management, cloud resource scheduling, cloud resource deployment, etc.

At the same time, the semantic web based on extensible markup language (XML) and resource description framework (RDF) runs through the whole decision support system based on cloud services, providing standardized metadata syntax specification and metadata semantic description specification for the whole technical architecture and describing the relationship between resources and resources at all levels.

3.2 Decision Task Submission and Decomposition Model

In the process of solving the decision task, firstly, the decision task should be gradually decomposed into sub problem units and the action sequence of the decision task should be assigned; Then, each sub problem unit is assigned to each calculation node, and the solution results of sub problem units are gradually summarized and synthesized according to the decomposition level; Finally, the reference results or solution resources of decision-making tasks at all levels are obtained.

There are decision task sets d = {D1, D2,..., Dn} (n ∈ R) and calculation node sets s = {S1, S2,..., Sm} (m ∈ R), as shown in Fig. 3.

(1) When the user inputs the decision task, the platform decomposes the decision task according to the solution logic of the model management method, sorts it, and selects the first action sequence D1.
(2) D1. Inform D2 and D3 of the status of the whole operation and that they are one of the sequences of the current decision-making operation. At the same time, D2 and D3 regularly detect whether D1 and D3 are still working normally.
(3) D1 obtains the available set of computing nodes by querying the system, and selects all or part of the slave nodes to perform decision computing tasks.
(4) When D1 fails, D2 and D3 will continue to detect the job status and select a new master node through the distribution process.

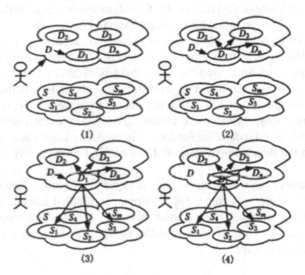

Fig. 3. Struts frame structure

Decision task submission and decomposition model of cloud storage in order to verify the construction method and related construction technology of decision support system based on cloud service proposed in this paper, with the support of the National 863 plan, the Key Laboratory of modern design and integrated manufacturing technology of the Ministry of education of Northwest University of technology, based on the research in related fields such as networked manufacturing, knowledge management and decision grid, combined with the preliminary research results of the author's team, Taking a university in Guangdong as the service object, this paper preliminarily designs the education management decision support system model of cloud storage technology. The decision support system platform based on cloud service provided by the platform mainly includes four subsystems, namely virtualization support subsystem, cloud service management subsystem, knowledge base management subsystem and complex product design subsystem based on cloud service.

4 Conclusion

From the basic idea and technical framework of decision support system based on cloud service, combined with cloud storage technology and semantic rich cloud service, this paper discusses and studies the model of education management decision support system based on cloud storage technology. Compared with the traditional decision model, the introduction of cloud service concept and semantic technology has brought many new characteristics to the decision support system, such as intelligent service matching and model mapping algorithm, systematic networked manufacturing service mode, distributed, real-time and dynamic service composition, which effectively strengthens the decision-making ability of decision-makers when solving complex problems.

The most fundamental factor leading to the chaos of competition in the cloud storage industry is the confusion of the profit model. Cloud storage is a large market and a market with great potential. It can be said that whoever wins cloud storage will win the future. In order to attract more users, cloud storage service providers must provide more free storage space. However, as the storage space increases, the number of users paying for upgrades will decrease. Some small service providers without other sources of income are bound to be unable to bear such a large investment, and they have to find other sources of revenue. As an enterprise, SSP's ultimate goal is to make money, while customers want to get more, better, cheaper and even free services. At present, enterprises can only increase advertising and reduce the burden on users. As for other value-added services, they are still in the development stage and can not find a better way out for the time being.

Natural disasters such as tsunamis and earthquakes or human factors such as war will bring many uncertain factors to the development of cloud storage. Although there is no need to worry too much about human factors such as war in China, the review in all aspects and the shielding of some sensitive content also increase the time cost and uncertainty of cloud storage.

References

1. Mutao, H., Yong, T.: Research and application of combined intelligent decision support system. Syst. Eng. Theory Pract. 27(4), 14–119 (2007)
2. Ming, Z.: On cloud storage technology and application. Inf. Technol. 39(3), 15–17 (2010)
3. Lu, X., Cao, W., Yu, Y.: Discussion on network problems of telecom operators developing cloud storage services. Telecomun. Sci. 26(6), 71–75 (2010)

4. Gao, H.: Decision Support System (DSS): Theoretical Method Case. Tsinghua University Press (2000)
5. Nagahara, S., Nonaka, Y.: Product-specific process time estimation from incomplete point of production data for mass customization. Procedia CIRP **67**(000), 558–562 (2018)
6. Xiong, X.Q., Wu, Z.H.: Development and application technology the mass customization furniture. J. Nanjing Forestry University (Nat. Sci. Ed.) **37**(4), 156–162 (2013)
7. Choi, T.-M., Ma, C., Shen, B., Sun, Q.: Optimal pricing in mass customization supply chains with risk-averse agents and retail competition. Omega **88**(10), 150–161 (2019)
8. Martin, C., Hoy, M.K., Murayi, T., Alanna, M.: Nutrient intake and dietary quality among children and adolescents by fast food consumption status: what we eat in America. Current Dev. Nutr. **4**(2), 235 (2020)
9. Zhu, X.-J., Lu, H., Rätsch, M.: An interactive clothing design and personalized virtual display system. Multimedia Tools Appl. **77**(20), 27163–27179 (2018)
10. Wang, Z., Suh, M.: Bra underwire customization with 3-D printing. Clothing Text. Res. J. **37**(4), 08 (2019)
11. Riedelsheimer, T., Dorfhuber, L., Stark, R.: User centered development of a Digital Twin concept with focus on sustainability in the clothing industry. Procedia CIRP **90**(000), 660–665 (2020)
12. Virtanen, J.-P., Antin, K.-N., Kurkela, M., Hyyppä, H.: The feasibility of using a low-cost depth camera for 3D scanning in mass customization. Open Eng. **9**(1), 450–458 (2019)
13. Obeidat, A.M., Nabawi , H.,. Hashem, O., El-Said, H.M.: The impact of using interactive interior design on enhancing the performance of clothing shop. J. Des. Sci. Appl. Arts **1**(1), 146–153 (2020)
14. Mosleh, S., Abtew, M.A., Bruniaux, P., Tartare, G., Xu, Y., Chen, Y.: 3D digital adaptive thorax modelling of peoples with spinal disabilities: applications for performance clothing design. Appl. Sci. **11**(10), 4545 (2021)
15. Xu, Z., Xu, L., Fan, Y., Guo, X., Li, J.: Study on the influence of yi handmade embroidery and fast fashion clothing combined development on the achievements of poverty reduction in liangshan area. Open J. Soc. Sci. **09**(6), 407–417 (2021)

Data Mining Analysis Based on Business Administration Data

Pengfei Ma[✉]

Nanchang Institute of Technology, Jiangxi 330044, China
416930145@qq.com

Abstract. With the advent of the era of big data, the utilization value of data has been paid more and more attention by various industries. Data mining shows its superiority in the secondary utilization of existing data, which can produce great economic benefits to our life. In order to improve management efficiency and adapt to modern management, the industrial and commercial administration department has gradually established its own business management system and realized the digitization of economic household registration. However, its current business system can only provide daily transaction management. It is becoming more and more difficult to obtain useful information from the business system, which seriously affects the full utilization of data. Therefore, based on the data mining of business administration data, this paper makes an in-depth understanding and analysis of business administration data.

Keywords: Business administration · Data mining · Data analysis

1 Introduction

The great changes in information technology in recent years have greatly improved people's ability to collect data. All industries will involve the use and storage of data, and the use of database is inevitable. As a government agency, the Administration for Industry and Commerce in all parts of China is of course essential to use the database system to improve the normal office efficiency. So what benefits can mining and analyzing business administration data bring us?

The industrial and commercial administration department is in charge of all the information of the market subject, and a large amount of such information is the basis for the state to judge the macroeconomic trend. The development of market subjects is a very important part of economic development. The change of market subjects will not only directly affect the operation state of the national economy, but also reflect the characteristics of national economic development. Therefore, it is very important to fully control and effectively use the information of market subjects for the study of Macro-economy.

From a macro perspective, if business big data can effectively predict the macroeconomic trend under the current severe fluctuations in the global economy and China is

M. A. Jan and F. Khan (Eds.): BigIoT-EDU 2022, LNICST 465, pp. 394–399, 2023.
https://doi.org/10.1007/978-3-031-23950-2_42

facing deepening economic reform, it can not only enhance the influence of the business management system in economic development, but also effectively affect the country's economic decision-making, so that the country can avoid detours in the process of economic development, Give full play to the effectiveness of industrial and commercial administration [1]. From a micro perspective, the functions and responsibilities of the industrial and commercial administration department determine that a large number of economic data such as market subject change, annual inspection information, investment situation and reporting information have been accumulated in the database of the current industrial and commercial administration department. If big data technology can be fully used in the industrial and commercial system, It can not only support government departments at all levels to formulate effective economic policies and improve the administrative effect of industrial and commercial administration departments from data and theory, but also make a qualitative leap in the work efficiency of industrial and commercial administration departments themselves.

2   Overview of Data Mining

2.1   Basic Concepts

Knowledge discovery in databases (KDD) is a complex process of extracting potentially useful, effective, novel and ultimately understandable patterns from databases. Data mining is the most important component of KDD. Nowadays researchers usually don't make a specific distinction between data mining and KDD. In Data Mining: (1) data is a combination of a group of facts, which can come from different data sources, either regular data or irregular data; (2) pattern is an expression described in a language about a data subset or an applicable model, also known as knowledge; (3) evaluate the effectiveness and innovation of the reliability evaluation model respectively The usability of the usability evaluation model and the comprehensibility of the simplicity evaluation model.

There are many kinds of knowledge or patterns produced by data mining, but they can be divided into five categories: (1) generalized knowledge that can reflect the common properties of similar things; (2) Correlation knowledge reflecting the interdependence between things: (3) classification knowledge reflecting the differences of different things; (4) predictive knowledge that can predict the future trend; (5) Biased knowledge that reflects deviations from conventional phenomena.

2.2   Data Mining Steps

The flow of data mining is shown in Fig. 1, which mainly includes the following contents:

(1)   Research problem domain: defining a problem domain is actually to clarify the mining requirements. Only with goals can there be directions. Therefore, this is the most important first step in mining operations.
(2)   Select target dataset: select the mining target and select some data from the data source according to the demand.

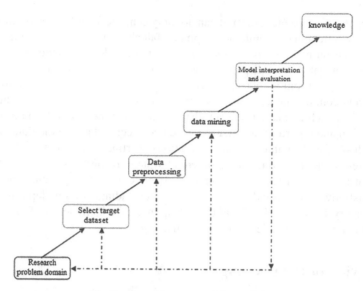

Fig. 1. General process of data mining

(3) Data preprocessing: purposefully process the target data set to turn it into high-quality data that can be mined directly.

(4) Data mining: this stage is simply a pattern generated by actual operation according to mining requirements. A more realistic problem is algorithm matching. This problem usually considers two points: one is the characteristics of data, and the other is the requirements of running system.

(5) Pattern interpretation and evaluation: This is the work that needs to be done before submitting the final results to the user. It is necessary to filter a large number of patterns formed in the previous mining stage and eliminate some useless patterns or patterns that the user is not interested in. If no patterns available to the user are found in these patterns, it is necessary to return to the initial problem domain description stage, Repeat the excavation operation [2].

(6) Knowledge: the final model obtained by using the above steps is to apply useful knowledge to practical problems and guide people's behavior.

3   Application and Prospect of Data Mining in Business Management System

In recent years, the data of business administration system has increased rapidly. In this large amount of data, there is huge information value such as industrial and commercial supervision and market development trend. If we can quickly and effectively analyze and process these data and mine useful knowledge that can guide us to make decisions, it will more effectively help the industrial and commercial system to carry out supervision and decision-making. The application model of data mining in industrial and commercial system is shown in Fig. 2.

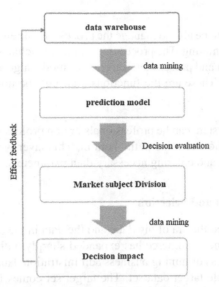

Fig. 2. Application model of data mining in business management system

From the perspective of business administration system, the main goal of business administration is to improve the modernization level of market supervision and understand the economic trend of the development of market subjects. Business administration data mining should mainly solve the above problems. Data mining can help industrial and commercial administrations clearly understand the current market supervision, and also help industrial and commercial administrations determine the development trend of market subjects, so as to master the mode and law of economic development, help the government correctly understand and understand the future direction of economic development, and provide strong data support for the formulation of economic policies.

4   Architecture and Data Preprocessing of Business Administration Data Mining System

4.1   Architecture of Business Administration Data Mining System

The architecture of business administration data mining system is based on the general process of data mining, and refers to the construction method of conventional application platform.

The architecture mainly includes the following three levels:

(1) Basic database layer.

This layer should include source database, mining requirement dictionary, model algorithm base and knowledge base. The source database comes from the business system of the industrial and commercial administration department. It is the accumulated data for the daily management and use of the industrial and commercial administration department [3].

(2) Functional layer.

The system needs to be able to manage the process, requirements, model algorithms and results of data mining. The process management includes requirements description, data selection and processing, selection of model algorithms and management of mining results. These are the functions that must be involved in the design of function layer.

(3) User layer.

The users of the system can be professionals or non professionals. There is no need to know in detail how to mine at the bottom. This layer is responsible for system permission setting and entering necessary data parameters.

4.2 Data Preparation and Selection

At present, it has entered the era of big data, and the data in the database of the Administration for Industry and Commerce has expanded sharply with the advent of the era of big data. In the process of mining business administration data, it is a very important step to establish a usable target data set. The target set comes from the original data, that is, the data in the business system of the industrial and commercial administration department. These data are huge and messy, and there must be problems such as attribute value vacancy, data noise and so on. Moreover, these data may come from different levels of industrial and commercial management systems, that is, different data sources. The data of each data source is large, including redundancy and scattered data [4]. It is often stored in a heterogeneous environment lacking unified design and management. It is difficult to access comprehensive query. In addition, many historical data cannot be stored and queried online. These factors will affect the efficiency of data mining. Therefore, it is very difficult to mine high-quality knowledge or patterns from these low-quality and non-uniform data sources. Thus, data preparation and selection is the most important part in the whole mining process.

5 Conclusion

With the realization of the digitization of economic household registration, the current database business system shows some deficiencies in the in-depth statistical analysis, and it becomes very difficult to obtain useful decision-making information. It is urgent to develop a new data analysis system by using emerging technologies. As a fresh blood in the field of data analysis, data mining gradually shows its superior practicability. At present, it has been applied to many industries, showing its wide application range and huge potential economic value. Although the application technology and concept of data mining in China are far from foreign advanced technology, great progress has been made. Although the domestic research on data mining of industrial and commercial big data is still in its infancy, it is believed that it will be more and more perfect and in-depth in the future, which is also the development direction of data analysis of industrial and commercial management system in the future.

References

1. Wang, L.: Overview of data mining research. Libr. Inf. **5**, 41–46 (2008)
2. Chen, F.: Try to describe the application of data mining in business administration under the network economy. Res. Urban Constr. Theory (Electronic version) **34**, 14 (2013)
3. Yan, W.: Application of data mining in business administration under network economy. Comput. Knowl. Technol. **8**(21), 5261–5263 (2012)
4. Xianhua, L.: On data mining technology and its research status. Mod. Inform. **30**(3), 167–169 (2010)

Application of Stochastic Simulation Algorithm in Evaluation of PE Training

Jie Zhang[✉]

Shaanxi University of Chinese Medicine, Xianyang 712046, Shaanxi, China
zhangj8708@126.com

Abstract. At present, there are many studies on the evaluation of primary physical education teaching ability, but most of them are constructed before the implementation of the new curriculum standard. This relatively old evaluation system is difficult to objectively and accurately evaluate the teaching ability of physical education teachers at this stage. Due to the inaccurate evaluation, teachers may lead to psychological imbalance and can not devote more energy to the improvement of teaching ability. Therefore, in order to improve the scientificity and objectivity of physical education teachers'teaching ability evaluation, this paper studies the application of random simulation algorithm in physical education teaching evaluation.

Keywords: Random simulation algorithm · Physical education · Teaching evaluation

1 Introduction

Physical education teachers' classroom teaching ability is the core ability in physical education, because physical education teachers'comprehensive classroom teaching ability determines students'learning effect, so as to determine the core quality of the whole physical education teaching, which is also the fundamental task and main goal of physical education teaching. The evaluation of physical education teaching ability can promote physical education teachers to improve teaching methods and teaching quality, and it is also an important basis for assessing the performance of physical education teachers. However, from the current situation of the evaluation of physical education teachers'teaching ability, various educational units often ignore the evaluation of Physical Education Teachers' teaching ability; From the research results, the evaluation of physical education teaching ability by scholars is mostly limited to the overview of theory, and there is no specific operation model of evaluation [1]. The evaluation of PE Teachers' teaching ability belongs to the research category of uncertain content of fuzzy theory. Only through fuzziness, PE Teachers' teaching ability belongs to a certain area of the set level.

Therefore, this paper constructs an independent advantage evaluation method that "highlights its own advantages". In the evaluation, a probability based random simulation

M. A. Jan and F. Khan (Eds.): BigIoT-EDU 2022, LNICST 465, pp. 400–405, 2023.
https://doi.org/10.1007/978-3-031-23950-2_43

algorithm is used to evaluate the advantages of the evaluation objects by calculating the degree of superiority between the evaluation objects. This method can produce evaluation conclusions in the form of probability (reliability) and have stronger explicability to practical problems. This method is proposed from the perspective of innovation The comprehensive evaluation method of "from base to top" has high independence. The evaluation link is added in the form of "component" to convert the information of the evaluation data. An example is given to verify the effectiveness of the method.

2 Stochastic Simulation Algorithm

2.1 Concept of Stochastic Process

In nature, the change process can be broadly divided into two types: one is deterministic process, and the other is uncertain process, also known as random process. Generally speaking, the so-called process is a change related to time. For example, for the motion of a free falling body in a vacuum, assuming that the initial velocity is 0 and the falling time of the object is t, the falling height $X(t) = \frac{1}{2}gt^2$ is determined by this functional relationship There is a certain causal relationship when leaving the exact position of the initial point at any time. Obviously, the falling height x is related to the time t, forming a process, which is called a deterministic process. The other kind of process has no definite change form and no inevitable change law. For example, the total daily turnover m of the mall is obviously an uncertain quantity, that is, a random variable, which is further improved The analysis shows that M is also related to time t, thus forming a process m(T), which is also called a random process. For example, the number of times x received by the paging team of the paging station every day is obviously uncertain, that is, it is a random variable. Further analysis shows that x is also related to time 1, so x(T) Similarly, air temperature, air pressure and daily customer flow of stores constitute a random process.

$$\begin{cases} E(t)\dot{x}_k(t) = f(t, x_k(t)) + B(t)u_k(t) \\ y_k(t) = C(t)x_k(t) \end{cases} \tag{1}$$

3 Development History of Stochastic Process

Stochastic process theory was born in the early 20th century. It is closely related to other branches of mathematics. It is an important tool to study stochastic phenomena in the fields of social science, natural science and so on. In the study of random processes, people measure the inevitable internal laws through the superficial view of contingency, and describe these laws in the form of probability. The greatest charm of this discipline is to realize necessity through contingency.

The development of stochastic process theory has a history of more than 100 years, which originated from the study of physics. Every new theory has its historical opportunity, and random process is no exception [2]. The earliest scientists paid attention to a part of the stochastic process associated with other disciplines, such as the characteristics of the independent incremental process discovered by Bachelier when analyzing the fluctuation of the stock market in 1900, the Markov chain studied by Markov, the findings of Gibbs et al. On statistical mechanics and Einstein et al. On Brownian motion. But in the real sense, the systematic and rigorous research on stochastic process theory began in the 1930s.

In the 1960s, on the basis of Markov process and potential theory, French scholars used some of their ideas and results to further expand the general theory of random process to a great extent, including section theorem, projection theory of process and so on.

In the development history of stochastic process, Chinese scholars have also done a lot of work and achieved good results. Theory comes from practice. In the development history of stochastic process, we study the actual phenomena deeply, put forward the theory to explain the phenomena, and finally verify the theory with phenomena, which is also the development process of most theories from special cases to general theories. In fact, many research directions have their practical background. When these directions are deeply studied and verified, they are used to guide practice and further expand and deepen the scope of application.

4 Construction of Evaluation Index System of Physical Education Teachers' Teaching Ability

4.1 Basic Principles of Constructing Evaluation Index System

When constructing the evaluation index system, we should strictly screen the selected indexes on the basis of following the theoretical knowledge of physical education, pedagogy, psychology and new curriculum standards. At the same time, the construction of evaluation index system must follow certain guidelines and principles.

First, the principle of integrity: that is, the constructed evaluation index system should be able to comprehensively evaluate the teaching ability of primary physical education teachers, and ensure that the selected indexes will not reappear, so as to construct hierarchical indexes at all levels, and then form a complete evaluation index system. In addition, in the process of constructing the evaluation index system, we should not only follow the commonness of the teaching ability of PE teachers in junior middle schools in the teaching process, but also highlight the characteristics of this special stage of junior middle schools.

Second, the principle of scientificity: scientificity means that the indicators should be selected on the basis of theoretical knowledge such as pedagogy and physical education. The selected indicators should not only conform to the objective truth, but also stand the test of practice [3]. They cannot be selected arbitrarily according to subjective judgment. The construction of evaluation index system is mainly to guide the teaching process scientifically and systematically, so as to improve the overall physical education teaching quality and improve teachers' teaching ability. Therefore, when constructing the evaluation index system, we should fully combine the characteristics of sports events and the actual situation of students to select the indexes at all levels.

Third, the principle of testability: testability means that the selection of indicators should be able to carry out specific operation and quantitative analysis, and make accurate judgment on the tested object through indicators. Therefore, when constructing the evaluation index system, the selection of indicators must be easy to understand and measure, reduce some vague indicators, and make each indicator reflect teachers'teaching ability in essence.

4.2 Basic Process of Constructing Evaluation Index System

The construction of evaluation index system has guiding significance for improving the teaching ability of physical education teachers and the judgment of school managers on Teachers' teaching ability. Therefore, when constructing the evaluation system, in addition to the above principles, we should also follow the strict sequence and process, so as to ensure the rationality of the evaluation system.

As shown in Fig. 1, the basic steps of constructing the evaluation index system are: (1) determine the object and goal to be evaluated; (2) Determine indicators at all levels; (3) The indexes were screened by Delphi method; (4) Calculate the weight ratio of indicators at all levels (analytic hierarchy process); (5) Complete the evaluation index system; (6) Verify the evaluation index system.

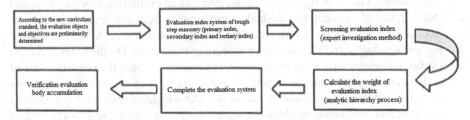

Fig. 1. Basic steps of establishing evaluation indicators

5 Application of Random Simulation Algorithm in Physical Education Teaching Evaluation

5.1 Random Simulation Algorithm is the Most Appropriate Method to Evaluate PE Teachers' Teaching Ability

The evaluation of PE Teachers' teaching ability belongs to the research category of social science, unlike the fixed data support in the evaluation standards of natural disciplines. Moreover, there is no obvious boundary for the evaluation level of physical education classroom teaching ability. In the ordinary physical education classroom evaluation, most of them make self judgment based on the evaluator's overall feeling of the main physical education classroom teaching, and sometimes there is a large gap in the evaluation level. The fuzzy matter-element clustering method solves the subjective defect in the evaluation through the qualitative and quantitative dimensions of physical education teachers'teaching ability. Therefore, the method of random simulation mathematics is feasible and the evaluation result is more reasonable.

In the calculation method, the sum of the simple difference and weight product of the two related matter elements is used as the distance between the matter element to be evaluated and the evaluation grade " In principle, the grade of the matter element to be evaluated is judged and clustered, so the calculation method is simple and easy to operate [4]. At the same time, the clustering ranking is arranged according to the distance from small to large, which makes it easy to compare the position of each physical education teacher's teaching ability in the whole and the ranks of the grade, so as to position the ability of education and teaching workers, and provide a good way to better promote the improvement of physical education teaching ability Evaluation method.

5.2 Suggestions for Model Improvement

(1) Appropriately increase the number and grade of evaluation indicators of physical education teachers'classroom teaching ability.

In this study, the author only designs the evaluation indexes of one level dimension. However, in the actual social science evaluation model, in order to better reflect the scientificity and authenticity of the evaluation model, multi-level evaluation indexes can be designed to form an interrelated evaluation index system, and then calculated by using the method of progressive from low level to high level. Such a fuzzy evaluation model, with the refinement of indexes, On the one hand, it is more conducive to the quantitative scoring of evaluators. On the other hand, the evaluation results will be more objective. For example, under the primary index of action demonstration ability, secondary indicators such as action accuracy, action effectiveness and action economy can be set. The weight of each level of index is a key step, and the method of obtaining index weight can also be based on the expert weighted statistics method in this model, or Analytic hierarchy process (AHP).

(2) Try to increase the number of experts who obtain the index weight.

In fuzzy evaluation, the index weight is obtained by human subjective scoring, with strong personal subjective judgment, but the weight is a key link in the implementation and operation of the evaluation model and a data-based performance that directly affects the evaluation results. In the method of obtaining the weight, first try to select well-known experts with deep academic attainments to obtain a relatively reasonable weight value. Secondly, in the number of experts It is better to select more than 30, and the more the number, the more reasonable the index weight value tends to be.

6 Conclusion

Teachers and students are the two necessary factors to constitute the physical education classroom. The role of physical education teachers has become the leader of the physical education classroom. It can even be said that the words and deeds of physical education teachers will have a profound impact on all aspects of students. This impact is reflected through the teaching ability of physical education teachers, so the teaching ability of physical education teachers is the guarantee A reasonable and sound evaluation index system can not only promote the progress of PE Teachers' teaching ability in all aspects, but also facilitate school managers to accurately judge PE Teachers' teaching ability, so as to complete the evaluation of PE Teachers' teaching ability under the new curriculum standard New requirements of physical education in junior middle schools.

References

1. Cai, W.: Matter Element Model and its Application. Science and Technology Literature Press, Beijing (1994)
2. Chen, G., Li, M.: Research on the integration of comprehensive evaluation methods based on method set. Chin. Manage. Sci. **12**(1), 101–105 (2004)
3. Yi, P., Guo, Y.: Negotiation combination method of multiple evaluation conclusions under the characteristics of bilateral conflict. Syst. Eng. Theory Pract. **26**(11), 63–72 (2006)
4. Yi, P., Zhang, D., Guo, Y.: Stochastic simulation algorithm for comprehensive evaluation and its application. Oper. Res. Manage. **18**(5), 97–106 (2009)

Course Recommendation Method and System of Education Platform Based on Deep Learning

Jingbin Zhang[✉]

Xi'an FanYi University, Xi'an 710061, Shaanxi, China
ruibin321@163.com

Abstract. Course recommendation is a service mode that recommends personalized learning resources to users according to their historical behavior information. Traditional recommendation methods can not effectively use auxiliary information and its potential relationship, resulting in problems such as cold start and sparse data. With the growth of data and the progress of computing power, the combination of deep learning and course Recommendation provides a new idea to solve the above problems. The research on in-depth learning methods for education platform curriculum recommendation has become a research hotspot in the field of education. In view of the challenges faced by the current curriculum recommendation, this paper studies the curriculum recommendation method and system of the education platform based on deep learning.

Keywords: Deep learning · Education platform · Course recommendation

1 Introduction

With the popularity of the Internet, great changes have taken place in learners' learning methods, which helps to promote the development of personalized education and promote the reform of education system and education model. The individualized education concept that varies from person to person breaks the traditional education and teaching methods, so that the education and teaching goal of "teaching students according to their aptitude" is no longer just a slogan. In the Internet environment, a large number of high-quality curriculum resources are widely spread and shared, which provides convenience for learners. Learners can arrange learning according to their own time to meet their personalized learning needs.

At present, the development of course recommendation applications is relatively slow, and most of them use the traditional collaborative filtering recommendation algorithm. Collaborative filtering recommendation algorithm has some problems, such as cold start, data sparsity and scalability, which can not meet the needs of current education platform course recommendation. How to help learners obtain appropriate curriculum resources and carry out personalized learning has become an important research topic in the field of intelligent education. With the popularization of online education and the rapid development of education information system, a large number of education and

M. A. Jan and F. Khan (Eds.): BigIoT-EDU 2022, LNICST 465, pp. 406–415, 2023.
https://doi.org/10.1007/978-3-031-23950-2_44

teaching data can be presented and saved, including learners' majors, interests, learning conditions, curriculum feedback and other records [1]. By analyzing the historical web page information that learners have browsed, we can obtain learners' interest preference information. At the same time, comprehensively considering the factors such as learning background, personal interest and major, recommending suitable courses to learners to meet learners' personalized learning needs has important theoretical research significance and practical application value.

Personalized recommendation is based on users' historical access data for analysis and calculation. The personalized recommendation in the system is based on Web log data mining and is implemented by using ALS machine learning algorithm in spark. ALS algorithm is based on collaborative filtering for course recommendation.

The recommendation algorithm is mainly based on the relationship between users. The required data includes user ID, course ID and course score. However, there is no user rating data for the course in the web log data, only the course content accessed by the user. Therefore, the system uses the number of times the user watches the course video as the rating for the course.

This paper counts the times each user watches each video from the web log data, and reflects the user's preference for the course according to the user's access times to the course. The more you watch, the more you like it, and vice versa. ALS algorithm can find similar users according to their favorite course videos, and there must be an intersection between their favorite videos. Then, it analyzes the favorite course videos of similar users, and removes the course videos that users have seen to recommend them. It can be seen that the algorithm is based on other existing user preferences to predict the user's rating or liking for the video they have not watched, and can not make personalized recommendations to new users.

The user information is saved in the MySQL database. When logging in, the user checks the account and password by accessing the database.

On the other hand, since the log automatically generates 200000 lines using scripts, the effect recommended here is not very obvious.

Hot spot analysis includes two parts: hot word analysis and regional analysis. First, extract the course name from the web log data, and use the jiebar extension package for word segmentation. During word segmentation, it is necessary to establish a course dictionary and a stop vocabulary for the system, because the course name in the web log contains some special nouns, such as "the Belt and Road". Using the system dictionary, it will be divided into two words: "the belt and road" and also contains a large number of stop words, such as "de" and "yes". In this way, the accuracy of word segmentation can be effectively improved.

Hot word analysis is to recommend some keywords to users. Users can search and view through the search function, which is also a potential recommendation method.

This function module extracts the user's access IP from the web log. Through the crawler, you can use the API provided by the data science toolkit website to obtain the geographical location according to the IP. According to the geographic coordinates, the remaph function of remap extension package is used for geographic data visualization. Remap extension package can draw excellent geographic heat map and migration map.

The results returned by the API provided by the data science toolkit are stored in the form of Josn and need to be processed with regular expressions. R language regular expression gsub function can complete the replacement of regular expression. The results returned by the API include country, city, operator, geographic coordinates, etc. By observing the data, it can be found that only the geographical coordinates are of numeric type, and the rest are of string type. Therefore, the data processing process obtained by using the web crawler is relatively simple. You can directly replace the non numeric string with null. After the replacement, the rest are numeric types, that is, longitude and latitude. However, it seems that this API can not be accessed directly now. It is estimated that you need to climb over the wall to use it.

However, what I need to explain here is that the geographical heat map is drawn through the remap package. However, due to the conflict between the CSS of the remap package and that of shiny, there are some failures in the system interface, because I save the geographical heat map as a picture for display.

2   Relevant Theories and Technologies

When a new user or an unlisted user enters the learning platform, the system cannot know the specific information of the user, so it does not know the interests of the user, so it cannot use the conventional recommendation algorithm for recommendation. Generally, at this time, it is only before recommending items that are generally well reflected to users. In the face of this situation, the project extracts courses that have been viewed more times and recommends them on the home page through web log analysis.

Home page recommendation is to extract the course IDS accessed by users from the preprocessed data, then count the number of times these course IDS appear, sort them according to the number of times they appear, and recommend the most popular and visited courses to users.

The search function can help users quickly find all courses related to search keywords. These course name data are extracted from the web log using R language, so all courses existing in the web log can be searched. The search engine is based on regular expressions. By performing regular expression matching in the course name in the course data through the grepl function, you can search all courses containing keywords and obtain their serial numbers. When the search is completed, the serial number collection is returned. The found courses are displayed in the front end according to the serial number and ID number of the courses.

Users can use the search function to complete the course search. On the other hand, this function improves the hot word analysis function in hot spot analysis. Users can view hot words and then use the search function to view courses.

Course classification mainly uses manual methods to add labels to each course in the course information summary file, which can be displayed according to the labels in the front display. Course classification can help users view courses according to categories. The design includes 13 categories, such as "office", "examination", "foreign language", "construction", "finance", etc.

At the beginning of crawling data, I didn't expect that there would be a course classification function in the later stage, so no classification labels were added to the data, so the data classification labels were added manually in the later stage.

2.1 Recommended System Definition

Wikipedia interprets recommendation system as an application of information filtering. In his book "practice of recommendation system", Xiang Liang explained the recommendation system as an information filtering and information push tool that automatically contacts users and projects. Adomavicius et al. Gave a formal definition of recommendation system. Suppose u represents the user set and V represents the set of items (such as books, movies and restaurants), and the number and scale of users and items are large. F represents a utility function used to calculate the recommendation of item V to user u, then the utility function f can be defined as: F: u v r, where R represents a fully ordered set of real numbers or non negative integers in a limited range. The task of the recommendation system is to find the item V with the highest recommendation for any user u U. the formal definition formula is as follows:

$$u, U, v_u \ arg \ maxf(u, v) \tag{1}$$

By modeling user preferences, the recommendation system obtains the potential characteristics of users and projects, predicts users' scores on projects, or forms a recommendation list. Goldberg gives a general process of recommendation system, which is divided into three modules, as shown in Fig. 1.

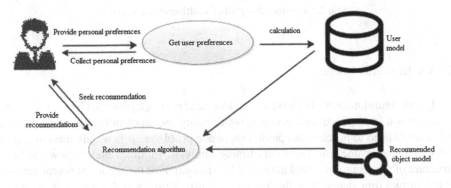

Fig. 1. General structure of recommendation system

2.2 Deep Learning Technology

In recent years, deep learning has made rapid development in the field of recommendation system. The performance of deep learning largely depends on the network structure. In order to adapt to different types of data and problems, various types of neural network structure models are applied to recommendation system. The following will describe in detail the two network model structures of multi-layer perceptron and long-term and short-term memory network.

1) Multilayer perceptron

Multilayer perception (MLP) is a basic neural network model. Because information propagates forward in MLP, and any two layers of neurons are connected with each other, MLP is also called forward propagation network and fully connected neural network. MLP network structure mainly includes input layer, hidden layer and output layer. The hidden layer can have one or more layers, and each layer is composed of several neurons, as shown in Fig. 2.

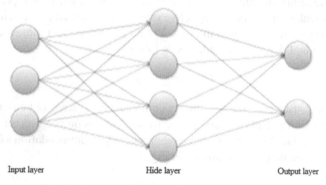

Input layer   Hide layer   Output layer

Fig. 2. Structure diagram of multi-layer perceptron

2) Cyclic neural network

Cyclic neural network is derived from Hopfield network proposed by saratha satha-sivam. It is a kind of artificial neural network using sequence information. At present, it is mainly used to process and predict sequence problems. It is widely used in speech recognition, machine translation and timing analysis. Figure 3 and 4 show the basic structure of the recurrent neural network [2]. The output of the recurrent neural network at the current time depends on the input at the current time and the state at the previous time. We can use the following formula to descript it.

$$x = \sum_{i=0}^{n} \sqrt{\frac{(X-\overline{X})^2}{n-1}}$$
$$x = \sum_{i=0}^{n} \frac{(X-\overline{X})^2}{n-1}, \tag{2}$$
$$x = \sum_{i=0}^{n} \frac{(X-\overline{X})(X-\overline{X})}{n-1}$$

where x is the network layer.

In order to realize the neuron network with deep learning. The formula of the algorithm is following:

$$T = (t_1, t_2, \ldots, t_n)$$
$$i_t = \sigma\left(w_i \cdot [h_{t-1}, x_t] + b_i\right)$$
$$f_t = \sigma\left(w_f \cdot [h_{t-1}, x_t] + b_f\right)$$
$$O_t = \sigma\left(W_0 \cdot [h_{t-1}, X_t] + b_0\right)$$
$$\tilde{c}_t = \tan h\left(w_c \cdot [h_{t-1}, x_t] + b_c\right)$$
$$C_t = f_t \cdot C_{t-1} + i_t \cdot \tilde{C}_t \tag{3}$$
$$h_t = o_t \cdot \tan h(c_t)$$
$$u_t = \tan h(w_s h_t + b_s)$$
$$a_t = \text{soft} \max\left(u_t^T, u_s\right)$$
$$v = \Sigma_t a_t h_t$$
$$y = \text{soft} \max(v)$$

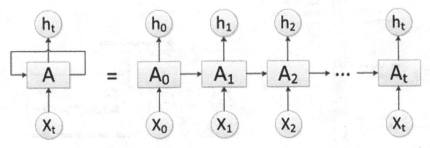

Fig. 3. Structure diagram of cyclic neural network

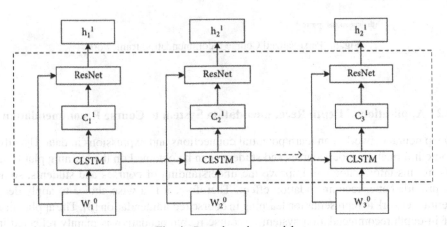

Fig. 4. Deep learning model

3 Curriculum Recommendation Method and System of Education Platform Based on Deep Learning

3.1 Personalized Course Recommendation Framework

As shown in Fig. 5, firstly, multi-source heterogeneous data fusion is carried out for book borrowing information, students' basic information, students' history course selection information and students' course selection behavior information, so as to absorb the characteristics of different data sources and enrich students' information, which is conducive to the expression of students' interest preference vector in model learning. Secondly, personalized course recommendation is carried out through deepafm model, and the combination of high-order and low-order features is integrated to improve the prediction ability of the model. Finally, the personalized course recommendation results are presented in the hot areas concerned by students to improve the course click through rate.

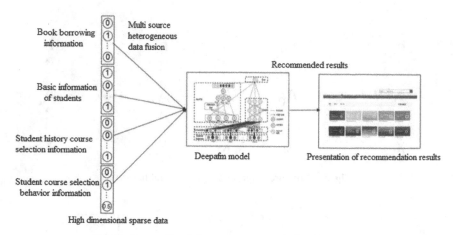

Fig. 5. Personalized Course recommendation framework

3.2 Application of Depth Recommendation System to Course Recommendation

Deep neural networks can learn potential connections and expressions in data. Usually, some information about courses and students can be obtained on the learning platform. Using this information can improve the understanding of courses and students, so as to provide better recommendation effect. Therefore, it is a wise choice to apply deep neural network to representation learning in course recommendation [3]. The application of in-depth recommendation system in course recommendation is mainly reflected in the following four levels:

(1) Improve the representation learning ability: the deep neural network can use the nonlinear activation function to model the nonlinearity in the data. This attribute can capture complex student course interaction patterns, and can effectively learn potential connections and useful feature representations from input data by using the powerful nonlinear fitting ability of deep learning, which is shown in Fig. 6.

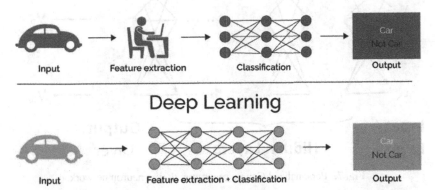

Input   Feature extraction   Classification   Output

Deep Learning

Input   Feature extraction + Classification   Output

Fig. 6. Personalized Course recommendation deep learning network

(2) Deep collaborative filtering: the classical matrix decomposition model can be considered as a simple neural network. Through the interaction of the neural network of the deep learning model, more nonlinear feature interaction can be introduced to improve the fitting ability of the recommended model which is shown in Fig. 7.

(3) Deep interaction between features: in order to improve the accuracy of the model, some features will be artificially interactive in the traditional recommendation system to improve the expression ability of students' preferences, which requires a lot of artificial feature engineering, and the effect also has great limitations. The deep neural network can automatically learn feature interaction from the original data by unsupervised or supervised methods. It not only improves the efficiency, but also greatly improves the recommendation effect of the model.

(4) High flexibility: with the support of many popular deep learning frameworks, the model of deep learning has a high degree of flexibility. The deep learning model can flexibly adjust its own structure according to the course recommendation scenario and data characteristics to adapt to the application scenario [4]. For example, different neural network structures are usually combined to establish a powerful hybrid model or replace one module with other modules. Therefore, it is easy to build hybrid and composite recommendation models to capture different features and factors at the same time.

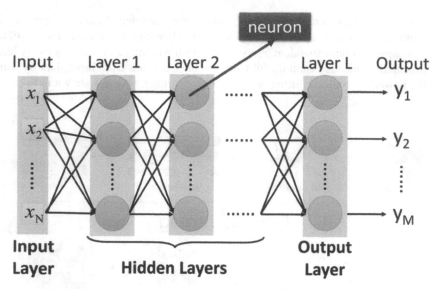

Fig. 7. Personalized Course recommendation neuron network

4   Conclusion

In the recommendation system based on deep learning, the commonly used deep learning technologies include neural networks such as RBM, MLP, AE, CNN and RNN. Among them, CNN, AE and their variants are often used in feature engineering to extract features from multimodal data such as text, image and video, RBM and MLP are often used in potential factor model, and RNN and its variants (such as long-term and short-term memory network, gated loop unit, etc.) are often used in recommendation based on sequence information. The curriculum recommendation method of education platform based on deep learning aims to better express how the time sequence of courses affects students' performance. From the initial method based on collaborative filtering, to machine learning method and matrix decomposition method, and then to the recommendation method based on deep learning, it is to realize personalized current course recommendation and gradually improve the effect of course recommendation.

Acknowledgements. 1. Xi'an Translation College 2021 University-level Online Curriculum Construction Project (ZK2143) "Introduction to Mao Zedong Thought and the Theory System of Socialism with Chinese Characteristics (Special School)".

2. The first batch of research projects and practical projects of online ideological and political work in Shaanxi universities (2021SPWSXM-Z-8) "Practice Innovation and Exploration of Shaanxi Local Party History Network Education in Colleges and Universities".

References

1. Li, Y.: Solving high dimensional partial differential equations based on deep learning method. Wang Lulu, Wuhan University (2019)

2. Yan, T.: Research on network representation learning method and application of multi-mode data fusion. Li Jiayi, Taiyuan University of Technology (2019)
3. Li, W.: Research on network representation learning method maintaining generalized structure. Zhu Sinan, Beijing Jiaotong University (2019)
4. Xi, X.: Research on emotion dictionary construction algorithm based on depth representation. Wang Leyi, Nanjing University of Technology (2018)

Design and Research of College Students' Comprehensive Quality Evaluation System Based on Evolutionary Algorithm

Ang Li[✉]

Sichuan University of Media and Communications, Chengdu 611745, Sichuan, China
lee_1008@sina.cn

Abstract. This paper studies the design of College Students' comprehensive quality evaluation system based on evolutionary algorithm. The current evaluation system mainly focuses on quantitative evaluation, displays the results in the form of summary evaluation, and lacks qualitative evaluation and process evaluation. The comprehensive quality of college students has increasingly become the focus of social attention. Colleges and universities are important places for cultivating high-quality talents. Therefore, strengthening comprehensive quality education is not only the need of the times, but also the need of China's higher education reform. Combining evolutionary algorithm with college students' comprehensive quality evaluation, a college students' comprehensive quality evaluation system based on electronic archives is developed, which better unifies qualitative evaluation and quantitative evaluation, process evaluation and summary evaluation.

Keywords: Evolutionary algorithm · Evaluation system · Comprehensive quality of College Students

1 Introduction

The word "quality" is originally a physiological concept. In the field of higher education, quality can be understood as "the basic conditions necessary to complete a certain activity". Comprehensive quality is the subjective quality formed by the educated on the basis of innate genetic quality, through receiving education and participating in social practice. It is the systematic integration of human physiology, psychology, culture, ability and moral quality.

With the rapid development of social productive forces, the demand for talents from all walks of life is increasing day by day. How to comprehensively and evenly evaluate personal comprehensive quality and realize the needs of talents? How to cultivate high-quality and high-level talents requires comprehensive consideration of teaching quality and students' quality level evaluation. Therefore, for students' comprehensive quality evaluation, we need a comprehensive and targeted evaluation system. At present, most colleges and universities conduct comprehensive quality evaluation based on students' academic performance and school performance, but is the evaluation method appropriate,

M. A. Jan and F. Khan (Eds.): BigIoT-EDU 2022, LNICST 465, pp. 416–422, 2023.
https://doi.org/10.1007/978-3-031-23950-2_45

comprehensive and targeted? Whether the quality of talents screened through evaluation basically meets the requirements of units at all levels of society.

At present, most colleges and universities have initially implemented the comprehensive evaluation of college students. There are many differences in the content, procedures and methods of the evaluation. Some of the evaluation items are divided into excellent, good, medium and poor grades under the moral, intellectual and physical modules. Some of them take the form of evaluation regulations as the evaluation implementation method, and the evaluators and the evaluated give static judgment on each item with reference to their behavior; Some of them only display extended articles in the aspects of "morality, intelligence and physique"[1]. Characteristics of comprehensive evaluation method: the comprehensive evaluation is divided into moral, intellectual and physical parts, each accounting for a certain score proportion; Weighted average of academic performance of each course in academic performance, reflecting the proportion of different courses; Moral performance is changed from voting to scoring or students' scoring is adjusted; The performance of students in the school is reflected separately in the form of addition and subtraction or in the individual items of morality, intelligence and sports. Problems in comprehensive evaluation: the weight relationship of moral, intellectual and physical sub items is artificially determined, which is lack of scientific basis; Academic achievement only focuses on examinations and examination courses, which can not reflect the needs of the new employment situation; The scoring of moral evaluation is arbitrary, without definite basis, only based on personal impression; The daily performance bonus is not standardized, so that each proportion can not reflect the real behavior of the evaluated person.

Colleges and universities are the national garden for cultivating all kinds of specialized talents and the cradle for the growth and success of college students. It is the central task of colleges and universities to cultivate millions of college students into useful talents with high comprehensive quality and solid professional knowledge. To judge the quality of college students, we must use scientific methods to make a comprehensive evaluation of college students. This is not only an important part of college student management, but also the need for college students' evaluation and graduation assignment. Especially after the merger of colleges and universities, the graduation distribution of college students will implement independent job selection and two-way selection. Each employing unit will select talents suitable for the needs of its own department according to the nature of work and business content. To this end, schools have to provide employers with all kinds of information about students so that each student's strengths can be brought into play. This information is based on the evaluation of College Students' comprehensive quality.

2 Relevant Overview

2.1 Evolutionary Algorithm

First, it is necessary to establish a first-class weight system, and finally determine the number and name of weights by means of questionnaire survey, consulting materials and referring to the existing evaluation standards of colleges and universities. Each index of the primary weight system is subdivided, and each primary index is divided into a secondary weight system. Similarly, the secondary weight system is subdivided to finally form a tertiary weight system. The weight values of the whole tertiary weight system are confirmed by expert evaluation method to obtain a complete tertiary weight system, It is used for the comprehensive quality evaluation system of college students. Then, the student's performance is evaluated through the student's comprehensive quality evaluation algorithm based on three-level fuzzy comprehensive evaluation. The algorithm is comprehensively displayed in the form of B / s system. The evaluator inputs various data representing the student's level, the system calculates the secondary comprehensive quality level coefficient, and then calculates the secondary coefficient and the primary weight value, Finally get the comprehensive quality level of students [2].

At present, there are many software related to students' comprehensive quality evaluation system. The final function of the software is the same. The only difference is that the students' evaluation indexes and the quantitative analysis of each index are different, but their purpose is to more effectively reflect the students' comprehensive quality of the University. In order to realize the quantification of comprehensive quality, we need to base on the different characteristics of each evaluation index, At present, the more commonly used methods are AHP, fuzzy comprehensive evaluation method, etc. the system uses evolutionary algorithm to calculate the weight of each evaluation index, which is the uniqueness of the system. The evolutionary algorithm code is shown in Fig. 1 below.

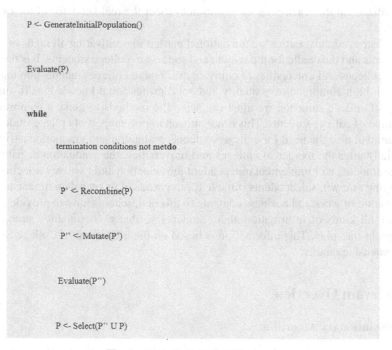

```
P <- GenerateInitialPopulation()

Evaluate(P)

while

    termination conditions not metdo

        P' <- Recombine(P)

        P" <- Mutate(P')

        Evaluate(P")

        P <- Select(P" U P)
```

Fig. 1. Evolutionary algorithm code

2.2 Evaluation Theory

System evaluation theory regards the evaluation object as a system, and the evaluation index, evaluation weight and evaluation method should operate according to the system optimal method.

(1) System behavior structure

Any system is a conversion mechanism, that is, it converts a certain input into a certain output, and then further feeds back to the input, so it operates repeatedly. In this way, all the activities of the system can be divided into four parts: input, operation, output and feedback. The structure description of "system behavior" is shown in Fig. 2 below:

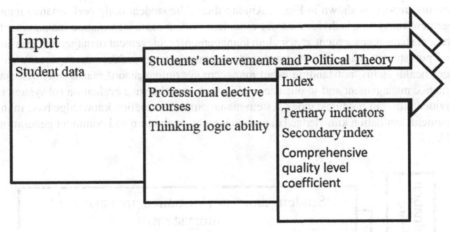

Fig. 2. Overall structure diagram

(2) Methods of systematic evaluation

As can be seen from the above description, there are many uncontrollable factors in the process of system conversion activities. It is difficult to deal with it directly, and the output of the system is the result of the established process. Different methods and means can be used to evaluate the system. Therefore, when evaluating the system, directly evaluate the output results rather than the conversion activity itself. On the other hand, the output result of the system is affected by two factors: the system environment and the internal state of the system, and the internal state of the system plays a decisive role, that is, it depends on the conversion ability and level of the input within the system, and finally depends on the optimization degree of the structure. In this way, through the evaluation of the output, it also indirectly evaluates various specific activities of the transformation work, so as to achieve the purpose of the evaluation work.

Evaluation is to evaluate the output of the system according to the principle of system integrity, not just one aspect or some parts of the work results. According to the principle of system optimization, the sum of the optimal individuals is not equal to the optimization of the system. The result of optimization is to establish the best combination of various elements, which is greater than the algebraic sum of parts, which requires a comprehensive evaluation process.

3 Design of College Students' Comprehensive Quality Evaluation System

According to the requirements of the system and combined with previous development experience, the system is designed into four subsystems: student daily performance management, comprehensive evaluation, intelligent analysis and interpretation subsystem and report, as shown in Fig. 3. Among them, the student daily performance management subsystem is divided into 11 modules: student basic information management, student status management, curriculum management, achievement management, reward and punishment management, community management, attendance management, student health status, outstanding event management, online record management, social practice management and so on; The intelligent comprehensive evaluation subsystem is divided into four modules: index system management, evaluation knowledge base management, evaluation knowledge base management, evaluation and comment generation [3].

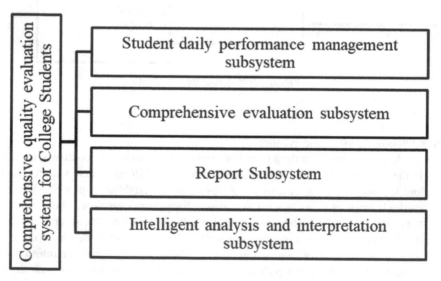

Fig. 3. System function structure diagram

4 Design of Comprehensive Quality Evaluation System Based on Evolutionary Algorithm

The design method of the index system of this system is: firstly, according to the requirements and characteristics of talent training objectives, on the basis of full investigation and research, carefully analyze the basic quality structure of all kinds of college students, extract the main aspects, and establish a more comprehensive and objective evaluation index set respectively. Secondly, Delphi is used to scientifically classify various indicators, establish a hierarchical structure, and determine the connotation and evaluation grade standard of various evaluation factors. Finally, on the basis of fully soliciting the opinions of all parties, the relative weight of each evaluation factor is calculated by Delphi.

Calculate relative weights:

According to the characteristics of the system, the following Delphi method is used to determine the relative weight a. Take the secondary indicators of ideology and morality as an example:

Set the corresponding weight of each index as a_1, a_2, a_3, a_4, that is, factor importance fuzzy subset a,

$$A = u_{11} + u_{12} + u_{13} + u_{14} \tag{1}$$

$$\sum_{A_{\max}} = \max\left\{\sum A_1, \sum A_2, \sum A_3, \sum A_4\right\} \tag{2}$$

$$\sum_{A_{\min}} = \min\left\{\sum A_1, \sum A_2, \sum A_3, \sum A_4\right\} \tag{3}$$

(1) The evaluation model is divided into three levels: intelligent single factor judgment, two-level fuzzy comprehensive evaluation and one-level fuzzy comprehensive evaluation.

(2) Single factor judgment uses the expert database in artificial intelligence to judge the impact of students' performance on each evaluation index. Usually, a student's performance record has an impact on more than one index of evaluation. For example, the first prize of the group in the student city mathematical modeling competition can at least show that students have strong mathematical application ability (belonging to the intellectual part) and strong teamwork ability (pioneering ability). Using the expert system, this influence relationship is stored in the system as expert knowledge, and mapped to the index system of the system when making single factor judgment [4].

The knowledge in the evaluation knowledge base is used to associate the daily performance of students with the secondary indicators of evaluation. As mentioned earlier, the relationship between students' daily performance and indicators is not a one-to-one relationship, but a one-to-many relationship; In addition, students' daily performance is easy to change compared with the evaluation model. For example, a new reward category can be added as needed; The relationship between indicators and students' daily performance often changes according to the needs of evaluation. Based on the above considerations, enhance the function of the system, increase the recording activity of the system, and establish an evaluation knowledge base.

5 Conclusion

This paper is completed on the basis of the actual project of "College Students' quality intelligent comprehensive evaluation system". This system is an information management system. As one of its subsystems, intelligent comprehensive evaluation collects students' moral, intellectual, physical and aesthetic information from multiple channels to realize multi-directional analysis, query, statistics, evaluation, annual assessment Comprehensive evaluation, score report, Graduate recommendation form and other functions comprehensively include student education and management.

References

1. Satty, T.L.: The Analytic Hierarchy Process, pp. 16–48. MeGraw Hill, New York (1980)
2. Zhengjun, P., Lishan, K., Yuping, C.: Evolutionary Computation. Tsinghua University Press, Beijing (2000)
3. Wang, S., Huang, Z., Zhang, G.: Research on humanistic evaluation system of scientific and technological development. China Sci. Technol. Forum 6, 132–135 (2003)
4. Xie, J., Liu, C.: Fuzzy Mathematics Method and its Application. Huazhong University of science and Technology Press (2000)

Design of Business Administration Professional Shared Whiteboard Teaching System Based on BS Data Mining Architecture

Min Chen[✉]

Nanchang Medical College School, Nanchang 330000, China
709124931@qq.com

Abstract. This paper is based on efficient background data support, the application of Ajax framework and B/S architecture and other advanced technologies. During the implementation of online experiment function, for business administration teaching real-time distance education system in the process of using, lecture notes, electronic induction whiteboard and other data content of large-scale broadcast and free preservation method. The purpose is to make full use of the advantages of the network in real-time distance teaching, and to display diversified teaching contents; The use of electronic whiteboard module can not only make teachers and students interact better, but also greatly enhance the interest and efficiency of teaching; The construction of business administration scene completed in the online experiment is an important innovation of traditional teaching methods, and the resulting teaching system can make users experience more real and effective visual effects.

Keywords: B/S framework · Sharing whiteboard · Teaching system design · Business administration

1 Introduction

With the continuous and rapid development of social economy, the world has entered the era of rapid progress of information technology. The strong information technology has impacted the traditional education, which makes the present education work have changed greatly both in the teaching methods and the teaching composition [1]. To do a good job in the education modernization and improve the quality of teaching work, we need to enhance the information of teaching process. According to the relevant investigation, the focus of the web technology support of distance education is to deal with the interaction between teaching work, resource reserve and quality management. With the development of computer network technology, especially the realization of individual interaction function led by Web2.0 technology, the operating efficiency and service quality of the new system which provides various technical services for education work are rapidly improved. The effect of teaching interaction between teachers and

M. A. Jan and F. Khan (Eds.): BigIoT-EDU 2022, LNICST 465, pp. 423–432, 2023.
https://doi.org/10.1007/978-3-031-23950-2_46

students in the network situation is more remarkable, These are in line with people's expectations of the development of modern education.

B/s architecture refers to the "browser/server" architecture, which is a network architecture mode. It can concentrate the core part of the system function realization into the server, and simplify the development, maintenance and use of the system. It can run through the browser without installing other clients.

B/s architecture (browser/server Architecture) is a network architecture mode, which centralizes the core part of the system function implementation into the server and simplifies the development, maintenance and use of the system. It can run through the browser without installing other clients.

B/s architecture is a browser server architecture. With the continuous development of new technologies, it is a change or improvement of c/s architecture.

B/S structure refers to the browser/server structure, that is, only one server needs to be installed and maintained, and the client uses the browser to run the software. With the development of Internet technology, it is a change and improvement of C/S structure. It mainly uses the WWW browser technology, combined with a variety of script languages and new technologies, centralizes the core part of the system function realization to the server, and simplifies the development, maintenance and use of the system. Is a new software system construction technology. It only needs to install a browser and database, so that the browser can interact with the database through the web server.

Advantages of B/S architecture:

(1) This architecture does not need to install the client and can run directly in the web browser
(2) B/s architecture can be directly placed on the Internet network, so as to achieve the purpose of controlling multi client access and interaction mode through some privileges.
(3) The b/s architecture does not need to install clients, so there are no problems such as updating multiple clients and upgrading servers

Disadvantages of B/S architecture:

(1) B/s architecture is not the most satisfactory architecture in cross browser
(2) It takes a lot of effort to reach the level of CS program
(3) In terms of speed and security, it still needs to spend a huge design cost, which is the biggest problem in b/s architecture.
(4) The client server interaction is a request response mode, which usually needs to refresh the page, which is unwilling to see the client. But this shortcoming has been alleviated to some extent after Ajax became popular. Figure 1 shows B/S data mining architecture.

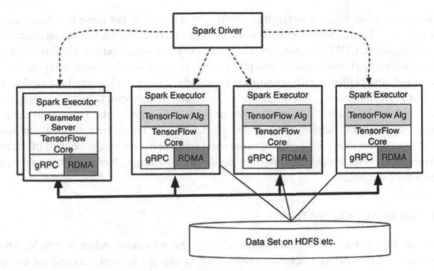

Fig. 1. B/S data mining architecture

2 Theoretical Basis and Technical Points

2.1 Browsing of Online Courseware for Business Administration

This operation can help users to browse the courseware effectively without downloading the courseware according to their own needs. Its function implementation involves three aspects: client part, network system part and service end part, as shown in the following figure. At this time, users can use the network system to realize the outgoing of courseware browsing request, then the server part will find and process the courseware, and finally build the information flow path of the contact server part and the client part, which is shown in Fig. 2.

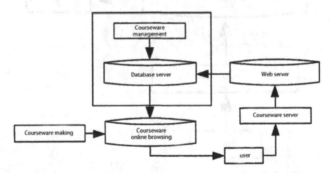

Fig. 2. The process of browsing Business Administration online courseware

The key point of this operation technology is to transform the online courseware effectively, so as to get the resource form which is convenient for users to consult in time. At this time, office programming interface is involved, but these interfaces are all existed by work card. No matter what kind of program, it can complete relevant operations by calling office COM components Net framework is a development platform that can realize high-speed development and processing, network service content layout, etc. it is a brand-new platform with revolutionary value for Microsoft to easily complete the program Net framework can complete the construction and operation of Web programs and windows programs. It uses the standard content given by the Internet to achieve integration. With the help of standard communication protocols such as XML and soap, it can realize the integration of programs and components under the control of various environments. The whole program only needs to call a single. Net assembly to process the COM component.

2.2   Shared Whiteboard Design

To develop a set of shared whiteboard teaching system with independent copyright, which is suitable for the current teaching environment, so that it can meet the needs of modern distance education. The shared whiteboard teaching system is based on the network and WCB. It uses handwriting electronic induction whiteboard writing, handwriting pen input, material introduction and web courseware synchronous browsing as a variety of teaching means. Through the same shared whiteboard, it provides all students in all classrooms with synchronous or asynchronous teaching content sharing. Each student can see the teaching content on the PC in front of him, take notes online and save the content he cares about. Through the way of server group distribution and cascade connection, it can support large-scale users online at the same time. It has the main characteristics of many concurrent numbers, display synchronization, stable operation, security, expandable function and so on. The composition is shown in Fig. 3, which is the flow of the operation of the electronic whiteboard.

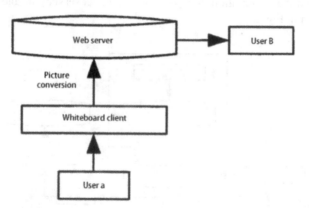

Fig. 3. Implementation process of whiteboard operation

As can be seen from the above figure, during the interaction between user a and user B relying on the electronic whiteboard, first of all, user a needs to make the graphics to be displayed by the client where the whiteboard is located. When the sending is selected, the client can display the complete data stream in the form of pictures. At this time, the PNG encoder plays a role; Then, with the help of Base64 encoding, it completes the encoding processing in order to get better transmission effect. The electronic whiteboard here will use JavaScript given by fabridge technology to complete the acquisition operation of the generated complete picture information, and then use ajax technology to convey the obtained information to the server. At this time, the server needs to complete the decoding process with the help of Base64, and then get the PNG image that can be recognized, and finally deliver it to user B, and the whole communication work is completed.

3 Business Administration Teaching System Design

3.1 B/S Framework

The structure of business administration course involves three aspects: background database, web server and user browser. At this time, the browser can complete the interactive processing with the database in the background with the support of the web server. There are many differences between B/S structure and CIS structure. The most important thing is that the former does not need to maintain the client's browser after updating. The requests from the client can act on the server with the help of the browser, and the processed information can be fed back to the client. The following figure shows the operation structure of this model (Fig. 4).

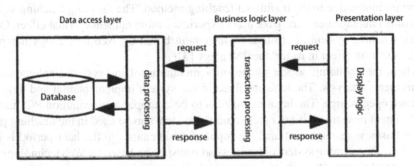

Fig. 4. B/S framework

As is easy to know from the above figure, the implementation of this structure involves the following three levels:

(1) The presentation layer, which is located at the outermost position of the whole system, has the smallest spacing with the user, and can display and receive the information input from the user, and facilitate the user to perform interactive processing operation page [2];

(2) Business logic layer, which is in the middle of the whole system, plays an extremely important role, and can relay the data involved in the system. Only because of the poor coupling effect here, the mutual information can only be reflected to the lower

level, but can not process the information from the upper position. Therefore, in the case of considering all aspects of factors, the drawer architecture which can be inserted instead of processing is used here, which is convenient to realize the efficient transformation of two types of roles.

(3) Data access layer: complete the access control of database, and access to common binary information and text information.

All business processing in b/s structure is implemented in the server location, so it is better than CIS structure in the aspect of maintenance and upgrade. And the efficient interconnection with web technology makes the program based on this completion have stronger extension effect. So here the system design chooses b/s architecture to complete the mode construction.

3.2 Demand Analysis

First, the technical aspect of the implementation of the system implementation requirements analysis. In the aspect of pattern, we choose the more widely used b/s architecture, and combine with the anthem.net which is implemented in Ajax framework by asp.net to build a better performance model. The online experiment part is realized by compiler and Microsoft, which ensures that the system users can display the various teaching contents well without installing the compiler; The introduction of electronic whiteboard module can make the whole teaching work more interesting and improve the teaching efficiency; The scene construction of business management completed in online experiment is an important innovation to the traditional teaching method. The resulting teaching system of business management can make users experience more authentic visual effect. Overall, the teaching system of business management based on Web technology has good implementation effect in its technical strategy [3].

Then, the economic aspect of the implementation of the system implementation requirements analysis. The tools involved in the system implementation and development are open source. The input only needs to be equipped with common PC, and the development investment is not much. And the system can be used in the teaching practice of business management, and the input of maintenance in the later period is low. Therefore, the teaching system of business administration based on Web technology has a good development effect in its economic investment.

Finally, the implementation requirements of the system are analyzed from the operation aspect. The analysis shows that the contents of the system are extremely simple, the early installation and the later maintenance and operation. As long as the instructions given can be well executed by the personnel, both the teachers and the teachers can perform the operation in a very short time. Therefore, the teaching system of business administration based on Web technology has good implementation effect in its operation and implementation.

The b/s layered model is selected in the system architecture of the teaching system for business administration. It can support the system to build online services such as video and experiment for users, and also help teachers and students realize real-time interaction in online situations, so as to facilitate users to get better service. The system combines the breakthrough of Web2.0 visualization technology, which can make the teachers and students more effective in the implementation of communication and inter-action, facilitate the realization of instant interaction function, and provide the auxiliary functions such as electronic whiteboard, teaching management and resource display, so as to improve the interest effect and interaction process of the whole teaching period, and the user can feel more clear visual effect. The introduction of online experiment function can make the whole system display more diverse contents. With the help of online experiment operation, it is convenient for all users in the system to complete the editing of language practice without equipping programming program in advance at any time, and enhance the flexible effect of students' learning tasks, and improve the practical level. Moreover, the system can achieve a significant functional with the help of this operation, users can get more authentic visual experience, business management teaching work more practical effect.

The overall goal of the implementation and development of the business management teaching system is to build a better online learning platform for students by means of online video viewing, courseware browsing, experimental operation and teacher-student interaction.

4 Concurrent Control Under Shared Whiteboard

At present, with the popularization of computers and networks, there are more and more digital devices, such as personal computers, laptops, personal digital assistants (PDA), mobile phones, set-top boxes, MP3 players, digital cameras, digital video cameras, electronic whiteboards, etc.; These devices can provide some services, but may have some limitations in other services; If we can make full use of the advantages of these devices while avoiding their disadvantages, that is, using the service composition of devices, we can create some new, easier to use and more powerful services. For example, the electronic whiteboard can receive the point signals drawn on the whiteboard, and then send these point signals to the computer, which can reproduce the contents of the electronic whiteboard. In this way, the difficulty of meeting minutes can be greatly simplified and the effect of the meeting can be enhanced. However, since the electronic whiteboard can only be used on one computer at present, it is obviously impossible to use it when holding a network conference, or if multiple users can see the contents of the electronic whiteboard on their own computers, mobile phones or PDAs.

In order to solve this problem, it is necessary to establish a software layer between users and different devices. This layer hides the underlying network protocols, devices and operating systems, and only provides electronic whiteboard services in the user range and operating LAN. Users can transparently use the electronic whiteboard devices and services in the network environment, regardless of the device where the electronic whiteboard is located and the operating system of the device.

MCU, a multi-point control unit, solves the problem of data multicast transmission among nodes in different subnets, and on the other hand, it solves the problem of concur-rent data transmission among multiple nodes. At present, most MCU is implemented by hardware based on H.320 standard, which is oriented to private network and centralized control mode. The main reason is related to circuit alternating pull mode and physical star topology [4–7].

However, in tcp/ip packet switching, it is not realistic to adopt hardware MCU centralized mode. In addition, hardware MCU has some problems, such as poor scalability, high cost, poor compatibility with tcp/ip protocol, etc. Therefore, in the design of this system, we propose a software MCU implementation technology suitable for tcp/ip packet switching, and adopt the realization method based on COM technology. The specific principle is: in the distance education network, a data server is set up for each subnet, and the distributed multi-point control and management method of tree structure is adopted. In the hierarchical control center, a dynamic IP address table of all data servers in the whole network is maintained, and MCU is dynamically created to connect several data servers to realize the connection and data forwarding between them. Thus, multiple MCU and data servers can jointly complete the receiving and forwarding, converging and switching, addressing and routing of media flows between multiple communication terminals, The utilization of network bandwidth is greatly improved [8, 9].

In the synchronous teaching or synchronous discussion mode, multiple members edit and access the shared whiteboard at the same time, which will lead to access conflicts, which will cause the inconsistency of whiteboard content. Therefore, a certain concurrency control strategy should be adopted. Combined with the characteristics of the distance teaching process, the centralized control mechanism of the chairman system is adopted, that is, through teachers, the normal initiation and implementation of the whole teaching process is maintained until the end. Teachers manage the students' speech right by maintaining the statement status table of Zhang students and allocate the students' speech rights through a priority queue, which is shown in Fig. 5.

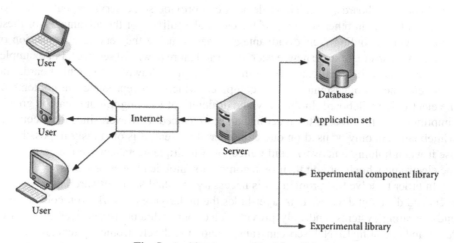

Fig. 5. Architecture used in this article

5 Conclusion

This paper introduces a design of the shared whiteboard teaching system for business management specialty based on b/s architecture. It adopts multi-layer b/s architecture, uses advanced component development ideas, supports synchronous teaching, asynchronous discussion, synchronous recording and other teaching modes. This system is specially aimed at the specific problems encountered in the process of distance teaching of video conference system, which has strong practical significance.

The b/s mode does not require a special client, as long as the browser, and the browser comes with the operating system. Convenience is its advantage. Moreover, b/s is based on Web Language and has nothing to do with the operating system, so cross platform is also its advantage. In the future, with the progress of web language and browser, b/s will be faster and faster in terms of performance and running speed, and its shortcomings will be less and less. Especially with the popularity of HTML5, it has been very powerful in graphics rendering, audio and file processing.

The software system is improved and upgraded more and more frequently, and the products of b/s architecture obviously embody more convenient features. For a slightly larger company, if the system manager needs to run back and forth between hundreds or even thousands of computers, the efficiency and workload can be imagined. However, the b/s architecture software only needs to manage the server, and all clients are just browsers, which do not need any maintenance at all. No matter how large the size of users and how many branches there are, the workload of maintenance and upgrading will not be increased. All operations only need to be carried out for the server; If it is a remote location, you only need to connect the server to the private network to realize remote maintenance, upgrade and sharing. Therefore, the client is becoming thinner and thinner, while the server is becoming fatter and fatter, which is the mainstream direction of information development in the future. In the future, software upgrading and maintenance will become easier and easier to use, which will obviously save users' manpower, material resources, time and cost. Therefore, the way to maintain and upgrade the revolution is "thin" client and "fat" server.

As we all know, windows almost dominates the world on desktop computers, and the browser has become the standard configuration. But on the server operating system, windows is not in the absolute dominant position. The trend of the software is that the application management software using b/s architecture only needs to be installed on the Linux server with high security. Therefore, there are many choices of server operating system. No matter which operating system is selected, most people can use windows as the desktop operating system, and the computer will not be affected. This makes the most popular free Linux operating system develop rapidly. In addition to the free operating system, Linux also has free databases. This choice is very popular.

Since the b/s architecture management software is only installed on the server, the network manager only needs to manage the server. The main transaction logic of the user interface is fully implemented through the WWW browser on the server, and a few transaction logic is implemented in the front browser. All clients only have browsers, and the network manager only needs to do hardware maintenance. However, the data load of the application server is heavy. Once the server "crashes", the consequences will be unimaginable. Therefore, many units have database storage servers in case.

References

1. Wu, W.: Research on distributed multi task cooperation mechanism of CSCW. Comput. Eng. **23**(5) (1997)
2. Huang, Y.: Research on agent based distributed intelligent collaborative design system. Comput. Eng. Appl. 1998-08
3. Yunhui, L.: On the structure and function of virtual teaching system. Continuing Educ. Res. **6**, 171–172 (2012)
4. Wu, W.: Research on the application of VRML based virtual reality technology in distance virtual experiment teaching. Shaanxi Normal University, Shaanxi, pp. 1–51 (2013)
5. Diao, T., Zhang, J., Yao, C., Li, W.: Application of Chinese text sentiment classification based on recurrent neural network. Wireless Internet Technol. **18**(19), 96–97 (2021)
6. Yuan, Y.: Research on sentiment classification of online review texts based on Naive Bayes. Inner Mongolia Sci. Technol. Econ. **18**, 91–94 (2021)
7. Zhang, H., Huang, H., Li, W.: Speech emotion database for emotion change detection. Comput. Simul. **38**(9), 448–455 (2021)
8. Wang, Y.: On the emotional penetration and integration in the process of Chinese teaching in higher vocational colleges. University **35**, 128–130 (2021)
9. Huang, Z., Wu, X., Wu, Y., Ling, J.: Chinese text sentiment classification combined with BERT and BiSRU-AT. Comput. Eng. Sci. **43**(9), 1668–1675 (2021)

Design of Education Management System Based on Cloud Storage

Haidan Xu[✉]

Qujing Medical College, Qujing 655000, Yunnan, China
`Wanglei18291826361@126.com`

Abstract. Information construction in Colleges and universities is the key factor to realize modern education. In the process of information construction in Colleges and universities, due to the similarity of teaching data, there are a lot of duplicate data between the education management systems independently built by colleges and universities, resulting in a great waste of storage resources, and the teaching data is growing exponentially, which brings great storage pressure to the traditional data center. All users share a resource pool, resulting in low resource search efficiency. Moreover, due to the unclear role and authority of users, teaching resources can not be safely shared among college users.

Keywords: Cloud storage · Management system · Resource sharing · Role

1 Introduction

With the rapid development of information technology and the popularity of personal computers and intelligent machines, more and more users begin to communicate with the outside world through the Internet, understand and obtain all kinds of information resources they need, and manage their own data through network storage. In the environment of colleges and universities, realizing the scientization and automation of daily education management is an important symbol of realizing education modernization. Campus network is a key factor in the modernization and information construction of colleges and universities. Relying on the convenient campus network, using advanced computer technology, implementing more scientific, effective and convenient online management of teaching work, and establishing a series of education management systems matching with college education can further accelerate the work efficiency of colleges and universities and improve the teaching level.

Analyzing the current process of University modernization, we can find that there are many problems in its education management system. For example, the education management system used by each university is generally built, operated and maintained independently. Due to the existence of a large number of similar resources or the use of the same teaching data among colleges and universities, the direct consequence is that the data between colleges and universities is highly repeated, resulting in a waste of a large number of storage resources and increasing the capital investment in network teaching

M. A. Jan and F. Khan (Eds.): BigIoT-EDU 2022, LNICST 465, pp. 433–438, 2023.
https://doi.org/10.1007/978-3-031-23950-2_47

of major colleges and universities. Moreover, most colleges and universities may have multiple education management systems at the same time. A variety of teaching systems lead to complex campus system maintenance and a great waste of human and financial resources. At the same time, this paper analyzes the current resource sharing strategies of colleges and universities. In order to obtain relevant shared resources, users often need to consume a lot of search time, resulting in the slow progress of campus digitization, so that the rapidly developing computer network technology can not timely serve today's teaching work, which seriously hinders the process of college education modernization [1].

In the past two years, cloud computing technology has developed rapidly. Its core idea is to provide software, platform and it equipment resources in the form of services. The goal is to integrate a large number of cheap physical computing resources with low performance into a powerful computer system with high computing power, large storage capacity, and provide a unified service interface. Users can pay for software, platform or underlying hardware equipment according to their actual needs.

2 Overview of Key Technologies

2.1 Cloud Storage Technology

With the emergence of cloud computing technology, cloud storage technology provides a new solution for massive data storage. The cloud storage platform has the advantages of storage space Virtualization (by aggregating the space of multiple storage devices, flexibly allocating and deploying storage space, avoiding unnecessary hardware device costs and improving the utilization of storage space), and dynamic scalability of storage capacity (on the premise that the original storage system is not affected, storage nodes are dynamically added or deleted to meet the needs of dynamic changes of data) and data security (ensure the continuity and integrity of data and ensure that users can obtain the data they want anytime, anywhere) Based on the above characteristics, cloud storage platform can provide enterprises with cheap, dynamically scalable storage capacity and safe and complete data, and provide a method to reduce the pressure of massive data storage for traditional data centers.

2.2 Data Layout Algorithm

Cloud storage platform is composed of a large number of heterogeneous storage devices. How data is stored and arranged in these storage nodes not only affects whether the storage devices can be fully utilized, but also affects the access efficiency of cloud storage platform. At the same time, cloud storage platform has dynamic scalability, and storage nodes can be dynamically added and removed. When the storage capacity of cloud storage platform changes, it is better Xiu's data layout algorithm can reduce the amount of migrated data and improve the performance of the cloud storage platform. Therefore, it is necessary to study the data layout algorithm to build the cloud storage platform.

The data layout algorithm mainly solves the two major problems of fairness and adaptability. The actual amount of data obtained by each device in the system is related to its performance, and the amount of data obtained by different devices is directly proportional to its performance. If - data layout algorithms meet the above relationship, it is considered that this layout strategy meets the fairness requirements. The adaptability of the layout strategy can be achieved by adding or removing device nodes It can be measured by the ratio of the actual amount of data migrated to the optimal amount of data that needs to be migrated in theory, or if it can be ensured that data migration only occurs between old equipment and new equipment, it can also be said that the corresponding strategy can well meet the requirements of self adaptability.

1. Assign a weight value to all devices according to their performance (storage location, storage capacity, network bandwidth, etc.):

$$\sum_{i=1}^{n} w_l = 1 \tag{1}$$

2. Assume that the minimum weight value of all devices is w_m. Allocate $k\log n$ virtual storage nodes to the storage node, where k is a constant and N is the number of actual storage nodes. For other storage nodes, the weight is assumed to be w_i. The algorithm will assign n to the device node N_i virtual storage nodes:

$$N_i = (w_i/w_m) \cdot k \log n \tag{2}$$

Therefore, a total of N storage locations are required in the ring to map all storage nodes (including physical storage nodes and virtual storage nodes) [2].

The algorithm can solve the fairness problem of the data layout algorithm. Its disadvantage is that it introduces a large number of virtual nodes, increases the storage overhead and increases the complexity of the algorithm. Especially in the case of large performance differences between devices, the number of virtual storage nodes introduced by the algorithm will be huge, resulting in serious storage overhead. At the same time, the algorithm still does not consider redundancy The remaining problem is that only one piece of data is stored in the storage space. When a storage node fails, the data stored in this node will not be recoverable.

3 Design of Education Management System Based on Cloud Storage

With the deepening of the process of educational modernization, the amount of data in the educational management system has increased exponentially, which has brought severe challenges to the traditional data center. The most direct way to store massive data is to increase the number of storage devices in the data center. However, relying solely on the addition of storage devices to solve the storage problems caused by the explosive growth of data will make college storage a success In the face of the explosive growth of data, how to realize the efficient storage of this part of data is an urgent problem to be solved in Colleges and universities.

Through the analysis and research of various data layout algorithms in cloud storage technology, an improved data layout algorithm is proposed to meet the requirements of fairness and adaptability at the same time. In addition, according to the characteristics of college teaching data, a local duplicate data deletion algorithm based on the characteristics of teaching data is proposed to minimize data redundancy and reduce the pressure of network bandwidth, so as to reduce the cost The storage pressure of massive data on the traditional data center and the complexity of system upgrading and maintenance in the future.

The construction of digital campus has achieved initial results in Colleges and universities. The use of network, multimedia and other high-tech means for auxiliary teaching or online teaching has been gradually carried out "By analyzing the current daily teaching process in Colleges and universities, it can be found that although the campus network has been built, the actual utilization rate of each teaching system is not high, and the auxiliary role for daily teaching work is not complete. For example, there are two common teaching activities: teaching courseware sharing between teachers and students and online submission of students' classroom homework. At present, there are three main ways: one is Copy through USB flash disk, that is, students use USB flash disk to copy teachers' teaching courseware in spare time such as recess; second, teachers share teaching resources by sending e-mail, that is, teachers uniformly set and publish a shared mailbox, and student users in a specific class use password to share teaching resources and submit classroom homework by logging in to the shared mailbox; third, FTP server is used.

There are two main backup strategies for information data backup using backup system: real-time backup and regular backup. Both strategies have their own advantages and disadvantages. In comparison, real-time backup has the advantages of high data integrity and good security. The disadvantage is that for the large storage system such as teaching system, real-time storage consumes too much resources and there is a great waste of resources At present, it is the most widely used. Its advantage is that it can make more full use of system resources. Its disadvantage is that when the timing policy is not set properly, it may cause the loss of data information.

Based on the frequency characteristics of data resources in the education system, the strategy of combining real-time backup, regular backup and manual backup is designed to back up the education system. In addition, the backup mode is dynamically and flexibly adjusted according to the semester characteristics of school teaching activities [3]. For example, the frequency of courseware resources in different chapters of curriculum courseware is different in the semester of the beginning of the course With the increase of class time, the use frequency of new courseware resources is high, and the use frequency of courseware resources in historical chapters is reduced. Therefore, different backup strategies need to be adopted for courseware resources in different chapters. The real-time backup strategy is adopted for courseware resources in new chapters. When the use frequency is reduced, the backup mode is dynamically changed to regular backup mode, so as to realize dynamic adjustment of storage Storage strategy to increase storage efficiency and resource utilization.

4   Cloud Storage Platform Implementation

The cloud storage platform is further modified and implemented on the basis of Apache Cassandra program, which is mainly composed of three parts: external interface, HTTP server and back-end storage device group. External interface: the system provides storage, reading and deletion interfaces for the upper layer developers. Developers can call the interfaces provided by the platform to complete the storage, reading, modification and deletion of data The main implementation interfaces include:

1. Performput (string nativepath) / L storage interface. The parameter is the local storage path;
2. Performget (string nativepath, string remoteobjectname) / / read interface. The parameters are the data storage path and the ID of the read data;
3. Performmodify (string objectname) / / modify the data interface. The parameter is the ID of the modified data;
4. Performdelete (string objectname) / / delete the data interface. The parameter is the ID of the deleted data.

HTTP server: this server completes the parsing of data packets transmitted between the upper layer developers and the back-end storage node. The interfaces involved include get, put, post and delete. The get interface encapsulates the back-end data and returns it to the upper layer developers. The put interface stores the front-end data in the back-end storage node. The post interface is based on the needs of the front-end developers It is required to modify the data stored in the back-end. The delete interface is responsible for data deletion.

The system realizes the classified storage of all data and stores the structured data in the database. The design of each data table is shown in Fig. 1.

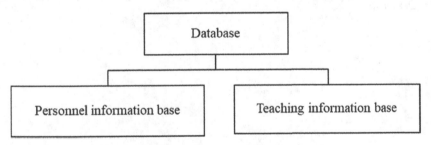

Fig. 1. Database implementation

The administrator first imports the question bank into the system and establishes the index of the question bank [4]. When a new question is added to the question bank, only one index record needs to be added; According to the item bank index, each item tester needs to save a mapping table. Mapping the item to the electronic item bank can complete the recording of an item; For students' answers, judge the correctness of the answers based on the question bank index and the test paper mapping table. For correct answers, they are mapped to the standard answer location of the question record by default. Only the wrong answers are stored, and the mapping between the storage location of the wrong answers and the students' test paper can be completed.

5 Conclusion

This paper deeply studies the problems of massive data storage and resource security sharing, and puts forward the corresponding solutions combined with the current popular technologies. On this basis, an education management system based on cloud storage is developed and implemented. Research and propose solutions to the problem of massive data storage. The cloud storage technology and data deduplication technology are deeply studied respectively. According to the advantages and disadvantages of each data layout algorithm in cloud storage technology, an improved data layout algorithm is proposed to better meet the performance requirements of fairness and adaptability in data layout algorithm at the same time. Research and propose solutions to the problem of resource security sharing. Based on the study of various resource sharing methods in Colleges and universities, a resource sharing strategy based on college resource space and role is proposed and implemented.

References

1. Wang, Y., Sun, W., Zhou, S., Pei, X, Li, Y.: Key technologies of distributed storage in cloud computing environment. J. Softw. **23**(4), 926–986 (2012)
2. Guo, Y., Yan, J.: Research on massive data storage mode. Comput. Digit. Eng. **36**(11), 153–169 (2008)
3. Luo, J., Jin, J., Song, A., Dong, F.: Cloud computing: architecture and key technologies. J. Commun. **32**(7), 3–21 (2011)
4. Dean, J., Ghemawat, S.: MapReduce: a flexible data processing tool. Commun. ACM **53**(1), 72–77 (2010)

Design of Information Teaching Management System Integrating Association Rule Mining Algorithm

DongHong Zhang[⊠]

Medical College, University of Business Management, Kunming, Yunnan, China
zdh123450701@163.com

Abstract. Teaching management informatization is an important part of campus informatization construction. How to use advanced network information technology to implement scientific and effective management of teaching and students' learning and make it give full play to its maximum benefits is an important topic of teaching management in Colleges and universities. In order to improve the level and efficiency of teaching management in Colleges and universities, this paper designs an information-based teaching management system based on association rule mining algorithm to improve the efficiency and management level of teaching management in Colleges and universities, so as to lay the foundation for scientific and comprehensive management of teaching in Colleges and universities.

Keywords: Merging association rules · Promotion of information technology · Teaching system

1 Introduction

Teaching management informatization is to use information management theory and information management methods, take modern information technology as the core, fully consider external variables and information, organize and allocate teaching information resources, and carry out information-based teaching management activities, so as to achieve the established teaching objectives efficiently. Teaching management information system is not only the most important part of teaching management information, but also the basis of education information. Its connotation includes teaching plan management, organization and management of teaching process, teaching quality management, teaching administration, teaching equipment management, laboratory management, discipline construction, specialty construction, curriculum construction, teaching material construction, faculty construction, student status management, scholarship management, management system construction, etc. [1]. Use information technology, network technology, multimedia technology and other information means to carry out teaching management activities. The basic characteristics of teaching management informatization are digitization, networking, multimedia and intelligence.

M. A. Jan and F. Khan (Eds.): BigIoT-EDU 2022, LNICST 465, pp. 439–445, 2023.
https://doi.org/10.1007/978-3-031-23950-2_48

2 Association Rule Mining in Data Mining

Mining association rules is the process of discovering interesting associations or related relationships between itemsets in a large amount of data. It is an important topic in data mining. In recent years, it has been publicly studied by the industry, has become a hot spot and is widely used in a variety of applications. At first, the research of association rules was only to help find the relationship between different commodities (items) in the transaction database and find out the customer purchase behavior pattern, such as the impact of buying a certain commodity on buying other commodities. The analysis results can be applied to commodity shelf layout, inventory arrangement and user classification according to purchase mode. At present, it has been widely used in various fields. As the world's largest "database" - network, association rule mining technology is also integrated into it.

Agrawal and others first proposed the problem of mining association rules between itemsets in customer transaction database in 1993 [2]. After that, many researchers have done a lot of research on the problem of mining association rules. Their work includes optimizing the original algorithm, such as introducing the idea of random sampling and parallelism, so as to improve the efficiency of algorithm mining rules and promote the application of mining association rules.

2.1 Simple Definition and Application of Association Rule Mining

At present, in the research of data mining, the research on association rule mining is more active and in-depth. The mathematical model given below is used to describe the discovery of association rules.

Let $I = \{I_1, L_2, \ldots, L_m\}$ be a set of items, where each transaction t is a set of items, obviously t L. Let X be a group of items. If and only if $x \subseteq T$, transaction t contains X. An association rule is an implication in the following form: $X \rightarrow y$, where $X \subseteq I, Y \subseteq L$ and $X \cap y = \varphi$. If s% of the transactions in D contain xuy, the support $(xuy) = s$ of rule $X \rightarrow Y$ on transaction set D. The confidence level is C. if C = support (xuy) * 100/support (x), it means that C% of the transactions containing x in D also contain y. Credibility indicates the strength of implication, while support indicates the frequency of patterns in rules. Rules with high reliability and strong support are called "strong rules". The essence of association rule discovery task is to find strong association rules in database. Using these association rules, we can understand the behavior of customers, which is very helpful to improve the decision-making of business activities such as retail. For example, it can help to improve the placement of goods (placing goods that customers often buy at the same time together), help how to plan the market (purchase goods with each other), etc. In the research field of data mining, the research on association analysis is relatively in-depth. People have proposed a variety of association rule mining algorithms, such as apriori, FP growth, AIS, DHP and so on.

2.2 Process of Association Rule Mining

As one of the most important tools in data mining, association rules have a wide application prospect. Generally, it can be divided into two parts:

(1) Mining frequent sets: find frequent sets that meet a given degree of support. Frequent sets: sets of items that meet the minimum degree of support.

K-frequent sets; Refers to a frequent set containing K items.

[property 1]: subsets of frequent sets must also be frequent.

For example, if {AB} is a frequent set, then {a} {B} must also be a frequent set

(2) Generate association rules with the obtained frequent sets

The basic idea is: if ABCD and ab are large itemsets, we can determine whether the rule ab-cd is established by calculating the reliability, that is, conf = support (ABCD) 1 support (AB), and conf $\geq$ miniconf (because ABCD is a large itemset, the rule must have the minimum support). The second step is actually a simple statistics and calculation, so the mining of association rules mainly focuses on the key step of mining frequent sets. Many data mining researchers focus on the algorithm of mining and bundling frequent itemsets, so there are many excellent algorithms for generating frequent itemsets. This paper also focuses on this problem.

3 Demand Analysis of Teaching Management Information System

(1) Demand analysis of educational administration subsystem. Educational administration is the center of school work, the premise of the normal operation of school teaching, and the guarantee of standardizing teaching order and improving teaching quality. Its contents include training objectives, enrollment objects and school system, ability structure, quality structure and knowledge structure, curriculum and content requirements, teaching organization and implementation, etc. The term teaching plan is the overall design and arrangement of the course by the teacher, including the class hour arrangement of the course, the description of the teaching content and method, the teaching schedule, etc. it is the basis for the teaching management department to check the teaching situation, teaching content and progress. The management of teachers by the teaching management department mainly includes teachers' basic information, teaching qualification, business learning, teachers' performance, annual assessment, etc., and submits the main information to the personnel department for archiving, or the content of teachers' management is directly carried out by the personnel department. Teacher management is not only an important indicator of teacher work assessment, but also a sensitive issue involving teachers' vital interests. At the same time, due to the large statistical workload and imperfect data accumulation, errors often occur, resulting in adverse effects.

(2) Demand analysis of student management subsystem. Student management is an important part of teaching management and an important part of cultivating comprehensive quality and comprehensive professional ability. Under the realistic situation of large number of students, wide professional coverage and few full-time staff, it is particularly important to adopt network and information management. Its management contents include: admission and registration, class management, student status management, etc. After electronic registration, freshmen will generate a sequence number according to each student in the class, which is the order of the list of students in the class, the basis for relevant departments to print attendance

sheets and transcripts, and it is also convenient for teachers to record their grades [3]. Class management is to form classes according to the predetermined number of students. In the database, class information includes specialty, class name, head teacher's name and contact information, class number, number of male and female students, classroom location, dormitory distribution, etc. at the same time, a class reward and punishment database is established.

(3) Demand analysis of student status management subsystem. Student status management is a complex and tedious task. Under the condition of manual management, the workload is huge, which often leads to the lack of some data. Supported by a powerful database system, the teaching management system directly links the registration of freshmen, the registration of teachers' achievements in the scholarship list and the formulation of make-up examination rewards and punishments with the student database. In case of class transfer and suspension, the student number remains unchanged. All records can truly record the overall situation of the student's study in school without conversion. When students graduate, according to the corresponding printing function, the student's personal transcript, rewards and punishments and other related contents will be printed directly. After being signed and sealed by the school, they will be put on file. The work is very simple.

(4) System management subsystem requirements analysis. System management is an important part of the teaching management clearing system. The security of the whole system depends on whether the design of the system management subsystem is scientific or not. It mainly involves user management, password management, data backup, data deletion and so on. The teaching management information system should set up a very flexible interface for the permissions of users at all levels. Therefore, the system management subsystem should set user permissions, password complexity, database backup mechanism, data deletion management mechanism and so on according to the different working characteristics of various users.

4 Information Teaching Management System Integrating Association Rule Mining Algorithm

4.1 System Architecture

The architecture of management information system mainly includes client 1 server (is) mode and browser 1 server (BS) mode. CIS mode divides the processing tasks of the system between the client and the server to optimize the overall performance. Under this architecture, the server is successively installed with multi-user or multi task operating system, network communication software and sqldbms, and the data processing part is shared by the client and server, which makes the performance of the system qualitatively improved compared with the previous structure. The disadvantage is that the development cost is high and there are many components of the system, so the possibility of failure increases. Moreover, it is difficult to locate the fault and maintain it. BIS mode is a new MIS system platform mode based on Web technology. Remote data service realizes the logical separation and independent encapsulation of user interface logical rules and data services. It can be reused, easy to manage and upgrade, and cross platform. Therefore, the teaching management information system should adopt browser server (B/S) mode, As shown in Fig. 1.

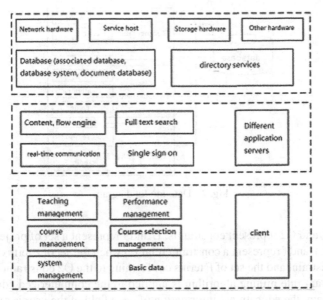

Fig. 1. System overall structure

4.2 Database Management System

Database management system. Database management system (DBMS) is a software system that manages data. It is the core of database system. It is closely related to all parts of database system. All operations on the database are completed under the control of the database management system. The main purpose of database management system is to make data as a controllable and manageable resource, so as to be shared by various users, improve the security, integrity and availability of data, and improve the independence of data. It is also a bridge between user's application and physical database [4]. SQL language has simple structure, powerful function and easy to learn. It is a general and powerful relational database standard language. Through the analysis and comparison of the above database management systems, according to the specific characteristics and requirements of the teaching management information system, the system adopts the relational database management system SQL, As shown in Fig. 2.

The appriori algorithm is improved, the association rules based on the constraints are acquired, the set of n different items is set to $J = \{j_1, j_2,\ldots, j_n\}$, the management set for J is B, the JV including the plurality of items is managed every time, and Ji and related rules are as follows.

$$E \cap Q_e \Rightarrow F \cap Q_f \tag{1}$$

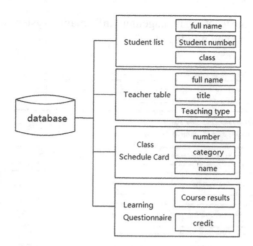

Fig. 2. Data model diagram

Food: Q1 and Q2 represent constraints. E and f represent a set of projects. E μ,μ In management, e and f represent a constraint relation when the set of e terms that conform to the Q1 constraint and the set of F terms conforming to the Q2 constraint are included.

The relevant rule mining algorithm is applied to the computerized education management system, the educational information of each field of the user is excavated, and the management is carried out according to the related information excavated, and the management performance of the system is improved.

5   Conclusion

In order to ensure system safety and stable operation, the system design process is very important to the safety of the system. This system has been designed and developed from three aspects of safety and database safety of cyber security data storage. The process segment management is designed, the shared hub is completely replaced with the exchange, the algorithm is excavated through the related rules, the molecular network is built in the national network, the firewall is installed between the host and the LAN, and the safety barrier is constructed Set filtering rules. Scientific settings monitor data packets in real time for workstations and prevent illegal data filtering. In this method, information necessary for education and management is extracted from the database. We verify the performance of this system's query process, client compatibility, and data mining.

References

1. Ronghuai, H.: Information Technology and Education. Beijing Normal University Press, Beijing (2002)
2. Wang, D., Zhou, J., Li, Q.: Fast association rule mining algorithm. J. Huazhong Univ. Sci. Technol. (Nat. Sci. Edn.) **30**, 12 (2002)

3. Cao, Y.: Selected Practical Engineering Cases of ASP/asp.net Database Development. Renmin Langdian Publishing House, Beijing (2004)
4. Li, S.: Design and practice of educational administration management information system. J. Wuhan Shipbuild. Vocat. Tech. Coll. **9** (2004)

On the Influence of Computer Digital Animation Technology on Film Style

ChunLiang Wang[✉]

School of Film and Television Media, Wuchang University of Technology, Wuhan 430223, Hubei, China
chunliang120150284@163.com

Abstract. With the advent of the new information age, film is more and more popular. The film industry is developing very rapidly. From the development of the film industry, film language, creative techniques and technical means have different forms in different periods For the film industry entering the information age, it will face more challenges. The film industry needs to absorb more and better elements in the new era and constantly innovate in order to face these challenges and achieve artistic breakthroughs. For the film itself, the main factors affecting its development are technical means. As a product of the information age, computer digital animation technology has a far-reaching impact on film style. According to the computer digital animation technology applied in today's films, this paper analyzes the impact of computer digital animation technology on film style.

Keywords: Computer · Digital animation technology · Film style

1 Introduction

In recent years, with the rapid development of digital technology, the digital industry has shown more and more vigorous vitality. Digital technology not only accelerates the output of digital resources, but also creates new opportunities for the development of film and television production in China. A number of excellent domestic animation film and television works came into being. Grasping the development opportunities of the times and strengthening the diversified application of digital animation technology is not only a necessary condition for building and improving the digital animation film technology system in the future, but also the top priority to improve the quality of animation film and television works and the level of film creation.

In the new century with the increasing development and improvement of science and technology, computer digital animation technology has been gradually integrated into every link of film creation. The application of computer digital animation technology not only enriches the form of expression of the film, but also affects the creative style of the film. It allows directors to present the film picture more intuitively, concretely and reasonably in front of the audience. At the same time, film is an artistic creation [1]. We can't take it as the expression space of emotional art and the performance occasion of

M. A. Jan and F. Khan (Eds.): BigIoT-EDU 2022, LNICST 465, pp. 446–455, 2023.
https://doi.org/10.1007/978-3-031-23950-2_49

director technology, which not only wastes film resources, but also ignores the artistic creation value of film. Therefore, a correct, scientific and reasonable view of the impact of computer digital animation technology on the film style and its artistic expression in the film can make the film embark on a correct development track. This paper attempts to explore the impact of computer digital animation technology on film style as a whole, in order to encourage with film peers.

The teaching of digital animation is guided by tasks. Through wonderful and rich task cases, starting with the basic theory of introduction to animation, this paper introduces in detail the production process of animation, the basic principle of animation production, the creation of animation script, animation lens language, and drawing techniques and laws. At the same time, through excellent lens dividing examples at home and abroad, it describes in detail the techniques of picture lens dividing from theory to practice. With comprehensive explanation of digital animation knowledge, rich task cases and strong operability, it can not only improve the theoretical level of readers' relevant industries, but also improve their application and operation skills.

"CG" was originally the English abbreviation of computer graphics. With the formation of a series of related industries that use computer as the main tool for visual design and production, it is customary in the world to call the field of visual design and production using computer technology CG. It includes both technology and art. It almost covers all the visual art creation activities in the computer age, such as the design of print, web design, three-dimensional animation, film and television special effects, multimedia technology, computer-aided design based architectural design and industrial modeling design.

In Japan, CG usually refers to digital works. The content is from pure artistic creation to advertising design, which can be two-dimensional and three-dimensional, static or animation. In a broad sense, it also includes dip and CAD. Now the concept of CG is expanding. The media culture produced by CG and virtual reality technology can be classified into CG. They have formed a considerable economic industry. Therefore, when referring to CG, it can be generally divided into four main areas:

1. CG art and design
   Including two-dimensional and three-dimensional, still pictures and animation (movies), from free creation, fashion design, industrial design, TV advertising (CM) to web page design, it can be said to be all inclusive.
2. Game software
   Electronic games began in the United States, and Japanese software has swept the world. Nintendo launched an 8-bit dedicated game console in 1993, which reached 64 bits in 1996. However, no matter how good the performance of the hardware is, there is no interesting software. With the cultural accumulation of Japanese animation and comics, game companies have made full use of CG to form a world-renowned game industry. In less than 20 years, it has grown to a scale of tens of trillion yen. Nintendo, Sega, Sony and other internationally renowned enterprises have become synonymous with video games
3. Animation
   Since the "Astro Boy" of Tezuka, Japanese animation has been widely known in the world. Before the popularity of computers, hand drawn animation has become a

sunrise industry in Japan. However, in the rising labor costs, it is difficult to imagine the scale of the animation industry today without the introduction of computers. The new works of animation master Hayao Miyazaki have repeatedly created new records at the box office. Although there are large companies producing 'cinema animation' such as Dongying in Japan, most of the works come from small companies, which also entrust zero detail processing professionals and individual producers in many aspects of production. There are about 34000 employees in the whole industry. More than 30 animation serials are shown on Japanese TV every week. With the addition of image products and customized works, their output reaches almost 200 every month. Although some of them are processed overseas, the quality and output of Japanese animation industry under simple conditions (compared with other manufacturing industries) are amazing. Without CG, the mass production of animation is unimaginable.

4. Comics

Before the introduction of CG, comics had become a mature cultural industry in Japan and a popular culture deeply loved by men, women and children. There are children's comics, young men's comics, young women's comics, youth comics, women's comics, etc., and there are contents and styles covering all age levels. As readers grow older, old age comics also begin to appear. Although cartoonists mainly use hand drawing and then use scanners for digitization, many techniques such as stickers use software such as Photoshop. The younger generation is becoming more and more accustomed to creating directly with software such as digital input boards and illustrator painer, or processing materials from digital cameras into cartoons which is shown in Fig. 1.

Fig. 1. Design of computer graphics

2   Application of Computer Digital Animation Technology in Film and Television

2.1   Visual Effects

Digital special effect technology is embodied in the visual effect of film and television animation, which mainly completes the designer's imagination of the work, and digital technology can save the cost of animation production. Through digital special effects technology, the scenes that cannot be displayed or the scenes that have invested a lot of money in scene construction are digitally presented in people's vision, and the post production is completed in combination with acoustics, lighting and other technologies, so as to give people visual impact. With the continuous improvement of digital technology, the technologies that can be integrated are also expanding. This plays an important role in promoting the development of animation industry. It can blur objects and rely on powerful special effects technology to meet shooting needs. When shooting works with common science fiction or myth themes, using digital stunt technology can fully realize the diversification of shooting angles, and using digital stunt technology to complete the superposition of shooting angles can undoubtedly speed up the shooting progress, as shown in Fig. 2. For designers, it saves shooting costs.

Fig. 2. Digital animation

2.2   Application of Digital Special Effect Technology in Video Application of In

In the traditional film and television production process, most applications are shot separately at the beginning, end and in the film, and then edited as a whole at the end. Such videos can only realize the splicing of scenes, but can not explain the consistency of stories. Digital stunt technology can save many intermediate links and directly complete video production. For the combination of digital technology, adding scenes and other actual shooting contents can achieve effective combination and promote the integrity of video. In terms of the aesthetic value of video, the application of digital technology can more vividly show the special effects, and it also has important practical significance for the narrative integrity of the whole story. At present, most of the image and text editing in most industries are completed through post production and repair. At the same time, a large number of digital models must be established. In practical application, all original products such as animated films and online games are based on three-dimensional animation technology, which is a new development method and expression of Chinese cultural and creative products [2]. Because most Chinese cartoon works have profound cultural heritage and unique opinions, they have their own thoughts and considerations on the display of works, and play a certain role in promoting the creator's cultural creation and emotional expression. Only through the organic integration of art, emotion and technology can we truly realize the perfect presentation of animation works.

3 The Influence of Computer Digital Animation Technology on Film Style

3.1 From Emotional Expression to Visual and Content Expression

Film works have made great changes with the changes of the times. Before and after the birth of digital animation technology, there are obvious differences in the style of film. Traditional films impress the audience through the setting of actors and plots. Current films do not pay much attention to the emotional factors such as whether the script content is exquisite and whether the actors' acting skills are in place, while films with computer digital technology impress the audience through more three-dimensional and more realistic picture scenes and three-dimensional effects, It will focus more on whether the film scene is grand and whether the visual effect is more in line with the audience's visual experience. This is the essential difference of film style. This change of focus angle makes the film present a different experience to the audience. The application of computer digital animation technology in movies can have a good positive significance for movies.

On the basis of paying attention to the film content, contemporary films have added more means of expression, making the film content richer and the visual effect more prominent. The defects of traditional films in film scene production and visual effect are made up by today's computer digital animation technology, which actively promotes the development of the film industry. Movies using computer digital technology show more real film content in this form, so that the audience can enjoy a better viewing experience. For example, in the well-known 3D film Titanic, the viewers can't forget the emotional world of the two protagonists, but the use of 3D technology to show the scene of the capsizing and sinking of the Titanic sublimates the feelings of the two protagonists. It cooperates with the plot of the film in a more real form, so that the film viewers can enjoy it and have endless aftertaste. Thus, the use of computer digital animation technology has enriched the film content and visual effects, and emotional communication is no longer the key point to move the audience. This transformation is very conducive to the development of the film industry (see Fig. 3).

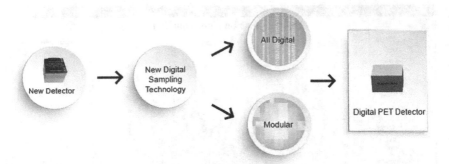

Fig. 3. The transformation for film industry

3.2 From Virtual to Realistic

Looking at the development process of the film, due to the limited technical level in the traditional film, the effect of the virtual plot set in the film plot to the audience is not ideal. The production of these scenes is relatively troublesome. For some scenes that will not appear in real life, these virtual plots have a very important impact on the quality of the whole film in film production. The traditional scene production adopts the mode of shooting foreground action and background action separately. The visual image of this mode will not be so prominent in the application process, and the effect will not be very real. After the application of computer digital technology, the complex mode of synthesis operation is implemented by using the projector equipment on the back of the screen and the foreground screen. Through special technical means, the workflow of synthesizing unrealistic scenes is no longer so cumbersome and complex [3]. The content shown to the audience in the film will be more realistic and give the audience an immersive feeling. For example, "the earth adventure", this film is mainly about the hero's journey in Egypt, accidentally falling into an abyss, and finally his fantasy journey. Among them, the strange creatures he met are difficult to show by real shooting. The tracking technology in computer digital animation technology can make the objects that need to move move move move flexibly. Under the careful processing of computer software, the whole animated film will be synthesized and produced in the future. This organic combination will make the audience see the film picture more intuitively and accurately. The quality of film works can not only be guaranteed, but also the time of film production can be shortened. Another example is the movie "speed and passion", in which the cool driving skills and other plots also need special effects to show, and its visual effect will be better. Through the above two examples, we can see that the application of computer digital animation technology can not only shorten the time of film production, but also make the visual effect of film screen more prominent.

Also, we can use the MATLAB to simulate the 3D digital animation which is shown in Fig. 4.

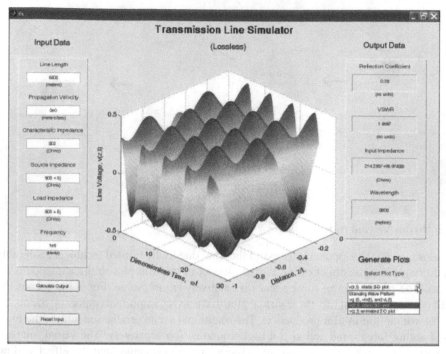

Fig. 4. Simulation for 3D digital animation

3.3 From Realism to Abstraction

If you look at traditional movies, you will find that most of the interpretation content is scenes in real life, and the content is more realistic. Due to the Limited traditional film production technology, there are problems in the expression of abstract content, and there will be a great lack of surreal scene production. After the application of computer digital technology, the advantages of 3D technology gradually show. In the process of film production, some abstract content or surreal content will be more integrated. With the application of 3D technology, the fantasy scenes in people's minds can be presented in a real way, so that people can see more specific abstract concepts. This transformation from realism to abstraction not only enriches the content level of the film, but also makes the film achieve a new breakthrough on the road of development. For example, the movie "biochemical crisis: punishment" will involve some sci-fi film scenes. Without the application of computer digital technology, it will not be able to show the fierce gun battle plot. In order to give the audience a shocking visual effect, many special effects lenses such as character animation, digital scene drawing, particle special effects and so on are applied in the film to show the surrealism of the film. Because this film will involve hundreds of special effects, it is very cautious in the production process. Before making special effects shots, first confirm the story frame of the whole film and arrange the rehearsal plan according to the story frame of the film. Arranging the rehearsal plan is very beneficial to the completion of post production. One scene involved is the tentacle in the mouth of the zombie. Because it is relatively subtle, it needs to be designed according to the physical model made by the special effects makeup artist. In addition, in order to make it more realistic, the filmmakers have remade the model and improved its texture effect. In order to highlight its tongue, the "licker" part applies many special effects techniques to perfectly shape such an image that makes the audience feel real. In addition, there is the film Spartan 300 warriors, which uses a lot of special effects. Without the application of computer digital technology, the artistic style of the film is difficult to fully show and the sense of fantasy is difficult to express. In the process of watching the film, the audience will not feel the reality of the film in the surreal picture. Through the above two films, we should integrate personal innovative thinking and ideas in the process of broadcasting and hosting, so as to make the program more attractive to the audience and reflect our unique charm [4]. Of course, this kind of innovation ability is not produced in vain. The author believes that in order to comprehensively cultivate the comprehensive innovation ability of broadcasting and hosting, we can create a certain broadcasting and hosting situation for them, so that they can give play to association and innovation in the process of actual broadcasting and hosting. At the same time, we need to cultivate them to widely read materials and absorb a lot of experience, and improve their ability of active learning, Realize the improvement of comprehensive innovation ability.

Combined with the development experience of the United States, Japan and other major animation industry countries, China needs to make efforts to practice the following contents in the development of the digital animation industry pattern: first, in terms of animation content, China's animation industry should always adhere to the originality of the content. Generally speaking, the originality of the content can be regarded as the core element of animation, and it is also the common element of the cultural industry. In terms of animation content setting, China's animation industry should be fully based on the content of Chinese traditional culture and deeply explore the theme of animation. For example, it can be combined with fairy tales and traditional cultural content. At the same time, the animation industry should be based on the changes of global digital animation target audience. That is to say, from the original audience group with children as the mainstream, it has gradually shifted to the audience group with the public as the mainstream. In other words, in terms of the setting of animation content, we should make appropriate adjustments according to the actual needs of the audience to ensure that the animation content produced meets the needs of the audience. Secondly, in the application of science and technology, the animation industry should actively promote the integration of high-tech and animation industry. Generally speaking, the application of high and new technology can be planned and reasonably applied from two aspects: animation products and new forms of services. For example, the U.S. animation industry has effectively broadened the service content of the animation industry by actively using high technology, and further promoted the economic development of the domestic animation industry. At the same time, new technology also effectively promotes the integrated development of the animation industry chain. In view of this, it is suggested that China's animation industry should be actively based on the development of new technology. Properly learn from the advanced development experience of the United States and other major animation industry countries, properly adjust the current animation industry model, and realize the transformation and upgrading of the entire animation industry chain. Finally, in terms of capital and international cooperation, it is suggested that Chinese government departments should strengthen policy support for the development of animation industry. At the same time, our government departments should strengthen the protection of intellectual property rights in the animation industry. By continuously strengthening the protection of intellectual property rights in the animation industry, China's animation industry market has always maintained a sound development. In addition, in terms of international cooperation, China's animation industry should be based on the development trend of international digital animation industry. Timely correct and optimize the existing deficiencies in the country. Although from an objective point of view, the output of China's animation industry is relatively high, there are still major deficiencies compared with the United States and other animation industry countries in terms of quality and influence. In view of this, it is suggested that China's animation industry should strengthen foreign exchange. Actively learn from the business development model of the United States and Japan, and appropriately optimize and improve the development pattern of China's animation business.

4   Conclusion

Science is developing and technology is innovating. Computer digital animation technology will further improve and progress with this development and innovation. At present, computer digital animation technology has fully covered the whole process of film production. Whether it is film planning, film shooting, film special effects production or film distribution, the film industry has completely entered the era of computer digital animation. In the future development process, this advantage will be further expanded. We should reasonably combine new technology with traditional digital technology and use their respective advantages to create more films with artistic charm.

As the second largest animation culture consumption market in the world, China has a strong consumption demand for animation, especially for the new generation. In view of this, China's animation market should firmly seize the opportunity of the times, actively meet the development requirements of the digital animation industry, and constantly activate the growth momentum of the animation industry. At the same time, China's animation industry should accurately grasp the development needs of market players, and promote the transformation, upgrading and innovative development of the entire industry chain of China's animation industry in accordance with the principles of overall planning and reasonable deployment. I believe that in the near future, China's digital animation industry is bound to get good development and occupy the leading position of the global animation industry.

References

1. Wang, Y.: The application of computer digital animation technology in today's films. Henan Sci. Technol. **21**, 11 (2014)
2. Song, D.: On the influence of computer digital animation technology on film style. Contemp. Educ. Pract. Teach. Res. **6**, 109 (2015)

3. Sun, X.: On the influence of computer digital animation technology on film style. J. Nanchang Inst. Educ. **8**, 48–49 (2013)
4. Huang, H.: Analysis of the influence of digital technology on film art. Examin. Weekly **32**, 123–124 (2012)

Discourse Analysis of Chinese Culture Translation Based on Crawler Algorithm

Rui Zhang[✉]

Xi'an Fanyi University, Xi'an 710105, Shaanxi, China
61663111@qq.com

Abstract. This paper studies the discourse analysis of Chinese cultural translation based on crawler algorithm. In recent years, the research of cultural translation has gradually become one of the research hotspots and difficulties in the field of translation. In order to improve the efficiency of discourse analysis of cultural translation and filter out most foreign translations with similar structure, an intelligent crawling algorithm is proposed. This paper first defines the concept of cultural translation, and then systematically combs the research of cultural translation. According to the location of nodes, the depth of DOM tree and the number of nodes with the same depth, the weight is assigned to each node, and then the similarity of cultural translation is calculated according to the given formula; On the basis of similarity, using the idea of aggregation hierarchical clustering, the cultural translation with similar structure is clustered into a group, leaving only one cultural translation in each group, so as to remove most cultural translation with similar structure. The experimental results show that the intelligent crawling algorithm can effectively reduce the cultural translation with similar structure and improve the inspection efficiency of vulnerability inspection system. On the basis of relevant data statistics, this paper summarizes the context, trend and existing problems of domestic research, and finally analyzes and prospects its current situation and work.

Keywords: Crawler algorithm · Cultural translation · Similarity

1 Introduction

Cross cultural communication and translation involve many important aspects, such as diplomacy, national image, cultural output and so on. Foreigners' misunderstanding of China's image caused by the wrong translation of Chinese Dragon into Western evil beast dragon has to make us deeply realize that cross-cultural communication and translation are indispensable. If cross-cultural communication and translation are not done well, we will be misunderstood, our culture will be plundered, and ill intentioned people will be given the opportunity to tamper with our national image [1]. In the field of cross-cultural communication, the practice of our ancestors is very brilliant. China's top strategy one belt, one road jointly built by China and other countries, has to thank Zhang Qian, who has opened up the Silk Road and the foresight of Emperor Han Wu. The silk road

M. A. Jan and F. Khan (Eds.): BigIoT-EDU 2022, LNICST 465, pp. 456–466, 2023.
https://doi.org/10.1007/978-3-031-23950-2_50

is not only the exchange of products, but also the dissemination of culture. China's four great inventions, advanced handicraft technology, advanced ideas and practical technology are disseminated to the world through this channel. The intersection with the Silk Road reflects Zheng He's feat of going to the West. Facing the open mind of the sea, the desire to share peace, the peaceful diplomatic policy of good neighborliness, leaving a civilized, friendly, generous and inclusive image of a big country to foreign countries, and spreading our most advanced technology and splendid culture are the cultural diplomacy that made the Ming Dynasty famous. There is no doubt about the great achievements of cross-cultural communication in ancient China, which makes foreign friends' impression of China still stay in the past. On the other hand, it also reveals the shortcomings of cross-cultural communication in today's China.

Our country's progress in military, economy, science and technology is indeed commendable, but the cultural and cross-cultural communication that affects the national accumulation is lacking. Our film market has become commercialized, bad films are popular, no acting skills, no connotation, let alone spreading culture. Chinese people still scold, not to mention foreigners. Plagiarism scandals are common in our academic circles. Cross cultural communication has a long way to go. In addition to learning from our ancestors' spirit of openness, inclusiveness and bold going out. In reality, we can also learn from European and American blockbusters, TV dramas, Japanese animation and Korean variety shows that are very popular with Chinese people, and integrate our own culture into spiritual production [2]. The popularity of these foreign cultures in China can be said to be cultural infiltration or even cultural invasion to a certain extent. If cross-cultural communication does not attract attention, let alone spread culture to the world, the status of Chinese culture in the country will also be threatened.

In view of the above situation, this paper proposes an intelligent crawling algorithm based on URL de duplication and aggregation hierarchical clustering based on cultural translation similarity for Chinese cultural translation discourse analysis, which can effectively remove repeated URLs and a large number of cultural translations with similar structure, minimize the test target of inspection system and improve the detection efficiency.

2 Related Technologies

2.1 Crawler Algorithm

Friends who have studied website design know that websites are usually designed in layers. The top-level domain name is followed by sub domain names, and there are sub domain names under sub domain names. At the same time, each sub domain name may have multiple domain names at the same level, and there may be mutual links between URLs, so as to form a complex network. When a website has many URLs, we must design the URL well, otherwise it will be very chaotic in the later understanding, maintenance or development process. After understanding the above structural design of cultural translation, the depth first algorithm in web crawler is formally introduced, as shown in Fig. 1 below.

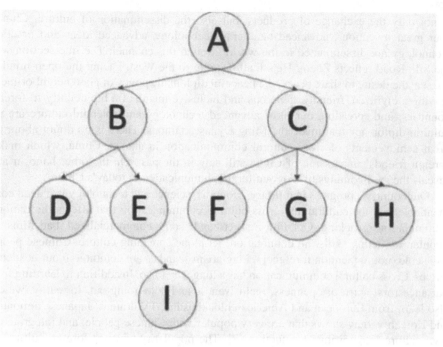

Fig. 1. Depth first algorithm tree structure in crawler

The above figure is a tree structure. Through the traversal of this tree, we can compare the external translation of grasping culture to deepen the understanding of reptile strategy [3]. The main idea of the depth first algorithm is to first start with the top-level domain name a, and then extract two links B and C. after the capture of link B is completed, the next link to be captured is d or E, not to grab link C immediately after the capture of link B. After capturing link D, we find that all URLs in link d have been accessed. Before that, we have established a list of accessed URLs, which is specially used to store the accessed URLs. When link D is completely crawled, link e will be crawled next. After the crawling of link e is completed, you will not climb link c, but continue to climb link I in depth. The principle is that the link will climb down step by step. As long as there is a sub link under the link and the sub link has not been visited, this is the main idea of the depth first algorithm. Depth first algorithm is to let the crawler go down step by step. After the crawl is completed, it will step back step by step and give priority to depth. After understanding the depth first algorithm and looking at the figure above, we can get that the order of crawler crawling links presented by the binary tree is: A, B, D, e, I, C, F, G and H (here, it is assumed that the links on the left will be crawled first). In fact, we often use this algorithm in the process of web crawler. In fact, our commonly used scrapy crawler framework is also implemented by this algorithm by default [4]. Through the above understanding, we can think that the depth first algorithm is essentially implemented by recursion. Figure 2 shows the code implementation process of the depth first algorithm.

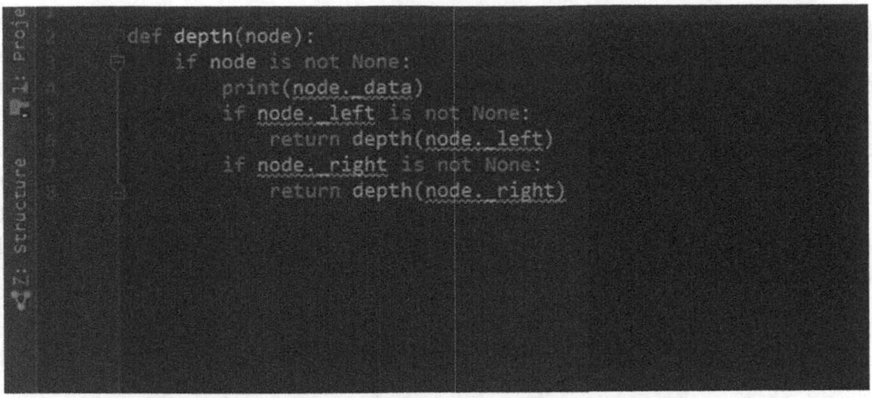

```
    def depth(node):
        if node is not None:
            print(node._data)
            if node._left is not None:
                return depth(node._left)
            if node._right is not None:
                return depth(node._right)
```

Fig. 2. Code implementation process of depth first algorithm

The depth first process is actually implemented in a recursive way. Looking at the code in the figure above, first define a function to implement the depth first process, and then pass in the node parameters [5]. If the node is not empty, print it. It can be compared with the top point a of the tree. After printing the node, check whether there are left node (link b) and right node (link c). If the left node is not empty, return it, call the depth first function itself again for recursion, and get new left node (link d) and right node (link E), and so on, It will not stop until all nodes are traversed or meet the established conditions.

2.2   Analysis of Cultural Translation

In a narrow sense, cultural translation is an activity to spread national cultural forms and products to target language countries through the medium of target language. In a broad sense, because language and culture are inseparable, all translation activities are essentially social and cultural communication activities. Therefore, all translation activities can be regarded as cultural translation activities (Zhong Weihe, Feng man 2014:57). The going out of Chinese culture requires not only the foreignization translation of Chinese translators, but also the domestication translation of foreign sinologists (Wang Qinghua 2015:100). In short, in the current situation of China's "going global", foreign translation is an export-oriented communication activity that takes the world as the development space and exchange platform for China's "going global" [6], translates China and Chinese culture into the target language and carries out cross-border, cross language and cross-cultural communication to the target language countries.

In order to facilitate analysis and comparison, based on relevant materials and data, this paper divides the existing situation of cultural translation research into three main aspects: scientific research institutions, talent training and academic achievements, in order to have a panoramic overview of cultural translation research in China.

In short, cultural diplomacy is a diplomatic activity in which independent sovereign states use cultural means to achieve specific purposes. It is an international activity. Its goal is to carry out peaceful and warm persuasion with the help of humanistic care and emotional investment, in order to establish a lasting and far-reaching international friendship with foreign people and government officials, so as to obtain their sympathy, understanding and support [7]. This requires us to face up to and respect national differences, language differences and cultural differences, and pay more attention to the ways and skills of persuasion. In order to attract the foreign public and make it easy for them to understand what we think, it is wise to adopt the strategy of peaceful and flexible publicity of cultural truth. Our cultural diplomacy should maintain cultural security; Our cultural diplomacy should help to establish a positive national image all over the world; Our cultural diplomacy should be neither humble nor arrogant. All these constitute the spirit of cultural diplomacy.

3   Discourse Analysis of Cultural Translation

As culture going out is a national strategy advocated by the Chinese government and an important way to enhance China's overseas cultural soft power and shape the image of China's cultural power, domestic scholars have focused on the new academic field of cultural external communication and published many research results. Looking at the research articles on translation communication at home and abroad since the new century, it can be seen that scholars' research attention is shifting from the study of translation ontology to the cross-border study of translation and communication. In the face of so many research literatures, four different approaches can be explored, namely: 1) research on translation strategies; 2) Research on the quality of translated works; 3) Research on external communication channels: 4) research on the communication effect of translation. This paper discusses the gains and losses of each research path, so as to correct the deviation, promote the academic achievements, better guide China's foreign translation practice and communication, and improve the communication effect.

3.1   Research on Foreign Translation Strategies

Huang Youyi believes that foreign translation should be close to the reality of China's development, the needs of foreign audiences for Chinese information and the thinking habits of foreign audiences; Wang Ning believes that the translation style advocated by the English world is "domestication". Whether it is literal or not, if it cannot be understood by ordinary readers, it will be ignored by the book market; Zhang Jian believes that in foreign translation, the translator should make necessary adaptations to the original text according to the specific context of the reader, and the adaptation strategies include addition and supplement, interpretation and adaptation and reasonable deletion; Xie Tianzhen believes that due to the phenomenon of "time difference" and "language difference" in cultural exchanges between China and the west, translators should adopt domestication strategy or abridge the original work to varying degrees to meet the readers' reading acceptance context: LV Shisheng believes that Lin Yutang's unique cross-cultural interpretation of a dream of red Mansions enlightens us that Chinese cultural translation must be adjusted and flexible, To reduce the resistance to entering the Western cultural framework. Scholars have brought the reader's cultural acceptance context into the research field of vision, realized that foreign translation is the collision of two languages and cultures, and need to take the reader's reading habits and cultural acceptance context into consideration in foreign translation. They emphasize that the reader's understanding and acceptance of the translation should be taken as the focus in foreign translation, which highlights that translation is a cross language, cross-cultural Cross social communication behavior. If the target language readers are difficult to understand the semantics of the translation, or do not recognize the ideological content of the translation, the translation will not achieve the purpose of cross-cultural communication. From this point of view, focusing on the target language readers and strengthening the research on the target language readers' reading expectations, cultural context and the mentality of accepting foreign cultures will help to improve the quality and communication effect of foreign translation.

3.2 Research on the Quality of Translated Works

Taking the translation of classics as an example, Wang Xiaonong analyzes the shortcomings of translation and editing in English translation, and discusses how to improve the quality of translation, editing and publishing; Ren Dongsheng investigated the phenomenon of incomplete correspondence between the two language texts in the typesetting of the English translation of Jin Ping Mei, and put forward some suggestions on bilingual translation, editing and publishing from the perspective of national translation practice. From the discussion of these two scholars, the translation quality of foreign translation works involves many factors, and the focus has shifted to the factors of editing and publishing outside the text. The author believes that the acceptability, comprehensibility and accuracy of the translated works will affect the communication and acceptance effect of the translated works among readers. Sometimes, the translator's Chinese-English bilingual skills are profound, and the translated content is faithful and smooth, which can stimulate the readers' reading desire. However, in the printing and publishing process, if the editing and typesetting of the translation are poor, the binding is not good, or the cover picture copy violates the readers' cultural acceptance taboos, these will directly reduce the communication effect of the translated works among the target language readers, Serious will also be resisted by readers. Therefore, the quality of translated works is determined by two links: 1) the quality of the original translation; 2) the layout and binding design in the process of printing and publishing. The first link requires the translator to have good bilingual control ability and be familiar with bilingual cross-cultural knowledge, so as to better ensure the quality of translation. Sometimes, on the premise of correctly conveying the semantics of the original, it is necessary to make appropriate cross-cultural obstacles to the original, so as to make the translation conform to the reading acceptance habits and cultural context of the target language readers; The second link concerns whether the translated works can capture the readers' eyes and enhance the attention of readers when readers quickly scan a wide range of books, which is one of the key factors for the translated works to be selected and read by readers. If the cover design is novel, beautifully bound and in line with the readers' aesthetic and cultural context, it will help the dissemination of the translated works. On the contrary, it will hinder the dissemination and acceptance of the translated works. In other words, the quality of the translated works is determined by the translation quality of the translation and the design of the translation typesetting.

3.3 Research on External Communication Channels

Zhang Kun believes that the multi-channel characteristics of the external communication of the national image can not be ignored. The bridge crowd, organizations and media can play the channel function of external communication; Zhang Menghan analyzed that foreign young netizens like to use new media platforms, and believes that external communication should pay attention to short video channels and mobile communication, so as to comply with the trend of integrated communication; Xu Jun believes that in addition to book translation and publishing, we should also integrate various media such as digital publishing, film and television, and the Internet, and give full play to the role of new media and integrated media in foreign cultural communication. From these representative results, scholars believe that the external communication channels are not limited to traditional newspapers, periodicals and radio stations. They need to explore the integration of new and old media and multi-channel simultaneous interpreting so as to achieve full coverage of readers' and audience's information Qu Daojin's coverage and increase the breadth and depth of readers' access to relevant information. Especially at present, with the popularity of mobile Internet in the world, readers or audiences can log in to the Internet anytime and anywhere and retrieve a large amount of relevant information. The Internet and mobile clients are becoming the main channels for people to obtain information. Therefore, exploring the communication role of new media in external communication is becoming the focus of scholars today.

At present, the media communication in western countries has changed from traditional paper media to network media and digital media. Therefore, China's external communication should conform to the information society, the fast speed of information communication, the readers' pursuit of information timeliness and the information publisher Characteristics of interaction with readers. This requires that the communication of cultural translation works should turn to the external communication situation dominated by network media and supplemented by paper publishing and communication. In addition, the foreign communication channels should not ignore the localized communication of overseas Chinese associations, Chinese overseas culture and Confucius Institutes. They are familiar with the customs, cultural taboos and communication skills of foreign countries. To sum up, the external communication channels of China's cultural translation works can include traditional paper media communication, network media communication, overseas Chinese community communication, China's overseas cultural center communication and overseas Confucius Institute communication. These five external communication channels can form a situation of multi-channel collaborative communication dominated by network media communication, supplemented by other channels, This can enhance the external dissemination of Chinese culture.

3.4 Study on the Communication Effect of Translation

There are few studies on the communication effect of foreign translation works by domestic scholars. The following are three representative research results: Li Ning believes that the circulation and retention of Chinese classics translation is too small and the attention is not high, which affects the communication effect of the translation among American readers; Bao Xiaoying analyzes all links in translation communication and believes that all links in communication are an organism that jointly affect the communication effect of the translation; Liu Yameng and Zhu Chunshen believe that the translation needs influential book reviews to guide overseas readers' reading choices, which will help to improve the communication effect of the translation in the target country. The above-mentioned scholars' research on the communication effect focuses on various factors affecting the communication effect, and the analysis is justified. However, the communication effect of the translated works is an abstract concept [8]. To what extent can the translated works be considered to have the communication effect when they are spread and accepted abroad? At present, there is no quantitative index to evaluate the communication effect. Generally, the academic circles believe that if the translated works are spread to the overseas target country, even if they enter the country's libraries and bookstores, they will achieve the purpose of communication. In fact, this understanding is wrong. If the translated works are published and distributed in the target country, it can only show that the translated works are likely to be read and accepted by the target language readers, and it can not ensure that the translated works will be read and understood by the readers, Even if the reader has read and understood the content of the translated works, it does not mean that the reader has accepted the content of the translated works. The ultimate purpose of our foreign translation, introduction and communication is to make the target language readers understand and accept the ideas, views, value orientation and Chinese culture of the translated works. Therefore, the communication effect of foreign translation and introduction can be divided into two levels: primary communication effect and advanced communication effect. The level of primary communication effect is that the translated works are read and understood by the target language readers. Whether the readers agree with the ideological content and values of the translated works is not within the scope of primary communication effect; The advanced communication effect is that the translated works are read and understood by the target language readers, and at the same time, the readers can recognize and accept the ideological content, values or Chinese culture carried by the translated works. At present, foreign translators and foreign translation publishing departments should correct the cognitive errors of foreign translation effect, improve the reading rate and understanding of target language readers of foreign translation works, and make foreign translation works widely spread among readers [9]. On this basis, let the translated works be read by the target language readers, recognize and accept the ideological content or values of the translated works, which is the ultimate goal of the study of external communication effect. Therefore, foreign translation and communication should focus on the above two levels of research in order to truly improve the effect of foreign communication.

4 Discourse Analysis of Chinese Culture Translation Based on Crawler Algorithm

The translation of Chinese books into foreign languages is a controversial topic. If anyone needs someone to translate, then Chinese people have no qualification and right to engage in Chinese foreign translation. It's possible that Chinese people's English level is lower than that of native English speakers, but who can guarantee that English scholars' Chinese understanding ability will be better than that of Chinese scholars?

Professor Xu Yuanchong proved that the English translation of classics is first-class in China with his rich practice [10]. At the same time, he also pointed out the limitations of foreign translators' understanding.

With the development of web applications, crawler technology is also improving. From the early general crawler to the current theme crawler and deep crawler, it meets the different needs of different users. The crawling process of the general crawler is relatively simple. Generally, the crawler starts from the initial URL, takes out the new URL from the 1-L list and starts crawling, and cycles in turn until the list to be crawled is empty or meets the set stop conditions. This method is simple and commonly used, but this kind of crawler only crawls the URL, which can not meet the additional needs of users.

Compared with the URL of the general psychological element, the deep crawler not only extracts the URL, but also parses it to remove the duplicate of the URL, which improves the crawling efficiency and avoids falling into a dead cycle. On the basis of deep crawler, this paper proposes an intelligent crawler to crawl all relevant cultural translations, and then use the intelligent crawling algorithm to crawl the website [11]. Finally, no duplicate URL is obtained, and the cultural translation corresponding to the URL pairs the URL to discard the duplicate URL. Next, the page similarity formula is used to calculate the similarity value of the pages corresponding to the two URLs in turn. Specifically, the page is parsed into a DOM tree [12]. Root zhe t allocates the depth of each section and the number of nodes with the same depth from he, allocates the weight to each node, and then calculates the similarity of cultural translation according to the given formula. Finally, based on the similarity, the cultural translation with similar structure is clustered into a group by using the idea of aggregate hierarchical clustering, and only the representative URL is selected for subsequent testing.

The calculation process of the intelligent crawling algorithm proposed in this paper is divided into three stages, as shown in Fig. 3. In the first stage, the URL needs to be de duplicated; In the second stage, cultural translation is analyzed and the similarity of cultural translation is calculated [13]; In the third stage, the cultural translations whose similarity meets the set threshold are clustered, and a URL is selected from each category as a representative for subsequent detection. The whole calculation process is called intelligent crawling algorithm.

Recognition conditions in international academic circles The development of translation theory and cultural intervention in translation have strongly criticized the view of some scholars at home and abroad, represented by British Sinologist Graham [14], that Chinese-English translation can only be "translated into" by English translators but not "translated out" by Chinese scholars It is emphasized that Chinese-English translation is not the patent of foreigners, and Chinese scholars and translators should boldly undertake this work.

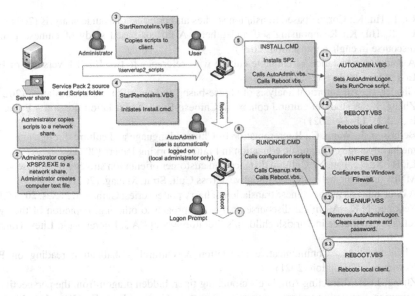

Fig. 3. Calculation process of intelligent crawling algorithm

5   Conclusion

In this paper, an intelligent crawling algorithm is proposed. In the crawling process, the Rabin fingerprint algorithm is used to remove the duplicate of the URL, which has fast retrieval speed and high efficiency, and avoids the crawler from wasting unnecessary time or even falling into a dead cycle; Before calculating the cultural translation similarity, the cultural translation is preprocessed, the DOM tree is constructed, and the text is uniformly represented by text, only the cultural translation label is retained, which simplifies the cultural translation, and the structural similarity of cultural translation is calculated by evenly distributing the weight, so as to make the calculation of cultural translation similarity more efficient; The aggregated hierarchical clustering algorithm is used to cluster the similar cultural translations into a group, which improves the efficiency of the inspection system. This paper solves the problem of a large number of similar cultural translation structures, and improves the efficiency of safety inspection. Moreover, this method has the advantages of simple idea, easy implementation, strong universality, high recognition rate of cultural translation with similar structures, and improves the accuracy of reptiles.

References

1. Wang, C., Pedrycz, W., Li, Z., et al.: Residual-driven fuzzy C-means clustering for image. Segmentation. **8**(4), 14 (2021)
2. Xuelei, W.: Advances in discourse analysis of translation and interpreting: linking linguistic approaches with socio-cultural interpretation. J. Commun. (2021)
3. Shaheen, F., Ali, G., Zahra, K.: Translating feminist identities: a critical discourse analysis of urdu translation of brown's work 'The Dancing Girls of Lahore' (2021)

4. Li, T., Hu, K.: Corpus-based translation studies and political discourse analysis (2021)
5. Li, T., Hu, K.: Reappraising self and others: A corpus-based study of chinese political discourse in english translation (2021)
6. A study on translation of etiquette culture with reference to two English versions of Hong Lou Meng. **28**(3), 8 (2021)
7. Ghader, H.: An empirical analysis of phrase-based and neural machine translation (2021)
8. Zhang, X.: A study of cultural context in Chinese-English translation. Region – Educ. Res. Rev. **3**(2), 11–14 (2021)
9. Bellassen, J., Wang, C.: Representation of Chinese language and culture through analysis of media coverage of linguistic education in France. Working Papers (2021)
10. Li, H., Xu, L., Fan, Y.: Cultural distance and customer orientation strategy of chinese service MNEs under the belt and road initiative. Cross Cult. Strat. Manag. (2021)
11. A brief analysis on the chinese translation of harry potter series: Gains and losses. **20**, 3 (2021)
12. Yetkiner, N.K.: A critical discourse analysis approach to othering: depiction of the syrian refugee experience in Turkish children's literature. [Sic] - A J. Literat. Cult. Liter. Transl. **2**, 11 (2021)
13. Alahyane, L.M.: Communicative translation & cultural globalization reading on Peter Newmark's Perception (2021)
14. Zhang, J.: Re-dissecting Ang Lee's crouching tiger, hidden dragon from the perspectives of cognition, translation and reconfiguration of culture. Compar. Liter. East West **1**, 1–20 (2021)

Optimization Models and Educational Teaching Research in Agricultural Logistics System

Jingjun Shu(✉)

Wuhan Business University, Wuhan 430056, Hubei, China
hubeiwuhansjj@icloud.com

Abstract. Logistics science is a new comprehensive discipline. It plays a very important role in the development of national economy and the improvement of production and management level. The task of cultivating new agricultural business entities is an important measure to build a strong agricultural industry. This paper studies and expounds the significance of the connection between the new agricultural management subject and the agricultural logistics system; Analyze the problems of coordination between the logistics system and the fresh characteristics of agricultural products, the docking between the main bodies of agricultural circulation channels and the control of production, supply and marketing costs in the docking process between new agricultural business entities and agricultural logistics; How to effectively optimize and allocate logistics operation and reduce logistics cost is of great significance not only to enhance the international competitiveness of enterprises, but also to promote the rapid development of the whole national economy.

Keywords: Agricultural logistics system · Optimization model · Research on Logistics algorithm

1 Introduction

Cultivating new agricultural business entities and strengthening their organic connection with agricultural logistics system are powerful measures to implement the strategy of strengthening agriculture. At this stage, it is increasingly urgent to achieve the strategic goal of building a well-off society in an all-round way. Comprehensively promoting agricultural modernization and fundamentally resolving the "three rural issues" restricting China's economic and social development are the basis to ensure the realization of this strategic goal.

Supply chain is a functional network chain structure mode that connects suppliers, manufacturers, distributors, retailers and end users into a whole by focusing on core enterprises and controlling information flow, logistics and capital flow, starting from purchasing raw materials, making intermediate products and final products, and finally sending products to consumers through the sales network.Agricultural supply chain is an advanced management model of modern agriculture based on the study of modern

M. A. Jan and F. Khan (Eds.): BigIoT-EDU 2022, LNICST 465, pp. 467–477, 2023.
https://doi.org/10.1007/978-3-031-23950-2_51

agricultural logistics. It not only studies the logistics allocation of agricultural production itself, but also studies the scientific flow of agricultural pre production and post production logistics, so as to achieve the organic connection of supply, production, transportation, processing and marketing, so as to connect the pre production, production, post production and market into a satisfactory system optimization operation state [1]. The model of agricultural supply chain management is a network composed of various entities and information, on which agricultural logistics, capital flow and information flow. These entities include some agricultural companies, subsidiaries, farms, processing plants, manufacturing plants, warehouses, external suppliers, transportation companies, distribution centers, retailers and farmers- A complete agricultural supply chain starts from the suppliers of agricultural means of production and ends at the end users of agricultural products (including processed finished products).The agricultural supply chain consists of three basic links: pre production, in production and post production. Pre production mainly refers to the supply of seeds, feed, fertilizer and other means of production for the production of agricultural products. In production refers to the planting and production of agricultural products, and post production refers to the grading, packaging, processing, transportation, storage and sales of agricultural products.

With the development of the national economy, the development of agriculture, as the basis of the national economy, has been paid more and more attention by the government. In addition to technological progress and policy guidance, a very important factor in the prosperity of agricultural economy is the circulation of agricultural materials and agricultural products, that is, agricultural logistics. To do a good job of agricultural logistics in a region, we must first have a better understanding of the existing logistics situation, and the selection of evaluation methods has become an indispensable step. By evaluating the advantages and disadvantages of agricultural logistics system, we can find out the shortcomings of the current situation of local agricultural logistics, so as to make reasonable decisions. How to evaluate agricultural logistics system? How to optimize the agricultural logistics system in a region? The research on these problems has certain application value.

Optimization theory and method is an important branch of mathematics. The problem it studies is how to find the optimal scheme and calculate the optimal solution among many schemes. Evaluation is indispensable for decision optimization, and its result is the basis of decision. Some of the traditional evaluation methods are subjective and lack of quantitative analysis in actual decision-making. Although some evaluation methods are based on quantitative analysis, due to the complexity and fuzziness of practical problems, the effect of these methods directly used in decision-making is not ideal. How to quantify qualitative problems better? How to apply optimization method in large-scale system modeling? The research on these problems has certain theoretical significance.

At present, there are few systematic studies on agricultural logistics system in China. This paper provides an optimization model and algorithm. Through systematic evaluation and optimization, taking the agricultural logistics system as the research object, this paper discusses the regional agricultural logistics problems.

2 Related Work

2.1 Agricultural Logistics System Control

Both producers and consumers of agricultural products are dissatisfied with the price of domestic agricultural products. Producers think the purchase price is too low, consumers think the retail price is too high, and the profit space of bulk circulation of agricultural products is very large. For example, in the first half of 2002, the lowest purchase price of banana producing areas in Hainan fell to about 0.09–0.1 yuan/kg, while the retail price of bananas in major cities in North China is about 1.5–2 yuan. In addition to reasonable transportation and marketing costs, there is a huge profit space for wholesale and retail sales. But on the other hand, the bulk logistics of agricultural products is actually risky, and there is a problem of uneven distribution of logistics profits and risks in all links of the supply chain. Shortening circulation channels is an effective way to solve this problem.

(1) Circulation channels. The bulk logistics of agricultural products generally goes through the following main links: suppliers - producers - wholesalers - land markets - retailers - consumers. In the whole logistics chain, because the unprocessed fresh selling products of agricultural products account for the vast majority, and such a multi link circulation chain, whether in terms of time and circulation efficiency, or the existing fresh-keeping means, cannot adapt to the fresh selling form of agricultural products, so a considerable number of new fresh products suffer huge losses due to freight rates, transportation capacity, basic traffic conditions and product fresh-keeping technology. When agricultural products are centrally listed, logistics is not smooth, The processing capacity is insufficient, the production and marketing are seriously disconnected, and the loss is more prominent. According to the statistics of relevant departments, the annual losses caused by the decay of fresh commodities such as fruits and vegetables in Guangdong reach 750million yuan. At present, the circulation channels of agricultural products are relatively single, and there is no multi-channel marketing system.

(2) Logistics cost. In the supply chain of agricultural products, the combination of production and marketing is one of the bottlenecks of current procurement and operation, and it is also the hot spot of future market investment. The current circulation cost is still high and unstable, and the transportation and marketing cost fluctuates greatly; In addition, the time cost of poor road conditions, card fees and other issues have virtually increased the circulation cost and increased the operational risk of bulk logistics of agricultural products.

(3) Logistics technology. Transportation and marketing fresh-keeping technology is one of the prominent problems affecting the fresh management of supermarkets at present. "Fresh" is the life and value of fresh agricultural products. However, due to the high water content, short fresh-keeping period and extremely perishable deterioration of fresh agricultural products, it will greatly limit the transportation radius and transaction time, so it puts forward high requirements for transportation efficiency and circulation fresh-keeping conditions.

At present, the logistics of agricultural products in China is mainly in the form of normal temperature logistics or natural logistics, and the losses of agricultural products in the logistics process are great. According to statistics, the loss rate of agricultural and sideline products such as fruits and vegetables in the logistics links such as picking, transportation and storage is about 25–30%, that is to say, more than 1/4 of agricultural products are consumed in the logistics links. While the loss rate of fruits and vegetables in developed countries is controlled below 5%, and the logistics of vegetables and fruits in the United States is more typical. Products can always be in the low temperature state of post harvest physiological needs and form a cold chain: pre cooling after harvest in the field – cold storage – refrigerated truck transportation – cold storage in wholesale stations – supermarket freezers – consumer refrigerators. The loss rate of fruits and vegetables in the logistics link is only 1–2%, which is shocking in comparison.

Agricultural logistics system is a limited resource temporarily stored to meet future needs. The agricultural logistics system is divided into two types according to the state. One is the static agricultural logistics system stored in the warehouse and the other is the dynamic agricultural logistics system during transportation.

Traditionally, agricultural logistics system plays a long-term storage place for raw materials, semi-finished products, products in process and finished products. The manufacturer produces for the agricultural logistics system and tries to sell out the agricultural logistics system in the warehouse. With the advent of real-time supply (Zero agricultural logistics system), partnership and supply chain, in order to achieve the logistics objectives of faster and shorter agricultural logistics system turnover time and lower cost, the position of warehouse in material flow system has been unprecedentedly increased and attracted the full attention of logistics experts. The warehouse is no longer regarded as a long-term goods storage facility, and its logistics activity level has made great progress. For many international logistics companies, the storage time of products in the warehouse is usually only a few days or only a few hours. In the macro-economic sense, warehouse plays an essential role and creates the time utility of products. Warehousing improves the utility value of goods by increasing the supply time of goods to customers. In short, by using the warehouse to store goods, enterprises can meet the needs of users anytime and anywhere. The value-added role of warehousing in the logistics system is reflected in: integrated transportation, mixed products, customer service, prevention of uncertain factors, stable supply and demand, etc. As shown in Fig. 1.

The purpose of agricultural logistics system control system is to decide when to order and how much to order [2]. The controlled ordering decision depends on the current situation, expected demand and different cost factors of agricultural logistics system. The current situation of the agricultural logistics system here is not only the so-called existing agricultural logistics system, but also includes the order quantity ordered from the outside but not yet arrived, the unfinished order and the backorders ordered by customers. It is described by the location of the agricultural logistics system.

The decision-making depends on the location of the agricultural logistics system, but the storage cost and shortage cost all depend on the level of the agricultural logistics system: the level of the agricultural logistics system = the existing agricultural logistics system - delayed delivery.

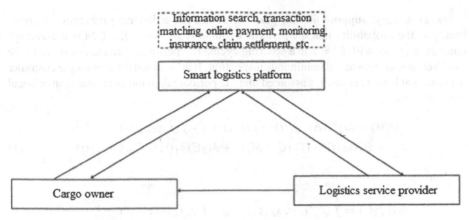

Fig. 1. Agricultural logistics system

2.2 Periodic Inspection Strategy

Periodic inspection of agricultural logistics system is to detect the quantity of agricultural logistics system at the beginning of each cycle. The decision of the whole cycle also depends on the value of agricultural logistics system detected this time. When the cycle is very small, the cycle detection can be approximated by continuous detection.

Assuming that the time unit is the inspection cycle of the agricultural logistics system and the order lead time l is an integer cycle, the agricultural logistics system level used to calculate the agricultural logistics system cost, shortage cost or service level is the IL at the end of each cycle, that is, the L after the demand of each cycle occurs, so it is not necessary to specify the time of the cycle when the demand occurs.

If the demand of a cycle is distributed at any position of the cycle, the level of agricultural logistics system can be considered at the end of the cycle or in the middle of the cycle. The assumptions here are the standard methods for modeling this problem, which is equivalent to that the demand occurs at the beginning of the cycle and after the replenishment decision is made. In this case, the level of agricultural logistics system is constant in the whole cycle [3].

Now consider that the position of the agricultural logistics system at the beginning of any cycle T and after replenishment is IP. At the end of cycle $T + L$, all replenishments occurring before cycle T and before cycle t have arrived, and the replenishment after cycle T has not arrived. There are $L + 1$ cycles from the beginning of cycle T to the end of cycle $T + L$, The level of agricultural logistics system at the end of cycle $T + L$ is as follows (discuss the (R, q) strategy and (s, s) strategy respectively):

(R, 2) strategy: the transition condition of agricultural logistics system state is the beginning of each cycle, not the trigger of customer arrival in continuous inspection. If the periodic demand is used to replace the demand of each customer in the continuous state, the relevant Markov chain is the same as the continuous inspection state.

(*s, s*) strategy: suppose that the periodic demand is a discrete probability distribution, g = the probability that the periodic demand is J ($J = 0, 1,...$), M is the average number of cycles with $IP = J$ in a ordering cycle. The periodic demand is similar to the single customer demand of continuous inspection. It is assumed that the single customer demand is at least 1. Here, it is assumed that the periodic demand is greater than or equal to 0, so:

$$(E(t) - M_2 C)\Delta \dot{x}_{k+1}(t) = f(t, x_d(t)) - f(t, x_{k+1}(t))$$
$$+ B\Delta u_k(t) - (\Gamma_{p1} C + M_1 C + M_2 C)\dot{x}_d(t) + \Gamma_{p1} C \dot{x}_{k-1}(t) \tag{1}$$

So:

$$\Delta x_{k+1}(t) = \int_0^t Q^{-1}(f(t, x_d(\tau)) - Q^{-1} f(t, x_{k+1}(\tau)))d\tau$$
$$+ \int_0^t Q^{-1} B\Delta u_k(\tau)d\tau - \int_0^t Q^{-1} Z\dot{x}_d(\tau)d\tau + \int_0^t Q^{-1} F\dot{x}_{k-1}(\tau)d\tau \tag{2}$$

3 Research on Some Optimization Models and Algorithms in Agricultural Logistics System

The current logistics system is designed for the storage and transportation characteristics of a chemical industrial product. Compared with industrial logistics, agricultural products show different characteristics because of their unique natural attributes and supply and demand characteristics [4]. The key point of realizing the value of agricultural products lies in "preservation", but most agricultural products have the characteristics of high water content, easy decay, easy deterioration and high requirements for storage and transportation environment, which puts forward the requirements for a large number of agricultural logistics enterprises to innovate the storage and transportation technology of agricultural products, so as to solve the problem of high "cargo damage rate" of agricultural products in storage, packaging, transportation and other links. Moreover, the production activities of agricultural products have significant seasonal characteristics, which determines that the operation of the logistics system of agricultural products should also have obvious seasonality. However, there is a lack of effective matching between the logistics capacity allocation of existing agricultural product logistics enterprises and the seasonal storage and transportation demand of agricultural products, which increases the logistics cost of agricultural products.

Set up agricultural logistics system processing station j the use and operation expenses during the planning period are C_j; $j \in S \cup K$. It has nothing to do with the processing quantity, but only with whether to use the station. The construction cost of the new agricultural logistics system processing station is apportioned to the planning period according to the depreciation method. If the new agricultural logistics system processing station is added, In addition to the transportation cost, the new cost also includes the construction and operation cost of the new agricultural logistics system processing station. Suppose that the agricultural logistics system processing station s is the closest to the new recycling station h in the original agricultural logistics system processing station, the unit freight rate from the recycling station h to the agricultural logistics system processing station s is k, and the unit freight rate from the recycling station h to the alternative agricultural logistics system processing station J is k_j; $j \in K$. If the recycling quantity of recycle bin h in the planning period is labor, the transportation cost borne by agricultural logistics system processing station s of recycle bin h is KGZ, and the cost borne by alternative agricultural logistics system processing station J is KGZ $C_j + k_j x$; $j \in K$. The 1-bit improved model is shown in the Fig. 2 below.

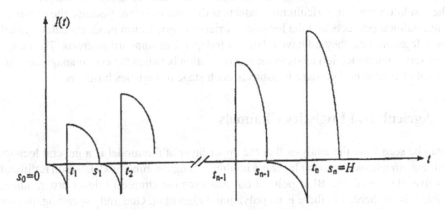

Fig. 2. Periodic improvement model of logistics system

Comparing the smallest of these costs is the optimal adjustment scheme:

$$F_j(x) = \begin{cases} k_j x, j \in S \\ k_j x, j \in K \end{cases} \tag{3}$$

There are problems in the connection between cost management and control of agricultural product circulation channels [5]. The channel structure among traditional agricultural product suppliers, logistics enterprises, chain supermarkets and consumers is too complex, usually including multiple contracts between farmers and agricultural product collection and storage enterprises, agricultural product collection and storage enterprises and logistics enterprises, chain supermarkets and distribution companies, which lengthens the circulation chain of agricultural products and increases the residence time of agricultural products in the circulation channel, It reduces the "freshness" of agricultural products, and then increases the cargo damage rate and logistics cost of agricultural products. Specifically, there are the following problems in the cost control of agricultural production, supply and marketing. First, the information search cost of agricultural product logistics business. The cost of agricultural product producers searching for terminal market demand is high, and the supply and marketing sides of agricultural products are unable to negotiate directly with the counterparty, which makes it impossible for each party to grasp the supply and demand information of the other party, thus lacking the necessary market bargaining power. Second, the long chain of agricultural product channels [6, 7]. It is difficult for shippers and distributors of agricultural products to reach a transportation contract with short channel chain, economies of scale and high cost performance price ratio. It is difficult for farmers and consumers to bear the problem of high circulation price and sales price of agricultural products caused by the problem of long channel chain of agricultural products. Third, the cost of agricultural product distribution business. The distribution channels of distribution channels in the terminal market are not smooth, the distribution cost remains high, and the problem of "the last kilometer" of agricultural products is difficult to solve. Because the producers of agricultural products and the logistics carriers of agricultural products belong to different legal entities, they all have relatively independent standard interests. The lack of necessary communication leads to the disconnection between the cost management and control of agricultural product logistics in each stage of logistics business.

4 Agricultural Logistics Channels

It can be seen from the analysis that the upper layer of the model is a general location problem model, and the lower layer is a nonlinear programming model, which is difficult to solve. Berr ayed and Blair pointed out that even the simplest bilevel programming problem is NP hard, and there is no polynomial algorithm. Generally speaking, the non convexity of bilevel programming is an important reason for the complexity of Solving Bilevel Programming problems. Even if the upper level problem and the lower level problem are convex, the whole problem is still very likely to be non convex. Because of its non convexity, the local optimal solution is usually obtained instead of the global optimal solution. Some scholars have discussed the relationship between multi-level planning and multi-objective planning, which is still inconclusive in academia. Therefore, for the bilevel programming model obtained in this paper, the heuristic algorithm proposed by sun Huijun and other scholars is called method one, which uses the algorithm as a heuristic to solve. Sun et al. Verified the feasibility of this method.

It should be noted that considering the seasonal characteristics of agricultural products, this model assumes that agricultural products The production, supply and sales of the factory in a certain period of time meet the conditions of the model. In addition, without considering the inventory factor, it is assumed that the inventory and additional losses are very small. Only one agricultural product logistics system is optimized at a time.

The key to solve the bilevel programming problem is to find the specific form of the response function, which is obviously difficult. For the case of continuous variables, the derivative relationship between variables can be obtained through the sensitivity analysis method. In this way, the Taylor expansion can be used to approximate the response function, so as to simplify the response function to solve the bilevel programming problem. This is the heuristic algorithm SAB (sensitivity analysis basedalgorithm) based on the sensitivity analysis method. Yang and yagar applied the sensitivity analysis method to solve the traffic control problem, and Gao Ziyou and others used the sensitivity analysis method to solve the bilevel programming model of traffic continuous balance network design. However, because some variables in this paper are discrete variables, the sensitivity analysis method of continuous variables cannot be applied.

First, eliminate the information asymmetry in the circulation channels of agricultural products. Cultivate a number of information intermediaries for the circulation of agricultural products to reduce the asymmetry in the collection of agricultural products. Local governments should vigorously support information intermediaries in the circulation of agricultural products [8].

Support the development of logistics information intermediary organizations and reduce the transaction costs paid by new agricultural business entities in the agricultural logistics market. Different from the general agricultural products circulation subjects, the new agricultural management subjects have strong price influence in the agricultural products market. It realizes the business goal of optimizing its profits by buying out specific categories of agricultural products in specific areas, and feeds back ordinary farmers through mechanisms such as agricultural cooperatives and agricultural land circulation, So as to realize the cross integration of the interests of new agricultural management subjects and ordinary farmers.

Second, establish a "tripartite contract" to optimize the channel structure. The value of agricultural products is reflected in the word "fresh", which is the key to ensure the value of agricultural products at the channel terminal. Therefore, the new agricultural management subject needs to strengthen the cooperation with the agricultural logistics subject to shorten the logistics time of agricultural products "from agricultural land to dining table" [9]. The traditional single door and single family discrete planting and breeding model usually lacks the necessary price negotiation ability in the face of large terminal retailers. In view of the complex channel structure among traditional agricultural product suppliers, logistics enterprises, chain supermarkets and consumers, new agricultural business entities such as farmers' professional cooperatives and large planting and breeding households need to establish strategic cooperative relations and sign "tripartite contracts" with third-party logistics and chain supermarkets, Integrate the interests of the business entities involved in the production, supply and marketing of agricultural products into a unified contract structure [10]. This can shorten the circulation chain of agricultural products from the level of system design, effectively reduce the retention time of agricultural products in the circulation channels, strictly control the damage rate and logistics cost of agricultural products from agricultural land to consumption, effectively ensure the "freshness" of agricultural products on consumers' tables, and then increase the income level of various stakeholders.

The operation process of agricultural logistics system is shown in Fig. 3.

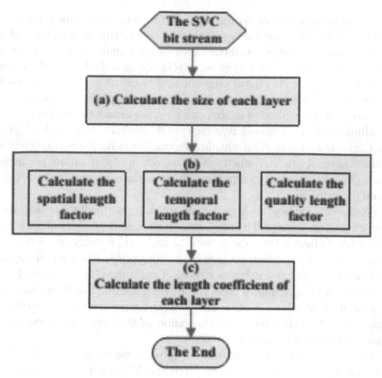

Fig. 3. Logistics system operation flow chart

5   Conclusion

This paper studies several optimization models and their algorithms in the agricultural logistics system, makes a detailed analysis on several problems of the logistics of the agricultural products agricultural logistics system in the agricultural logistics system, and improves the traditional logistics model to make it more suitable for solving the actual agricultural products logistics problems. The specific performance is as follows:

The classification criteria of supply chain structure are given. The corresponding classification methods are proposed from four aspects: the complexity of supply chain, the concentration of supply chain node enterprises, the reliability of supply chain and different optimization objectives. The seasonality of agricultural products, its demand rate and agricultural logistics system will also change periodically. Therefore, this paper improves the classical EOQ problem.

Acknowledgements. Provincial Scientific Research Projects, Research on the development path and countermeasures of agricultural logistics driven by big data (2021CSLKT3-205, China Society of Logistics).

References

1. Su, J.: Coastline climate environment and e-commerce logistics system development: a GIS perspective. Arab. J. Geosci. **14**(9), 1–17 (2021)
2. Li, Q., Xiao, R.: The use of data mining technology in agricultural e-commerce under the background of 6G Internet of things communication. Int. J. Syst. Assur. Eng. Manag. **12** (2021)
3. Reardon, T., Minten, B.: Agricultural development: New perspectives in a changing world. Food value chain transformation in developing regions. In: IFPRI Book Chapters (2021)
4. Ilesanmi, F.F., Ilesanmi, O.S., Afolabi, A.A.: The effects of the COVID-19 pandemic on food losses in the agricultural value chains in Africa: The Nigerian case study. Publ. Health Pract. **2**, 100087 (2021)
5. Saputra, R.P., Rijanto, E.: Automatic guided vehicles system and its coordination control for containers terminal logistics application (2021)
6. Sun, X., Shu, K.: Application research of perception data fusion system of agricultural product supply chain based on Internet of things. EURASIP J. Wirel. Commun. Netw. **2021**(1), 1–18 (2021)
7. Rani, N., Goyal, V., Gupta, D.: Multi-level multi-objective fully quadratic fractional optimization model with trapezoidal fuzzy numbers using Rouben Ranking function and fuzzy goal programming. Mater. Today: Proc. **2** (2021)
8. Srinivas, R., Aggarwal, S., Singh, A.P.: Detecting SARS-CoV-2 RNA prone clusters in a municipal wastewater network using fuzzy-Bayesian optimization model to facilitate wastewater-based epidemiology. Sci. Total Environ. **778**(9), 146294 (2021)
9. Scheller, C., Schmidt, K., Spengler, T.S.: Decentralized master production and recycling scheduling of lithium-ion batteries: a techno-economic optimization model. J. Bus. Econ. **91** (2021)
10. Singh, B., Knueven, B.: Lagrangian relaxation based heuristics for a chance-constrained optimization model of a hybrid solar-battery storage system. J. Global Optim. **80**(4), 965–989 (2021)

Practical Research on the Form of Art Undergraduate Education in Cultural and Creative Industry Under the Background of Big Data

Chen Zhou[✉]

Hangzhou Normal University, Hangzhou 311121, Zhejiang, China
zchxtt@126.com

Abstract. In recent years, China's cultural and creative industries have developed rapidly. Under this condition, most provinces and cities have begun to pay attention to the development of cultural and creative industries. As an emerging industry with creativity as the core, cultural and creative industries are being needed by people and filling our lives. In order to make art education in Colleges and universities better adapt to the development of cultural and creative industries and promote the integration of corresponding favorable factors in the context of cultural and creative industries, this paper analyzes the general situation of cultural and creative industries, and deeply analyzes the status and role of art education in cultural and creative industries based on ant colony algorithm, How to optimize the development of art education in Colleges and universities in the context of cultural and creative industries.

Keywords: Cultural and creative industries · Ant colony algorithm · Art Education in Colleges and Universities

1 Introduction

Cultural and creative industry refers to the industry that can make creativity become the most economic value after it is widely industrialized. Industry is known as the sunrise industry with the most development potential in the 21st century. When the cultural industry develops to a certain extent, the creative economy will develop vigorously, and the creative industry will also appear. In the information age, China's cultural and creative industry develops rapidly, and there is a great demand for professional art and design talents in the market, All countries are sparing no effort to encourage and support each other, in order to remain invincible in the future competition. For the cultural and creative industry which highly emphasizes creative ability, the cultivation of cultural and creative talents is of great importance.

With the increasingly stringent demand for talents in art design and the vigorous development of cultural and creative industries, art design education in Colleges and

M. A. Jan and F. Khan (Eds.): BigIoT-EDU 2022, LNICST 465, pp. 478–484, 2023.
https://doi.org/10.1007/978-3-031-23950-2_52

universities can provide talents for cultural and creative industries. At present, although the enrollment of talents in art design major is increasing gradually, there are still many problems and great pressure in talent training. Colleges and universities have to constantly meet the needs of industrial development, Only in this way can we help the development of cultural and creative industries. As the forefront of personnel training, colleges and universities have great advantages in scientific research, and should play a good role in the supply of talents in the development of cultural creativity. Therefore, to further clarify the relationship between art education and cultural and creative industries, to explore the development path of art education, to make it adapt to the needs of the development of cultural and creative industries, and to promote the development of art education, has become a new topic of art education in Colleges and universities [1].

2   Ant Colony Algorithm

2.1   Basic Principle

Artificial ant colony algorithm (ACA) is the principle of simulating the real ant colony foraging process to find the shortest path. ACA absorbs the typical characteristics of ant colony behavior: first, it can detect the situation in a small area and judge whether there is food or other similar pheromone trajectory; Second, it can release its own pheromone; Third, the number of pheromones left behind will gradually decrease at any time.

Ant algorithm seeks the optimal solution through the evolutionary process of candidate solution organization group, which includes the adaptation stage and the cooperation stage. In the adaptation stage, each candidate solution adjusts its structure according to the accumulated information; In the cooperation phase, the candidate solutions communicate with each other to produce better performance solutions.

In ant colony algorithm, a limited artificial ant colony finds the optimal solution to the problem through cooperative search. Each ant establishes a feasible solution or a component of the solution from the selected initial state according to the problem dependency criteria. In building their own solution, each ant collects information about the characteristics of the problem and its own behavior, and uses this information to modify the representation of the problem, as other ants see. Ants can not only act together but also work independently, which shows a kind of cooperative behavior. They do not use direct communication, but use pheromone to guide the information exchange between ants.

Ants use a structured greedy heuristic to search for feasible solutions. According to the constraints of the problem, a solution is listed as the minimum cost (shortest path) through the problem state. Every ant can find a solution, but it may be a poor one. Individuals in the ant colony have established many different solutions at the same time, and finding high-quality solutions is the result of global cooperation among all individuals in the colony [2].

In addition to finding the shortest path between the nest and the food source, the ant colony also has a strong ability to adapt to the environment. As shown in Fig. 1, when there are obstacles on the route, the ant colony can quickly find the optimal path.

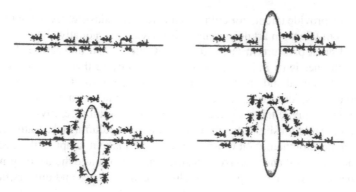

Fig. 1. Adaptive behavior of ant colony

2.2 Mathematical Model

For the sake of understanding, the ant colony algorithm model is usually illustrated by taking the ant system (AS) to solve the TSP problem of a city on a plane as an example. Firstly, the following notation is introduced: let m be the number of ants in the ant colony, dij $(i, j = 1, 2, ..., n)$ denote the distance between city i and j, $b(t)$ be the number of ants in city i, $m = \sum_{i=1}^{n} b(t)$, $\tau_{ij}^{\alpha}(t)$ is the amount of information left on the line at time t. Let $\tau_{ij}(0) = c$, where c is a constant. The ant k $(k = 1, 2, ..., m)$. In the process of movement, the direction of transfer is determined according to the amount of information on each path. $p_{ij}^{k}(t)$ represents the probability of ant k transferring from position i to position j at time t.

$$p_{ij}^{k}(t) = \begin{cases} \frac{\tau_{ij}^{\alpha}(t)\eta_{ij}^{\beta}(t)}{\sum \tau_{is}^{\alpha}(t)\eta_{is}^{\beta}(t)}, j \in allowed_k, s \in allowed \\ 0, otherwise \end{cases} \tag{1}$$

2.3 The Advantages of Ant Colony Algorithm

Ant colony algorithm is a kind of bionic optimization algorithm based on the collective foraging behavior of the biological ant colony system. Therefore, the algorithm must have many advantages of the real ant colony system. The summary is as follows:

(1) Parallel distributed computing. All ants search for many points in solution space independently and unsupervised, which is very suitable for parallel implementation. Therefore, it is an efficient parallel search algorithm in essence. The distribution calculation characteristics of ant colony algorithm are shown in two aspects: one is that pheromone is distributed on each side of the structure map. Each ant constructs the solution according to the information element condition of the current location, and does not need control center; On the other hand, when one or several ants stop working, the whole ant colony system can still keep normal function, so the algorithm has strong robustness.

(2) Strong global optimization capability. The probability of finding global optimal solution is increased by using the randomly generated ant group instead of single ant; In addition, probability rules are used instead of deterministic rules to guide search; The algorithm can escape local optimization. The traditional optimization algorithm is sensitive to the selection of initial value and iteration step, and it is difficult to escape once it is trapped in local optimization.

(3) It has strong adaptability. The ant colony algorithm has no special requirements for search space, such as the continuity, differentiability of objective function and accurate mathematical description of objective function and constraint function, which has wide adaptability.

(4) Polysolubility. Because ant colony algorithm uses population method to calculate evolution, when the population is solved once, it can provide multiple approximate solutions, which is very useful for multi-objective search or need more approximate solutions as reference.

(5) It is easy to combine with other algorithms. The construction process of ant colony algorithm solution is completed gradually, which can be combined with prior knowledge in this field conveniently. The deconstruction mechanism of ant colony algorithm has a very good advantage, that is, it can handle constraints conveniently. Ants can dynamically adjust the next accessible nodes in the process of solution construction to ensure the feasibility of the solution. However, the processing of complex constraints is a weak link of other algorithms.

3 The Current Situation of Art Undergraduate Education in Colleges and Universities

3.1 Unreasonable Curriculum and Teaching Mode

In the present art design education, many colleges and universities ignore the cultivation of students' design ideas and the overall logical thinking. Many colleges and universities are not clear about the relationship between art design courses, and the courses are scattered. Many colleges and universities only pay attention to the formal effect, and do not really cultivate the design thinking of students. It is difficult for students to understand the course deeply because of the content of the course which is too scattered and independent, and it does not form a certain design ability. Moreover, teachers are too single in teaching mode, according to the traditional teaching mode, so the students trained lack innovative thinking, so the talents trained by such art design education are difficult to meet the needs of cultural and creative industries in the market [3].

3.2 The Talent Training Mode is Out of Line with the Market Demand

Nowadays, many colleges and universities have opened art design majors to train design talents. But now many colleges and universities cultivate design talents can not meet the real needs of the market. Nowadays, the demand of design talents is not only to have professional design skills, but also to have excellent practical ability and professional design literacy. So many colleges and universities are training design talents and the market needs of design personnel is out of line. On the one hand, most of the students in our country are trained by traditional teaching ideas. The mode is too single, only focusing on textbooks, and there is no chance of practice; On the other hand, some young teachers are directly left in school for teaching, without practical experience, so they can not teach more practical experience to students. Therefore, the talents cultivated in art education in Colleges and universities are out of line with the market demand.

3.3 Lack of Creativity and Innovation Ability

According to the survey, many colleges and universities are backward in talent training of art design specialty, whether it is education concept or training plan, which is not in line with the current trend, has not kept pace with the times, and does not match the development of cultural and creative industries. We can see that many colleges and universities lack the atmosphere of innovation and creativity. A small number of colleges and universities ignore the education of human quality, and do not pay attention to the cultivation of students' humanistic quality. Moreover, for the talents in the cultural and creative industry, many colleges and universities have not carried out special curriculum and professional training, mainly art design professional education.

At present, the practitioners of cultural and creative industries in the market generally lack the ability of innovation, so it is more necessary for colleges and universities to exert their own strength to train professional talents for the society. At present, many schools of art design in China are still in the stage of introduction, and the relevant research institutions of creative science are also in the stage of introduction. There is a lack of people involved in creative research, and some platforms for creative research are also very lacking. And whether it is the art education major in colleges or some institutions studying creative science, they have not studied the overall development strategy of creative science, but only introduce the layout of talent creative industry and the theoretical basis of creative science [4].

4   Research on Art Undergraduate Education in Colleges and Universities Based on Ant Colony Algorithm

4.1   Combining Art Education with Creative Talent Training Mode

The original art education mode is easy to ignore the humanistic quality. Once it ignores the humanistic quality, it will be contrary to the central content and thought. This is also one of the important contents of Chinese cultural industry, which is of great significance. Art Education in Colleges and universities should be based on humanistic quality education, provide innovative hardware support for students through the form of the second classroom, and edify students' emotion and wisdom by creating a humanistic environment conducive to cultural innovation.

4.2   Closely Linked with the Cultural Industry Market

The development concept of business model innovative education model and the development of cultural industry are mutually adaptive, especially in the aspect of market development, which will continue to give play to the advantages of art education. At the same time, training methods and education contents should be adjusted in time. Art Education in Colleges and universities should be closely combined with real life. Art education in Colleges and universities should be closely connected with the essence of art creation, and better combine production, learning and research. Art Education in Colleges and universities is the practice base of integrating with the market and actively integrating into the industrial market. The development direction of art education is multi angle, and has made great contribution in the reform and development, but the development of art education needs to increase the pace, take the cultivation of innovative talents as the goal, highly combine with the market of cultural industry, and attach importance to the all-round development of students, so that art education can have fresh vitality and vitality, and cultivate innovative talents with high cultural quality.

4.3 Consolidate the Quality Foundation in the Era of Cultural and Creative Industries

Art Education in Colleges and universities should first establish the basic position of humanistic quality education in art education. To renew the curriculum of art education major, the curriculum should aim at cultivating students' artistic quality and aesthetic ability, strengthen the infiltration and construction of humanities courses and theoretical courses, and improve students' humanistic cultivation; Secondly, we should make full use of the second classroom. Carry out campus innovation activities, combine the first classroom with the second classroom, form a strong cultural innovation atmosphere, stimulate students' creative passion, establish innovation incentive mechanism, encourage students' innovation activities, strengthen the construction of innovation base, and provide hardware support for students' innovation; Third, it is necessary to create a campus humanistic environment conducive to cultural innovation. Campus culture has a subtle influence on the cultivation of students' temperament, the promotion of their realm, the sublimation of their emotions, their behavior and value orientation. It is an effective way to hold all kinds of humanities lectures and actively promote elegant art into campus.

4.4 New Requirements of Art Education in Colleges and Universities for Teachers' Teaching Idea and Teaching Level

The cultivation of creative thinking has a great relationship with teachers' teaching methods. Teachers should guide students' thinking towards divergence, flexibility and originality. At the same time, teachers should consciously add some exploratory topics in teaching to stimulate students' emotions and develop their creative potential. Innovative art education requires teachers to have innovative quality. Teachers should not only have solid and generous professional knowledge, but also master the latest knowledge and research results of various disciplines. The role of teachers should also be changed. Teachers should be changed from the past simple imparter to the information resource allocator and guide.

5 Conclusion

The industrialization of cultural creativity not only provides a broad space for the future of art education, but also points out the direction of reform and development for art education. China's art education should speed up the pace of reform, take the cultivation of innovative talents with high cultural quality as the goal, change the traditional concept of art education, maintain a high degree of integration with the cultural industry market, and pay attention to the overall development of students' innovation consciousness, innovation ability and humanistic quality, Make art education continuously inject new vitality and vigor into the development of cultural and creative industries, and cultivate innovative and compound talents with high cultural quality.

Acknowledgements. 2017 College of Cultural Creativity of Hangzhou normal university Research on Excellent Courses.

References

1. Liu, Y.: Division and reflection on research paradigm of cultural and creative industries in China. Mod. Commun. **1** (2007)
2. Li, S.: Ant Colony Algorithm and its Application. Harbin Institute of Technology Press, Harbin (2004)
3. Li, Y.: Current situation and countermeasures of humanistic quality education for college students. Vocat. Technol. **1**, 53 (2005)
4. Yu, Z.: Research on Zhang Daoyi's art education thought. Design Art **2**, 10–12 (2005)

Prediction of English Major Training Model in Higher Vocational Education Based on Fuzzy Neural Network Algorithm

Liang Gu[✉]

Maanshan Teacher College, Maanshan 243000, Anhui, China
941433604@qq.com

Abstract. The prediction of English major training model in Higher Vocational Education Based on fuzzy neural network algorithm is the process of using a neural network to predict the future. The main function of this method is to analyze and understand the human brain and its characteristics. This method can be used as an effective tool for predicting or analyzing any kind of data, such as finance, economics, psychology, medicine etc. In addition, it can also be used for understanding people's behavior and their reactions towards various situations. Higher Vocational and technical education, the importance of talent planning in Higher Vocational and technical education has become increasingly prominent, The premise of each higher vocational and technical talent planning is to make a reasonable prediction of each higher vocational and technical talent and professional training. Fuzzy neural network can effectively deal with nonlinear and fuzzy problems, and plays a great role in intelligent information processing. Therefore, this paper studies the prediction of English professional training model in Higher Vocational Education in fuzzy neural network algorithm.

Keywords: Talent training forecast · Higher vocational and technical · Fuzzy neural prediction

1 Introduction

Facing the fundamental change of economic growth mode, the economic structure is also facing strategic adjustment. The quantity and quality of highly skilled talents can not meet the needs of industrial structure transformation and upgrading, and the knowledge and skills of graduates do not match the job needs. In recent years, the graduation rate of domestic vocational college students is more than 99% and the employment rate is more than 80%, but the overall quality of students, the satisfaction of employers and society are not high. Higher vocational colleges are the cradle and important position for cultivating high skilled talents. The quality of talent training is related to their survival and development [1]. Therefore, colleges should have the problem of teaching quality, feel the urgency of survival crisis, and have a clear quality consciousness and the standard and power of quality construction. To correctly evaluate the teaching quality of higher

M. A. Jan and F. Khan (Eds.): BigIoT-EDU 2022, LNICST 465, pp. 485–496, 2023.
https://doi.org/10.1007/978-3-031-23950-2_53

vocational colleges, the author believes that while paying attention to "quantity" and "rate", we should pay more attention to "quality". The teaching quality directly affects the employment quality and social recognition [2]. Through the ways to improve and monitor the teaching quality in the process of training high skilled talents, form a perfect quality management mechanism, promote the training of high skilled applied talents, and give full play to the role of Vocational Education in industrial upgrading.

With the rapid development of international trade, higher vocational English continues to grow and deepen. At present, English majors are developing towards professional quality management and discipline establishment and improvement, realizing the high-quality quantification of professional talents, positioning and curriculum system, and then improving the value of English majors. Based on the talent training model of English major in Higher Vocational Education in fuzzy neural network algorithm, English major in higher vocational colleges can continuously improve curriculum evaluation, teaching team, teaching conditions and quality monitoring, improve the development level of business major in Higher Vocational Colleges and improve the quality of talent training [3]. In order to meet the sustainable development of English major, higher vocational colleges need to actively strengthen the training mode of professional talents, and realize the high-quality development of business English Major Based on the needs of social talents and the current situation of industry development.

People are the core elements of national development. Talents are the strategic resources to promote national economic development, and the cultivation of talents depends on education. In recent years, the scale of personnel training in Higher Education in China has been continuously expanding, and now it has entered the stage of popularization of higher education. The expansion of talent training scale makes the quality of education and training become the focus of social attention. In September 2016, the research results conference of Chinese students' development core literacy was held in Beijing, which defined the personality qualities and key abilities that students should have, and put forward new requirements for talent training. The cultivation of students' core literacy is mainly realized through the education and teaching of various disciplines. English, as one of the necessary professional skills under the background of economic globalization, has attracted much attention for its educational and teaching quality [4]. At present, most of the researches on the core competence of English discipline focus on the curriculum setting and textbook development, and lay particular emphasis on basic education. Few articles combine the core competence of English discipline with the cultivation of College English majors from a macro level. Under this background, the author was inspired and decided to choose the topic of "Research on the prediction of training mode of Higher Vocational English Majors Based on fuzzy neural network algorithm" to explore the training mode of College English Majors under the background of subject core quality based on fuzzy neural network algorithm.

2 Fuzzy Neural Network

2.1 Fuzzy Theory

As another focus of this paper, fuzzy neural network will be used to establish the network operation situation awareness model. As for the study of fuzzy neural network learning algorithm, in 1993, JYH Shing and Roger Fang proposed an adaptive fuzzy neural network model that uses gradient descent and least square method to learn parameters; A. In 1999, ntimberger et al. Proposed a reinforcement learning algorithm and improved the learning algorithm of sub parameter learning; Buckley et al. Proposed a hybrid learning algorithm combining BP algorithm and genetic algorithm to learn the parameters in 1996. In recent years, a large number of scholars have used some non derivative learning methods as algorithms, such as genetic algorithm and particle swarm optimization algorithm. Some researchers at home and abroad are also constantly using improved GA and improved psof to learn the network parameters and improve the performance of fuzzy neural networks [5]. Most of the improved ideas of the hybrid learning algorithms designed in these studies are to use different algorithms to realize the learning of nonlinear antecedent parameters and the learning of linear antecedent parameters, and fix one parameter to learn the best value of another parameter. The gradient descent method and the partial least square method are used to learn the rules. The researchers improved the fuzzy neural algorithm based on genetic algorithm and proposed an improved crossover operator, which can simultaneously optimize the structure and weight parameters of the fuzzy neural network [6].

Fuzzy neural networks (FNN) is a kind of neural network which combines fuzzy information processing. The first research began in 1987 when B. Kosko introduced the idea of neural network into the fuzzy system. Since then, many scholars have continuously studied and improved this field, including various improvements in the structural design of fuzzy neural network and the output principle between layers. This paper will briefly explain the principle and concept of FNN.

Fuzzy neural network has the advantages of fuzzy theory and neural network. It can not only complete the processing of fuzzy information, reflect the uncertainty of characteristics, but also use the structure of neural network to complete the learning and adaptation of models.

Each basic unit of the fuzzy neural network is composed of fuzzy neurons, and the following fuzzy neurons are included in the fuzzy neural network:

(1) Fuzzy neuron: this kind of fuzzy neuron is used to convert the determined value into the fuzzy output value:

$$y = \mu(x) \tag{1}$$

In the above formula, X is the input of the determined value, y is the output of the fuzzy value, and U (.) is the membership function.

(2) Defuzzification neuron: this type of neuron is similar to the former type in form but has the opposite effect, which is to transform the fuzzy value into

The defuzzification relationship is expressed as:

$$y = f(x_1, x_2, ..., x_n,)$$ (2)

At present, the widely used models are T-S model and Mandani model.

(1) T-S model. When dealing with linear data, T-S model has unique advantages. It divides variables into independent individuals. In logical reasoning, the rules are simple and the matching speed is fast. However, when the nonlinear characteristics of data are obvious, T-S model will produce a large number of fuzzy rules, which greatly affects the operation efficiency of the algorithm and increases the difficulty and complexity in the reasoning process [7].

(2) Mandani model. The core of the model is fuzzy rule base and fuzzy inference engine. The input data is fuzzified through membership function, then the rules in the rule base are matched, and the fuzzy inference engine performs logical reasoning. Finally, the results are clarified and output. The working principle of Mandani model is shown in Fig. 1.

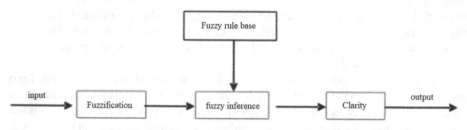

Fig. 1. Schematic diagram of Madani model

2.2 Fuzzy Neural Network Type

Fuzzy theory and artificial neural network together constitute fuzzy neural network. According to different combination methods, the types of fuzzy neural network are different, which are mainly divided into the following five types:

(1) Indirect connection type: each independent part is responsible for its own work, which is not directly related in the overall network model, that is, when processing data, the part that can be expressed by fuzzy logic is processed by fuzzy theory; The parts that cannot be processed by fuzzy theory are expressed by neural network. This network model structure only uses the two methods to deal with different data, and does not carry out intelligent fusion. It can not give full play to the advantages of the two algorithms at the same time, and it is easy to cause large data deviation during operation, which affects the accuracy of the overall structure [8]. The type of fuzzy neural network is shown in Fig. 2 below.

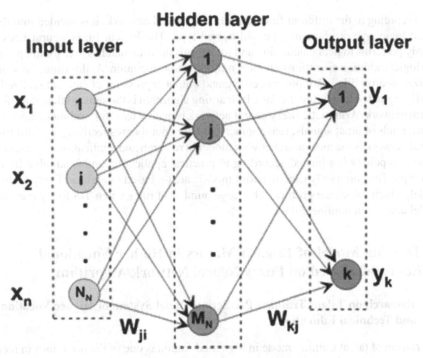

Fig. 2. Types of fuzzy neural networks

(2) Series type: the fuzzy system is used as the input (output) of the network model, and the neural network is used as the output (input) of the overall network model. Compared with the non direct connection type, this connection method has a great improvement in system efficiency and accuracy. First, the data is processed through one technology, and then output and expressed through another technology. Compared with the non direct connection type, The series type ensures the advantages of the two algorithms at the same time.

(3) Parallel type: take the fuzzy system and neural network as the input and output of the overall network model at the same time, so that the two methods can process the input data and output results in parallel. This model can process data more accurately, give full play to the reasoning advantages of fuzzy system, and ensure the learning efficiency of neural network.

(4) Network type: the neural network is introduced into the fuzzy reasoning system to learn and control the fuzzy rules through the neural network, determine the corresponding membership function and adjust the error, so that the overall network model has the ability of self-learning and self-adaptive.

(5) Equivalence: in fuzzy neural network, all neurons are fuzzy neurons, and all nodes have fuzziness. They participate in the process of learning and error adjustment. They are more suitable for intelligent reasoning of complex data and have been widely used in the field of fault detection.

According to the different functions of fuzzy neural network, it is divided into three types: logic type, arithmetic type and hybrid type. The logical fuzzy neural network mainly performs logical calculation and transforms the rule matching reasoning process into logical addition operation or logical multiplication operation. At this time, the neuron is fuzzy neuron [9]. The input processing and output expression of data are realized by fuzzifying and defuzzifying the data. Its learning algorithm is the same as that of artificial neural network; Arithmetic fuzzy neural network is mainly used for arithmetic operation of two kinds of input signals, real number and fuzzy number respectively; Hybrid fuzzy neural network is the most used network model in research and application at present. Its network topology is adjusted according to practical application and is suitable for any data type. The commonly used network models are t-s-based model and fuzzy modular model, which solves the problem of a large number of rules when T-S fuzzy reasoning model deals with nonlinear data.

3 Training Model of English Majors in Higher Vocational Education Based on Fuzzy Neural Network Algorithm

3.1 Research on Talent Training Prediction Model System of Higher Vocational and Technical Education

The reform of talent training mode in higher education is one of the hot topics in recent years. However, what is the talent training mode? What does it include? There is still no unified conclusion on these issues. According to the interpretation of modern Chinese dictionary, "mode" refers to the standard form of something or the standard form that people can follow. The "training mode" was first proposed in China in 1994 in the "reform plan of teaching content and curriculum system of higher education for the 21st century" comprehensively launched and implemented by the former State Education Commission. However, the "training mode" was not defined at that time. In 1998, the Ministry of Education issued the opinions on deepening education reform and cultivating high-quality talents to meet the needs of the 21st century, The talent training mode is expressed as: "The structure of knowledge, ability and quality built by the University for students, as well as the way to realize this structure. It fundamentally defines the characteristics of talent training and embodies the educational thoughts and concepts. Scholars also have different views on how to define the talent training mode. Zhou Yuanqing believes that the so-called talent training mode refers to the talent training objectives, training specifications and basic training methods. It embodies higher education in a concentrated way The basic characteristics of the trained talents are determined by the educational thoughts and educational concepts of the University. Song Huiling believes that the "talent training mode" is "a standard structure style and operation mode formed by designing the whole process of talent training activities around the center of talent training objectives with a certain educational ideology as the soul, higher education talent training activities as the ontology or prototype." Thus, the talent training mode is a stable education and teaching structure organized by the school to achieve the training objectives [10].

From the definition, we can see that the talent training mode is an educational and teaching structure composed of different parts. Gong Yizu believes that the talent training mode includes three parts: training objectives, training process and operation mode; Zhou Yuanqing believes that the talent training mode is composed of training objectives, training specifications and training methods; Bian Jing thinks that the talent training mode is an organic combination of educational ideas, educational concepts, curriculum system, teaching methods, teaching means, teaching resources, teaching management system, teaching environment, etc. This study draws on the views of various scholars and believes that the training mode is composed of three parts: training objectives, training process and training evaluation. The training process specifically involves three parts: curriculum setting, teaching form and student management.

Based on the diversity and dynamics of training types and educational levels of higher vocational education talents, the interpretability and quantifiability of training higher vocational education talents are constantly changing with the passage of time and the change of environment, and the collectability of data This paper qualitatively analyzes the influencing factors of talent training in Higher Vocational and technical education from the four aspects of science and technology environment.

(1) Social environment. The talent training of higher vocational education will be affected by national policies, regional social development level, population status and national education level. This topic selects the total population at the end of the year, the natural growth rate of population, the number of students in Colleges and universities per million population and the national financial expenditure on education as the measurement indicators,

(2) Economic environment. Based on the measurement of the impact of economic development on the talent training of higher vocational education, the main indicators of the most direct impact of economy on the talent training of Higher Vocational Education under the market-oriented environment are as follows:

Industrial structure: different industries cultivate higher vocational education talents with different material capital scale: material capital scale is the basis of economic development, and its changes lead to different cultivation of higher vocational education talents. Economic aggregate and quality: economic growth can promote the promotion and improvement of the total amount and structure of higher vocational education talents.

(3) Foreign related economy. With the acceleration of economic globalization and integration, the exchanges between countries in economy, science and technology are becoming closer and closer. Therefore, the economy outside Saudi Arabia covers a wide range. Considering the collectability of data and the quantification of indicators, this topic mainly analyzes the impact of foreign-related economy on Higher Vocational educators from three aspects: foreign-funded enterprises, foreign economy and import and export Impact measure of talent training.

(4) Science and technology environment. In the information age, the development of science and technology not only promotes the development of economy, but also shortens the knowledge renewal cycle and speeds up the training of Higher Vocational and technical education talents in emerging industries or industries, which

has a great impact, especially on the training of Higher Vocational and technical education talents.

3.2 Research on Fuzzy Neural Network Model

On this basis, this paper proposes to apply the fuzzy logic evaluation method to the network situation evaluation, and analyze the types of characteristics. The specific method is to divide each feature of the data into multiple fuzzy types, calculate the probability that the feature belongs to each type, obtain the fuzzy relationship matrix, obtain the fuzzy evaluation result through fuzzy operation, and then calculate the network operation situation value by synthesizing the weight of the feature itself.

The fuzzy comprehensive evaluation method is a comprehensive evaluation method that makes use of fuzzy logic to fuzzify certain characteristics. The method steps for calculating the situation value by the fuzzy comprehensive evaluation method are as follows:

a) Determine the characteristic domain of network situation u = {u, UZ,... UN}, i.e. n indicators to be evaluated; And determine the modulus
     The hierarchical domain of fuzzy evaluation, i.e. the number of fuzzy subsets v = {V, VZ,... VM} J;
b) Determine the membership function Uij of each fuzzy subset (I = 1, 2,..., N; J = 1, 2,..., m);

The membership function UX represents the degree of membership of the ith evaluation index in the j-th hierarchy. The expression of the membership function UX is often obtained by fuzzy statistical method or direct empirical assignment method. This paper proposes a method to obtain the number of membership functions m and the expression UG through clustering for network perception. The type number and function formula of membership functions will be discussed in detail in 3.3.2.2.

c) The membership degree of each feature on each fuzzy subset is calculated.

The fuzzy neural network, which combines the fuzzy system and the neural network, combines the advantages of the two in terms of characteristics. On the one hand, it can be used to deal with the related problems of fuzzy information, construct and imitate the fuzziness of human thinking judgment, and on the other hand, it can imitate the principle of neural network to complete the analysis of a large amount of data information and establish an independent learning model. From the previous evaluation methods of network situation awareness in this paper, the fuzzy neural network is very suitable for establishing the network situation awareness learning model, further solving the consistency and stability problems in situation awareness, and completing the function of situation analysis and prediction in the network situation model, as shown in Fig. 3:

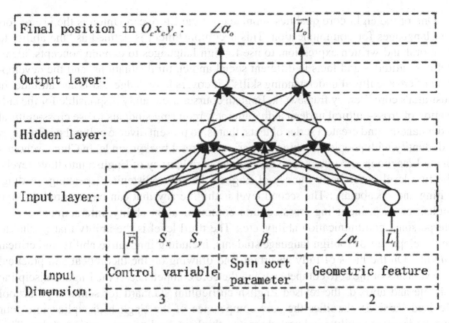

Fig. 3. Fuzzy neural network model

The higher vocational technical education in the fuzzy prediction model has the talent training influence factor XI, and we can obtain its value x = (x1, X2,..., xn) for m consecutive years; The time series value x = (x1, X2,..., xn) of the impact factor XI is structured according to the following model:

$$E(t)\dot{x}_{d+1}(t) - E(t)\dot{x}_{k+1}(t) = E(t)\Delta\dot{x}_{k+1}(t) = f(t, x_d(t)) + B(t)u_d(t)$$
$$-f(t, x_k(t)) - B(t)u_k(t) = f(t, x_d(t)) - f(t, x_{k+1}(t)) + B(t)\Delta u_{k+1}(t)$$
(3)

$$\begin{cases} E(t)\dot{x}_d(t) = f(t, x_d(t)) + B(t)u_d(t) \\ y_d(t) = C(t)x_d(t) \end{cases}$$
(4)

4 Prediction of Training Mode of English Major in Higher Vocational Education

The core literacy indicator system for the development of Chinese students developed by experts organized by the Ministry of education also includes foreign language literacy, and defines foreign language literacy as "being able to realize understanding, expression and communication in other languages through oral or written language forms according to one's own wishes and needs". This definition breaks through the "instrumental" definition of language. As the most widely circulated language in the world, the cultivation of English core competence has also attracted the attention of many scholars at home and abroad.

One of the eight core qualities stipulated by the European Union is the use of foreign languages for communication. This accomplishment is defined as "the ability to learn oral and written expression, to use foreign languages to explain concepts, ideas, feelings, attitudes and facts in different social and cultural situations, and the development of cross-cultural understanding skills". It covers knowledge, skills and attitude. In Australia's core literacy framework, English courses are mainly responsible for the cultivation of cross-cultural understanding literacy, requiring students to use cross-cultural understanding and create a series of texts, that is, to present diverse cultural perspectives and identify with people and things of various cultural backgrounds. In China, scholars Zhang Lianzhong and others have divided the core literacy of English into three levels. The first level is the basic literacy of English, including listening, speaking, reading, writing and vocabulary; The second level is the literacy that can be acquired through English courses, including cross-cultural communication ability, international career, interpersonal communication ability, etc.; The third level is the ability that is vital to the development of foreign language students, including innovative ability and critical thinking. On the basis of fully absorbing and drawing on the theoretical and practical achievements of the core competence and the core competence of the English discipline at home and abroad, the revised English curriculum standard for senior high school (Revised Version) classifies the core competence of the English discipline into four aspects: language ability, cultural character, thinking quality and learning ability. This is also the commonly recognized classification of core competence of English subjects in China. The core competence model of College English professionals in this study is based on this.

Specifically speaking, language competence is the most important part of the core competence of English discipline, which includes not only basic language skills such as listening, speaking, reading and writing, but also language understanding, language awareness and communicative identity awareness. According to the existing literature, this paper divides language competence into three parts: language knowledge, language cognition and language application.

In the aspect of "cultural character", the goal of cultural character has significantly enhanced the educational value of English curriculum. Cultural character accomplishment not only refers to understanding Chinese and foreign cultural phenomena and values, but also emphasizes the evaluation of cultural traditions and social cultural phenomena. In this paper, it includes three parts: cultural identity, cultural discrimination and cross-cultural communication ability.

Thinking quality is a quality that is easy to be neglected in traditional English disciplines, but it is a dimension that is closest to the development of the core quality and personality of English majors, and is closely related to the fundamental task of "cultivating morality and cultivating people". The thinking quality is manifested in the level and characteristics of students' logical criticism and creativity through discrimination, generalization, inference and analysis. In this paper, it is divided into three indicators: understanding, inference and creativity.

Thinking quality is a quality that is easy to be neglected in traditional English disciplines, but it is a dimension that is closest to the development of the core quality and personality of English majors, and is closely related to the fundamental task of "cultivating morality and cultivating people". The thinking quality is manifested in the level and characteristics of students' logical criticism and creativity through discrimination, generalization, inference and analysis. In this paper, it is divided into three indicators: understanding, inference and creativity.

Citizens in the 21st century must have the consciousness of lifelong learning and the ability of self-learning. Learning ability is essential for every discipline. Learning ability in English core competence is not limited to learning methods and strategies, but also includes understanding and attitude towards English and English learning, specifically including active learning ability, cooperative learning ability and deep learning ability.

To sum up, the training mode prediction of English Majors in Higher Vocational Colleges Based on fuzzy neural network algorithm is shown in Fig. 4.

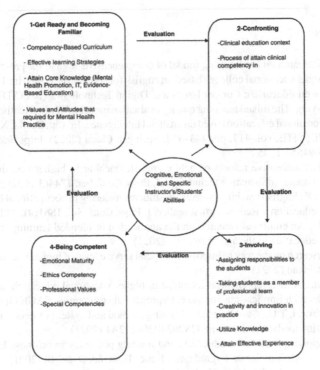

Fig. 4. Fuzzy neural network algorithm

5   Conclusion

Based on the prediction of talent training of Higher Vocational and technical education in China, most of the research still stays at the enterprise level. Market oriented specialty setting and adjustment are imminent. The premise is to carry out scientific and reasonable prediction research on talent training of socialized higher vocational education. Fuzzy neural network model structure. Aiming at the problem of network situation awareness, this paper constructs a running situation awareness model based on fuzzy neural network. In the model structure design, a nonlinear output activation layer is added to improve the expression ability to form an improved FNN. At the same time, an initialization method that is consistent with the actual problem is proposed. According to the survey results of core competence of English Majors in higher vocational colleges, the development level of English Majors' learning ability is the highest, but among the three indicators of learning ability, cooperative learning ability is the worst. This is related to the students' learning habits and normal teaching forms. In order to improve students' cooperative ability, teachers should consciously adopt the methods of group discussion and cooperative inquiry in teaching. Teamwork is one of the most important abilities in contemporary society. It is not only an essential skill in the undergraduate stage, but also in the workplace.

References

1. Zeng, Y.: Research on the teaching model of comprehensive english for preschool education major in higher vocational colleges based on english for specific purposes. In: 1st International Conference on Education: Current Issues and Digital Technologies (ICECIDT 2021) (2021)
2. Chen, Hai-ying: The mixed teaching quality evaluation model of applied mathematics courses in higher vocational education based on artificial intelligence. In: Liu, S., Ma, X. (eds.) ADHIP 2021. LNICSSITE, vol. 417, pp. 443–454. Springer, Cham (2022). https://doi.org/10.1007/978-3-030-94554-1_35
3. Yue, C.: The innovative reform of public english teaching in higher vocational education based on computer information technology. J. Phys. Conf. Ser. **1744**(3), 032050 (5pp) (2021)
4. Wen, J., Fu, F.: English teaching courses for students majoring in occupational health in higher vocational education based on virtual reality. J. Phys. Conf. Ser. **1881**(4), 042020 (2021)
5. Yanbing, L.: An empirical research on the application of blended learning model in higher vocational education in the age of internet (2021)
6. Yue, S.: Research on the way to improve the social service level of higher vocational education based on demand (2021)
7. Li, Z., Islam, A.: Entrepreneurial intention in higher vocational education: an empirically-based model with implications for the entrepreneurial community. SAGE Open **11** (2021)
8. Luo, Y., Weiwei, T.U., Cao, R., et al.: Training method and system of neural network model and prediction method and system, US20210264272A1 (2021)
9. Xie, Q.: Applying vocational education and training pedagogy in business English courses for China's English major undergraduates. Educ. Train. **63**, 292–312 (2021)
10. Wang, Y., Zheng, Y., Jia, Q., et al.: Prediction algorithm of regional lymph node metastasis of rectal cancer based on improved deep neural network. J. Med. Imaging Health Inf. (2021)

Professional Course System of Film and Television Photography and Production Under Data Technology

Hongxing Qian[✉]

Changchun Humanities and Sciences College, Jilin 130117, China
334842896@qq.com

Abstract. With the rapid development of technology, digital technology has become an important tool for film and television photography and production in China, and university students, as future film and television professional practitioners, should be fully familiar with the digital technology context during their school years. This paper is based on the reform of the curriculum system of film and television photography and production under the background of ant colony algorithm. This paper briefly describes the changes brought by digital technology to film and television photography and production, followed by the analysis of the main points of the construction of the curriculum system of film and television photography and production industry under the background of ant colony algorithm. Finally, the ideas for the construction of a specific professional curriculum system are elaborated. Through this paper, we hope to provide educational administrators and teachers of film and television photography and production with some reference materials for curriculum reform.

Keywords: Ant colony algorithm · Film and television photography and production · Curriculum reform

1 Introduction

After 2000, the 16th National Congress explicitly proposed the development of cultural industries, of which the film and television cultural industry is an important part, and the large-scale education and training of arts and communication talents at this time not only led to the formal establishment of the film and television photography and production major, but also the education and training of film and television talents to meet the needs of the film and television industry. 2012, the state adjusted the catalogue of undergraduate majors, for the first time in several major universities to create a new major–Film and Television Photography and Production. At this stage, as an emerging speciality, the construction of this speciality is still being explored by universities, and a systematic and theoretical curriculum has not yet been formed.

Digital technology and electronic computer technology go hand in hand to produce different forms of graphics, sound and image. Digital technology has a wide range of

M. A. Jan and F. Khan (Eds.): BigIoT-EDU 2022, LNICST 465, pp. 497–505, 2023.
https://doi.org/10.1007/978-3-031-23950-2_54

applications, both in the professional computer field and in the film and television photography and production industry. The world's film and television industry has entered a new phase of development, with creators choosing advanced digital technologies to create new categories of films in order to present complex images. Categories such as magical films, science fiction films and fictional films are recognized by the public [1]. The importance of applying digital technology to update the actual value of the film and television production industry has been established as indispensable. With the goal of cultivating talents to adapt to society and the industry, domestic institutions should create courses in film and television photography and production with a focus on digital technology in response to this situation where the digital technology context continues to mature. This paper explores the reform of the professional system of film and television photography and production based on the background of the ant colony algorithm.

The learning system is shown in Fig. 1.

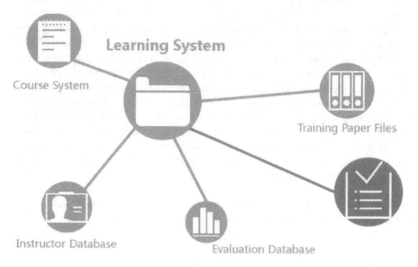

Fig. 1. The learning system

2   Ant Colony Algorithm

2.1   Description of the Ant Colony Algorithm

The ant colony algorithm can be seen as a probabilistic search algorithm that guides the search by parameterising the solution space of the problem in terms of the pheromones released by the ants. Each ant constructs a feasible solution, or part of a solution, from the initial state according to the criteria given by the problem. The parameters of the solution space are updated with the solutions already produced, allowing subsequent ant searches to focus on a range of high quality solutions. The following four components play a decisive role in modelling the ant colony algorithm:

(1) Description of the problem solution space

Since computers deal with discrete events, they cannot completely describe a continuous plane. This requires that the continuous plane must be discretized into a discrete plane consisting of a set of points, so that the artificial ants can move freely on the abstracted points. Since ants moving on a continuous plane always pass through discrete points, the problem space solved by an ant colony algorithm can be described by a data structure called a graph. Since graphs are suitable for describing many problems, this makes possible a wide range of applications of ant colony algorithms.

(2) Construction of feasible solutions

While ants determine the direction of their progress during the search for a food source based on the pheromones on the path, artificial ants move on the nodes of a plane, so the process of moving from the anthill to the food source can be abstracted as the construction of a solution in the algorithm by abstracting the pheromones as trajectories that exist on the edges of the graph. At each node, the artificial ant sense calculates the probability of moving towards the next node based on the magnitude of the concentration of pheromone trajectories on the edges connected to that node. The artificial ant selects the next node from the initial node according to certain state transfer rules, and so on until it reaches the target node, thus obtaining a feasible solution to the desired problem.

(3) Pheromone trajectory update

In the ant colony algorithm, the decision of when and how much pheromone to release into the environment should be designed according to the problem to be solved. Ants can release pheromones immediately after they have constructed a feasible solution, i.e. after moving from one node to another, using local information; or they can release pheromones after they have already constructed a feasible solution, i.e. after they have reached the target node, using global information. The positive feedback mechanism plays an important role in the ACO: the more ants an edge selects, the more the edge is rewarded (through pheromone release), and the more attractive the edge is to the next ant. The amount of pheromone released is proportional to the quality of the solution constructed by the ant. If an edge contributes to the generation of a high quality solution, then its pheromone will grow and be proportional to its contribution.

2.2 Ant Systems (AS)-Prototype Ant Colony Algorithm

The ant colony algorithm has evolved over the years into various versions, but these algorithms are still largely similar to the AS. The program flow diagram for the ant system is shown in Fig. 2.

Flowchart of the ant System algorithm is shown in Fig. 2.

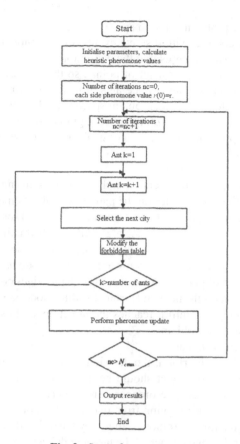

Fig. 2. Struts frame structure

3 Changes Brought About by Digital Technology for Film and Television Photography and Production

3.1 Computer Compositing has Become an Important Tool in Film Production

The industry related to film and television photography and production has been in a constant state of renewal for many years. The content of work in the film and television industry is inherently creative in nature. The value of the work is related to the talent and ideas of the creator. Some creators specialise in creating realistic work, which corresponds to the art of cinematography and production, with a bias towards techniques such as editing and articulation. Some creators are more imaginative, and are able to create film and television material that is beyond the real world, either through their scripts or their artistic perception. Such creators therefore need to use digital technology to restore their inner film images. Digital technology can be used to synthesise virtual film images by capturing realistic material. The collision of the virtual and the real clearly creates a strong visual impact for the viewer. And the successful sell-out of films such as Star Wars once again proclaims the epoch-making value of the integration of digital technology with the film and photography industry [2]. Digital technology not only brought visual impact to audiences, but also had a direct impact on the film production industry. Since then, the filmmaking industry has officially embraced computer technology as a key tool in the production of films. This has had a disruptive effect in terms of the innovative changes that digital technology has brought to the film and television photography and production industry (Fig. 3).

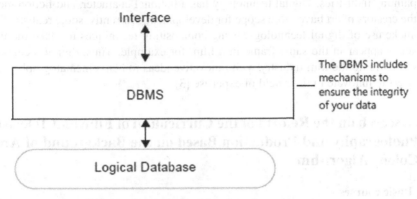

Fig. 3. The structure of data base for course system

3.2 Digital Technology Presents Transformational Challenges for the Film and Television Industry

The profession of cinematography and production is essentially a service to film and television productions, but in reality it is the audience that the profession serves. The audience is the main audience for film and television, and it is the audience that decides whether a film is a hit or whether a television series is a ratings winner. However, some filmmakers believe that while the audience plays a judging role, as thinking filmmakers, filmmakers should play a role in leading the aesthetic direction of the art of film. And when digital technology was not integrated into the film and photography industry decades ago, people could only keep making films within the known limits and valuing the content of the film. This in turn prevented the profession of cinematography and production from exercising its professional competence. And when digital technology officially entered the film and television production industry, the capabilities of the photography and production profession were officially opened up. At the same time, the profession of photography and production had to be transformed, retaining traditional production techniques and photographic thinking, but also incorporating the modern features of digital technology to become a film and television technology that could stand on its own.

3.3 Digital Technology Provides Innovative Ideas for the Film and Television Industry

In the course of its development, the film and television industry usually makes every effort to avoid entering into the genre film creation trend. In reality, however, after many years of development, the choice of subjects and forms of filmmaking is largely based on a fixed range. This is an inevitable situation for the art industry, as it is for the music and painting industries. Digital technology has a fictional character, and fiction means that the creators of art have more scope for development. Currently, some realistic films also make use of digital technology, using compositing techniques to make the main characters appear in the same frame in a film, for example. Thus, digital technology is also providing the film industry with innovative ideas to help cinematographers and producers to innovate in their field of expertise [3].

4 Research on the Reform of the Curriculum of Film and Television Photography and Production Based on the Background of Ant Colony Algorithm

4.1 Basic courses

(1) Confirmation of teaching objectives and curriculum goals

The basic courses mainly run within the first and second semesters, and it is necessary to confirm the talent training objectives of the film and television photography and production major first. With the digital technology context as the main focus, the talent cultivation goal of the film and television photography and production major is to cultivate film and television photography and production professionals with digital technology application thinking, and professional practical ability. To address this, the university should offer courses in art and design, photography, directing, sound and editing creation at the foundation course stage. The foundation courses should be characterised by the need to be detailed but not repetitive. Different skills should be divided into different course structures, but there also needs to be some connection between the different courses. In this way, students can link the different knowledge points as they engage with the individual courses. Each institution has a different teaching style, and the school can choose different main courses as a basis on top of the in-school teaching, and then add digital technology-related content.

(2) Curriculum construction

It is important to update the equipment or tools used in the school as part of the foundation programme. Each activity room can be equipped with functional computer equipment, and the value of the equipment can be guaranteed. Each class that enters the activity room to participate in the exercises should be reported in advance to the activity room manager. In order to achieve a high quality of supervision, a schedule of times for each class to use the activity room could be set in advance and given to the manager, who would then be responsible for monitoring that the room is used in the required manner. Students in Film and Video Photography and Production will enter the activity room at a set time and, after watching the teacher in action, edit the video according to the textbook or task list. However, it is clear from observing the actual teaching process that most students' main activity time is concentrated outside of class, i.e. they will work on the basics of photography skills and modelling techniques after completing their classroom learning tasks. Therefore, teachers should also be required to set staged learning tasks when conducting foundation courses. This means that teachers can use a semester as a limit for different course content and ask students to complete tasks individually or in small groups. Tasks could be set as simple photo competitions, or short videos with a fixed theme, etc. Students must use digital technology to populate the video work, making sure to apply their knowledge of digital technology, to the work. This form of education and teaching can, on the one hand, consolidate students' mastery of the basic knowledge of film and television photography and production, and, on the other hand, exercise their practical skills and help them to become familiar with the professional working mode of film and television photography and production in the context of digital technology.

4.2 Professional Practice Courses

(1) Confirmation of teaching objectives and curriculum goals

Professional practice teaching courses refer to the practical courses conducted within the campus. The teaching objectives of professional practice courses are to develop students' mastery of professional practice skills in film and television photography and production in an on-campus environment. For example, camera skills, directing skills, editing skills and a sense of the application of digital technology. The course is characterised by two things. One, the in-school practical course is run by in-school teachers. Teachers use contextual or task-based teaching methods more often in the course of delivering the course. Teachers provide more assistance to students and can fully exercise their practical skills. Secondly, the on-campus practical course is based on studios and laboratories, which can exercise students' professional skills but cannot develop students' practical experience in film and television photography and production [4]. The course is set up with the objective that students need to really exercise their professional practical skills. Teachers need to reduce their own dominant role in the course and make students the central members of the practical teaching. The number of practical courses can be limited to a certain number, and the practical teaching can be in the form of integrated teaching mode, so as to exercise the comprehensive strength of students in a limited time.

(2) Construction of the curriculum

The professional practice courses are basically carried out in the studio or in the editing laboratory. Teachers are responsible for consolidating theoretical knowledge for students and setting learning objectives for them. Students need to be taught or guided by the teacher to complete the practical objectives set by the teacher. Teachers can set practical sessions using digital technology and students can use their own artistic aesthetics to engage in practice. In addition to retaining some basic practical courses, teachers can also include some new practical courses in media management, or new media practice courses on the internet, etc. This will enable students to develop their professional skills in the new media environment, and will enable them to develop a stronger grasp of professional application skills in a digital technology context. In practical courses, teachers can include simulations, for example, by asking students to form specific film and television photography and production teams to work with other students in the school. In the process, students can gain real work experience. Students can work for students on campus, opening up avenues of work on campus. They can also provide short video services or photography services for various departmental events. By combining practical courses with real work, students can develop their practical skills as well as their language coordination skills. However, the teacher needs to play the role of a monitor during the students' creative process, i.e. to regularly observe the progress of the students' work, remind them to use digital technology to create, etc. The students need to be able to create new ideas in the practical sessions, not just the same ones.

4.3 Industrial Practice Courses

Industrial practice is directly oriented towards internships, i.e. students are required to work in film and television companies or other internal partners to participate in actual film and television photography and production work. The university has two types of industrial practice courses, one of which is conducted within the school's training base. The second is an in-company practical training course. To conduct the practical training courses within the school, the school and the enterprise can run in a co-operative way, i.e. the courses within the school will be integrated with the actual work in the society, but managed by the school alone, with the enterprise as the supervisor for the co-operation. The enterprise is responsible for docking the work with the teachers. After the enterprise has given the work objectives or work instructions, the students in the school will complete the work project within a specified period of time. The work project is professionally appraised by the enterprise after it has application value. A professional work team consisting of students in film and television photography and production can formally complete the docking with the enterprise. The enterprise will send special educators and staff into the institution to play a management and industry practice education role. Helping students within the school to better integrate with the digital technology context.

5 Conclusion

In summary, this paper has conducted a more in-depth research and analysis of the idea of reforming the curriculum system construction of film and television photography and production based on the background of ant colony algorithm. The research results show that the school curriculum is divided into basic courses, professional practice courses and industrial practice courses. Based on the ant colony algorithm, it has a positive impact on improving the standard of education and teaching in film and television photography and production.

With the continuous development of information technology, there are some evaluation systems supported by computers. For example, the automatic scoring system for programming test developed by Harbin Institute of technology can carry out on-board tests at the middle and end of the term. It can not only test the students' program running results, but also analyze some errors in the process and give reasonable scores, which is very close to the scoring results of teachers' personnel. This is similar to the way coursera and others use simple online testing, and udacity and EDX use the combination of online testing and training and examination center. Through the collection and analysis of students' learning process data, they can timely feed back evaluation opinions on students' learning situation, so as to truly test students' learning effect.

References

1. Chulei, Z.: Reflections on the core strategies of brand construction of film and television photography and production in private independent colleges. Talent **27**, 59 (2018)
2. Haojie, Y., Jining, L., Mo, M.: Reform of the curriculum system of film and television photography and production based on the CDIO concept. China Educ. Technol. Equip. **22**, 116–118 (2015)
3. Chuncheng, A.: Exploring the integration of learning and production in film and television photography in local applied colleges and universities. West. Radio Telev. **4**, 22–23 (2016)
4. Wei, S.: Exploration of internationalized teaching of media art in art colleges and universities_Taking the cooperative school project of Nanjing Arts College School of Media as an example. Young J. **35**, 117–118 (2017)

Quality Evaluation Model of Preschool Art Education Based on Deep Learning Theory

Lijuan Zhong(✉)

Xianyang Normal University, Xianyang 712000, Shaanxi, China
holyzhong@163.com

Abstract. In order to solve the problem that the expression ability and generalization ability of shallow learning network to complex functions are limited, and to improve the accuracy of preschool art education quality evaluation, a preschool art education quality evaluation method based on deep learning network is proposed. Starting from the creation of preschool art education environment, the quality of preschool art education and children's development, this paper constructs a preschool art education quality evaluation index system including three primary indicators and nine secondary indicators. Take the secondary index in the evaluation index system as the input of the deep learning network, optimize the weights of each layer of the deep learning network by using the unsupervised pre training model, determine the conditional probability distribution and joint probability distribution of each layer in the restricted Boltzmann machine based on the bottom-up unsupervised learning process, and the output layer optimizes the parameters of each layer according to the input DMOS value, Build a regression model between the abstract primary index and DMOS value, and predict and obtain the objective evaluation results of the quality of preschool art education according to the regression model.

Keywords: Deep learning network · Preschool art education · Quality assessment · Index system

1 Introduction

With the development of the times, people increasingly realize the importance of preschool education to children. Preschool art education is related to children's future development. Enlightening children's artistic talent is the first and key step in children's art growth. Nowadays, the development of psychology and physiology is no longer a new product, and gradually makes early childhood education perfect. People have a further understanding of children's art education. The educational goal of early preschool art takes professional skills as this standard and ignores children's development in other fields, which is reflected at home and abroad. Art class is not simply to let children draw and cultivate children's imagination and aesthetic ability [1]. For example, some parents believe that art can calm ADHD children. These art classes can be done, but the real art class is more than that. Until the end of the 19th century and the beginning of the

M. A. Jan and F. Khan (Eds.): BigIoT-EDU 2022, LNICST 465, pp. 506–517, 2023.
https://doi.org/10.1007/978-3-031-23950-2_55

20th century, some people began to pay attention to children's preschool art education. With the continuous efforts of educators studying children's art, children's preschool art class was gradually valued, and then began to pay attention to children's imagination and creativity. Today's preschool art education is not only a single subject, but also applicable to other fields, and can help children in need. Children's art education can also treat autistic children, and has a certain effect. In foreign countries, art learning has been regarded as a means of treating autism. The performance of autistic children is to close themselves and do not communicate with the outside world, but they can express their hearts and convey their inner world to the outside world through painting.

The basic goal of preschool art in kindergarten is to "learn and master simple art knowledge and skills, cultivate children's preliminary expressiveness, and make children germinate aesthetic interest". Mastering art knowledge and painting skills is a necessary condition for art teachers to engage in art teacher profession. Through preschool art education, children's cognitive ability, emotion and attitude have been developed [2]. In the outline of the national medium and long-term education reform and development plan, it is pointed out that it is necessary to guide kindergartens and families to implement scientific education, promote the comprehensive and harmonious development of children's body and mind, and formulate the learning and Development Guide for children aged 3–6, which is referred to as the guide, which lists in detail what goals should be achieved at each stage.

Preschool art education includes aesthetic perception and expression education, creativity education, aesthetic culture education, social and life education and personality growth education. The purpose of setting up art courses in preschool art education major is to train preschool teachers and students to make full use of the art knowledge and skills learned in the future education and teaching work to guide children to feel and create beauty and stimulate the all-round development of children's mind [3]. The teaching quality of art education of preschool art education specialty directly affects the overall level of early childhood education in the future, and is the premise and guarantee for the all-round development of children in the future.

At present, the worldwide attention to preschool art education has generally increased, the development speed and school scale of preschool art education have continued to increase, and the construction modes of preschool art education institutions are more diverse. The national guidance direction for preschool art education becomes clearer with the increase of attention. On the basis of improving the development speed of preschool art education and improving the difficult problems of preschool art education for preschool children, we pay more attention to the quality of preschool art education [4]. Therefore, it is of great significance to study a systematic, scientific and complete evaluation method for the educational quality of preschool art education institutions.

As an important part of machine learning, deep learning network is based on the neural network description data of constructing and simulating human brain analysis and learning. Its main advantages are strong modeling ability and high representation accuracy. It can effectively solve the problem that the expression ability and generalization ability of the commonly used shallow learning network for complex functions are limited under the condition of limited samples and calculation units. Based on this, this paper studies the quality evaluation method of preschool art education based on deep learning network.

2 Overview of Deep Learning Algorithms

Deep learning was first proposed in 1986. It extends from the field of machine learning. Its powerful representation learning ability and automatic feature mining ability can get good results. Therefore, it is widely used in computer vision, natural language processing and other fields, and has developed rapidly in recent ten years.

In natural language processing tasks, more and more studies use deep learning to represent text, and apply the training results to downstream tasks. Traditional natural language processing tasks often represent words by means of independent hot coding. This high-dimensional representation method is very easy to cause dimensional disaster when there are many kinds of words in the corpus. Because deep learning abstracts the original data such as multilinear and nonlinear changes, its representation learning ability is much stronger than the traditional representation method, which can greatly improve the problem of dimensional disaster. In recent years, in the research of natural language processing, the use of deep learning for distributed representation is more widely applicable than the traditional single hot and word bag representation [5]. At the same time, using deep learning to pre train word vectors for a large number of texts such as Wikipedia has also been verified to speed up the training convergence and improve the universality of word vectors in natural language processing tasks.

As the basic unit of neural network, neuron plays an important role in understanding the concept of neural network. Neurons, also known as perceptrons, were very popular in the 1950s and 1960s and successfully solved many problems at that time. The mathematical model of a neuron is shown in Fig. 1.

As can be seen from the above figure, a neuron consists of the following three parts:

Input weight: a neuron can receive multiple inputs, each input corresponds to a weight, and there is also a bias term.

Activation function: there are many kinds of activation functions of neurons. The neurons in Fig. 1 choose step function. In addition, relu function and sigmoid function are often used as activation functions of neural networks.

Output: the output of neurons can be calculated by the following formula

$$y = f(w \cdot x + b) \tag{1}$$

where W is the weight, X is the input, B is the offset term, and F is the activation function.

2.1 Artificial Neural Network

The development history of artificial intelligence can be summarized as three waves, and the first wave can be called artificial neural network. Artificial neural network is the cornerstone of deep learning. Its original inspiration comes from the work of mathematician Pitts and psychologist mcculloch l26) in biological neurons. Hopfield put forward the neural network model and the application of back propagation in training and learning in the 1920s, which solved the problem that the neural network perception layer can

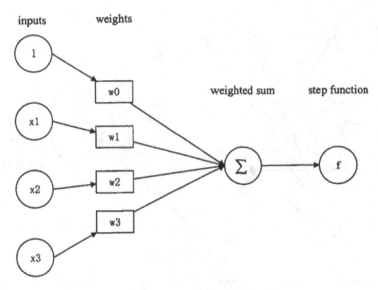

inputs   weights

Fig. 1. Neuron mathematical model

not be trained and the linear propagation information gain is poor, and greatly promoted the development of neural network [6]. This is the second wave of artificial intelligence, as shown in Fig. 2.

However, artificial neural networks also have many fatal problems, which are mainly divided into: the nonlinear propagation of multi-layer perception leads to a large number of local optima, and the gradient descent becomes extremely difficult; With the accumulation of network layers, the memory consumed by model training is too large, and the training time is difficult to accept; The gradient dissipation of multilayer neural network leads to the failure of complete back propagation of error, and the model iteration lacks the most critical gradient descent direction, which makes it difficult to converge to the stable value [7]. The development of artificial intelligence fell into silence due to the harsh hardware environment and the bottleneck of mathematical computing research at that time.

2.2 Deep Confidence Network

At the end of last century, the classical machine learning algorithm SVM (support vector machines) was born. The algorithm has the advantages of low training complexity, low parameter adjustment requirements and high discrimination ability of small samples. The algorithm has quickly become the mainstream research direction of machine learning and guided the deep learning to rise again.

In 2006, with the development of machine learning and the improvement of mathematical theory, the training algorithms of deep belief network (DBN) and restricted Boltzmann machine (RBM) were proposed. The founder Hinton made use of the advantages of supervised learning and unsupervised learning to coordinate the advantages and disadvantages of supervised and unsupervised learning during initialization parameters

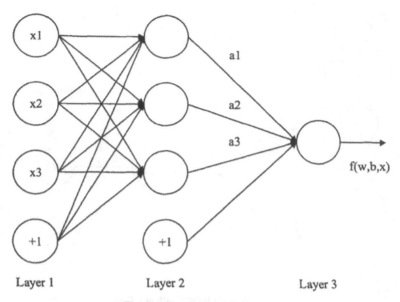

Fig. 2. Neural network diagram

and network training, which made the model converge rapidly, and solved the problems that the iteration of the model left over by artificial neural network in the last century lacked the most critical gradient descent direction, resulting in difficulty in converging to the stable value [8]. At the same time, people have gradually found the importance of data for training network. Scholars in the early 20th century began to accumulate a large amount of data silently, and artificial intelligence is waiting for his third climax.

2.3 Deep Convolution Neural Network

With the rise of the big data era and the vigorous development of basic matrix computing hardware GPU, artificial intelligence finally shines brightly in the Imagenet competition in 2012. Krizhevsky et al. Won the competition with convolutional neural network and beat other traditional image processing algorithms and traditional machine learning algorithms, For the first time, the interactive shallow model training and learning algorithm is greatly developed. Four years later, alphago, developed by Google, was invincible in the go competition with a variety of in-depth learning algorithms. It successively challenged the top go players and won results, and even changed the pattern and competition mode of the whole go competition. So far, artificial intelligence has become a household name. Major business circles, industrial circles and academic circles have made every effort to develop in-depth learning algorithms [9]. At the same time, people outside the industry began to pay attention to and look forward to the improvement of life brought by artificial intelligence.

Because the structural characteristics of cyclic neural network and long-term and short-term memory network can solve most of the problems of processing language sequences, most of the current research work adopts this chain structure neural network.

However, because their state at each time depends on the input at that time and the state at the previous time, they can only process language sequences serially, which greatly reduces the efficiency [10].

As a typical parallel feature processor, convolutional neural network is widely used in image processing tasks, but it was first proposed for natural language processing tasks in 2014.186. The network structure of convolutional neural network includes convolution layer, pooling layer and full connection layer. The changes to its network structure when processing language sequences are shown in Fig. 3.

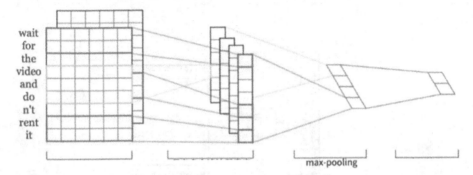

Fig. 3. Convolutional neural network structure

Compared with cyclic neural networks and long-term and short-term memory networks, convolutional neural networks have the following advantages: 1) because convolution operations can be carried out in parallel, its parallel ability is higher; 2) Due to the structural characteristics of sliding window, it can capture more context information; 3) Due to the characteristics of sequential sliding of sliding window, it can record the information of relative position in text. However, because the size of the sliding window directly determines the distance to capture word dependencies, dependencies between words beyond the window cannot be captured. In order to break through the limitation that convolutional neural network can not capture long-distance dependence characteristics, relevant studies have improved convolutional neural network from two aspects: one is to change the sliding window of continuous coverage into discontinuous coverage without changing the depth of convolution layer, that is, void convolution [11]; The second is to deepen the depth of the convolution layer so that the upper and lower coverage windows are superimposed. At present, in addition to text classification, convolutional neural network is also widely used in natural language processing tasks such as relationship extraction and sentence repetition recognition.

3   Evaluation Method of Preschool Education Quality Based on Deep Learning Network

3.1   Construction of Quality Evaluation Index System of Preschool Art Education

The construction of preschool art education quality evaluation index system is the basis of preschool art education quality evaluation. Build a preschool art education quality evaluation index system composed of three primary indicators: the creation of preschool art education environment, the quality of preschool art education and child development, as shown in Fig. 4.

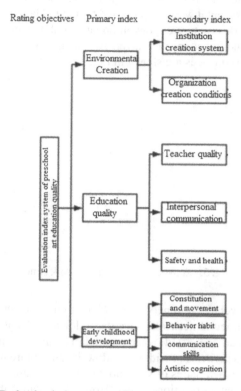

Fig. 4. Evaluation index system of preschool art education quality

The creation of preschool art education environment includes two secondary indicators: the creation system of preschool art education institutions and the creation conditions of preschool art education institutions, which respectively describe the school running mode adopted by preschool art education institutions and the hardware and software facilities used in preschool art education and teaching activities. The establishment system of preschool art education institutions includes two main contents: the establishment thought and management mechanism of preschool art education institutions; The establishment conditions of preschool art education institutions include three main contents: infrastructure and equipment, staffing, scale and class [12].

The quality of preschool art education includes three secondary indicators: Teachers' quality, interpersonal communication and safety and health. Teacher quality refers to the working ability of preschool art educators, including teacher qualification, teaching skills, professional ethics and curriculum management. Interpersonal communication refers to the ability of pre-school art educators to communicate and interact with preschool children and parents. Safety and health refers to the ability of preschool art education institutions to meet the most basic physiological and safety needs of preschool children, including education/health care management, traffic safety management and meal management. Early childhood development includes four secondary indicators: physique and movement, behavior habits, communication skills and artistic cognition. Physique and movement refer to the normal development level of physiological function of preschool children; Behavior habit refers to the self-care ability of preschool children in their daily life; Communication ability refers to the ability of preschool children to convey their emotions through their accumulated vocabulary; Artistic cognition refers to the ability of preschool children to appreciate the beauty and artistic expression of simple natural phenomena around them based on the mastery of basic knowledge.

3.2 Evaluation Method Based on Deep Learning Network

(1) Deep learning network

The deep learning network has an input layer, multiple hidden layers and an output layer, and its hierarchical structure is very similar to that of human brain. In the deep learning network, there is only connection between adjacent nodes, and there is no connection between nodes in the same layer or different layers. Each layer in the deep learning network can be defined as a logistic regression model [13]. The hidden layer in the deep learning network model contains several restricted Boltzmann machines. By superimposing several restricted Boltzmann machines, the deep Boltzmann machine learning network can be constructed, as shown in Fig. 5 (a). When the structure closer to the visual layer and the structure farther from the visual layer are built using Bayesian belief network and restricted Boltzmann mechanism respectively, the constructed network is depth information network, as shown in Fig. 5 (b).

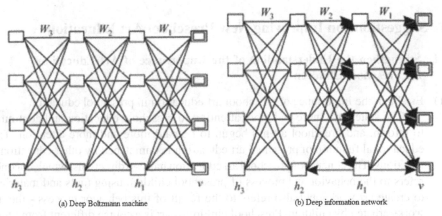

(a) Deep Boltzmann machine   (b) Deep information network

Fig. 5. Depth Boltzmann machine and depth information network structure

In Fig. 5, V and H represent the visible layer and the hidden layer, respectively. The restricted Boltzmann machine is trained layer by layer in a bottom-up manner, the weights w are obtained through pre training, and the weights of each layer of the deep learning network are optimized by using the unsupervised pre training model, which can abstract the simple features. The input of the visual layer is each secondary index a in the preschool art education quality evaluation index system, and the number of nodes of the input layer and the output layer is set. The nodes of the hidden layers H1, H2 and H3 are 100.

In the bottom-up unsupervised learning process, each layer is defined as a restricted Boltzmann machine. The greedy learning method is used to train the weight of each layer layer layer by layer from bottom to top. The first layer and other layers construct Gaussian binary restricted Boltzmann machine and binary binary restricted Boltzmann machine respectively. There is no correlation between the visible layer nodes and the hidden layer nodes in the restricted Boltzmann machine, which describes the conditional probability distribution and joint probability distribution of each layer in the restricted Boltzmann machine.

$$\begin{cases} E(t)\dot{x}_d(t) = f(t, x_d(t)) + B(t)u_d(t) \\ y_d(t) = C(t)x_d(t) \end{cases} \tag{2}$$

(2) Evaluation process

In the training stage, the in-depth learning network is used to abstract describe the input's preschool art education evaluation indicators, and the in-depth learning network of each indicator is constructed according to the input's preschool art education evaluation indicators, using dbna, DBN. And dbnag. In the testing stage, the characteristics of each index of any preschool art education institution to be tested are defined. Dbna, dbna, and DBN obtained through training. Predict and obtain the evaluation results Q*, q "and Q% of each index respectively, and combine the evaluation results of three indexes to obtain the evaluation results of preschool art education quality of preschool art education institutions to be tested.

4   Suggestions on Improving New Preschool Art Education

4.1   Strengthen the Understanding of the Importance of Art Education for Preschool Children

(1)   Establish the importance of preschool art education in preschool education

The state pays more and more attention to preschool education and continues to reform, and preschool art has begun to be paid more and more attention. The educational function of preschool art education is unmatched by other educational functions. The concept of preschool art education has two directions, which not only refers to the behavior and process of preschool children using tools and materials to create art works, but also refers to the result of this behavior process - the art works created by children. Preschool children's art is a course different from other education. It really takes children as the main body. Among many disciplines, it is difficult to divide disciplines according to age. Therefore, it is difficult for you to hear children's Chinese, children's mathematics, children's physics and so on. The recipient of children's art is children, and the creator is also children. This is something that other disciplines cannot ignore. Such as children's music, the receiver is children, but the creator is adults; The same is true of children's dance. Although the performers are children, the choreographers are adults. Therefore, the creator of children's art is children, which is different from other children's disciplines.

(2) Increase investment in preschool art education

1) Investment in educational talents. Talents are the most scarce in the 21st century. With the development of science and technology society, talents are becoming more and more scarce. The teacher team of preschool children's art education also needs teachers with certain professional level and teaching quality. Therefore, the key to preschool art is to increase the investment of children's art teachers. Teachers are the foundation of education. A good teacher will affect a child's life. Kindergartens should first carry out subject teaching for teachers, have professional art teachers to teach, introduce art teachers with art skills and educational theory, and try to avoid the phenomenon that one teacher in one class takes all courses. As mentioned above, art courses are different from other courses. The theme of children's art is children, which is the works created by children themselves. Professional teachers are needed for guiding education, which can not be replaced by any other curriculum teachers. Children are at different ages and have different courses, so how to learn and how to teach needs a professional teacher to guide education. To understand the importance of teachers' talents, we should increase investment in time, which can not only improve the teaching quality of kindergarten art education, but also cultivate children's correct art concept and contribute to children's art road in the future.

2) Investment in environmental creation. Through this survey, we know that the amount of art investment in a kindergarten directly affects the teaching quality of children's art. Under the guidance of the idea that the environment plays an educational role in children, kindergartens continue to study and explore how to provide children with a high-quality educational environment. The good art environment provided by the kindergarten should not be simply understood as the simple furnishings of items in the kindergarten. The environment of the kindergarten should be a place to stimulate children's imagination and artistic creation. The creation of environment should be arranged according to different age stages, and timely change according to the changes of four seasons or popular culture, local history and culture or characteristic food, so as to give children a different art atmosphere and imperceptibly edify children's artistic aesthetic ability. The creation of the environment is not only simple and understandable life common sense and theoretical knowledge, but also artistic lines, color blocks and handicrafts. Fully involving children in creation can not only exercise children's subjective initiative, but also promote children's desire to protect handmade and wall paintings. Environmental innovation is not only the personal responsibility of teachers, but also the common responsibility of all children.

4.2 Improve the Strength of Teachers

The role of teachers is the expected behavior of teachers related to their social status and identity. In society, teachers are given a high status. Teachers' educational background, teaching experience and teaching ability are regarded as the capital of teachers' employment. No parents choose teachers without considering these problems. Teachers' words and deeds will affect the development of students. In teaching activities, teachers teach students art knowledge and affect students' understanding of art. At the same time, the emotion, attitude and values of art teachers will imperceptibly penetrate into the classroom. A qualified art teacher should have rich art knowledge and theory, comprehensive art skills, extensive scientific and cultural knowledge, energetic creativity, and certain teaching ability. Schools can take this as a standard to strictly require teachers to keep learning and reading. So as to improve their teaching ability and professional knowledge.

5 Conclusion

Preschool art education is the main part of early childhood education and the basis of art education. It can realize all the educational values contained in art education to the greatest extent and give full play to the educational function of beauty. The comprehensive quality of preschool art teachers directly affects the overall level of early childhood education, so it is particularly important to cultivate the comprehensive quality of preschool art teachers. This paper studies the quality evaluation method of preschool art education based on deep learning network, inputs the quality evaluation index of preschool art education into the constructed deep learning network for training, and uses the trained deep learning network to obtain more accurate quality evaluation results of preschool art education. In the follow-up research process, we will continue to optimize the method in this paper Gradually improve the teaching quality of preschool art education institutions and realize the dream of strengthening education.

Acknowledgements. 2019 Xianyang Normal University Education and Teaching Reform and Research Project "Art Curriculum System Reform and Innovation Research of Preschool Education under the Background of Excellent Preschool Teachers Training" Project No.: 2019Y17.

References

1. Ge, D., Wang, X., Liu, J.: A teaching quality evaluation model for preschool teachers based on deep learning. Int. J. Emerg. Technol. Learn. (iJET) **16**(3), 127 (2021)
2. Wiggins, L.D., Rubenstein, E., Windham, G., et al.: Evaluation of sex differences in preschool children with and without autism spectrum disorder enrolled in the study to explore early development. Res. Dev. Disabil. **112**(2), 103897 (2021)
3. Cattani, B.C., Lago, V., Bandeira, D.R.: The evaluation of preschool children in family courts: expert practices of judicial psychologists. Quaderns de Psicologia **23**(1), 1648 (2021)
4. Tafiadis, D., Zarokanellou, V., Voniati, L., et al.: Evaluation of Diadochokinesis in Greek preschoolers with speech sound disorders using a Diadochokinetic rates protocol. Commun. Disorders Q. **43**, 152574012110170 (2021)

5. Piffer, S.: Outcome evaluation of the visual preschool screening in the province of Trento North East Italy. Biomed. J. Sci. Techn. Res. **35**, 27956–27961(2021)
6. Basaran, M., Dursun, B., Yilmaz, G.: Evaluation of Preschool education program according to CIPP model. Pedagogical Res. **6**(2), 91 (2021)
7. Kse, M., Koyiit, M., Erdem, C., et al.: An evaluation of accessibility to preschool education institutions using geographic information systems. Educ. Inf. Technol. **26**(7), 4307–4328 (2021)
8. Daniels, B., Bender, S.L., Briesch, A.M., et al.: Expanding daily report card intervention to the preschool setting: evaluation of effectiveness and usability for teachers and parents. Contemp. School Psychol. (2021)
9. Bauminger-Zviely, N., Shefer, A.: Naturalistic evaluation of preschoolers' spontaneous interactions: The Autism Peer Interaction Observation Scale. Autism **25**, 136236132198991 (2021)
10. Zhang, H., Li, J., Su, X., et al.: Growth charts for individualized evaluation of brain morphometry for preschool children (2021)
11. Ylmaz, A., Akar, N., Yldz, E., et al.: Evaluation of 2013 preschool curriculum objectives and indicators according to revised Bloom's taxonomy. Uluslararas Eitim Programlar ve retim almalar Dergisi (2021)
12. Kuset, S., Zgem, K., Amacolu, E., et al.: Evaluation of the impact of distance education on children in preschool period: teachers' opinions. Near East Univ. Online J. Educ. **4**(1), 78–87 (2021)
13. Wha, B.C., Kim, S.Y., Uk, L.S., et al.: Quality evaluation model of artificial intelligence service for startups. Int. J. Entrepreneurial Behav. Res. **12**, 255–283 (2021)

Education Targeted Poverty Alleviation System Under Cloud Computing

Wang Yaoqing[✉]

Xi'an Polytechnic University, Xi'an 710600, Shaanxi, China
18234507281@163.com

Abstract. At present, all parts of China are vigorously carrying out targeted poverty alleviation through education. Poverty alleviation is an important measure for the country to promote the construction of a well-off society in an all-round way and plays an important role in improving people's livelihood and promoting economic development. However, there are still many problems in poverty alleviation, especially in education. Most of them pay more attention to the construction of hardware, but ignore the improvement of software, pay more attention to theoretical education, but ignore the practical application of education. This paper mainly studies the problems existing in education targeted Poverty alleviation, and puts forward some solutions based on cloud computing technology, so as to provide reference for domestic education targeted poverty alleviation.

Keywords: Targeted poverty alleviation · Education cloud computing

1 Introduction

Building a well-off society in an all-round way is the common expectation of individuals, society and even the country. Since the 19th CPC National Congress, China's poverty alleviation and development has entered a decisive period. This is not only a great leap forward in China's poverty alleviation, but also a strong push forward in realizing the great rejuvenation of the Chinese nation. The promotion of targeted poverty alleviation is an important layout for the country to build a well-off society in an all-round way. The 19th National Congress to the 20th National Congress is an important node in the objectives of the "two centenaries" (the 100th anniversary of the founding of the Communist Party of China and the 100th anniversary of the founding of new China). The first Centennial plan is about to end. At the same time, it is also necessary to start a new journey of a socialist modern country and start towards the second Centennial plan. Poverty alleviation is an important starting point for the realization of the two Centennial plans.

Poverty alleviation and development is a social project that the Chinese government has paid close attention to and vigorously promoted since the early stage of reform and opening up. In many poverty alleviation and development studies, there is the most lasting and close relationship between education and poverty alleviation. In practice, poverty

M. A. Jan and F. Khan (Eds.): BigIoT-EDU 2022, LNICST 465, pp. 518–529, 2023.
https://doi.org/10.1007/978-3-031-23950-2_56

alleviation through education first means "supporting the poverty of education", that is, education has always been the main position and key field of poverty alleviation and development, It regards education as the goal, task, content or field of poverty alleviation, and finally realizes poverty reduction and poverty alleviation in the field of education through various means and methods such as policy preference, increasing investment and adjusting structure.

Looking at the past and present, looking at China and foreign countries, it is difficult to eliminate poverty from its root if we only rely on material poverty alleviation. Spiritual poverty makes poverty factors more stubborn in poor families, and the intergenerational transmission of poverty is difficult to disintegrate. In order to control poverty, we should help the poor objects economically and improve their lives. More importantly, we should cut off the growth context of poverty factors from the root and level the soil for poverty growth [1]. Education has improved the professional consciousness and life concept of the poor people and solved the problem of insufficient subjective initiative. Poor people can absorb the energy of production and life in education and get rid of poverty by relying on their own knowledge and skills. At the same time, we can also consolidate the achievements of vocational skill learning and prevent the phenomenon of returning to poverty by participating in lifelong education training. Therefore, this paper is based on cloud computing technology education targeted poverty alleviation research.

2 Related Work

2.1 Cloud Computing Concept

Cloud is a metaphor of network and Internet. In the past, cloud was often used to represent telecom network in images, and later it was also used to represent the abstraction of Internet and underlying infrastructure.

Cloud computing is a dynamic and scalable network application infrastructure based on Internet services, with virtualization technology as the core and low cost as the goal. Users pay for relevant services according to their use needs.

The cloud computing mode is very similar to the centralized power supply mode of national power plants (power plants provide points and users pay for them). In the cloud computing mode, cloud computing provides hardware facilities (server, memory, hard disk) and various application software that users can't see or touch. Users only need to access the Internet, pay for the resources they need, and then send instructions and receive data to the "cloud" through the browser. Basically, they don't have to do anything. They can use the computing resources, storage space, various application software and other resources of the cloud service provider to meet their needs.

These resources in the cloud computing mode can be provided quickly, requiring little management work by users or little interaction with service providers. Cloud computing allows you to experience the computing power of 10 trillion times per second. With such powerful computing power, you can simulate nuclear explosions, predict climate change and market trends.

Cloud Computing Goals

The ultimate goal of cloud computing is to provide computing, services and applications to people as a public facility, so that people can use computer resources like water, electricity, gas and telephone.

Users do not need to have visible and tangible hardware facilities, nor do they need to pay for equipment power supply, air conditioning and refrigeration, special maintenance and other expenses for the computer room, nor do they need to wait for a long supply cycle, project implementation and other lengthy time. They only need to remit money to the cloud computing service provider, and they will get the required services immediately.

In the cloud computing environment, users' use concept has also changed from "purchasing products" to "purchasing services", which also promotes the development of the business model of cloud services.

Cloud Computing Features

Cloud computing is to distribute computing on a large number of distributed computers rather than local computers or remote servers. The operation of enterprise data center will be more similar to the Internet. This enables enterprises to switch resources to needed applications and access computers and storage systems according to their needs.

It is like changing from the old single generator mode to the centralized power supply mode of the power plant. It means that computing power can also be circulated as a commodity, just like gas and hydropower, with convenient access and low cost. The biggest difference is that it is transmitted through the Internet. The cloud computing system is shown in Fig. 1 below.

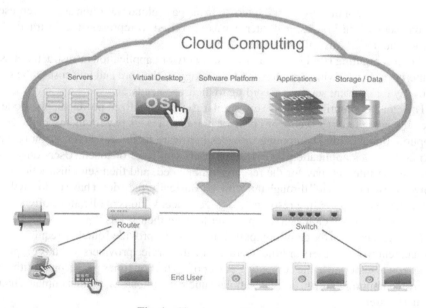

Fig. 1. Cloud computing system

2.2 Targeted Poverty Alleviation in Education

1. Remote schools or teaching sites mainly radiate the economically underdeveloped areas in rural areas, with poor students, poor school buildings, inconvenient transportation and meager wages. Their value and welfare are greater than education itself, so it is difficult to attract teachers to work for a long time.

2. For remote schools and teaching sites, the State implements various standard thinning projects, mainly allocating certain funds to strengthen school buildings and replace teaching equipment. Generally speaking, it is certainly good, but it is also a plan to kill many birds with one stone: strengthening school buildings and improving the campus environment can generate income for local migrant workers, but the projects can only be contracted by a few teams, and the project quality is not flattered, One can't say it's fishy; The replacement of teaching equipment, such as old equipment eliminated by urban schools, outdated products that are unsalable by enterprises, all kinds of inferior teaching aids, stationery, desks and chairs, pulling network cables, and purchasing all kinds of online school services, are all public procurement prices. Although they are not better than replacement, there is no need to say that they are fishy [2]; For the construction of teachers, the investment is mainly focused on various short-term training, mainly looking for online schools, urban schools and lecturers with high professional titles, and doing many kinds of inefficient and ineffective things at the price of public services purchased by the government. The problem of increasing the income of rural teachers is basically unchanged. The final result is that everyone has increased the income except rural teachers, There is no end to the fishiness.

3. Old rural teachers will not use new equipment, new teachers who can use new equipment can not stay, and the phenomenon of idle equipment is very common. In addition to going to the peak to check and take photos for political achievements, it is basically not used at other times.

4. The attempt to replace teachers with equipment, implement distance education and improve remote rural education with weak teachers is a bubble blown by the capital of online schools, which is specially used to cooperate with the peak promotion eager for quick success and instant benefit. Unwilling to spend a lot of money to build a stable and high-quality team of rural teachers, but using this kind of commercial marketing, money making feast and political achievement project, it is really limited and pitiful to improve the declining rural education.

5. It's just pity for most of these children who can't go to high school. When they were young, they had to endure the company of their parents or poverty. They received an education far inferior to their peers in urban areas, but they had to accept a unified standard of social division of labor in adulthood. Everything, roughly speaking, is decided at the moment of birth.

2.3 Cloud Computing

Cloud computing is the product of the integration and development of parallel computing, grid computing, virtualization, distributed computing, network storage, load balancing and other technologies. The most key technologies include data management technology, parallel programming model, data storage technology, cloud computing platform management technology, virtualization technology and so on. The data storage technologies widely used in cloud computing systems mainly include Google File System (GFS), BigTable, HDFS, the open source implementation of GFS developed by Amazon dynamo and Hadoop team. BigTable is a distributed storage system designed to manage structured data. The most widely used model in parallel programming model is MapReduce proposed by Google. MapReduce can process TB or Pb level massive data concurrently [3]. At present, MapReduce is the most widely used representative Hadoop and spark, as a typical data batch processing technology, are widely used in the fields of big data mining, data analysis, machine learning and so on. The virtualization technology of cloud computing can enable a single server to support multiple virtual machines and run multiple operating systems and applications, so as to greatly improve the utilization of the server.

One of the important applications of cloud computing technology is to build a big data mining platform. Virtualization technology in cloud computing technology can divide a single resource into a splitting mode of multiple virtual resources, or integrate multiple resources into an aggregation mode of virtual resources. It is a key technology for the full integration and efficient utilization of various computing and storage resources, which can maximize the data processing speed and improve the mining efficiency. The data storage technology in cloud computing technology uses tens of thousands of cheap storage devices to form a huge storage center. These heterogeneous storage devices aggregate scattered and low reliable resources into a whole with high reliability and high scalability through their respective distributed file systems, which can effectively solve the problem of big data storage [4]. Parallelizing data mining algorithms through the parallelization programming model in cloud computing is the mainstream idea of fast big data mining.

The transfer of applications, data, information and other resources from the cloud to end users (regional security communication control administrators and controlled users) requires a highly secure transmission channel to prevent data loss, data leakage and manipulation in the transmission process, and ensure the safe and effective transmission of cloud services. It mainly consists of the following parts: LAN security isolation and threat prevention, Wan and extranet connection isolation and monitoring. To isolate and monitor different services/systems on WAN, the most effective way is to distinguish services through MPLS VPN, and use firewall and intrusion detection to provide virtualized detection services. In the LAN, the protection of packet confidentiality and integrity is integrated into the network matrix, and the internal data of the enterprise is encrypted and secure by using the macsec protocol built in the switch. Linksec (IEEE 802.1ae) provides line speed link layer encryption at all ports, as shown in Fig. 2. Packets are encrypted at the exit and then decrypted at the entry, so they remain in clear text inside the device. This method allows the insertion of network services transmitting unencrypted traffic, while ensuring the integrity and confidentiality of traffic when transmitted over the line.

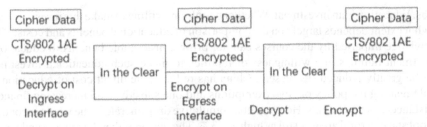

Fig. 2. Schematic diagram of cloud computing linksec

3 Analysis on Poverty Alleviation Defects of Current Precision Education

3.1 Pay Attention to Hardware Construction and Ignore Software Construction

In the current process of poverty alleviation through education, many places attach great importance to hardware construction, mainly in the following ways: first, strengthen the maintenance and transformation of school buildings, add tables and chairs, maintain the lighting of school buildings, etc.; Second, strengthen the construction of relevant hardware facilities, such as investing a lot of money to purchase classroom computers, refitting multimedia classrooms, adding zhihuiyun classroom equipment, etc. In addition, many places have increased financial support for rural poor students in the process of targeted poverty alleviation through education, such as food subsidies, or reduction and exemption of health care and education fees and miscellaneous fees for rural preschool students [5]. Although the improvement of hardware facilities and strong financial support for poor students can provide some support and guarantee for the development of rural education, domestic and foreign experience has repeatedly proved that the development and quality improvement of education are inseparable from a stable, well-trained, highly motivated and reliable team of teachers. Therefore, education targeted poverty alleviation should pay more attention to the construction of "software", that is, we must strengthen the construction of teachers in rural areas.

At present, the weakness of teachers has become the biggest bottleneck restricting the development of rural education. The survey of rural teachers shows that there are some problems in rural teachers, such as insufficient quantity, unstable team, serious aging, resulting in aging knowledge, lagging renewal of educational ideas, lack of educational and teaching ability and so on. According to statistics, at present, the proportion of rural teachers with senior professional titles is only 4.2%, 6.6% points lower than the national average of 10.8% and 12% points lower than the 16.2% of urban teachers; In the primary professional titles, the proportion of rural teachers is 44.9%. This means that the titles of rural teachers are more at the primary and intermediate levels, and the gap between urban and rural teachers is obvious [6].

3.2 Attach Importance to Theoretical Education and Ignore Applied Education

Poverty alleviation through education should also focus on "what to learn", that is, what kind of education, what type of knowledge and what courses should be offered in poor areas. Education is an investment. Whether people are willing to make this investment and to what extent depends largely on the comparison of educational benefits and costs. If the knowledge imparted by the courses can not bring considerable benefits to educational investment families, the willingness of families to make such educational investment will be greatly reduced. At present, China has reduced the direct cost of education by implementing the policy of "two exemptions and one subsidy" and increasing financial assistance to poor students. However, the cumulative drop out rate in the whole secondary school stage in rural areas is still as high as 63%. The reason is that the income and cost of general theoretical knowledge education to rural families are not proportional. At present, China formulates rural education policies according to the model of urban education, but the income brought by this education model to rural families is much lower than that of urban families [7]. According to the "follow-up survey on employment, life and values of Chinese college students" by the Chinese Academy of Social Sciences, compared with ordinary college graduates from urban families, The employment rate and quality of graduates from rural families are much worse. In the case of low return on education investment, the cost of rural education investment is relatively high. The same amount of university education cost is not a heavy burden for an urban family, but it is heavier for a rural family. Therefore, in the face of the reality full of uncertainty, due to the high opportunity cost of sending children to school and the uncertainty of the expected income from school, rational choice makes rural families tend to a short-term behavior.

3.3 Neglect of Mental Health Education for Students

The realization path of education targeted poverty alleviation is to "enable children of poor families to receive fair and quality education", but learning must first give full play to students' own initiative. If students are unwilling to learn or even give up learning opportunities, targeted poverty alleviation cannot be realized. The survey shows that at present, rural education evaluation students focus on scores, and humanistic care is not enough. Students with poor academic performance can not get the care of teachers and the respect of students for a long time, and their self-esteem has been seriously hit. Finally, they are tired of learning and even impulsively choose to drop out of school regardless of the future.

3.4 Poor Groups Have Weak Awareness of Education, Which Makes it More Difficult to Provide Accurate Assistance

In order to "enable children from poor families to receive fair and quality education", it is also required to obtain the active cooperation of students' parents in the process of education targeted poverty alleviation, and parents should enlighten and urge children to actively learn [8]. In China, affected by the long-term influence of traditional ideology and culture, many parents of students in poor areas do not understand the long-term role of education, or just because education does not see a return in the short term, they think that reading is a waste of time, and even the view of "reading is useless" appears in some areas. The lack of active cooperation of students' families makes it impossible to establish a systematic funding platform in the process of poverty alleviation through education, which seriously increases the difficulty of targeted poverty alleviation through education.

4 Education Targeted Poverty Alleviation Under Cloud Computing

4.1 We Will Strengthen Precise Assistance to Rural Teachers and Improve Teaching Quality and Educational Attraction

First, vigorously develop internet education, transfer high-quality educational resources in urban areas to rural poor areas through Internet technology, strengthen the training of teachers' teaching informatization, make teachers fully understand the functions of teaching research, electronic lesson preparation, courseware production, electronic teaching materials and lesson drying in the platform, and incorporate the application of Teachers into the school quality assessment system. These measures can effectively and quickly change the unbalanced distribution of educational resources between urban and rural areas, improve the quality of rural education, and then improve the attraction of rural education to rural families. Second, strengthen the rotation and training of teachers in the targeted poverty alleviation through education [9]. Restricted by the overall economic and social environment, it is still difficult for poor areas to attract excellent teachers even if they increase financial subsidies. Based on this, on the one hand, rural teachers can be organized to conduct remote training in cities with superior educational resources to continuously improve the teaching skills of rural teachers; On the other hand, we can also learn from the practices of South Korea, Japan and other countries to implement the teacher exchange rotation system. For example, in order to ensure the equal level of teachers in different regions, South Korea requires public school teachers to work in rural schools for 3–4 years after working in cities for 8–10 years. Third, we must pay attention to the treatment of rural teachers in the process of education targeted poverty alleviation. It should be introduced and implemented as soon as possible Strong and substantially attractive policies to ensure the treatment and status of teachers, and attract and retain excellent teachers to teach in poor areas through policies, so as to improve and improve the quality of rural teaching.

4.2 Vigorously Develop Rural Vocational Education

One side, Urbanization of rural education The low rate of return on investment in rural education affects the investment enthusiasm of rural families; on the other hand, the development of rural economy urgently needs a large number of trained primary and intermediate professional and technical talents. Therefore, we must change the current single structure and school running mode of higher education in rural education, and vigorously develop rural vocational education in the future. Rural vocational education is mainly for all kinds of education Production skills training directly applied to agricultural production and life, such as breeding technology [10]. The great difference between this vocational education and academic education is that its investors and beneficiaries can be organically unified to a great extent, which can directly improve agricultural production efficiency and increase rural family income. Therefore, farmers are also willing to invest in this aspect. In China, rural vocational education plays a significant role in rural family income. The average rate of return is about 27% (annual average rate of return 9%), which is basically consistent with the international average rate of return of 10%. Therefore, in the future, the government should appropriately increase the investment in rural vocational education, implant the mature vocational education model in cities and towns into rural areas, and improve the vocational skills of rural teenagers.

5 Implement Cloud Computing Precision Education Poverty Alleviation

First of all, we need to know what the purpose of cloud computing education poverty alleviation is.

In order to thoroughly implement the poverty alleviation spirit of cloud computing education, ensure the effective implementation of cloud computing education targeted poverty alleviation, and ensure that students from poor families can normally receive all kinds of cloud computing education at all levels. Develop pre-school cloud computing education, consolidate and improve compulsory cloud computing education, and popularize cloud computing education in senior high school. By 2020, the overall development level of cloud computing education in poor areas will be significantly improved, and the basic public services of cloud computing education for the poor such as filing and card establishment will be fully covered [11].

We will ensure that all cloud computing education stages are fully funded from enrollment to graduation, that children from poor families can go to school, and that no student is allowed to drop out of school due to family difficulties. Everyone has the opportunity to lift their families out of poverty through vocational cloud computing education, higher cloud computing education or vocational training. The ability of cloud computing education to serve regional economic and social development has been significantly enhanced. This is the purpose of cloud computing education poverty alleviation.

Secondly, we should know why we should implement cloud computing education to help the poor.

Poverty alleviation through cloud computing education is the main way to get rid of poverty and become rich. Combined with the local reality, we should earnestly study and solve the problems such as the lack of pre-school cloud computing education, the shortage of high-quality resources in ordinary high schools and the weak ability of vocational cloud computing education and training, give full play to the role of cloud computing education in poverty alleviation, and lay the foundation for the overall local poverty alleviation [12].

Then we need to know how to implement cloud computing education.

"Helping the poor first helps the wise, and treating the poor must cure the foolish" and if we want to carry out cloud computing education to help the poor, we must do the following:

First: improve the teaching environment on campus and cultivate a stable and capable team of teachers.

Second: we should take practical measures to let the lost children return to school.

Third: carry out vocational cloud computing education to enable students to master "- skills".

Finally, it is worth mentioning that the poverty alleviation of cloud computing education can not let the cloud computing education department "pick one shoulder" and get "people pick up firewood and fire". Xiaobian suggested that we should establish a cloud computing education poverty alleviation mechanism led by the state, linked by local governments and jointly participated by all sectors of society. "Only when we pay attention to cloud computing education can we win the battle of poverty alleviation through cloud computing education." As a public welfare platform in Hunan, shangxuequ has done its best in cloud computing education poverty alleviation and targeted poverty alleviation. At present, the "still learning" public welfare platform is helping more children in need to return to school.

People are the sum of all social relations and people in the specific environment. Rural students have a natural disadvantage of growth environment. This disadvantage is very obvious compared with developed regions [13]. This disadvantage comes from cloud computing education environment, social environment and family environment. In most cases, family cloud computing education accounts for the main negative impact, which is also the conclusion drawn from their own personal experience.

In terms of cloud computing education environment, the level of rural teachers and campuses is generally low. Recently, it has been greatly improved with the support of thousands of countries. However, the overall level is still low. However, the impact of school is not the main one, but more on society and family. Rural children are rarely strictly controlled. They have the opportunity to contact all kinds of social idlers and all kinds of bad habits and let themselves go, so they have a great chance of learning bad, especially in learning. Learning itself naturally has the nature of anti-human nature for dry students. Every child wants to maximize freedom, so he is unwilling to accept the constraints of learning, unless learning can make them feel the joy of learning or be affected accordingly. Students will learn a lot of bad habits and some bad ideas in society.

Among these three types of factors, the core is the family factor. In the early stage of personal growth, family is the most influential factor. What parents are like has a crucial impact on children's cloud computing education. The learning and living environment and corresponding concepts created by parents have become a crucial factor in children's growth [14]. Most rural family cloud computing education is free range cloud computing education, and children are often lack of binding force, which is easier to develop in negative factors. For most rural students, home is a place to live, not a place to study. Therefore, we can find that the place where students live is full of books. We can basically conclude that their cloud computing education will be very good in the future. However, the proportion of rural students is very low. Most of these students are not affected by their families, but by other factors.

Rural parents have great randomness to their children's cloud computing education, and there will be many problems in cloud computing education methods, methods and concepts. The initial stage of personal growth is the golden period of personal plasticity, so we will find that once the ideas, concepts and habits of Japanese children are stereotyped, they are basically difficult to change, Therefore, we will find that many children have the shadow of their parents, and even some of them are completely reprinted [15]. Most rural parents do not know much about cloud computing education, nor do they understand the ways and methods of cloud computing education. Most of them directly let students grow up by themselves. In addition, there are some problems in cloud computing education poverty alleviation. For example, the focus of social cloud computing education poverty alleviation is the cultivation of selected students. Like Guohua Memorial Middle School, these schools are more to cultivate students who have higher learning ability and have been found, but more are ordinary students.

6 Conclusion

As a concept innovation of China's targeted poverty alleviation development, targeted poverty alleviation through education has become a stabilizer, a fundamental plan for the realization of targeted poverty alleviation, and the key to blocking the intergenerational transmission of poverty. Historical development shows that poverty is not only the poverty of economic material level, but also the poverty of social resources, including intellectual poverty, information poverty, concept poverty, cultural poverty and many other factors. The lack of material and the restriction of natural conditions only cause the superficial phenomenon of poverty. The delay of education level is the most fundamental reason for poverty. It takes ten years to cultivate trees and a hundred years to cultivate people. Targeted poverty alleviation through education, as the most important play of "targeted poverty alleviation", is of great significance. Ideas lead to behavioral poverty, which is a myoma restricting people and children in poor areas. Only with the accurate development of education can it be eliminated. Education prospers, the country prospers, education is strong, and the country is strong. We should make educational poverty alleviation work effectively in targeted poverty alleviation, and gather great forces for China to build a well-off society in an all-round way and realize the great rejuvenation of the Chinese nation.

References

1. Kanwal, S., Iqbal, Z., Irtaza, A., et al.: Head node selection algorithm in cloud computing data center. Math. Probl. Eng. (2021)
2. Zheng, P., Wu, Z., Sun, J., et al.: A parallel unmixing-based content retrieval system for distributed hyperspectral imagery repository on cloud computing platforms. Remote Sens. 13(2), 176 (2021)
3. Li, J., Qiao, Z., Zhang, K., et al.: A lattice-based homomorphic proxy re-encryption scheme with strong anti-collusion for cloud computing. Sensors 21(1), 288 (2021)
4. Kovalets, I.V., Maistrenko, S.Y., Khalchenkov, A., et al.: Adaptation of the web-service of air pollution forecasting for operation within cloud computing platform of the Ukrainian National Grid Infrastructure. Sci. Innovat. 17(1), 78–88 (2021)
5. Elrotub, M., Bali, A., Gherbi, A.: Sharing VM resources with using prediction of future user requests for an efficient load balancing in cloud computing environment. Int. J. Softw. Sci. Comput. Intell. 13(2), 37–64 (2021)
6. Maelah, R., Lami, M., Ghassan, G.: Usefulness of management accounting information in decision making among SMEs: The moderating role of cloud computing (2021)

7. Yang, H.: Research on the new model of education precision funding under the model of precision poverty alleviation (2021)
8. Yong, M., Zhang, Y.: Poverty alleviation by education: Exploration and experience from China – analysis based on China's policy of poverty alleviation by education (2021)
9. Xu, C., Sun, Y.: Mechanism of vocational education promoting precision poverty alleviation. Int. J. Electric. Eng. Educ. 002072092098350 (2021)
10. Davie, G., Wang, M., Rogers, S., et al.: Targeted poverty alleviation in China: A typology of official household relations. Progr. Develop. Stud. **21** (2021)
11. Shepherd, D.A., Parida, V., Wincent, J.: Entrepreneurship and poverty alleviation: The importance of health and children's education for slum entrepreneurs (2021)
12. Liao, C., Fei, D., Huang, Q., et al.: Targeted poverty alleviation through photovoltaic-based intervention: Rhetoric and reality in Qinghai, China. World Dev. **137**, 105117 (2021)
13. Zhang, P.: On the construction of higher vocational teachers' ethnics in education poverty alleviation. J. High. Educ. Res. **2**(2) (2021)
14. Tq, A., Lh, A., Yang, L..B.: Does targeted poverty alleviation disclosure improve stock performance? Econ. Lett. **201** (2021)
15. Cheng, X.Y., Wang, J.Y., Chen, K.Z.: Elite capture, the "follow-up checks" policy, and the targeted poverty alleviation program: Evidence from rural western China. **20**(4), 11 (2021)

Research and Construction of University Sports Decision Support System Based on Extraction Algorithm and Big Data Analysis Technology

Liang-kai Guan[✉]

Shandong University of Management, Jinan 250357, Shandong, China
guanliangkai@126.com

Abstract. The era of big data puts forward intelligent requirements for university sports decision support system. The characteristics of big data and its function and influence on University intelligent decision support system are analyzed; This paper analyzes the process of university sports intelligent decision support system based on big data intelligence analysis. On this basis, the big data technology and artificial intelligence technology are integrated into the construction of university sports decision support system, and the system framework and its composition structure are put forward. Finally, the related key technologies are analyzed, which can provide reference for the construction of this kind of system.

Keywords: Big data analysis · College physical education · Decision support system

1 Introduction

Decision support system (DDS) is an application system based on management science, operations research, control and behavior science, with computer technology, simulation technology and information technology as means to assist command and decision-making in the form of human-computer interaction. Since Scott Morton, an American management scientist, first put forward the concept of decision support system in management decision system in the 1970s, decision support system has been widely used in many fields such as business administration, finance, health care and government departments, and has achieved extensive application results. Decision making refers to making decisions on future actions after analyzing, calculating, judging and selecting the best factors affecting the realization of objectives based on objective possibility, certain information and experience and with the help of certain tools, skills and methods, including "decision" and "policy". Decision making is a common behavior in politics, economy, technology and daily life. It is an activity that often occurs in management.

With the advent of the era of big data, the existing decision support systems based on the idea of small data, including decision support systems based on abstract mathematical models, expert knowledge in application fields and local sampling data, have

© ICST Institute for Computer Sciences, Social Informatics and Telecommunications Engineering 2023
Published by Springer Nature Switzerland AG 2023. All Rights Reserved
M. A. Jan and F. Khan (Eds.): BigIoT-EDU 2022, LNICST 465, pp. 530–536, 2023.
https://doi.org/10.1007/978-3-031-23950-2_57

the following shortcomings: (1) they can not effectively process big data, especially rheological unstructured big data (2) The decision object is required to be fixed (3) Mostly offline decision-making (4) It is often a single objective decision (5) The depth of data intelligence mining is insufficient.

It is also an urgent problem to be solved in college physical education. In the process of deepening the development of the new curriculum reform, although the physical education reform in Colleges and universities has made some achievements, the teaching thought has not changed, and the serious separation between theory and practice always exists [1]. In addition, limited by the teaching environment and conditions, the actual teaching environment has been affected, so that college physical education has always been the weakness of higher education. Therefore, with the advent of the era of big data, there is an urgent need to build a university sports decision support system based on big data information analysis and processing based on new design concepts, so as to realize the university sports intelligent decision support system of "from data to decision".

2 Big Data and Its Characteristics

2.1 Concept and Connotation of Big Data

Big data is a new concept with the rapid popularization of the Internet. The original meaning of data is known, can be understood as facts, and represents an objective description of something or phenomenon. Ancient Greek philosopher Pythagoras believed that number is the origin of all things. Big data is a huge amount of data, or massive data. According to Wikipedia's definition of big data, big data refers to the huge amount of data involved, which can not be intercepted, managed and processed in a reasonable time through conventional labor and technology, and sort out the information that can be interpreted by adults. The huge number is only a representation of big data. In essence, the value of big data lies in that it implies information at all levels of the world system, organization, movement and state, and provides a way to understand, discover and insight into the world. Its strategic significance lies not in mastering huge data, but in deepening cognition. Through specialized storage and processing of a large number of data, mining and extracting required knowledge and information, discovering higher-level laws and deepening understanding of the world. In other words, if big data is compared to an industry, the key to the profitability of this industry is to improve the multi-dimensional and multi angle analysis and processing ability of data, and realize the value and value-added of data through analysis, processing and application. Therefore, big data not only refers to the large amount of data, but also refers to the high speed and excellent quality of data processing. Big data does not use random analysis sampling survey to process all data [2]. Therefore, the famous big data research institute Gartner defines big data as a massive, high growth rate and diversified information asset that requires a new processing mode to have stronger decision-making power, insight and discovery power and process optimization ability.

2.2 Big Data Features

To sum up, big data has multiple and multi angle values. It is a massive complex data set (commonly used 4V description in the industry) that cannot be extracted, stored, searched, shared, analyzed and processed by classical localization methods. It is an objective and true reflection of things, phenomena and laws. It has the characteristics of integrity, holography, dynamics and growth.

(1) Integrity: big data refers to all data across multiple domains. The units of volume range from Pb, EB and ZB to Nb and DB. For example, in 2016, the total amount of global digital content reached 16.1 ZB. Although the scale is huge, due to the universal connection of the objective world, the seemingly mixed big data in different fields and levels are interrelated and are a whole, so it is holistic. Therefore, big data has overall application advantages.

(2) Holography: the term holography comes from the concept of holography in laser physics. Big data is a reflection of the real world. Big data contains all the knowledge and structure of the world. If it is considered that big data is equivalent to holographic recording of the world, then big data analysis is equivalent to holographic reconstruction of the world, which has the holographic nature of reflecting the essence and phenomenon of the world. ① Big data as a whole truly reflects the essence and phenomena of the world from different perspectives and levels; ② Each part of big data reflects the essence and phenomenon of the world from different attributes and aspects, and the contents reflected and reflected by the whole and part are interconnected, complementary and mutually confirmed.

(3) Dynamic: ① the amount of large data is constantly changing. With the extensive deepening of human activities and the application and development of high and new technology, the amount of big data increases exponentially with time. According to IDC, the new data increases at a rate of more than 50% every year, doubles every less than two years, and the data scale is constantly refreshed. At present, the magnitude of big data has developed from massive TB to huge Pb, and even ZB. ② The type, attribute, content and proportion of data change with the movement of the real world. Compared with the traditional relational data based on text, the semi-structured and unstructured information data such as sensor information, audio, video, pictures, text, XML, HTML, web log and geographical location generated by natural and human social activities are growing explosively. These types of semi-structured and unstructured data from a wide range of sources and multimedia unstructured fast flowing data account for an increasing proportion and are dominant.

3   Role and Impact of Big Data on Combat Intelligent Decision Support System

Traditional decision support systems make decisions based on small data world models, knowledge and data, that is, they rely on existing knowledge, abstract models and sample data for limited deduction and decision-making. They can be divided into model-based, knowledge-based and data-based, including collecting necessary information and processing and analyzing the collected information. There is no doubt that the comprehensiveness and integrity of the collected information will directly affect the scientificity and accuracy of decision-making.

As we all know, college physical education does not simply cultivate students' physical quality and skill exercise, but still needs to be continuously expanded and extended to effectively cultivate students' social adaptability and psychological quality, so as to realize the comprehensive expansion of the connotation of physical education. In physical education classroom teaching, we should appropriately introduce localized content, always run through health ideological education, skillfully master physical health knowledge and sports technology, and cultivate students' most basic physical quality and skills, so as to lay a solid foundation for fitness.

Big data is a massive complex data set with multiple and multi angle values that cannot be extracted, stored, searched, shared, analyzed and processed by classical localization methods. It is a vivid representation and embodiment of nature and human society. Big data is not random samples, but all data; Not precise, but mixed; Not causality, but correlation. Big data hides the knowledge and laws of the world and pays attention to related relationships. Big data from different perspectives and dimensions will help to grasp problems more systematically, comprehensively and deeply, reveal knowledge, and provide new ideas for combat intelligent decision support.

In the big data environment, in addition to the static historical big data, University Sports decision-making is faced with a large amount of real-time intelligence, information and data. The emergence of big data has changed the thinking mode and decision-making driving mode of the small world in the past, and has played a significant role and impact on the decision-making basis, knowledge source, decision-making mode and driving mode of decision support system. Big data has transformed the traditional linear, top-down and reason based decision-making model into a nonlinear, uncertainty oriented and bottom-up decision-making model. The decision-making driving mode has changed from model experience driven to big data driven, and the decision-making process has changed from post decision-making to ex ante prediction [3]. It really enables decision-makers to predict in advance, perceive in the process and feedback after the event, which greatly enhances the foresight and effectiveness of decision-making. In application, it is necessary to integrate causality into human correlation, and find hidden knowledge and laws through correlation analysis, so as to make the data "speak".

4 Design of Combat Intelligent Decision Support System Based on Big Data Analysis

4.1 System Design Requirements

College physical education is also full of uncertainty. The physical condition and training information of each student have increased sharply in physical education teaching, and the multi-source, complexity and real-time of data have been greatly enhanced. The university sports intelligent decision support system based on big data intelligence analysis (hereinafter referred to as intelligent decision support) should be able to timely provide the required knowledge at all stages of big data collection, access, processing, analysis and application, and deepen the training situation awareness, Integrate the intelligent cognition of physical education teaching situation, provide big data university physical education intelligent decision support guarantee including the whole process of intelligent decision-making such as the formulation, implementation and evaluation of university physical education decision-making, and realize decision support driven by big data. Specific requirements are as follows:

(1) It can not only process historical big data, but also process rheological big data online and in real time;
(2) It can not only provide global decision support, but also provide decision support for the whole process;
(3) It can not only provide multi task decision support, but also flexibly provide ex ante and ex post decision support according to the changes of decision tasks and environment;
(4) It can be applied not only to the decision support for the static target object, but also to the dynamic university sports decision support.

4.2 Intelligent Decision Support Process

Information and cognition are the basis of intelligent decision-making. The essence of intelligent decision support is the process of analyzing, absorbing knowledge and acquiring wisdom from big data. The process of decision support system refers to the systematic analysis of decision objectives and training situation prediction, putting forward countermeasures and schemes for decision makers to optimize schemes, and finally put them into action [4]. Intelligent decision support refers to the decision analysis of big data intelligence by using appropriate data analysis technology in the whole battle decision-making process through model, knowledge and learning, so as to obtain ideal scheme optimization results and present them to decision makers for selection in an appropriate way. The system decision-making process is shown in Fig. 1.

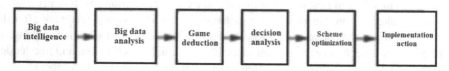

Fig. 1. System decision process

4.3 Composition

The traditional decision support system has continued the n-base structure and three system functional system in terms of composition and functional structure. It can not fully and effectively analyze and process big data, especially real-time rheological big data, and can not meet the requirements of system intelligence. It needs to change the structure, content and form. The decision support system of n-base structure and three system function system is shown in Fig. 2 respectively. In terms of architecture, it is necessary to develop and discard the n-base structure and knowledge-based functional system.

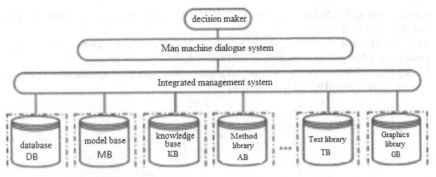

Fig. 2. Decision support system with n-base structure

Based on big data intelligence analysis, the system adopts MapReduce parallel computing and storm stream computing dual-mode cloud computing platform architecture to process static historical big data and real-time rheological big data in time. At the same time, the parallel simulation deduction system is embedded in the intelligent decision support system to form a multi-module and multi-functional hierarchical structure in the cloud computing environment. The top level is the physical training task given by the superior leaders. Physical education teachers form decision-making through the centralized selection of winning schemes provided by the system through the human-computer interaction system (Human-Computer Interface). Matched with it is the problem consultation and interpretation system, which includes intelligence database, expert system and knowledge base, and provides the functions of consultation, interpretation and problem reservation description of the mission, task and implementation scheme of the interactive parties.

5 Conclusion

Aiming at the current demand of intelligent development, this paper puts forward the university sports intelligent decision support system based on the big data analysis technology of extraction algorithm, introduces the big data analysis of extraction algorithm, embeds the parallel simulation deduction system into the university sports intelligent decision support system, and organizes an intelligent decision network for real-time mission and task requirements on this basis, Then an intelligent decision support system for physical education teaching based on big data information analysis is formed. Each intelligent decision support system has different intelligence levels, relatively different application requirements and interactive environment. Therefore, in the construction of specific system, it is necessary to conduct in-depth research on specific scenarios, algorithm design and software application.

References

1. Jian, L.: Research and practice on the construction of university sports fitness ability training system. Sports Sci. Technol. **4**, 142–145 (2011)

2. Luoxi, L., Jiang, W.: Summary and prospect of decision support system development. Comput. Sci. **43**(10), 27–32 (2016)
3. Man, C., Huifeng, X.: Research on intelligent decision support system based on cloud computing. Manag. Modernization **2**, 72–74 (2014)
4. Chongdong, L.: Research on the construction of military decision system based on big data support. Softw. Eng. **19**(3), 21–23 (2016)

Research and Design of Education Management System Based on Cloud Storage

Qingyan Cheng(✉)

Nanchang Institute of Technology, Jiangxi 330044, China
ck123456m@163.com

Abstract. Information construction in Colleges and universities is the key factor to realize modern education. In the process of information construction in Colleges and universities, due to the similarity of teaching data, there are a lot of duplicate data between the education management systems independently built by colleges and universities, resulting in a great waste of storage resources, and the teaching data is growing exponentially, which brings great storage pressure to the traditional data center. All users share a resource pool, resulting in low resource search efficiency. Moreover, due to the unclear role and authority of users, teaching resources can not be safely shared among college users.

Keywords: Cloud storage · Management system · Resource sharing · Role

1 Introduction

With the rapid development of information technology and the popularity of personal computers and intelligent machines, more and more users begin to communicate with the outside world through the Internet, understand and obtain all kinds of information resources they need, and manage their own data through network storage. In the environment of colleges and universities, realizing the scientization and automation of daily education management is an important symbol of realizing education modernization. Campus network is a key factor in the modernization and information construction of colleges and universities. Relying on the convenient campus network, using advanced computer technology, implementing more scientific, effective and convenient online management of teaching work, and establishing a series of education management systems matching with college education can further accelerate the work efficiency of colleges and universities and improve the teaching level.

Analyzing the current process of University modernization, we can find that there are many problems in its education management system. For example, the education management system used by each university is generally built, operated and maintained independently. Due to the existence of a large number of similar resources or the use of the same teaching data among colleges and universities, the direct consequence is that the data between colleges and universities is highly repeated, resulting in a waste of a large number of storage resources and increasing the capital investment in network teaching

M. A. Jan and F. Khan (Eds.): BigIoT-EDU 2022, LNICST 465, pp. 537–542, 2023.
https://doi.org/10.1007/978-3-031-23950-2_58

of major colleges and universities. Moreover, most colleges and universities may have multiple education management systems at the same time. A variety of teaching systems lead to complex campus system maintenance and a great waste of human and financial resources. At the same time, this paper analyzes the current resource sharing strategies of colleges and universities. In order to obtain relevant shared resources, users often need to consume a lot of search time, resulting in the slow progress of campus digitization, so that the rapidly developing computer network technology can not timely serve today's teaching work, which seriously hinders the process of college education modernization [1].

In the past two years, cloud computing technology has developed rapidly. Its core idea is to provide software, platform and it equipment resources in the form of services. The goal is to integrate a large number of cheap physical computing resources with low performance into a powerful computer system with high computing power, large storage capacity, and provide a unified service interface. Users can pay for software, platform or underlying hardware equipment according to their actual needs.

2 Overview of Key Technologies

2.1 Cloud Storage Technology

With the emergence of cloud computing technology, cloud storage technology provides a new solution for massive data storage. The cloud storage platform has the advantages of storage space Virtualization (by aggregating the space of multiple storage devices, flexibly allocating and deploying storage space, avoiding unnecessary hardware device costs and improving the utilization of storage space), and dynamic scalability of storage capacity (on the premise that the original storage system is not affected, storage nodes are dynamically added or deleted to meet the needs of dynamic changes of data) and data security (ensure the continuity and integrity of data and ensure that users can obtain the data they want anytime, anywhere) Based on the above characteristics, cloud storage platform can provide enterprises with cheap, dynamically scalable storage capacity and safe and complete data, and provide a method to reduce the pressure of massive data storage for traditional data centers.

2.2 Data Layout Algorithm

Cloud storage platform is composed of a large number of heterogeneous storage devices. How data is stored and arranged in these storage nodes not only affects whether the storage devices can be fully utilized, but also affects the access efficiency of cloud storage platform. At the same time, cloud storage platform has dynamic scalability, and storage nodes can be dynamically added and removed. When the storage capacity of cloud storage platform changes, it is better Xiu's data layout algorithm can reduce the amount of migrated data and improve the performance of the cloud storage platform. Therefore, it is necessary to study the data layout algorithm to build the cloud storage platform.

The data layout algorithm mainly solves the two major problems of fairness and adaptability. The actual amount of data obtained by each device in the system is related to its performance, and the amount of data obtained by different devices is directly proportional to its performance. If - data layout algorithms meet the above relationship, it is considered that this layout strategy meets the fairness requirements. The adaptability of the layout strategy can be achieved by adding or removing device nodes It can be measured by the ratio of the actual amount of data migrated to the optimal amount of data that needs to be migrated in theory, or if it can be ensured that data migration only occurs between old equipment and new equipment, it can also be said that the corresponding strategy can well meet the requirements of self adaptability.

1. Assign a weight value to all devices according to their performance (storage location, storage capacity, network bandwidth, etc.):

$$\sum_{i=1}^{n} w_l = 1 \tag{1}$$

2. Assume that the minimum weight value of all devices is w_m. Allocate $k \log n$ virtual storage nodes to the storage node, where k is a constant and N is the number of actual storage nodes. For other storage nodes, the weight is assumed to be w_i. The algorithm will assign n to the device node N_i virtual storage nodes:

$$N_i = (w_i/w_m) \cdot k \log n \tag{2}$$

Therefore, a total of N storage locations are required in the ring to map all storage nodes (including physical storage nodes and virtual storage nodes) [2].

The algorithm can solve the fairness problem of the data layout algorithm. Its disadvantage is that it introduces a large number of virtual nodes, increases the storage overhead and increases the complexity of the algorithm. Especially in the case of large performance differences between devices, the number of virtual storage nodes introduced by the algorithm will be huge, resulting in serious storage overhead. At the same time, the algorithm still does not consider redundancy The remaining problem is that only one piece of data is stored in the storage space. When a storage node fails, the data stored in this node will not be recoverable.

3   Design of Education Management System Based on Cloud Storage

With the deepening of the process of educational modernization, the amount of data in the educational management system has increased exponentially, which has brought severe challenges to the traditional data center. The most direct way to store massive data is to increase the number of storage devices in the data center. However, relying solely on the addition of storage devices to solve the storage problems caused by the explosive growth of data will make college storage a success In the face of the explosive growth of data, how to realize the efficient storage of this part of data is an urgent problem to be solved in Colleges and universities.

Through the analysis and research of various data layout algorithms in cloud storage technology, an improved data layout algorithm is proposed to meet the requirements of fairness and adaptability at the same time. In addition, according to the characteristics of college teaching data, a local duplicate data deletion algorithm based on the characteristics of teaching data is proposed to minimize data redundancy and reduce the pressure of network bandwidth, so as to reduce the cost The storage pressure of massive data on the traditional data center and the complexity of system upgrading and maintenance in the future.

The construction of digital campus has achieved initial results in Colleges and universities. The use of network, multimedia and other high-tech means for auxiliary teaching or online teaching has been gradually carried out By analyzing the current daily teaching process in Colleges and universities, it can be found that although the campus network has been built, the actual utilization rate of each teaching system is not high, and the auxiliary role for daily teaching work is not complete. For example, there are two common teaching activities: teaching courseware sharing between teachers and students and online submission of students' classroom homework. At present, there are three main ways: one is Copy through USB flash disk, that is, students use USB flash disk to copy teachers' teaching courseware in spare time such as recess; second, teachers share teaching resources by sending e-mail, that is, teachers uniformly set and publish a shared mailbox, and student users in a specific class use password to share teaching resources and submit classroom homework by logging in to the shared mailbox; third, FTP server is used.

There are two main backup strategies for information data backup using backup system: real-time backup and regular backup. Both strategies have their own advantages and disadvantages. In comparison, real-time backup has the advantages of high data integrity and good security. The disadvantage is that for the large storage system such as teaching system, real-time storage consumes too much resources and there is a great waste of resources At present, it is the most widely used. Its advantage is that it can make more full use of system resources. Its disadvantage is that when the timing policy is not set properly, it may cause the loss of data information.

Based on the frequency characteristics of data resources in the education system, the strategy of combining real-time backup, regular backup and manual backup is designed to back up the education system. In addition, the backup mode is dynamically and flexibly adjusted according to the semester characteristics of school teaching activities [3]. For example, the frequency of courseware resources in different chapters of curriculum courseware is different in the semester of the beginning of the course With the increase of class time, the use frequency of new courseware resources is high, and the use frequency of courseware resources in historical chapters is reduced. Therefore, different backup strategies need to be adopted for courseware resources in different chapters. The real-time backup strategy is adopted for courseware resources in new chapters. When the use frequency is reduced, the backup mode is dynamically changed to regular backup mode, so as to realize dynamic adjustment of storage Storage strategy to increase storage efficiency and resource utilization.

4 Cloud Storage Platform Implementation

The cloud storage platform is further modified and implemented on the basis of Apache Cassandra program, which is mainly composed of three parts: external interface, HTTP server and back-end storage device group. External interface: the system provides storage, reading and deletion interfaces for the upper layer developers. Developers can call the interfaces provided by the platform to complete the storage, reading, modification and deletion of data The main implementation interfaces include:

1. Performput (string nativepath) / L storage interface. The parameter is the local storage path;
2. Performget (string nativepath, string remoteobjectname) / / read interface. The parameters are the data storage path and the ID of the read data;
3. Performmodify (string objectname) / / modify the data interface. The parameter is the ID of the modified data;
4. Performdelete (string objectname) / / delete the data interface. The parameter is the ID of the deleted data.

HTTP server: this server completes the parsing of data packets transmitted between the upper layer developers and the back-end storage node. The interfaces involved include get, put, post and delete. The get interface encapsulates the back-end data and returns it to the upper layer developers. The put interface stores the front-end data in the back-end storage node. The post interface is based on the needs of the front-end developers It is required to modify the data stored in the back-end. The delete interface is responsible for data deletion.

The system realizes the classified storage of all data and stores the structured data in the database. The design of each data table is shown in Fig. 1.

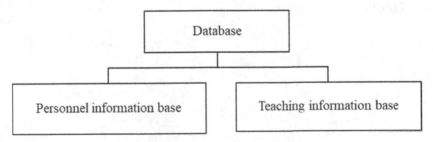

Fig. 1. Database implementation

The administrator first imports the question bank into the system and establishes the index of the question bank [4]. When a new question is added to the question bank, only one index record needs to be added; According to the item bank index, each item tester needs to save a mapping table. Mapping the item to the electronic item bank can complete the recording of an item; For students' answers, judge the correctness of the answers based on the question bank index and the test paper mapping table. For correct answers, they are mapped to the standard answer location of the question record by default. Only the wrong answers are stored, and the mapping between the storage location of the wrong answers and the students' test paper can be completed.

5 Conclusion

This paper deeply studies the problems of massive data storage and resource security sharing, and puts forward the corresponding solutions combined with the current popular technologies. On this basis, an education management system based on cloud storage is developed and implemented. Research and propose solutions to the problem of massive data storage. The cloud storage technology and data deduplication technology are deeply studied respectively. According to the advantages and disadvantages of each data layout algorithm in cloud storage technology, an improved data layout algorithm is proposed to better meet the performance requirements of fairness and adaptability in data layout algorithm at the same time. Research and propose solutions to the problem of resource security sharing. Based on the study of various resource sharing methods in Colleges and universities, a resource sharing strategy based on college resource space and role is proposed and implemented.

References

1. Yijie, W., Weidong, S., Song, Z., Xiaoqiang, P., Yong, L.: Key technologies of distributed storage in cloud computing environment. J. Softw. **23**(4), 926–986 (2012)
2. Yanxia, G., Jun, Y.: Research on massive data storage mode. Comput. Digital Eng. **36** (11), 153–169 (2008)
3. Junzhou, L., Jiahui, J., Aibo, S., Dongfang.: Cloud Computing: architecture and key technologies. J. Commun. **32**(7), 3–21 (2011)
4. Dean, J., Ghemawat, S.: MapReduce: a flexible data processing tool. Commun. ACM **53**(1), 72–77 (2010)

Research and Design of Information Teaching Management System Integrating Association Rule Mining Algorithm

Chengli Zhao(✉)

Ya'an Polytechnic College, Ya'an City 625000, Sichuan, China
zhaochengli1984@163.com

Abstract. The main purpose of this research is to design and implement an information teaching management system integrating association rule mining algorithm. The process is divided into two parts: the first part is about the design model, and the second part is about implementing it. Research and design of information teaching management system integrating association rule mining algorithm In this research, we are trying to develop an information teaching management system, which can be applied to college students studying in the field of computer science. The purpose is to provide teachers with a tool that can help them work. We also hope to use it as a learning tool for students so that they can acquire more knowledge about how computers work and what they need to learn when using computers. Combine the research and design of information teaching management system with association rule mining algorithm. This algorithm can be used to find the most important rules in a given dataset, which are related to each other. It can then be used to select the best rule from the rules found using this method. It will help teachers choose the best teaching methods or skills to improve their skills and knowledge.

Keywords: Teaching management · Association rules · Mining algorithm · Data mining

1 Introduction

The term "knowledge discovery from databases" (KDD) first appeared at the 11th International Joint Academic Conference on artificial intelligence held in 1989. After that, the research focus gradually shifted from discovery methods to system applications, focusing on the integration of multiple discovery strategies and technologies, and the mutual penetration of multiple disciplines. Among the database research projects of the National Science Foundation (NSF), KDD was listed as the most valuable research project in the 1990s. Scientists in the field of artificial intelligence research also generally believe that one of the important topics of the next artificial intelligence application will be large-scale database knowledge discovery with machine learning algorithm as the main tool [1]. Although data mining is still a very new research topic, its inherent

M. A. Jan and F. Khan (Eds.): BigIoT-EDU 2022, LNICST 465, pp. 543–553, 2023.
https://doi.org/10.1007/978-3-031-23950-2_59

potential to create huge economic benefits for enterprises has made it quickly have many successful applications. The representative application fields include market prediction, investment, manufacturing, banking, communications and so on [2].

American Iron and steel company and Kobe iron and steel company use ISPA system based on data mining technology to study and analyze product performance laws and carry out quality control, and have achieved remarkable results. General Electric Company (GE) and French aircraft engine manufacturing company (SNECMA) developed Cassiop by using data mining technology EE quality control system has been used by three European airlines to diagnose and predict the fault of crossover 737, which has brought considerable economic benefits. In 1996, the system won the European first-class creative application award [3].

Recently, a senior technology survey of Gartner Group listed data mining and artificial intelligence as the top of the "five key technologies that will have a profound impact on industry in the next three to five years", and also listed parallel processing system and data mining as the top two of the ten emerging technologies that will be the focus of investment in the next five years. According to the recent Gartner HPC research, "with the rapid development of data capture, transmission and storage technologies, users of large-scale systems will need to adopt new technologies to tap the value outside the market, and adopt broader parallel processing systems to create new business growth points." At present, several hotspots in the future include web site data mining, bioinformatics / genomics data mining and text mining.

At present, the key point in the management of colleges and universities is teaching management. Effective teaching management not only requires managers to set a good management system, but also should have an ideal information management system. Because the management methods and teaching modes of colleges and universities are different, the teaching management systems applied by colleges and universities are also different. Data information such as teacher information, student information, course information and achievement information is cumbersome for teaching managers, However, if the teaching management system combines such information data with different management directions according to their respective management characteristics, it can effectively reduce the pressure of managers and give full play to the effect of the teaching management system to the greatest extent [4]. As a new way of teaching management, information-based teaching management has been gradually introduced into the university management center, which can fundamentally simplify the work content of managers. Therefore, the design of information-based teaching management system has become the top priority of university management.

Data mining refers to extracting interested knowledge from the database. Association rule mining is the research focus in the field of data mining. Association rule refers to the rule of some relationship between a group of objects in the database. Its mining object is usually transaction database. Due to the continuous accumulation of a large number of historical data in the teaching management of colleges and universities, including a lot of valuable information, the application of association rule data mining in the information-based teaching management of colleges and universities can analyze and mine the useful information in the teaching management, and provide help for the teaching managers the foundation for the scientific and comprehensive management of college teaching.

2   Fusion Association Rule Mining Algorithm

2.1   Overview of Data Mining

Data mining, It was once called "fishing", "snooping" and "fishing". A considerable number of people regard data mining as another commonly used term, knowledge discovery in database or KDD (knowledge discovery in database). In short, data mining It is a process of extracting potentially useful information and knowledge hidden in a large number of incomplete, noisy, fuzzy and random practical application data that people do not know in advance. The object of data mining must be real, massive and noisy; What is discovered is the knowledge that the user is interested in; The discovered knowledge should be acceptable, understandable and applicable; Data mining technology involves database, artificial intelligence, neural network, prediction theory, machine learning and statistics [5].

With the maturity of database technology and the popularization of data application, the amount of data accumulated by human beings is growing rapidly at an exponential rate. In the 1990s, with the emergence and development of the Internet, the emergence and application of Intranet, extranet and VPN (virtual private network), the whole world is connected into a small global village. People can exchange data information and work together on the Internet across time and space. In this way, what is displayed in front of people is not limited to the huge database of the Department, the unit and the industry, but the vast ocean of information, and the data flood is coming to people [6]. When the amount of data grows extremely, if there is no effective method to extract useful information and knowledge with computer and information technology, people will feel helpless in the face of the information ocean like looking for a needle in a haystack. It is estimated that only 7% of the data in a large enterprise database is well used. In this way, compared with "data surplus" and "information explosion", people feel "information poverty" and "data locked in a cage", just as John naisbett exclaimed "well dropping in information, but standing for knowledge".

Faced with the boundless data, people call for a technology and tool to remove the essence, eliminate the false and preserve the true from the vast ocean of data, that is, KDD. Knowledge discovery in databases. In this way, data mining (DM) is born. The general process of data mining technology is shown in Fig. 1.

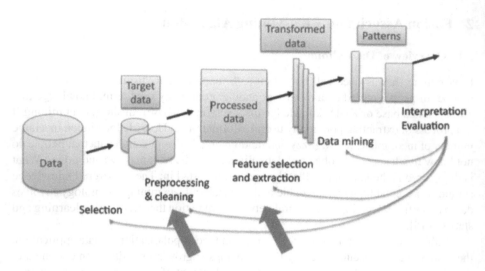

Fig. 1. General process of data mining technology

2.2 Association Rule Mining in Data Mining

Integrated association rules are rules involving multiple attributes or predicates. The mining of integrated association rules does not search for frequent item sets like the mining of single dimension association rules. In the mining of integrated association rules, we search for frequent predicate sets. The k-predicate set is a set containing K conjunctive predicates. Integrated association rule mining methods can be divided into the following three types according to their processing of quantitative attributes:

(1) Integrating association rules with static discretization mining based on quantitative attributes

i.e. discretizing the quantization attribute using a predefined concept hierarchy. This discretization is carried out before mining. The value of the numerical attribute is replaced by an interval, such as "O~20", "21~30", "31~40", etc., to replace the original value of the attribute. If the result data related to the task is stored in the relational table, the Apriori algorithm can find all the frequent predicates rather than the frequent itemsets (that is, by searching all the related attributes instead of only one attribute) with a slight modification [7]. Finding all frequent k-predicate sets will require K or K + 1 table scans. Other strategies, such as hashing, partitioning, and sampling, can be used to improve performance, as shown in Fig. 2.

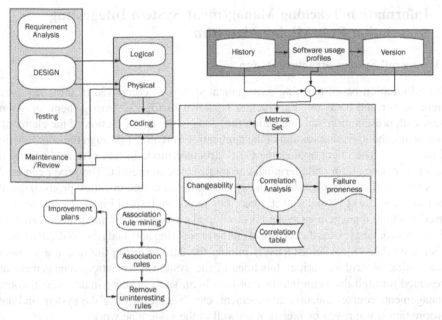

Fig. 2. Integrated association rule mining algorithm flow

(2) Mining quantitative association rules

Quantitative association rules are integrated association rules, in which numerical attributes are dynamically discretized to meet certain mining standards. This method discretizes the quantitative attributes into "boxes" according to the distribution of data. These boxes may be further combined during excavation. For example, the method used by the system arcs (association rule clustering system) is to map the quantitative attribute pairs to the 2-D grid that meets the given classification attribute conditions, and then search for the clustering of grid points to generate association rules.

(3) Mining distance based association rules

This method is the discretization of quantitative attributes to closely follow the semantics of interval data, and does not allow the approximation of data values. This process takes into account the distance between data points, so it is called distance based association rules. The two pass algorithm can be used to mine such association rules. The first time use clustering to find intervals or clusters. The second pass searches for frequently occurring cluster groups to obtain distance based association rules.

3 Information Teaching Management System Integrating Association Rule Mining Algorithm

3.1 Overall System Structure Design

The information-based teaching management system is composed of three key parts: client, server and database. Its structure is shown in Fig. 2. Among them, providing users with presentation and interaction functions is the core function of the client, and completing the logical operation of the application is realized through the core function of the server. The client applies the C / S structure mode in this system, focusing on the smart phone and mobile terminal commonly used at present; The server can apply B / s and C / S structure modes in the system, and the communication protocol can be compatible with HTTP and socket. According to the analysis of Fig. 3, the information-based teaching management system is developed on the basis of the layering principle. The system database uses the relational online processing and analysis (ROLAP) method to store all data [8]. After effectively mining the data by using the fusion association rule mining algorithm, various functions of the system information management are presented through the main interface of the client, such as score management, course management, course selection management, etc., The security of the system and data information is improved by means of firewall in the system network.

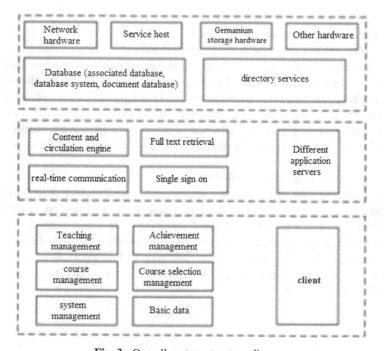

Fig. 3. Overall system structure diagram

3.2 Application of Association Rule Mining Algorithm

The data mining process determines the data type to be mined. The data in the database is transformed and cleaned up. The mining algorithm of association rules is used to destroy the data according to the correct data type. After mining, the mining results are analyzed and evaluated and displayed to users through customers. The detailed data mining process of the system is shown in Fig. 4.

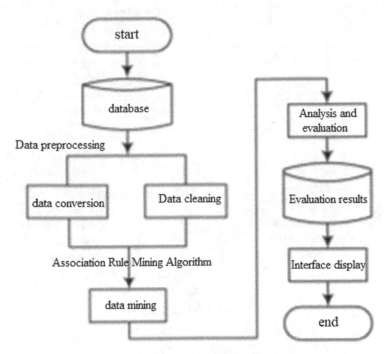

Fig. 4. System data mining process

(2) Apriori algorithm core.

In order to generate all frequent sets, Apriori algorithm uses recursive method, as follows:

Ki = (large I-itemsets}
For(1 = 2;K1-1, μ;1++) do begin
Ar = apriori-gen(K.-)
For all transactions ijB do begin
A, = subset(A,t)
For all candidates cj A, do
c.count++
End
K={cjA,l c.count minsup)
End
Reply= I ∪ Kr

The first frequent itemset K1 and the second frequent itemset K2 are generated successively until a U value makes K null, and the algorithm terminates. In the 1st cycle, the set al of candidate 1 item set is generated. The function of each set in Al is to generate the candidate set of frequency set. As shown in Fig. 5 below.

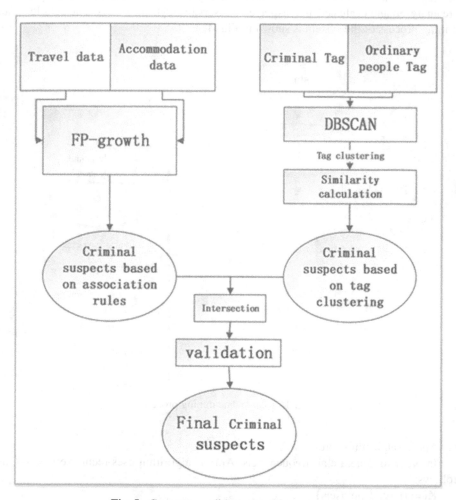

Fig. 5. Generate candidate sets of frequency sets

The generation of each set is completed by (I-2) connecting the KR-1 frequency set with only one different item, and the finally generated frequency set K must be a subset of A. Each element in a needs to be verified in the database to determine whether each element can add people to K. during verification, the database needs to be scanned several times. If there are at most 12 items in the frequency set, the database should be scanned 12 times, which requires a large I/0 load, and a large number of candidate sets will be produced several times. Therefore, the database still needs to be scanned many times during verification [9]. Therefore, the disadvantage of Apriori algorithm is that the amount of candidate set generation is too large and the scanning time is too long due to repeated scanning of the database, which is the bottleneck of Apriori algorithm.

4 Information Teaching Management System Based on Integrated Association Rule Mining Algorithm

4.1 Overall Objectives and Project Requirements of the System

The overall goal of the teaching management system based on DM is to establish a unified teaching management decision support system based on data warehouse, with the database of the teaching management system and other business systems as the data source, supplemented by the external data related to the business such as the student source database and the examination database, so as to realize the comprehensive and centralized management of the business data; Take the teaching management system as the platform, provide management reports, information query and data analysis services for personnel at all levels, and adopt or develop specific tools to provide information decision support for leaders of various departments and school administrators [10]. The teaching management decision support system based on data warehouse shall meet the following requirements:

(1) It can realize automatic data collection and centralized management
   It can automatically collect, store, apply and manage raw data (data source) according to conditions. The design of the system is based on the B / S structure of the web. Users should be able to operate according to their different permissions to ensure the security of the whole system.
(2) Friendly human-machine interface for data input
   The system can provide a flexible and convenient data entry method, and the new data can be input into the management analysis database through a friendly human-machine interface. Some data are entered manually.
(3) Flexible dynamic report function
   Reports are indispensable auxiliary tools in financial business activities. The system should be able to generate reports flexibly and quickly according to user requirements and report requirements, so as to improve the work efficiency of business personnel.
(4) Decision analysis function
   The decision analysis function is divided into three types of methods. In addition to data mining analysis and sensitivity analysis, it also includes graphical comparative analysis. Through the processing and integration of the original business report data, the deep and detailed business analysis is carried out on student information, teacher information, examination results, course selection information, etc.
(5) Scalability

The amount of data in teaching management is very large. In the process of construction, business expansion and analysis elements should be considered. Therefore, maintaining the relative independence and redundancy of the database is very beneficial to the expansion of the data warehouse in the future.

4.2 System Functional Architecture

The data mining system based on teaching management system is composed of five parts: basic system network, data source, warehouse management, data warehouse and data presentation. They interact with each other to form a teaching management decision support system, as shown in Fig. 6.

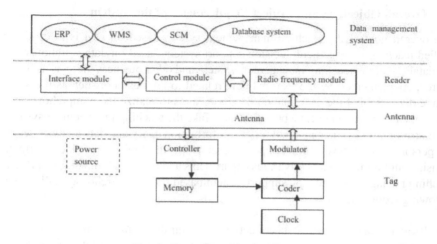

Fig. 6. System functional architecture

The lowest layer is the data acquisition layer, including a series of software and hardware data. Data sources include databases and non-traditional data. Due to the heterogeneity and autonomy of the underlying data, in order to maintain the data consistency and the data quality of data mining, it is necessary to clean up, extract and transform the data in the data source, generate a unified data and store it in the data warehouse.

The data storage layer is mainly used to store and manage the processed comprehensive data oriented to the decision theme, and reorganize it according to the requirements of the decision theme to provide a large amount of data basis for decision support. In order to mine the data of data warehouse, the data warehouse needs to provide complex data transformation functions.

The data processing layer includes data mining, OLAP and its corresponding management system.

The data access layer provides the decision maker with an access to interact with the system. After the decision-maker sends a decision request, the data mining tool mines the data related to the task from the data warehouse and stores it in the knowledge base. The online analysis tool further analyzes and processes these data, and generates data that is helpful to the decision-maker in combination with the knowledge base. The human-computer interaction system presents the results to the decision-maker, and the decision-maker solves the problem accordingly.

5   Conclusion

The research and design of integrated association rule mining algorithm in information teaching management system is a research problem, that is, in order to store information about teaching courses, students' learning ability and achievements, we need to use data mining technology. This is a new way for us to collect data from different sources, such as student records, teacher records and other related documents. It can also be used as a tool to analyze students' learning ability using statistical methods (such as association rules). In this paper, we will introduce a system design integration method based on association rule mining algorithm. The main purpose of this study is to find out how to use this algorithm in the process of information management, and what are its advantages and disadvantages. In order to answer these questions, we used a university database containing more than 20000 records to conduct experiments. For each record, we examined two types: people not affected by any rules and people affected by rules. We also compared them with other databases that do not use rules but only have data preprocessing methods (data cleaning).

References

1. Li, M., Li, J., Chong, R.: Research and application of flipped classroom in the information teaching module of interior design course. In: ICIMTECH 21: The Sixth International Conference on Information Management and Technology (2021)
2. Li, Y., Chen, L., Yu, D., et al.: Research and developing of evaluation information system using B/S structure and SQL server technology. J. Phys. Conf. Ser. **1952**(4), 042088 (2021). (6pp)
3. Zhang, X.: Research and Design of Intelligent Detection System in Teaching Manner Training of Normal School Students (2021)
4. Li, B.: Design and research of computer-aided english teaching methods. Int. J. Humanoid Robot. (2022)
5. Beidelschies, M., Cella, D., Katzan, I., D'Adamo, C.R.: Patient-reported outcomes and the patient-reported outcome measurement information system of functional medicine care and research. Phys. Med. Rehabil. Clin. North Am. **33**(3), 679–697 (2022)
6. Jing, R., Wang, H., Gao, G.: Research on integrated management of sales and inventory information in circulation enterprises based on case-based learning. Int. J. Inf. Technol. Manage. **21**, 153–168 (2022)
7. Park, H., Kang, S.H., Lee, Y.S., et al.: global trends of regional health information systems and suggested strategic utilization of their medical information. Healthcare Inform. Res. **27**(3), 175–181 (2021)
8. Lin, J.: Design and research of inverted classroom teaching of information technology integrating into the major of finance and economics. In: IPEC 2021: 2021 2nd Asia-Pacific Conference on Image Processing, Electronics and Computers (2021)
9. Jin, Z., Zou, W.: Research on the design of online teaching system of basketball basic technology. J. Phys. Conf. Ser. **1992**(3), 032080 (2021)
10. Yan, Y., Zhou, F., Zhang, X., et al.: Research and Design of ACM-oriented C Language Experimental Teaching (2021)

Research Design of English Teaching Resource Management System Based on Collaborative Recommendation

Wang Aju[✉]

School of Foreign Languages, Dalian Polytechnic University, Dalian 116034, Liaoning, China
tsingxiaozhu@sina.com

Abstract. Aiming at the "lost" and "waste" of current English teaching resources In order to realize the system, firstly, the use cases of the system are analyzed. Based on the use case analysis, the functions and overall architecture of the system are designed respectively, and the collaborative recommendation module is designed. The combination of For the professional attributes and other attributes of old users, the hybrid recommendation algorithm is used to recommend learning resources. Finally, the partially implemented interface is given.

Keywords: Collaborative recommendation · Resource management · English teaching

1 Introduction

Although English, as a highly professional language discipline, has been very common in all stages and fields of education in China, especially when higher vocational English education has made some achievements, there are still many problems, such as poor practical oral ability and dumb English, which hinder the further improvement of teaching quality. This is mainly because, on the one hand, the teaching means are relatively limited and can only use the traditional classroom time to interact with students. Students have less time to learn consciously after class. Compared with other skill-based disciplines, English learning is not skilled and it is difficult to play an "immediate" role in learning effect. Therefore, students tend to have their own interests and have low enthusiasm for learning after class, It is difficult to improve English teaching continuously; On the other hand, teaching resources are scattered, which makes it difficult for teachers and students to adapt. As a basic subject, there is a wide range of English learning materials to choose from. Students do not know how to choose their own English teaching resources. The individual training of oral English and grammar is also stretched, which further affects their enthusiasm [1, 2]. At the same time, teachers know how to select appropriate English learning materials, but due to the limited sharing means, It is difficult to share English resources to each student in time. It can only be shared and taught in English classes once a few days, which makes good English learning materials

M. A. Jan and F. Khan (Eds.): BigIoT-EDU 2022, LNICST 465, pp. 554–562, 2023.
https://doi.org/10.1007/978-3-031-23950-2_60

"overqualified and underused" in a certain range [3, 4]. Students want to learn but can't find English resources, and teachers want to teach but can't share English resources, which makes it difficult to promote the work of English teaching management smoothly. In this regard, there are similar problems in English teaching at home and abroad. Based on this background, it is particularly meaningful to study and analyze English teaching management system which is shown in Fig. 1.

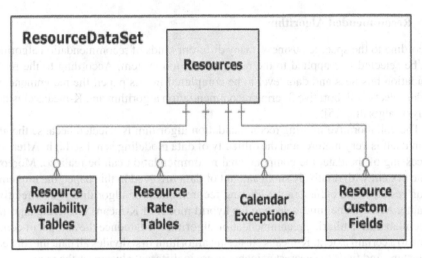

Fig. 1. Relationship for English teaching management system

2 Related Work

(Wu, 2020) introduce the research status of big data and ideological and political education in colleges and universities at home and abroad, USES big data to promote the ideological and political education in colleges and universities, advances the application of big data to college education, and finally summarizes the results and prospects. In order to solve the problems of orderly management, disclosure and evaluation of digital teaching resources, a QR code-based Digital teaching resource navigation system construction plan is proposed (Li et. al., 2020). (Ge, 2020) introduce the design and implementation of new media film and television aesthetics teaching information management system based on Web. In order to improve the management of computer-aided dance teaching resources (Huang, 2021) obtain the key point position coordinates of the human body; The inverse kinematics calculation of the robot obtains the angle values of each joint of the robot, and the angle values of the lower body joints are adjusted to maintain the balance of the robot. Through literature research (Zhu, 2021) find the matching point between constructivism theory and artificial intelligence-assisted teaching, and through the second language acquisition theory and communicative teaching method to summarize the language acquisition process assisted by artificial intelligence. In order to improve the storage and sharing of teaching video resource system in colleges and universities (Yan, 2021) design a teaching video resource management system based on micro grid technology. (Zhu, 2021) propose the design of constructing English teaching resources information management system based on artificial intelligence technology. Other influential work includes (Yang, 2018), (Zong et. al., 2018), (Zhu, 2021).

3   Collaborative Recommendation Algorithm

3.1   Recommended Algorithm

According to the specific business, many different kinds of recommendation algorithms can be selected and applied to the recommendation system. According to the recommendation business and data level to be completed in this paper, the recommendation model selects collaborative filtering recommendation algorithm and K-means clustering analysis algorithm [5].

The collaborative filtering recommendation algorithm is selected because the algorithm itself is very mature, and the difficulty of data modeling is not so high. After some processing of the data, the computational recommendation can be realized. Moreover, in the system with relatively small amount of data involved in this paper, the implementation result of the collaborative filtering recommendation algorithm is also relatively reliable. At the same time, selecting the hybrid model of K-means clustering algorithm and collaborative filtering recommendation algorithm will reduce the amount of computation to a certain extent. K-means clustering algorithm first divides all data into different K clusters, and finds the nearest neighbor users in different clusters as the recommended objects. The collaborative filtering recommendation algorithm is shown in Fig. 2 below.

The most commonly used collaborative filtering recommendation algorithms are user based collaborative filtering recommendation and Project-based Collaborative filtering recommendation [6]. The related algorithms of collaborative filtering recommendation have been well verified and recommended in the recommendation system. Firstly, the similarity between users is calculated through the user's historical behavior data, and the most similar users are found according to the similarity ranking. The result obtained through the weight of the item is the item recommended to the target user. Collaborative filtering recommendation system can deal with unstructured complex data objects, and is often used in film and music recommendation.

3.2   Collaborative Filtering Recommendation Algorithm

Collaborative filtering recommendation algorithm has been applied to real life for a long time, and has been very perfect. The purpose of collaborative filtering recommendation is to recommend information to users. Its core is to calculate and analyze the user's historical behavior data through relevant algorithms, divide different users into groups, and recommend the products liked by users with higher similarity to the group users. The two most commonly used algorithm models of collaborative filtering recommendation algorithm model are user based collaborative filtering recommendation algorithm and Project-based Collaborative filtering recommendation algorithm [7]. The two recommended algorithms will be described and explained in detail below.

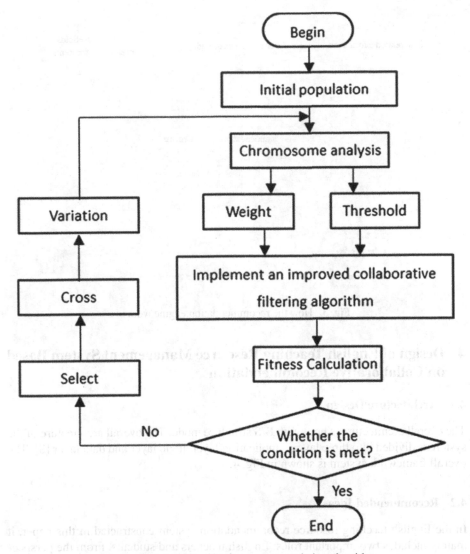

Fig. 2. Collaborative filtering recommendation algorithm

The recommendation algorithm is the core of the recommendation system, but the whole model of the recommendation system must be considered for specific business selection, but the core recommendation engine of the recommendation system will not change. Figure 3 shows the working principle of the recommendation engine:

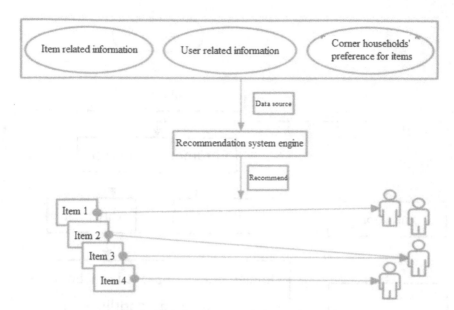

Fig. 3. How the recommendation engine works

4 Design of English Teaching Resource Management System Based on Collaborative Recommendation

4.1 Architecture Design

The overall architecture is built with B/S structure mode. The overall architecture of the system is divided into three layers: application layer, logic layer and data layer [8]. The overall framework system is shown in Fig. 4.

4.2 Recommended Ideas

In the English teaching resource recommendation system constructed in this paper, it mainly includes two important roles: English teachers and students. From the perspective of teaching resources, it contains many types, such as image, audio, video and so on. Therefore, if the traditional association rule algorithm is used to recommend these English teaching contents, it is difficult to make cross domain recommendation. Therefore, the collaborative recommendation model is selected in the recommendation algorithm. In addition, English teaching resources are usually composed of specialty name, resource type, content profile, author profile, upload time and other attributes, while students mainly include student number, specialty code, education type and other attributes. In the recommendation process, it is also considered that students may be interested in teaching resources of other majors in addition to their own majors. Therefore, the recommendation of teaching resources is divided into professional and non professional [9]. At the same time, the score between new and old registered users shall be considered. Different methods are used to recommend different users. In the past

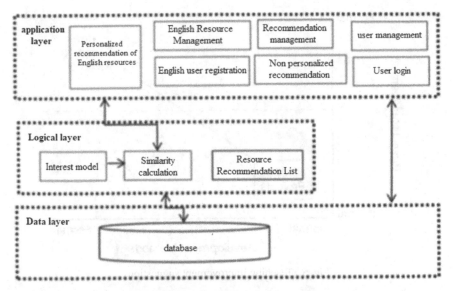

Fig. 4. Overall system architecture

school information construction, schools often only pay attention to the investment of hardware equipment, and the plan and budget are also done according to the hardware investment, and the software cost is rarely included. Due to the lack of attention to the construction of educational software environment, the application level of many built information hardware is not high, and it is not closely combined with teaching practice, so it is difficult to play its due role. The school cannot inherit the effective teaching resources summarized by teachers and students in the past [10]. The following Fig. 5 shows the teaching improvement suggestions.

Therefore, we propose that the construction of teaching resource database system is very important in the process of school information construction. Teaching resource database is not simply collecting and managing text, articles and images. In schools, the teaching resource database is the material basis for education stakeholders to carry out education and teaching work, covering a large number of school administrative documents, teaching materials, courseware, student homework, dynamic materials and so on. And it needs to do orderly classification management, which is convenient for later use.

The construction scheme of mobox teaching resource database system is recommended.

The construction of teaching resource database system is an important part of school informatization [11]. The basic characteristics of school informatization are digitization, networking, intelligence and multimedia; The basic attributes include openness, usability, interactivity and collaboration. So how can we further improve the informatization of education?

There are many practical difficulties in the management and utilization of teaching resource database:

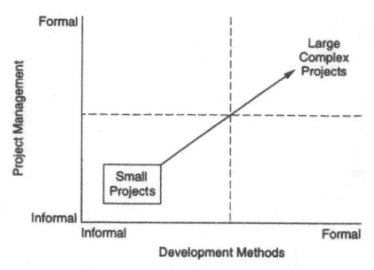

Fig. 5. Teaching improvement suggestions

1) There are many materials in various disciplines and offices of the school, most of which exist in paper form, which is difficult to keep for a long time and find. The time cost of management and application by managers and actual users is very high.
2) The exchange of teaching resources between students and teachers is almost blank. Although there is also the emergence of personal space, the realization of deep-seated sharing and free management of teaching resources has not really been realized.
3) The form of teaching resource database transmission between the majority of teaching staff and management departments is too simple, and it still stays in QQ, email, wechat and other ways. When there are many participants and a large amount of information, the cost of information transmission and management increases sharply. In addition, the statistical cost is unimaginable, and there are great security risks.

The process of building teaching resource database system.

The difficulties in the construction, management and use of teaching resource database platform have become prominent. How to solve them?

After testing, research and demonstration of several private cloud platforms, our school has adopted mobox shared private cloud disk to build the teaching resource database platform, which has achieved good results and greatly improved the management efficiency [12]. The specific performance is as follows:

1) Unified identity authentication
   Mobox can go to the school's ad or LDAP for integrated authentication
   After mobox logs in, it can be integrated with the third-party campus information software. After mobox logs in, it does not need to log in again to enter the third-party information system (the same as the integrated information system).

Mobox has personnel management and authentication services, which can provide each teacher with an independent personal account. Teachers can directly log in to the platform through the link of the portal to carry out relevant work.

2) A simple and easy-to-use hierarchical and decentralized data authority management system

The administrator creates document cabinets of each discipline, grade and department, and assigns the administrator of the document cabinet. In this way, the administrator only creates a large classification, and the detailed directory in each grade or discipline is managed by the administrator of the document cabinet [13].

The management of each document cabinet is subdivided into categories according to the management needs of their own disciplines or grades. When it is complicated, you can assign a directory to a teacher to manage it by yourself.

Relevant access permissions can be set for each document cabinet or directory. (for example, who can see, who can download, who can modify, who can upload, etc.)

There are management and sharing problems that cloud disk cannot solve.

3) Management and use of teaching resource database

It is very convenient to solve the difficulties in the distribution, recovery, download, statistics, sharing and other links of traditional teaching resources [14]. The cost of teaching resource database management is greatly reduced, and teachers' enthusiasm to use teaching resource database for teaching is increasing day by day, which is more convenient than the traditional one. Figure 6 below shows the load organization of the resource manager system.

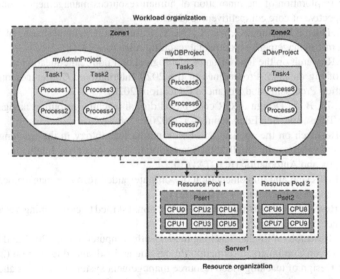

Fig. 6. The workload organization for resource manager system

5 Conclusion

To sum up, a teaching resource management system with collaborative recommendation function is the key to solve the current excessive accumulation and low efficiency of teaching resources. This paper introduces the collaborative recommendation algorithm into the teaching resource management system to recommend different types of teaching resources to applicable users. The collaborative recommendation teaching resource management system is composed of personal space management, resource management, recommendation module and system management to meet the different functional requirements of users in different roles, so as to improve the sharing and utilization of teaching resources.

References

1. Haitao, L., Xiaofang, D., Sunan, D.: On intelligent recommendation technology machine of teaching resources in open education. J. Yancheng Inst. Technol. (Soc. Sci. Ed.) **30**(4), 81–84 (2017)
2. Qihua, L.: Research on hybrid recommendation based on interest community and trusted neighbors. Inf. Sci. **34**(2), 65–69 (2016)
3. Qingxia, L., Wenhong, W., Zhaoquan, C.: E-commerce personalized recommendation algorithm for hybrid user and project collaborative filtering. J. Sun Yat sen Univ. (Nat. Sci. Ed.) **55**(5), 37–42 (2016)
4. Ma, R., Bian, Y., Chen, C., Wu, H.: E-commerce personalized recommendation algorithm based on Hadoop – Taking film recommendation as an example. Comput. Syst. Appl. **24**(5), 111–117 (2015)
5. Yan, Y.: Exploration of the innovation of human resources management in university from the perspective of core competitiveness (2018)
6. Zong, Y., Huang, X., Wang, G., Wu, X., Hu, X.: Research on regional sharing platform system of economic management experimental teaching resources (2018)
7. Wu, X.: Research on the innovation of ideological and political education in universities in the era of big data. In: Proceedings of the 2020 International Conference on Computers, Information Processing and Advanced Education (2020)
8. Li, J.-Y., Li, B.-J.: Design of QR code-based digital teaching resources navigation system. Destech Trans. Soc. Sci. Educ. Hum. Sci. (2020)
9. Ge, S.: Research on the application of new media technology in the teaching of film and television aesthetics. In: 2020 13th International Conference on Intelligent Computation Technology and Automation (ICICTA) (2020)
10. Huang, P.: Design and implementation of computer aided resource management system for dance teaching. J. Intell. Fuzzy Syst. (2021)
11. Zhu, Y.: Research on English teaching of professional skilled talents training based on artificial intelligence. J. Intell. Fuzzy Syst. (2021)
12. Zhu, M.: Research on English teaching model with computer aid. In: 2021 2nd International Conference on Computers, Information Processing and Advanced Education (2021)
13. Yan, Q.: Design of teaching video resource management system in colleges and universities based on microtechnology. Secur. Commun. Networks (2021)
14. Zhu, Y.: Design of integrated management system for English teaching resources based on artificial intelligence. In: 2021 2nd International Conference on Artificial Intelligence and Education (ICAIE) (2021)

Research on Art Design Education Based on Genetic Algorithm

Xi Tian[✉]

Xi'an Academy of Fine Arts, Xi'an 710001, Shaanxi, China
tianxi3707054@163.com

Abstract. In today's society, with the improvement of people's living standards and the acceleration of the pace of life, people's consumption concept is gradually changing. Consumers pay more and more attention to the appreciation of works of art. The beautiful appearance and shape of the art improve the value of the art in people's mind. Now the artistic feeling is mainly based on the long-term experience. In order to realize the innovation of art design, designers must broaden their thinking and try their best to tap creative inspiration. How to tap creative inspiration and bring forth the new has become the key to art design. This paper attempts to use genetic algorithm to study it, and obtain more design schemes through the replacement and iteration of genetic algorithm, so as to broaden the thinking of designers and realize the innovation of art design.

Keywords: Art design · Genetic algorithm

1 Introduction

The research on art design education based on genetic algorithm is a research aimed at improving the performance of the system. The optimization of the system can be completed by using genetic algorithm, which is an evolutionary technology to solve optimization problems. This technology was first used in biology, and then in computer science, engineering, economics and other fields. It has been found that this technique provides better results than other techniques such as linear programming or simulated annealing. Genetic algorithm is also called GA (genetic algorithm), GA (genetic algorithm) or GA (growth algorithm).The so-called art design is to combine the form and beauty of art with the design related to society, culture, economy and our life, so that it has not only aesthetic function, but also use function. In other words, art design first serves people (from space environment to clothing, food, housing, transportation and use). Art design should be the perfect combination of certain material functions and spiritual functions of human society. It is necessary in the development process of modern society [1]. Art design is an independent art discipline, Its research content and service object are different from traditional art categories. At the same time, art design is also a highly comprehensive discipline, which involves many factors such as society, culture, economy, market, science and technology, and its aesthetic standards change with the

M. A. Jan and F. Khan (Eds.): BigIoT-EDU 2022, LNICST 465, pp. 563–573, 2023.
https://doi.org/10.1007/978-3-031-23950-2_61

changes of these factors. The value of art design lies in creative activities and practice. Art design is actually the embodiment of the designer's own comprehensive quality (such as expression ability, perception ability and imagination ability). Although each major has different emphasis on design knowledge, the requirements for beauty, rhythm, balance and rhythm of the concept of "big design" are the same. Whether it is plane or three-dimensional design, candidates must first face an understanding of the designed object - an understanding of the background culture, geography, history and humanistic knowledge related to the design object. Natural products. Art comes from life and in turn acts on life.

Swarm intelligence algorithm is constructed from the simulation training of swarm biological movement, foraging attack, reproduction and other processes. Swarm algorithm has been favored by scholars in many fields, such as path optimization, data clustering, search optimization and so on. In art design, swarm intelligence algorithm also shows certain advantages, especially in design [2]. In art design, the character modeling is complex, the roles are diverse, and the design process is complex. Therefore, the efficiency of manual design is generally low, and intelligent algorithm is urgently needed for auxiliary design. Genetic algorithm shows good convergence and high efficiency in data design. The elements of persona are simulated and trained by this algorithm, and finally the persona modeling is obtained, in order to improve the efficiency of art design.

2   Related Work

2.1   Basic Principle of Genetic Algorithm

The main difference between NSGA and simple genetic algorithm is that the algorithm is layered according to the dominant relationship between individuals before the selection operator is executed. Its selection operator, crossover operator and mutation operator are no different from simple genetic algorithm. Before the selection operation is performed, the population is sorted according to the dominant and non dominant relationships between individuals: first, all non dominant individuals in the population are found and given a shared virtual fitness value. Get the first non dominated optimal layer;

Then, ignore this group of stratified individuals, continue to layer other individuals in the population according to the dominant and non dominant relationship, and give them a new virtual fitness value, which should be less than the value of the previous layer. Continue the above operations for the remaining individuals until all individuals in the population are stratified [3].

The algorithm reassigns the virtual fitness value according to fitness sharing: for example, specify that the virtual fitness value of the first layer individual is 1, and the virtual fitness value of the second layer individual should be reduced accordingly, which can be taken as 0 9, and so on. In this way, the virtual fitness value can be normalized. Maintain the advantage of good individual fitness to obtain more replication opportunities, while maintaining the diversity of the population. The flow chart of genetic algorithm is shown in Fig. 1 below.

(1)   Coding mechanism. The process of transforming the solution of the problem into an object that can be operated by genetic algorithm is called coding. Coding is

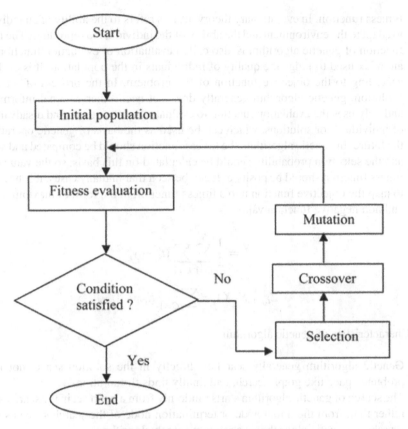

Fig. 1. Flow chart of genetic algorithm

a mapping of solutions to individuals, solution space to chromosome space, and phenotypes to genotypes. Common coding methods are as follows:

1) Binary encoding. Binary is a coding method composed of 1 and 0. It was originally proposed by Holland. This coding method is the most commonly used coding method in genetic algorithm. Binary coding adopts the principle of minimum character to encode. The coding and decoding of this coding method are relatively simple and easy, which is very helpful for the smooth realization of crossover and mutation. At the same time, this method can also be analyzed theoretically by mode theorem. However, when this coding method is used in multi-dimensional and high-precision numerical problems, the effect is not ideal, and it can not reflect the inherent structure of the problem. It has low accuracy, large individual length and occupies more memory. 2) Decimal encoding. This method uses decimal coding to control parameters, which alleviates the problem of "combination explosion" and premature convergence of genetic algorithm. 3) Gray code. Binary coding has some shortcomings in discretization of continuous functions. In order to overcome this deficiency, gray code method is proposed, which is a deformation of binary coding form [2].

(2) Fitness function. In evolutionary theory, fitness refers to the ability of an individual to adapt to the environment and the ability of the individual to reproduce. The fitness function of genetic algorithm is also called evaluation or evaluation function. It is an index used to judge the quality of individuals in the population. It is evaluated according to the objective function of the problem. In the process of searching evolution, genetic algorithm generally does not need other external information, and only uses the evaluation function to evaluate the advantages and disadvantages of individuals or solutions, which can be used as the basis of genetic operation in the future. In genetic algorithm, the fitness function should be compared and sorted, and the selection probability should be calculated on this basis, so the value of the fitness function should be positive. It can be seen that in many cases, it is necessary to map the objective function into a fitness function in the form of maximum value and non negative function value.

$$E^N = \frac{1}{2} \sum_{n=1}^{N} \sum_{k=1}^{c} (t_k^n - y_k^n)^2 \tag{1}$$

$$Z_{i,j,n}(K,X) = \sum_{C=1}^{C} K_{cn} \bullet X_{i,j,n} \tag{2}$$

Characteristics of genetic algorithm

(1) Genetic algorithm generally searches directly in the solution space, not in the problem space like graph search, and finally finds the solution.
(2) The search of genetic algorithm starts randomly from a point set in the search space, rather than from the initial node or termination node of the search space as graph search, so genetic algorithm is a random search algorithm.
(3) Genetic algorithm is always looking for the optimal solution, unlike graph search, which does not always require the optimal solution, but generally tries to find the solution as soon as possible, so genetic algorithm is an optimization search algorithm [4].
(4) The search process of genetic algorithm is to search from one point set (population) to another point set (population) in space, rather than from one point to another in space as graph search. Therefore, it is actually a parallel search, which is suitable for large-scale parallel computing, and this population to population search has the ability to jump out of the local optimal solution.
(5) Genetic algorithm has strong adaptability. In addition to the fitness function, it hardly needs other prior knowledge.
(6) Genetic algorithm is good at global search. It is not constrained by the restrictive assumption of search space and does not require continuity. It can find the global optimal solution from discrete, multi extreme and noisy high-dimensional problems with great probability.

The step flow of genetic algorithm is shown in Fig. 2.

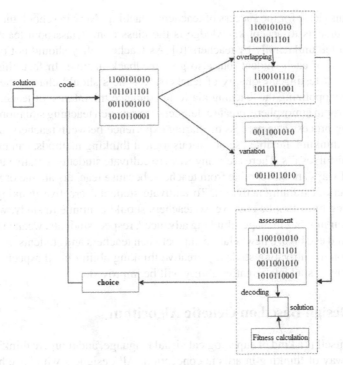

Fig. 2. Genetic algorithm step flow

2.2 Art Design Teaching

Art design is an independent art discipline. Its research content and service object are different from traditional art categories. At the same time, art design is also a highly comprehensive discipline, which involves many factors such as society, culture, economy, market, science and technology, and its aesthetic standards also change with the changes of these factors. The value of art design lies in creative activities and practice. Art design, in fact, is the embodiment of the designer's own comprehensive quality (such as performance ability, perception ability, imagination ability). Although each major has different emphasis on design knowledge, the requirements for beauty, rhythm, balance, rhythm, etc. of the concept of "big design" are the same. Whether it is plane or three-dimensional design, creative thinking ability plays a decisive role. In art design teaching, it is very difficult for students to carry out art design, because most of their homework is completed by copying. In this way, after a period of time, students' creative ability gradually weakens in copying, and they are used to copying others' mode [5]. Therefore, when teachers set questions for students to create, students will say, "how can I design it" "it's too difficult", and they are eager to find information to move things around. Such development will only make students become conformist and lack personality and imagination The students trained can only be "artistic craftsmen".

In the teaching of art design, teachers play a major role, not only in imparting knowledge, but also in leading thinking. Therefore, teachers' own quality has become an important factor for the success of teachers' teaching. Now in school, the most direct place for students to accept knowledge is the classroom. Classroom teaching should not be instilled unilaterally by teachers [6]. As teachers, they should not only observe the reflection of each student, but also give feedback in time. In fact, this process is the process of testing the quality of teachers. Teachers should change the concept of teachers monopolizing the teaching platform, enhance the interest of teaching, create a lively classroom atmosphere, create a democratic and open teaching situation, and regard the teaching process as a process of sharing experience between teachers and students. Innovative thinking, flexible use of various logical thinking methods, can be found and achieve fruitful results. There are many ways to cultivate students' creative thinking, but all kinds of ways are inseparable from teachers, because teachers are the organizers and implementers of training activities. To cultivate students' creative thinking, teachers' own thinking must first be creative, so teachers should continue to study, work hard to "change their minds", manage "thinking advance", respect students, weaken the sense of authority, and establish a new relationship between teachers and students. As long as we pay attention to cultivating students' creative thinking ability in all aspects of teaching and at all times, students' creative ability will be improved.

3 Art Design Based on Genetic Algorithm

Art design itself is a kind of super logical visual language, and intuitive thinking is a very important way of thinking in artistic conception. All designers who have had creative experience in design have had such experience. Although they have carried out comprehensive and rational analysis and long-term and arduous thinking on the design theme, the idea of satisfaction has not appeared yet, As the saying goes, "there is no way out of doubt". At this time, a wonderful idea was born through the induction of some accidental factors, which is the typical application of intuitive thinking in design. Intuition means "a way of understanding or knowing that occurs directly and instantaneously without conscious thinking and judgment" [7].

This paper studies art design. The solution of art design is a combination of different types and types. Based on the practical problems of this paper, this paper adopts binary coding. There are many coding methods in genetic algorithm, and binary coding is a commonly used coding method. In this coding method, 0 and 1 are the symbols of the individual, and the whole individual is the symbol string of 0 and 1 composed of several 0 and several 1. The symbol precision of the problem to be solved by genetic algorithm determines the length of binary coding string. Suppose there is a parameter whose value range is [UMIN, Umax]. If the parameter is represented by a binary string with length L, it can generate 2L codes. Figure 3 below shows the art design parameterized binary code.Then the binary encoding accuracy is:

$$u_{max}(t) = u_{min}(t) + L(t)(\dot{e}_{k+1}(t) + e_{k+1}(t)) \tag{3}$$

The advantages of this coding method are as follows:

(1) For genetic algorithm, the important genetic operations are crossover and mutation, which are easy to realize by binary coding;

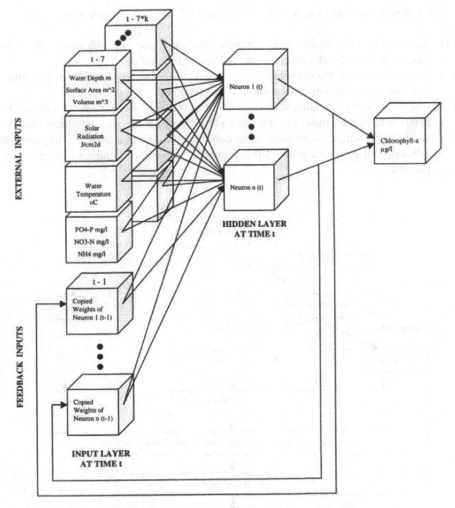

Fig. 3. Art design parametric binary coding

(2) Encoding and decoding are relatively simple and easy to operate;

(3) Binary coding conforms to the coding principle of the minimum character set in the coding principle;

(4) The binary coding method is more convenient to analyze by using the pattern theorem.

Genetic algorithm basically does not use external information in evolutionary search, only based on fitness function. The value of individual fitness function in genetic algorithm is the basis of population search. Whether the fitness function is properly selected is very important for the whole algorithm to find the optimal solution at a faster speed. The selection of fitness function is generally transformed from the objective function of the problem objective [8].

The fitness function design shall mainly meet the following conditions:

(1) Reasonable and consistent. The fitness function value is required to reflect the advantages and disadvantages of the corresponding solution;
(2) Adapt to as many problems as possible. For a class of specific problems, the fitness function should be universal without much change;
(3) The amount of calculation shall be as small as possible. Because genetic algorithm needs to search for many generations and has a large time cost, the fitness function should be as simple as possible, reduce the amount of calculation and improve the efficiency of genetic algorithm [9]. Figure 4 below shows the art design coding process.

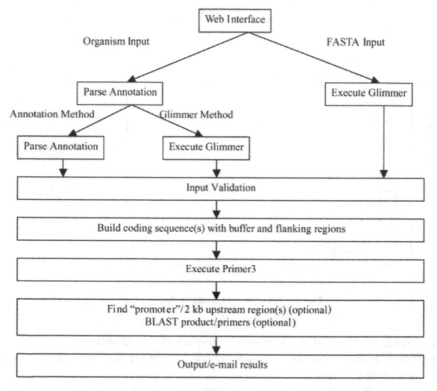

Fig. 4. Art design coding process

K-means algorithm is a method of clustering with the help of the center of data. Therefore, when the distribution of some data is very special, such as some data is large, it will affect the center position of the data, thus affecting the results of the whole clustering. In order to overcome the shortcomings of K-means algorithm, we can consider using medoid as a clustering center to replace the average center of the previous k-means algorithm. The data can be classified according to the principle of minimizing the sum of the distances between each data object and medoid. This is the basic idea of k-medoids algorithm [10].

Because the value of an abnormal data may be very large, which will affect the estimation of data distribution (the calculation of clustering mean in k-means algorithm), K-means mean algorithm is very sensitive to abnormal data. Therefore, it is envisaged to use medoid as a reference point to replace the mean value of each cluster in the k-means algorithm (as the cluster center). Thus, the division method can continue to be applied according to the principle of minimizing the sum of the distances (differences) between each object and each reference point. This constitutes the k-medoids algorithm.

The basic idea of k-medoids method is to randomly select a data to represent a certain class, so that K clustering centers can be found from n clustering data (which needs to be repeated). According to the distance from these clustering centers, other objects are classified into their corresponding categories (according to the principle of minimum distance). If you change a clustering center, you can get a better clustering result, It is proved that the new cluster center is better, and the original cluster center can be replaced. The quality of clustering will be evaluated by a cost function, which can express the distance between each data and the cluster center.

In artistic creation, intuition is the direct understanding and Revelation of the inside story or essence of things by omitting the reasoning process. Inspiration and intuition are the same word inspi ratio in English. The ancient Greeks believed that "inspiration is a sudden understanding of the fundamental nature of something". Psychology believes that although inspiration is sudden and unexpected, it is positive after the excitement of the advantage of brain concentration. That is to say, although its occurrence is accidental, it must be an instant manifestation of the barrier between long-term ideation and sexuality. Cheng needs to transform design concepts into design images, which is the key point of creative thinking. From design concepts to Jun's fear, we must first help intuition and inspired thinking activities to achieve. The designer should first explore and establish the forms and models of W countless possibilities, and the bridge from here to there. Then repeated logical inference and test are carried out [11]. Finally, T2 image appeared Excellent designers strive to design the "bird's nest", the National Swimming Center "Water Cube", the British Pavilion of the Shanghai WorldExpo "seed Temple", and so on. These five are not from concept to image It is derived from the design process of intuition and inspiration, and the spirit of allowing full officials to be creative.

The algorithm flow of this paper is as follows:

(1) Coding: binary coding.
(2) Generation of initial population;
(3) Determination of fitness function. The fitness function is designed according to the artistic characteristics;
(4) Implementation of selection operator: using tournament method to select operator;
(5) Implementation of crossover operator: single point crossover is adopted for the first 1/3 individuals with fitness function value, and three-point crossover is adopted for the last 2/3 individuals;
(6) Implementation of mutation operator: set individual mutation probability threshold a and gene mutation threshold β Two parameters, according to which the selected individuals are mutated.

4 Creative Thinking in Art Design Emphasizes Intuition and Inspiration

Art design itself is a kind of super logical visual language, and intuitive thinking is a very important way of thinking in artistic conception [12]. All designers who have had creative experience in design have had such experience. Although they have carried out comprehensive and rational analysis and long-term and arduous thinking on the design theme, the idea of satisfaction has not appeared for a long time, which is the so-called "no way out". At this time, induced by some accidental factors, a wonderful idea was born, which is the typical application of intuitive thinking in design. Intuition means "a way of understanding or knowing that occurs directly and instantaneously without conscious thinking and judgment". In artistic creation, intuition is the direct understanding and Revelation of the inside story or essence of things by omitting the reasoning process. Inspiration and intuition are the same word inspi ratio in English[13]. The ancient Greeks believed that, "Inspiration is a sudden understanding of the fundamental nature of something". Psychology believes that although inspiration is sudden and unexpected, it is certain after the advantage of brain concentration. That is to say, although its occurrence is accidental, it must be the result of long-term thinking. Therefore, inspiration and intuition are, to some extent, a breakthrough in the barrier between rationality and sensibility, and an instant manifestation of the high integration of the two.

Art design is a subject that uses image thinking. The creative process needs to transform design concepts into design images, which is the key point of creative thinking. The transformation from design concepts to design images needs to be realized with the help of intuitive and inspirational thinking activities. Designers should first explore and establish the design concept, which is the starting point of creativity. Then build countless possible forms and models in the mind with intuition, and constantly try to build a bridge between subjective concepts and objective images. Then repeated logical inference and test are carried out [14]. Finally, with the outbreak of inspiration and intuitive judgment, the idea is connected, creative artistic images appear, and excellent design schemes are born. This creative design process represents the creative process in almost all design fields. We are familiar with the "bird's nest" of the National Stadium of the Olympic Games, the "Water Cube" of the National Swimming Center, the "seed Temple" of the British Pavilion of the Shanghai WorldExpo, and so on. All these design works with profound ideological connotation, dreamlike beauty and wonderful creativity came from this design process from conception to image, with the help of intuition and inspiration, full of adventure and creativity.

5 Conclusion

The research on art design education based on genetic algorithm is the research on the relationship between art design and genetic algorithm. The main purpose of this study is to find out the most effective method of using genetic algorithm to design art. The purpose of this article is to better understand how these two areas work together to create more effective products, which is beneficial to both students and designers. In this research, we are using genetic algorithm to design art education courses. The main goal is to find a course that can be used in art schools. In other words, our goal is to find out what kind of art education courses are most effective for students and teachers. We want to know which type of course is more efficient than others. The study was conducted by the University of California, Davis, through its neural computing center (CNC). CNC aims to develop neural networks that can solve problems related to computer vision, speech recognition, natural language processing (NLP) and machining.

Art design has always been one of the art design themes widely concerned by people, and has also added color to people's life. Because of its variety, or elegant, or gorgeous, or fresh, it has been widely selected by people in life and career to beautify the environment and improve the quality of the environment. Based on the research of genetic algorithm, this paper uses heritage algorithm to study art design, which can open up ideas for designers and improve the efficiency and quality of art design.

References

1. Huang, R.: Exploration of practical teaching method of art design education based on new media technology under Internet plus background (2021)
2. Alyabieva, L., Sakhno, I., Fadeeva, T.: Innovative forms of education in art and design: overview and prospects. Sci. Anal. J. Burganov House Space Cult. **17**(1), 126–144 (2021)
3. Hafsha, A.: Study of Creative Thinking in Digital Media Art Design Education (2020)
4. Xiao, Y.Y.: The development space of university art design education in the era of big data. J. Phys: Conf. Ser. **1648**(4), 042088 (2020)
5. Zou, J., Lin, F., Gao, S., et al.: Transfer learning based multi-objective genetic algorithm for dynamic community detection (2021)
6. Sun, Y., Xue, B., Zhang, M., et al.: Automatically designing CNN architectures using the genetic algorithm for image classification. IEEE Trans. Cybern. **99**, 1–15 (2020)
7. Huang, X., Li, K., Xie, Y., et al.: A novel multistage constant compressor speed control strategy of electric vehicle air conditioning system based on genetic algorithm. Energy **241**, 122903 (2022)
8. Liu, R.: Innovation Mode of Art Education in Colleges and Universities Based on Big Data. J. Phys: Conf. Ser. **1852**(3), 032027 (2021)
9. Toshiya, A., Sugimori, J.: Practice of Manufacturing Education Using an Art Work Based on design thinking (2020)
10. Ukovi, A.V., Mrvo, I.D., Radovanovi, I.V.: Education Based on Art as Inclusive Education. Inovacije U Nastavi **33**(2), 1–14 (2020)
11. Liu, Q.: Application and exploration of online education of art and design subjects. In: 2020 International Conference on Big Data and Informatization Education (ICBDIE) (2020)
12. Xu, C., Huang, Y., Dewancker, B.: Art Inheritance: an education course on traditional pattern morphological generation in architecture design based on digital sculpturism. Sustainability **12** (2020)
13. Zhang, W., Shankar, A., Antonidoss, A.: Modern art education and teaching based on artificial intelligence. J. Interconnection Netw. **22**, 2141005 (2021)
14. Yu, H.C.: Development of multidisciplinary learning model of maker education based on design thinking for technology education. Korean Soc. Sci. Art **38**(2), 323–335 (2020)

Research on Channel Optimization Strategy Based on Data Mining Technology

Dan Wang[✉]

Sichuan University of Media and Communications, Chengdu 611745, China
286212023@qq.com

Abstract. In recent years, the rapid application and popularization of e-commerce generated by the development of information technology and network technology. After the combination of e-commerce and traditional banking, emerging self-service channels such as self-service bank, online bank, telephone bank, mobile bank and TV bank have emerged. Compared with traditional banking service channels, these emerging banking service channels have more advantages, lower cost, no time and space constraints, service differences, innovation advantages, scale and scope economy advantages, etc. Therefore, how to use data mining technology to reduce the excessive use of counter and other channels, alleviate the phenomenon of network queuing, give full play to the maximum efficiency of various service channels, improve the bank service quality, so as to improve customers' satisfaction and loyalty to bank services has become one of the key concerns of commercial banks.

Keywords: Data mining technology · Channels · Optimization strategy

1 Introduction

With the rapid development of China's financial industry, the competition among commercial banks is becoming more and more fierce, and all kinds of businesses and products are becoming more and more homogeneous. For ordinary customers, it is difficult for them to see how excellent the internal background system of a bank is, and the perceptual understanding of the channel as the "medium" basically determines the customer's satisfaction and loyalty, so the construction and optimization of the channel is directly related to the customer's feeling of the bank's service; At the same time, the complexity of banking operations has also become an important factor for customers to choose banks and service channels, which is also the key for banks to occupy the market and win customers. Through the optimization of service channels, commercial banks can achieve good results in business operation, service optimization and the expansion of new channels and new businesses [1]. Therefore, the optimization of service channels has become an urgent work for commercial banks in the current market competition.

By optimizing service channels, developing multi-channel operation and realizing the diversion of counter business has become an important means for commercial banks

M. A. Jan and F. Khan (Eds.): BigIoT-EDU 2022, LNICST 465, pp. 574–579, 2023.
https://doi.org/10.1007/978-3-031-23950-2_62

to improve service competitiveness and product competitiveness, which is related to the business development and operation development of grass-roots outlets. In order to give better play to the main channel role of outlets, it has become an urgent task for the banking industry to improve the competitiveness of outlets to divert counter business, alleviate counter pressure and improve the proportion of channel transactions. At the same time, the diversion of counter business is of far-reaching significance for banks to release the pressure of counter personnel, effectively save operating costs and cultivate customers' habit of consciously using self-service equipment and electronic channels. Its advantages are reflected in:

First, optimize the structure of customer transaction channels, and further tilt the counter channels to target customers by reducing the volume and proportion of individual customers' counter business; Low star customers are more diverted to electronic channels, which can improve the activity level of electronic channel customers. Second, promote the improvement of bank service level, reduce the proportion of customers waiting overtime and the average queuing time of customers, and improve customer satisfaction. Third, optimize the personnel structure. The diversion of counter business can release the labor force of grass-roots temporary counter personnel and improve the proportion of sales personnel. Fourth, promote the improvement of operational risk management level. With the decrease of diversion rate, the work pressure of front-line tellers is reduced, which can greatly reduce the occurrence of operational risk events.

2 Data Mining Technology

Data mining (DM) is a process of extracting hidden, unknown but potentially useful information and knowledge from a large number of incomplete, noisy, fuzzy and random data. At the beginning, data mining technology was mainly application-oriented. It can process structured or semi-structured data, from simple retrieval and call of data to micro or macro analysis, statistics and reasoning of these data, so as to seek the basis for solving practical problems and find the internal relationship between events, Finally, the existing data can be used to make decisions on future activities.

2.1 Analysis Method of Data Mining

The more tools and methods the data mining system uses, the higher the accuracy of the results, because one way can't be used for the same problem, and another way can be used. It all depends on the type of problem and the type and scale of data. There are many classification methods of data mining technology. According to the mining tasks, it can be divided into classification, clustering, association, pattern recognition, visualization, decision tree, genetic algorithm and so on.

(1) Classification analysis

The prediction of the model often aims to obtain other data through some data in the database. If the predicted data volume is discrete, it is called classification; If the amount of data is continuous, it is called regression [2]. The model constructed by this description is generally represented by rules, decision trees and neural network patterns.

If you want to analyze the credit risk of a user's credit, you must make a comprehensive analysis of its debt, income and stability of work. For the classification algorithm, the result is given through the relationship between the above attributes and the risk degree in the data. This approach can be implemented using a decision tree. Analyzing the data and taking the most important attribute in risk prediction as the first branch point is a sufficient condition for large credit risk. For those with high credit risk, it can be used as the second judgment condition, and so on. In fact, each user applicant has many other different attributes, and the number of applicants is very large. It will be very difficult to seek judgment manually, and the classification algorithm can complete the decision tree of the rule.

(2) Cluster analysis

Clustering is to classify data into several groups according to similarity. It is different from the prediction model, and the data attributes of target variables in clustering are not obvious. The algorithm judges its "hidden attributes" through the detection of data, and divides the customer database into multiple similar groups by grouping. Each group contains multiple similar customers, and corresponding strategies can be formulated for different groups. There are a variety of data classification methods. The commonly used methods are k-means algorithm, hierarchical aggregation method and estimation maximum method. In practical application, the dimension should be defined. When the dimension is 2, the division of groups is relatively simple and can be realized manually; However, if the dimension becomes larger, it will be quite difficult to classify manually, because simple data division is meaningless. With the increase of divided data points, the situation becomes quite complex. In this case, the clustering algorithm can handle it well. It will classify the data and produce the corresponding aggregate values.

(3) Correlation analysis

The purpose of association analysis is to generate a summary of some data information and obtain the correlation between data sets or the derived relationship between data. The technology used is usually association rules. The calculation of association rules mainly depends on the data set in the relevant data, which is composed of the data in the transaction. The measurement of its relevance can usually be realized by two thresholds: support and credibility. At the same time, the parameters such as interest and relevance are further introduced to make the mined rules more in line with the actual needs.

2.2 Data Mining Process

The process of data mining is not a linear process, but an iterative process, in which there are many feedback loops. As shown in Fig. 1, it can be roughly divided into problem determination, data preparation, data mining implementation and result expression and evaluation.

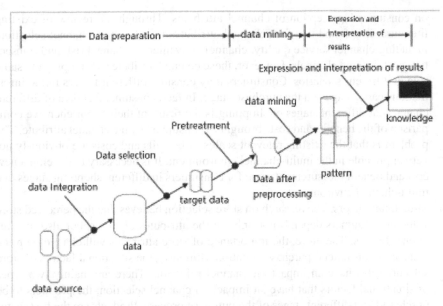

Fig. 1. Data mining process

3 Channel Selection

3.1 Channel Selection Behavior

The so-called channel is the channel or way for consumers to obtain products (or services) from manufacturers or retailers. It is the organization on which products or services are transmitted from production or retail to consumption. Some scholars also define the channel as the specific way or channel formed by connecting all links in the process of transferring products (or services) from the production field to the consumption field. Channel is not only the contact point between consumers and enterprises, but also the medium for interaction between enterprises and consumers.

With the development of network technology, more and more enterprises integrate the network into multi-channel marketing strategy by using existing resources, and carry out marketing activities through a variety of sales channels such as traditional physical stores, mail orders, TV shopping channels and e-commerce websites. Moreover, consumers make complex shopping choices in a variety of channel environments, obtain products and experience a high level of customer service. From the perspective of bank service channels, with the development of information technology, the service channels provided by banks have also developed from the traditional counter to multi-channel such as self-service bank, online bank and telephone bank [3].

3.2 Influencing Factors of Channel Selection

(1) Channel factors. Channel selection mainly comes from the costs and benefits brought by the channel to its users. In other words, channel selection depends

on consumers' perception of channel attributes. Through the review of existing literature, it is found that four channel attributes mainly affect channel selection, including channel service quality, channel convenience, channel risk and transaction cost through channels. However, these channel attributes do not play the same role in different scenarios. Consumers may consider different factors in the information search stage and the purchase stage. In fact, consumers' choice of different channels at different stages of shopping is the result of their comprehensive comparison of the benefits and costs brought to consumers by the channel attribute. The problem is that the existing relevant scales of benefits and costs are obviously not very applicable in the multi-channel environment, It is necessary to develop a new cost and benefit measurement scale for consumers in different shopping stages in a multi-channel environment.

(2) Situational factors. The research on store selection believes that the perceived store value of consumers depends not only on the attributes of stores, but also on situational factors. Therefore, the importance of store attributes will change with the change of consumers' purchase situation. Similarly, the situational factors of store selection also have an impact on channel selection. There are mainly two types of situational factors that have an impact on channel selection: the products to be purchased and different stages of the purchase process. Products are the first factor that consumers consider when choosing channels [3]. Chiang et al. (2006) found through experiments that the factors affecting consumers' choice of traditional and virtual channels will show differences due to different product categories. Generally speaking, the Internet is more suitable for the sales of search products, while complex and high involvement products are suitable for traditional channels. Balasubramanian et al. (200) and Baal and Dach (2005) believe that channel selection also depends on different stages of the shopping process. For example, a consumer uses the Internet to search for product information, then buys in a physical store, and finally uses a call center to obtain services. In other words, the importance of channel attributes in the channel selection decision-making process will change with different stages of the shopping process [4].

(3) Consumer factors. Consumers' demographic characteristics (gender, age, income and education), psychological characteristics (lifestyle, innovation characteristics) and behavioral characteristics (previous shopping experience) will affect consumers' choice and preference for channels. The early literature mainly focused on demographic characteristics. Later, with the increasing popularity of Internet applications, many scholars also began to explore the impact of psychological and behavioral characteristics such as lifestyle, innovation characteristics, channel tendency and shopping experience on online channel selection.

4 Conclusion

Therefore, based on data mining technology and with the help of the characteristics and advantages of various channels, some innovative businesses are launched. For example, the business that meets the installment payment of credit card can be marketed to customers in the form of external dialing by telephone bank. With the consent of customers, it can be handled directly for customers through relevant background transactions; Through the outbound call of telephone banking, you can also market some specific financial products to customers, and subscribe to customers first with the consent of customers. Then, customers complete this transaction through the verification and confirmation of U shield of online banking, so as to expand innovative business by combining the respective channels of telephone banking and online banking.

References

1. Fengjing, S., Zhongqing, Y.: Data Mining Principles and Algorithms. China water resources and Hydropower Press, Beijing (2003)
2. Jiawei, H., Bo, K.: Concept and Technology of Data Mining. Machinery Industry Press, Beijing (2007)
3. Yaqin, C.: Empirical Analysis on Influencing Factors of bank customer service channel selection. Financial circles (Academic Edition), No. 06 (2013)
4. Jingdong, C.: Research on customer behavior in the environment of diversified banking service channels. International financial research, No. 08 (2005)

Research on College Chinese Online Learning System Based on Content Recommendation Algorithm

Liang Chen[✉]

Gongqing College of Nanchang University, Jiangxi 332020, China
yuerushui@163.com

Abstract. With the development of Internet scale, recommendation algorithm is widely used in e-commerce, advertising, community and so on, and collaborative filtering algorithm is also widely used because of its simple implementation and clear process. However, the traditional recommendation algorithm has the problems of long cold start time, insufficient suppression of Matthew effect and insufficient utilization of item information. In the existing methods for cold start problems, the recommended contents are not fully utilized. If we want to use the recommended content as the information source of the recommendation system, we need an appropriate modeling method to analyze the content. Therefore, the focus of this paper is how to analyze and model the College Chinese online learning system, and finally use this information for recommendation.

Keywords: Content recommendation algorithm · College Chinese · Online learning system

1 Introduction

The emergence of recommendation system has a great impact on the traditional information retrieval business and traditional Internet services. Due to the penetration of recommendation algorithm, it is an active mining of content and information in the Internet. In other words, the recommendation algorithm is a more accurate automatic search, because it does not require user intervention. In the traditional e-commerce model, there are only two ways for users to retrieve the goods they want to buy: classified catalog and search. When user needs are not clear, search cannot work. On the other hand, the huge directory tree will make users lose patience. While increasing the time cost, users are unlikely to buy their favorite items. After the rise of recommendation system, e-commerce websites can establish user preference model for each user by using recommendation system. When the user's operation and data are more detailed, the accuracy of the model will be better. When the recommendation system generates a recommendation list for users, users can browse and buy goods that meet their interests in the list. These goods often meet the needs of users [1]. There are many information sources in the recommendation system, among which the most common is user history

M. A. Jan and F. Khan (Eds.): BigIoT-EDU 2022, LNICST 465, pp. 580–585, 2023.
https://doi.org/10.1007/978-3-031-23950-2_63

data, including user browsing, clicking, downloading, comments and so on. At the same time, the information source also has historical data of items, such as click through rate, sales volume, etc. After many optimization and changes, more and more data are also used to recommend algorithms, such as labels, time, geographical location and other additional information.

In order to better improve contemporary college students' Chinese learning ability, this paper takes the popular wechat applet for college students' Chinese online learning as the research carrier, takes the frequent and compulsory Chinese test types at the university stage as the direction, pursues objective reality, and constructs a self-defined and improved recommendation system to make personalized recommendation for college students in Chinese learning. The recommendation system mainly focuses on content-based recommendation algorithm, supplemented by user based collaborative filtering algorithm And make appropriate amendments and improvements according to the type framework of College Students' Chinese test questions, so that it can make corresponding personalized recommendations to college students more effectively, so as to effectively improve college students' Chinese learning ability.

2 Content Based Recommendation Algorithm

Content based recommendation (CB) is a recommendation algorithm proposed and used earlier, even earlier than user based collaborative filtering. This recommendation method is to recommend corresponding items or contents for users according to the items or contents users use or click, which was first applied to information retrieval system.

There are three main steps of CB algorithm:

(1) Item representation: extract some features (that is, the content of the item) for each item to represent the item. For an item, the data contained in it is divided into two categories: structured data and unstructured data. Taking text as an example, its structured data includes such as title, label, length, publishing time, etc., while the text itself is unstructured data. Because of its content and ideas, we can't store it directly through a simple data structure. In the object representation, we need to extract these two parts of the object at the same time and make a unified structured representation. In text analysis, the familiar vector space model (VSM) and term frequency inverse document frequency (TF IDF) are a kind of modeling after extracting features from text documents in the field of information retrieval. Music can be recommended based on metadata, such as common writers, albums, release dates, etc., which is the earliest content-based recommendation method involving music. However, this has great limitations [2]. The reason is that the styles of these composers and singers are relatively changeable, which are affected by their own conditions such as their experience, times and age. If you make recommendations based solely on this information,

The results obtained are not entirely accurate.

(2) User learning: use the feature data of a user's favorite (and disliked) content in the past to learn the user's preference profile. There are many different methods to learn

user preferences, such as k-nearest neighbor (KNN), Rocchio algorithm and so on. The former is a clustering method. For a new item, the algorithm finds K items that user u has scored and similar to this item, and judges the preference for the new item according to U's preference for these K items. The difference from the collaborative filtering algorithm is that the KNN method here is the preference calculated according to the item attribute vector, not the user score. Rocchio algorithm is an algorithm for dealing with relevance feedback in information retrieval. The feedback data generated by the user's behavior in the operation process constantly modifies the vector representing the user's preference to approximate the real result. The formula is as follows:

$$u_{k+1}(t) = u_k(t) + \Gamma_{l1}\dot{e}_k(t) + \Gamma_{l2}\dot{e}_{k+1}(t) + \Gamma_{p1}\Delta\dot{e}_k(t) + \Gamma_{p2}\Delta\dot{e}_{k+1}(t) \tag{1}$$

(3) Recommendation generation: by comparing the user profile obtained in the previous step with the characteristics of candidate items, recommend a group of items with the greatest relevance for this user. The method used in this step depends on the type of model used in step 2). If the learning method is used, the algorithm will return K items most related to the user's attributes to the user as recommendations; If the traditional classification method is adopted, the algorithm will directly predict K users' favorite items through the model and recommend them to users. The specific similarity measurement can be obtained by calculating cosine similarity or Euclidean distance, and the formula is as follows:

$$(E(t) - M_2C)\Delta\dot{x}_{k+1}(t) = f(t, x_d(t)) - f(t, x_{k+1}(t)) + B\Delta u_k(t)$$
$$- (\Gamma_{p1}C + M_1C + M_2C)\dot{x}_d(t) + \Gamma_{p1}C\dot{x}_{k-1}(t) \tag{2}$$

CB algorithm has advantages, such as independence between users, generating a user's recommendation list does not depend on the behavior of other users. For example, it is better interpretive because it models items and users separately and quantifies some specific attributes, which can well explain the reasons for the recommendation results.

3 College Chinese Online Learning System Based on Content Recommendation Algorithm

3.1 Overall Structure

The composition of convolutional neural network crnn is divided into two main parts: one is feature learning layer and the other is feature mapping layer. The crnn structure designed in this paper has four hidden layers, plus the input layer and output layer, there are six layers. The first layer is the input layer. As mentioned above, we process the text into 96 × Mel spectrum of 1366, which will be directly used as the input of the network.

The next 2 to 5 layers are hidden layers. The hidden layer is the main component of convolutional neural network, which is also the difference between it and general depth neural network. The hidden layer is composed of neurons in accordance with the number of pixel points. The convolution kernel scans and learns the features on the plane of each layer. After pooling, the features are mapped to the next layer, which is a layer by layer mapping process from low-level features to high-level features. Finally, we access an output layer in the form of full connection, and the output layer is also a classifier. The results we get can be classified and recommended [3].

Each H × W × The convolution layer of D will learn D features from the image with width of W and height of H. each convolution layer is followed by a pool layer, which reduces the number of feature maps of each layer. If it is the maximum pool, it means that the internal maximization function is adopted to screen the most significant features.

The model structure diagram of crnn is shown in Fig. 1:

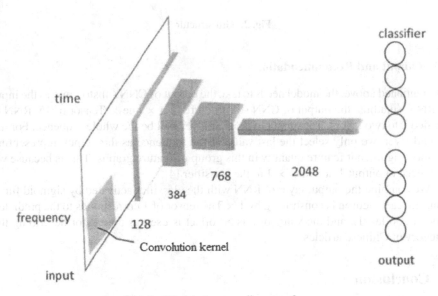

Fig. 1. Model structure diagram of crnn

3.2 Dropout Optimization and Regularization

As mentioned above, over fitting and gradient disappearance are easy to occur after the model is complicated. According to statistics, if the content of the article is too long, it will be divided into two parts in the Chinese text processing stage and processed into a Mel spectrum. Therefore, for a music, in the tensor diagram of n × 1 × 15 output in the CNN substructure of crnn, the maximum value of n is 2, so the number of layers of RNN is finally two. The RNN substructure adopts Gru structure (as shown in Fig. 2), because its required number of iterations and convergence speed are better than the LSTM model with the same function.

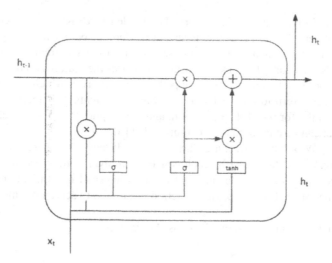

Fig. 2. Gru structure

3.3 Output and Recommendation

As mentioned above, the model needs to take the output of CNN substructure as the input of RNN, so adjust the output of CNN substructure to n × one × Tensor of 15. RNN is divided into two layers. The output of the first layer will be the whole sequence. For the second layer, we only select the last value of the sequence as the output, representing the most significant feature quantity in this group of feature graphs. This is because we only need to output 1 at a time × 1 to the classifier [4].

We combine the output layer of RNN with the classifier activated by sigmoid function, and each neuron is constrained by 1 × The tensor of 1 corresponds to the predicted offset of 50 labels, and the value of this 50 offset is used as the vector describing the category of Chinese articles.

4 Conclusion

In the analysis and comparison of the existing methods to optimize the recommendation algorithm, it is found that the traditional methods generally do not pay enough attention to the information contained in the recommended content itself. This part of information can not be used as the information source of the recommendation algorithm effectively and completely, which is actually one of the reasons for the cold start. When a new item is added to the database, there is no user data, so it is difficult to be scanned by the traditional collaborative filtering algorithm. If the recommendation algorithm can use the information of the content itself to analyze the "semantics" of the content, it can define the nature of a content and directly make basic recommendations when new content is added. Based on this, taking the College Chinese online learning system as an example, this paper puts forward a recommendation method to analyze the content semantics.

References

1. Liang, X.: Practice of recommendation system. People's Posts and Telecommunications Press (2012)
2. Shuying, Y., Hua, Z.: Pattern recognition and intelligent computing. Electronic Industry Press (2015)
3. Yuhang, Z., Wenjuan, Y., Shan, J.: Overview of personalized recommendation system. Value Eng. **39**(02), 287–292 (2020)
4. Bing, S., Pengfei, D.: Speech emotion recognition method based on convolutional neural network. Sci. Technol. Innov. Guide **13**(6), 87–90 (2016)

Research on College Students' English Online Autonomous Learning Based on ID3 Algorithm

Zhangyan Li[⊠]

Guilin University, Guilin Guangxi 541006, China
115249936@qq.com

Abstract. The purpose of this project is to study the use of ID3 algorithm in online learning environment. The purpose of this study is to study whether autonomous learning based on ID3 algorithm can be used as an effective tool for College English teaching. This research will provide us with information about how students learn and use their online resources, what impact it has on them, and whether there are any negative effects of using these tools. This study aims to determine whether students can learn English more effectively when they are able to work by themselves, rather than when they are assigned tasks that require them to complete in a group environment. The study will involve two groups: one group will work independently, and the other group will work together using an online program called English Online Autonomous Learning (eoal). We intend to provide an effective and efficient English teaching method by using ID3 algorithm. The main purpose of this study is to find out how ID3 can be used as an autonomous learning system for English teaching through web-based multimedia tools such as video clips and audio files.

Keywords: ID3 algorithm · Online learning · College English · Reform in education

1 Introduction

Autonomous learning has become a hot topic in the field of social research since the 1950s. With the development and progress of Chinese society, communication with foreign countries has become increasingly close, and English autonomous learning has been paid more and more attention by English learners. Henry holee once pointed out in 1981 that learner autonomy is the ability of students to manage language learning. In this situation, the majority of English educators began to pay attention to and actively engage in the research of autonomous learning. This paper will study college students' English Online Autonomous Learning Based on ID3 algorithm [1].

According to the spirit of the outline of basic education curriculum reform (for Trial Implementation), it can be understood that we just want to change the past tendency of "overemphasizing acceptance learning", rather than completely denying the acceptance learning method, and advocate students to learn how to study independently.

M. A. Jan and F. Khan (Eds.): BigIoT-EDU 2022, LNICST 465, pp. 586–595, 2023.
https://doi.org/10.1007/978-3-031-23950-2_64

Meanwhile, in the process of foreign language teaching, when we advocate cultivatingcollege students'autonomous learning ability,we cannot ignore the factors of Englishclassroom environment.The factors that affect the students'autonomous learning mainlyinclude three categories: physical environment,social environment and psychologicalenvironment. In terms of physical environment, the campus environment and hardwarefacilities can affect students'autonomous learning. The social environment mainly includesteachers' support, harmonious relationship between teachers and students. The psychologicalenvironment involves class involvement, teachers'innovation and so on.

So far, researchers have carried out a great deal of studies on college students'perception of classroom environment and the autonomous learning ability, but most of thestudies only tend to one aspect of them.Among these studies, some are about the relationshipbetween classroom environment and learning achievement, or classroom environment itself inuniversities or senior high schools, others are about the correlation between the autonomouslearning ability and achievement or its influence in the process of English learning.However,the analysis of the correlation between the classroom environment and the students'autonomous learning ability is relatively few. Thus, this paper aims to investigate the potentialcorrelation between these two aspects. Figure 1 below shows the flow chart of autonomous learning.

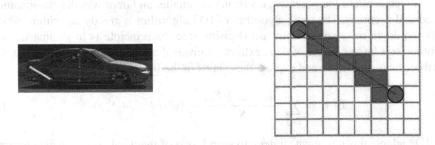

Fig. 1. Autonomous Learning flow chart

2   Data Mining and Decision Tree

2.1   ID3 Algorithm

ID3 (iterative dichotomizer 3) algorithm was proposed by Quinlan in 1986. Based on the theory of information entropy, Fig. 2 below shows the ID3 algorithm judgment process.

ID3 is a typical decision tree learning system. Its core is to select attributes on all levels of nodes of the decision tree, and use information gain as the attribute selection standard, so that when testing on each non leaf node, the largest category information about the tested example can be obtained [2]. After using this attribute to divide the instance set into subsets, the entropy of the system is the smallest. It is expected that the average path of the non leaf node to each descendant leaf node is the shortest, which makes

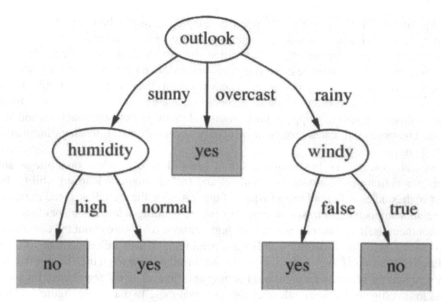

Fig. 2. ID3 algorithm judgment process

the average depth of the generated decision tree smaller and improves the classification speed and accuracy. The basic algorithm of ID3 algorithm is greedy algorithm, which uses top-down recursion to construct decision tree. Its principle is to summarize and summarize a large number of data, extract a universal and general description (i.e. the attribute laws of things), and express these laws in the form of decision tree.

$$E(A) = \sum_{i=1}^{v} \frac{S_{1i} + \dots + S_{mi}}{S} - I(S_{1i} + \dots + S_{mi}) \tag{1}$$

ID3 adopts this top-down strategy to search part of the whole space, which ensures that fewer tests are done, so the classification speed is also fast. ID3 learns by constructing a decision tree from top to bottom [2]. All current training samples are used in each step of the search. Because the statistical attributes of all samples are used, the sensitivity to errors of individual training samples is greatly reduced, so the algorithm is suitable for learning with errors in training samples. The effectiveness of ID3 on autonomous learning is shown in Fig. 3 below.

2.2 Improved ID3 Algorithm

Set a as the selection attribute, a has v attribute values, and the corresponding weight is ω_1, $\omega_2, \dots, \omega_i$. The attribute a is extended according to ID3 algorithm, and the corresponding information entropy is $E(B1), E(B2), \dots, E(Bv)$. Then the weighted entropy is defined as:

$$E(A)^* = \sum_{i=1}^{v} \omega_i \times E(B_i) \tag{2}$$

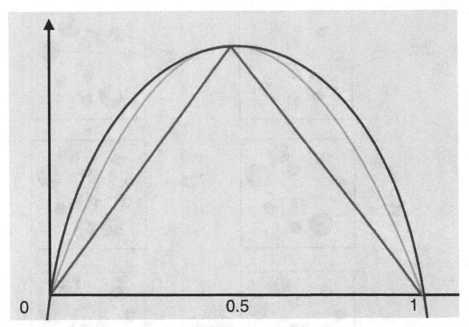

Fig. 3. The effectiveness of ID3 for autonomous learning

Directly copying a data set takes a lot of memory. If the depth of a tree is k, the data star of the original data set is n, and the dimension of each data is m, when the data itself is big data, M may be very large, then the total spatial complexity of the whole decision tree is O (n*k*m) (the worst case is a full tree with depth K, that is, all leaf nodes are at the bottom level, and each level is a division of the whole data set at this time) [3]. The robustness of ID3 algorithm framework is shown in Fig. 4 below.

(1) .n refers to the data scale. If the amount of data is large enough, the method of importing memory in batches can be adopted, but the reading operation of data sets on the Weka platform is transparent to learners. This point is difficult to import memory in batches without looking at the underlying code of the data import implementation mechanism, so it is not optimized here

(2) K is the depth of the tree obtained according to the established decision tree algorithm ID3, which can be optimized in combination with the decision tree algorithm taught by the teacher, such as 4.5 and 4.8 algorithm, which many students have done here, and there is ready-made code on the Weka platform [4]. I think it is absolutely effective to invent a new algorithm that can significantly shorten the depth of the decision tree theoretically, and the effect is immediate, but for beginners, my theoretical knowledge reserve is insufficient, It is difficult to find a universal algorithm that abandons experience and avoids generalizations, but rises to the theoretical level. This can be achieved by teachers, so I won't teach others. I will talk about how to optimize the spatial complexity of the algorithm from the perspective of a programmer. Of course, I will start from the perspective of algorithm implementation

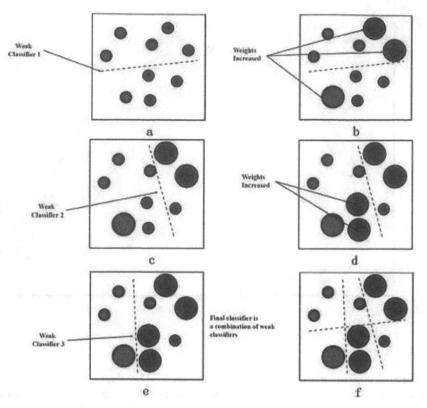

Fig. 4. Robustness of ID3 algorithm framework

based on details.

$$\pi(\theta|x) = \frac{p(x|\theta)\pi(\theta)}{m(x)} = \frac{p(x|\theta)\pi(\theta)}{\int_{\emptyset} p(x|\theta)\pi(\theta)d_\theta} \tag{3}$$

(3) .m is the dimension, which is an important factor affecting the spatial efficiency of the algorithm when the data is complex. Imagine that M is 101001000... Then the space consumption of the corresponding algorithm should be increased by 10 times, 100 times, 1000 times. Opening memory on all nodes to store the corresponding data sets is very memory consuming. How to optimize it? It is absolutely feasible to store only the index of the corresponding data set in the original data set on all nodes, and determine which data is divided into the corresponding child nodes through the index. In this way, the spatial complexity of the algorithm is effectively reduced to o (n*k), which can completely avoid the risk of insufficient memory caused by excessive data dimension in the data set, and improve the robustness and robustness of the program. Moreover, it is faster to find corresponding elements and divide elements into corresponding subtrees through subscript indexing than to directly operate the whole element, because what we directly operate is an index (probably an int type data), rather than a user-defined object with complex structure with large

dimensions [5]. There is no need to participate in the preparation of constructors, copy constructors, assignment functions, etc. related to object initialization, which simplifies programming; Moreover, the instantiation of objects requires the new operator, which consumes computer resources in any programming language. Why not optimize the execution time and space of the algorithm?

3   College Students' English Autonomous Learning Under the Network Environment

3.1   Current Situation of College Students' English Autonomous Learning

(1) Positive results. By using network information, students' learning efficiency is greatly improved. The application of network technology in English teaching provides real communication needs and language learning atmosphere, and transforms abstract and boring learning contents into vivid and vivid learning contents [6]. Therefore, it enhances students' interest in learning English. At the same time, through the resource sharing on the network, if students encounter problems in the process of autonomous learning, they can query relevant information on the Internet at the first time, which is conducive to obtaining a large amount of knowledge and cultivating autonomous learning ability [7]. Multimedia and network technology provide students with a relaxed learning environment. Without face-to-face communication, students are more likely to release emotional anxiety. Therefore, learning efficiency has been improved and the effect is more positive. Figure 5 below shows the English autonomous learning process.

(2) Existing problems. Influenced by the traditional teaching mode, many students have poor autonomous learning ability and can not adapt to the teaching mode of autonomous learning. This means that the teaching mode of teachers' autonomous learning in the classroom is difficult to get the cooperation of students. Some students have utilitarian motivation to learn English. Their motivation to learn English is to get CET-4 and CET-6 certificates. This utilitarian motivation is not conducive to cultivating students' autonomous learning ability in the network environment. At the same time, under the influence of this traditional education model, not only students do not adapt to the teaching model of autonomous learning, but also teachers can not adapt to the transformation of roles in the autonomous teaching model [8]. This also hinders the implementation of the autonomous learning teaching model to a great extent. Some teachers go too far, directly abandon the traditional teaching platform and completely rely on network resources. In this way, all learning tasks are pressed on students, ignoring the guiding role of teachers in the whole autonomous teaching model, which will make students learn blindly and find no learning direction.

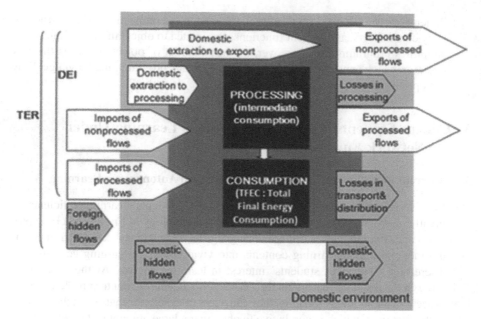

Fig. 5. English autonomous learning process

3.2 Countermeasures for Cultivating College Students' English Autonomous Learning Ability Under the Network Environment

(1) Create a good e-learning platform. An advanced e-learning platform is an important guarantee to improve the efficiency of College Students' English autonomous learning [9]. The platform can adopt a more advanced, efficient and humanized software system. Its function should include the retrieval of curriculum learning resources, have a good interactive function between teachers, students and students, and can reflect all links of the teaching process. In the learning process, it can retrieve problems at any time, has flexible and convenient upload and download methods, and establishes an effective test and Q & a system. Quickly enrich teaching resources in multiple ways, so that all kinds of course materials can be uploaded and updated in time.

(2) Cultivate students' ability to correctly use e-learning. Most students are influenced by the traditional teaching mode and are used to "walking" passively with teachers in the classroom [10]. Therefore, we should pay attention to correcting students' bad habits, encourage them to give full play to their main role in the classroom, change their utilitarian learning motivation, and formulate learning objectives and learning plans in line with students' reality under the guidance of teachers. At the same time, guide students to use network resources for independent learning, so that students can achieve the purpose of full preparation before class and full review after class through the network.

(3) Change the role of teachers in College English classroom. As the manager of e-learning platform, teachers should not only make full use of and master the functions

of the platform, but also constantly optimize and improve the platform [11]. In College English classroom, teachers should let students play the main role of learning, and can not exaggerate the role of network resources, completely rely on network resources, and ignore their guiding and supervising role for students.

3.3 Using ID3 Algorithm to Study College Students' English Autonomous Learning

This paper analyzes and Studies College Students' English autonomous learning by selecting the five attributes of the longest login time, the cumulative online time, the number of visits to the learning resource network, questions and posts, and the progress of autonomous learning as candidate attributes and autonomous learning results as class label attributes. The data records are from the College English learning database, which holds the learning records of College English in general liberal arts and science and Engineering in the past two years [12].

The decision tree generated by ID3 algorithm is shown in Fig. 6:

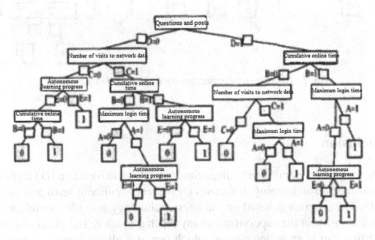

Fig. 6. Decision tree generated by ID3 algorithm

Using analysis of variance (ANOVA) to learn college students' English Autonomous Learning in a classroom environment the purpose of this chapter is to provide you with an overview of ANOVA. It also provides you with a brief description of the software that can be used for statistical analysis and how to apply it to all aspects of learning classroom teaching. English classroom teaching is a unique and effective way to teach English to non-native speakers [13]. It combines the best aspects of traditional classroom teaching with the latest research on language learning, which shows that students will learn more effectively when they actively participate in the learning process.

College English Online Autonomous Learning (oalce) is based on ID3 algorithm, which is used to identify and mark audio files. The ID3 standard was developed by Michael sweet in 1994 as a way for digital music players to recognize tracks and make them available for playback. Since then, it has been adopted by many other applications, including software that can automatically recognize speech from microphones or video files. The oalce system works on a similar principle: it uses its own proprietary technology to identify spoken words in recordings, and then marks them with metadata that describes their meaning so that they can be searched later [14].The decision tree generated by the improved ID3 algorithm is shown in Fig. 7:

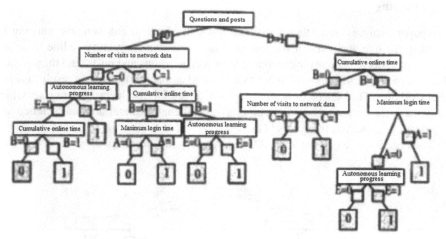

Fig. 7. Decision tree generated by improved ID3 algorithm

4   Conclusion

Online Autonomous Learning of College Students' English based on ID3 algorithm is a unique way of English learning. It focuses on students' ability to learn and use English in real life. The program is based on the latest technology and allows students to learn by themselves without the supervision of any teacher or tutor. The plan consists of two parts: the first part is an online course, which contains all the necessary materials for self-study; The second part is an interactive learning environment, which helps students master new skills through practice and interaction with other learners. Students use this program to learn language and improve their speaking, listening, reading and writing skills. Students can use this program to learn more effectively because it is designed by experts who know how to teach people how to speak English. Based on the latest technology, Online Autonomous Learning of College Students' English based on ID3 algorithm enables learners from all over the world to connect with each other through video conferences and chat rooms.

References

1. Lu, Y.U.: Investigation and analysis of college students' English autonomous learning based on online open courses. J. Changzhou College Inf. Technol. (2019)

2. Wu, C.: Effect of online and offline blended teaching of college english based on data mining algorithm. J. Inf. Knowl. Manag. **21**(Supp02) (2022)
3. Ma, X.: Study on college English online teaching model in mixed context based on genetic algorithm and neural network algorithm. Discr. Dyn. Nature Soc. 2021 (2021)
4. Wang, Q.: Construction of two way interactive and cooperative teaching mode between college English teachers and students under the network autonomous learning platform. In: ICIMTECH 21: The Sixth International Conference on Information Management and Technology (2021)
5. Sang, H., Jiang, M., Lu, Z., et al.: Data mining algorithm for influencing factors of university students' position promotion based on decision tree. J. Beihua Univ. (Nat. Sci.) (2019)
6. Zhang, B., Fang, J., Xiong, Z.: Online English vocabularies autonomous learning model based on EM algorithm. J. Phys. Conf. Ser. 1168 (2019)
7. Qian, W.: Challenges and strategies of online English learning for college students in the post epidemic era **12**(2), 5 (2022)
8. Li, J.: Mobile-assisted autonomous English learning in college students' extra-curriculum time: a case study in China. Technium Soc. Sci. J. 19 (2021)
9. Chen, L., Bai, J.L.: Research on the training mode of "the Combination of College Students'Extracurricular English Autonomous Learning and Chinese Culture" based on WeChat platform. Overseas English (2019)
10. Ding, J.: A study on vocational college students' English learner autonomy based on three-dimensional conceptual model. J. Ningbo Inst. Educ. (2019)
11. Zhang, F.: A study of college students' autonomous learning based on project-based learning. J. Qiqihar Junior Teachers' College (2018)
12. English hybrid teaching model analysis teaching based on association algorithm. J. Phys. Conf. Ser. **1881**(2), 022041 (2021). (7pp)
13. Li, M., University, J.: A study on strategies of training college students' English learning autonomy based on network environment. J. Heihe Univ. (2019)
14. Xiao-Fan, L.I.: Research on college english autonomous learning model under the background of big data. J. Hubei Open Vocational College (2019)

Research on Computer Aided English Curriculum Design in Higher Vocational Colleges

Lei Zhao[✉]

Shandong Technician College of Water Conservancy, Shandong 255130, China
767580360@qq.com

Abstract. Strengthening the connection between secondary and higher vocational education is one of the primary tasks of current vocational education, which is of great significance to improve the quality of vocational education. Computer aided English curriculum design has been more and more developed and applied in higher vocational colleges. In view of the problems and misunderstandings in the process of practice, this paper proposes that English teachers should have a unified understanñding and correct attitude, improve the quality of English teachers in higher vocational colleges, and strengthen the construction of infrastructure in higher vocational colleges, It aims to promote the development of computer aided English curriculum design in higher vocational colleges.

Keywords: Computer-aided · Higher vocational English · Curriculum design

1 Introduction

The basic task of higher vocational education is to cultivate applied talents with certain practical ability. As a public basic course in higher vocational colleges, higher vocational English should also serve this goal. However, the effect of English Teaching in many vocational colleges is not optimistic. Due to the lack of pertinence in teaching concept, teaching content and teaching mode, it is difficult for teachers; Teachers and students want to learn, but the effect is not good, can not meet the needs of employers and other issues. Higher vocational English teaching should be committed to the cultivation of students' professional ability, reflecting the characteristics of vocational education application, practicality and professionalism. First of all, it needs to consider and grasp from the macro perspective of curriculum design.

With the increasing importance of higher vocational education, the traditional teaching mode can not meet the needs of students to adapt to social development and work competition. At present, English Teaching in Higher Vocational Colleges urgently needs to explore a set of teaching mode suitable for higher vocational education, which aims at cultivating skilled talents, takes application ability as the main line, strengthens the basic knowledge and skills of English language education, and pays attention to cultivating

M. A. Jan and F. Khan (Eds.): BigIoT-EDU 2022, LNICST 465, pp. 596–602, 2023.
https://doi.org/10.1007/978-3-031-23950-2_65

students' communication in English. Computer assisted language learning (call) refers to the use of computers to comprehensively process and control multimedia information such as symbols, language, words, sound, graphics, images, etc., and organically combine them according to the teaching requirements, and then display them through screen or projector projection, through human-computer interaction between users and computers, The teaching mode that completes the process of teaching or training. Multimedia Assisted English teaching is a new breakthrough in the field of English language teaching. By changing the traditional teaching mode, it provides a dynamic teaching environment in which students can actively participate in the teaching process, reflects the teaching concept of "teachers play a leading role, students play a dominant role", and greatly improves the quality of English Teaching in higher vocational colleges. Computer aided English teaching has developed into a new mode of English Teaching in higher vocational colleges[1].

2 The Advantages of Computer Aided Learning of English Curriculum Design

Computer aided English teaching includes network resources aided English curriculum design, CAI multimedia teaching software, e-mail, distance education, pictures and audio-visual materials display with the help of slides and recordings, etc. Computer aided English teaching has the following characteristics.

2.1 Improve the Vividness of English Class and Stimulate Students' Learning Enthusiasm

Computer aided curriculum design has a variety of information functions including sound, image, text and animation. It can provide a lot of non-verbal materials, such as the background of the times, roles, psychological activities and so on, and mobilize students' attention and interest from multiple angles. Computer aided English teaching can make students in vocational colleges who are not good at English participate in teaching activities more actively. Students can not only read words, listen to recordings, see pictures and animations, do exercises, but also answer questions, so that they are willing to learn, able to learn and good at learning. In this way, English classroom teaching can become interesting, so that the original rigid English knowledge can be presented to students vividly, effectively stimulate students' thirst for knowledge, make students more in a positive learning state, so as to improve the effect of English Teaching in higher vocational colleges.

2.2 The Learning Environment of Human-Computer Interaction Can Create Individual Learning Conditions

Interactivity is an important feature of computer aided English teaching. This characteristic makes the teaching process become the communication process between students and teachers, students and students, students and computers. Teachers can understand the students' mastery of the teaching materials according to the situation of each student completing the exercises; Students can also test their learning effect through man-machine dialogue. Students can also discuss and express their opinions through virtual classroom Multimedia computer provides a new way of human-computer interaction, which is rich in pictures and text, and can give immediate feedback. Interactivity makes multimedia computer an effective teaching method Especially in the interactive environment formed by computer-aided English teaching, students can choose what they want to learn according to their own learning basis and learning interest, and students' initiative and enthusiasm can be brought into full play, which provides the best way for individual teaching and hierarchical teaching to achieve individualized teaching. For example, the Art Department of Nantong Vocational University students, College English class class is not divided into single enrollment and general enrollment, the class students' English level is uneven, to teach English class has brought some difficulty. With the help of computer, Multimedia Assisted English teaching not only solves the problem of different learning needs of students with different cognitive levels, but also cultivates students' autonomous ability and enhances students' self-confidence in learning English. Let students constantly improve their English level in the process of "learning" to "learning".

2.3 Help English Teachers Update Their Teaching Concepts

The emergence of computer-aided English teaching has put a lot of pressure on English teachers in higher vocational colleges, forcing them to change the traditional teaching mode they have been used to and re-establish the information-based teaching concept. Teachers should organize the design, production and processing of teaching information before class, operate and control teaching courseware in class, answer questions well, enrich teaching means and improve teaching effect [2].

In the traditional classroom teaching mode, teachers spend little time on a single student, especially in the current higher vocational colleges, which generally expand enrollment. Most of the public English classes adopt the way of class sharing, which leads to poor communication between students and teachers, and teachers can not grasp the learning situation of students. But in the computer-aided English teaching mode, the interaction between teachers and students, students and students is always maintained. Teachers have changed from the authority of teaching activities to teaching partners. Students can choose their own teaching content, and the problems encountered, the feelings of timely feedback to teachers. Teachers and learners become a cooperative relationship. Although computer-aided English teaching has many advantages, we should also be aware of some problems and shortcomings in computer-aided English teaching.

3   The Tendency to Avoid in the Design of Higher Vocational English Curriculum

3.1   Focus on Language Knowledge

Due to the late start of Vocational Education in China, the lack of experience in vocational education, the imperfection of higher vocational education ideas, and the need to update the curriculum concept, it is inevitable to be affected by the traditional undergraduate education ideas, and the higher vocational English curriculum design is still based on the knowledge-based curriculum concept. The purpose and starting point of the course teaching is to impart language knowledge, highlight the goal of knowledge training, and emphasize the natural improvement of English level through the systematic study of language knowledge and language skills; The content of the course is mainly mechanical knowledge such as grammar, vocabulary and sentence pattern, supplemented by certain language skills training, focusing on the comprehensiveness, integrity and systematicness of knowledge; The teaching process is only regarded as the process of language knowledge accumulation, and the teaching method of "one speech" and intensive training is adopted. Through the teacher's intensive teaching of the textbook word by word and sentence by sentence in the classroom, the students accept it step by step, and realize the mastery and consolidation of knowledge through classroom questions and answers and a large number of exercises and exercises after class; And take the mastery of mechanical language knowledge as the evaluation standard [3].

This kind of curriculum design mode is convenient for teachers to control the whole teaching process and to learn systematic knowledge. However, it only focuses on students' development at the level of "knowledge", but ignores students' "practice", which does not reflect the practical, applied and professional characteristics of higher vocational education, and is difficult to meet the needs of Higher Vocational English teaching. First of all, the teaching time of higher vocational education is limited, so it is impossible for students to have enough time in class to systematically and deeply learn all kinds of basic language knowledge; Secondly, compared with the students in academic universities, higher vocational students are deficient in knowledge learning ability. If teachers ignore the actual situation and instill systematic language knowledge blindly, it will inevitably cause students' weariness; Thirdly, the mastery of knowledge is not equal to the ability to use. If there is no chance of practice, which separates the students' knowledge and behavior, it will not be able to achieve the purpose of Higher Vocational English teaching to help students to communicate in English in their daily life and foreign business activities. The idea of language knowledge centered English curriculum design is deeply rooted and needs to be avoided.

3.2 Focus on Skill Training

At present, the concept of vocational education has been widely accepted by the educational circles. Many curriculum researchers and teachers are discussing how to carry out the curriculum reform of vocational education. How to highlight the practicality and operability of vocational education curriculum has become a hot topic in the research. Sometimes, in order to reflect the characteristics of higher vocational education, the curriculum design has gone to the other extreme and fallen into the pattern of pure vocational skills training. English course teaching aims at serving the needs of students' future jobs. There is no teaching part of English for general purpose in the course content, and English for occupational purpose is directly learned after learning. According to the major, determine the possible positions, analyze the post's demand for English, extract and summarize the key employment skills, and carry out the training of listening, speaking, reading, writing, translation and other practical skills. The classroom teaching mainly uses the teacher to explain and demonstrate first, then the students imitate and practice repeatedly until they form the conditioned skills. Basic language knowledge is no longer the focus of the course. The cognitive difficulty of the selected teaching materials is greatly reduced. There is little time to explain the knowledge points. A lot of time is spent on the repeated practice of related sentences in the workplace, so that students' skills can reach the degree of coordination, proficiency and perfection[4].

4 The Overall Design of Higher Vocational English Course Based on Computer Aided

Before making the overall plan of the course, we first analyze the various conditions of students' learning, such as the needs of the society, the training objectives of higher vocational schools, students' learning needs, attitude, experience, level and interest, learning environment, the nature of the course, the relevant situation of teachers, teaching conditions and other factors inside and outside the school, so as to ensure more targeted and effective teaching.

4.1 Course Objectives

In view of the fact that higher vocational English is a compulsory public basic course for non English Majors in higher vocational colleges, the course objectives must be in line with the objectives of personnel training in Vocational Colleges and adhere to the principle of basic courses serving the major. Therefore, the overall goal of the course teaching is to establish the basic professional quality and English communication ability required by the cultivation of vocational talents. Through the study of the course, students will master certain basic English knowledge, have certain listening, speaking, reading, writing and translation skills, be able to read and translate relevant English business materials with the help of dictionaries, and conduct simple oral and written communication in daily activities and business activities of foreign communication. At the same time, we should learn good language learning methods to lay a foundation for further improving our English communicative competence and enhance cross-cultural awareness, so as to meet the needs of social development and economic construction.

4.2 Course Content

The purpose of course teaching is to help students to use English to complete the communicative tasks in daily life and foreign business activities. Therefore, the course content should also reflect the communicative contents in life and professional situations. Students will study general English for two semesters first, and then enter the part of Vocational English for one semester. The teaching content takes the theme as the unit, dividing the common topics in daily life and foreign business communication into thematic learning units, and determining the knowledge, ability and quality objectives in each learning unit according to the actual situation of students (such as language level, professional characteristics, etc.), As shown in Fig. 1. Around the theme, we will carry out various language practice activities such as listening, speaking, reading, writing and translation, so as to help students master practical knowledge, train comprehensive language education skills and improve general foreign business communication ability. The teaching of basic language knowledge does not emphasize the integrity of the system, but focuses on the ability to use.

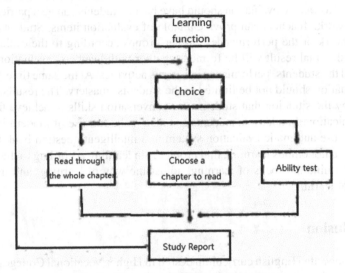

Fig. 1. Computer aided English learning

Language practice activities such as listening, speaking, reading and writing related to computer-aided design enable students to experience perception, discover the rules of language knowledge through reflection and summary, and internalize knowledge through the specific application of language skills. For example, when learning the topic of "advertisement", students first listen to, watch or read some English advertisements, then discuss in groups and summarize the language features of English advertisements; Then, the reading students select a product as the object of advertising, set the target group, write the advertising copy or slogan, and demonstrate it. In the "experience mode", students are the main body of learning activities, through active exploration to achieve the construction of knowledge. In this process, the role of teachers is not weakened, but more reflected in the ability to create supportive learning situations and provide more learning resources to promote students' learning according to the characteristics of students' learning psychology.

4.3 Evaluation of Learning Effect

Computer aided learning evaluation is a means of testing learning achievements and promoting learning. Therefore, learning evaluation is constantly carried out in the whole teaching process, and the learning process and learning strategies are regulated according to the evaluation results. Before the beginning of English Teaching in higher vocational colleges, students can be tested to understand the basic situation of students' English level, which can be used as the basis for graded teaching, so as to help teach students in accordance with their aptitude. At the same time, the proportion of process evaluation accounts for 40% of the total score. Homework, dictation, attendance, report and participation in extracurricular language activities (such as various English competitions) can be included in the formative assessment. In order to make the score more objective, the results of formative evaluation should have basis. Students can also participate in the evaluation work. Teachers can provide a table of evaluation items. Students can judge their homework or the performance of other groups according to the evaluation standards, and the final result will be formed together with teachers' evaluation. Teachers must record the students' performance in various activities. At the same time, the content of the evaluation should not be limited to the students' mastery. The results are mainly evaluated by the situation that students use conversation skills to achieve the purpose of communication. In addition, students can also make full use of modern information technology, use automatic evaluation system and intelligent question bank to evaluate the effect of autonomous learning, find problems in learning according to the evaluation results, determine the focus of learning, adjust the way of learning, and improve the efficiency of learning.

5   Conclusion

The computer-aided English curriculum design in Higher Vocational Colleges advocates changing "teaching" into "learning", attaches importance to the status of students as the main body of learning, and emphasizes that students' cognitive ability is conducive to the formation of students' knowledge ability and method ability. Integrated teaching can fully mobilize students' learning enthusiasm, make students from passive acceptance to active participation, complete their understanding of work and experience accumulation in the process of learning while doing, so as to obtain the improvement of comprehensive vocational ability including key ability, meet the requirements of students' all-round development, and improve the competitiveness of higher vocational students.

References

1. Jiyue, H., Guoying, Z., Lanping, S.: Research on teaching mode of English network development. Audio Visual Foreign Language Teaching (1) (2003)
2. Ran, R.: Advantages of computer aided English Teaching. J. Zhengzhou Railway Inst. Technol. (12) (2008)
3. Yang, Q.: Multimedia computer aided English Teaching. J. Xianning Univ. (5) (2006)
4. Zhang, Y.: Dewey. A brief discussion on "new vocational education view". Primary Vocational Tech. Education (11) (2005)

Research on Computer Network Information Security Protection Strategy and Evaluation Algorithm Education

Meng Teng[✉]

Hunan Foreign Language Vocational College of China, Changsha 410008, Hunan, China
tmeng123@sina.com

Abstract. Computer network information security management is an important problem to be solved in China. The effective protection of computer network information security depends on the perfect deployment of computer network security information protection strategy. Computer network security information protection strategy is one of the key research projects in China. According to the relevant standards and regulations, this paper analyzes the current situation of computer network information security protection strategies, studies several common security protection strategies and the evaluation algorithm of relevant computer network information security insurance, so as to guide and prevent the security management of public network information system.

Keywords: Computer network · Information security · Protection strategy

1 Introduction

We are in the information age of the 21st century. Information security, especially network information security, has been closely related to everyone's daily life. More and more companies use the Internet to operate their business. Administrative organs and government departments use computers to store important information and data, and individuals use computers and diversified terminal devices to enjoy the speed and convenience of the Internet. However, due to the openness, interconnection and anonymity of the network, all kinds of sensitive information, ranging from important administrative and military information to personal privacy information, are inevitably transmitted and stored on the Internet, as shown in Fig. 1. These are the targets of computer criminals and hackers. If these information is not properly protected to meet its security requirements, individuals, companies, various organizations and even countries will face huge economic risks and trust risks [1]. As computer workers, deepening the exploration of network information security protection technology is the guarantee of citizens' information security. Therefore, the security and reliability of modern network information has become the focus of common concern all over the world, and has also become a new field of hot research and talent needs.

© ICST Institute for Computer Sciences, Social Informatics and Telecommunications Engineering 2023
Published by Springer Nature Switzerland AG 2023. All Rights Reserved
M. A. Jan and F. Khan (Eds.): BigIoT-EDU 2022, LNICST 465, pp. 603–613, 2023.
https://doi.org/10.1007/978-3-031-23950-2_66

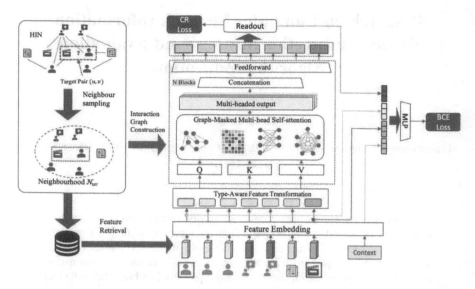

Fig. 1. Computer network information

The processing and storage of cloud computing data are carried out on the cloud platform. The separation of the owner of computing resources from the user has become an inherent feature of the cloud computing model. As a result, users' concerns about the secure storage and privacy of their data are inevitable.

Specifically, user data, including even privacy related content, may be intentionally or unintentionally disclosed in the process of remote computing, storage and communication. There are also data loss problems caused by power failure or downtime. Even for unreliable cloud infrastructure and service providers, they may learn the user's privacy information through the analysis and speculation of user behavior. These problems will directly lead to contradictions and frictions between users and cloud providers, reduce users' trust in the cloud computing environment, and affect the further promotion of cloud computing applications.

The access control policy of "all" only explicitly opens the corresponding port or opens the relevant access policy when there is a data access demand [2]. In the virtual application environment, the logical boundary security access control strategy in the virtual environment can be set, such as the refined data access control strategy between virtual machines and within virtual units by loading virtual firewalls.

2 Concept and Technical Characteristics of Network Information Security

2.1 Concept of Network Information Security

The so-called computer network security refers to ensuring the confidentiality, integrity, availability and auditability of data and information on the network by relying on network management control and technical measures. The essence of network security is network information security. Therefore, protecting network information security is the ultimate goal and key of network security. Information security is to ensure that information is not leaked or destroyed in the process of generation, transmission, storage and processing. The conceptual process of network information security is shown in Fig. 2 below.

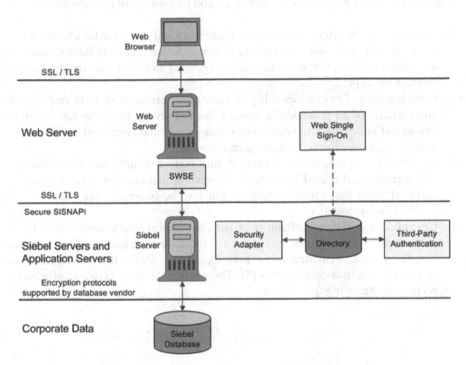

Fig. 2. Conceptual process of network information security

The model of communication security includes three aspects: one is physical security, that is to protect information and valuable resources, which can only be physically accessed with permission. In other words, security service personnel must protect these data information from being moved, tampered with or stolen by unauthorized persons [3]. The second is operation safety, which refers to the work required to deal with security threats. It mainly includes: network access control (protect the security of network information resources from unauthorized persons), identity authentication (ensure the authenticity and reliability of user identity using information), network topology (set the network physical location of each device according to its own needs). The third is security management, which is to effectively manage the safe operation of information and systems by using comprehensive measures.there must be a "back door" opened for them in our system. As long as we block it and let hackers have nowhere to start, isn't it beautiful!

2.2 Technical Characteristics of Network Information Security

The integrity, confidentiality, availability, controllability and non repudiation mentioned in the meaning of network security are the basic characteristics and objectives of network information security, of which the first three are the basic requirements of information security. The five characteristics of network information security reflect the important characteristics of the basic elements, attributes and technology of network security.

(1) Integrity. The integrity of network information security refers to the characteristics of non modification, non-destructive and non look at each link of information storage, transmission, exchange and processing, so as to ensure that the information remains intact [4].

(2) Confidentiality. The confidentiality of network information security refers to the strict control of all possible disclosure links to prevent the disclosure of private and useful information to unauthorized individuals and entities in the process of generation, transmission, processing and storage.

(3) Availability. The availability of network information security means that network information can be used by authorized users, which can not only be correctly accessed when the system is running, but also be restored when the system is attacked and damaged.

(4) Controllability. The controllability of network information security refers to the characteristics that can effectively control the dissemination of information and specific content circulating in the network system. Resist the unauthorized use of network information resources [5]. The controllability of network information security is shown in Fig. 3 below.

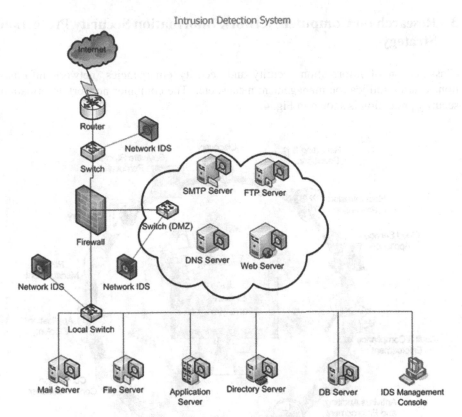

Fig. 3. Controllability of network information security

(5) Non repudiation. The non repudiation of network information security, also known as censurability, refers to the two sides of network communication in the process of information exchange to ensure that participants can not deny their true identity, the authenticity of the information provided, as well as the completed operations and commitments [6].

For an open Internet system, it is extremely necessary to take security measures, otherwise any end user connected to the network can access the information resources in the network. In today's information age, network information has penetrated into all fields of society and is used more and more widely. It not only brings convenience and development opportunities, but also provides possibilities for all kinds of computer crimes [3]. Typical threats in network systems include information disclosure, integrity infringement, denial of service and illegal use [7].

3 Research on Computer Network Information Security Protection Strategy

Classification of information security and security emergencies, network information security notification management means, etc,. The computer network information security protection is shown in Fig. 4.

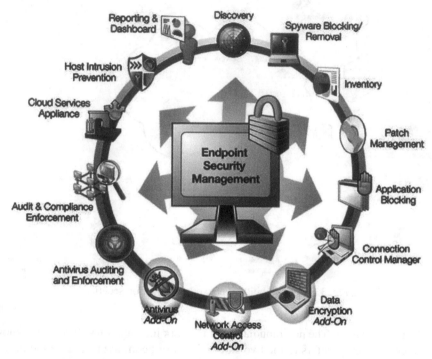

Fig. 4. Computer network information security protection

3.1 Safety Technology

Physical security technology. In order to comprehensively improve the computer network information security protection level, the whole computer room needs to be improved in strict accordance with the relevant specifications of the computer room construction technology [8]. The technical framework of network security is shown in Fig. 5 below.

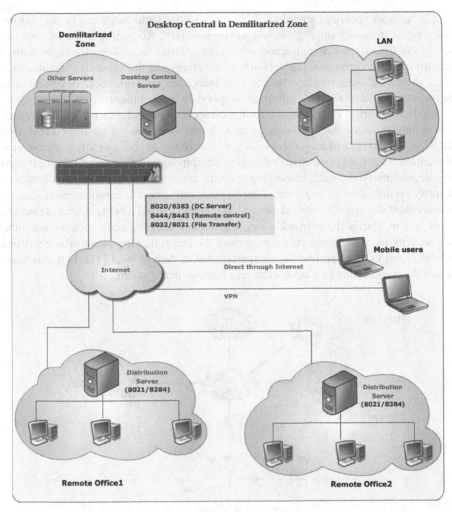

Fig. 5. Network security technology framework

The construction of the computer room should not only meet the requirements of fire prevention and waterproof, but also evaluate the computer network information security problems from the perspective of physical security, such as physical access In the control stage, we need to focus on the following contents[9]: ① special personnel must be assigned to take charge of the exit location of the computer room, and the personnel information of each exit computer room shall be recorded; ② For visitors to the computer room, strictly implement the application and approval process, and control the scope of activities of visitors; ③ Pay attention to avoid the theft and damage of the machine room, keep the main equipment during work, and fix it on the basis of proper placement; Mark each equipment for easy search; At the same time, pay attention to the storage location of communication cables, such as indoor underground and pipeline location [4].

(2) Network security technology. Network security technology can be divided into many types, including sub regions and sub regions [10]. According to the relevant regulations of China, the sub region and sub region security technology should be defined according to the corresponding network architecture, and the security guarantee measures should be taken to pass the first step Integrated network security system, after constructing an ideal network information operation environment.

(3) Host security. The network information security protection strategy of host security mainly includes the following points: ① anti-virus. Based on the current virus database, form a virus management system to realize comprehensive virus detection and prevention from the perspectives of system equipment and Intranet; ② desktop security, depending on the habit of desktop security management, hardware configuration, security optimization strategy, etc. Face to face, implement a comprehensive desktop management strategy; ③ Network access management Build a network access management system, clarify the network access regulations, identity authentication and other key security management regulations, ensure the controllability of the whole terminal behavior, and finally improve the computer network Safety level [11]. Figure 6 below shows the construction of a network access management system.

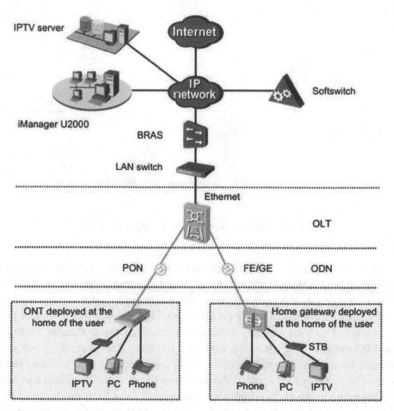

Fig. 6. Build a network access management system

4 Analysis of Computer Network Information Security Evaluation Algorithm

4.1 Comprehensive Grey Correlation Clustering Method Analysis

In this study, the comprehensive grey relational clustering method will be adopted. This method mainly includes three functional modules: data acquisition, data preprocessing and comprehensive query. In this technology, it can be further refined according to the relevant contents, and by adding auxiliary processes, It can obtain network security data resources more effectively.

$$Delta\{x\} = m(distance) \tag{1}$$

$$delta\{x\} = m - max \tag{2}$$

when studying related problems, relevant technicians can form a comprehensive information security strategy by extracting the security management information of multiple time periods [12]. It can also be combined with the Grey Correlation Clustering safety evaluation system to evaluate various safety events and find solutions from the perspective of safety evaluation (Fig. 7).

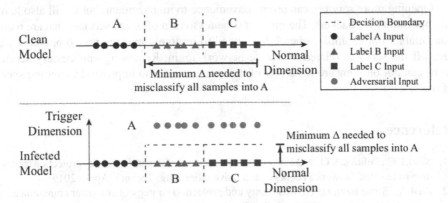

Fig. 7. Grey relational clustering analysis framework

4.2 Grey Relational Clustering

The basic concept of grey correlation clustering is: assuming that the correlation degree of the two indicators is matched, it can be regarded as the same type. The key of the specific operation process is to classify the indicators according to the correlation between the calculated indicators The principles to be followed in the classification process are: assuming that the selected indicators do not appear in the divided groups, they can form - a new independent group; If a selected indicator appears in the divided group, you need to add another indicator to the group [13].

From the application effect, many grey factors in computer network information security evaluation can be processed quantitatively through grey correlation clustering, in which all evaluation index parameters will affect the evaluation results; In the evaluation process, there will be no loss of information, so the feasibility of the analysis results can be guaranteed However, it should be noted that in the network information security evaluation algorithm of Grey Correlation Clustering, it is also necessary to build a static network information module and a dynamic network firewall module [14], which is an inevitable requirement for the whole network security supervision.

5 Conclusion

Computer network information security protection involves a wide range. Therefore, for relevant personnel, in the next stage of work, they must deeply understand the needs of network information security management and improve it from the aspects of host security, network technology and physical security. At the same time, from the case enterprise selected in this paper, The grey relational cluster analysis method can evaluate the level of network information security, which is worthy of further promotion.

By default, any user can connect to the server through an empty connection, enumerate accounts and guess passwords. Therefore, we must prohibit the establishment of empty connections.

Opening more services can bring convenience to management, but it will also leave an opportunity for hackers. Therefore, it is better to turn off some services that are really unavailable. For example, when I don't need to remotely manage my computer, I will turn off the services related to remote network login. Removing unnecessary service stops can not only ensure the safety of the system, but also improve the running speed of the system.

References

1. Xiao, F.C., Politics, S.O., ND University: Research on information security protection strategy of private cloud network in colleges and universities. Dig. Technol. Appl. (2019)
2. Zhai, Y.: Some thoughts on the security and protection strategy of computer communication network. Wirel. Internet Technol. (2018)
3. Gao, F., Mu, J., Han, X., et al.: Performance limit evaluation strategy for automated driving systems 5(1), 12 (2022)
4. Shandilya, S.K., Upadhyay, S., Kumar, A., et al.: AI-assisted computer network operations testbed for nature-inspired cyber security based adaptive defense simulation and analysis. Futur. Gener. Comput. Syst. 127, 297–308 (2022)
5. Chen, T., Kong, D., Hong, Y.: Development and implementation of anti phishing wi-fi and information security protection APP based on android. In: IOP Publishing Ltd. IOP Publishing Ltd, 032109 (2021). (7pp)
6. Xu, Y., Lan, S.: The detection and evaluation strategies for critical information infrastructure. Inf. Technol. Network Secur. (2019)
7. Li, Y.: Relevant thoughts on computer communication network security and protection strategy. Electronic Test (2018)

8. Zheng, X., Xiao, Q.: Coupling physical information channels and building a practice design and evaluation system:thoughts on the reconstruction strategy of physical problems under the condition of information technology (2018)

9. Ge, S.: Risk and preventive strategy of network information security in public library. Library Theory and Practice (2018)

10. Cheng, X., Zhang, P.: Information security and adoptable solutions in the implementation of industry 4.0 strategy for the fourth-generation industrial revolution. J. Phys. Conf. Ser. **1682**, 012087 (2020)

11. Yu, L.: Analysis of computer software security and protection strategy. China Computer & Communication (2019)

12. Liu, X., Zheng, A., Zhu, E., et al.: Application of the whole life cycle cloud platform of electric energy metering equipment and security protection strategy. Electr. Energy Manage. Technol. (2018)

13. Wei, C., Feng, T., Li, X., et al.: Computer network security and network security technology strategy research. Electronic Test (2019)

14. Yang, C.H., Zhou, H.F., Jun, M.A., et al.: Research and implementation of beidou short message security protection system based on national secret algorithm. Comput. Modernizat. (2019)

Research on Computer Software Teaching Method of Digital Media Art Theory Under the Background of Big Data

Lujun Cao[✉]

Software Engineering Institute of Guangzhou, Guangzhou City 510990, Guangdong, China
caolujun520@163.com

Abstract. With the advent of the Internet era, enterprises put forward higher requirements for the comprehensive quality of talents. However, in the traditional computer software teaching, teachers carry out relatively few software teaching contents, and most of them focus on the teaching of computer history evolution and other related contents, resulting in the lack of outstanding computer software application ability of most students, which seriously affects the teaching effect. Based on this, this paper analyzes the application of digital media art theory in computer software teaching based on Apriori algorithm, in order to further improve the quality of computer software teaching.

Keywords: Apriori algorithm · Digital media · Computer software

1 Introduction

At present, computer software teaching usually focuses on classroom demonstration, which leads to the loss of students' dominant position in the classroom, which is not conducive to improving students' software operation ability. According to the traditional vocational education model, the teaching purpose is mainly to let students learn professional knowledge, systematic knowledge and cultural basic knowledge, take professional knowledge as the basis of students' learning, and pay attention to the systematicness and coherence between disciplines, learning and memory. Despise the cultivation of students' ability and creative ability; Emphasis on Teachers' classroom as the main body. Students follow the teacher's baton, weaken students' personal ideological performance, lack of initiative, catch up with the progress in teaching methods, instill the whole class, and students lack discussion and interaction time. This can not be unified with the practical skills advocated by today's society, and it is difficult to make it better meet the needs of social development. Based on this, the in-depth analysis of computer software teaching method based on digital media art theory under Apriori algorithm has important practical significance.

M. A. Jan and F. Khan (Eds.): BigIoT-EDU 2022, LNICST 465, pp. 614–619, 2023.
https://doi.org/10.1007/978-3-031-23950-2_67

2 Apriori Algorithm

2.1 Description of Apriori Algorithm

In the Apriori algorithm, the basic idea of finding the maximum item set is that the algorithm needs to process the data set in multiple steps. The first step is to simply count the frequency of all item sets containing one element, and find out those item sets that are not less than the minimum support, that is, one-dimensional maximum item sets, Starting from the second step, the cycle process is: in step k, a k-dimensional candidate item set is generated according to the (k-1) dimensional maximum item set generated in step k-1, and then the database is searched to obtain the item set support of the candidate item set, which is compared with the minimum support, so as to find the k-dimensional maximum item set.

For the convenience of the following description, it is hereby agreed as follows:

(1) The items in database transactions are arranged in alphabetical order. Each item is identified by <TID, item>, where TID represents the identifier of the corresponding transaction and item represents the item name.
(2) The number of items in each item set is called the size of the item set. When the size of the item set = k, the item set is called k-itemset (k-dimensional item set).

The following symbols encountered below represent the corresponding contents
K-itemset k-dimensional itemset
LK maximum k-i temset with minimum support
CK candidate k-itemsets (potential maximum item set).

2.2 Description of Apriori Algorithm

The first step of Apriori algorithm is to simply count the frequency of all itemsets containing one element to determine the largest one-dimensional itemset. In step k, it is divided into two stages. Firstly, a function SC is used_ Candidate: generate the candidate item set CK through the maximum item set LK-1 generated in step (k-1). Then search the database to calculate the support of the candidate item set CK. In order to calculate the support of the items in CK more quickly, the function count is used in this paper_ Support calculates support.

Apriori algorithm is described as follows
   (1) C1 = {candidatel-i temsets};
   (2) L1 = {c ∈ C1|c. count ≥ minsupport};
   (3) For(k = 2, Lk-1 ≠ φ, k++) //Until the maximum project set can no longer be generated
   (4) Ck = sc_ candidate(Lk-1); //Generate a candidate project set with k elements
   (5) for all transactions t ∈ D //Handling
   (6) Ct = count_ support (Ck, t); //The set of candidate items included in the transaction t
   (7)for all candidates c ∈ Ct
   (8) c. count = c. count +1;

(9) next.

(10) Lk = {c ∈ Ck|c. count ≥ minsupport};

(11) next

(12):resultset = resultset ∪ Lk

Where, D represents the database; Minsupport represents the given minimum support; Resultset represents all the largest itemsets. Sc_ Candidate function.

The parameter of the function is LK-1, that is, all the maximum k-1-dimensional itemsets, and the result returns the candidate itemset CK containing K items. In fact, CK is a superset of the maximum k-dimensional itemset. Through the function count_ Support calculates the support of the project, and then generates LK.

The advantage of Apriori algorithm is that when the support is not too low, the number of database scans is not much, and the spatial complexity of the algorithm is small. Disadvantages: the algorithm may generate a large number of candidate sets and may need to scan the database repeatedly.

Apriori algorithm is the basic algorithm of association rule mining. Although it has been optimized to some extent, there are still unsatisfactory places in practical application. Therefore, people have proposed some methods to improve Apriori algorithm from different angles. Including: ① reduce the amount of scanned data, ② improve the search speed by using the prefix tree, ③ reduce the number of scans, and ④ reduce the number of candidate itemsets.

3 Digital Media Art Theory Under Apriori Algorithm

With the continuous progress of computer technology, communication technology and digital broadcasting, digital media art with Internet and wireless communication as the communication carrier and traditional media content and innovative content mode as the core is rising rapidly all over the world, and is changing people's way of information hunting and the form of leisure and entertainment. Its industries cover information services, communication, advertising Communication, electronic entertainment, animation, games, online education, publishing and other fields.

3.1 Overview of Digital Media

Digital media refers to the information carriers that record, process, transmit and acquire the process in the form of binary numbers. These carriers include digital sensory media such as text, graphics, images, sound, video images and animation, and the presentation media (coding) representing these sensory media. They are commonly referred to as logical media, as well as physical media for storing, transmitting and displaying logical media. But in the general sense, the so-called digital media often refers to sensory media.

Digital media is a highly integrated interdisciplinary subject of science and art, which is dominated by information science and digital technology, based on mass communication theory and guided by modern art, and applies information communication technology to the fields of culture, art, commerce, education and management. Digital media includes various forms such as image, text, audio and video, as well as digitization in communication form and content, that is, the digitization process of information collection, access, processing and distribution. Digital media has become the latest information carrier after language, text and electronic technology.

3.2 Types of Digital Media

Digital media can be divided into many kinds according to different classification methods. If divided by time attribute, digital media can be divided into still media and continuous media. Still media refers to digital media whose content will not change over time, such as text and pictures. Continuous media refers to digital media whose content changes over time, such as audio and video.

According to the source attribute, it can be divided into natural media and synthetic media. Among them, natural media refers to the digital media obtained after digitization and coding by special equipment, such as photos taken by digital cameras. Synthetic media refers to the text, music, voice, image and animation generated (synthesized) by computer with computer as a tool and expressed by specific symbols, languages or algorithms, such as animated characters produced by 3D production software.

If divided by constituent elements, it can be divided into single media and multi media. As the name suggests, single media refers to the carrier composed of a single information carrier; Multimedia refers to the forms of expression and transmission of a variety of information carriers.

What we usually call "digital media" generally refers to "multimedia", and "multimedia" is also a technology that is talked about a lot now.

3.3 Classification of Digital Media

(1) Perception refers to the media that can directly act on people's sensory organs and make people produce direct feelings (vision, listening, smell, taste, touch), such as language, music, various images, graphics, animation, text, etc.

(2) Presentation refers to the media artificially researched to transmit sensory media. With the help of this media, sensory media can be stored more effectively or transmitted from one place to another, such as language coding, telegraph code, bar code and language coding, Still and moving image coding, text coding, etc.

(3) A display is a device that displays sensory media. Display media can be divided into two categories. One is input display media, such as speech brief, camera, light pen and keyboard, and the other is output display media, such as speakers, displays and printers. It refers to the media used in communication to generate conversion between electrical signals and sensory media.

(4) Storage media is used to store presentation media, that is, the media that stores the digitized code of sensory media, which is called storage media. For example, magnetic disk, optical disc, magnetic tape, paper, etc. In short, it refers to the carrier used to store certain media.

(5) Transmission media refers to the physical carrier of signal transmission, such as coaxial cable, optical fiber, twisted pair and electromagnetic wave

Digital media technology is the software and hardware technology to realize the representation, recording, processing, storage, transmission, display and management of digital media (sensory media, i.e. text, graphics, image, sound, video image and animation). It is generally divided into digital media representation technology, digital media storage technology, digital media creation technology, digital media display application technology Digital media management technology, etc.

4 Research and Application of Computer Software Teaching Method of Digital Media Art Theory Under Apriori Algorithm

In view of the above, the project teaching method can be used in the actual teaching of various computer software. Different from the tutorials of other disciplines, computer teaching is more practical. The application of project teaching method must run through the whole teaching process of computer software course, and build various knowledge points into multiple small projects, so that students can master the knowledge points by completing one small project by one.

For example, in the teaching of Visual FoxPro 6.0 programming course, before teaching, first let students create their own database through preview, and input the corresponding data into the table created in the library. Finally, submit the previously built database and table to the teacher for review in the form of homework. Although the operation is simple, in the past, the classroom has always been teaching first and then practicing. At first, students still had no way to start. After students' independent study and group discussion with their classmates, many students can establish databases independently. As a result, more and more students have mastered these basic operations. At the same time, the table structure has gradually changed from meaningless English field names and arbitrary data types to meaningful Chinese field names and purposeful data types. In addition to the payroll and students' learning transcripts, some students also integrated their own innovative ideas and created a variety of information tables, such as star information tables, which brightened people's eyes and virtually improved the quality of teaching.

In addition, through students' own active learning, they can not only broaden their horizons of knowledge, but also make their knowledge more solid. More importantly, students have developed good learning habits and greatly improved their learning ability.

5 Conclusion

In conclusion, the research on computer software teaching method of digital media art theory under Apriori algorithm can promote the innovation of teaching mode and provide students with more significant teaching effect, more profound memory, effective learning methods and good learning environment. At the same time, we must give full play to the leading role of teachers, comprehensively show the value orientation of people-oriented and ability-based in modern vocational education, change the quality of classroom teaching, and improve the learning efficiency faster.

References

1. Chen an, C.N.: Data Mining Technology and Application. Science Press, Beijing (2006)
2. Xiao, S.: Research on project teaching method in Computer Course Teaching. Res. Audio Visual Educ. (2003)
3. Yayuan, H.: Application of project teaching method in computer language teaching – Taking VB programming course as an example. Occupation **10**, 59–60 (2020)
4. Lei, S.: Application of project teaching method in computer aided design practice teaching – taking computer aided product design course teaching as an example. Comput. Prod. Circul. **3**, 138143 (2020)

Research on Design of English Teaching Resource Management System Based on Collaborative Recommendation

Huang Hua[(⊠)]

Changde Vocational Technical College, Changde 415000, Hunan, China
935748819@qq.com

Abstract. The design of English teaching resource management system based on collaborative recommendation is a research aimed at designing and implementing an e-learning environment for teachers to recommend materials to students. The main purpose of this study is to develop a recommendation system to help teachers recommend textbooks with high efficiency and quality. This study also aims to develop an effective recommendation system to improve the quality of students' English learning materials. Researchers are interested in finding out what recommendations can be made by using collaborative recommendation systems (such as wikis or social networks) and how to use these tools to improve.

Keywords: Business English · Decision tree · Practical teaching · Effectiveness evaluation

1   Introduction

Business majors and has strong practicality. However, influenced by China's traditional educational concepts, there of business English teaching level. Firstly, at this stage, most of China's on theoretical teaching, which mainly explains the basic knowledge of English, vocabulary and grammar and business English knowledge to students. There is less practical teaching for students, which leads to the separation of students' theory and practice. Students are unable to apply the theoretical knowledge to practice, which affects students' learning enthusiasm. Secondly, the business English teaching curriculum is unreasonable, most of which are mainly English courses, supplemented by business English courses. Moreover, many colleges and universities set professional business English courses as elective courses, which shortens the time for students to learn professional business English, and students can't learn business English knowledge comprehensively and systematically, resulting in low business English level, Unable society [1]. Finally, majors not only include the knowledge of English majors, but also include the finance, law, trade, economic management and so on. They cover a wide range, so they have high requirements for business English teachers. Business professional English knowledge, but also need to master other relevant professional knowledge. However,

M. A. Jan and F. Khan (Eds.): BigIoT-EDU 2022, LNICST 465, pp. 620–630, 2023.
https://doi.org/10.1007/978-3-031-23950-2_68

most business English teachers do not have these abilities and have no relevant experience in Business English practical teaching, learn more useful knowledge and students' business English practical ability can not be improved.

When making teaching plans, teachers begin to establish [2]. Through practice to help students combine their theoretical knowledge with practice and promote their all-round development. In Business English teaching, in order to improve students' professional quality, we should let students participate in practice [3]. However, in the actual teaching practice. In order to enable the school to cultivate talents who meet the needs of the society, we should establish an evaluation system for the effectiveness. The effectiveness evaluation system is shown in Fig. 1 below.

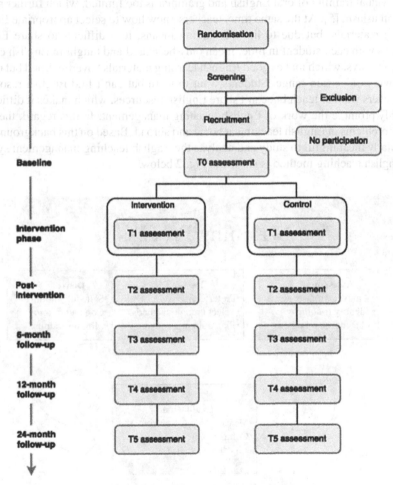

Fig. 1. Effectiveness evaluation system

English, as a highly specialized language discipline, has been very popular in all stages and fields of education in China, especially in Higher Vocational English education. At the same time, there are still many problems, such as poor oral ability and dumb English, which hinder the further improvement of teaching quality. This is mainly because, on the one hand, the teaching means are relatively limited, and students can only use traditional classroom time to interact with students. Students have less time to consciously learn after class[4]. Compared with other skills based subjects, English learning is not highly skilled, and it is difficult to play an "immediate effect" on learning results. Therefore, students tend to have their own interests and are not enthusiastic about learning after class, which makes it difficult to continuously improve English teaching; On the other hand, teaching resources are scattered, which is difficult for teachers and students to follow. As a basic subject, there is a wide range of English learning materials to choose. Students do not know how to choose suitable English teaching resources, and the individual training of oral English and grammar is too limited, which further affects their enthusiasm [5]. At the same time, teachers know how to select appropriate English learning materials, but due to limited sharing means, it is difficult to share English resources with each student in time, It can only be shared and taught in English classes once a few days, which makes good English learning materials "overqualified but under-used" within a certain range. Students want to learn but can't find English resources, and teachers want to teach but can't share English resources, which makes it difficult to smoothly promote the work of English teaching management. In this regard, there are similar problems in English teaching at home and abroad. Based on this background, it is particularly meaningful to study and analyze the English teaching management system. The English teaching method is shown in Fig. 2 below.

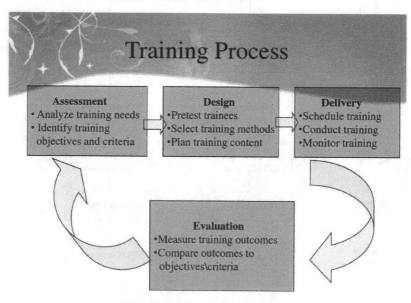

Fig. 2. English teaching methods

English teachers should cultivate students' autonomous inquiry learning strategies, problem-based learning strategies, collaborative communication learning strategies, resource utilization learning strategies, planning and monitoring learning strategies and self-evaluation learning strategies[6]. Based on Oxford's classification of learning strategies, this paper combines the use of direct and indirect strategies to solve the problems of English teaching.

2   Generation Process of Decision Tree

From the perspective of supporting networked collaborative design, collaborative design resources can be divided into six categories: design parts resources, standard parts resources, document resources, material resources, design instance resources and design specification resources, and corresponding resource databases are constructed to organize and manage them, because these resources are widely used in the process of collaborative design.

1) Design parts library: used to store the product or parts information of cooperative enterprises, so that collaborative designers can apply or deform the designed product or parts information.
2) Standard parts library: it is used to store all kinds of standard parts information. When designers in different places develop products according to the design requirements, they can get rid of the manual and query, retrieve, access and extract the required part (product) information from the standard parts library for use in design, manufacturing and other processes[7].
3) Design document library: the final product design information of most manufacturing enterprises is mostly stored in various CAD file formats, so a large number of drawing documents including CAD files formed in the design process most directly describe the design idea of products. The document library can effectively manage these CAD drawing documents, design calculations, technical standards, simulation animation and other documents from different sources and in different formats[3].

The conditions for the decision tree to stop segmentation are: the data on a node belongs to the same category; No attributes can be used to segment data. Figure 3 briefly describes the process of decision tree generation.

3   The Guiding Significance of Decision Tree Practical Teaching Effect Evaluation Model to Business English Practical Teaching

IT is conducive to assisting teachers in practical teaching. Decision tree evaluation model of practical teaching effectiveness is helpful to assist teachers in practical teaching. Teachers can evaluate students according to the decision tree, so that the whole English practice teaching can be carried out step by step. In English practice, teachers can reasonably arrange practical posts for students and improve the quality of practical teaching. Decision tree business English is helpful for teachers to guide students' learning in practice and promote students' all-round development [8].

It is the integration of practical teaching evaluation system and management system. Under the business English practical teaching system based on decision tree, teachers are

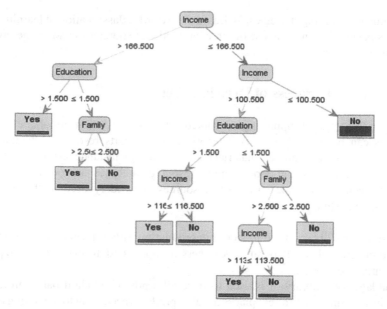

Fig. 3. Decision tree generation process

conducive to the combination of practical teaching evaluation system and management system. On this basis, effectively use the data provided by the decision tree to evaluate and integrate the whole management system, reasonably analyze the learning situation of each student, and manage according to the amount of knowledge that students master, so as to make the evaluation and management of students in the same data system, as shown in Fig. 4, effectively carry out educational work for each student [9]. The detailed level division in the evaluation system can evaluate students' learning and the ability to complete practical assignments, so that students can clearly recognize their short-comings. According to the samples provided by the decision tree, supervise students' learning and make rational use of the resources of the evaluation system. This interaction not only makes the whole practical teaching management system more perfect, but also makes the practical teaching system of business English more perfect.

The teaching effect feedback business flow consists of two sub businesses: obtaining English teaching feedback and teachers' viewing feedback. The management personnel of the Academic Affairs Office prepare the feedback form of the teaching information of the course, print out the feedback form in batch after review, and distribute it to the students to fill in. The students fill in the teaching feedback on the spot, which is collected by the class leaders, and assist the teachers to sort out the feedback [10]. The teachers of the academic affairs office are responsible for reviewing the feedback, and the English teachers are responsible for reviewing the feedback, summarizing and analyzing the English course teaching according to the feedback, and putting forward targeted rectification measures for the teaching effect.

In the above analysis of the original business process, we can see that each business process is basically in the manual operation stage. The process is relatively simple, the

Fig. 4. Student practical teaching evaluation system

human subjective factors are strong, and the work efficiency is not high [11]. The error in one link often delays the processing of subsequent business. In addition, English teaching resources cannot be effectively accumulated and managed, and teachers' teaching and students' learning cannot be interconnected and online shared, which makes English teaching work slow. If the information system is not used for effective optimization, it will seriously restrict the development of English teaching work. The development of English teaching is shown in Fig. 5 below.

English teaching resources suitable for students of this grade shall be compiled by foreign language teachers in a unified way, and these teaching resources must be classified and reviewed by teachers of specific teaching and research departments [12]. Teachers of foreign language professional courses shall set system parameters of relevant query conditions, and catalog them according to the established rules of each professional course. The director of the teaching and research department can upload them only after confirmation. The teaching and research department is responsible for the warehousing of classified teaching resources of English majors, The vice president in charge of teaching regularly checks to obtain feedback. Only when the teaching and research office manages the teaching resources of the discipline in a reasonable and orderly way can the safety review, uploading, warehousing, retrieval and downloading of the resources be ensured. The corresponding teaching resources shall be issued and the number of the resources shall be recorded and sorted out for reuse by the foreign language teaching personnel of each batch. The resource type can be a single foreign language reading, writing and other resource files, a composite audio resource file in listening and speaking, or a URL link. Relevant personnel of foreign teachers [13]. The uploaded documents also

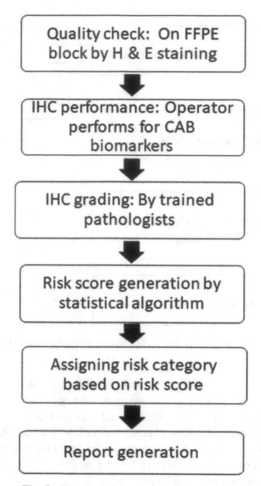

Fig. 5. The development of English Teaching

need to go through the above-mentioned relevant review processes before entering the foreign language resource library for reference by the college's foreign language teaching personnel or students' reading and learning.

4 Effectiveness Evaluation of Business English Practical Teaching Based on Decision Tree

4.1 Composition of Effectiveness Evaluation System of Business English Practical Teaching

IS established to make statistics on the students majoring in Business English. Collect the scores of business English majors. Assuming that C is a collection, it is the scores of business English majors. Arrange each of them according to their student number, in which the student number can be represented by A1 and A2, and set their expectations at the same time. Teachers can evaluate each student's ability in English practice according to the data in the decision tree. The formula is

$$u_{k+1}(t) = u_k(t) + \Gamma_{l1}\dot{e}_k(t) + \Gamma_{l2}\dot{e}_{k+1}(t) + \Gamma_{p1}\Delta\dot{e}_k(t) + \Gamma_{p2}\Delta\dot{e}_{k+1}(t) \qquad (1)$$

However, in practical teaching, there are still some problems. For example, with the increase of business English practice content, the amount of calculation of the evaluation system will increase, and the decision tree will be difficult to bear a lot of data. As a result, when dealing with data, the decision tree needs to constantly establish a new decision tree, which brings some troubles to teachers in evaluation teaching. The algorithm flow is shown in Fig. 6 below.

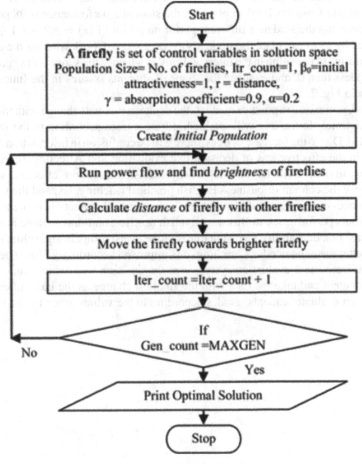

Fig. 6. Algorithm flow

4.2 Improvement of Decision Tree Practical Teaching Effect Evaluation Model

First, optimize the teaching data. When using the decision tree, in order to ensure the performance of business English majors, repeated operations are required, which brings a certain burden to teachers in the evaluation and reduces the efficiency of decision tree operation to a certain extent. Especially when the teaching data increases, the operation speed of decision tree will become very slow, which increases the cost of data operation. In order to optimize the decision tree, the data can be processed intensively according to the data in practical teaching to reduce the time consumption [14]. During data processing, the data can be limited to a fixed value, and the fixed value interval is [C, D]. Teachers can use the computer to process the data, such as marking the floating of the current data. When $f(x) > 0$, the data will appear concave in the function table. When $f(x) < 0$, the data will appear convex in the function table. When estimating a student's performance, the teacher can select a value and bring it into the (C, d) range. For example, in Business English practice, the student's performance is 98 points. The teacher can bring the student's different performance into $f(x) = A0 + A1 + A2 + ...$ An divided by an to calculate the student's average score. Check whether the calculated value conforms to the value in the interval. Look at whether the score is $f(x)$ greater than 0 or $F(x)$ less than 0, and evaluate the shape of students' scores in the function table. As shown in Fig. 7.

Second, optimize the practice content, the decision tree will change with the increase of practice times. In the tree will establish different trees according to the increase of content [15]. Due to the increase of trees, there will be confusion in information exchange, resulting in the effectiveness of decision tree evaluation and Affecting Teachers' data processing. In order to make the evaluation of decision tree more effective, we should first improve the content of business English practical teaching. Expand the memory of the data processing system and comprehensively process the practical content. Evaluate each student's performance in Business English practice, and draw a table according to the students' practical ability. Decision tree is prone to instability in algorithm. In order to make it better meet the needs of teaching, it is improved accordingly [16]. The practical teaching effectiveness evaluation system uses the decision tree, which can carry more practical content and take the data with the smallest change as the basis of evaluation. Teachers can evaluate students' grades according to the values given by the evaluation system.

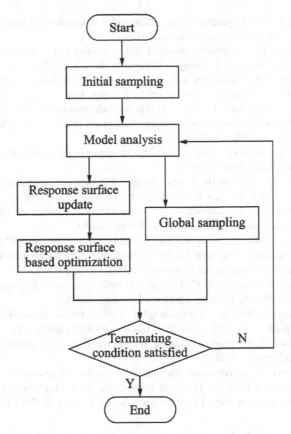

Fig. 7. The process of assessing student scores in the menu.

5 Conclusion

As mentioned above, the relevant personnel of the school can analyze and improve the existing teaching system according to the decision-making principles in Business English teaching, and make reasonable and effective use of the existing teaching resources for specific teaching. The organic combination of theory and practice emphasizes the cultivation of students' professional skills and practical skills to promote.

References

1. Wei, L., Lin, W.: Design of the teaching demonstration system for the course of measurement and control circuit. China Mod. Educ. Equip. (2018)
2. Hao, J.: Design of university academic management cloud system based on openstack. China Comput. Commun. (2019)
3. Rao, H., Gu, Y., et al.: Design of Teaching Resource Management Platform Based on MVC (2018)
4. Wang, B., Jianling, H.U., Zhou, M., et al.: Design of cloud-based signal processing virtual experiment system. Modern Electron. Technique (2019)

5. Tao, T., Yuan, J., H.R. Department: Innovation and demonstration of university teaching staff management system. Exp. Sci. Technol. (2018)
6. Chen, K., Bai, Q.: The study on systematic design of training and development for international Chinese language teachers. J. Chengdu Univ. (Soc. ences) (2019)
7. Liu, L.F., Wang, C.L., Chun-Sen, Y.E., et al.: Teaching mode design of project management course by SPOC and flipped classroom method. Logist. Eng. Manage. (2018)
8. Fang, L.I., Liu, Q.Y., Guo, K., et al.: Public English teaching hypothesis with the core of vocational demand: human resource management major in Guangzhou Donghua College. J. Chengde Petroleum Coll. (2019)
9. Liu, Y.: Research on course design of hotel human resource management in higher vocational colleges. Educ. Teach. Forum (2019)
10. Lian, N.Y.: Exploration on the course design of human resource management under art management major. Educ. Teach. Forum (2018)
11. Sun, Z.G.: Research on teaching model composition and elements of human resource management major course. Educ. Teaching Forum (2018)
12. Zhu, J.: Research on resource equilibrium scheduling of massive MOOC teaching resources information management system. In: Proceedings of the 2018 International Symposium on Social Science and Management Innovation (SSMI 2018) (2019)
13. Liu, X., Zhang, W., Polytechnic, C.: Design and implementation of data visualization teaching system based on Web technology. Electron. Des. Eng. (2019)
14. Su, F.: Application research of college English teaching resources based on knowledge base management platform. J. Phys. Conf. Ser. **1345**(5), 052072 (2019). (7pp)
15. Yang, S.: Research on human resource management research course teaching system. Education Modernizat. (2018)
16. Bai, Y.: Research on experimental teaching reform of human resource management course in Higher Vocational Colleges. In: Proceedings of the 2018 5th International Conference on Education, Management, Arts, Economics and Social Science (ICEMAESS 2018) 2018

Author Index

Printed in the United States
by Baker & Taylor Publisher Services